Let's Talk...

WITH READINGS

100
W. W. NORTON & COMPANY
Celebrating a Century of Independent Publishing

Let's Talk...

WITH READINGS

Andrea Lunsford
Stanford University

Michal Brody

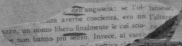

dell'angoscia; se l'oli lattete,
za averne coscienza, ero un l'altare
pazzo, un uomo libero finalmente le cui scia
non hanno più senso. Invece, al varco
la coscienza ntiva
di pazzo ed Ritorno

W. W. NORTON & COMPANY has been independent since its founding in 1923, when William Warder Norton and Mary D. Herter Norton first published lectures delivered at the People's Institute, the adult education division of New York City's Cooper Union. The firm soon expanded its program beyond the Institute, publishing books by celebrated academics from America and abroad. By midcentury, the two major pillars of Norton's publishing program—trade books and college texts—were firmly established. In the 1950s, the Norton family transferred control of the company to its employees, and today—with a staff of five hundred and hundreds of trade, college, and professional titles published each year—W. W. Norton & Company stands as the largest and oldest publishing house owned wholly by its employees.

Copyright © 2023, 2021 by W. W. Norton & Company, Inc.
All rights reserved
Printed in Canada

Editor: Marilyn Moller
Project Editor: Christine D'Antonio
Assistant Editor: Emma Peters
Managing Editor, College: Marian Johnson
Production Manager: Jane Searle
Media Editor: Joy Cranshaw
Media Editorial Assistant: Maria Qureshi
Media Project Editor: Diane Cipollone
Managing Editor, College Digital Media: Kim Yi
Ebook Production Manager: Sophia Purut
Composition Marketing Research Manager: Michele Dobbins
Design Director: Rubina Yeh
Design and Illustrations: Doyle Partners
Director of College Permissions: Megan Schindel
College Permissions Specialist: Josh Garvin
Photo Editor: Melinda Patelli
Composition: Achorn International
Manufacturing: Transcontinental—Beauceville

Permission to use copyrighted material is included in the Credits section, which begins on page 809.

ISBN 978-1-324-04214-3

W. W. Norton & Company, Inc., 500 Fifth Avenue, New York, NY 10110
www.norton.com

W. W. Norton & Company Ltd., 15 Carlisle Street, London W1D 3BS
1 2 3 4 5 6 7 8 9 0

I could spend the rest of my life
reading, just satisfying my curiosity.

MALCOLM X
(1925–65)

Preface

This book began as an attempt to write a really brief rhetoric, one that would be short and sweet and inexpensive—and would address the pressing needs of today's college writers. But as I thought about those needs, I was humbled and also challenged by what I saw: students overwhelmed by information that they could scarcely process, much less trust. Social media bubbles in which they heard only views like their own. Civil discourse replaced by relentless tweets, retweets, and rants that crowded out any room for critical thought or dialogue, let alone conversation. So I knew I wanted to write a book that would cover more than just writing and research: that it also needed to help students resist clickbait and the lure of echo chambers, to help them listen to and engage perspectives other than their own. And that's why we called it *Let's Talk*.

That little book seems to have struck a chord with teachers and students, who tell us it provides "just enough" of information and guidance, and it's already being used in more than 200 colleges and universities. But while many instructors have praised it, many others have said—loud and clear—that they wished it included readings. And so—ta da!—welcome to *Let's Talk with Readings*! Please welcome Michal Brody as well, my coauthor who has cast her wide and ingenious net to find the readings.

This is still a compact **rhetoric**, one that will help students do the kinds of writing and research that they're expected to do in college. But it now includes a **reader** that focuses on five issues and topics that I think students will want to read about, talk about, and write about:

The Inequities That Bedevil Us

What's Language Got to Do with It?

What's News, and How Do We Know What to Trust?

Who Owns Nature?

Do Sports Matter?

And—it comes with its own **library**! The *LetsTalkLibrary* is an online collection of essays, speeches, videos, and more that invites students to read, listen, talk, and write about the same issues that are covered in the readings in the book. Plus, we'll be updating this library with new readings twice a year, making it a collection that will never grow old.

So. It's a rhetoric, a reader, and a library—and we've built in links throughout to help you use all three. That's *Let's Talk with Readings*! Read on to learn about some of its highlights.

Let's Talk is short for "let us talk," a title that assumes more than one voice—and more than one point of view. And *talk* assumes that there's someone listening. But what does it mean to talk or to listen in such a contentious environment? One thing it means is that we all need to do more listening, and to see if we're doing more talking than listening: as Epictetus put it, "We have two ears and one mouth so we can listen twice as much as we speak." This book begins, then, with **a chapter on listening**, which shows students how listening purposefully and with an open mind can build empathy and understanding—and provides clear guidelines for how to do so. This kind of listening, identified by Krista Ratcliffe as *rhetorical listening*, paves the way for student writers and speakers to engage critically and ethically with others—especially those with whom they may disagree.

Let's Talk with Readings aims to teach student writers to seek out multiple perspectives and to practice the kind of civil discourse that can build common ground and bring people together across differences. Chapter 3 provides concrete guidance for **engaging respectfully with others**, and short chapters on arguing, analyzing, summarizing and responding, and other genres will help students add their own voices to what Kenneth Burke called "the conversation of humankind," in messages informed by careful research and delivered with a sense of responsibility. To that end, the readings in both the book and the *LetsTalkLibrary* include a question that prompts students to discuss the reading with several classmates and offers explicit guidance for engaging thoughtfully and respectfully with what others think and say.

Writing a book that not only encourages but demonstrates critical and ethical engagement also calls for some difficult introspection, for looking squarely at my own biases and preferences. As a result, *Let's Talk with Readings* works hard to bring in **many, many perspectives**, not shying away, for example, from quoting Condoleezza Rice—or Ibram X. Kendi—and agreeing with Janet Yellen that none of us has "a monopoly on the truth." The same goes for the readings, where you'll find an op-ed making a conservative case for environmentalism along with a comparative analysis of rap and poetry, advice for getting along with people whose political views you hate— and more. These are only some of dozens of viewpoints given voice in essays and epigraphs and examples and more, throughout the book. In short, this book not only encourages students to listen to others, but it tries hard to take its own advice.

Attending to multiple perspectives means recognizing the full linguistic repertoire student writers bring to class, from multiple languages to a wide range of dialects and ways with words that enrich their messages and help them connect to various audiences. This book celebrates **stylistic and linguistic diversity**, particularly in Chapter 24, Mixing Languages & Dialects, and Chapter 32, What's Language Got to Do with It?, which includes readings on standardized English, Black English, *Latinx*, and more.

Our **attention to inclusion and diversity** continues throughout the book, beginning with an opening note to students that contextualizes the controversies surrounding standard English, especially in the ways it privileges some and silences others, and in Chapter 31, The Inequities That Bedevil Us.

The student writing in this book also helps to underscore this focus. These students come from a wide range of colleges and universities—two-year and four-year, public and private, HBCUs and schools with religious affiliations, Hispanic-serving and NASNTI-serving institutions. And you'll see what students have on their minds today, from an essay on civil rights rhetoric, to an argument about minority clubs on campus, to a summary/response essay on getting into college without having rich parents to buy a spot, to a proposal for improving the working conditions of hospital nurses, to a podcast about being first-gen students—all showing students doing what John Lewis asked young people everywhere to do: "stand up, speak up, and speak out." This book aims to make sure their voices are heard and appreciated.

The ability to stand up and speak out, to get our messages across, is—according to Aristotle—one of two key reasons to know and understand rhetoric. The other reason is for self-defense, to be able to recognize and resist manipulation by others. Today, this ability is perhaps more important than ever before, as we face a tsunami of misinformation and even outright lies every hour of every day. So *Let's Talk with Readings* provides two chapters to help students read defensively—Chapter 6 on **distinguishing facts from lies and misinformation** and Chapter 15 on **evaluating sources and checking facts**—along with a reading by Sam Wineburg in Chapter 33 on navigating the dangers of the web.

As I developed these chapters, however, I kept my eyes focused on that original goal: to write a *brief* rhetoric, a handy little book that would speak to students who are increasingly busy—with work, families, and so many other pressing responsibilities. I kept thinking of my east Tennessee granny who often responded to my rambling stories with a curt "get to the point, Andrea, get to the point." So these chapters try hard to provide **just enough detail**, to "get to the point"—but then to link to a glossary/index where students can find more detail *if* they want or need it. And throughout the book they'll find **prompts for reflection**, questions to get them thinking about their own use of rhetoric and writing.

If this little book has a mission (and it does!), it is to embody the lesson John Lewis's mother taught him when he was young: "once you learn something, once you really get it into your head, no one can take it away from you." The gift of learning, which no one can take away: that's a lesson to hold on to, and to pass on to others. I hope this book will help you do that—and so much more.

Acknowledgments

One set of voices echoing in the pages of this book is those of the many friends, colleagues, and reviewers who have prodded, questioned, sometimes heckled, and ultimately inspired me to think harder and more deeply, to identify weak spots (and to improve them), to meet students where they are and to recognize and to honor the wisdom and the strengths they bring with them into our classrooms. In fact, one hallmark of this book is its multivocality, its inclusion of and attention to a wide range of diverse and lively voices. Chief among these in *Let's Talk with Readings* is that of my coauthor, Michal Brody, curator of the readings in both the book and the *LetsTalkLibrary*. As a sociolinguist and a coauthor of several other important composition books, Michal is also my partner in searching for quirky stories about language—and for the perfect burger! You'll find her wit and wisdom throughout this book. Next comes our editor, Marilyn Moller: for thirty-five years and counting, Marilyn's ingenuity, tough-minded persistence, and sheer brilliance have inspired me to reach farther and to try harder. One of her many moments of brilliance led us to the world-renowned graphic designer Stephen Doyle, whom she somehow convinced to design *Let's Talk*. His consummate artistry and razor-sharp wit are on display throughout this book, and we are profoundly grateful for his contributions to this project.

We are also fortunate to have the support of a magnificent Norton team, starting with Christine D'Antonio, who consistently goes above and beyond—and has skillfully guided the book from manuscript to final pages, improving it immensely along the way; and Jane Searle, who has produced this book beautifully and, miraculously, on time. Thanks also go to Alice Vigliani for her very careful copyediting.

And very special thanks to Debra Morton Hoyt, Rubina Yeh, and Michael Wood for overseeing the entire design of this book—and to Tyson Cantrell for the whimsical interior design, one that has made this book easy to use, Rhoan O'Connell for the playful trailers, and Rosemarie Turk for keeping it (and us) all on track.

Many others have given their time and talent to this project. Special thanks to Josh Garvin and Melinda Patelli for securing permission for the many texts and images. And we owe an especially big thank-you to Claire Wallace for truly heroic work on the MLA and APA chapters and to Emma Peters for her help finding good examples and images—and for help in so many other ways. And high five to Claire, Emma, and Vinny Yu for sharing their tweets about Stomper and Split. #letsgooakland #thesavbananas

We're similarly grateful to Kim Yi, Sophia Purut, and Diane Cipollone for their meticulous work on the ebook; to Joy Cranshaw and Maria Qureshi for all they've done on behalf of the *LetsTalkLibrary*, *Let's Teach*, and *InQuizitive for Writers*; and to Evan Yamanishi for his very helpful advice about alt text.

Thanks as well to Michele Dobbins, Heidi Balas, Sarah Purnell, and Ryan Schwab for all they will be doing to introduce *Let's Talk with Readings* to teachers across the country—and to Lib Triplett for her help making sure that this book will serve *all* teachers and students. And what can we say about the fabled Norton travelers: A. MA. ZING. They rock!

As always, we are very grateful to Mike Wright, Ann Shin, Roby Harrington, and Julia Reidhead for their unwavering and enthusiastic support for this new book. And we're especially grateful to the many colleagues who reviewed *Let's Talk* and its readings for their generous and astute comments and suggestions:

Michael Anderson, Northwestern Michigan College; Jessica Lynn Bannon, University of Indianapolis; Nicole Bishop, Prince George's Community College; Kelly Blewett, Indiana University–East Campus; Kristie Boston, Lone Star College—University Park; April Bristow-

Smith, Nash Community College; Kendra Bryant, North Carolina A&T State University; Margarette Christensen, University of Nebraska–Omaha; Scott Compton, Midlands Technical College; Ginny Crisco, California State—Fresno; Kimberly Crowley, Bismarck State College; Gabriel Cutrufello, York College of Pennsylvania; Laura Davies, SUNY Cortland; Miranda Egger, University of Colorado–Denver; Michael Faris, Texas Tech University; David Gooblar, University of Iowa; John Goshert, Utah Valley University; Jane Greer, University of Missouri–Kansas City; Kay Halasek, The Ohio State University; Amora Hand, Norfolk State University; Marie Hannan-Mandel, Corning Community College; Rodney Herring, University of Colorado–Denver; Shaye Hope, Delgado Community College; Heather King, Ivy Tech Community College–Indianapolis; Danielle Klafter, Southeast Community College–Lincoln; Paul Madachy, Prince George's Community College; Faye Maor, North Carolina A&T State University; Adam Mekler, Morgan State University; Annie Mendenhall, Georgia Southern University; Leigh Ann Moore, Alvin Community College; Patrick Nevins, Ivy Tech Community College–Columbus; Meagan Newberry, College of Western Idaho; Carolyn Nolte, Southeast Community College–Lincoln; Monica Norris, Texas Tech University; Jon Ostenson, Brigham Young University; Staci Perryman-Clark, Western Michigan University; Richard Potsubay, Green River College; Abraham Romney, Michigan Technological University; Sherry Rosenthal, College of Southern Nevada; Anthony Sams, Ivy Tech Community College–Sellersburg; Dagmar Scharold, University of Houston–Downtown; Kaia Lea Simon, University of Wisconsin–Eau Claire; Elizabeth Starr, Ivy Tech Community College–Bloomington; Doug Swartz, Indiana University–Northwest Campus; Renee Scariano Willers, Oxnard College; Danielle Williams, Baylor University; Jewon Woo, Lorain County Community College; Maria Zlateva, Boston University. We hope that this book responds to everything these instructors have told us they want and need.

And special thanks to the many students whose writing appears in this book. We thank Wesley Cohen and Stephanie Pomales, both of UC Davis; Colin Flanagan, Brandon Hernandez, and Jack Long, Ohio State; Sam Forman, Grinnell; Emma González, Marjory Stoneman Douglas High School; Rosa Guevara, LaGuardia Community College; Erin Hawley, East Carolina University; Brandon Hayden, Georgia State; Melissa Hicks, Lane Community College; Julia Johnson and Taylor Jordan, both of North Carolina A&T; Isaac Lozano, Bonita Vista High School; Gabriela Moro, Notre Dame; Olivia Steely, University of Missouri–St. Louis; Henry Tsai, Vrinda Vasavada, Trey Connelly, and Jackson Parell, all of Stanford; and Eli Vale, Texas A&M–San Antonio.

Michal would like to thank her many students in the United States and Mexico for asking all the good, hard questions. She'd also like to thank her own teachers and models of teaching excellence: Judith Kaplan-Weinger, Teddy Bofman, Carlota Smith, Nora England, and Keith Walters.

Finally, I want to offer thanks to those whose scholarship and leadership I deeply admire and from whom I have learned so much over the years—and particularly over this last year: brilliant friends and colleagues Lisa Ede, Cheryl Glenn, Melissa Goldthwaite, Shirley Brice Heath, Shirley Logan, Faye Maor, Beverly Moss, Roxanne Mountford, Krista Ratcliffe, Jackie Royster, Geneva Smitherman. Brilliant partners at Stanford Adam Banks and Marvin Diogenes and Christine Alfano. The whole brilliant Bread Loaf/NextGen group and La Casa Roja, inspired by Dixie Goswami, Lou Bernieri, Tom McKenna, Ceci Lewis, and Rex Lee Jim. The amazing and brilliant DBLAC (Digital Black Lit and Composition) group, and especially Khirsten Echols and Lou Miraj; and brilliant writers and thinkers whose work has challenged me in all the best ways: April Baker-Bell, Ta-Nehisi Coates, Lorena German, Ibram X. Kendi, Carmen Kynard, and Shauna Shapiro. With your help and guidance, I am learning still.

A Note to Students: Can We Talk?

This is not a trivial question. In fact, can we begin to talk, right now, by taking a closer look at these three little words?

CAN we talk? That is, do we have the ability to communicate, through spoken words or with the use of some technology—print, audio, video or some other media? Today, more than ever before, we certainly have the capacity to talk—to communicate, to reach others both near and far. Whether we *will* talk—well, that's another question.

Can WE talk? This raises the question of just who *we* refers to. First of all, it includes everyone who is using this book, in print or online. But for the authors, it means much more than that, reaching out to include anyone now or in the future who may come across this book, in English or in translation to another language. More important, *we* suggests, at the very least, a two-way conversation, a dialogue, and one that, we hope, is fair and open and involves a lot of listening.

Can we TALK? This is the most challenging of our three words, because *talk* encompasses not just what we are talking about, but what we are using to do so—in this case, language. Stop for a moment and imagine a world without language of any kind: no spoken words, no sign language, not even any pictures. Or try going even a few hours without any language. You'll find it nearly impossible. Language is what allows us to know the world and one another, and to share what we know with others. But because we don't all speak the same languages (there are currently over 7,000 languages spoken in the world!), understanding one another is often easier said than done. Even within a single language, getting to understanding can be hard, because words can have many different shades of meaning—and because most languages include many different regional, ethnic, and other dialects.

Such difficulties are exacerbated by hierarchies that have developed over time to differentiate various languages and dialects, marking some as more prestigious and acceptable and others as less so. In ancient China, the prestige language was so oppressive that it led women to create a secret language of their own. From 1945 to 1987, students in Taiwan were forbidden to speak their regional dialects, and punished for doing so. In France, the Académie Française, made up of forty scholars known as "the immortals," continues to lay down the law on all things having to do with usage, vocabulary, and grammar of the French language—and as recently as 2008 sought to block the recognition of regional languages. In England, George Bernard Shaw's *Pygmalion* features the pompous linguist Henry Higgins mercilessly drilling Eliza Doolittle's cockney accent out of her—all to win a bet that he could teach her to speak "proper" English.

And in the United States, the dialect of English used by those in power gradually came to be considered the "standard," taught in schools and expected (or required) in all professional communication. Anxious to establish a national literature and an English that was every bit as proper and prestigious as the "King's English" spoken by the upper class in England, schools and other US institutions adopted a standard American English. Proponents of this standard argue that it has some benefits: it allows for stability, for efficiency, and for ease of communication across differences. It is also easier, they say, to learn one standard than many varieties.

In the abstract, these benefits make some sense. But in promoting a standard dialect, powerful US institutions also *ranked* the various dialects of English—privileging the standard and considering all others nonstandard, and inferior. And then, by association, those using nonstandard dialects came to be considered "inferior." It's a short jump from this conclusion to the kind of linguistic discrimination that then labels languages other than the standard as "deficient," "ignorant," or worse. Today, the vestiges of such discrimination are still all around us: any of us who has ever been made fun for the way we speak has felt its effects. And since standard English has been the dialect used by the elite and powerful, it has worked to reinforce the power and prestige of this particular group—and to disempower and even silence many others.

This is the great *dis*advantage of standardized English, one that has taken a toll on generations by failing to recognize a central fact of life endorsed by linguists around the world: that *all languages and dialects are equally vital and valid forms of expression.* The debate over the advantages and disadvantages of standardized languages is ongoing. You can read about several aspects of this debate in Chapter 32.

Yet in spite of ongoing attempts to impose a standard dialect, languages have their own ways of evolving—and people have their own ways of resisting standardization. We can see such evolution at work in the words from Spanish and many other languages that have entered English vocabulary. In the United States, Black English has evolved partly as a result of the systemic segregation of Black Americans from the mainstream as well as the inherent creativity and genius of the people. Hundreds of years of teaching—and requiring—standard English have not erased or even diminished the richness and sophistication of Black English, which sociolinguist John Rickford describes as "spoken soul." And today many linguists and instructors are resisting and even pushing back against standard English.

Linguist and rhetorician Geneva Smitherman has been a leader in demonstrating the validity and power of all languages and dialects and in calling for a national language policy urging that all Americans become fluent in multiple languages and dialects. Half a century ago, she was a major force in developing the *Students' Right to Their Own Language,* a policy statement adopted by NCTE, the largest organization of English teachers in the United States. Her advocacy of multilingualism and of resisting a standard continues today, with scholars such as April Baker Bell, Carmen Kynard, and Missy Watson contesting standardized English and the role it plays in composition classes.

And while these and other scholars have been working at the level of theory, many other writers continue to explore, innovate, and experiment brilliantly with language, and do so in a way that not only resists any one single "standard" but expands the boundaries, even of academic discourse. Author and teacher Lou Tonouchi uses

Hawaiian Pidgin to write powerful academic articles, as do acclaimed writers Joe Balaz and Lois-Ann Yamanaka in their poetry and novels, demonstrating the vibrancy and richness of this language. And Lin-Manuel Miranda mixes languages in many of his songs, noting that "It's enormous fun to write songs where we rhyme Spanish and English." Many other writers, from historian Cristína Ramirez to novelists Sandra Cisneros and Junot Díaz provide other powerful examples. They and many others are not just rethinking but also remaking what constitutes good writing, and they are doing so in a way that may well inspire you to do the same.

Writers who resist using a single standard language and choose to write in multiple languages and dialects can tell us that such choices have consequences: many have faced resistance or worse, especially in schools and other institutions. So our language choices often come with very high stakes. You can turn to June Jordan's haunting essay "Nobody Mean More to Me Than You and the Future Life of Willie Jordan" on p. 647 to read about the decision one group of students faced about what variety of English to use in a particularly difficult situation.

In describing why and when they choose to mix languages and dialects, professors Geneva Smitherman and H. Sammy Alim say they draw on their own knowledge of "Latin, Arabic, Spanish, and so-called standard English and . . . flex these linguistic muscles according to the rhetorical situation"—and to argue that "it is a decided benefit for American citizens to be able to speak in more than one tongue." And, we would add, to *write* in more than one tongue. Chapter 24 says much more about when and how to mix languages and dialects.

Today, our language(s) are changing and growing, as language always does, and along with it, our choices are expanding too. If it has been elite, powerful people and institutions that have defined what counts as "good" language, it is important to remember that language in and of itself offers the possibility of power to all of us—the power to raise our voices and to say what we want to say. *Let's Talk with Readings* is a book dedicated to helping you negotiate the many choices you have that will allow you to do just that.

Resources

Like the book itself, the resources that accompany *Let's Talk with Readings* provide just enough detail, for instructors and students alike, while remaining brief and to the point.

 THE LETSTALKLIBRARY offers a wealth of online readings on the same themes covered in the book, sortable by theme, genre, and medium. Curated by Michal Brody, each reading is accompanied by a headnote and prompts that guide students to analyze, to discuss, to reflect, and to respond to in writing. Designed to complement the readings in the book, the *LetsTalkLibrary* offers readings in a variety of media, with new, up-to-the-minute selections posted twice per year. Updates to the ebook will provide new study questions that help students to make connections between readings in the book and those added to the *LetsTalkLibrary*.

 THE EBOOK allows highlighting and note-taking to help students understand, engage with, and respond to what they read, and instructors can share their own models of engaged reading with students using the instructor annotation tool. New animated videos are embedded within the ebook to reinforce the guidance provided in the text, and study questions prompt students to make connections with readings on the *LetsTalkLibrary*. Norton ebooks can be viewed on all devices and are born-accessible, with content and features designed from the start for all learners. Ebook access comes with all new print copies of this book or can be purchased directly from **digital.wwnorton.com/letstalkreadings**.

INQUIZITIVE FOR WRITERS allows students to practice writing skills in a low-stakes, feedback-driven environment. Interactive questions help students to explore writing processes and genres, practice sentence editing, and apply good research habits, building their confidence at all stages of the writing process. The activities are adaptive, so students receive additional practice in the areas where they need more help; and explanatory feedback and direct links to relevant sections in the *Little Seagull Handbook* offer advice precisely when it's needed. Access to *InQuizitive for Writers* and the *Little Seagull Handbook* is included with all new copies of *Let's Talk with Readings* and can be integrated directly into most campus learning management systems.

 **THE LITTLE SEAGULL HANDBOOK.** Access to the *Little Seagull* ebook is included with all new copies of *Let's Talk with Readings*—or the print book can be packaged with *Let's Talk with Readings* for only $10 more, providing the help all students need on punctuating and editing what they write—and the help L2 students need on using articles, prepositions, phrasal verbs, and idioms. Whether they need help analyzing a text, creating a works-cited list, or knowing where to put a comma, these two little paperbacks will be there to help.

 VIDEOS. A new collection of videos includes short author videos linked to from the ebook, as well as charming animations that are available online, through a campus LMS, and in new *InQuizitive for Writers* activities. Informed by feedback from hundreds of composition instructors, topics include writing processes, rhetorical situations, specific kinds of writing, critical reading strategies, and more.

 A PLAGIARISM TUTORIAL explains why plagiarism matters, what counts as plagiarism, and how to avoid plagiarism—and concludes with a short quiz to assess what students have learned.

LET'S TEACH! Available in both print and PDF formats, with teaching advice for each chapter and reading in the text. Brief like the student book, this guide includes: classroom activities and sample writing assignments for every chapter in the rhetoric and brief guides to the readings. Written by Andrea Lunsford herself, this little book is full of stories, suggestions, and advice from her own 50 years in the classroom.

QUIZZES. More than 150 ready-to-use quizzes on sentences, language, punctuation/mechanics, paragraph editing, plagiarism, and MLA and APA documentation are available for import into your LMS, where you can customize them for your course.

All resources can be found at **digital.wwnorton.com/letstalkreadings**.

Contents

1 RHETORIC / Join the Conversation

3 **Engaging Respectfully with Others**   29

4 **Developing Academic Habits of Mind**   42

8 Arguing   99

4 RESEARCH / Find Out

7 MEDIA / A Portfolio

8 READINGS / Let's Read!

How to Use This Book

YOU COULD LOOK IT UP.

—JAMES THURBER

Many people attribute the above statement to Casey Stengel, the late great manager of the New York Yankees. But if in fact you do look it up, you'll find that it comes from the title of a short story written by James Thurber. Whoever said it first, it works for this book. Whether you're trying to figure out how to conclude an essay, fact-check an outlandish statement, or come up with a good title, *Let's Talk with Readings* is here to help. And whatever the advice or help you're looking for, here are various ways you can look it up.

Brief menu. If you're looking for a specific chapter, check the Brief Menu on the inside front cover. If you're looking for a specific section of a chapter, look in the Contents on pages xxii–xxxv.

Directory of readings. You'll find a list of all the readings on the inside back cover of the book.

Glossary/index. The fastest way to find something in any book is with the index, and this book combines the glossary and the index where you'll find both the definitions of key terms and concepts and the pages where you'll find more detail. Words highlighted in RED are all defined there, and many of the definitions include enough detail that you'll find all you need there.

Color-coded organization. The various parts of this book are color-coded for easy reference: green for the INTRODUCTION, turquoise for the RHETORIC chapters, orange for the WRITING chapters, gold for the READING chapters, blue for the RESEARCH chapters, pink for MLA, light blue for APA, blue-green for

LANGUAGE & STYLE, tan for DESIGN, purple for MEDIA, gray-green for the READINGS, and red for the GLOSSARY/INDEX.

Writing guides. Chapters 8 to 13 cover six kinds of writing that college students are often assigned to do, along with essays written by students demonstrating each kind of writing.

Index of common kinds of writing. Whatever kind of writing you are assigned or simply decide to do, you'll find guidance in this book. Inside the front cover flap, you'll see a list of commonly assigned kinds of writing and where you'll find help in this book.

A *roadmap for doing research* on the back flap refers you to pages in the book you'll want to consult when doing research.

MLA and APA guidelines. If you need to document sources, turn to Chapters 20 for MLA style and 21 for APA. Each chapter provides color-coded templates that show what information to include, along with documentation maps showing where to find that information. Directories in the back of the book will lead you to the specific examples you need. You'll also find a full MLA-style research essay on page 348 and an APA-style essay on page 390.

The LetsTalkLibrary. Here you'll find an online collection of essays, articles, op-eds, videos, speeches, and more—all searchable by theme, genre, and medium. Check it out at **letstalklibrary.com**.

Editing what you write. This book comes with digital access to both *The Little Seagull Handbook* and *InQuizitive for Writers*. You'll find help with sentence-level editing in the *Little Seagull* and game-like practice editing common errors and working with sources in *InQuizitive*. Access is free with all new print copies and can be activated on the registration card included in the book. You can also purchase access at **digital.wwnorton.com/letstalkreadings**.

Introduction:
Stop! Look! Listen!
and Write!

**BIG TEN, PAC-12 PULL PLUG ON FALL FOOTBALL
AMID COVID-19 PANDEMIC**

—ASSOCIATED PRESS

**HOW THE BLACK LIVES MATTER MOVEMENT
WENT MAINSTREAM**

—WASHINGTON POST

WILDFIRES RAGING IN CALIFORNIA AND COLORADO

—NPR

Headlines like these jostle with hundreds of others vying for our attention, all too often leaving us out of breath just trying to keep up with "breaking news." And while these three headlines report actual, factual information, much of the "news" that reaches us is based on misinformation and oddball conspiracy theories that aim at nothing so much as creating divisiveness, stoking fears, and inciting distrust. It's enough to make us want to throw up our hands and just tune out. But I say: resist that urge!

If we have ever needed to put our critical thinking caps on, to take a deep breath, to *stop, look*, and *listen*, this is it. For all the junk that clogs our news feeds and inboxes, there's much of real importance to think about, to read about, to talk about—and yes, to write about. And that's what this book will help you do. To talk about these and other important issues with others, including those whose views differ from yours—and to listen to what they say, respectfully and with an open mind. To research topics and issues you care about as a matter of inquiry, searching for multiple perspectives rather than just for data to support what you already believe. And of course to write—as a way to explore ideas, to respond to something you've read or heard, to report on a topic you've researched or argue a position you want others to think about. In fact, thinking and writing almost always go hand in hand: as one of my students put it, "I really can't think without a pen in my hand—or a mouse." This book is here to help you do all that.

Stop!

In the face of so many urgent issues, it seems especially important to hit the pause button long enough to look very closely at these issues in all their immediate complexity. In other words, to resist the urge to rush from one tweet to another, one headline to the next. Instead, we need to slow down to a crawl, and then to a halt: close observation and real understanding take time and patience—they can't be done on the fly. So turn off your devices, put distractions aside, and practice being still and open to what is happening around you.

> Take a moment, pause, and look at things from all perspectives.
> MELANIA TRUMP

Look!

We all have ways of seeing the world, some of which are so deeply ingrained that we're not even aware of them. So it's especially important to understand them, to look at where they come from, and to ask if they really reflect values we want to embrace. *We need to look at ourselves as clearly as possible*—our age, race, ethnicity, religion, gender identity, sexual orientation, political affiliation; where we live, where we work and play, where we go to school, what interests we pursue—and ask how these factors lead us to see and understand the world from a certain position, and how that position keeps us from seeing the world as others from different backgrounds see it. This kind of up close and personal looking at ourselves is not easy. But it is necessary if we are to recognize and understand—and acknowledge—the role we may be playing in going along with the status quo, and even in perpetuating unjust systems.

> Your assumptions are your windows on the world. Scrub them off every once in a while, or the light won't come in.
> —ALAN ALDA

Consider the coronavirus pandemic, for instance. How do we understand competing policies and narratives about protecting people's health versus protecting the nation's economy, about how best to combat the virus, about something as simple as whether or not to wear a mask? What are our responsibilities in such a time—to ourselves, our families, and our fellow citizens? And what will we actually do, what specific actions will we take?

Such choices, though often unconscious, reveal what we pay attention to and how they affect and limit what we see—and also what we read. So as a reader, you first need to be aware of how your preferences and ways of seeing the world lead you to value (and trust) some things and not others, and to think critically about what that means for what you know—and what you don't know. Second, you need to learn to pay close attention to what you read, especially when the stakes are high. Most of all, you need to read with an open mind, saying "maybe" to ideas you're not sure about and attempting to understand them before saying "no" or rejecting them. It means looking closely at texts you might once have rejected, giving them a chance to make their points to you, and being open to the idea that they just might be right. When you read in this way, you are actively reading to understand, to learn, and to respond thoughtfully to what someone else thinks.

Listen!

Where do you get most of your news? *Facebook*? *Twitter*? Take some time to switch gears and listen for half an hour or so to a news source you don't normally pay attention to—or even resist listening to (MSNBC, say, or Fox News). *Pay attention to* how *you are listening*: With sources you like, do you accept what you hear without questioning or even thinking about what they say? And with sources you don't like, are you listening with a chip on your shoulder, looking for ways they're wrong? All of us have such patterns of listening, so it's important to get a sense of where your listening biases lie and to keep them from clouding your good judgment.

In addition, we all need to listen consciously and critically, doing the kind of listening that rhetoric professor Krista Ratcliffe calls "rhetorical listening." This kind of listening means opening yourself up to the views of others, even those with whom you disagree, and really hearing what they have to say. It means taking their views seriously, listening to really understand what they're saying.

> We have to listen to other people, so that *we* and *they* may lay *our* stories alongside one another's.
> KRISTA RATCLIFFE

This is the kind of listening that one student did when he read a series of *Facebook* posts attacking a politician in his Navajo community who "proudly supports" Donald Trump. Rather than joining them and screaming out "hate speech," he responded to those posts with a call for listening and understanding. As he listened more carefully to this politician, he said:

> I began to understand more about why she supports what we don't like. In her positions, I have to applaud her for having a clear and civil stance. She doesn't come off to me as aggressive like the comments have labeled her. We need to remember that she is also a loving mother, aunt, and relative in the community. Creating memes to "Put her in her own casket" is taking it too far! You don't understand what this kind of a violent witch hunt can do to a person. I am certain she means good.
>
> Furthermore, social media has its good and bad sides, and learning more about an issue before posting that next hate speech is the

best method for starting a proper conversation. I know that discussing politics is not all rainbows and butterflies. I get it. She is controversial. But taking time to at least know where she's coming from may help you understand her politics (even if, like me, you disagree). After understanding her stance, you can proceed to make a critique that's not violent or threatening.

—KYLE WHITE

This post is a product of sound rhetorical listening, of listening as a way of coming to understand another person. So the next time you're talking with someone with whom you deeply disagree, take a tip from Kyle White: don't attack, don't insult, don't hate. It's always better to stop and listen.

Think!

The listening and reading this book advocates, and the writing that grows out of them, go hand in hand with *thinking*—not just skimming over words and passages, but putting your mind to it and asking questions at every turn. But what does that really mean? It means paying very close attention and then asking serious and often detailed questions about what you are hearing or reading. In other words, it means not just agreeing or going along with it, but challenging it to convince you.

> I don't write to make readers think like me. I write to make them think.
>
> —ANNA QUINDLEN

One student who was taking a course examining cultural stereotypes started wondering where his own largely negative impressions of Iran as a country of religious zealots came from. Since he was reading Marjane Satrapi's *Persepolis* for another course, he decided to make some notes about how Satrapi represents Iran, her home country—and he quickly saw that her perceptions of Iran differed from those he held. This careful reading led him to dig further, looking back to the time of the 1979 Iranian revolution, which overthrew the US-backed regime of the shah. Carefully and methodically, he read coverage of Iran in national newspapers and found that

New York Times reporting from 1979 reveals a narrative emphasizing a solidly unified, radical religious movement that brought the Islamic Republic into reality. Such a narrative laid the foundation for characterizations of Iran by future leaders, whether by President Bush in his famous claim that Iran was part of an "axis of evil" or by Iranian Mahmoud Ahmadinejad when he spoke of Holocaust denial in the name of Iran.

—DREW AGUILAR

This analysis led to further reading on Iranian history and especially on the diversity within Iran, a diversity that contradicted the monolithic stereotype he saw reflected in the *Times* coverage. At the end of his investigation, this student had not only learned a great deal about Iran; he had also thought about how narratives about entire countries can build up in our minds almost without our even noticing—and he was able to bring this new understanding to his reading of Satrapi's famous graphic novel as well. Best of all, he was well prepared to write essays in both of his classes that drew on the knowledge he had gained and on his growing understanding of how cultural stereotypes get established and reinforced.

Act!

Taking time to stop, look, listen, think, and write can bring us only so far. Sooner or later we need to roll up our sleeves and do something—to take some kind of action. When 17-year-old Trayvon Brown, who had organized a protest following the death of George Floyd, found a burning cross propped up on the lawn of his home in Monroe, Virginia, he was so shocked and taken aback that the event stopped him in his tracks. What deeply held beliefs could have propelled such a hateful and violent attack? As he looked at the situation in his community and listened to those on both sides of the debate surrounding police violence, Brown came to the conclusion that he had to do something—to lead a second protest. Here's what he said to those who joined him as the protest began:

Stand up, speak up, and speak out!
—JOHN LEWIS

> This is your chance, young people. Y'all complain about the laws? Go change those laws. You don't have to destroy anything. You don't have to tear down statues.
>
> —TRAYVON BROWN

As news of that second protest march had spread, counterprotesters were there as well, some waving Confederate flags, some armed. Law enforcement officials gathered to try to keep the two sides apart, as those on both sides began shouting angrily at each other. With tensions at a boiling point, Brown took another action: he knelt, raised his arm, and began shouting "I love you" to those on the other side. He was soon joined by the rest of the protesters, who did the same—thus defusing the situation and leading to a peaceful conclusion to the march.

Remember the Golden Rule

Trayvon Brown's actions call to mind the old Golden Rule, of "doing unto others as you would have them do unto you." Showing respect for others and for their views will encourage them to reciprocate, and in so doing will pave the way for establishing common ground that can move a conversation forward. And doing so is pretty simple, even if sometimes challenging: you demonstrate respect when you take other people's feelings and thoughts seriouly, when you acknowledge them as equals in conversation, when you listen to what they say carefully and with an open mind, and when you are truthful.

Such respect is especially necessary now, in the summer of 2020, as the coronavirus pandemic takes hundreds of thousands of lives, as millions of Americans are out of work and suffering, and as the deep inequities built into our institutions are more visible and disturbing than ever. Such times call for us to think beyond our individual selves, to recognize that we are all in this together, and to take action not just for ourselves but for the greater good of all. In short, we need to focus less on "I" and more on "we," knowing that in helping—and respecting—others we will in the long run be helping everyone.

When "I" is replaced with "we," even illness becomes wellness.
—MALCOLM X

Respect, in other words, is the very opposite of the kind of trolling, cyberbullying, and harassment that often takes place online—actions that seek to disrupt, to attack, to sow discontent and distrust and even fear. This is not to say that you cannot disagree with someone; just keep in mind that you can disagree without being disagreeable, much less frightening or disruptive.

We all need, then, to stop, look, and listen—to step back and think hard about how we communicate with others, about how well and how respectfully we listen. But we can't stop there. Eventually, we will need to engage with the issues most important to us and with other people, including those who do not share our views as well as those who do.

Write!

This kind of engagement will often involve writing. Taking notes and trying to capture in words what you've heard someone say, for example, is a very good way to help understand it better, and to remember it. And just think of the role that writing plays in the courses you're taking, from preparing reports to analyzing issues, summarizing and synthesizing information drawn from many sources, developing a script to use in an important oral presentation, and reflecting on the ideas and perspectives of others—all writing. And don't be surprised if you find that as you write, your thinking gets sharper, your ideas more focused, your message more clear: you are, in fact, writing yourself into the role of a college student. Then, as you move toward your major, absorbing its vocabulary and methods and style, you are writing yourself into that discipline, becoming a member of its intellectual community.

> How can I know what I think till I see what I say?
>
> —E. M. FORSTER

And then there's the role that writing plays well beyond the classroom. Think about posters and signs proclaiming No Justice, No Peace! Make America Great Again! I Can't Breathe! Vote!—these are all words, yes, but they are actions as well. Think about the writing you do on social media—*Instagram*, *Facebook*, and *Twitter* all connect you to friends and family as well as to people you might never otherwise know. Podcasts and *YouTube* videos—these allow you to put the power of your spoken voice and your personality to work in getting your messages across.

No matter what kinds of writing you do, you'll be aiming to reach particular audiences in particular contexts and for particular reasons. That means you'll be listening and thinking hard about what others say. Thus moving purposely from listening to thinking, and from thinking to writing, is a kind of dance that good communication calls for—and the more we practice that dance, the better we will get.

Stopping, looking, listening, thinking, taking action. None of the steps in this dance are easy or simple, especially in times as contentious as those we face today. But we need to try—and to recognize that our differences are some of our most valuable assets. We won't know about those differences, however, without being open to them, without opening ourselves to the thoughts and ideas and beliefs of others. This book is one attempt to begin and sustain such conversations. So—let's talk!

REFLECT! Fox News host **Laura Ingraham** once famously criticized **LeBron James** for commenting on political issues, saying that he should "shut up and dribble." Her comment got instant blowback from many, including James and other athletes, who posted on social media with the hashtag #wewillnotshutupanddribble. Ingraham and James are coming from completely different places in terms of their personal beliefs and ideologies, but how might this exchange have gone differently had they at least attempted a face-to-face conversation—and first taken time to stop, look, listen, and think?

Let's Talk...

WITH READINGS

1 Listening

LISTENING TO OTHERS, ESPECIALLY THOSE WITH WHOM
WE DISAGREE, TESTS OUR OWN IDEAS AND BELIEFS.
IT FORCES US TO RECOGNIZE, WITH HUMILITY,
THAT WE DON'T HAVE A MONOPOLY ON THE TRUTH.

—JANET YELLEN

IF YOU WANT TO BE LISTENED TO,
YOU SHOULD PUT IN TIME LISTENING.

—MARGE PIERCY

Why would a book titled *Let's Talk* begin with a chapter on listening? That's a good question, and it has an important answer. Talking is (at least) a two-way street: when you talk, you're talking *to* someone, and you want that someone to listen, to hear what you're saying, whether it's calling a clinic to make a doctor's appointment or talking confidentially with your best friend about whether to break off a relationship. You want—and sometimes need—to be listened to. You can probably think of times when you've felt like you *weren't* being listened to, or when the person you were talking with was only halfway listening.

4

Elizabeth MacGregor certainly has such memories. As the first person in her family—and one of only two students in her high school graduating class—to go to college, she remembers feeling insecure when she first arrived at college. "Do I really belong here?" she wondered. Faced with some daunting assignments in the first weeks of fall term, she asked for advice from an older student in her dorm. That person was sympathetic, but he was checking email and was somewhat distracted, responding "don't worry; you'll be fine." She also went to her history instructor's office hours, hoping to get some guidance for doing the first assignment. He merely encouraged her to "start on the assignment early" and wished her luck; he didn't seem to hear what she was really asking for, which was concrete advice on how to address the assignment. Reflecting on these experiences two years later, MacGregor said, "They were well meaning, but they just weren't listening to me."

Or you may be part of a group that feels ignored or not listened to. After the 2018 shootings at Marjory Stoneman Douglas High School in Parkland, Florida, when a group of predominantly white students started a protest that went viral and led to a huge rally against gun violence, a "march for our lives," students of color at that school pointed out that they'd been talking persistently about gun violence

Students at
Marjory Stoneman
Douglas High School.

Listening is the ultimate sign of respect. What you say when you listen says more than any words.

—THOMAS FRIEDMAN

for years and years—but no one was listening to them. Tyah-Amoy Roberts made this point, saying that students of color had "never seen this kind of support" and that they didn't feel as if their voices were "valued as much as those of our white counterparts." In other words, they were speaking up—but no one was listening.

Or sometimes you may be the one who is not listening. During the 2019 NBA finals, Draymond Green—known for his constant chatter on and off the court—decided he'd been doing too much talking and not enough listening. In particular, he decided to listen to his mother and his fiancée, both of whom told him he needed to learn some self-discipline and especially to stop screaming at the referees. As Green put it:

> Sometimes I'm not mindful, and I'll get a tech and that will just kill the energy of our team. I've really been focused and locked in on that, and I realized I got to a point where I was doing more crying than playing. I'm sure it was disgusting to watch, because I felt disgusting playing that way.
>
> —DRAYMOND GREEN

Draymond Green, frustrated by getting a tech for yelling.

Sometimes we all need to take a good look at our behavior to see if we are doing more talking than listening.

Certainly, careful listening has been in short supply in the last few years, as the divisions in our society have grown deeper and more entrenched and as many people have retreated into their own bubbles or echo chambers where they hear only what they already agree with—and have stopped listening to anyone else. Yet if we don't learn to listen openly and carefully to one another, including those whose views differ from our own, we can't hope to gain understanding and insight into their motivations, hopes, and goals. So that's why this book opens with a chapter calling on you to start by listening and calling on all of us to pay attention to the words of others—and be willing to *hear* what they say.

Robin Kimmerer opens her essay with a sentence about listening. You may be interested in what exactly she's listening to. Find out on p. 731.

Think of the times when you have most needed someone to listen—openly and carefully and intently—to something you needed to say: when you were talking through a serious conflict with a family member, for instance, or when you were trying to explain to a professor something you didn't understand about a complex topic. On occasions like these, you want the person you're addressing to really listen—to look up from what they're doing and pay attention to what you're saying. And in return, you'll want to reciprocate, listening—really listening—to what others are saying. At times you may be tempted to jump into a conversation and say what you think; but think again: it's often much more effective to find out what others think before doing so.

Whether you're writing an essay or participating in a face-to-face discussion, you'll need to engage with other people's views. In order to do so, you'll need to listen to what they say—and even to repeat what they say as a way of making sure you've understood before responding with what *you* want to say. This kind of listening is what rhetorician Krista Ratcliffe dubs RHETORICAL LISTENING—opening yourself to the thoughts of others and making the effort not only to hear their words but to take those words in and fully understand them. It means paying attention to what others say as a way of establishing

We have two ears and one mouth so we can listen twice as much as we speak.

—EPICTETUS

See p. 31 for advice on getting to know people different from you.

good will and acknowledging the importance of their views. And yes, it means taking seriously and engaging with views that differ, sometimes radically, from your own.

Rhetorical listening is what middle school teacher Julia Blount asked for in a *Facebook* post following the 2015 riots in Baltimore after the death of Freddie Gray, who suffered fatal spinal injuries while in police custody:

> Every comment or post I have read today voicing some version of disdain for the people of Baltimore—"I can't understand" or "they're destroying their own community"—tells me that many of you are not listening. I am not asking you to condone or agree with violence. I just need you to listen. . . .
>
> —JULIA BLOUNT, "Dear White *Facebook* Friends:
> I Need You to Respect What Black America Is Feeling Right Now."

Turn to p. 539 to see how one writer's thinking changed once he started paying attention—listening—to views different from his own.

Blount went on to call for her friends to expose themselves to unfamiliar perspectives, and to engage in conversation—in other words, to listen rhetorically. Learning to listen this way takes time and attention and practice, but it is a skill you can develop and one that will pay off in better and more effective communication. There aren't any magic bullets for becoming a good listener, but here are some tips that should put you on your way to achieving that goal.

- **Listen with an open mind** and without an agenda. Listen to learn, and with the goal of understanding.
- **Let others speak** before stating your own opinions or asking questions. And be sure that any questions you ask are respectful, not judgmental. Ask questions that are open-ended ("What do you think we should do?") or that clarify, not challenge ("Are you saying—?" rather than "Don't you think—?").

- **Turn off your phone**, and don't be checking email. Let the other person have your full attention.
- **Listen with empathy** to try to see things from the other person's point of view. Make it a goal to understand their perspective, where they're coming from. Be on the lookout for COMMON GROUND, things you can agree on: "I can see where you're coming from."
- **Pay attention to body language** and TONE of voice— yours and theirs. These can give you insight into the message the other person is trying to send. And maintain a respectful tone and posture yourself: lean in, nod your head.
- **Don't interrupt**, and don't be thinking about what you're going to say in response.
- **Summarize** what the other person says to make sure you understand what they're saying.
- **Offer affirmation** when possible: "Good point; I hadn't thought of that."
- **Make it a point to listen to people whose views differ from yours**—and whenever possible, talk with them in person. It's much harder to be dismissive (or mean-spirited, as so often happens online) when you're speaking face-to-face.

What's listening got to do with writing?

That's a good question, and it has a good answer: whatever you're writing, you need to start by doing your homework—reading up on your topic, doing research, maybe conducting some interviews. That means listening.

And whatever your topic, it's unlikely that you'll be the first to write about it. In fact, when it comes to academic writing, what you write will usually respond to something that others have already said

Writing doesn't begin when you sit down to write. It's a way of being in the world, and its essence is paying attention.
—JULIA ALVAREZ

about your topic: they say this, you think that. So after introducing your topic, one effective way to proceed is to SUMMARIZE, QUOTE, or PARAPHRASE what other credible sources have said about your topic and then to present your ideas as a response. And that means listening carefully to what's already been said, not just launching into what you have to say.

So writing is actually a way of participating in a larger conversation, of engaging with the ideas of others. When you quote or summarize or paraphrase sources, you're weaving their words or ideas in with yours—and hopefully responding to them in some way. You can't do that unless you've listened closely to those words and ideas.

Like writing, reading demands listening, really hearing what an author has to say. And if you read rhetorically, not just to absorb information but also to question and respond to the text, you are entering into a dialogue with the author. That too starts with listening.

Listening to views that differ from yours

Fortunately, there are now a number of organizations that provide guidance for listening respectfully and with an open mind, along with opportunities to meet up with people who think differently than you do.

One such organization is the Listen First Project, founded by Pearce Godwin with the goal of "mend[ing] the frayed fabric of America by bridging divides one conversation at a time." Listen First has launched the National Conversation Project, which helps people start new conversations, ones dedicated to moving "from *us vs. them* to *me and you*." In 2018, hundreds of schools, libraries, faith communities, and other groups hosted conversations "grounded in a commitment to 'listen first to understand.'" Go to listenfirstproject.org or www.nationalconversationproject.org if you're interested in joining or hosting such a conversation.

When you look at election results, the color red doesn't necessarily mean white power. It can also mean there are people who want the world to pay attention to them.
—TREVOR NOAH

A Listen First poster at a rally during the 2016 presidential election.

I hope you'll take the advice in this chapter to heart, seeking to understand those with whom you may disagree, and learning to become a better listener as you do.

REFLECT! Think of a time when you felt you were being ignored, or not listened to. Why were others not listening—or not listening well enough? Did you try to do something about that, to get them to hear you? If not, why not? Then think of a time when you yourself failed to really listen to someone else. What caused you not to listen carefully? What would you do differently if you could go back and re-live that encounter?

2 Thinking Rhetorically

THE ONLY REAL ALTERNATIVE TO WAR IS RHETORIC.

—WAYNE BOOTH

WE DIDN'T BURN DOWN ANY BUILDINGS. . . .
YOU CAN DO A LOT WITH A PEN AND PAD.

—ICE CUBE

Wayne Booth made the above statement at a conference of writing teachers held only months after 9/11, and it quickly drew a range of responses. Just what did Booth mean by this stark statement? How could rhetoric—usually thought of as the art, theory, and practice of persuasion—act as a counter to war?

A noted critic and scholar, Booth explored these questions throughout his long career, identifying rhetoric as an ethical art that begins with intense listening and that searches for mutual understanding and common ground as alternatives to violence and war. Put another way,

two of the most potent tools we have for persuasion are language—
and violence: when words fail us, violence often wins the day. Booth
sees the careful and ethical use of language as our best approach to
keeping violence and war at bay.

In the years since 9/11, Booth's words have echoed again and again
as warfare continues to erupt in Syria, Yemen, Afghanistan, and elsewhere. And in the United States, people have protested the deaths of
George Floyd, Breonna Taylor, and other Black people at the hands
of police. Protesters have held up signs saying "I Can't Breathe" and
"No Justice, No Peace," and "Black Lives Matter" has been written in
large yellow letters on streets in Washington, DC, and other cities.
And after way too many other such killings, protesters have taken to
social media as well, using similarly dramatic and memorable statements as rhetorical strategies that have captured and held the attention of people around the world.

Aerial view
of Fulton Street
in Brooklyn,
New York.

Rhetoric as an ethical art

Note that while Booth speaks of rhetoric as an "ethical" art (based on good intentions), rhetoric can also be used for unethical purposes (with bad or evil intent)—as Hitler and other dictators have done. In fact, rhetoric used in unethical ways can itself lead to violence. That's why the ancient Greek philosopher Aristotle cautioned that we need to understand rhetoric both to communicate our own ethical messages *and* to be able to recognize and resist unethical messages that others attempt to use against us. That's also why this book defines rhetoric as the practice of ETHICAL communication.

So how can you go about developing your own careful, ethical use of language? One short answer: by developing habits of mind that begin with listening and searching for understanding before deciding what you yourself think, and by thinking hard about your own beliefs before trying to persuade others to listen to and act on what you say. In other words, by learning to THINK RHETORICALLY.

Learning to think rhetorically can serve you well—at school, at work, even at home. After all, you'll need to communicate successfully with others in order to get things done in a responsible and ethical way. On the job, you and your coworkers might do this kind of thinking to revise a shift schedule so that every worker is treated fairly and no one is required to work double shifts. Or in your college courses, you'll surely encounter class discussions that call for rhetorical thinking—for listening closely and really thinking about what others say before saying what you think.

When a group of college students became aware of how little the temporary workers on their campus were paid, for example, they met with the workers and listened to gather information about the situation. They then mounted a campaign using flyers, social media, speeches, and sit-ins—in other words, using the available means of persuasion—to win attention and convince the administration to raise the workers' pay. These students were thinking and acting rhetorically—and doing so responsibly. Note that these students worked together, both with the workers and with one another. After all, none of us can manage such actions all by ourselves; we need to engage in conversation with others and listen hard to what they say. Perhaps that's what philosopher Kenneth Burke had in mind when he created his famous "parlor" metaphor:

> Imagine that you enter a parlor. You come late. When you arrive, others have long preceded you, and they are engaged in a heated discussion, a discussion too heated for them to pause and tell you exactly what it is about.... You listen for a while, until you decide that you have caught the tenor of the argument; then you put in your oar.
>
> —KENNETH BURKE

In this parable, each of us is the person arriving late to a room full of animated conversation; we don't understand what's going on. Yet instead of butting in or trying too quickly to get in on the conversation, we listen closely until we catch on to what people are saying. And *then* we join in, using language and rhetoric carefully to engage with others as we add our own voices to the conversation.

This book aims to teach you to think rhetorically:

- To listen to others carefully and respectfully
- To try to understand what they think, and why—and then to think hard about your own beliefs and where they come from
- To do these things before deciding what you yourself think and trying to persuade others to listen to what you say

Pay attention to what others are saying— and think about why

Thinking rhetorically begins with a willingness to hear the words of others with an open mind. It means paying attention to what others say before and even *as a way* of making your own contributions to a

> The simple act of paying attention can take you a long way.
> —KEANU REEVES

conversation. More than that, it means being open to the thoughts of others and making the effort not only to hear their words but also to take those words in and fully understand what they are saying. It means paying attention to what others say as a way of establishing good will and acknowledging the importance of their views. And most of all, it means engaging with views that differ from your own—and being open to what they say.

When you enter any conversation, whether at school, at work, or with friends, take the time to understand what's being said rather than rushing to a conclusion or a judgment. Listen carefully to what others are saying, and think about what motivates them: Where are they coming from?

Developing such habits of mind will be useful to you almost every day, whether you're participating in a class discussion, negotiating with friends over what movie to see, or thinking about a local ballot issue to decide how you'll vote. In each case, thinking rhetorically means being flexible, determined to seek out varying—and sometimes conflicting—points of view.

In ancient Rome, the great Roman statesman and orator Cicero argued that considering alternative POINTS OF VIEW and COUNTER-ARGUMENTS was key to making a successful argument, and it is just as important today. Even when you disagree with a point of view—perhaps especially when you disagree with it—force yourself to see the issue from the viewpoint of its advocates before you reject their

REFLECT! Blogger **Sean Blanda** warns that many of us gravitate on social media to those who think like we do, which often leads to the belief that we are right and that those with other worldviews are "dumb." He argues that we need to "make an honest effort to understand those who are not like us" and to remember that "we might be wrong." Look at some of your own posts. How many different perspectives do you see represented? What might you do to think—and listen—more rhetorically?

positions. Say you're skeptical that hydrogen fuel will be the solution to climate change, for example: don't reject the idea until you've thought hard about what those in favor of it say and carefully considered other possible solutions.

Consider the larger context

Thinking hard about the views of others also means considering the larger CONTEXT and how it shapes what they're saying. When you think rhetorically, you may need to do some research, to investigate whether there are any historical, political, or cultural factors that might account for where someone's beliefs are "coming from."

In analyzing the issue of gun rights, for instance, you would not merely consider your own thinking or read about what others think. In addition, you would look at the issue in a larger context by considering what the US Constitution says about gun ownership and how it's been interpreted over time, thinking about the broader political agendas of both those who advocate for and those who oppose stricter gun control, asking what the economic ramifications of adopting—or rejecting—new gun restrictions might be, and so on. In short, you would try to see the issue from as many different perspectives and in as broad a context as possible before formulating your own stance. And in writing about this issue, you'll draw on these sources—what others have said about the issue—to support your own position and to help you consider other positions.

Thinking rhetorically leads one sportswriter to defend Naomi Osaka and others for prioritizing their mental health. Read Jemele Hill's essay on p. 786.

What do you think, and why?

Examining all points of view on any issue will involve some tough thinking about your own STANCE—literally, where you yourself are coming from—and why you think as you do. Such thinking can help you define your stance or perhaps even lead you to change your mind; in either case, you stand to gain. Just as you need to think hard about the motivations of others, it's important to examine what's motivating you, asking yourself what influences in your life lead you to think as you do or to take certain positions.

Ibram X. Kendi offers an example. When a student from Ghana gave a "monologue" in class detailing negative and racist ideas about Black Americans, Professor Kendi provided data to counter his views, to no avail. After class, however, the discussion continued, with Kendi asking the student if he could name "some racist ideas the British say about Ghanaians." The student hesitated, but then came up with a list of such ideas, which he vehemently agreed were not true. Then Kendi returned to the student's earlier statements about Black Americans, asking him where he got those ideas. On reflection, the student said he got them from his family, friends, and his own observations. And where did he think those people get their ideas about Black Americans? "Probably American Whites," the student said.

> His mind seemed open, so I jumped on in. "So if African Americans went to Ghana, consumed British racist ideas about Ghanaians, and started expressing those ideas to Ghanaians . . . What would you think about that?"
>
> He smiled, surprising me. "I got it," he said, turning to walk out of the classroom.
>
> "Are you sure?" I said. He turned back to me. "Yes, sir. Thanks, Prof."
>
> —IBRAM X. KENDI, *How to Be an Antiracist*

Examining your own stance and motivation is equally important outside the classroom. Suppose you're urging fellow members of a campus group to lobby for a rigorous set of procedures to deal with accusations of sexual harassment. On one level, you're alarmed by the statistics showing a steep increase in cases of rape on college campuses, and you want to do something about it. But when you think a bit more, you begin to consider the rights of those who stand accused. Maybe a close friend has been a victim of sexual harassment—and maybe another friend has been falsely accused.

You begin to realize that the issue of sexual harassment on campus is more complex than you thought. Your commitment to reduce sexual violence still holds, but thinking rhetorically has led you to a more nuanced understanding of what it means to have fairness and justice for all.

Find out what's been said about your topic

Rhetorical thinking calls on you to do some homework, to find out everything you can about what's been said about your topic, to ANALYZE what you find, and then to use that information to inform your own ideas. In other words, you want your own thinking to be well informed and to reflect more than just your own opinion.

To take an everyday example, you should do some pretty serious thinking when deciding on a major purchase, such as a new laptop. You'll want to begin by considering the purchase in the larger context of your life. Why do you need a new laptop right now? If you're considering buying the newest model, is it for practical reasons or just because it seems likely to be the best? Do you want it in part as a status symbol? If you're concerned about the environment, how will you dispose of your current laptop? Analyzing your specific motivations and purposes this way can guide you in drawing up a list of laptops to consider.

Then you'll need to do some RESEARCH, checking out product reports and reviews. Don't just trust the information provided by the company that manufactures and sells the laptops you're considering. Instead, you should consult multiple sources and check them against one another.

You'll also want to consider your findings in light of your priorities. Cost, for instance, may not be as high on your priority list as something else. Such careful thinking will help you come to a sound decision, and then explain it to others. If your parents are helping you buy the laptop, you'll want to consider what they might think, and to anticipate questions they may ask.

You'll also need to recognize and analyze how various rhetorical strategies work to persuade you. You may have been won over by a funny Apple commercial you saw on Super Bowl Sunday. But what made that ad so memorable? To answer that question, you'll need to study it closely, determining just what qualities—a clever script? memorable music? celebrity actors? cute animals? a provocative message?—made the ad so persuasive. Once you've determined that, you'll want to consider whether the laptop will actually live up to the advertiser's promises. This is the kind of research and analysis you will do when you engage in rhetorical thinking.

Give credit

Part of engaging with what others have thought and said is to give credit where credit is due. Acknowledging the work of others will show that you've done your homework and that you want to credit those who have influenced you. The great physicist Isaac Newton famously and graciously gave credit when he wrote to his rival Robert Hooke in 1676, saying:

> You have added much in several ways.... If I have seen a little further it is by standing on the shoulders of giants.
>
> —ISAAC NEWTON

In this letter, Newton acknowledges the work of Hooke before saying, with a fair amount of modesty, that his own contributions were made possible by Hooke and others. In doing so, he is thinking—and acting—rhetorically.

You can give credit informally, as Newton does in this letter, or you can do so formally with a full CITATION and DOCUMENTATION. Which method you choose will depend on your purpose, genre, and the rest of your RHETORICAL SITUATION. Academic writing, for instance, usually requires documentation, but if you're writing for a personal blog, you might embed a link that connects to a work you've cited—or simply give an informal shout-out to a friend who contributed to your thinking. In each case, you'll want to be specific about what words or ideas you've drawn from others, and to be sure it's clear what they say and what you're saying. Such care in crediting your sources contributes to your credibility—and is an important part of ethical, rhetorical thinking.

Be imaginative

Remember that intuition and imagination can often lead to great insights. While you want to think carefully and analytically, don't be afraid to take chances. A little imagination can lead you to new ideas about a topic you're studying and about how to approach it in a way that will interest others. Such insights can often pay off big-time. One student athlete was interested in how the mass media covered the Olympics, and he began doing research on the coverage in *Sports Illustrated* from different periods. So far, so good: he found plenty of information for an essay showing that the magazine had been a major promoter of the Olympics.

While looking through old issues of *Sports Illustrated*, however, he kept feeling that something he was seeing in the early issues was different from current issues . . . though he couldn't quite articulate what. This hunch led him to make an imaginative leap, to study that difference even though it was beyond the topic he had set out to examine. On closer inspection, he found that over the decades *Sports Illustrated* had slowly but surely moved from focusing on teams to depicting only individual stars.

This discovery led him to make an argument he would never have made had he not followed his creative hunch—that the evolution of sports from a focus on the team to a focus on individual stars is reflected in the pages of *Sports Illustrated*. It also helped him write a much more interesting—and more persuasive—essay, one that captured the attention not only of his instructor and classmates but also of a local sports newsmagazine, which reprinted his

A hunch is creativity trying to tell you something.
—FRANK CAPRA

The cover on the left shows the 1980 US ice hockey team's "miracle on ice" victory over the USSR; the one on the right shows the 2018 MVP in the Stanley Cup playoffs.

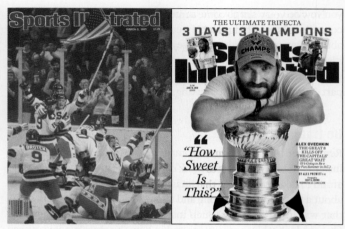

essay. Like this student, you can benefit by using your imagination and listening to your intuition. You just might stumble on something exciting.

REFLECT! Think about a topic you'd like to explore or a question you'd like to answer. You could do some research . . . or you could begin by thinking *beyond* the box. Draw a picture that captures your topic, or compose a brief rap, or create a meme. If you made a movie about your topic, what would the title be—and who would star in it? In other words, use your imagination!

Put in your oar

So rhetorical thinking offers a toolkit of strategies for entering a conversation, strategies that will help you understand the situation and "put in your oar" and make your voice count. Whatever you say, give some thought to how you want to present yourself and how you can best appeal to your audience. Following are some tips that can help.

- How do you want to come across—as thoughtful? serious? curious? something else?
- What can you do to represent yourself as knowledgeable and CREDIBLE?
- What can you do to show respect for your AUDIENCE?
- How can you show that you have your audience's best interests at heart?

Imagine you want to create a campus food pantry and are preparing a presentation for your meeting with the dean and the director of food services. You'll want to come across as knowledgeable and well informed, to show them that you've done your homework. You'll need to present evidence of food insecurity on your campus and of what other colleges have done—statistics about how many students often go hungry, anecdotes about students you know, examples of food pantries that similar schools have created, and so on. You might want to put this information on a PowerPoint slide to reinforce the points you are making.

You'll also want to be careful to demonstrate respect for your audience. That means thanking them for meeting with you, being well prepared, and keeping to the time allotted for the meeting. And you'll want to show that you're aware of the stakes involved and to acknowledge that they have many other issues to deal with. Finally, you'll want to listen carefully to what they say, and with an open mind.

In other words, you'll want to think and act rhetorically—and to use language that shows you have the best interests of the college and its students in mind. You might say you "wish to suggest" that "opening a food pantry is one way to help students who are food insecure"—rather than expecting your audience to come up with a solution and insisting, perhaps too strongly, that something "needs to be done right now." This is not to say that you should underestimate the problem; but better to focus on your proposed solution, on how the college can help students who are food insecure.

This kind of rhetorical thinking will go a long way toward making sure you will be listened to and taken seriously.

As the examples in this chapter illustrate, rhetorical thinking involves certain habits of mind that can and should lead to something—often to an action, to making something happen. And when it comes to taking action, those who think rhetorically are in a very strong position. They have listened attentively, engaged with the words and ideas of others, viewed their topic from many alternative perspectives, and done their homework. This kind of rhetorical thinking will set you up to contribute your own ideas—and will increase the likelihood that your ideas will be heard and will inspire real action.

Indeed, the ability to think rhetorically is of great importance in today's global world, as professors Gerald Graff and Cathy Birkenstein explain:

> The ability to enter complex, many-sided conversations has taken on a special urgency in today's diverse, post-9/11 world, where the future for all of us may depend on our ability to put ourselves in the shoes of those who think very differently from us. Listening carefully to others, including those who disagree with us, and then engaging with them thoughtfully and respectfully . . . can help us see beyond our own pet beliefs, which may not be shared by everyone. The mere act of acknowledging that someone might disagree with us may not seem like a way to change the world; but it does have the potential to jog us out of our comfort zones, to get us thinking critically about our own beliefs, and perhaps even to change our minds.
>
> —GERALD GRAFF and CATHY BIRKENSTEIN,
> *"They Say / I Say": The Moves That Matter in Academic Writing*

In the long run, if enough of us learn to think rhetorically, we just might achieve Wayne Booth's goal—to use words (and images) in thoughtful and constructive ways as an alternative to violence and war.

REFLECT! Spend a half hour or so looking back over the above tips for thinking rhetorically, and then make some notes about how many of those tips you currently follow—and to what effect.

THINK ABOUT YOUR OWN RHETORICAL SITUATION

Whatever you're writing—a text to a friend, a job application, an essay exam, a script for a presentation—will call for you to consider your rhetorical situation: your *purpose* for writing, your *stance* toward your topic, the *audience* you want to reach, a *genre* and *medium* for doing so. In addition, you'll want to consider the larger *context*, about both the topic and what you'll need to know to write well about it. These are all things to think about early in the process of writing. The following guidelines will help you do so:

What is your purpose for writing, and what motivates you to do so?

What drives you to write? In college, it may be an assignment. Even then it's likely that you'll write about something that matters, that grabs your attention. But beyond an explicit assignment, what gives you the itch to write? Most likely it will be some issue you're passionate about, and that inspires you to speak up, to add your voice to the conversation. It's worth taking time to explore your purposes for writing: Do you want to explain a topic, to help others understand it? To persuade someone to agree with your position on an issue? To fulfill an assignment? To entertain, or bring a smile to those who read what you write? Whatever your purpose, it affects your choice of genre, medium, design, and content: the material needed to entertain is not the same as that needed to explain a theory or to persuade an audience to support a certain cause. So your purpose becomes your guiding light, one that helps you stay on track.

What audience do you want to reach?

Before starting to write, take some time to think about your potential audiences. Today, that audience might be as narrow as your instructor or as wide as anyone with access to the internet; but the more you can know about who you're writing to, the better chance you have of connecting with them. If your audience is an instructor, for instance, you know that they value clarity, so you should choose your words carefully and make sure that your points are clear. If you're tweeting to friends, however, you can probably assume that they want information about you and your thoughts—and that they won't hold you to a high bar in terms of correctness or precision. Here are some questions for thinking about your audience:

- What do you and your AUDIENCE have in common? Where do you differ?

- What values do they hold, and what kinds of EVIDENCE will they accept? How can you build on any COMMON GROUND you share with them and appeal to their values?

- What do they know about your topic, and how much background information will they need? Can you assume they'll be interested in what you say—and if not, how can you get them interested?

- What do you want your audience to think or do in response to what you say—take your ideas seriously? Take some kind of action?

If your audience is largely unknown, be careful not to assume that they think as you do, value what you value, or have the same cultural and linguistic background as you do. For these audiences, best to take a calm and respectful stance, hoping that they will respond to you in the same way.

What is your stance on your topic, and what do you want to say about it?

Think of stance as your attitude toward the topic. If your topic is one about which you have some depth of knowledge, you may take an authoritative stance: you've done your homework and know what you're talking about. Or you might take a reporter's stance, laying out information you've researched so that others can understand it. Or your stance may be that of a critic who analyzes a text and raises questions about it. On other occasions, you may take up the stance of an advocate, a skeptic, even a cheerleader for an issue you're passionate about. In each case, your stance will guide the TONE you adopt in your writing: whether passionate, objective, curious, outraged, or something else, you'll want to make sure that it reflects your stance and is appropriate to your AUDIENCE and PURPOSE.

What genre(s) will you use?

Academic genres include many of the assignments you regularly receive: REPORTS, ANALYSES, close readings, ANNOTATED BIBLIOGRAPHIES, research-based ARGUMENTS. All genres. In some cases, you may be assigned to write in a specific genre ("Write an argument related to the maker movement"). But if not, you'll need to decide which genre best matches your purpose, audience, and stance. Then you'll have to make sure that you understand the characteristic features of your chosen genre, including format.

What media will you use, and how will you design what you write?

Closely aligned to the genre you choose are questions of MEDIA and DESIGN. Do your purpose, stance, and audience call for a written print text, perhaps with illustrations? a password-protected website? an oral presentation with slides or handouts? Whether your medium is oral, print, or digital, you'll need to consider questions of design: what you want the "look" of your text to be—informal or formal, eye-catching or subdued, serious or humorous, and so on. What use of headings, fonts, color, or white space will help achieve your purpose? What VISUALS, video clips, or audio clips might enhance your text?

Consider context: What do you need to know?

Answering this question calls for taking an inventory of what you know about your issue topic. For an assignment that asks you to ANALYZE a text or image, you'll need the ability (and the time) to do a detailed close reading that will uphold your interpretation. For an ARGUMENT on Bollywood films, you might need to research the history of Bollywood, its rise in popularity, and what's already been said about it. For a presentation on the need for more lighting on campus to make it a safer place, you might conduct a survey of student opinion, carry out observations on poorly lit areas of campus, interview campus officials, or track changes to lighting over the years. In all these instances, you would also need to decide whether you need illustrations. Consider your answer to this question in context: How much time do you have to complete the project, and what sources will you need and find available in that time frame?

If you've thought about the questions in this chapter for considering your own rhetorical situation, you should have a pretty good grasp of the circumstances within which you write. It's important to recognize that your writing doesn't come out of nowhere but rather occurs in a particular time and place, in response to particular things others have thought and said, and in relation to those who will be receiving your message.

It's also important to recognize that the advice offered here is itself part of a particular context—of college writing in English-speaking countries. But writing and rhetoric differ across contexts and cultures. That's one more reason to analyze the contexts you're working in as well as the audience you're trying to reach.

Wherever you are, think of yourself as being at the center of an ongoing conversation, one in which what you have to say matters. Then start to write!

REFLECT! Look over something you've written, and think about the rhetorical situation in which you wrote it—your intended audience and purpose, the genre and medium, and so on. Choose one of those elements, and think about how well you addressed it. Then think about what you would have done differently if your rhetorical situation had been different—for example, if you'd written in a different genre or medium—and write a paragraph or two about how your writing would have been different, and why.

3 Engaging Respectfully with Others

LET US TALK WITH—NOT AT—EACH OTHER—
IN OUR HOMES, SCHOOLS, WORKPLACES, AND
PLACES OF WORSHIP.

—CONDOLEEZZA RICE

WHERE SOMETHING STANDS,
SOMETHING ELSE STANDS BESIDE IT.

—IGBO PROVERB

I n the late spring of 2017, Oprah Winfrey stood
before a cheering crowd of graduating students
at Agnes Scott College, urging them to learn
to engage respectfully with others. She told the
assembled crowd that "two weeks after the election
last year" she had invited a group of women voters—
half on the right and half on the left, politically—to
join her at a diner for "great croissants with jam."
But no one wanted to come, saying they'd "never
sat this close" to someone from the other side and
didn't want to be around them. Winfrey eventually
prevailed and brought the women together, even
though they came in "all tight and hardened." But
as she goes on to say in her speech, it worked.

Watch Oprah Winfrey's speech at letstalklibrary.com.

After two and a half hours . . . the women were sitting around the table, listening to each other's stories, hearing both sides, and by the end they were holding hands, exchanging emails and phone numbers, and singing "Reach Out and Touch." . . . Which means it's possible; it can happen. So I want you to work in your own way to change the world in respectful conversations with others. . . . And I want you to enter every situation aware of its context, open to hear the truths of others and most important open to letting the process of changing the world change you.

—OPRAH WINFREY, Agnes Scott College commencement address

You have probably encountered views that differ a great deal from your own in your college classes: after all, that's one good reason for going to college—to learn about people and cultures and places other than those you call home. And some of your instructors may have focused on how to engage in critical conversations without being belligerent or disrespectful. But consider this incident that took place some years ago in one writing class at Ohio State.

Students who were serving as peer reviewers were reading a narrative essay called "The Little Squirrel" in which the author described finding a "small, helpless squirrel" caught in a trap on his family farm. His descriptions of the squirrel were empathetic and emotional as he contemplated his choices: "What should I do now?" he asked. The peer reviewers, expecting him to free the little squirrel, were quite startled when he continued the essay by saying that with only a few seconds hesitation, he pulled out his gun and killed the squirrel. "How could you do that to a little squirrel?" two students demanded, one coming just short of calling him a murderer.

The author responded defensively and said he thought they were being "wimps." At this point, they weren't even talking about the essay anymore, until another student who'd been quietly observing the scene said, "Hold on now! This isn't getting us anywhere. We need to step back and give each other a little space—and a little respect." This intervention allowed the writer to say he thought he had made the ethical decision because the squirrel had a broken leg and wasn't going to survive. In his view, he had done the right thing. Giving him their attention enabled the group to understand his motives better. In addition, they noted that if the author had explained his rationale in the narrative, rather than arousing their empathy for the little squirrel, they might still disagree with his decision but wouldn't have been so horrified and antagonistic to him. In this case, paying respectful attention didn't lead to unanimous agreement, but it did lead to defusing a very contentious situation and to learning about differing views of responsibility and action.

The goal of this chapter is to encourage and guide you as you engage with others: respectfully listening to their stories, their truths—and contributing to a process that may, indeed, change the world. Here are some steps you can take to realize this goal.

Get to know people different from you

It's a commonplace today to point out that we often live and act in "silos," places where we encounter only people who think like we do, who hold the same values we do. Even though the internet has made the whole world available to us, we increasingly choose to interact only with like-minded people—online and in person. We operate in what some call "echo chambers," where we hear our views echoed back to us from every direction. It can be easy, and comforting, to think this is the real world—but it's not! Beyond your own bubble of posts and conversations lie countless others with different views and values.

So one of the big challenges we face today is finding ways to get out of our own echo chambers and make an effort to know people who take different positions, hold different values. But simply encountering people who think differently is just the start. Breaking out of our bubbles calls for making the effort to understand those different perspectives, to listen with empathy and an open mind, and to hear where others are literally coming from. As we see in the story Oprah Winfrey tells in her commencement address, even the first step is hard: she had to work to convince the women to simply meet one another, and then she had to persuade them to listen, as she says, with respect. Once they did, things changed: they realized that it's not as easy to dislike or dismiss someone when you're sitting face-to-face.

> To make sense of the world, look to those who see it differently.
> —*THE ATLANTIC*

That's certainly what one Canadian student found when she spent a semester in Washington, DC. She had expected the highlights of her semester to be visiting places like the Smithsonian museums or the Library of Congress, but her greatest experience, as she describes it in a blog post, turned out to be an "unexpected gift: While in DC, I became close, close friends with people I disagree with on almost everything." As she got to know these people, she found that they were

> funny, smart, and kind. We all really liked music. . . . We even lived together. We ate dinner together, every single night. So I couldn't look down on them. I couldn't even consider it. And when you can't look down on someone who fundamentally disagrees with you, when you're busy breaking bread, sharing your days, laughing about the weather . . . well.
>
> —SHAUNA VERT, "Making Friends Who Disagree with You (Is the Healthiest Thing in the World)"

During a conversation with one of her housemates, a deeply conservative Christian from Mississippi, Vert mentioned that she was "pro-choice," realizing as she did so that this was "dangerous territory." To her surprise, she met not resistance or rebuke but—curiosity:

She wanted to know more. Her curiosity fueled my curiosity, and we talked. We didn't argue—we debated gently, very gently. . . . We laughed at nuance, we self-deprecated, we trusted each other. And we liked each other. Before the conversation, and after the conversation. To recap: Left-wing Canadian meets Bible Belt Republican. Discusses controversial political issues for over an hour. Walks away with a new friend.

Read Shauna Vert's full blog post at letstalklibrary.com.

This kind of careful, responsible, respectful exchange seems particularly hard in today's highly polarized society, where anger and hate are fueled by incendiary messages coming from social media and highly partisan news organizations. Just finding people outside our silos to talk with can be hard. But, like Vert, some people have taken up the challenge and acted to find ways to bring people with different views together.

One group aiming to create conversation rather than conflict is the Living Room Conversations project, which offers guidelines for engaging in meaningful discussions on more than fifty specific topics—free speech on campus, the opportunity gap, and more. The founders want these conversations among people who disagree to "increase understanding, reveal common ground, and allow us to discuss possible solutions." Visit livingroomconversations.org to find the resources to start a "living room" conversation yourself.

The point is that it's worth making the time to find and engage with those who hold different ideas and values than you do. And this means becoming familiar with sources other people read, too. Get out of your comfort zone, and look beyond the sources you know and trust; look carefully at what "the other side" is reading. Sites like allsides.com that present views from left, right, and center can help. It's time to shut down the echo chambers, seek out people outside of our silos, and engage respectfully with others.

We may have all come on different ships, but we're in the same boat now.
—MARTIN LUTHER KING JR.

Practice empathy

How can you engage respectfully with someone whose political views you detest? See what an ethicist advises on p. 587.

Many of the examples above suggest the power of EMPATHY, the ability to share someone else's feelings. Dylan Marron is someone who directly addresses empathy and shows how it works. As the creator and host of several popular video series on controversial social issues, Marron has gained quite a bit of attention and, he says, "a lot of hate." Early on, he tried to ignore hateful Comments, but then he started to get interested and began visiting Commenter profiles to learn about the people writing them. Doing so, he said, led him to realize "there was a human on the other side of the screen"—and prompted him to call some of these people and talk with them on the phone. He shares these conversations on his podcast *Conversations with People Who Hate Me.*

In one of these talks, Marron learned that Josh, who in a Comment had called Marron a "moron" and said that being gay was a sin, had recently graduated from high school, so Marron asked him "how was high school for you?" Josh replied that "it was hell" and elaborated by saying that he'd been bullied by kids who made fun of him for being "bigger." Marron went on to share his own experiences of being bullied, and as the conversation progressed, empathy laid the groundwork that helped them relate to each other.

Dylan Marron, host of a podcast of conversations among people who disagree.

At the end of another conversation, a man who had called Marron a "talentless hack" reflected on the ubiquitous Comment fields where such statements often appear, saying that "the Comment sections are really a way to get your anger at the world out on random strangers"—an insight that made him "rethink the way I interact with people online." Marron's work shows that Comment sections are sometimes used to release anger—and often hate, the very opposite of the kind of empathy that can bring people together. More than that, his work demonstrates the power of practicing empathy and how it can help us to see one another as human, even in the most negative and nasty places.

In his 2018 TED Talk, Marron stresses the importance of empathy, noting, however, that "empathy is not endorsement" and doesn't require us to compromise our deeply held values but, rather, to acknowledge the views of "someone raised to think very differently" than we do. That's the power and the promise of practicing empathy.

Watch Dylan Marron's TED Talk and listen to his podcast at letstalklibrary.com.

Demonstrate respect

If you've never heard Aretha Franklin belt out the lyrics to "Respect," take time to look it up on *YouTube*. Franklin added two now-famous lines along with a chorus to Otis Redding's original song, transforming it into an anthem for all those who are demanding R-E-S-P-E-C-T.

Franklin's message is still a timely one today, when *dis*respect seems so common, especially among those who don't agree. But respect is a two-way street: if we need to stand up and ask for the respect of others, then we also need to respect them. Moreover, we need to invite (and deserve!) respect. Easy to say, but harder to do. So just how can you demonstrate respect for others?

- *Listen* with genuine interest and an open mind, and without interrupting or making snap judgments.
- *Be helpful* and cooperative.
- *Build bridges* instead of shutting others out.

Aretha Franklin onstage in 1968.

- ***Represent other people's views fairly*** and generously—and acknowledge their accomplishments whenever you can.
- ***Ask questions*** rather than issuing orders or challenges.
- ***Apologize*** if you say something you regret. We all make mistakes!
- ***Be sincere***, and remember to say "thank you."
- ***Be on time***: even that is a sign of respect.
- ***Do what you say you'll do***. Keep your promises.

This advice largely holds for writing as well as speaking. Whether online or in print, our written words will usually be more effective if they come across as sincere, cooperative, and fair—and if we acknowledge viewpoints other than our own and consider them evenhandedly. These acts help build bridges in our writing, connecting us to members of our audience, including those who may not agree with us on all things.

If you respect others in these ways, in both writing and speaking, it's more likely that you'll earn their respect in return. Remember that respect can engender respect in return and thus lead to common ground, compromise, and understanding. As the French philosopher Voltaire is reported to have said, "I may disapprove of what you say, but I will defend to the death your right to say it."

Search for common ground

Even children learn pretty early on that digging in to opposing positions doesn't usually get very far: "No you can't!" "Yes I can!" can go on forever, without getting anywhere. Rhetoricians in the ancient world understood this very well and thus argued that for conversations to progress, it's necessary to look for and establish some COMMON GROUND, no matter how small. If "No you can't!" moves on to "Well, you can't do that in this particular situation," then maybe the conversation can continue.

This was a strategy that members of a book group used when they were discussing Michelle Obama's *Becoming*. One member set off alarm bells when she said she was shocked by the glossy cover photo, showing the former First Lady with "one shoulder bare." Another member of the group responded, saying she was equally shocked that anyone would make a fuss about what's on the cover rather than focusing on what's inside the book—and went on to say she found the book "deeply moving." Conversation could have stopped right there, at an impasse. But then someone said, "Well, like it or not, it's a story well worth reading." That comment established some common ground they could all agree on—and the conversation continued.

In this case, the stakes were not high: all members of the group were friends, and whether or not they all liked the book, they liked and respected one another. But sometimes the stakes can be very high, and even potentially dangerous. That was certainly the case when Daryl Davis, a Black blues musician, decided to do some research on the history of the Ku Klux Klan, a white supremacist group that had terrorized—and lynched—Black people in the past. Davis's research led him to decide to try to meet with some Klansmen, and to listen to them and try to engage with what

> You like dogs? So do I.
>
> —TRISH HALL, *How to Persuade*

they said. He was well aware of the risks he was taking but persevered. Davis has written and lectured widely about these experiences (which eventually led over 200 members to leave the Klan), about the importance of finding common ground, and how the rest of us can go about doing so:

> Look for commonalities. You can find something in five minutes, even with your worst enemy. And build on those. Say I don't like you because you're white and I'm black. . . . And so our contention is based upon our races. But if you say "how do you feel about all these drugs on the street" and I say "I think the law needs to crack down on things that people can get addicted to very easily." . . . and you say " Well, yeah I agree with that." You might even tell me your son started dabbling in drugs. So now I see that you want what I want, that drugs are affecting your family the same way they affect my family. So now we're in agreement. Let's focus on that. And as we focus more and more and find more things in common, things we have in contrast, such as skin color, matter less and less.
>
> —DARYL DAVIS, "How to Argue"

We're in this boat together. We sink or swim together. And when there's a leak in the boat and people are at risk, it puts all of us at risk.

—SUSAN RICE

Davis reports that he was not always successful—there were some people he met with whom it was impossible to find common ground. Yet he urges us whenever possible to seek out areas of agreement and then areas of compromise, all the while listening carefully and respectfully to one another. And he reminds us that argument doesn't need to be abusive, insulting, or condescending—stances that usually only make things worse. But he notes as well that looking for areas of compromise doesn't mean giving in to ideas you know are not right. As Davis says, "You are going to hear things that you know are absolutely wrong. You will also hear opinions put out as facts." In such cases, he suggests offering facts or other EVIDENCE that disprove the opinion being put forward. Then, if the person still holds to the opinion, try saying something like "I believe you are wrong, but if you think you're right, then bring me the data."

Daryl Davis with Scott Shepherd. Because Davis was willing to listen, respect, and talk with him, Shepherd listened, respected, and talked with Davis, a process that led to his leaving the KKK.

Such a response invites the other person to bring information that may actually carry the conversation forward. So when you hear things you believe to be wrong, be careful to respond in a civil way, showing data that refutes what the other person says or asking them to show you evidence that *you* are wrong—with the hope of continuing the conversation based on data and evidence rather than mere opinion.

If you sense danger. It's important to remember that some situations may not allow for you to engage with those who disagree vehemently with you—or who perhaps even threaten you. Some social media threads are so hateful and toxic that you'd be wise *not* to engage in the discussion. Remember as well that in the case of clearly dangerous exchanges, simply not engaging isn't enough, especially if the discussion is one that could lead to violence. In such cases, you must remove yourself from the situation as quickly as possible, and then alert the police or a faculty member—or both.

Souad Kirama, who is Muslim, described being confronted by teenage girls in New York who screamed curses and charges of "terrorist" at her, definitely targeting and endangering her. Such a situation allows for little or no possibility for discussion. Kirama had very little choice then but to get to safety, and quickly.

So if you encounter a situation in which all the empathy and efforts to find common ground you can think of fail to work, remember: your own physical safety is paramount.

REFLECT! Some would say it's pointless or even wrong to try to find common ground with people whose views they find hateful or dangerous. **Daryl Davis** would probably disagree. Based on your own experiences, what do you think—and why?

Invite response

Note that all the examples we've provided in this chapter feature dialogue and conversation; the road to understanding and change is never a one-way street. That's why long harangues or speeches—monologues—often have little effect on anyone who doesn't already agree with you. But as Dylan Marron discovered, tuning out is a lot harder in "live" conversations—face-to-face or on the phone. So if you want to engage successfully with people who think differently from you, then inviting them to respond, to join the conversation, is a good way forward. To invite response, you have to make time for it. Rather than rushing forward, hogging the air space, or talking over others, make a space for them to chime in: pause, make eye contact, even ask for response directly—"So how do you feel about what I've just said?"

You can invite response to your writing as well as to your spoken words. Especially online, you can turn on Commenting features and ask explicitly for responses to tweets or social media posts—and then respond (respectfully) to those who leave Comments for you. In doing so, you show that you value what others think and that you really want to hear and understand their views.

Join the conversation: collaborate! engage! participate!

Especially in times of such deep societal divisions, it may be tempting to retreat, to put our heads in the sand and hope that somehow things will get better. But don't give in to that temptation. Your voice is important, your thoughts are important, and you can best make them heard if you engage with other people. That may mean working with groups of like-minded people to speak out—for or against—contentious social issues such as immigration, guns, or environmental protections. That kind of civic engagement and participation is important in a democracy.

We cannot do democracy without a heavy dose of civility.

—MIKE PENCE

But there are smaller ways, too, like looking beyond those who think as you do, collaborating with them, listening to them, understanding their reasons for thinking as they do—and then searching for a shared goal you can work toward together. As a country, as a world, we have a lot riding on being able to reach across barriers and work together for the common good and to keep on trying even in the most difficult circumstances. And as writers, readers, and thinkers, we all have much to offer in this endeavor. So let's get going!

REFLECT! "Throughout history, generalizations have been made about 'other people,' but the only true generalization you can say about other people is that they are not you. They have done different things than you have. They were raised differently, maybe, or they have seen or heard things, perhaps, about which you don't know. They have different thoughts. Listen to them, and you may find out what everyone is arguing about." That's what **Lemony Snicket** has to say about "other people." Think about your own experiences interacting with people who think differently from you. How much listening have you done, and how much talking? Have you been satisfied with the results? What might you try to do differently next time?

4 Developing Academic Habits of Mind

YOU CAN'T BE AFRAID TO FAIL.
IT'S THE ONLY WAY YOU SUCCEED—
AND YOU'RE NOT GOING TO SUCCEED ALL THE TIME.

—LeBRON JAMES

JUST TRY NEW THINGS. DON'T BE AFRAID.
STEP OUT OF YOUR OWN COMFORT ZONE AND SOAR,
ALL RIGHT?

—MICHELLE OBAMA

Have you given some thought to what exactly you want to accomplish in college? What do you want to learn, but more than that: What do you hope to gain from your time in college? When a group of Howard University students asked Michelle Obama what she got from her college experience, she could hardly contain herself. "College did everything for me," she said. And then she offered some advice, saying that going to college "opens up a world of opportunity" and urging them to be open to trying new things, to move out of their comfort zones in order to "soar." That's pretty darned good advice. And it turns out that a nationwide group of writing teachers have figured out some more detailed advice—and identified several habits of mind that are essential for that kind of success in college. This chapter provides guidelines for developing ten habits of mind as you travel the path toward being an active, curious, and engaged reader, writer, and thinker.

Be curious

Inquire, investigate, ask questions. Poke and pry until you find answers. Explore the college catalog, looking for courses you *want* to take, even if they're not required. If you're assigned to do reseach, don't think of it just as an assignment you've got to "get done." Take it as an opportunity to learn something that you don't already know. And do the same with any writing assignments. Whatever position you take in an essay, find out about other POSITIONS—and take them seriously. Be curious about what others think: they just might change your mind. You can practice curiosity by asking questions: What? What *if*? Why? Why *not*? Who? How? Where? When?

Two students at Ohio State were tired of walking fifteen minutes through rain and snow from the parking lot to class and wondered why student parking was outdoors rather than in a garage. And why was it so far from the classrooms? Could it be located any closer, and in a garage? They were curious about who makes such decisions and whether students are ever consulted—and so they drafted an op-ed for the student newspaper raising their concerns.

Be open to new ideas

You're sure to encounter all kinds of new ideas in college, and new perspectives. In class or elsewhere, you'll have occasion to discuss ideas with others, including people whose views differ from yours. Make it a goal to understand their views, to try to see the world from their perspective. Ask questions, and be interested in what they say. Resist the temptation to respond too quickly with your own opinions. Remember that they just might be right. And even if they aren't, they'll get you thinking. New ideas do that.

The writing and research you'll do will be all about ideas. Here too you'll need to start by seeking out multiple positions on your topic—and to do so before even thinking about where you stand. What you don't want to do is to start with an idea you already have and simply look for sources that support that idea; you'll never learn anything new if you do that. Seek out ideas and viewpoints that differ from yours. In a campus discussion about anti-racism, for example, be sure to examine your own assumptions and biases and try to put yourself in the position of people with different perspectives—a student from Kenya or Brazil, a descendant of Japanese grandparents who were incarcerated during World War II, a victim of police violence. They'll all have different viewpoints, ones that should be part of the discussion.

Engage

Grapple with ideas: focus. To really focus on something—reading, writing, listening to a lecture, whatever—you need to clear your mind of everything else and pay attention to what you're doing, 100 percent. Turn off your monitor; stop checking email or *Twitter*. ANNOTATING as you read can help you engage with the text: underline key points, scribble questions in the margins. SUMMARIZING can help you understand and remember a difficult or complex text.

If you're in a class that doesn't engage your interest, look for an angle that does. That's what one student did in a physics for nonmajors course. She found physics hard, and abstract—and boring. Then one day her instructor mentioned the physics of *Angry Birds*. That was one of her favorite video games, and calculating acceleration and velocity became much less abstract when it helped her launch the birds. Soon she was knocking over the pig like a champ—and finally enjoying physics.

Be creative

Explore new ideas, try out new methods, experiment with new approaches. Play around with ideas, and see where they take you. Try

Angry Birds.

BRAINSTORMING and **FREEWRITING**. If you're struggling to write an essay, for instance, try expressing your ideas in a different **MEDIUM**. One of my students was taking a course on ancient religious texts, primarily to fulfill a requirement, and when he was assigned to read the Samson and Delilah story in different religious traditions, he used his keen interest in comics to create a graphic narrative of his favorite version. His creative approach to the assignment made it one that he was excited about.

If you think about your most successful school endeavors, you'll probably find that creativity played an important role: the science project you created and presented that was unlike anything anyone else imagined; those hip-hop lyrics you wrote to illustrate a point in a history presentation; the marathon you weren't thoroughly prepared for but that you managed to finish—which led to a fascination with effective training processes, which in turn might lead to a senior thesis in human biology.

> Creativity is intelligence having fun.
> —ALBERT EINSTEIN

Be flexible

Whether you're at a small college or a large university, there will be a lot to deal with—classes in multiple fields that call for various kinds of work (labs and lab reports in science classes, long reading lists and essays in English, large textbooks and online homework in Econ), much more work than you've had before now, and maybe you have a part-time job and a young child. Or maybe you're caring for a sick or elderly parent. It's a lot to juggle, and *you* are the one who's responsible for doing all that. This means you need to develop strategies for managing your time, planning for due dates, and keeping yourself on task—and that you'll need to be flexible.

Perhaps you prefer to do your serious reading early in the morning, but one term you have early classes every day. Rather than getting up earlier and earlier, try to stay flexible and find a time later in the day you can devote to your reading assignments. One student was so determined to write a summary of an assigned article that she told herself she couldn't get up from her desk until it was done. Hours later, she was still sitting there, praying for inspiration that just wouldn't come. A little flexibility—getting up and taking a walk, doing another task that she could accomplish easily, or just taking a brief break—would probably have helped her make a fresh start.

Be persistent

It's hard to beat a person who never gives up.
—BABE RUTH

Keep at it. Follow through. Take advantage of opportunities to revise and improve. Keep track of what's challenging or hard for you—and look for ways to overcome those obstacles. You've probably already seen the positive effects of persistence in your life, and these effects will double (or triple) in college: successful students don't give up but keep on keeping on.

One student who was searching for information on a distant relative who had played a role in the civil rights movement kept coming up empty-handed and was about to give up on the project. But she decided to try one last lead through ancestry.com—and discovered a crucial piece of information that led to a big breakthrough and a sense of personal satisfaction. Her persistence paid off, and it eventually led her to write a profile of her relative introducing that person to the rest of her large extended family.

Take responsibility

The work you do in college will call on you to take responsibility for what you say and write and do. You'll need to take charge of your learning and make the most of your education. That means not just being engaged with the topics you're writing or speaking about, but "owning" what you say about them, standing behind your words. And that also means being able to vouch for the sources you use.

One student who was very interested in the right-to-die movement in his state began researching arguments on all sides of this debate. Coming to the conclusion that those arguing in favor of the movement were persuasive, he began incorporating some of their arguments into an essay. But something began nagging at him when he realized that several of his sources were saying pretty much exactly the same thing. He traced these sources back to one single source— a website owned by the Euthanasia Society, a group dedicated to assisted suicide. And that discovery led him to do additional research, including sources by groups that oppose assisted suicide and explain their reasons for doing so. This additional research then led him to qualify his conclusions—and to present a more balanced argument about this volatile issue. In short, he was taking responsibility for what he was writing—and for the sources he was using.

Chapter 15 provides tips for determining if a source is reliable.

Collaborate

Remember to work with others. When it comes to solving problems or coming up with new ideas, two heads are better than one—and more than two is often better still. Lots of your college work will call for collaboration, from conducting an experiment with a lab partner to working with a team to research and present a report. As a writer you're in constant collaboration with those who read and respond to your ideas. Then there's all you'll do online—on *Zoom*, or *Twitter*. All collaboration. And all important: learning to work well with others is as important as anything else you learn in college.

Talk to the person next to you, make a network, have an open mind, and don't be ashamed to ask for help.

—GAIL MELLOW

Reflect

Think about how you learn, and make it a habit of doing so often. *Where* do you do most of your learning—in class? at the library? at home? *How* does your learning take place—from lectures? textbooks? doing research? talking to others? writing? *Who* takes charge of this learning—instructors? your mom? you? Several major studies identify this kind of purposeful reflection as instrumental to becoming well educated. And many students find that keeping an informal journal to write about what they're learning, how they're learning it, and how they're learning to overcome obstacles leads to better comprehension and better success. One group of students used *Twitter* to share what they were learning, saying that doing so helped them "learn it better."

Don't be afraid to fail

And what is "failure," anyway? One parent of a severely disabled child faces that question daily. See what she has to say about that on p. 580.

You may remember your grandmother or some other wise person saying "nothing ventured, nothing gained," and they were right! After all, we all learn from our mistakes, from doing something wrong and then keeping at it until we get it right. The first time I tried to ride a bike, I promptly fell off. But with encouragement and a little instruction from my dad, I got back on and kept trying until I was zooming around the neighborhood like an ace. When Philadelphia Eagles quarterback Nick Foles was asked about his amazing career, from barely a starter to a backup, and then eventually to MVP in the 2018 Super Bowl, here's what he said:

> I think the big thing is, don't be afraid to fail. In our society today—*Instagram, Twitter*—it's a highlight reel. It's all the good things. And then . . . when you have a rough day . . . you think you're failing. Failure is a part of life . . . a part of building character and growing. . . . I wouldn't be up here if I hadn't fallen thousands of times. Made mistakes. [So] if something's going on in your life and you're struggling? Embrace it. Because you're growing.
>
> —NICK FOLES, 2018 Super Bowl press conference

Nick Foles scoring on fourth-down-and-goal in the 2018 Super Bowl, the first player in Super Bowl history to both throw and catch a touchdown.

It's no coincidence that all these habits of mind go along with what it means to think and act rhetorically. The same practices that make us careful, ethical, and effective communicators (listen, search for understanding, put in your oar) also lead to success in college—or in the Super Bowl. You'll have plenty of opportunities to practice and develop these habits in the writing and reading and speaking and listening you'll do in college. I bet you'll enjoy the ride—and if, like Michelle Obama, you work at it, you too can soar!

REFLECT! What new things have you tried so far in college? And what other new things do you hope to try? Make a bucket list of all that you hope to experience and accomplish before you graduate. Then get started—and remember: don't be afraid to make mistakes. That's just part of trying new things!

黒
black

fish

父
use

使

大
big

巣

PALAMEDE, REMIGIA ED IO   61

giva per suo conto. Ero lì lì su quel-
limite: v'ero giunto senza saperlo,
dall'incalzare dell'angoscia: se l'ol-
avo, senza averne coscienza, ero un
un uomo libero finalmente le cui scia-
on hanno più senso. Invece, al varco
rio, la coscienza m'avvertiva ch'io
pazzo... ed era finita! Ritorna

con le scarp Ma
bisbiglio de sacerd
lamede, ch
l'altare
ne

PROVENCE TED

CHEMINS

GET THE MESSAGE

5 Reading to Understand, Engage & Respond

THE WORDS ON THE PAGE ARE ONLY HALF THE STORY.
THE REST IS WHAT YOU BRING TO THE PARTY.

—TONI MORRISON

Chances are, you read more than you think you do. You read print texts, of course, but you're probably reading even more on a phone, a tablet, a computer, or other devices. Reading is now, as perhaps never before, a basic necessity. In fact, if you think that reading is something you learned once and for all in the first or second grade, think again. Today, reading calls for strategic effort. As media critic Howard Rheingold sees it, literacy today involves at least five interlocking abilities: attention, participation, collaboration, network awareness, and critical consumption. Of these, attention is first and foremost. In short, you need to work at paying

52

attention to what you read. In *The Economics of Attention*, rhetorician Richard Lanham explains: "We're drowning in information. What we lack is the human attention needed to make sense of it all."

When so many texts are vying for our attention, which ones do we choose to read? In order to decide what to read, what to pay attention to, we need to practice what Rheingold calls "infotention," a word he coined to describe a "mind-machine combination of brain-powered attention skills and computer-powered information filters." In other words, it helps us to focus. And while some of us can multitask (fighter pilots are one example Rheingold gives of those whose jobs demand it), most of us aren't good at it and must learn to focus our attention when we read.

READING TO UNDERSTAND

Your first job as a reader is to make sure you understand what you are reading, and why you're reading it.

Start by previewing

Reading experts tell us that it's best to begin not by plunging right into a text but by previewing it to get a sense of what it's about.

- ***Look at the title*** and any subtitle, the first paragraph, and any headings to get a sense of what the text covers.
- ***What do you know*** (and think) about the topic? What do you want to learn about it?
- ***Who are the authors***, and what's their expertise? Where do you think they're coming from? Might they have an agenda?

- *Who's the publisher* or sponsor, and what does that tell you about the text's intended audience and purpose?
- *Consider any sources* that are cited. Are they credible?
- *Look at any visuals*—photos or drawings, charts, graphs. What information do they contribute?
- *Consider the design.* How does it affect the way you understand the text? What do the fonts and any use of color suggest about the text's TONE? Are there any sidebars or other features that highlight parts of the text?
- *What's your first impression* of the text, and what interests you the most?

Think about your rhetorical situation

Once you have a sense of what the text is about, think about why you're reading it and the rest of your rhetorical situation.

- What's your PURPOSE for reading? To learn something new? To fulfill an assignment? To prepare for a test? Something else?
- Who's the intended AUDIENCE for the text? What words or images in the text make you think so? Are you a member of this group? If not, there may be unfamiliar terms or references that you'll need to look up.
- What's the GENRE? An argument? A report? A narrative? An annotated bibliography? Knowing the genre will tell you something about what to expect.
- How does the MEDIUM affect the way you will read the text? Is it a written print text? a podcast? a visual or MULTIMODAL text, such as an infographic?
- Think about the larger CONTEXT. What do you know about the topic and what others say about it? What do you need to find out?
- What's your own STANCE on the topic? Are you an advocate? a critic? an impartial observer?

Read difficult texts strategically

You'll surely encounter texts and subject matter that are hard to understand. Most often these will be ones you're reading not for pleasure but to learn something. You'll want to slow down with such texts, to stop and think—and you might find this easier to do with print texts, where paragraphs and headings and highlighted information help you see the various parts and find key information. Here are some other tips for making your way through difficult texts:

> Reading is an active, imaginative act; it takes work.
> —KHALED HOSSEINI

- Read first for what you can understand, and simply mark places that are confusing, things you don't understand, words or concepts you'll need to look up.

- Then choose a modest amount of material to reread— a chapter, or part of a chapter. Figure out how it's organized and see its main points—look at headings, and any THESIS and TOPIC SENTENCES.

- Check to see if there's a SUMMARY at the beginning or end of the text. If so, read it very carefully.

- Reread the hard parts. Slow down, and focus.

- Try to make sense of the parts: this part offers evidence; that paragraph summarizes an alternative view; here's a signal about what's coming next.

- If the text includes VISUALS, what data or other information do they contribute to the message?

> Is equality "simple and self-evident"? Then why does Joshua Rothman call it a "conundrum"? See what he says on p. 527. The strategies here will help.

- Resist highlighting: it's better to take notes in the margins or on digital sticky notes.

- Get together with one or two classmates, and read together, talking through anything you find difficult to understand.

ENGAGING WITH WHAT YOU READ

Engagement is one of the habits of mind that are crucial to success in college and to the reading you do there. You're "engaged" as a reader when you approach a text with an open mind, ready to listen to what it has to say. This kind of engagement may come naturally when you're reading something you want to read. But what about texts you're assigned to read, ones you wouldn't read otherwise? How do you engage productively with them? There's no magic wand you can wave to make this happen, but here's a little advice, based on what students have told me about how they can get "into" an assigned text.

First, find your comfort zone, a place where you can concentrate. A comfy lounge chair? A chair with good back support? Starbucks? Wherever it is, getting up to stretch every half hour or so will help you maintain focus. Then choose the medium or device that helps you focus. Some readers like print text best for taking notes. Others prefer ebooks, which can be read on a Kindle or similar device to avoid the distractions phones and computers have.

And consider reading with a classmate. Particularly with difficult texts, two heads are usually better than one—and discussing any text with someone else will help you both to engage with it. Try to explain something in the text to a friend: if you can get the major points across, you've understood it!

Annotate as you read

Annotating enables you to note the key points in the text. Do what literary critic Anatole Broyard once recommended: "Stomp around in it . . . underlining passages, scribbling in the margins, leaving [your] mark." Broyard's point echoes what reading experts say: the more you "stomp around" in a text, the better you'll understand it and engage with what it says. Here are some points to look for as you read and annotate:

- What CLAIMS does the text make? Note any THESIS statement.
- What REASONS and EVIDENCE are offered to support any claims—examples, DEFINITIONS, and so on?
- Identify any key terms (and look them up if necessary).

- Note places in the text where the author demonstrates AUTHORITY to write on the topic.

- What is the author's STANCE toward the topic—passionate? skeptical? neutral? something else? Note any words that reflect the author's stance.

- How would you describe the author's STYLE and TONE— formal? conversational? skeptical? something else? Mark words that establish that, and think about how they affect the way you react to the text.

- Mark any COUNTERARGUMENTS or other perspectives. How fairly are those views described, and how does the author respond to them?

- Consider any sources cited in the text and think about whether you can trust them. If you have any doubts, FACT-CHECK.

- Pay attention to the DESIGN and any VISUALS, and think about how they affect the message.

- Underline any points that are unclear or confusing, and jot down your questions in the margins.

- Note anything you find surprising—and why. Chapter 6 provides tips for checking anything that's questionable.

- Give some thought to anything in the text that you question or disagree with; keep an open mind!

A sample annotated text

On the following page is the opening of an essay about minority student clubs on college campuses written by Gabriela Moro, a student at the University of Notre Dame. See how one reader has annotated her text—and how it helped that reader engage with her argument. You can read Moro's full essay on page 123.

Minority representation on US college campuses has increased significantly in recent years, and many schools have made it a priority to increase diversity on their campuses in order to prepare students for a culturally diverse US democratic society (Hurtado and Ruiz 3–4). To complement this increase, many schools have implemented minority student clubs to provide safe and comfortable environments where minority students can thrive academically and socially with peers from similar backgrounds. However, do these minority groups amplify students' tendency to interact only with those who are similar to themselves? Put another way, do these groups inhibit students from engaging in diverse relationships?

Many view such programs to be positive and integral to minority students' college experience; some, however, feel that these clubs are not productive for promoting cross-cultural interaction. While minority clubs have proven to be beneficial to minority students in some cases, particularly on campuses that are not very diverse, my research suggests that colleges would enrich the educational experience for all students by introducing multicultural clubs as well. To frame my discussion, I will use an article from *College Student Journal* that distinguishes between two types of students: one who believes minority clubs are essential for helping minority students stay connected with their cultures, and another who believes these clubs isolate minorities and work against diverse interaction among students. To pursue the question of whether or not such groups segregate minorities from the rest of the student body and even discourage cultural awareness, I will use perspectives from minority students at Notre Dame to show that these programs are especially helpful for first-year students. I will also use other student testimonials to show that when taken too far, minority groups can lead to self-segregation and defy what most universities claim to be their diversity goals. Findings from research will contribute to a better understanding of the role minority clubs play on college campuses and offer a complete answer to my question about the importance of minority programs.

—GABRIELA MORO,
"Minority Student Clubs: Integration or Segregation?"

Good question! What's the answer?

Is this her thesis?

She's going to consider more views. I like that.

I need to check out this source—are these real students or just stereotypes?

I wonder who these students are and how she found them. What does she mean by "minority" students?

Looks like her stance will be to take the middle ground in this debate. Let's see if this holds true.

Consider the larger context

All texts are part of some larger conversation, and one reason academic writers document their sources is to acknowledge an awareness of that conversation. Considering that larger context will help you understand the text and shed light on issues that you may not have known about.

When Secretary of Education Betsy DeVos said that Historically Black Colleges and Universities (HBCUs) stand tall as "pioneers of school choice," her words sounded like a compliment and testimony to the work of HBCUs. But putting that claim into context helps to assess—or reassess—what she said. After all, HBCUs arose in response to Jim Crow segregation at many colleges and universities, from which Black students were excluded. Putting DeVos's statement in context, then, calls it into question, revealing that in fact students of color had very few choices in terms of higher education.

Here are some tips to help you consider the larger context of texts you read:

- What else has been said about this topic? What's the larger conversation surrounding it, and how does this text fit into that conversation?
- Is the writer's point confirmed (or challlenged) by what others say?
- Is the author responding to what someone else has said— and if so, what?
- Who's cited, and what does that tell you about the author's STANCE?
- Does the text consider COUNTERARGUMENTS and multiple PERSPECTIVES on the topic fairly and respectfully?
- Who cares about this topic, and why does this topic matter in the first place?
- How does the larger context inform your thinking about the topic?

RESPONDING TO WHAT YOU READ

Whenever you actively engage with a text, annotating and "stomping around" in it, you are already responding, talking back to it, questioning it, assessing its claims, and coming to conclusions about whether or not you accept them. There are many ways to respond more explicitly—from jotting a quick reply to a blog post, to writing in the comment space following a news article, to writing a full-blown review. Following are three kinds of writing you may be assigned to do when responding to something you've read.

Summarize

Summarizing something you've read in your own words can help you understand and remember its main points. Following are some tips for doing so:

- Keep your summary short and sweet, capturing the text's main ideas but leaving out its supporting information.
- Take care that your summary is fair and accurate—and uses neutral, nonjudgmental language.
- Use your own words and sentence structure; if you do QUOTE any words from the original text, be sure to enclose them in quotation marks.
- DOCUMENT any texts you summarize in academic writing of your own.

Here's a summary of Gabriela Moro's essay:

See Moro's full essay on p. 123.

In a time of increasing diversity on US college campuses, Gabriela Moro asks whether minority student clubs and programs help minority students succeed and have a good "college experience," or whether they result in separation and even segregation. Moro considers the pros and cons of each position and concludes that while these clubs and programs are "especially helpful for first-year students," they can work against college goals for inclusiveness.

If you're assigned to write a SUMMARY/RESPONSE essay, there are various ways to respond. Two ways that are often assigned are by arguing with what the text says and analyzing the way it says it.

Respond to what the text says

Agree or disagree—or even agree with some parts and disagree with others. However you respond, you'll be making an ARGUMENT for what you say. Following are some tips to help you do so:

See an essay that responds to an op-ed on p. 217.

- What does the text CLAIM, and is it stated explicitly in a THESIS? Does the claim need to be QUALIFIED—or stated more strongly?

- What REASONS and EVIDENCE does the author provide? Are they sufficient?

- Does the author acknowledge any COUNTERARGUMENTS or other positions? If not, what other views should be addressed?

- Has the author cited any sources—and if so, how trustworthy are they?

- Do you agree with the author's position? disagree? both agree and disagree? Why?

Analyze the way the text is written

How does the text work? What makes it tick? ANALYZING how a text is written can help you to understand what it's saying. Here are some questions to consider:

See an essay that analyzes a magazine on p. 148.

- What does the author CLAIM about the text? Is it stated explicitly in a THESIS—and if not, should it be?

- Is the text DESCRIBED or SUMMARIZED in enough detail?

- What EVIDENCE is provided in support of the claim? Is it sufficient? If not, what additional evidence would help?

- What insight does your analysis lead to? How does the way it's written affect the way you understand it?

READING ON-SCREEN AND OFF

Once upon a time "reading" meant attending to words on paper. But today we often encounter texts that convey information in images and in sound as well—and they may be on- or off-screen. Whatever texts you're reading, be sure to think carefully about how the medium may affect your understanding, engagement, and response.

Researchers have found that we often take shortcuts when we read online, searching and scanning and jumping around in a text or leaping from link to link. This kind of reading is very helpful for finding answers and information quickly, but it can blur your focus and make it difficult to attend to the text carefully and purposefully. Here are a few tips to help you when reading on a screen:

- Be clear about your PURPOSE for reading. If you need to remember the text, remind yourself to read very carefully and to avoid skimming or skipping around.
- Close *Facebook* or any other pages that may distract you.
- Try taking notes on PDFs or Word documents so that you can jot down questions and comments as you read. Alternatively, print out the text and take notes on paper.
- Look up unfamiliar terms as you read, making a note of definitions you may need later.
- For really high-stakes reading, consider printing out the text to read and take notes on.

The pervasiveness of reading on-screen may suggest that many readers prefer to read that way. But current research suggests that most students still prefer to read print, especially if the reading is important and needs to be internalized and remembered. Print texts, it's worth remembering, are easy to navigate—you can tell at a glance how much you've read and how much you still have to go, and you can move back and forth in the text to find something important.

In addition, researchers have found that students who read on-screen are less likely to reflect on what they read or to make connections in ways that bind learning to memory. It's important to note, however, that studies like these almost always end with a caveat: reading practices are changing, and technology is making it easier to read on-screen.

It's also important to note that online texts often blend written words with audio, video, links, charts and graphs, and other elements that can be attended to in any order you choose. In reading such texts, you'll need to make decisions carefully. When exactly should you click on a link, for example? The first moment it comes up? Or should you make a note to check it out later, since doing so now may break your concentration—and you might not be able to get back easily to what you were reading? Links can be a good thing in that they lead to more information, but following them can interrupt your train of thought. In addition, scrolling seems to encourage skimming and to make us read more rapidly. In short, it can be harder to stay on task. So you may well need to make a special effort with digital texts—to read them attentively, and to pay close attention to what you're reading.

We are clearly in a time of flux where reading is concerned, so the best advice is to think very carefully about *why* you're reading. If you want to find some information quickly, to follow a conversation on *Twitter*, or to look for online sources on a topic you're researching, reading on-screen is the way to go. But if you need to fully comprehend and retain the information, you may want to stick with print.

READING VISUALS

Visual texts present their own opportunities and challenges. As new technologies bring images into our phones and lives on a minute-by-minute basis, visual texts have become so familiar and pervasive that it may seem that "reading" them is just natural. But reading visual texts with a critical eye takes time and patience—and attention.

Take a look at the advertisement for a Shinola watch on the next page. You may know that Shinola is a Detroit-based watchmaker

A WATCH SO SMART
THAT IT CAN TELL YOU THE TIME
JUST BY LOOKING AT IT.

THE RUNWELL. IT'S JUST SMART ENOUGH.™

SMART ENOUGH THAT YOU DON'T NEED TO CHARGE IT AT NIGHT. SMART ENOUGH THAT IT WILL NEVER NEED
A SOFTWARE UPGRADE. SMART ENOUGH THAT VERSION 1.0 WON'T NEED TO BE REPLACED NEXT YEAR,
OR IN THE MANY DECADES THAT FOLLOW. BUILT BY THE WATCHMAKERS OF DETROIT TO LAST
A LIFETIME OR LONGER UNDER THE TERMS AND CONDITIONS OF THE SHINOLA GUARANTEE.

SHINOLA
DETROIT

Where American is made.™

NEW YORK 177 FRANKLIN ST.
DETROIT • MINNEAPOLIS • CHICAGO • WASHINGTON DC • LOS ANGELES • LONDON

SHINOLA.COM

proud that its watches are "built in America"; if not, a quick look at Shinola.com will fill in this part of the ad's CONTEXT. But there's a lot more going on in terms of its particular rhetorical situation. The ad first ran in 2015, when it was clearly responding to smart watches in general and to the launch of the Apple Watch in particular, with its full panoply of futuristic bells and whistles. "Hey," the Shinola ad writers seemed to be saying, "our watch is just smart enough."

Thinking through the rhetorical situation tells us something about the ad's purpose and audience. Of course its major PURPOSE is to sell watches; but one other goal seems to be to poke a little fun at all the high-tech, super-smart watches on the market. And what about its AUDIENCE—who do you think the ad addresses most directly? Perhaps Americans who think of themselves as solid "no frills" folks?

Reading a visual begins, then, with studying its purpose, audience, message, and context. But there's a lot more you can do to understand a visual. You can look closely, for instance, at its DESIGN. In the Shinola ad, the stark, high-contrast, black-and-white image takes center stage, drawing our eyes to it and its accompanying captions. There are no other distracting elements, no other colors, no glitz. The simplicity gives the watch a retro look, which is emphasized by its sturdy straps, open face, and clear numerals, its old-fashioned wind-up button and second hand.

You'll also want to take a close look at any words. In this case, the Shinola ad includes a large headline right above the image, three lines of all-caps, sans serif type that match the simplicity of the image itself. And it's hard to miss the mocking TONE: "A WATCH SO SMART THAT IT CAN TELL YOU THE TIME JUST BY LOOKING AT IT." The small caption below the image underscores this message: "THE RUNWELL. IT'S JUST SMART ENOUGH." Take that, Apple!

READING ACROSS ACADEMIC DISCIPLINES

Differences in disciplines can make for some challenging reading tasks, as you encounter texts that seem almost to be written in foreign languages. As with most new things, however, new disciplines and their texts will become familiar to you the more you work with them. So don't be put off if texts in fields like psychology or physics seem hard to read: the more you read such texts, the more familiar they'll become until, eventually, you'll be able to "talk the talk" of that discipline yourself.

Pay attention to terminology

It's especially important to read carefully when encountering texts in different academic fields. Take the word *analysis*, for instance. That little word has a wide range of definitions as it moves from one field to another. In *philosophy*, analysis has traditionally meant breaking down a topic into its constituent parts in order to understand them—and the whole text—more completely. In the *sciences*, analysis often involves the scientific method of observing a phenomenon, formulating a hypothesis about it, and experimenting to see whether the hypothesis holds up. In *business*, analysis often refers to assessing needs and finding ways to meet them. And in *literary studies*, analysis usually calls for close reading in order to interpret a passage of text. When you're assigned to carry out an analysis, then, it's important to know what the particular field of study expects you to do and to ask your instructors if you aren't sure.

Know what counts as evidence

Beyond knowing what particular words mean from field to field, you should note that what counts as EVIDENCE can differ across academic disciplines. In literature and other fields in the *humanities*, textual evidence is often the most important: your job as a reader is to focus on the text itself. For the *sciences*, you'll most often focus on evidence gathered through experimentation, on facts and figures.

Some of the *social sciences* also favor the use of "hard" evidence or data, while others are more likely to use evidence drawn from interviews, oral histories, or even anecdotes. As a reader, you'll need to be aware of what counts as credible evidence in the fields you study.

Be aware of how information is presented

Finally, pay attention to the way various disciplines format and present their information. You'll probably find that articles and books in *literature* and *history* present their information in paragraphs, sometimes with illustrations. *Physics* texts present much important information in equations, while those in *psychology* and *political science* rely on charts, graphs, and other visual representations of quantitative data. In *art history*, you can expect to see extensive use of images, while much of the work in *music* will rely on notation and sound.

So reading calls for some real effort. Whether you're reading words or images or bar graphs, literary analysis or musical notation, in a print book or on a screen, you need to read attentively and intentionally and with an open mind. On top of all that, you need to be an active participant with what you read. As Toni Morrison says: "The words on the page are only half the story. The rest is what you bring to the party."

REFLECT! The next time you read a text online, pay attention to your process. Do you go straight through, or do you stop often? Do you take notes? Do you turn away from what you're reading to look at or attend to something else? What do you do if you don't understand a passage? How long can you read at a stretch and maintain full concentration? Then answer the same questions the next time you read a print text. What differences do you notice in the way you read each kind of text? What conclusions can you draw about how to be a more effective reader, both on- and off-screen?

6 Recognizing Facts, Misinformation & Lies

FACTS ARE FACTS AND WILL NOT DISAPPEAR
ON ACCOUNT OF YOUR LIKES.

—JAWAHARLAL NEHRU

YOU KNOW WHERE I'M COMING FROM,
BUT YOU CAN FACT-CHECK ANYTHING I SAY.

—RACHEL MADDOW

Palestinians Recognize Texas as Part of Mexico." "Pope Francis: God Has Instructed Me to Revise the Ten Commandments." "Canada Bans Beyoncé after Her Superbowl Performance." Really? Well, no. While these are in fact actual headlines, none is anywhere near the truth. But being false hasn't kept them from being widely shared—and not as jokes, but as facts. With so many people spreading misinformation, unsubstantiated claims, and even outright lies today, it can be hard to know who and what to trust, or whether to trust anything at all. The good news, however, is that you don't have to be taken in by such claims. This chapter provides strategies for navigating today's choppy waters of news and information so that you can make confident decisions about what to trust—and what not to.

Facts, misinformation, fake news, and lies

Some say we're living in a "post-truth" era, that the loudest voices take up so much airtime that they can sometimes be seen as telling the "truth" no matter what they say. A 2018 study by MIT scholars examined tweets about 126,000 major news stories in English and came to the conclusion that "the truth simply can't compete with hoax and rumor." In fact, the study says, "fake news and false rumors reach more people, penetrate deeper into the social network, and spread much faster than accurate stories."

It's worth asking why misinformation and even lies outperform real news. While it is notoriously difficult to establish an airtight cause-and-effect relationship, these researchers suspect that several reasons account for their "success." First, they're often outlandish and novel in a way that attracts attention. Second, the content of such stories is often negative and tends to arouse very strong emotions. Third, they use language that evokes surprise or disgust, and seems to lead to the information going viral. Accurate tweets, the researchers found, use words associated with trust or sadness rather than surprise or disgust—and as they note, "the truth simply does not compete."

Lies and misinformation are nothing new. What's new is that anyone with an internet connection can post whatever they think (or want others to think) online, where it can easily reach a wide audience. And unlike mainstream newspapers and other such publications, online postings go out without being vetted by editors or fact-checkers.

Perhaps it's time to step back, take a deep breath, and attend to some basic definitions. Just what is a fact? What's fake news? And what about misinformation and lies? Both misinformation and lies give false or inaccurate information. The difference is that *misinformation* is not necessarily intended to deceive, whereas *lies* are

A lie can travel halfway around the world while the truth is putting on its shoes.

—MARK TWAIN

always told deliberately, for the purpose of giving false information. *Fake news* stories are fabricated and false articles are made to look authentic. Often they're used to spread conspiracy theories or deliberate hoaxes—the more bizarre, the better. In addition, many people simply dismiss anything they don't like or agree with as fake news. *Facts*, on the other hand, can be verified and backed up by reliable evidence—that the Washington Capitals won the 2018 Stanley Cup, for example, or that the consumption of soft drinks in the United States has declined in the last five years. Unlike claims about what God has instructed Pope Francis to do, these statements can be checked and verified; we can then trust them.

Think about your own beliefs

It's one thing to be able to spot misinformation, unsubstantiated claims, and exaggerations in the words of others, but it's another thing entirely to spot them in our own thinking and writing. So we need to take a good look at our own assumptions and biases. We all have them!

Attribution bias is the tendency to think that our motives for believing, say, that the Environmental Protection Agency (EPA) is crucially important for keeping our air and water clean are objective or good, while the motives of those who believe the EPA is unnecessary are dubious or suspect. We all have this kind of bias naturally, tending to believe that what we think must be right. When you're thinking about an argument you strongly disagree with, then, it's a good idea to ask yourself *why* you disagree—and why you believe you're right. What is that belief based on? Have you considered that your own bias may be keeping you from seeing all sides of the issue fairly, or at all?

Confirmation bias is the tendency to favor and seek out information that confirms what we already believe and to reject and ignore information that contradicts those beliefs. Many studies have documented this phenomenon, including a university experiment with student participants, half of whom favored capital punishment and thought it was a deterrent to crime and half of whom thought just the opposite. Researchers then asked the students to respond to two studies: one provided data that supported capital punishment as a deterrent to crime; the other provided data that called this conclusion into question. And sure enough, the students who were pro capital punishment rated the study showing evidence that it was a deterrent as "more highly credible," while the students who were against capital punishment rated the study showing evidence that it didn't deter crime as "more highly credible"—in spite of the fact that both studies had been made up by the researchers and were equally compelling in terms of their evidence. Moreover, by the end of the experiment, each side had doubled down on its original beliefs.

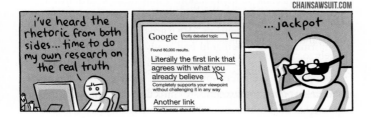

That's confirmation bias at work, and it works on all of us. It affects the way we search for information and what we pay attention to, how we interpret it, and even what we remember. That's all to say you shouldn't assume a news story is trustworthy just because it confirms what you already think. Ask yourself if you're seeing what you want to see. And look for confirmation bias in your sources; do they acknowledge viewpoints other than their own?

REFLECT! Where do you get the news? Whatever your sources, what do you pay attention to, and why? What are you most likely to click on? What, on the other hand, are you likely to skip, or ignore? Can you see confirmation bias at work in the choices you make?

Read defensively

Reading defensively is a good idea. Sam Wineburg offers another one: learning what to ignore. You can find his suggestions on p. 689.

Well over 2,000 years ago, the philosopher Aristotle said that one reason people need rhetoric is for self-defense, for making sure we aren't being manipulated or lied to. Today, the need for such caution may be more important than ever—especially in social media and elsewhere online, where false stories may look authentic and appear right next to accurate, factual information. These times call, then, for *defensive reading*—that is, the kind of reading that doesn't take things at face value, that questions underlying assumptions, that scrutinizes claims carefully, and that doesn't rush to judgment. This is the kind of reading that media and technology critic Howard Rheingold calls "crap detection." Crap, he says sardonically, is a "technical term" he uses to describe information "tainted by ignorance or deliberate deception." He warns us not to give in to such misinformation. As Rheingold and many others note, there is no single foolproof way to identify lies and misinformation. But the following discussion offers some specific strategies for determining whether—or not—a source can be trusted.

Triangulate—and use your judgment

If you have any doubts, find three different ways to check on whether a story can be trusted. Google the author or the sponsor. Consult fact-checking sites such as *Snopes.com* or *FactCheck.org*. Look for other sources that are reporting the same story, especially if you first saw it on social media. If it's true and important, you should find a number of other reputable sources reporting on it. But however carefully you check, and whatever facts and evidence you uncover, it's up to you to sort the accurate information from the misinformation—and often as not that will call on you to use your own judgment to do that.

See p. 269 for more tips on triangulating.

Before reading an unfamiliar source, determine whether it can be trusted

Take a tip from professional fact-checkers, who don't even start to read an unfamiliar website until they've determined that it's a trustworthy site. If you have any doubts, here are some ways to proceed:

Do a search about the author or sponsor. If there's an author, what's their expertise? Do they belong to any organizations you don't know or trust? Be wary if there's no author. And do a search about the site's sponsor. If it's run by an organization you've never heard of, find out what it is—and whether it actually exists. What do reliable sources say about it? Read the site's About page, but check up on what it says.

If an organization can game what they are, they can certainly game their About page!
—SAM WINEBURG

Check any links to see who sponsors them and whether they are trustworthy sources. Do the same for works cited in print sources.

Be careful of over-the-top headlines, which often serve as CLICKBAIT to draw you in. Check to see that the story and the headline actually match. Question any that are over the top: look for words like *amazing*, *epic*, *incredible*, or *unbelievable*. (In general, don't believe anything that's said to be "unbelievable!")

Pay attention to design. Be wary if it looks amateurish, but don't assume that a professional-looking design means the source is accurate or trustworthy. Those who create fake news sites are careful to make them to look like authentic news sites.

Recognize satire. Remember that some authors make a living by writing satirical fake news. Here's one: "China Slaps Two-Thousand-Per-Cent Tariff on Tanning Beds." This comes from Andy Borowitz, who writes political satire in the *New Yorker*, which tips us off not to take it seriously by labeling it "not the news." The *Onion* is another source that pokes fun at gullible readers. Try this: "Genealogists Find 99% of People Are Not Related to Anyone Cool." This one's silly enough that it can't possibly be true. But if you're not sure, better check.

Ask questions, check evidence

Double-check things that too neatly support what you yourself think, or that seem too good to be true.

What's the CLAIM, and what EVIDENCE is provided? What motivated the author to write, and what's their PURPOSE? To provide information? Make you laugh? Convince you of something?

See p. 266 for more on fact-checking sites. *Check facts and claims* using nonpartisan sites that confirm truths and identify lies. *FactCheck.org, Snopes.com,* and *AllSides.com* are three such sites. Copy and paste the basics of the statement into the search field; if it's information the site has in its database, you'll find out whether it's a confirmed fact or a lie. If you use *Google* to check on a stated fact, keep in mind that you'll need to check on any sources it turns up—and that even if the statement brings up many hits, that doesn't make it accurate.

If you think a story is too good to be true, you're probably right to be skeptical. And don't assume that it must be true because no one could make up such a story. They can. Check out stories that are so outrageous that you don't believe them; if they're true, they'll be widely reported. That said, double-check stories that confirm your own beliefs as well; that might be confirmation bias at work.

Look up any research that's cited. You may find that the research has been taken out of context or misquoted—or that it doesn't actually exist. Is the research itself reliable? Pay close attention to QUOTATIONS: Who said it, and when? Is it believable? If not, copy and paste the quotation into *Google* or check *FactCheck.org* to verify that it's real.

Check any comments. If several say the article sounds fake, it may well be. But remember that given the presence of BOTS and TROLLS—not to mention people with malicious intent—comments, too, may be fake.

Fact-check photos and videos

Is a picture really worth a thousand words? In some cases, yes—but only if the picture is an accurate depiction. Today, it's never been easier to falsify photographs. Take the often-repeated, retweeted, and repurposed story of a shark swimming down a highway whenever a hurricane strikes or some other natural disaster causes flooding. A couple years ago, someone tweeted: "Believe it or not, this is a shark on the freeway in New Burn, North Carolina. #Hurricane Florence"—a message that was retweeted 88,000 times. But the same shark popped up on Twitter swimming down a road in Houston, Texas, and in many other cities. Easily done with *Photoshop*.

This 2017 photo looks real—but one of these men was photoshopped in.

And see the photo on page 75 that went viral in 2017, showing President Trump, Vladimir Putin, and others in conversation. A little investigation, however, showed that Putin had been photoshopped into the image; he wasn't actually at the table.

Again, there are no simple, foolproof ways to identify doctored photos, but experts in digital forensics recommend various steps we can take. Here's advice from Hany Farid, a computer science professor at the University of California at Berkeley:

- **Do a reverse image search** using *Google Images* or *Tin Eye* to see if an image has been recirculated or repurposed from another website. Both sites allow you to drag an image or paste a link to an image into a search bar to learn more about its source and see where it appears online.
- **Check Snopes.com,** where altered images are often identified, by typing a brief description of the image into the site's search box.
- **Look carefully at shadows:** an image may have been altered if you find shadows where you don't expect them or don't see them where you do expect them.

Farid goes on to say that the best defense against fabricated photos is "to stop and think about the source"—especially before you share it on social media. After a shooter killed seventeen people at a Florida school in 2018, an altered photo of Emma González, one of the students who protested the mass shooting, went viral, showing her tearing up a page of the US Constitution. In fact, she was actually tearing up a shooting target as part of her advocacy for gun control; the Constitution had been photoshopped in.

The same advice holds true for video, which is all too easy to falsify. Videos that flicker constantly or that consist of just one short clip are often questionable, as are videos of famous people doing things that are highly suspicious. How likely is it that Kobe Bryant could jump over a speeding Aston Martin? Not very—but a lot of us were fooled by a fake video made for Nike.

Such fabricated videos proliferate daily, especially on *YouTube*, now an extremely popular source of news. As *YouTube* has found in trying to control or ban fake videos, those who make them are getting more and more sophisticated. As the *Guardian* reports, artificial intelligence and computer graphics now make it possible to create "realistic looking footage of public figures appearing to say, well, anything."

Thanks to the internet, there's a lot of misinformation and fake news out there. But the fact-finding and defensive-reading strategies described in this chapter will help you sort out fiction from fact, falsehood from truth—and determine with confidence who and what you can trust. You may have to dig a little, but truth and the "good stuff" are out there. Take it from Elvis Presley: "Truth is like the sun. You can shut it out for a time, but it ain't goin' away."

REFLECT! Look for something that has been sent to you on social media—retweeted, forwarded, "liked," whatever. Then take the time to check out its source, using the help provided in this chapter on page 74. After checking, do you find that the information in the source holds up as credible and trustworthy? Why—or why not?

WRITING

MAKE YOUR POINT

7 Writing Processes

THE FUNCTION OF WRITING IS TO DO MORE THAN TELL IT
LIKE IT IS—IT IS TO IMAGINE WHAT IS POSSIBLE.

—BELL HOOKS

IF YOU'VE GOT A PROCESS . . . YOU HAVE A LIST
OF THINGS TO DO TO GET TO YOUR GOAL.

—NIPSEY HUSSLE

D o you knit? play video games? do yoga?
If so, you're probably accustomed
to following a process of some kind,
whether it's for making socks, playing *Fortnite*, or
doing a downward-dog yoga pose. The same goes
for writing: whether it's a thank-you letter after
a job interview, an email to a teacher, or an essay
for a class, you follow some kind of process. This
chapter will help you make your way through the
process of writing, from a blank page to a finished
text. Think of it as a GPS that will help you navigate
the many choices you have along the way—and
direct you to places in the book with additional
detail if you need it.

Start with questions

Whatever your topic or purpose, start out by asking questions. Even if your purpose is to solve some kind of problem, don't just go looking for answers. Whatever the task, approach it with an open mind. If you already have some ideas about your topic, expect to find new ideas. Be curious: inquire! explore! Here are some tips that can help:

Ideas come from curiosity.
—WALT DISNEY

If you already know something about your topic, what do you think about it, and why? What more do you want to find out? Be aware of CONFIRMATION BIAS, which can make you too quick to accept ideas that confirm what you already believe.

Keep an open mind, ready to be challenged. You're sure to encounter viewpoints that differ from yours—and if you don't, seek them out. Take them seriously and be open to the possibility that they just might be right. Even if that's not the case, they'll get you thinking!

Ask questions: What? Who? How? Where? When? Why? Why *not*?

What are others saying about your topic, and why? What else might be said? What do you want to say?

Think about your rhetorical situation

Whether you're writing a text or a tweet, an essay or a speech, you have a RHETORICAL SITUATION that you need to consider:

- A PURPOSE—what you're trying to accomplish by writing.
- An AUDIENCE—those who will be reading or seeing or listening to what you say.
- Your own STANCE, or attitude about the topic, which you convey in the TONE of your writing.
- A larger CONTEXT. What else has been said about your topic? If you're writing for an assignment, what are its requirements—and what can you accomplish in the time you have?

- One or more GENRES. You may be ARGUING a position, REPORTING information, SUMMARIZING a text, or something else. Whatever it is, your genre will determine the way you approach your topic.

- One or more MEDIA—print, oral, digital, and social. If you have a choice, choose the one(s) that best suit your purpose and audience.

- DESIGN. What fonts serve your purpose? Do you need headings? images? charts or graphs?

Chapter 2 provides detailed guidelines for thinking about each element of a rhetorical situation, but you'll want to keep your audience and purpose in mind from start to finish of whatever you're writing.

Generate ideas

I had an old typewriter and a big idea.
—J. K. ROWLING

Once you have a topic, it's time to learn what you can about it—to *think* about it and start writing about it. Here are several techniques that can help you think about and generate ideas.

Freewriting is a technique for exploring a topic through writing. Start by writing quickly, without stopping. Some writers find it useful to freewrite for five or ten minutes; others find it works better if they write until they fill a screen or a certain number of pages. Don't worry about your spelling or grammar; just write! Your goal is to come up with ideas, and the more the merrier!

Brainstorming is a process for generating as many ideas as you can, quickly. And don't worry about whether they're right or wrong, smart or silly. You can brainstorm on your own by simply writing down all the ideas you have, or you can work with a group, with everyone suggesting whatever ideas they have, as many as possible. The more brains the better—and the greater the likelihood that you'll discover a range of viewpoints. Alone or with others, the goal is to explore an idea and to be open to whatever it turns up.

Questioning is a good way to explore a topic and to get beyond what you already know or think about it. And it's easy: just ask *what, who, where, when, how,* and *why.* What happened (or happens)? Who's involved? Where and when did (or does) it take place? How does it happen? And why: what caused (or causes) it to happen?

Do some research

Unless your topic is a personal one, you'll probably need to do some research. *Wikipedia* can be a good starting point, likely to provide an overview of the topic, to give a sense of the various perspectives that exist on it, and to list sources you can check out. If you're writing about a current issue, you may want to check news articles or periodicals or do a KEYWORD search. If you're writing about a topic from the distant past, you'll need to look for older sources, but you may also need to see if there's any recent scholarship on the topic. And if you're writing about a local issue, you may want to interview experts or do some other kind of FIELD RESEARCH.

For more on finding sources, see Chapter 14.

Start by thinking about what you already know about the topic. What do you need or want to learn? What questions do you have?

What have others written about the topic? What are the various issues, and the different POSITIONS and viewpoints? Be sure to seek out a variety of perspectives, and read them all with an open mind.

Check FACTS *and* CLAIMS. If something seems questionable, check it out. If you see a claim that sounds too good to be true, chances are it's not true. Search the web to see if anyone else is saying the same thing; if not, it may not be true. Or maybe you find several sources that say exactly the same thing; check them out—are they all sponsored by a single organization? Even if sources *look* real, don't assume they are; fake sources are usually designed to look legitimate.

For more on checking facts, see Chapter 6.

Come up with a working thesis

At this point, you should be ready to write out a thesis, a sentence that identifies your topic and the point you want to make about it. Rarely if ever will you have a final thesis when you start drafting, but establishing a tentative one will help focus your thinking and any research you may yet do. Here are some prompts to get you started:

- **Write out the point you want to make**: "In this essay, I will present reasons to quit social media."

- **Plot out a working thesis in two parts**, first stating your topic and then making a claim about the topic:

  | TOPIC | CLAIM |

  Quitting social media will improve your ability to focus, eliminate stress, and make you happier.

- **Be sure your** CLAIM **is debatable—and that it matters**. There's no point in arguing for a claim that is a fact or that no one would disagree with—or that no one would even care about.

- **Think about whether you need to narrow or** QUALIFY **your thesis**. You don't want to overstate your case—or make a claim that you'll have trouble supporting. Adding words like *generally* or *sometimes*, or saying *might* or *could* rather than *will* can make your thesis easier to support: "Quitting social media *could* help you sleep better, *might* make you more productive, and *may* even make you happier."

- **Does the thesis tell readers what's coming?** Will it help keep you and your readers focused on your message? Will it interest your readers?

At this point in your process, this is a tentative thesis, one that could change as you continue to do research, write, and revise. Continue exploring your topic, and don't stop until you feel you understand it well. But once you're confident that your thesis makes a claim that you can support and that will interest your audience, gather up the notes from your research. This is the information you'll draw from as support for your thesis.

Write out a draft

Once you have a working thesis, you will need to organize the evidence that supports what you're claiming and to start drafting. If you're writing a narrative, you might tell the story in CHRONOLOGICAL ORDER. If you're making an argument, you might present your evidence in order of importance, starting with the information that's the most important, followed by the less important information. And if you're describing something, you might organize it SPATIALLY, from left to right or top to bottom.

Ways of beginning

The way you begin a text can grab an audience's attention, or not. Here are some ways of making them interested in what you've got to say—and want to read on:

See Chapter 22 for tips on writing powerful opening sentences.

- By QUOTING or SUMMARIZING something others have said about your topic
- By telling an ANECDOTE that will get your audience's attention
- By posing a provocative question
- By stating your THESIS
- By using a startling fact, statistic, or VISUAL

Ways of organizing your evidence

Whatever your thesis, you need to provide good, reliable evidence to support what you say. The good news is that the ancient Greek philosopher Aristotle long ago developed strategies for finding such support, strategies that will serve you well both for finding evidence and for organizing it into paragraphs in the body of your essay. Following are a number of familiar strategies that can help you find and present evidence for what you say.

Description. When we describe something, we say what it looks like—or how it sounds, smells, feels, or tastes. Good descriptions provide concrete details that create some kind of DOMINANT IMPRESSION that helps your audience imagine what you're describing—and engages their interest. See, for instance, how Maya Angelou describes a group of people gathered in a store to listen to a prize fight on the radio:

> Women sat on kitchen chairs, dining-room chairs, stools, and upturned wooden boxes. Small children and babies perched on every lap available and men leaned on the shelves or on each other.
>
> —MAYA ANGELOU, "Champion of the World"

She could have simply said "the room was full of women, children, babies, and men"—but her vivid descriptive writing brings the scene to life, helps us to picture the scene. You'll have reason to use description in almost all the writing you do: in a REPORT on climate change, you might describe some recent hurricanes or severe droughts that are thought to result; and in a NARRATIVE, you'd likely describe people, places, and things.

While you can sometimes describe something using words alone, there may be cases when you need to include an image to show what you're describing. If, for example, you were writing an art history essay about the architecture of Barcelona, you might describe the multicolored mosaics, stained glass, and glazed titles of its music hall, pictured on the next page. But could you do so in a way that would enable your readers to visualize it?

Narrative. Using narrative means telling a story. And according to Tyrion Lannister, "There's nothing in the world more powerful than a good story." Exactly! A good story well told can engage your readers and provide memorable support for an argument.

Facade of the
Palau de la Música
Catalana.

In a book called *The Years That Matter Most*, Paul Tough writes about the growing inequality in US colleges and universities, supporting his argument with stories about how this inequality affects several students he interviewed. He tells about Clara, whose parents pay $400 an hour for ACT tutoring to help her get into Yale; about Kim, who gets no support of any kind, financial or emotional, from her family when she goes to Clemson; and about many other students as well—all narratives that provide powerful support for Tough's argument.

You can use narratives to good effect in writing you do as well—in an essay ARGUMENT for universal early child education, you might include a brief narrative about your own childhood experience in preschool. Or you could add several ANECDOTES about athletes you know who've suffered concussions in a REPORT on head injuries in football. Be sure, however, that any story you tell supports your point, and that it is not the only evidence you offer.

See pp. 108–9 for an example of how narrative is used in an ad.

Comparison and contrast. When we compare things, we focus on their similarities; when we contrast them, we look at their differences. These strategies can help support what you say, explaining something that's unfamiliar by comparing (or contrasting) it with something more familiar. In a blog post arguing that the use of singular *they* is inevitable, for example, linguist Dennis Baron compares it with singular *you*, pointing out that it too was originally plural but eventually became singular as well. As a student, you'll often be assigned to compare and contrast things as a way of making some kind of point: the music of Philip Glass and Steve Reich, the political philosophies of John Locke and Thomas Hobbes, three poems by Adrienne Rich.

There are two methods you can use for making comparisons: the block method, in which you discuss everything you have to say about one item first and then everything you want to say about another item; or the point-by-point method, in which you discuss one point for both items and then do the same for another point.

Definition. A definition says what something is—and what it is not. As a writer, you'll often need to provide definitions for words you use that your audience may not understand. And definitions can play another role as well, especially when you're writing about controversial topics. If you define abortion as killing an unborn child but your readers define it as a right for women to have control over their own bodies, they are unlikely to agree with any arguments you make.

Example. Good examples bring a subject to life, making abstract ideas more concrete and easier to understand—and providing specific instances to back up a point. Here's Jose Antonio Vargas, someone who's won the Pulitzer Prize and "lived the American Dream," writing about how he is still undocumented:

See pp. 108–10 for more on using examples.

> But I am still an undocumented immigrant. And that means living a different kind of reality. It means going about my day in fear of being found out. It means rarely trusting people, even those closest to me, with who I really am. It means keeping my family photos in a shoebox rather than displaying them on shelves in my home, so friends don't ask about them. It means reluctantly, even painfully, doing things I

Gleaming Lights of the Souls (2008), an infinity room by Yayoi Kusama, at the Louisiana Museum of Modern Art in Humlebaek, Denmark.

know are wrong and unlawful. And it has meant relying on a sort of 21st-century underground railroad of supporters, people who took an interest in my future and took risks for me.

—JOSE ANTONIO VARGAS,
"My Life as an Undocumented Immigrant"

With one example after another, he helps us understand what it means to live in the United States as an undocumented immigrant.

Examples can often be presented visually, and sometimes need to be. You could, for example, describe Yayoi Kusama's famous infinity rooms with words: that they have mirrors on the walls and ceiling and a floor in a reflecting pool, that they include hundreds of lights that change colors, and so on. But if you want readers to get any sense of what an infinity room is, you would also want to provide a photograph.

With words or images, a good example can help you to explain a general statement or concept—and to support what you say about it.

Classification. When we classify things, we group them into categories. Books, for example, can be classified as fiction, nonfiction, fantasy, poetry, picture books, and so on. As a writer, you might use classification as a way to organize a text or to elaborate on a topic.

If you're writing a presentation ANALYZING films for a course on the history of films, you might organize your text by classifying the films by genre—dramas, thrillers, comedies, musicals, and so on—and then discuss them genre by genre. But you could classify them in many other ways as well. *Netflix*, for instance, now classifies TV shows into dozens of categories, among them Feel-Good TV shows, Crime TV shows, Family Watch Together TV, and Quirky Sitcoms. The categories you choose will depend on your AUDIENCE and PURPOSE.

Cause and effect. When we analyze causes, we try to understand and explain why something happened. Why have there been so many wildfires in recent years? Why did Tom Brady leave the New England Patriots? And when we think about effects, we speculate about what might happen. How will the COVID-19 pandemic affect the global economy? How will the Patriots do without Brady? As a writer, you'll sometimes need to cite causes or effects. In a LITERACY NARRATIVE about deciding to major in English, you might focus on the books that caused you to love literature, or on particular effects that will serve you well in the future—the ability to write well, for instance.

> When a national chain bought Elaine Godfrey's hometown newspaper, the effects on town life were dramatic. Read about what happened on p. 669.

Arguing about causes or effects can be tricky, because it's rarely possible to link a specific cause to a specific effect. Consider what we know about what's caused so many people to become ill from vaping, or the long-term effects of climate change: in each case, there are many *possible* or *probable* causes and effects. When you write about causes and effects, then, you can often only argue that they are likely, or probable—and one reason that you'll want to QUALIFY what you say by using words like *might* or *could* is to limit what you claim.

Consider counterarguments and other perspectives

Unless you're the first to write about your topic, many others will have opinions about it as well—and some of them will have ideas that differ from yours. If you've done your homework, you'll be aware of what else has been said and will have thought about it. You need to acknowledge other perspectives, and to do so respectfully and accurately. And you need to respond to any COUNTERARGUMENTS, objections that others may have to your position. Whether you provide evidence refuting ideas you take issue with, admit that some other position just might be right, or QUALIFY what you yourself say, acknowledging other perspectives demonstrates that you've done your homework and that you've considered opinions other than your own carefully.

In a newspaper profile of Adam Sandler, Jamie Lauren Keiles acknowledges that not everyone agrees with those of us who love *Big Daddy* and his many other zany films—and admits that such criticism is "sometimes" fair:

> Critics, as a group, hate Sandler comedies, sometimes fairly, but just as often because the movies undermine the project of close reading altogether. If you don't think a Sandler comedy is funny, no amount of thinking on the page is ever going to convince you otherwise. It either tickles your funny bone or it doesn't.
>
> —JAMIE LAUREN KEILES, "Adam Sandler's Everlasting Shtick"

Force yourself to consider opposing arguments, especially if they challenge your best-loved ideas.
—CHARLIE MUNGER

Cole Sprouse and Adam Sandler in *Big Daddy*.

Ways of concluding

Your conclusion is where you get to wrap things up and to leave your audience thinking about what you've said. Here are some ways of doing that:

See Chapter 22
for tips on
writing strong
closing sentences.

- By reiterating your main point
- By issuing a call to action
- By saying why your point matters
- By inviting response

Come up with a title

TITLES are important. On the one hand, they need to tell readers what your piece is about and give some sense of what you're going to say about it. As an author, however, you'll want to come up with a title that will get your readers' attention and make them want to read on. Whatever your purpose, you should always think about your rhetorical situation when deciding on a title, to be sure it will appeal to your AUDIENCE and reflect your STANCE.

Some titles simply indicate the topic:

- "When Doctors Make Mistakes"
- "The Sanctuary of School"
- "My Life as an Undocumented Immigrant"
- "Stop Coddling the Super-Rich"
- "How Junk Food Can End Obesity"

Other titles are more provocative, saying something surprising or asking a startling question. Such titles often reflect a strong point of view—and make readers want to read on (or not):

- "Well-Behaved Women Seldom Make History"
- "Have Smartphones Destroyed a Generation?"
- "What My Bike Has Taught Me about White Privilege"

- "Is Google Making Us Stupid?"
- "Get a Knife, Get a Dog, but Get Rid of Guns"

Some titles include a subtitle, usually to explain the title or indicate the author's stance:

- "For Better or Worse: *Spotify* and the Music Industry"
- "Minority Student Clubs: Segregation or Integration?"
- "Extra Lives: Why Video Games Matter"
- "Utopian Dream: A New Farm Bill"
- "To *Siri* with Love: How One Boy with Autism Became BFF with Apple's *Siri*"

Get response and revise

One good thing about writing, according to author Robert Cormier, is that "you don't have to get it right the first time, unlike, say, a brain surgeon. You can always do it better." That's for sure! And a good first step to doing it "better" is to get a little help from your friends. Once you have a draft, you'll want to get feedback from some readers. Here's a list of questions for reading a draft with a critical eye and thinking about how it might be revised:

- How does the OPENING get your AUDIENCE's attention? Does it make clear why your topic matters?
- Is your point stated explicitly in a THESIS—and if not, should it be?
- Have you provided sufficient REASONS and EVIDENCE to support your thesis? If not, do you need to find more evidence? Or do you need to QUALIFY your thesis to make it one you can support?
- Have you noted any COUNTERARGUMENTS or views other than your own—and represented them accurately and respectfully? What other positions should you consider?

- Have you cited any sources? If so, have you clearly distinguished what they say from what you say—and provided DOCUMENTATION? Are any QUOTATIONS introduced with a SIGNAL PHRASE?

- Is the text organized in a way that's easy to follow? Have you provided TRANSITIONS to help readers follow what you've written? Are there headings to help readers see the main parts—and if not, should you add some?

- Does the text include any VISUALS? Is there any data that would be easier to understand if you presented it in a pie chart or bar graph—or illustrated it with a photo?

- How does the text CONCLUDE? What does it leave readers thinking? Have you invited your readers to respond? How else might you conclude?

- Does your title announce the topic and give some idea of what you have to say about it—and will it get your audience's attention? If not, might it help to add a subtitle?

I try to leave out the parts that people skip.
—ELMORE LEONARD

Once you've gotten feedback and read over your draft yourself, put it aside for a day or two if you can. The above questions will have identified plenty of specific things to consider as you revise, but be sure to keep your RHETORICAL SITUATION firmly in mind as you work, especially your AUDIENCE and PURPOSE. You want to make your text as readable as possible, and to be sure that everything in the draft contributes to your point and purpose. Take seriously any advice you've gotten from other readers, but don't feel that you have to do everything they suggest. You're the author!

Edit!

Cheryl Strayed may be the author of a best-selling book called *Wild*, but it seems that she's rather cautious when it comes to her writing, saying that she writes to find out what she has to say—and that she *edits* "to figure out how to say it right." Good advice! So once you've written and revised what you want to say, you need to fine-tune your text to be sure that it says precisely what you want it to say, and that your readers will be able to follow and understand what you say. There's no single recipe for doing that, but here are some tips that can help guide you.

Editing paragraphs

- Check each paragraph to be sure it contributes to your point in some way.
- Does each paragraph focus on one point—and include a TOPIC SENTENCE that tells readers what it will focus on?
- Is each paragraph developed in enough detail?
- If any paragraphs are especially long, check to see if they might be split into two paragraphs.
- Pay special attention to your OPENING paragraph (will it grab your audience's attention?) and CONCLUDING paragraph (will it solidify your message?).

Editing sentences

- Be sure that your sentences *are* sentences, starting with a capital letter and ending with a period, question mark, or exclamation point; and including a subject and VERB.
- Check for sentences beginning with *it is* or *there is*. These can be good ways of emphasizing or introducing an idea, but often they simply add unnecessary words. Why say "It is essential that we speak up" rather than "We need to speak up"?
- Check to see if you've used any unnecessary words—words like *very* or *really*.
- Count up the words in each sentence. If too many are pretty much the same length, see if you can combine some sentences, add details, or vary the sentence structure in some other way.
- Pay attention to the way your sentences open. If sentence after sentence begins with a subject, try varying them by adding PREPOSITIONAL PHRASES or TRANSITIONS.

Chapter 23 offers advice for writing good sentences.

Editing words

- Have you used any terms that your readers may not understand? If so, be sure to include DEFINITIONS.

- Think about what TONE is most appropriate for your audience and purpose—serious? playful? casual? academic?—and be sure that the words you use reflect that tone.

Words matter, tone matters, civility matters.

—JEN PSAKI

- Check to be sure that your language is respectful. Especially when you're writing about a controversial topic or discussing positions you disagree with, use words that demonstrate RESPECT—and not disrespect. Civility matters!

- Pay attention to your use of gender pronouns. Use *he / him / his* to refer to someone who is male and uses those pronouns—and *she / her / hers* to refer to someone who is female and uses those pronouns. If, however, you're referring to someone who uses *they / them / their* or some other pronouns (*ze* or *hir*, for example), call them what they want to be called. And if you're writing about someone whose gender is unknown or not pertinent, use SINGULAR *THEY* (as in "Nobody would admit they were wrong.").

Give some thought to design

You're almost there: you've written out a draft, gotten response, and edited your text. It says what you want it to say. So now you need to think about what you want it to look like, and whether there are any design elements that will help your readers follow what you say. As usual, you'll need to think hard about what will work best for your AUDIENCE, PURPOSE, and the rest of your RHETORICAL SITUATION.

- Choose FONTS that suit your purpose and reflect the TONE you want to convey. And think about whether there are any words you want to emphasize with *italics* or **boldface** (or ***boldface italics***).

- Think about whether you should add headings to help readers see (or scan) your main points.

- Is there any text that would be easier to understand if it were set off in a list?
- If you're presenting numerical data, would it be easier to see in a pie chart or bar graph?
- Are you including any VISUALS—and if not, are there any images, charts, or other visuals that would help to illustrate a point? If so, be sure to include CAPTIONS.
- Be sure as well to refer to any images, charts, or graphs in the text so that readers know how they relate to your point.

Don't forget to proofread

Read over your text slowly, start to finish. If at all possible, print it out; mistakes can be hard to spot on a computer screen. Then read it aloud bit by bit.

- Read each sentence to be sure it begins with a capital letter and ends with a period, question mark, or exclamation point.
- If you've included headings, be sure they're all in the same font and with the same amount of space above and below.
- If you've included any VISUALS, be sure they are all referred to in the text.
- Check for PARALLELISM to be sure that all headings or all elements in a series or list have the same structure: all NOUNS, all GERUNDS, all PREPOSITIONAL PHRASES, all commands, and so on.
- Check your spelling. Use a spellchecker, but be aware that it won't catch wrong words that are spelled correctly. For example: if you write *principle* when it should be *principal*, a spellchecker would not likely catch the mistake.
- If your text is in MLA, APA, or another style, make sure that your title, margins, spacing, page numbers, and documentation follow the requirements of that style.

Take time to reflect on your own writing process

I think I did pretty well, considering I started out with nothing but a bunch of blank paper.
—STEVE MARTIN

Once you've finished writing something, it's a good idea to take stock of what you've written—and of your writing process. Here are some questions that can help you get started:

- What did you do well?
- If you could do one more draft, what would you change?
- What did you find challenging? easy? satisfying? fun?
- What response did you get from others, and how did it help?
- Did you do any research for this project? If so, how did it contribute to what you wrote? Did it change your mind in any way about your topic?
- If you cited other sources, how many different perspectives did you include? Did you incorporate positions that differed from your own, and how fairly did you represent those views?
- How did your audience affect what you wrote?
- What is your favorite sentence or passage, and why?
- What was your purpose for writing, and how well do you think you achieved that purpose?

Finally, think about what you've learned about yourself as a writer. What do you want to work on?

REFLECT! "Forget a room of one's own—write in the kitchen, lock yourself up in the bathroom. Write on the bus or the welfare line, on the job or during meals." Cultural critic **Gloria Anzaldúa** wrote these words in 1981, long before cell phones allowed us to write pretty much anywhere. Picture her on a bus, pad of paper in one hand and a pen in the other, *writing*. Where do you do most of your writing—on a bus or train? in an armchair? at breakfast? And how do you do it—on a laptop? a mobile phone? a pad of paper? Think about your circumstances today: where you write and how that allows you to do your best writing.

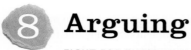

8 Arguing

FIGHT FOR THE THINGS THAT YOU CARE ABOUT.
BUT DO IT IN A WAY THAT WILL LEAD OTHERS TO JOIN YOU.

—RUTH BADER GINSBURG

COME NOW, LET US REASON TOGETHER.

—ISAIAH 1:18

College athletes should be paid. Climate change is a reality, and one cause is the burning of fossil fuels. Corporate tax cuts enable companies to pay their workers more. These are all arguments, not facts. They make claims that are debatable and with which we may agree or disagree—so anyone making such claims needs to support them with good reasons and evidence. Think for a moment about some of the claims that surround us, coming from social media, podcasts, newspapers, even song lyrics and movies (think "We Are the Champions" or *Parasite*). So we're surrounded by argument—what we read and see, what we hear, what we talk about, and especially what we write. We need to look and listen with an open mind but a critical eye, to present our own arguments carefully, and to respond to those of others respectfully. This chapter provides a roadmap for reading, writing, and thinking about the arguments you'll encounter in college, at work, and everywhere in between.

A GUIDE TO DEVELOPING AN ARGUMENT

You'll often be assigned to write an essay that argues a position of some kind—to stake a CLAIM that you then support with REASONS and EVIDENCE. Here now is some advice that will make you aware of the various choices you'll have and that will help you make good choices. It's designed to be used *as you write*. Keep it close at hand!

Identify a topic that matters

If you get to choose your topic, choose one that matters to you and will matter to others. But even if you're assigned to write about a specific topic, try to come up with some aspect that interests you—or that will be of interest to others.

Think about your rhetorical situation

Once you have a topic, give some thought to who your audience is, what you hope to accomplish, and the rest of your rhetorical situation.

Purpose. What do you hope to accomplish by writing about this issue? What do you hope to learn? What do you want to persuade your audience to think or do? How can you best achieve these purposes?

Audience. Whom do you want to reach? What do they know about your topic, and what if any background information will you need to provide? Are they likely to think your argument matters, or will you have to convince them? How sympathetic are they likely to be to your argument? What kinds of evidence will they find persuasive? What values do they hold, and how are they different from yours?

Stance. How do you want to come across as an author—as curious? well-informed? sympathetic?—and how can you establish your credibility to write on this topic? Why do you care about the topic? Do you have any preconceived ideas about it? Where did these ideas come from? How else might you think about it?

Context. What's motivating you to write about this issue? What is being said about it: what are the various perspectives? If you're writing in response to an assignment, what's your time frame and are there any requirements you need to keep in mind?

Medium and design. How will your argument be delivered—in print? online? as a speech? How does the medium affect the way it will be designed and the kinds of evidence you can provide—can you include images? audio? links to other sources?

Be sure the topic is arguable— and one you can approach with an open mind

Begin by making sure that the topic is arguable—not an easily verified fact or a mere opinion, but a subject about which there are a number of different perspectives. Think about whether it's worth discussing: Is it a topic that matters, and one that others (including your audience) will care about? Be sure the topic is manageable, given the time and resources you have. Finally, ask yourself whether it's a topic you can investigate with an open mind. If not, find another topic.

Let's assume you're intrigued by a topic you've read about in your campus newspaper: whether NCAA athletes should be paid. A quick search reveals a wide range of viewpoints on this topic, suggesting that it is timely and not a matter of simple facts or mere opinions. So this topic appears to be arguable; so far, so good. The sources you've identified in your quick search suggest that it's also manageable, that you'll be able to find informative arguments on all sides of the issue that will be readily available to you online or through your library. Finally, since you have no preconceived idea about whether or not athletes should be paid, you believe you can approach the topic with a fair and open mind.

In an interview about how he came to write his 2016 book *Indentured: The Rebellion against the College Sports Cartel*, Joe Nocera reflects on how he first became interested in the topic of pay for athletes in 2011, when he wrote an article in the *New York Times Magazine* arguing that college athletes should be paid:

> I got interested in this subject around rights, much more than the issue of pay. I did write the first story with an idea of how to pay the players, but it was more of a thought exercise. And I did it five years ago, when I was just starting to get into this, and before the widespread criticism of the NCAA really gained steam. So, I hadn't really thought much about it. And in the course of doing that story . . . I began to realize how pervasively the life of an athlete is controlled.
>
> —JOE NOCERA, "Let's Start Paying College Athletes"

Note that Nocera started with a question for which he had no answers, and one he hadn't "thought much about." So he began with

Like many of the most talented college athletes, Zion Williamson was "one and done" and left Duke to play for the New Orleans Pelicans.

a topic that intrigued him rather than one he had already made up his mind about. And the research he then did led him to understand how many perspectives there are on the topic and how many lives are affected by it.

Research your topic with an open mind

Start by thinking about what you already know about the topic—and what you don't know. What questions do you have? What do you think about the topic, and why? Finally, think again about whether you can explore this topic with an open mind.

Do some research

If you're exploring a current topic, you'll likely find a lot of sources online; but if you're studying a topic from the past, you'll probably find many of the sources you'll need in the library. And for some topics you may need to conduct interviews, observations, or other field research. Whatever research you do, keep in mind that your goal is to learn about the topic, not simply to find evidence to support ideas you already have.

Identify the various positions on the topic

You'll want to learn about all the PERSPECTIVES you can find. Especially if you have an idea of your own position on the topic, keep an open mind. What are some of the issues that are being discussed, and what are the various positions on those issues? What are others saying—and why?

Authors of a piece about an Amazon warehouse interviewed executives, managers, workers, and union leaders to get many perspectives on the situation. Read the article on p. 553.

Formulate an explicit position, and state it as a working thesis

When you feel you understand the topic well and have enough information to work with, you'll need to formulate a position that you'll be able to support. And once you can articulate your position, write it out in an explicit THESIS, one that clearly identifies your topic and makes a claim that will get your audience's attention. For example:

> Artificial intelligence will be the death of humans as we know them.
>
> Professional athletes today are shuffled around like pawns.
>
> COVID-19 will change every aspect of our lives.

Be careful, however, not to overstate your thesis: you may need to QUALIFY it using words like *sometimes*, *might*, or *in some cases*, which will limit your position to one that you'll be able to support. For example:

> Artificial intelligence *may well be* the death of humans as we know them.
>
> Today, professional athletes are *too often* shuffled around like pawns.
>
> COVID-19 will change *many* aspects of our lives.

See pp. 84–85 for more detail on coming up with a thesis. Such qualifying words and phrases show that you are arguing seriously and cautiously, rather than making absolute claims that you may not be able to substantiate. So be sure to ask yourself whether your thesis needs to be qualified—and if so, in what ways. And keep in mind that at this point in the process, this is a *working* thesis; it may change as you continue to work on your draft.

Here's how one author team stakes out their position on whether higher education is for everyone:

> Study after study reminds us that higher education is one of the best investments we can make. We all know that, on average, college graduates make significantly more money over their lifetimes than those with only a high school education. What gets less attention is the fact that not all college degrees are equal. There is enormous variation in the so-called return to education depending on factors such as institution attended, field of study, whether or not a student graduates, and post-graduation occupation. While the average return to obtaining a college degree is clearly positive . . . it is not uni-

versally so. For certain schools, majors, occupations, and individuals, college may not be a smart investment.

—STEPHANIE OWEN and ISABEL SAWHILL,
"Should Everyone Go to College?"

Their position is clear: higher education is not always a good investment. Notice, however, how careful they are to qualify their argument, noting that while college graduates earn more "on average," it is "not universally so," and that in certain cases college "may not be a smart investment." By saying that higher education *may* not be a good investment, the authors have limited their position to one they will be able to support.

Come up with support for your position

With so much misinformation flying around today, it's more important than ever for the arguments you make to be backed up by solid support. Even in everyday arguments—say over a claim that Impossible Burgers are ten times better than the real thing—you'd better be prepared to prove that the new meatless wonders are really, really good—or face skeptics who will say, simply, "Says who?" or "Can you prove it?" Answering such questions persuasively is the key to supporting your claim. The ancient Greek philosopher Aristotle long ago wrote that we should use "all the available means" we can to persuade an audience and suggested three in particular: providing good reasons and evidence, demonstrating credibility, and appealing to emotion.

You're entitled to your own opinions but not your own facts.

—DANIEL PATRICK MOYNIHAN

Provide good reasons and evidence

Whatever your thesis, it needs to be backed up by reasons *why* you take that position. One way to think about that is to write out your thesis and then answer the question *why?* For example:

Artificial intelligence may well be the death of humans as we know them. *Why?* Because robots will be able to do what humans now do—and more.

Too often today, professional athletes are shuffled around like pawns. *Why?* Because most contracts give more rights to teams and owners than to players.

COVID-19 will change many aspects of our lives. *Why?* Because experts including physicians and epidemiologists say that old behaviors won't work in a post-pandemic world.

If you can't come up with good reasons, you may need to revise your thesis—or find another topic. But once you have a list of reasons, think about which ones best suit your PURPOSE, and which ones your AUDIENCE is likely to accept. Then you need to provide evidence to support those reasons. While there are many kinds of evidence you can use to good advantage, we'll focus here on five common ones: facts and statistics, expert testimony, narrative, examples, and personal experience.

See pp. 85–90 for more on finding evidence.

Facts and statistics. Facts are ideas that have been proven to be true; because they can be verified, they serve as a kind of evidence that an audience will accept. Statistics are numerical data gathered from research or experimentation. See how a report about World Water Day provides both facts and statistics to support what it says about the importance of clean water:

A staggering 844 million people live without access to clean water. That's roughly 1 in 10 people on earth, or about twice the population of the United States. March 22nd is World Water Day 2018, a day to pause, consider the impact of clean water in the world, and make a difference.

A stunning statistic—that one in ten people in the world don't have access to clean water—leads to a description of ten facts about the water crisis:

1. 100 million families are stuck in a cycle of poverty and disease because they don't have access to safe water.
2. More people die from unsafe water than from all forms of violence, including war.
3. 2.4 billion people, 1 in 3, lack access to a toilet.

Women
in Tanzania
carrying water.

4. Water-borne diseases kill more children under the age of 5 than malaria, measles, and HIV/AIDS—combined.

5. In developing countries, as much as 80% of illnesses are linked to poor water and sanitation conditions.

6. Women and girls spend up to 6 hours every day walking to get water for their families.

7. The average distance that women in Africa and Asia walk to collect water is 3.7 miles. That is 19,500 steps, every day, just to get water that is making them sick.

8. 443 million school days are lost each year due to water-related diseases.

9. Time spent gathering water around the world translates to $24 billion in lost economic benefits each year, furthering the cycle of poverty.

10. Every dollar invested in safe water and improved hygiene and sanitation results in 8 dollars of increased economic activity.

—"World Water Day 2018: 10 Facts about the Water Crisis"

The writers of this report take care to show that these are indeed "facts" by linking to a Water Crisis Fact Sheet.

Facts and statistics like these can help you make sound and believable arguments. But you'll want to make sure that any facts or numbers you cite are accurate, and think about whether they'll be accepted by your readers. You'll want to be especially careful with statistics, which can all too easily be manipulated or taken out of context.

Expert testimony. One of the most persuasive kinds of evidence is the direct testimony of experts on the issue you're writing about. Citing authorities also demonstrates that you've researched the topic and know what you're talking about, adding to your CREDIBILITY as an author.

For an article on the dangers concussions cause to many athletes, Kristin Sainani, a professor of health policy, interviewed David Camarillo, a professor of bioengineering whose lab focuses on understanding and preventing head injuries. Throughout her article, Sainani cites information she learned from Camarillo as evidence that wearing a helmet does little to prevent concussions and to convince readers that equipment to protect against concussions "needs to be better." Even as a professor of health policy herself, Sainani made her argument more persuasive by citing someone with more expertise on her topic—and you can do the same by citing experts in fields you write about.

Narrative. We all know that stories matter—and that a powerful story can engage audiences and help support an argument. Be sure, however, that any story you tell is pertinent to your point—and that it is not the only evidence you provide. Advertisements often use narrative to get our attention, as in the ad on the next page from a bus stop in New York for Feeding America, an organization that provides a nationwide network of food banks. With just two sentences, the ad tells a story that supports the argument that hunger is something that needs to end.

Examples. Good EXAMPLES make abstract ideas more concrete and easier to understand—and can provide specific instances to back up a claim. See how one author uses a specific example to support his

argument that resolving lawsuits against opioid producers with large
cash settlements has made those drug companies "big winners":

> Consider the case of Florida, which in 2001 became one of the first
> states to investigate Purdue Pharma. Its attorney general at the time,
> Robert Butterworth, pointing to a growing number of overdose
> deaths, declared that he would discover when Purdue Pharma first
> knew about OxyContin's abuse.
>
> That never happened. Instead, state investigators interviewed only
> a single former OxyContin sales representative, and Mr. Butterworth,

who was running for a State Senate seat, ended the case soon after it was filed.

He lost his election and the case's settlement proved empty. While Purdue Pharma agreed to pay $2 million to fund a system that would monitor how Florida doctors prescribed opioids, state legislators blocked its creation. David Aronberg, the state attorney for Palm Beach County, told me that nearly all of the $2 million was returned to the drug company, and Florida went on to become a major center of the opioid crisis.

—BARRY MEIER, "Opioid Makers Are the Big Winners in Lawsuits"

This example provides concrete evidence to show one instance when a drug manufacturer actually benefited, unfairly and mightily, from a settlement—and how "Florida went on to become a major center of the opioid crisis."

Personal experience can sometimes provide powerful support for an argument since it brings a kind of "eyewitness" evidence. See how Louie Lazar, a journalist who's fascinated by both basketball and Buddhism, opens an article about the surprising popularity of

Buddhist monks shooting hoops in Tibet.

basketball in Tibet with a personal ANECDOTE about how he came to research that topic:

> A few years ago, while living in Queens, I began to wonder whether any Buddhist monks played hoops. I'd loved the sport since childhood and had recently become fascinated by practitioners of Buddhism. And while the pairing may seem far-fetched, it made a certain sense to me. Devotion to the sport involves countless hours in the solitude of echoing, dimly lit places . . . where one undergoes a genuinely meditative sensory experience: the rhythmic bounding of a ball, the mental focus and repetition essential for knocking down free throws, the visualizations, such as imagining oneself sinking a last-second shot. There's a reason Phil Jackson—a.k.a. the Zen Master—didn't coach football.
>
> I visited a few Buddhist monasteries in the New York area, where I was met with a consistent response from the polite but puzzled residents: *No, monks don't play basketball.* That seemed to be that.
>
> But there's always the Internet. Late one evening in 2017, I googled "basketball and Buddhist monk" and eventually found a *Facebook* page on which a grainy video had been posted. It showed a red-robed monk on an outdoor court effortlessly leaping up, grabbing the rim, and shattering the backboard.
>
> —LOUIE LAZAR, "How Tibet Went Crazy for Hoops"

This personal anecdote contributes to Lazar's article in two respects: by providing evidence that some Buddhist monks do in fact play basketball, and also by demonstrating that Lazar has done his homework and knows what he's writing about. In your own writing, make sure that any personal experience you cite is pertinent to your argument and will serve your purpose.

For another example, take a look at David French's article in the *National Review* about the virtues of traditional masculinity and his decision to become more fit. He describes being on a Cub Scout trip when his son suffered a serious head injury. When medics were unable to reach the bottom of the ravine, French picked up his son and ran up a steep incline, something he would have been unable to do had he not been so fit. Reflecting on this life-threatening event, French explains:

> But I answered the call of my "traditional masculinity" and got stronger not because I wanted to look good or attract women or "be fit" but because something inside me whispered that an able-bodied man should not be weak. In other words, I tried my best to become a true "grown man."
>
> —DAVID FRENCH, "Grown Men Are the Solution, Not the Problem"

Demonstrate your credibility

You need to establish your own AUTHORITY as a writer: to show that you know what you're talking about by citing trustworthy sources, and to demonstrate that you're fair by representing other positions evenhandedly and accurately. Be careful, though, not to overdo it, especially when you need to demonstrate respect as well as credibility. You don't want to come across as boastful. You might want to acknowledge those you've learned from, noting that you're "building on" their work.

When Jaron Lanier, often said to be the "father of virtual reality," decided that social media—for which he'd been an advocate—have become a monster we now can't control, he wrote a book called *Ten Arguments for Deleting Your Social Media Account RIGHT NOW*. Anticipating criticism of his position, Lanier acknowledged and addressed that criticism in the opening chapter:

> Plenty of critics like me have been warning that bad stuff was happening for a while now. . . . For years, I had to endure quite painful criticism from friends in Silicon Valley because I was perceived as a traitor for criticizing what we were doing. Lately I have the opposite problem. I argue that Silicon Valley people are for the most part decent, and I ask that we not be villainized; I take a lot of fresh heat

for that. Whether I've been too hard or too soft on my community is hard to know.

The more important question now is whether anyone's criticism will matter. It's undeniably out in the open that a bad technology is doing us harm, but will we—will you, meaning *you*, be able to resist and help steer the world to a better place?

—JARON LANIER, *Ten Arguments for Deleting Your Social Media*

In this passage, Lanier comes across as straightforward and honest: he's telling it like it is, even if he gets criticized for doing so. But then he takes an unexpected turn: rather than condemning "Silicon Valley," he argues that most people working there are in fact decent (and he includes himself in this "we") but then points to an even larger issue: Is it possible that by now, no one will be able to make "bad stuff" stop happening? Lanier suggests that such a goal can only be achieved if everyone who uses social media takes action, and he closes by addressing us directly—as *you*. Readers will know Lanier's credentials: they are detailed on the inside cover of the book. This passage increases his credibility by including himself in the group he's criticizing and by accepting responsibility, suggesting that we can trust him to be giving us his most thoughtful and best advice.

Appeal to your audience's emotion

Good reasons and evidence provide powerful support for an argument, but sometimes it helps to appeal to an audience's emotions as well—appealing to their hearts as well as their minds. Emotional appeals can be a powerful means of supporting an argument, stirring feelings and sometimes invoking values that those in your audience can be assumed to hold. Images are especially effective in conveying emotion and in stirring emotion in others, as did this photo of a dazed and wounded child, pulled from the rubble after air strikes in Aleppo. This photo galvanized millions to protest the war in Syria, to donate to charitable organizations trying to help, and to change their attitudes about the role the United States has played in that war.

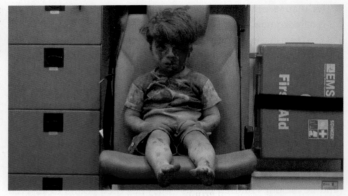

A young boy just rescued after an air strike in Aleppo, Syria.

Be careful when you make an emotional appeal that it suits your argument and purpose, and think about what you want your audience to think or do in response. Also, take care not to overdo it, pulling at their heartstrings so hard that your audience feels manipulated or that you have in some way taken advantage of your subject's vulnerability. Remember that if used inappropriately, emotional appeals may turn your audience off!

Consider other perspectives respectfully, and look for common ground

No matter what your position, others may have different views or even offer COUNTERARGUMENTS. You need to acknowledge views other than your own accurately and respectfully and to answer any objections—whether to explain why you disagree, concede that they have a point, or some of each. Doing so shows that you've done your homework and are aware of what else has been said, enhancing your authority to write on the topic and demonstrating to your readers that you're a writer they can trust. And including views that are contrary to your own shows you to be confident enough of your own views to acknowledge other perspectives that are also worth considering.

Acknowledging the views of others is also a way of establishing COMMON GROUND with those who hold positions different from yours—and showing that you're trying to understand where they're coming from will increase the likelihood that they'll take seriously what you say. And finding some point of agreement will always increase the likelihood that your own argument will be heard.

Sometimes building common ground is a matter of choosing the right words. Calling someone who doubts the existence of climate change a "climate denier," for example, is likely to end the conversation. Better instead to say they're skeptical of the scientific forecasts and to avoid any labels.

See how journalist Clive Thompson considers other points of view and builds common ground in arguing that technology is making our minds and our lives better:

> Some people panic that our brains are being deformed on a physiological level by today's technology: spend too much time flipping between windows and skimming text instead of reading a book, or interrupting your conversations to read text messages, and pretty soon you won't be able to concentrate on anything—and if you can't concentrate on it, you can't understand it either. In his book *The Shallows*, Nicholas Carr eloquently raised this alarm, arguing that the quality of our thought, as a species, rose in tandem with the ascendance of slow-moving, linear print and began declining with the arrival of the zingy, flighty Internet. "I'm not thinking the way I used to think," he worried.
>
> I'm certain that many of these fears are warranted. . . . Today's multitasking tools really do make it harder than before to stay focused. . . . One of the great challenges of today's digital thinking tools is knowing when *not* to use them, when to rely on the powers of older and slower technologies, like paper and books.
>
> —CLIVE THOMPSON, *Smarter Than You Think: How Technology Is Changing Our Minds for the Better*

Successful arguments include a healthy consideration for other views.

—JOHN DUFFY

The title of Thompson's book lets readers know that he is an advocate for new technologies: they are "changing our minds for the better." Yet he takes time to seek out those like Nicholas Carr who disagree with him, considering his opinion and quoting him, letting Carr speak for himself—a sign of respect. Thompson goes on to build common ground with those readers by acknowledging Carr's position as worthy of respect. He even heeds Carr's warning to some degree, noting that it's important to know when and when *not* to use digital tools.

Present your position as a response to what others say

Whatever your topic, you will rarely if ever be the first one to say something about it. What you say will be part of a larger conversation, one that began before you got there. It's a good idea, therefore, to start your essay by noting something else that has been said about the issue and then presenting your position as a response. Framing your ideas in this way is a means of engaging with the ideas of others, of weaving their ideas in with yours, and of entering that conversation.

In the following example from an op-ed column in the *New York Times* arguing that community colleges need more support, the president of LaGuardia Community College opens by noting something that many of those who read the *Times* probably assume about American college students: that they divide their time between "classes, parties, and extracurricular activities":

> You might think the typical college student lives in a state of bliss, spending each day moving among classes, parties and extracurricular activities. But the reality is that an increasingly small population of undergraduates enjoys that kind of life.
>
> Of the country's nearly 18 million undergraduates, more than 40 percent go to community college, and of those, only 62 percent

can afford to go to college full-time. By contrast, a mere 0.4 percent of students in the United States attend one of the ivies.

The typical student is not the one burnishing a fancy résumé with numerous unpaid internships. It's just the opposite: Over half of all undergraduates live at home to make their degrees more affordable, and a shocking 40 percent of students work at least 30 hours a week. About 25 percent work full-time and go to school full-time.

—GAIL O. MELLOW, "The Biggest Misconception about Today's College Students"

Mellow responds to what readers "might think" by questioning that assumption, noting that very few students live "that kind of life"—and that more than 40 percent attend a community college and work at least thirty hours a week. She then points out that public funding for community colleges is "significantly less than for 4-year colleges"—and states her position clearly and explicitly:

Community colleges need increased funding, and students need access to more flexible federal and state financial aid, enhanced paid internships and college work-study programs. . . . It's time to put public and private money where more and more students are

Students at LaGuardia Community College.

educated, and remove the real, but surmountable, obstacles that stand between them and a degree.

Whenever you argue a position, you're responding to something someone else said or did that has motivated you to speak up. Especially in academic writing, you're expected to do more than just assert your own position; you need to let your readers know what larger conversation you're responding to.

Establish a responsible stance and a trustworthy tone

In a time of arguments based on fake news, misleading headlines, and downright lies, it's more important than ever that you aim for honesty and truth, take full responsibility for what you say, and establish a reasonable, trustworthy tone. After all, your audience must trust that you know what you're talking about and believe that you have their best interests at heart if they're to listen carefully to what you say, much less accept what you want them to think or do.

See how Kamala Harris establishes a trustworthy tone in a commencement address at Howard University, a school that she herself attended:

> I've had the honor of speaking at many commencements. But this one is particularly special for me. Because decades ago, I sat just where you sit now, feeling the embrace of my Howard family.
>
> Our Howard family.
>
> And a family, at its best, shares common values and aspirations. . . . A family looks for ways to support and inspire one another. . . .
>
> You are . . . part of a legacy that has now endured and thrived for 150 years.
>
> Endured when the doors of higher education were closed to Black students. Endured when segregation and discrimination were the law of the land.

> But over the last 150 years, Howard has endured and thrived. Generations of students have been nurtured and challenged here—and provided with the tools and confidence to soar.
>
> —KAMALA HARRIS, Howard University commencement address

It's not hard for Harris to win her audience's trust, having graduated from Howard University herself. But she makes the most of it, noting that she's "had the honor" of speaking at many commencements, but that "this one is particularly special." In fact, she still recalls "feeling the embrace" of "Our Howard family." A family shares common values and aspirations, and her words suggest that she and her audience have much in common beyond having attended the same school. And when she tells them they have "the tools and confidence to soar," she speaks from personal experience: she's been where they are now and assures them that they have what it takes "to soar." Her words demonstrate that she knows what she's talking about—and both understands and cares about the members of her audience.

There are other ways to establish trustworthiness and credibility, of course. Harris could have, for example, cited statistics about how many generations of successful graduates Howard has sent forth to uphold its values. Or she could have drawn on testimony from other respected and knowledgeable scholars who can also speak to Howard's ability to help students "soar." But in this instance, she draws on her own authority—as a highly successful former prosecutor, attorney general of California, and senator—and her own experience to build a sense of trust with her audience.

REFLECT! Find a speech on *YouTube* given by someone who interests you, perhaps an author or a candidate for office, and listen for how that speaker establishes credibility—or not. What does the speaker do (or fail to do) to come across as trustworthy (or not)?

Invite response

Read how Benji Backer invites his fellow conservatives to become active in environmental issues on p. 746.

Whatever your topic, you are not likely to be the first one to write about it. If in writing about an issue, you're joining a larger conversation, then you should invite your readers to do the same—to respond to what you say and add their voices to that conversation. One way to do this is to conclude by calling on readers to do something specific, as civil rights activist Michelle Alexander does in the introduction to her book *The New Jim Crow*:

> A new social consensus must be forged about race and the role of race in defining the basic structure of our society, if we hope ever to abolish the New Jim Crow. This new consensus must begin with dialogue, a conversation that fosters a critical consciousness, a key prerequisite to effective social action. My writing is an attempt to ensure that the conversation does not end with nervous laughter.
>
> —MICHELLE ALEXANDER, *The New Jim Crow: Mass Incarceration in the Age of Colorblindness*

Here Alexander calls on readers to act, to join a conversation that she hopes her book will begin, one that she says is "prerequisite to effective social action."

Now see how she concludes an op-ed on the same topic published in the *New York Times*. Like many newspapers, the *Times* explicitly invites readers to respond by sending in letters to the editor or posting comments online, and Alexander concludes by naming specific goals and how they should be met—and then challenging her readers to respond to a direct question:

> If our goal is *not* a better system of mass criminalization, but instead the creation of safe, caring, thriving communities, then we ought to be heavily investing in quality schools, job creation, drug treatment and mental health care in the least advantaged communities rather than pouring billions into their high-tech management and control. Fifty years ago, the Rev. Dr. Martin Luther King Jr. warned that "when machines and computers, profit motives and property

rights are considered more important than people, the giant triplets of racism, extreme materialism and militarism are incapable of being conquered." We failed to heed his warning back then. Will we make a different choice today?

In this conclusion, Alexander calls directly on readers to reject mass criminalization and instead to invest in education, job creation, and health care as the best way to create "safe . . . communities." To underscore this position, she notes that citizens failed to act when Martin Luther King Jr. urged them to take action against the "giant triplets" that have led to mass criminalization, closing with a potent rhetorical question she very much hopes will be answered by a resounding "yes."

Read your draft with a critical eye, get response—and revise

Now's the time to read over what you've written to see that you've made your position clear, supported it with good reasons and evidence, and considered carefully what others have said—and then to ask a classmate to read it over as well. The following questions can help you or someone else to read over a draft that takes a position:

- Have you DESCRIBED the issue clearly and in a fair-minded way?

- Have you stated your POSITION explicitly and as a response to what others have said about the topic? Is there a THESIS—and if not, is one needed?

- What good REASONS have you given for your position, and what EVIDENCE have you provided as support? Is your evidence factually accurate? How likely is it that your AUDIENCE will find it persuasive?

- What's your STANCE? Is it trustworthy and appropriate to your audience and purpose?

- What background information have you provided? What more might your readers need?

- How reliable are any sources you've cited? What kinds of sources are they—scholarly? popular? Who published or sponsored them? What's their purpose—to inform? sell? persuade? entertain? What can you learn about them? Do other sources say the same thing?

- What COUNTERARGUMENTS and other perspectives have you considered, and have you described them fairly and accurately? How have you addressed what they say?

- How will your OPENING make your audience want to read on? How else might you begin?

- Is it clear why the issue matters? Why do you care, and who else should care?

- Does the CONCLUSION make clear what you want readers to think or do? Have you invited them to respond?

- Is your argument easy to follow? If not, would it help to add TRANSITIONS or headings?

- Consider your title. Does it tell readers what the topic is, and will it make them want to read on? Now's the time to think about whether there's a better title.

Now take a deep breath—and REVISE! If you've analyzed your draft and gotten advice from others, you've got a plan. You know what you need or want to do. But remember: you're writing an ARGUMENT, which needs to take a clear POSITION supported by REASONS and EVIDENCE—and to acknowledge other positions as well. That said, here's what *you* think and why!

REFLECT! Examine something that you've written—an essay, an email, a presentation, whatever. Have you made clear that what you wrote about mattered to you, and should matter to others? If not, how would you now revise what you wrote to make that explicit?

A STUDENT ARGUMENT

GABRIELA MORO
Minority Student Clubs: Segregation or Integration?

Gabriela Moro wrote this essay in her first-year composition class at the University of Notre Dame. It was later published in Fresh Writing, *an online archive of exemplary first-year writing by students at Notre Dame. Moro graduated in 2018 with a major in neuroscience and behavior and is pursuing a career in medicine.*

Minority representation on US college campuses has increased significantly in recent years, and many schools have made it a priority to increase diversity on their campuses in order to prepare students for a culturally diverse US democratic society (Hurtado and Ruiz 3-4). To complement this increase, many schools have implemented minority student clubs to provide safe and comfortable environments where minority students can thrive academically and socially with peers from similar backgrounds. However, do these minority groups amplify students' tendency to interact only with those who are similar to themselves? Put another way, do these groups inhibit students from engaging in diverse relationships?

Many view such programs to be positive and integral to minority students' college experience; some, however, feel that these clubs are not productive for promoting cross-cultural interaction. While minority clubs have proven to be beneficial to minority students in some cases, particularly on campuses that are not very diverse, my research suggests that colleges would enrich the educational experience for all students by introducing multicultural clubs as well.

To frame my discussion, I will use an article from *College Student Journal* that distinguishes between two types of students: one who believes minority clubs are essential for helping minority students stay connected with their cultures, and another who believes these clubs isolate minorities and work against diverse interaction

Provides background information and introduces topic.

Poses questions that guided her research.

Summarizes what others say.

States claim as a response to what's been said.

among students. To pursue the question of whether or not such groups segregate minorities from the rest of the student body and even discourage cultural awareness, I will use perspectives from minority students to show that these programs are especially helpful for first-year students. I will also use other student testimonials to show that when taken too far, minority groups can lead to self-segregation and defy what most universities claim to be their diversity goals. Findings from research will contribute to a better understanding of the role minority clubs play on college campuses and offer a complete answer to my question about the importance of minority programs.

Discusses opposing views.

Before I go further, I would like to differentiate among three kinds of diversity that Patricia Gurin and colleagues identify in their article "Diversity and Higher Education: Theory and Impact on Educational Outcomes." The first type is *structural diversity*, "the numerical representation of diverse [racial and ethnic] groups." The existence of structural diversity alone does not ensure that students will develop valuable intergroup relationships. *Classroom diversity*, the second type, involves gaining "content knowledge" or a better understanding about diverse peers and their backgrounds by doing so in the classroom. The third type of diversity, *informal interactional diversity*, refers to "both the frequency and the quality of intergroup interaction as keys to meaningful diversity experiences during college." Students often encounter this kind of diversity in social settings outside the classroom (Gurin et al. 332-33). Informal interactional diversity is the focus of my research, since it is the concept that leads colleges to establish social events and organizations that allow all students to experience and appreciate the variety of cultures present in a student body.

Defines key term, "diversity."

In a study published in *College Student Journal*, three administrators at Pennsylvania State University explore how biracial students interact with others on a college campus. The authors conclude that views of minority clubs and related programs, which the authors call race-oriented student services, tend to fall into two groups: "Although some argue that these race-oriented student services are divisive and damage white-minority relations, others support these services as providing a safe place and meeting the needs of minority students to develop a sense of racial pride, community and importance" (Ingram et al. 298). I will start by examining the point of view of those associate minority clubs with positive outcomes.

Cites evidence from published studies.

A study by Samuel Museus in the *Journal of College Student Development* finds that minority student programs help students to stay connected with their culture in college and help ease first-year minority students' transition into the college environment. The study also shows that ethnic student organizations help students adjust and find their place at universities that have a predominantly white student body (584). Museus concludes that universities should stress the importance of racial and ethnic groups and develop more opportunities for minority students to make connections with them. This way, students can find support from their minority peers as they work together to face academic and social challenges. Museus's findings suggest that minority student groups are essential for allowing these to preserve and foster connections to their own cultures.

Cites evidence showing benefits of minority clubs.

In another study, Wendell Hall and colleagues evaluate how minority and non-minority students differ in their inclinations to take part in diversity activities and to communicate with racially and ethnically diverse peers at a predominantly white university. These scholars conclude that "engagement [with diverse peers] is learned" (434). Students who engaged with diverse students before going to college were more likely to interact with diverse peers by the end of their sophomore year. Minority students were more predisposed than their white peers to interact with diverse peers during their freshman year (435). These findings indicate that minority student clubs can be helpful for first-year minority students who have not previously engaged with other minority students, especially if the university has a predominantly white student body.

Cites further evidence of positive effects.

Professors and scholars are not the only ones who strongly support minority clubs. For example, three students at Harvard College—Andrea Delgado, Denzel (no last name given), and Kimi Fafowora—give their perspective on student life and multicultural identity on campus to incoming students via *YouTube*. The students explain how minority programs on campus have helped them adjust to a new college environment as first-year students. As Delgado puts it:

Quotes student testimony on the benefits of such clubs.

I thought [cultural clubs were] something I maybe didn't need, but come November, I missed speaking Spanish and I missed having tacos, and other things like that. That's the reason why I started attending meetings more regularly. Latinas Unidas has been a great intersection of my cultural background and my political views. ("Student Voices")

Quotes student testimony on the benefits of such clubs.

The experiences these minority students shared support the scholarly evidence that minority clubs help incoming students transition into a new and often intimidating environment.

While the benefits of these clubs are quite evident, several problems can also arise from them. The most widely recognized is self-segregation. Self-segregating tendencies are not exclusive to minority students: college students in general tend to self-segregate as they enter an unfamiliar environment. As a study by Nathan Martin and colleagues finds, "Today, the student bodies of our leading colleges and universities are more diverse than ever. However, college students are increasingly self-segregating by race or ethnicity" (720). Several studies as well as interviews with students suggest that minority clubs exacerbate students' inclination to self-segregate. And as students become comfortable with their minority peers, they may no longer desire or feel the need to branch out of their comfort zone.

Considers problems with minority clubs.

In another study, Julie Park, a professor at the University of Maryland, examines the relationship between participation in college student organizations and the development of interracial friendships. Park suggests, "if students spend the majority of time in such groups [Greek, ethnic, and religious student organizations], partic-ipation may affect student involvement in the broader diversity of the institution" (642). In other words, if minority students form all of their social and academic ties within their minority group, the desired cultural exchange among the student body could suffer.

Cites research pointing out problems with many clubs.

So what can be done? In the Penn State study mentioned ear-lier, in which data were collected by an online survey, participants were asked to respond to an open-ended question about what they think universities should do to create a more inviting environment for biracial students (Ingram et al. 303). On one hand, multiple stu-dents responded with opinions opposing the formation of both biracial and multiracial clubs: "I feel instead of having biracial and multiracial clubs the colleges should have diversity clubs and just allow everyone to get together. All these 'separate' categorizing of clubs, isn't that just separation of groups?" "Having a ton of clubs that are for specific races is counter-productive. It creates segrega-tion and lack of communication across cultures" (304-05).

Considers views opposing biracial and multiracial clubs.

On the other hand, students offered suggestions for the forma-tion of multicultural activities: "Encourage more racial integration to show students races aren't so different from each other and to lessen stereotypes" (305). "Hold cultural events that allow students of different races to express / share their heritage" (306). Patreese Ingram and colleagues conclude that while biracial and multiracial student organizations are helpful in establishing an inviting college environment for minority students,

Cites student testimony in support of multicultural activities.

> creating a truly inclusive environment . . . requires additional efforts: these include multicultural awareness training for faculty, staff, and students, and incorporation of multicultural issues into the curriculum. In addition to the creation of biracial / mul-tiracial clubs and organizations, the students in this study want to increase awareness of the mixed heritage population among others on college campuses. (308)

Quotes research on the need for an inclusive environment.

The two very different opinions reported in this study point to the challenges minority student programs can create, but also suggest

Sums up evidence on both sides of the issue. Reiterates claim.

ways to resolve these challenges. Now that evidence from both research studies and student perspectives confirms that these clubs, while beneficial to minority students' experiences, can inhibit cultural immersion, I will continue with my original argument that the entire student body would benefit if campuses also implemented multicultural advocacy clubs, rather than just selective minority clubs. Gurin and colleagues, the researchers who identify the three types of diversity in higher education, contend that even with the presence of diverse racial and ethnic groups and regular communication among students formally and informally, a greater push from educators is needed:

> In order to foster citizenship for a diverse democracy, educators must intentionally structure opportunities for students to leave the comfort of their homogenous peer group and build relationships across racially/ethnically diverse student communities on campus. (363)

This suggestion implies that participation from students and faculty is needed to foster cultural immersion in higher education.

Another way to improve cross-cultural exchange is by developing a diverse curriculum. An article on multiculturalism in higher education by Alma Clayton-Pedersen and Caryn McTighe Musil in the *Encyclopedia of Education* reviews the ways in which universities have incorporated diversity studies into their core curriculum over the last several decades. The authors report that the numbers of courses that seek to prepare students for a democratic society rich in diversity have increased (1711, 1714). However, they recommend that institutions need to take a more holistic approach to their academic curricula in order to pursue higher education programs that prepare students to face "complex and demanding questions" and to "use their new knowledge and civic, intercultural capacities to address real-world problems" (1714). My research suggests that a more holistic approach to the importance of diversity studies in the college curriculum, as well as multicultural advocacy clubs, are necessary in order to prepare *all* students, not just minority students, for the diverse world and society ahead of them.

Thus, even though minority student clubs can lead to self-segregation among students and result in less cross-cultural interaction, their benefits to minority students suggest that a balance needs to be found between providing support for minorities and avoiding segregation of these groups from the rest of the student body. Besides sponsoring minority student programs, colleges and universities can implement multicultural events and activities for all students to participate in, especially during the freshman year. An initiative like this would enhance the diverse interactions that occur on campuses, promote cultural immersion, and garner support for minority student clubs.

Beyond the reach of this evaluation, further research should be conducted, specifically on the types of cultural events that are most effective in promoting cultural awareness and meaningful diverse interactions among the student body. By examining different multicultural organizations from both public and private institutions, and comparing student experiences and participation in those programs, researchers can suggest an ideal multicultural program to provide an optimal student experience.

Concludes by calling for response in the form of further research.

Works Cited

Clayton-Pedersen, Alma R., and Caryn McTighe Musil. "Multiculturalism in Higher Education." *Encyclopedia of Education*, edited by James W. Guthrie, 2nd ed., vol. 5, Macmillan, 2002, pp. 1709-16.

Gurin, Patricia, et al. "Diversity and Higher Education: Theory and Impact on Educational Outcomes." *Harvard Educational Review*, vol. 72, no. 3, 2002, pp. 330-63. *ResearchGate*, https://doi.org/10.17763/haer.72.3.01151786u134n051.

Hall, Wendell, et al. "A Tale of Two Groups: Differences between Minority Students and Non-Minority Students in Their

Predispositions to and Engagement with Diverse Peers at a Predominantly White Institution." *Research in Higher Education*, vol. 52, no. 4, 2011, pp. 420-39. *Academic Search Premier*, https://doi.org/10.1007/s11162-010-9201-4.

Hurtado, Sylvia, and Adriana Ruiz. "The Climate for Underrepresented Groups and Diversity on Campus." *Higher Education Research Institute*, 2012, heri.ucla.edu/briefs /urmbrief.php.

Ingram, Patreese, et al. "How Do Biracial Students Interact with Others on the College Campus?" *College Student Journal*, vol. 48, no. 2, 2014, pp. 297-311.

Martin, Nathan D., et al. "Interracial Friendships across the College Years: Evidence from a Longitudinal Case Study." *Journal of College Student Development*, vol. 55, no. 7, 2014, pp. 720-25. *Academic Search Premier*, https://doi.org/10 .1353/csd.2014.0075.

Museus, Samuel D. "The Role of Ethnic Student Organizations in Fostering African American and Asian American Students' Cultural Adjustment and Membership at Predominantly White Institutions." *Journal of College Student Development*, vol. 49, no. 6, 2008, pp. 568-86. *Project MUSE*, https://doi .org/10.1353/csd.0.0039.

Park, Julie J. "Clubs and the Campus Racial Climate: Student Organizations and Interracial Friendship in College." *Journal of College Student Development*, vol. 55, no. 7, 2014, pp. 641-60. *Academic Search Premier*, https://doi .org/10.1353/csd.2014.0076.

"Student Voices: Multicultural Perspectives." *YouTube*, uploaded by Harvard College Admissions and Financial Aid, 7 Aug. 2014, www.youtube.com/watch?v=djIWQgDx-Jc.

Thinking about the Text

1. What do you take away as the main CLAIM of Gabriela Moro's argument?

2. How well do you think she supports this claim? Show examples from the text that you find most persuasive.

3. How does Moro take COUNTERARGUMENTS into consideration? Do you think she deals fairly and evenhandedly with all sides? Cite examples from her text.

4. What does Moro do to convince you that she is CREDIBLE and trustworthy? What more might she have done?

5. Moro obviously cares deeply about this topic. Think of a topic that is equally important to you, and write a paragraph or two introducing the topic and summarizing an argument you'd most like to make about it.

9 Analyzing

HOPE IS NOT THE BASIS FOR POLICY.
WISE POLICYMAKERS ANALYZE ISSUES CAREFULLY
AND LOOK AT FACTS AND PROBABILITIES
INSTEAD OF JUST HOPING FOR THE BEST.

—LAURA INGRAHAM

I'M A HUGE FAN OF TEACHING YOU TO THINK,
ANALYZE, AND COMMUNICATE, THEN SENDING YOU OUT
INTO THE WORLD TO CAUSE TROUBLE.

—HILARY MASON

Why have you put on five pounds in the last month? What made *Tiger King* so popular? Which candidate should you vote for? Answering such questions calls for analysis, for examining something in detail in order to understand it in some way. In analyzing why you've gained five pounds, you might begin by detailing your eating patterns: At what time of the day do you eat? How often do you eat? What prompts you to eat—or not? What foods do you favor, and which ones do you avoid? As you gather data on what and when you eat, and on your reasons for eating as you do, you are generating evidence you can use to answer your original question.

132

Analyzing *Tiger King* will lead you to examine the features of that show that made it so popular: the eccentric characters, the tension and unpredictability, the setting, and so on. And in order to decide which candidate to vote for, you'll need to consider *all* the candidates, their policies, the issues you care about, and so on. Whatever your subject, conducting a detailed analysis—looking at "facts and probabilities" rather than "hoping for the best," in Laura Ingraham's words—will help you answer questions and understand your topic better as a result.

Every field uses analysis. *Engineers* carry out detailed analyses to understand whether a bridge can be built in a specific location. *Scientists* use quantitative data to analyze causes and effects. *Social scientists* use qualitative analysis to help them understand human behavior. *Literature students* analyze poetry in order to understand how various aspects of a poem lead us to understand it in a certain way. This chapter provides guidelines for doing a rhetorical analysis, focusing on texts of various kinds and how an author or artist communicates a message to an audience.

REFLECT! Think of an issue that's being discussed and debated now—on campus, in a local community, in the world. What are people saying? What do the various sides think, and why? What kinds of analysis are they doing or citing as support for what they think?

A GUIDE TO ANALYZING A TEXT

A speech, a novel, an ad, a painting, a contract: all are *texts*, and all are things that you might be assigned to analyze. Or just need to analyze, to figure out what it says and what you think about that. Here now is some advice that will help you analyze texts of various kinds. As you'll see, it's designed to be used *as you write*. Keep it close at hand!

Identify a text you want to understand

Whether you're assigned to analyze a specific text or get to choose one yourself, you'll do your best work if the topic or text is of interest to you. But all analysis is driven by a question of some kind, something you're curious about, so a good way to begin is by looking for a question that you really want to know the answer to: What was the best Super Bowl ad this year? What makes K-pop so popular? Why do so many people say that *Moby-Dick* is the greatest American novel? These questions all call for analysis, for looking closely at these texts to tease out answers.

Journalist Charles Duhigg asks such a question in "Why Are We So Angry?"—a lengthy essay that "unfolds the story of how we all got so mad at one another." Inspired by a "strange questionnaire" asking people in a small town in Massachusetts to recall the number of times they'd been angry in the past week and to describe "the most angry of these experiences," his essay opens by summarizing some of what they said. In his analysis, Duhigg shows that the United States has always been an angry country (it arose from an angry, violent revolution, after all) and then focuses on three kinds of anger—everyday or "ordinary" anger, "moral indignation," and "desire for revenge"—giving copious examples of each and showing how one can escalate into another. In his thesis, Duhigg previews the results of his analysis:

> We are further down this path [from moral indignation to desire for revenge] than you may realize, but it's not too late for us to reverse course. If we can understand anger's mechanisms, we might find a way to turn our indignation back into a strength.
>
> —CHARLES DUHIGG, "Why Are We So Angry?"

Analyzing "anger's mechanisms" becomes a major focus of the essay, helping Duhigg to answer why we are so angry and to suggest what we may be able to do about it.

Think about your rhetorical situation

Once you have a chosen a text to analyze, take time to consider your rhetorical situation.

Purpose. What do you want to happen as a result of your analysis—a more thorough understanding of a complex text? a certain interpretation of a poem? a decision about a proposal? How can you best accomplish your goals?

Audience. Who will be reading your analysis, and what do you know about them—their age, gender, cultural background? What are they likely to know about the text you're analyzing, and what background information will you need to provide? Can you assume they'll be interested in your subject? If not, how can you frame your analysis in a way that they will relate to? If you're analyzing some of the corporate statements professing solidarity with the Black Lives Matter movement for your composition class, for instance, you'd likely analyze any ethical and emotional appeals and look for evidence of what kind of support they plan to provide. If, however, you were writing on *Instagram*, you might simply post one corporate statement along with a question asking what else they can offer in addition to solidarity.

Stance. How do you want to come across to your readers—as well-informed? objective? enthusiastic? Whatever it is, how can your writing reflect your stance? And how are you approaching the text you're analyzing—as a student? a serious reader? a critic? something else?

Context. What else has been said about the subject of your analysis? What are the various perspectives? You'll need to provide some of that larger context in your analysis. And what's *your* context—if you're writing in response to an assignment, what's your time frame, and are there any requirements that you need to keep in mind?

Media and design. Think carefully about how you will deliver your analysis—will it be a print text? an online digital text? an oral or multimedia presentation? Your medium will affect the way it is designed and even the kinds of evidence you provide: for an oral presentation, you might use *PowerPoint* or *Prezi* slides; for a print text, you might include illustrations with captions as well as headings. Whatever the medium, your design should aim to help readers follow the major points of your analysis.

Be sure it's a text you can manage— and approach with an open mind

Think carefully about how much time you have to complete your analysis before you decide definitively on a text. A student in a course on the history of the Bible who was interested in the Book of Judges proposed doing an analysis of that book. This student quickly realized, however, that such a task was far from manageable given the due date, and so he chose to analyze one story in that book that he had always been curious about, the Samson and Delilah story. Consider as well what resources you may need to carry out your analysis—and whether you have access to them. The student analyzing the Samson and Delilah story had access to several different translations as well as to a bibliography provided by the instructor that included other scholarly analyses of this story. Finally, think about how open-minded you are about the subject of your analysis. The purpose of an analysis is to gain some kind of insight about the subject, not to confirm something you already believe about it.

Think about what you want to know about the text

You may need little but the text itself to conduct a rhetorical analysis, especially in cases where the text is assigned in class. Sometimes, however, you may need to do some research to find out more about the topic. Wesley Cohen grew up in a household that would never have subscribed to *Cosmopolitan*, a magazine she therefore assumed was all fluff and no substance—the kind of thing you'd pick up while waiting for a dental appointment. But once she got to college and was free to read anything, including *Cosmo*, she was surprised to see that it now includes articles about some very serious issues—domestic violence, equal pay—right alongside horoscopes and fashion advice. So for an assignment to write a feature in a journalism class, she decided to look at what was happening "over at *Cosmo*." Noting that "It's rare to find a magazine that covers domestic violence and celebrity fashion on equal footing," she set out to analyze the changes that have taken place there in recent years.

If you want to read about what's happening at *Cosmo*, see Wesley Cohen's essay on p. 148.

You might not always begin an analysis with an explicit question as Cohen did, but your analysis will always be prompted by a question of some kind, by something that you're curious about.

Conduct a preliminary rhetorical analysis

A rhetorical analysis looks closely at a text (verbal or visual) in order to see what it says and how it does so. When you analyze a text, you examine each of its parts systematically to show how they engage readers' attention and lead them to understand the text in a certain way.

If you take any humanities courses, you'll surely be asked to analyze various kinds of texts. Imagine, for example, how you might go about analyzing the following short but powerful poem:

> A word is dead
> When it is said,
> Some say.
> I say it just
> Begins to live
> That day.
>
> —EMILY DICKINSON

In analyzing this poem, you might begin by summing up the meaning as you see it and then showing how each line builds to that meaning. You'd consider why Dickinson breaks lines where she does, how rhyme and repetition contribute to the meaning, and what the contrast between living words and dead words suggests about spoken words.

You might also be assigned to analyze a visual text. One assignment I've often given to my first-year students asks them to analyze the campus map. Ours is a huge university, and they need to learn their way around campus. Analyzing the map gets them thinking about what's where and why. Why are certain buildings in one place rather than another? What is at the center of campus and what is on the periphery? What are the largest buildings? the smallest? Does one area of the map seem dominant? If so, what does that area represent—science and technology? the humanities? the administration? sports arenas? Analyzing the map reveals a lot!

Suppose you are working on a presentation for an environmental engineering course on what the city of New Orleans should consider doing to prepare for any future hurricanes. You might show a slide of a map in your presentation showing which areas of the city lie at or below sea level as part of your analysis of the potential problems along with specific suggestions for what needs to be done now to ensure the safety of those who live in those low-lying neighborhoods.

A map of New Orleans showing areas above sea level and those at or below sea level.

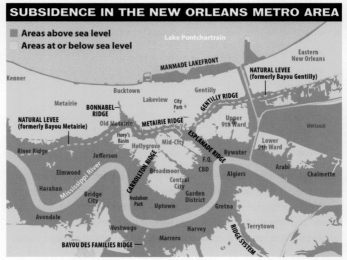

Whether the text you're analyzing is written or visual, you'll need to examine it carefully to see how it supports what it says. Asking the following questions will help you to do so systematically.

Analyzing a written text

- What is your overall impression of the text—and what specific elements lead you to that impression?
- What CLAIM is the text making, and how do you know?
- What REASONS and EVIDENCE does the writer provide to support the claim? How convincing do you find them?
- What has motivated the writer to take on this topic? What's the larger conversation this text is responding to?
- How has the writer acknowledged and responded to COUNTERARGUMENTS—other points of view on the subject? Are they presented fairly and honestly?
- Does the writer use any EMOTIONAL APPEALS?
- How does the writer establish AUTHORITY and CREDIBILITY to address this topic?

Analyzing a visual text

- What does your eye go to first, and why has the designer chosen to draw your eye to that spot?
- What seems most important or interesting?
- Who do you think the visual aims to reach—who is its AUDIENCE, and how do you know?
- What is its PURPOSE? How well does it achieve its goal?
- Even if there are no words, what does the visual *say*? What's its ARGUMENT (it may be implicit rather than explicit), and how do you know?
- If there are words, how do they help get the message across? What's the font, and how does it affect the TONE?

What does your preliminary analysis show?

By the time you've completed a preliminary analysis, you should be immersed in your subject, so it's time to step back and look not at the trees but at the forest: What does your analysis reveal about the text? What most interests you about what you've discovered, and why does it seem important? Begin by making notes answering these questions and looking for patterns that may emerge.

In studying the notes she had taken on our campus map, for example, one of my students found that the very center of the campus houses the administrative offices but that two very large areas, the medical complex and the sports complex, take up the biggest part of campus. She found that the engineering and science area is next in terms of space occupied and in prominence on the map, and that student dorms are on the outer periphery of the campus. These findings got her wondering if it had always been this way, so she went to the library and found the original campus map, showing classroom buildings in the center and only one small office devoted to administration. The library was the largest and most prominent building on campus. As she continued to think about the data she'd gathered, she thought hard about what her analysis revealed about the university and its values. How do these values play out in terms of campus layout and building design? Do changes in the development of the campus suggest a shift in what the university values?

See pp. 84–85 for more on coming up with a working thesis.

Come up with a working thesis

Once you've analyzed your subject, you need to determine what your analysis shows. What have you learned about the subject, and what can you now say about it? Try writing that out as a working thesis, saying what you've analyzed and what you can now claim about the subject. Here's what my student wrote: "Our campus map is a work in progress, constantly changing in ways that reflect shifting priorities and financial realities."

Remember that you may need to qualify your thesis

On reflection, my student worried that she was overstating her case, saying that shifting priorities are always linked to financial realities. Such overstatements can hurt a writer's credibility and make an analysis less persuasive, or perhaps not even taken seriously. Be careful to qualify if need be. Here's how my student did that: "Our campus map is a work in progress, constantly changing in ways that reflect shifting priorities that are often linked to financial realities."

Develop support for your analysis

Every textual analysis depends on support, and there are three questions you can ask to begin gathering support: What evidence supports the analysis? Is the author trustworthy? Does the text make any emotional appeals?

What evidence supports the analysis?

Any analysis of a text needs to examine its use of facts and other evidence. In *Dopesick: Dealers, Doctors, and the Drug Company That Addicted America*, Beth Macy analyzes the factors that led up to the current opioid epidemic in the United States. Macy, an award-winning journalist, has the credentials to make her account trustworthy and credible; and her interviews with addicted people and those who love them provide very strong emotional appeals. But she also relies on facts and other evidence drawn from research.

Consider how she uses facts presented in two research studies. The first, by researchers at Princeton, supports Macy's finding that opioid addiction has now reached a crisis point: this study found that mortality rates "had quietly risen a half-percentage point annually between 1999 and 2013 while midlife mortality continued to fall in other affluent countries." She then turns to results of a poll conducted by the Kaiser Family Foundation showing that today "56 percent of Americans now know someone who abused, was addicted to, or died

In her analysis of nature documentaries, Emma Marris presents evidence that many of them are, um, less than natural. Read her essay on p. 719.

from an overdose of opioids." Indeed, Macy's book-length analysis piles up facts and statistics that make her conclusions inescapable: America is "dopesick."

In addition to facts and statistics, Macy draws on the expert testimony of doctors and medical researchers, who support her analysis of the complicit role the medical community unwittingly played in exacerbating the opioid epidemic. And she provides one major example—Purdue Pharma, which introduced OxyContin after it gained FDA approval in 1995 and advertised it as completely safe: "If you take the medicine like it is prescribed, the risk of addiction is one half of one percent." Many people using OxyContin, however, ignored the "if." Within two months of its release, Macy shows, the drug was "on the streets" in large amounts, even as it was also being prescribed by doctors nationwide. This extended example supports Macy's analysis and the argument she is making about the opioid crisis.

The kinds of evidence that you provide as support for an analysis will depend on your topic, but could include ANALOGIES, ANECDOTES, COMPARISONS, examples, FACTS, QUOTATIONS, DEFINITIONS, statistics, personal experience, and so on.

Is the author trustworthy?

It may be a truism to say we tend to believe people who seem trustworthy, credible, and honest—but establishing such credentials has never been more important than it is today. Whatever kind of text you're analyzing, then, you should ask how the author (or speaker, or artist) manages to come across as believable, as someone whose work you can trust.

In an analysis of *How Change Happens: Why Some Social Movements Succeed While Others Don't*, law professor David Cole focuses on that book's author, Leslie Crutchfield, introducing her as someone who has studied social movements extensively over the last several decades. We learn that Crutchfield has analyzed campaigns against smoking and drunk driving, as well as both for and against gun control. Cole is careful, then, to provide credentials for the author of the text he is analyzing: she is experienced, deeply knowledgeable, and open-minded—thus, he suggests, readers can trust the advice she offers to those seeking to establish effective social movements. He himself is careful to QUALIFY his own conclusions about the viability of some social movements—noting, for instance, the following:

> Whether #MeToo and other movements will achieve lasting reform will depend on those organizations working collectively in multiple forums, including courtrooms, state legislatures, corporate boardrooms, union halls, and, most importantly, at the ballot box.

—DAVID COLE, "The Path of Greatest Resistance"

Cole uses Crutchfield's qualification of her claim as further evidence of her credibility: she is a careful researcher not given to exaggeration or to absolute conclusions.

Analyzing whether or not you can trust an author or speaker will lead you to look carefully at the words they use to see what kind of TONE they establish (careful and cautious? angry and belligerent? even-handed?). Likewise, in analyzing a visual text, the use of fonts and colors and even layout might give you a sense of whether it's taking its subject seriously or not.

Does the text make any emotional appeals?

Any rhetorical analysis should carefully consider whether the text appeals to its audience's emotions—and if so, to what effect. Emotional appeals are often misused: think of ads that suggest that buying a certain skincare product will make us as gorgeous as the model using it, for example. But appeals to emotion can also tug at our heartstrings in positive ways, persuading us to appoint a designated driver when we've been drinking, for instance, or to contribute to the life-saving work of Doctors without Borders.

See how Vanessa Friedman, a fashion critic at the *New York Times*, appealed to readers' emotions in her analysis of the role that clothing played at President Trump's 2019 State of the Union address:

Congresswomen in white at the 2019 State of the Union address.

When the television cameras came up on the buzzing House chamber as Congress awaited President Trump's entrance, the most striking sight was not the grandeur of the room (though it is pretty grand) or the nerves and excitement of the special guests, but rather <u>the unmistakable block of Congresswomen</u> practically aglow in white on the Democratic side of the aisle.

—VANESSA FRIEDMAN, "A Sea of White, Lit by History"

A photo underscores Friedman's point: no one, she said, could "miss the message in what they wore: one of gender equality and pride, the long arc of history and the fight for women's rights, commitment to an agenda and, in the background, joy." The photo captures that moment of joy and appeals to readers to share in that joy and the message it delivers.

When analyzing any text, look carefully for emotional appeals, and think about how they're used. Are they used to create empathy? to arouse outrage? to change minds? to help establish the author's credibility? Or are they used negatively, to call out or humiliate someone, or to stoke divisiveness or even hatred? Perhaps they're simply illustrating why readers should care about the topic. In each case, think about how any emotional appeal supports or relates to the argument the text is making, and whether it does so fairly.

Consider the larger context— and perspectives other than your own

If you're analyzing a text or topic that you think matters, chances are that you won't be the first one to do so. That means you should try to look *beyond* your own reaction and consider other perspectives. Being open to the ideas of others will help you produce a stronger analysis and will underscore your credibility as someone who's open to what others think and doesn't rush to judgment.

> For excellence, the presence of others is always required.
> —HANNAH ARENDT

In a lengthy analysis of American exceptionalism, Jake Sullivan, who is a senior fellow at the Carnegie Endowment for International Peace, sums up the perspectives of others before offering his own conclusion:

> Some argue that the United States is fractured beyond repair— . . . that you can no longer make arguments to the American people based on higher purpose—they are too angry or too cynical.
>
> I see it another way. . . . Let's not forget that, throughout American history, the path forward has been determined not in times of disruption but in their aftermath. . . . As for the American people, I believe that they would welcome a renewed form of exceptionalism that addresses their concerns, speaks to their aspirations, and restores confidence that their country can be a force for good in the world. . . . American exceptionalism is not a description of reality but the expression of an ambition. It is about striving, and falling short, and improving. This is the essence of a patriotism that every American can embrace.
>
> —JAKE SULLIVAN, "Yes, America Can Still Lead the World"

Thus does Sullivan's lengthy analysis of anger lead him to move beyond those who think we cannot recover from the current divisiveness, arguing that his analysis shows that Americans are very likely to keep working toward the goal of improving, always improving.

Invite response

Good analyses need to be able to withstand close scrutiny by others, so remember to ask for response to your draft. When ethnographer Patricia Lather carried out a study of women living with HIV, she used a series of interviews to analyze their experiences, which resulted in a book-length study called *Troubling the Angels*. Lather didn't publish her book, however, until she had asked the women she'd interviewed to read and respond to it. They did so, at length, and Lather then used their astute insights and criticisms to revise her analysis. You can benefit by following Lather's example and inviting response to what you write.

Read your draft with a critical eye, get response—and revise

Now's the time to read over what you've written to see that you've made clear what question has driven your analysis and that you've provided sufficient evidence to support the conclusion your analysis draws. Then you'll want to ask others to read over your draft. Here are some questions that can help you or others read over the draft.

- How will your OPENING grab readers' attention? If you aim to reach a specific AUDIENCE, will your opening make them want to read on? How else might you begin?

- Have you DESCRIBED the text in enough detail for readers to follow your analysis? Is there more background information you need to add?

- Have you made clear what your analysis revealed about the text—and have you stated it explicitly in a THESIS? If not, should you do so?

- What EVIDENCE supports your analysis? Is there any other evidence that could add to the strength of your analysis?

- Have you made any EMOTIONAL APPEALS—and if so, how do they support your analysis?
- How have you established your CREDIBILITY to write on this subject?
- Have you addressed PERSPECTIVES other than your own— and if not, should you do so? Have you considered such perspectives fairly? If you've cited any sources, have you DOCUMENTED them fully?
- How effective is your CONCLUSION? What does it leave your audience thinking? How else could you conclude?
- Consider your title. Does it make clear what your analysis is about, and will it engage readers' interest? How might you make the title more engaging?

Now's the time to REVISE! If you've analyzed your analysis (!) and gotten advice from others, you've got a plan. You know what you want to do. But remember what you *need* to do: to explain what your ANALYSIS shows and provide EVIDENCE that supports your conclusions. And as always, keep in mind your AUDIENCE and the rest of your RHETORICAL SITUATION.

REFLECT! Set your analysis aside for a few days. Then come back to it with fresh eyes and read it again. What do you find most effective about your analysis? What is your favorite sentence or passage—and why? What spots might call for further revision—and why? How well do you think you conveyed your point(s) to your audience? Write a paragraph or two in which you sum up what you've learned—both about the text, and the process of analysis itself.

A STUDENT ANALYSIS

WESLEY COHEN

What's Happening over at *Cosmo*?

Wesley Cohen wrote this essay for a journalism class at the University of California at Davis. It was later published in Prized Writing, *an annual book of exemplary writing from across the disciplines done by students at Davis. The version included here has been revised to include MLA documentation, something that was not required in her journalism class. She graduated in 2019 and is now working as a college sales representative at W. W. Norton & Company.*

The title and opening sentences capture readers' interest.

Open up *Cosmopolitan Magazine*'s March 2016 issue and you'll find tips for flirting with a guy at work ("Text him a funny follow-up!") and a fashion-infused profile of actress-slash-beauty mogul Jessica Alba (titled "Billion Dollar Babe").

Summarizes the contrast that she'll explore in her analysis.

Between these pieces is an eight-page feature on the intersection of gun rights and domestic violence in America. The article includes an eye-catching graphic of a chocolate gun in a candy box surrounded by brightly striped truffles, and a handy flowchart for talking with a new romantic partner about gun ownership. There are also stark warnings and statistics.

According to the piece's author, Liz Welch, "8,700 women were shot to death by their partners between 2000 and 2013" (162) and women are 200 percent more likely to be killed when a physically abusive relationship involves a gun. The article frames gun control as a women's issue, chronicling the stories of several young women who were murdered by abusive partners or ex-partners (Welch).

First claim.

It's rare to find a magazine that covers domestic violence and celebrity fashion on equal footing—and this wide editorial scope is largely the work of the former editor-in-chief Joanna Coles. *Cosmo*'s shift toward more diverse content goes against decades of editorial tradition in a brand famous for its focus on sex, celebrities, and fashion—and its racy covers, as figure 1 shows.

Cosmo started life in 1886 as a women's magazine that published Willa Cather, Upton Sinclair, and Kurt Vonnegut. Chief editor Helen Gurley Brown was brought on in the 1960s in response to weak sales, and she recreated the magazine as a sex-centered, single woman's guidebook to the fab life.

Provides background information.

Brown pledged to keep *Cosmo* "frisky and fresh" over her three-decade reign. She acknowledged in her November 1995 letter from the editor that women may be interested in subjects other than "sexual pleasure, passion, friendship, love, achievement," but told readers that "we let the newspapers, TV shows, and newsmagazines deal with them" (30). But Joanna Coles eschewed this either-or approach to writing for women, telling NPR's Rachel Martin, "I have no problem understanding that women are interested in mascara and the Middle East" (*Morning Edition*). (Indeed, figure 2 shows Coles speaking at a *Cosmo* event that was sponsored by Maybelline, a company known for its mascara.)

Fig. 1. 2006 cover names Beyoncé the "Fun, Fearless Female of the Year." www.getty.com

Fig. 2. Editor-in-chief Joanna Coles speaking at a *Cosmopolitan* event in 2015 that was sponsored by Maybelline. www.getty.com

Since 2014, *Cosmo* has endorsed political candidates based on whether they support equal pay, birth control access, and reproductive rights. Coles doesn't see a conflict in presenting pro-choice political endorsements alongside stiletto recommendations: "I feel that these are about lifestyle issues for women. The biggest single decision which will impact your life is when you have a child. I want women to have control over that" (qtd. in Gold).

Provides examples to support the claim that Cosmo *tackles serious issues.*

Coles's *Cosmo* is all about diversifying what counts as "women's interest." A new header, Cosmopolitan.com, next to "LOVE," "CELEBS," and "BEAUTY" reads—in appropriate millennial format— "#COSMOVOTES." Under this tab, readers can find *Cosmo*'s political endorsements, updates on polls and primaries, and opinion pieces on candidates and issues. It makes no secret of *Cosmo*'s political leanings.

In her same 1995 letter from the editor, Brown laid out her reasoning for leaving hard-hitting subjects out of *Cosmo*'s pages, writing, "We're not big on scaring you" (30). But Jill Filipovic's November 2015 piece about anti-abortion violence seems pretty scary to me.

Filipovic, a UN Foundation Fellow and award-winning contributor to *The Guardian*, *The New York Times*, *Al Jazeera America*, and *Time* magazine, is no lightweight. But in the margin by Filipovic's byline, there's a picture of Mary-Kate and Ashley Olsen as toddlers above a link offering to show me "A Photo from Every Year of Their Lives."

This new *Cosmo* balances pithy quizzes about Hanna Montana and critiques of the hypher-sexual portrayals of African American women in film and TV. How does one women's magazine make it all work?

Poses a question that will guide the analysis.

First of all, *Cosmo*'s new direction rejects the idea of women's-interest journalism as a niche market. On CNN's *Reliable Sources*, Joanna Coles pushed back against host Brian Stelter's suggestion that working with women's magazines to reach voters—instead of reaching out directly through social media or relying on hard news reporting—was a way that political candidates use "alternative media."

"Well, I don't think of women's magazines with 53 million readers as being 'alternative media,'" said Coles, nearly breaking into a laugh. "I think it might be as big, if not bigger, than the footprint of *Reliable Sources*, Brian" (Coles, *Reliable Sources*).

Coles noted instead that she believes her "very large" readership has been underserved by mainstream media. It's hard to argue with her. While men's-interest magazines like *Esquire* publish hard-hitting cultural essays alongside fiction by the likes of George Saunders and Stephen King, the news that *Cosmo* had won a National Magazine Award in 2014 for an extensive piece on contraception was met with astonishment. Coles seems to carry her sense of humor in her purse, however. About a story titled "It's Time to Start Taking *Cosmopolitan* Seriously," she tweeted "Start?????" (Coles, *Twitter*).

A different *Reliable Sources* interview featured host Brian Stelter asking two uncomfortable-looking female journalists "Are women's magazines serious?" Roberta Meyers, editor-in-chief at

Elle, was set up against *Rolling Stone* writer Janet Reitman, who worried aloud that female writers who focus on women's-interest writing often never "break out" of women-only journalism. Meyers noted that she started out at *Rolling Stone* before taking the lead at *Elle* and pointed out that many of her writers are also published in *The New Yorker, New York Magazine,* and *Rolling Stone*. Reitman responded by saying that she appreciates and reads women's magazines herself, but reiterated her earlier concern about the "ghettoizing" of female-interest journalists. This time, Reitman said, eyes focused and concerned, that many women journalists "just literally cannot, somehow, make it to write for larger men's magazines or general-interest magazines" (Meyers and Reitman).

Introduces another perspective: Can women's magazines be serious?

It seems that this, in Reitman's mind, is the ladder that female journalists must climb: women's magazines, men's magazines, then general-interest magazines. Or perhaps: women's magazines/general-interest magazines. Because in many ways, male interests are considered general interest.

While writing about romance or fashion puts a journalist into the "ghetto" of trivial feminine pursuits, typically masculine interests are widely considered respectable reading material. As Joanna Coles noted in her NPR interview, "Men are allowed to talk about sports relentlessly, and yet we still take them seriously. I don't understand why women can't talk about fashion, or sex, or love, or wanting more money and not be taken as seriously as men" (*Morning Edition*).

In her *Reliable Sources* appearance, *Elle*'s Roberta Meyers looked fabulous: her blow-out great, her makeup subtle and professional, her poise unshakeable. But she looked worn down, too. She spoke of a perceived gap between her readers and the rest of the world, "the idea that there's a divide between people who care about fashion and only fashion," and everybody else. She then went on to say "I find it sad . . . that we're still talking about women as a whole separate kind of people, you know?" (Meyers and Reitman). Meyers spoke brightly of her love for her readers, but to Reitman and Stelter, choosing to write for *Elle* instead of *Rolling Stone* is apparently a real comedown.

It's hard to find an article discussing *Cosmo*'s long history without reading contemptuous descriptions of its past content. As *Jezebel*'s managing editor Kate Dries said, *Cosmo*'s new focus on career advancement and female empowerment has been a "slow climb out of lipstick-and-lasagna land" ("The New *Cosmopolitan*").

Acknowledges Cosmo's earlier reputation.

Cosmo was forbidden to my sisters and me when we were growing up. My parents didn't want us encountering this male-centric view of sexuality or developing such a shallow image of female beauty. They even tried to ban Barbie from the premises before she snuck in inside wrapped birthday presents and well-meant hand-me-downs. I don't blame them.

Cites her own experience to support the claim that Cosmo once presented shallow views.

Cosmo still passes down narrow ideas of what a woman is and does and wants. Women of color, transgender women, and queer women are not addressed as *Cosmo*'s central audience, and the women who star on its covers month to month are overwhelmingly thin and pale and provocatively dressed. My parents didn't want to limit the type of woman I could be while I was still a girl.

Explores the view that Cosmo presents a narrow view of women.

So instead I learned how to be like a boy. I learned how to play hockey and laughed at the sorts of girls who wanted to be princesses. I learned not to cry when I got hurt, and I learned to love reading about boys, or girls who pretended to be boys, in *Eragon* and *To Kill a Mockingbird* and *The Woman Who Rides Like a Man*. And in many ways this was an honest expression of who I was and who I wanted to be.

Makes an emotional appeal.

But perhaps these behaviors also came from an understanding that it was possible—easy, even—to be too feminine. That uber-femininity could be shallow, or stupid, or mean. That it could be dangerous.

Now I am learning to look hard at the books that I read and the movies that I watch and the people that I admire. I am learning not to dismiss femininity for its own sake, but this is hard when feminine books and speech patterns and movies are constantly

Cites personal experience to establish her credibility to write on this topic.

dismissed by the cultural outlets I admire. The shock with which media outlets have responded to Joanna Coles's work at *Cosmo* is yet another example of this dismissal. But still I have learned to love Taylor Swift and horoscopes and eyeshadow, as well as weight lifting and science fiction and neuroscience, Walt Whitman and Suzanne Collins. And *Cosmo* has helped.

I am not saying that *Cosmo* is above critique. It continues to sideline the experiences of women who do not fit its target audience. It builds prehistoric concepts of femininity into its columns, and tells women implicitly or explicitly to trim down, dress up, and make themselves beautiful. Its advertisements and photosets build a fantasy of femininity in which woman is pale and thin and glossy. This does real damage.

But *Cosmo* is not beneath contempt. When we close the door to *Cosmo* for its perceived frivolity or irrelevance, we close the door to women's voices, their interests and concerns and desires. By assuming that women's journalism cannot be real journalism, Brian Stelter and others declare that women cannot know what journalism looks like, that we don't even know which stories are important and which are stupid. That we earn the right to tell our own stories only by making them unfeminine.

Why her analysis matters.

That femininity cannot be universal.

But femininity is universal. It always has been.

And universal experiences are feminine. As long as men are taught, like I was, that femininity is saccharine and silly and toxic, they are also taught to hate a part of themselves.

Nobody wins this fight.

Reiterates claim that Cosmo *can be both progressive and not progressive.*

Making room for femininity in feminism means recognizing that outlets like *Cosmo* can be progressive as well as problematic.

I want the right to criticize *Cosmo* when it writes harshly about female celebrities' bodies and the right to relish its fashion slideshows. I want to read about face gloss and I want to know about domestic terrorism. I want the right to be unfeminine without recourse, and the right to delight in my femininity. As a woman, and as a person, I should not have to choose just one story.

> Do I contradict myself?
> Well then I contradict myself,
> (I am large, I contain multitudes.)

Concludes on a personal note—and by echoing Walt Whitman's Song of Myself.

Works Cited

Brown, Helen Gurley. "Step into My Parlor." *Cosmopolitan*, Nov. 1995, pp. 28, 30.

Coles, Joanna. Interview with Brian Stelter. *Reliable Sources*, CNN, 7 June 2015. Transcript.

---. Interview with Rachel Martin. *Morning Edition*, NPR, 14 Oct. 2014. Transcript.

---. "Start?????" @JillFilipovic: Time to take @Cosmopolitan seriously." *Twitter*, 2 May 2014, twitter.com/joannacoles /status/462312728812863488.

Dries, Kate. "The New *Cosmopolitan* & the Slow Climb Out of Lipstick-and-Lasagna Land." *Jezebel*, 9 Dec. 2014, jezebel .com/the-new-cosmopolitan-the-slow-clim-out-of-lipstick -a-1666538526.

Gold, Hadas. "The New *Cosmo*: Love, Sex, Politics?" *Politico*, 9 Apr. 2014, www.politico.com/story/2014/09/the-new -cosmo-love-sex-politics-110586.

Meyers, Roberta, and Janet Reitman. Interview with Brian Stelter. *Reliable Sources*, CNN, 30 June 2013. Transcript.

Welch, Liz. "Love and Guns." *Cosmopolitan*, Mar. 2016, pp. 158-66.

Thinking about the Text

1. Wesley Cohen has a lot to say about *Cosmopolitan*, but what is her primary CLAIM about what's "happening over at *Cosmo*"?

2. How well do you think she supports that claim? Point out examples of the EVIDENCE she provides that you find most persuasive, and explain why you find them so persuasive.

3. Cohen includes a lot of personal information; how do you think it contributes to her analysis?

4. You might say that this essay analyzes more than one text—that which is found on the pages of *Cosmopolitan* and that which has been said (and written) about it. How effectively does Cohen weave it all together?

5. Go to cosmopolitan.com and see for yourself "what's happening" over there now. Find some examples that support—or contradict—what Cohen concludes about *Cosmo*, and draft an email to her about what you find.

10 Reporting

I LOVE THE ADVENTURE OF GOING OUT
AND REPORTING ON THINGS.

—TOM WOLFE

ANYONE CAN BE A REPORTER ON *TWITTER*,
AND THAT'S LED TO A UNIVERSE OF
DIVERSE VIEWPOINTS. . . .

—*WIRED*

R eporters often think of themselves as adventurers—on a quest to discover something important and to share that information with others. Some reports have galvanized the entire country, as was the case with Rachel Carson's report on the dangers of pesticides in 1962, a report that is again at issue this year in thousands of lawsuits against the weed killer Roundup. In the 1940s, the Kinsey Reports on human sexual behavior caused a national uproar of epic proportions—and led to changes in the way people think about sex. Much more recently, in 2018 an Intergovernmental Panel on Climate Change report led many Americans to purchase electric cars and install solar panels.

So reports—written or spoken accounts of some topic the author has thoroughly investigated—have been influential documents for a long time and continue in that role today. And you yourself may well be assigned to write reports in college—lab reports in *biology*, ethnographic reports in *sociology*, research reports in many classes. In many ways, then, Reports R Us, providing much of the information we rely on to get as close to the truth as possible, to make sense of the world, and to take effective action.

A GUIDE TO DEVELOPING A REPORT

Whatever kind of report you're writing, you'll need to think about who will be reading it, what they know about the topic, and what information you'll need to provide. And since reports are expected to provide factual information, you'll likely have to do some research— and to demonstrate that the information you report is accurate and trustworthy. Here now is a guide to the process of writing a report. It's designed to be used *as you write*, so keep it close at hand.

Choose a topic that interests you

In many instances, you may be assigned a specific topic. If so, find an angle that interests you—and one that you think will interest your audience. Say you're assigned to write a report for an economics class on supply and demand in a particular industry. Choose an industry you want to know more about—skin care, craft beer, whatever. On other occasions, you may be able to choose a topic to report on. If so, spend some time BRAINSTORMING about topics or issues that interest you, that you feel you can research with an open mind, and that you want to spend some time learning about. Here's a chance to do so!

Think about your rhetorical situation

Once you have a topic, spend some time thinking about the audience for the report, what you hope the report will accomplish, and the rest of your rhetorical situation.

Purpose. What do you want to accomplish with this report—provide information? inspire your audience to take some kind of action? What can you do in your report to achieve this purpose?

Audience. Who will be reading your report? Stakeholders of some kind? Your superiors in an organization? Fellow students? Think about what your target audience already knows about the topic and what background information you may need to provide. How interested will they be in the topic—or will you have to get them interested?

Stance. How do you want to be perceived as the author—as an authority on the topic? an interested and knowledgeable observer? How can you establish that stance—and how will you establish your credibility to report on this topic?

Context. What have others said about the topic, and do you need to take their perspectives into account in your report? How will your report contribute to the larger conversation about the topic? How much time do you have to complete the report, and what kind of research will you need to do? Reports are often written by a team. Will you be collaborating with other writers? Are there any other requirements you need to keep in mind?

Medium and design. How will your report be delivered—in print? as an oral report? online? How does the medium affect the way you'll design the report? If it will include information that's best presented in a graph or charts, will that affect the medium you use?

Research your topic and decide on a focus

The heart of most reports is in the information they provide, so a big part of your job as a report writer will be to gather as much relevant data as possible. Whatever your topic, your report will only be as strong as the information it provides. Begin with any information you already have about the topic, and make notes about what more you need to find out. What questions do you have? What will your readers want to know or need to be told?

Do some research

Start with REFERENCE WORKS that give an overview of the topic. If you're reporting on a current issue, you'll likely find a lot of sources online; sometimes *Wikipedia* can be a good place to start, for it often includes links to other sources. You'll also find help in this book—check out Chapter 14: Starting with Questions, Finding Sources.

What are the various perspectives on your topic?

What are others saying about it? Reporting calls on you to maintain a neutral, objective STANCE, but others are sure to have various viewpoints on the topic, and you need to be aware of them.

Focus on an angle that interests you

Once you have a broad understanding of the topic, what aspect do you want to focus on? Here's where you need to consider the constraints of your assignment: What can you do in the time you have? And think about your audience: What angle will interest them? Most of all, though, think about what interests *you!*

Formulate a working thesis

Say what you plan to report about the topic. For example, if you're reporting on food insecurity on campus, your working thesis might be something like this:

> Hunger is a big problem in the United States today.

Then think about whether you need to QUALIFY that statement—to make it one that you'll be able to support, and that will interest your AUDIENCE. Here's one way to qualify that statement:

> Hunger is a growing problem on our campus today.

If you're reporting on a controversial topic, your research may lead you to develop an opinion about the issue. But remember that your goal is to present information on the topic, not to tell readers what you think about it.

See how a report written for the general public summing up the findings of an annual survey presents its facts and data. The survey measured who people in 2019 trusted the most. Read on: you may be surprised by what it found.

Employers are now the most trusted institution, according to the 2019 Edelman Trust Barometer, with 75% of respondents saying they trust "my employer"—25 points more than business in general, 40 points more than government, 20 points more than a peer or expert and 10 points above traditional media.

Of the 33,000 people surveyed in 27 countries for the 19th annual Trust Barometer, more than three quarters (76%) say they want CEOs to take the lead on change instead of waiting for government. And 73% believe a company can take actions that both increase profits and improve economic and social conditions in the community where it operates.

A similarly high number of employees expect their employer to actively join them in advocating for social issues (67%), and 71% expect that their work will shape the future of society in a meaningful way.

Stephen Kehoe, Edelman's global chair of reputation, told the Holmes Report: "Overall, people are pessimistic about the future, and they are also concerned about fake news, and don't trust the media and government, so 58% say they are looking to their employer as being a trustworthy source of information about headline issues where there is not consensus in society, such as gun control, #MeToo, or immigration."

—MAJA PAWINSKA SIMS, *The Holmes Report*

Note how much data the reporter packs into this passage: we know that these findings are based on a survey of 33,000 people, for instance, from 27 countries. Note too the use of statistics to support the findings: 76 percent of those 33,000 people reported that they wanted CEOs "to take the lead on change," rather than "waiting for government." Finally, see how this reporter uses quotations to support the findings she reports, quoting the "chair of reputation" of the firm that conducted the original research. As readers, we know this is information we can trust.

Tailor your report to a target audience

Some reports are written for very specific audiences: a company's annual report to stockholders, for example, will address a group of people who have a stake in the company's performance, attempting to provide a clear and positive overview of the firm's accomplishments in the preceding year. A report to members of a synagogue on how their funds have been used to reduce poverty in a partner community will present data documenting the use of funds and may include photos showing the effect that the funds had on those in need. Whatever your audience, you'll want to think hard about what they already know about your topic and what information they'll be looking for.

The annual report for Girls Who Code, a national non-profit working "to close the gender gap in technology," addresses two audiences: contributors to the organization, and those people who might contribute in the future. See how the author of the report, the founder and CEO of the organization, speaks directly to these two audiences:

> When I started Girls Who Code, I never imagined that we would grow to become a movement reaching almost 90,000 girls of all backgrounds in all 50 states. And now, just six years into our work, we've reached a tipping point. We are on track to achieve gender parity in computer science by 2027. And we know why: because our work is as much about quantity as it is about quality. We scale our programs to reach more girls in more places, and to give them the chance to forge lifelong bonds so they may persist in computer science.

Joe Drape's report on e-sports offers abundant data and facts, along with profiles of 2 boys and their parents—members of his intended audience. Check it out on p. 770.

It's incredible. But for us, parity is really just the beginning.

We've reached a moment unmatched in our history, a moment as full of anger and anguish as it is promise and potential. Women and girls across the country are coming together to correct centuries-long power imbalances across lines of gender, race, sexuality, and more.

Girls Who Code is proud to be a part of this movement, and even prouder because our girls—girls of all races and ethnicities and abilities and zip codes—are leading it.

They are solving problems in their communities, empowering their friends, and defining the future of our world.

We're thrilled to be giving them the tools they need to get there.

I hope you'll join us and make sure every girl has the chance to change her world—our world—for the better. Thank you for your support.

—RESHMA SAUJANI, Annual Report of Girls Who Code

Here Saujani engages supporters and potential donors by summarizing the remarkable strides the group has made in its six years of

Girl coders.

Girls Who Code
is in every state.

PROGRAM MARKETS, 2017–2018

SIPs
1–10
11–50
51–100
101–150
>150

operation—now working with "girls of all races and ethnicities and abilities and zip codes"! And she includes a map showing that the organization now has programs in all 50 states. Note too that girls don't just get coding skills: they get coding skills that can help them "change our world." Finally, Saujani concludes her report with a thank-you, another way of acknowledging and encouraging donors.

Demonstrate your credibility, and that of the information you're reporting

In an age of misinformation and even outright lies, it's more important than ever to demonstrate that you are knowledgeable, trustworthy, and fair—and that the information in your report can be trusted as well. You can build credibility by demonstrating that you've read up on the topic, by citing reliable sources, and by documenting your sources. And you can demonstrate fairness by being evenhanded in the information you present—by citing sources that reflect various perspectives.

In an essay reporting on food production, Sam Forman compares two kinds of farms in Iowa—large industrial farms and small family-owned farms. As a student at Grinnell, a college in Iowa, he had some firsthand knowledge of both kinds of farms, but see how he presents information in ways that make readers feel we can trust both the author and what he reports:

Proponents of large-scale agriculture argue that it is cheaper and more efficient to produce food following an industrial model. Judging by price tags, they may be right. Often vegetables at a farmer's market fetch a higher price than those in the supermarket do. But the supermarket is not the only place we pay for industrially produced goods.

Iowa State professor Mark Honeyman pointed out to me, citing work by J. E. Ikerd, a professor of agricultural economics at the University of Missouri, that many of the costs of mass-produced agriculture are hidden. For instance, we all pay taxes to the government, which in turn spends billions of tax dollars a year subsidizing the industrial food system. Between 2003 and 2005 the government spent an average of $11.5 billion per year on crop subsidies, 47 percent of which went to the top 5 percent of beneficiaries ("Crop Subsidy"). This means we are subsidizing a lot, and mostly the biggest agri-businesses.

Most family farmers receive no government subsidies. So when I told Barney Bahrenfuse and Suzanne Costello, who run B & B Farms in Grinnell, that I repeatedly heard from people involved in large-scale agriculture that family farming is nice but ultimately not very profitable if even viable at all, Costello was quick to respond: "You take away the industrial farms' government subsidies—they don't work. We don't take any government subsidies, so who's viable?"

In fact, the CEO of Fremont Farms, which holds about 9 million hens, pointed out to me that they receive no government subsidies, which I verified online; according to the Environmental Working Group's website, which gets its statistics from the US Department of Agriculture, except for a paltry $5,361 in corn subsidies between 1999 and 2000, Fremont Farms has gotten no subsidies at all. No direct subsidies, that is. It is important to remember, however, that their operation is indirectly subsidized by the artificially low price of corn in their chickens' feed.

—SAM FORMAN, "The Future of Food Production"

Note that Forman interviewed and quotes an Iowa State professor, the owners of a small family farm, and the CEO of a large industrial farm—and that he even did the work of verifying what one of them told him. He also cites (and documents) data from a policy analysis database. He's clearly done his homework! See also how careful he is to qualify his information, noting that those who say food produced by large-scale farms is less expensive than food sold at farmer's markets "may be right" and that family farmers receive no subsidies "for the most part." And while he quotes one family farmer who says that industrial farms wouldn't work without government subsidies, he also notes that the CEO of a large-scale poultry farm said they get no government subsidies. Forman may well have his own opinions, but he's careful here to report only what he has learned about his topic, leaving readers free to reach their own conclusions.

> Without data, you're just another person with an opinion.
> —W. E. DEMING

It's important to note that reports are supposed to be objective, "just the facts." But while you should strive to be as objective as possible, most of the people you cite will have a particular point of view. And even as it's important to keep objectivity as a goal, it's also worth noting that reports are rarely if ever completely neutral: think of a fact-filled infographic reporting on the quality of local water sources, which will probably lead readers to draw conclusions that favor one viewpoint more than others. Remember, however, that readers will expect you to provide some kind of information, not to tell them what you think about it—or what they should think. Remember too that bringing in more than one viewpoint or perspective can help you aim for fairness and objectivity.

> **REFLECT!** Reread the excerpt from **Sam Forman**'s report on food production. How would you describe Forman's TONE? What words in his text help you decide what his tone is? And how would you describe his STANCE toward the topic: Can you spot any places where he is less than objective—and if so, does that affect how you respond to the report? Write a paragraph reflecting on the challenges of maintaining objectivity when you have your own opinions about a topic you're reporting on.

Establish a confident stance and an engaging tone

One of your tasks as a writer reporting information is to engage your readers, to make them interested in reading about your topic. In an era when we're all constantly bombarded with information, getting readers' attention is more important than ever. And then to keep their attention, you'll need to demonstrate confidence, to show that you know what you're talking about.

William Cronon makes some alarming assertions about nature and wilderness—but his engaging tone wins readers over. Check it out on p. 711.

Jean Twenge might have been thinking about this reality when she wrote an article for the *Atlantic* on the question "Have Smartphones Destroyed a Generation?" That's a title that grabs attention, and the article that follows includes some startling facts:

> The arrival of the smartphone has radically changed every aspect of teenagers' lives, from the nature of their social interactions to their mental health. These changes have affected young people in every corner of the nation and in every type of household. The trends appear among teens poor and rich; of every ethnic background; in cities, suburbs, and small towns. Where there are cell towers, there are teens living their lives on their smartphone. . . .
>
> You might expect that teens spend so much time [on their phones] because it makes them happy, but most data suggest that it

does not. The Monitoring the Future survey, funded by the National Institute on Drug Abuse and designed to be nationally representative, has asked 12th-graders more than 1,000 questions every year since 1975 and queried eighth- and tenth-graders since 1991. The survey asks teens how happy they are and also how much of their leisure time they spend on various activities, including nonscreen activities such as in-person social interaction and exercise, and, in recent years, screen activities such as using social media, texting, and browsing the web. The results could not be clearer: Teens who spend more time than average on screen activities are more likely to be unhappy, and those who spend more time than average on nonscreen activities are more likely to be happy.

There's not a single exception. All screen activities are linked to less happiness, and all nonscreen activities are linked to more happiness. Eighth-graders who spend 10 or more hours a week on social media are 56 percent more likely to say they're unhappy than those who devote less time to social media. Admittedly, 10 hours a week is a lot. But those who spend six to nine hours a week on social media are still 47 percent more likely to say they are unhappy than those who use social media even less. The opposite is true of in-person interactions. Those who spend an above-average amount of time with their friends in person are 20 percent less likely to say they're unhappy than those who hang out for a below-average amount of time.

—JEAN TWENGE, "Have Smartphones Destroyed a Generation?"

Twenge is clear, straightforward, and unequivocal, and she provides data to support the connection between time spent on phones and general unhappiness and stress. She tells it like it is, with confidence: "The results," she says, "could not be clearer: Teens who spend more time than average on screen activities are more likely to be unhappy." Her tone throughout is serious but not alarmist: she reports information her readers need to know, and she comes across as a confident, steady, reliable reporter who provides some very interesting and thought-provoking information.

Organize your report to suit your topic

The way you organize and design a report depends on the information you're presenting and the medium you'll use. Some topics call for COMPARISON, others call for you to present many examples, still others may lead you to present numerical data as a VISUAL in a bar chart or an infographic. So it's not possible to specify one generic way to organize all reports. Most reports, however, feature an organization their audiences can easily follow, whether it's using headings to guide readers from topic to topic, presenting some information in a list to make it easier to follow, and so on.

See pp. 85–90 on ways of organizing information.

Let's say you're writing a report comparing two teams in the NBA finals that are most likely to win the championship. You could organize your reports in two sections—one on Team A and the other on Team B—and for each team you would examine the star players, the postseason statistics, and other factors that point toward winning or losing. Or you might choose to organize the report around key statistics—rebounds per game, number of turnovers, and so on—and then look at both Team A and Team B in each of these categories. Each method of organization should yield a clear and reader-friendly result.

Take a look at part of a recent article from the *Washington Post* that uses classification as an organizing principle for reporting on the attitudes and feelings of people who have pets—in this case, those who have dogs, cats, cats and dogs, or no pets:

Dog or cat?

In 2018, the <u>General Social Survey</u> for the first time included a battery of questions on pet ownership. The findings not only quantified the <u>nation's pet population</u>—nearly 6 in 10 households have at least one—they made it possible to see how pet ownership overlaps with all sorts of factors of interest to social scientists.

Like happiness.

For starters, there is little difference between pet owners and non-owners when it comes to happiness, the survey shows. The two groups are statistically indistinguishable on the likelihood of

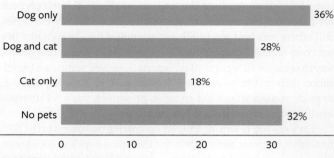

HAPPINESS IS A WARM DOG
Percentage saying they're "very happy," by type of pet owned

Dog only — 36%
Dog and cat — 28%
Cat only — 18%
No pets — 32%

Source: General Social Survey, 2018

identifying as "very happy" (a little over 30 percent) or "not too happy" (in the mid-teens).

But when you break the data down by pet type—cats, dogs or both—a stunning divide emerges: Dog owners are about twice as likely as cat owners to say they're very happy, with people owning both falling somewhere in between.

Dog people, in other words, are slightly happier than those without any pets. Those in the cat camp, on the other hand, are significantly less happy than the pet-less. And having both appears to cancel each other out happiness-wise. (Since someone's bound to ask, it isn't possible to do this same type of analysis for, say, rabbit owners or lizard owners or fish owners, since there aren't enough of those folks in the survey to make a statistically valid sample.)

—CHRISTOPHER INGRAHAM,
"Dog Owners Are Much Happier Than Cat Owners"

This article reports on a 2018 survey in which researchers set out to answer an age-old question—do dogs or cats make people happier?

And the answer is DOGS: "when you break the data down by pet type—cats, dogs or both—a stunning divide emerges: dog owners are about twice as likely as cat owners to say they're very happy, with people owning both falling somewhere in between." Notice that the writer classifies the pet owners in four categories: those with dogs, with cats, with both dogs and cats, and with no pets. He presents the findings in two different ways: with words, in paragraphs; and in a bar graph. Which of these two ways do you find easier to understand?

Finally, when it comes to organizing a report that you're assigned to do for a class, make sure to find out if there are any requirements for how to organize your work. Some fields in the sciences and social sciences require an organization known as IMRAD for the headings it includes: introduction, methods, results, and discussion. Engineering instructors may require you to include a title page and organize your report around methods, results, discussion, conclusions, and references. Other disciplines may require different organizations.

Consider whether to include any visuals

Many reports include information that is best presented in visual texts. The annual report for Girls Who Code, for example, includes a map to show all the states where that organization has chapters. And the *Atlantic* article on smartphones includes a number of graphs showing ways that smartphones have affected teenagers' behavior.

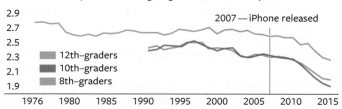

Not Hanging Out with Friends
Times per week teenagers go out without their parents

Joe Sacco's depiction of Sarajevo during the Bosnian war.

The one below shows how much less they've been hanging out with friends since the iPhone was released.

But there are many other ways to use illustrations in a report. Journalist and war correspondent Joe Sacco is well known for his graphic reporting on the horrors and heartaches of warfare. Reporting on the 1990s war in Bosnia in a series of reports later published in a book called *The Fixer*, Sacco describes what he saw when he entered the devastated city of Sarajevo:

> [P]ut yourself in my shoes: You've just arrived at the Great Siege . . . your teeth are still rattling from the ride over Mt. Igman . . . and someone has just pointed you down the road and into an awful silence.
>
> —JOE SACCO, *The Fixer*

The "awful silence" is surprising, given that the siege featured horrific noise—exploding bombs, gunfire, and what Sacco describes as a "very noisy media circus." But that has all given way to "an awful silence." At this point, Sacco includes a wordless, two-page image of his entry into Sarajevo.

Readers see Sacco, very small and hunched over and wearing a heavy backpack, walking past burned-out buildings, including a shelled Holiday Inn. No words. No sounds at all. Thus the illustration shows readers just what walking into an "awful silence" looked like.

Read your draft with a critical eye, get response—and revise

Once you have a draft, it's time to read over what you've written to be sure that your report will engage readers and tell them what you want them to know about your topic. If at all possible, get feedback from a classmate or friend. The following questions can help you or others read a report with a critical eye.

- Does the title make clear what the report is about—and will it engage readers' interest? What other title might you use?

- How well does the report address your intended AUDIENCE? Will they see why the topic matters?

- Have you indicated in a THESIS what the report is about and how it is organized?

- How have you established your CREDIBILITY? How many PERSPECTIVES does your report represent? Have you done your homework?

- How have you demonstrated that the information in your report is accurate and trustworthy? Have you FACT-CHECKED to be sure?

- How would you characterize the TONE? Does it reflect your STANCE and the way you want to come across to your readers? If you have an opinion about your topic, have you kept it out of the report?

- Is the organization clear and appropriate to the topic? Have you included headings and TRANSITIONS to help readers follow the report easily?

- Have you included any VISUALS or presented any text graphically? If not, is there any information that would be easier to understand in a chart or table or list?

- How does the report CONCLUDE? What do you want to leave readers thinking—and does the conclusion do that? How else might your report conclude?

And now it's time to REVISE. If you've analyzed your draft and gotten advice from others, you've got a plan. You know what you *want* to do—but think about what you need to do. Remember that you're writing a REPORT, and that means providing FACTUAL information—"just the facts," some would say. You're also writing to a particular AUDIENCE about something that you think matters, so now's your chance to make them care as well.

REFLECT! Choose a topic you are very interested in, and then browse the web to find someone who is reporting on that topic. Read the report carefully, and reflect on how effective the reporting is: How trustworthy is the information it provides? How objective is it? How credible is the author? How well does the report engage you and make you want to read on (or not)? If you could revise the report or give advice to the writer, what would you do or say?

A STUDENT REPORT

STEPHANIE POMALES

For Better or Worse: *Spotify* and the Music Industry

Stephanie Pomales wrote this essay for an introduction to computers class when she was a student at the University of Califoria at Davis, and it was a winner of the school's annual Prized Writing competition. She has a passion for communication and social media, and she has continued to pursue writing and research since her graduation. Her essay is documented using APA style.

When you want music, where do you turn? Are you a purist who demands vinyl? Or do you go online to *Pandora*? *YouTube*? *Apple Music*? *Tidal Music*? *Spotify*? If so, you are one of millions upon millions of people who access music digitally. But how much do you really know about the digital streaming services you are using? If streaming is the way most of us now listen to music, what issues does this shift raise for artists and the music industry? This report sets out to explore that question.

Opens with questions that engage her audience of college students.

Announces the purpose of her report.

Let's consider *Spotify*, the most popular streaming music service in the United States today. Founded in 2008 by Swedish entrepreneur Daniel Elk, *Spotify* was first made available here in 2011. Since then, *Spotify* has created a new way for people to consume music and has had a huge impact on the music industry's business model. With over 40 million paying subscribers, *Spotify* currently ranks number one as the most popular music service in the world, with more users than *Apple Music*, *Tidal*, or *Pandora*.

Establishes a conversational tone.

However, with popularity has come a critical backlash. The company, and its CEO, have been on defense ever since *Spotify* was first introduced into the US music marketplace, facing public opposition from recording artists, labels, and music industry executives. Piracy concerns, a decline in physical record sales, and *Spotify's* pay-per-stream model have been major points of discord between the music industry and streaming companies. Most everyone in

Provides background information.

the industry acknowledges that streaming services are not going away, but many are still concerned about the ethics of streaming and whether musicians, especially independent artists, are being treated fairly. Despite these criticisms, streaming services are likely here to stay—at least until a new technology that is better, faster, or cheaper comes onto the marketplace.

In fact, *Spotify* was once a new technology, one that was invented to be "better" than existing technology. You might say it all started with *Napster*, a peer-to-peer service that let people share and receive music files online or through email. It made music available for free, and thus was hugely popular. Its site was shut down after intense legal battles with copyright holders, but Napster had already changed the face of the music industry (Swanson, 2013). Apple's *iTunes*, *Rhapsody*, and *Pandora* all came shortly thereafter, each helping to further the digital music sphere into a more legitimate way of listening to music online (Marshall, 2015). And then, in 2008, along came *Spotify*.

Spotify is an "on demand" streaming service that operates on two plans. The first level, *Spotify Free* ("freemium"), lets users listen to music for free but with advertisements and with limited options. For example, they can listen to music only on shuffle mode and cannot access the higher quality sound that comes with a paid subscription. They also cannot listen to songs on demand and are limited to a certain number of skips in shuffle mode. For $9.99 per month ($4.99 for students), users can upgrade to the second tier, *Spotify Premium*, which gives them consistent, high quality, on-demand music. The music is considered "on demand" because users can listen to specific music that they choose instead of having music chosen for them by a computer-generated formula. *Spotify* licenses access to millions of songs by making deals with labels and independent artists for a certain percentage of its profits, money that comes from advertisements in the *Spotify Free* tier or from subscription fees in *Spotify Premium*. These funds go into a pool that is distributed based on how often songs are played and other

States thesis.

Provides a short narrative about the history of streaming.

Describes the services Spotify provides.

popularity factors; "think of it like having your paycheck fluctuate based not only on your own performance, but on the performance of everyone else in your industry as well" (Luckerson, 2019). According to an article in *Quartz*, song rightsholders make anywhere from $.006 to $.0084 cents per play, and these earnings can be divided up between the label, the producers, and the artists (Livni, 2018).

Streaming services are currently locked in a heated debate with music industry professionals over whether or not the pay-per-stream model is adversely affecting the industry and the artists. As the top streaming service in the world, *Spotify* takes up much of the spotlight, especially after Taylor Swift pulled all her music from *Spotify* in 2014. Swift added her albums back in 2017, but her absence on the site for many years raised serious questions about the ethics of *Spotify*'s free model. Many artists and music industry professionals believe that the backlash is warranted, while others argue that *Spotify* provides a legal alternative to pirating that justifies its existence (Swanson, 2013).

Provides statistics.

Introduces alternative views of streaming services.

Taylor Swift raised red flags about *Spotify* when she removed her albums from *Spotify* in 2014.

Spotify started with good intentions: to combat the music piracy that *Napster* had unleashed, as people began to see peer-to-peer sharing as a way of owning free music. Daniel Elk, *Spotify*'s founder, believed that streaming services could simply monetize already existing consumer behavior, and that it would be a legitimate alternative to the global issue of pirating.

In spite of the criticism, *Spotify* has lived up to much of its early promise. Streaming services are in fact saving music sales, which have been declining in recent years in part because of struggles with piracy (Shaw, 2016). Even Carl Sherman, the president of the Recording Industry Association of America, has spoken out on the subject. In a recent blog article reporting on the music industry midway through 2016, Sherman admitted that much of the growth in the music industry in recent years has been brought about by music subscription services (Sherman, 2016), saying that 2016 was the first time that music professionals had seen consistent sales since 1999, when record sales reached their peak (Singleton & Popper, 2016). Sherman even acknowledged that streaming had contributed a lot to these record-high sales numbers, noting that it "accounted for almost half of all recorded music revenue in the first half of 2016" (Sherman, 2016). Since *Spotify* is the streaming service with the most subscribers, and the main contributor to the industry's increased sales, its impact on the music marketplace is considerable. Approximately $1 billion was spent on streaming services in the first half of 2016, with more people than ever opting for paid subscription plans. Music spending in total for the same year, including record sales and online sales, was more than $3.4 billion according to industry statistics (Shaw, 2016). The three major record labels—Universal Music Group, Sony Music Entertainment, and Warner Music Group—have all seen improved sales, largely due to the popularity of streaming services in the United States (Shaw, 2016).

Many still believe, however, that *Spotify* is not doing enough to help musicians earn a living wage, especially in the case of indepen-

Provides evidence of Spotify's positive effects.

Spotify's billboards celebrate its listeners and inspire others to join the fun.

dent artists. Many common arguments state that music buying is decreasing. During the heydays of CDs and records, buying music was a more public, even social, experience. Now that big box stores are reducing their CD sections and there are fewer music stores around, music buying takes place mostly online and in the privacy of one's home. While it's easy to assume that fewer people are willing to pay for music, data shows that people who pay for streaming services will spend more over time than those who bought physical CDs in the 1990s (Shaw, 2016). A typical CD buyer in 1990 spent $50 per year on music, while a *Spotify* subscription could cost as much as $120 per year (Singleton & Popper, 2016). With 25% of all *Spotify* "freemium" users converting to paid subscriptions (Singleton & Popper, 2016), more people than ever before are paying for their music.

Many of *Spotify*'s defenders believe that critics are simply looking at streaming services in the wrong way, saying that streaming services and store-bought albums are different things. Streaming,

Provides evidence of Spotify's negative effects.

Notes counterarguments to Spotify's critics.

they say, needs to be taken seriously as a new technology that cannot be compared to previous technologies. Vinyl, cassettes, and CDs each had a moment in which they were the most in-demand technology, and streaming is now having its moment. This suggests that a major change is overdue concerning how people view the streaming model. When radio DJs play a song, they are sending music over airwaves to hundreds or even thousands of people at the same time. On the other hand, streaming occurs on a one-to-one basis with individual people accessing a song they want to hear whenever they want to hear it. This explains why the payment per stream is so low, and why *Spotify* simply can't be compared with *AirPlay*.

Spotify's Daniel Elk has a response to all the criticism that his company has faced. Most industry professionals see music sales on a per-unit basis, he says, like buying an individual song on an online music store. Elk suggests that the music industry needs to move away from a unit-based business model and to a streaming model. People do not buy music from streaming services—instead, they pay for access to music for a designated period. Over an extended period, the small payments for music access will result in more money for both artists and industry professionals (Marshall, 2015).

But *Spotify*'s biggest problem is not the complaints of artists or industry bigwigs. Indeed, it is piracy, in the form of illegal music downloading. The switch to streaming has many researchers trying to determine whether it has resulted in more or less music piracy. After all, one of the main reasons Elk started *Spotify* was to make streaming a viable alternative to piracy in the digital age. If piracy has decreased, then one could say that streaming services have fulfilled a valuable goal for the music industry; if piracy has risen, it may be that streaming services are adding to digital piracy.

The Federation of the Phonographic Industry estimates that 20 million Americans are pirating on a regular basis (Carman, 2016), and it seems that the "exclusives" that some streaming companies

Compares streaming with earlier technologies.

Introduces the music industry's main problem: piracy.

offer may be partly responsible. When popular music is available only on specific streaming services, users are less able to get all their music on one service, resulting in widespread pirating of that music (Singleton & Popper, 2016). For example, when Kanye West's *Life of Pablo* album was available only on *Tidal*, it is estimated that 500,000 people illegally downloaded the album from various file-sharing websites (Carman, 2016). Each of the illegal downloads resulted in loss of income for the artist, the streaming services, and the industry professionals behind the production and creation of the album. Although exclusive content may help to bring more business to a specific streaming service, ultimately, they may be doing more harm than good to the industry and to *Spotify*'s efforts to eradicate pirating.

Provides evidence of the damage done by piracy.

Academic research offers conflicting viewpoints about music streaming services and their influence on pirating. In their paper "Streaming Reaches Flood Stage: Does *Spotify* Stimulate or Depress Music Sales?" Aguiar and Waldfogel (2015) conclude that Spotify has been revenue-neutral for the music industry, stating that "losses from displaced sales are roughly outweighed by the gains in streaming revenue" (p. 1). Their research also shows that *Spotify* has helped to decrease the amount of music piracy in the United States and across the globe, but does not do much to raise the net profit of the music industry (Aguiar & Waldfogel, 2015). Borja and Dieringer (2016), however, conclude that streaming services like *Spotify* increase instances of pirating by 11%, with more streaming directly correlated with higher rates of music pirating. This might have to do with the fact that most people "do not view streaming as a low-price substitute for pirating," as many complain that streaming services are still too expensive (Borja & Dieringer, 2016, p. 91). In fact, Borja and Dieringer found that the two most predictive factors for pirating were peer pressure and a high tendency toward risk taking. College students seem to be the population most inclined to this behavior, as students have little income and many expenses.

Cites research about Spotify's effects on piracy.

Citing scholarly research helps build the author's credibility: she's done her homework!

With higher levels of risk taking, students are more likely to pirate from illegal file-sharing websites because they have less money to buy music and are more susceptible to the considerations of others.

While peer pressure surely plays a significant role in piracy behavior, internet users may have more complex reasons behind why they resort to pirating even when low-cost alternatives like streaming are available. In 2016, Russ Crupnick, a writer for MusicWatch .com, conducted a survey with 1,000 respondents between the ages of 13 and 50 and found that the reasons for music pirating are varied between different age categories. Some people surveyed simply stated that they want to own the music, rather than only have access to it for a brief period, while others only pirate music if they do not like the track enough to purchase it on a digital music site (Crupnick, 2016). Many of the respondents stated that they wanted to have "on demand" music on their smartphones, a feature that *Spotify Free* does not offer. Somewhat surprisingly, many of the people surveyed who pirated music claimed that they spend a fair amount of money buying music from legal sources; in fact, the amount they spend on legal music is only slightly less than the amount spent by average, non-pirating music buyers (Crupnick, 2016).

Although criticism of streaming continues and research gives conflicting information concerning piracy, streaming services have made their mark on the music industry. Those using these sites, including both premium and "freemium" subscribers, have grown accustomed to accessing large quantities of music for free, or for incredibly cheap prices. Music labels must adjust to these changes and work accordingly with streaming services in order to stay relevant into the 21st century, especially given the potential for streaming services to independently contract with musicians in the near future. The more subscribers join, the more money artists will see in their pockets and the less irritated music executives will be with *Spotify*'s cut of the profits. This not only applies to big name artists receiving millions of streams, but indie artists as well. Longer

Considers other perspectives on piracy.

Sums up the findings of her research.

free trials, special discounts, and family memberships are all ways that streaming services can get more paid subscribers. Any money that goes to the music industry is still better than having musicians' work be pirated. Marketing toward older generations on the benefits of streaming services may also prove to be useful in increasing the number of paid subscription members. With *Spotify* holding a high conversion rate of users from free to paid plans, it is likely that streaming services will become more normalized in music history and will begin to secure a stronger reputation in the eyes of industry professionals.

If you're someone who gets your music via *Spotify*, *Pandora*, or another streaming service, do you subscribe or take the freemium options? Or do you find a way to download what you want for free? What do you think you *should* do, and why? As subscribers, or potential subscribers, these are all issues that you should consider when you stream your next song. As this report has demonstrated, these are decisions we all need to think about.

States the conclusion supported by research.

Challenges readers to think about where they get music; invites response.

References

Aguiar, L., & Waldfogel, J. (2015). *Streaming reaches flood stage: Does* Spotify *stimulate or depress music sales?* (NBER Working Paper No. 21653). The National Bureau of Economic Research. http://doi.org/df3d

Borja, K., & Dieringer, S. (2016). Streaming or stealing? The complementary features between music streaming and music piracy. *Journal of Retailing and Consumer Services, 32,* 86–95. http://doi.org/gc8qv8

Carman, A. (2016, April 10). *How music streaming service exclusives make pirating tempting again.* The Verge. http://www.theverge.com/2016/4/10/11394272/music-streaming-service-piracy-spotify-tlop-tidal

Crupnick, R. (2016, February 22). *Bad company, you can't deny.* MusicWatch. http://www.musicwatchinc.com/blog/bad-company-you-cant-deny/

Livni, E. (2018, December 25). *Mariah Carey's record-breaking day shows how little musicians make from* Spotify. Quartz. https://qz.com/1507361/mariah-careys-record-breaking-day-shows-how-little-musicians-make-from-spotify/

Luckerson, V. (2019, January 16). *Is Spotify's model wiping out music's middle class?* The Ringer. https://www.theringer.com/tech/2019/1/16/18184314/spotify-music-streaming-service-royalty-payout-model

Marshall, L. (2015). "Let's keep music special. F—*Spotify*": On-demand streaming and the controversy over artist royalties. *Creative Industries Journal, 8*(2), 177–189. http://doi.org/gc3chw

Shaw, L. (2016, September 19). *The music industry is finally making money on streaming.* Bloomberg. https://www.bloomberg.com/news/articles/2016-09-20/spotify-apple-drive-u-s-music-industry-s-8-first-half-growth

Sherman, C. (2016, September 20). *The modern music business midway through 2016.* Medium. https://medium.com/@RIAA/the-modern-music-business-midway-through-2016-f74e22ecff42#.geo4odf4s

Singleton, M., & Popper, B. (2016, September 20). *The music industry is on the rebound thanks to paid streaming.* The Verge. http://theverge.com/2016/9/20/12986980/music-industry-apple-spotify-paid-streaming

Swanson, K. (2013). A case study on *Spotify*: Exploring perceptions of the music streaming service. *MEIEA Journal, 13*(1), 207–230. http://doi.org/gfvxmh

Thinking about the Text

1. Stephanie Pomales has obviously done a lot of research on *Spotify* and other streaming services. What is her major CLAIM and where is it stated?

2. What examples, facts, and reasons does she offer to support the major claim? How well do you think she supports that claim? What EVIDENCE do you find most informative and persuasive—and what leads you to that conclusion?

3. How does Pomales deal with COUNTERARGUMENTS and alternative viewpoints? Do you think she does so fairly?

4. Make a rough outline of this report. What does it reveal about how she has organized all her information? How effective is that organization? How else could it be organized?

5. Pomales concludes her report by asking readers how they get music—by subscribing to a streaming service, using a free streaming service, or downloading what they want for free—and then asking what they think they should do, and why. Write a paragraph or two describing how *you* get music, and reflecting on what you now think you should do—and why.

11 Narrating

WHAT UNITES PEOPLE? ARMIES? GOLD? FLAGS?
NAH. *STORIES*. THERE'S NOTHING MORE POWERFUL
THAN A GOOD STORY. NOTHING CAN STOP IT.
NO ENEMY CAN DEFEAT IT.

—TYRION LANNISTER

W hy would telling a story be "more powerful" than everything else in the world? Is it because millions of people watch *Game of Thrones*? Or read about the adventures of Odysseus, or Captain Underpants? It's much more than that. Storytelling is a universal genre: "the one true democracy we have," says novelist Colum McCann. "It goes across borders, boundaries, genders, wealth, race—everyone has a story to tell." A good story can even change minds. These are all reasons that stories mean so much to our lives and to the work we do as readers, writers, and speakers.

If you're a *biology* major, you'll learn a lot through stories about how major discoveries were made, from Watson and Crick's quest to solve the structure of DNA to the epic journeys that led Charles Darwin and Alfred Wallace to their theory of evolution. If you're a *business* major, you're likely to work with case studies, narratives about situations that real companies faced in which you might be assigned to be the CEO (the protagonist) and have to figure out how to deal with the situation. And if you watched the 2019 *Super Bowl*, you likely saw the Toyota ad that linked a vehicle to the powerful story about Toni Harris, the first woman to win a college football scholarship and who hopes someday to be the first woman to play in the Super Bowl.

So narratives are all around us, not just in literature and on TV. It's no surprise then that they will play a role in your composition class. You might open an argument with a personal narrative that makes a point about your topic—and perhaps return to that story in your conclusion. Or you might compose a narrative as a way to make a point. And sometimes you may be assigned to write a literacy narrative about how you learned to read or write or do something else. This chapter aims to guide you in creating a narrative of your own.

Toni Harris with her teammates.

A GUIDE TO DEVELOPING A NARRATIVE

Put most simply, a narrative tells about something that's happened in order to make a point of some kind. A personal narrative focuses on something that happened to the person writing it. That's you, and here are some steps to get you started.

Identify an event that matters

The first step is to come up with a topic that matters—to you, and hopefully to others as well. Think about what happened, and why. When and where did it happen? Who was involved, and what roles did they play? Why does it matter to you, and why have you chosen to write about it? How can you write about it in a way that will interest others—especially if it's something they wouldn't ordinarily read about?

If you're assigned to write a LITERACY NARRATIVE, you'll focus on how you learned to do something—read, write, knit, play the guitar, whatever. Just be sure it's something you care about. Start by thinking about what you learned, and who else was involved. Was it easy? challenging? fun? something else? Why has it mattered enough to write about it?

When Melissa Hicks was assigned to write a personal narrative for her writing class at Lane Community College, in Oregon, she found herself thinking over and over about making butter on her family's farm as a young girl and her fondness for butter now as an adult. Writing about those experiences prompted her to think about why they've been so important to her:

> I swear that it's the butter that makes everything taste so good. My
> favorite foods that remind me of my mother and my own childhood.
> In the grocery store aisle, I stand under the harsh white lights of the
> dairy case, margarine in one hand and butter in the other.... I weigh
> them in my mind, thinking of the high cost of butter. No matter how
> long I stand and weigh, I always put the butter in my cart. I remem-

ber the times when I was a girl—the taste of sweet, fresh butter melting on my tongue. I remember the work it took, and I know the price is more than fair.

—MELISSA HICKS, "The High Price of Butter"

The story Hicks goes on to tell moves back and forth between her present grown-up self and her past childhood. She meditates on the honest, hard work on the farm where she took care of the cow and made butter, and reflects on how those experiences shaped the values that she still holds today.

And here's Savion Glover, now a famous tap dancer, telling the story about how learning to play the drums at a young age got him started "making too much noise":

I started playing drums in Suzuki class when I was three or four. I'd go in there and start banging on some drum or on the piano or the xylophone, and they eventually moved me up a level into the regular drum class, I think because I was just making too much noise. I just couldn't stop banging around. Meanwhile at home I used to play everything, just everything, my mother tells me. I do remember putting

A close-up of Savion Glover, making music and noise with his feet.

on shows for her. She would come home from work, and I'd have the knives and forks out from the drawers and the pots and the pans set up like drums. I figured out you could get different tones out of the big pots and the little pots and the teakettle and the colander.

—SAVION GLOVER, *My Life in Tap*

Note that Glover's narrative implicitly tells readers that this sequence of events matters a great deal to him: it captures his commitment to and near obsession with making music (and noise!) since he was a toddler, using red highlighting to underscore that he "just couldn't stop banging around." Creating sound and performing for his mother seem like the most important things in his life! This paragraph draws readers in and invites us to find out what happens next.

Think about your rhetorical situation

When you've decided on the event(s) your narrative will focus on and considered the point you want the narrative to lead up to, it's time to consider your rhetorical situation.

Purpose. Think again about why you want to tell this story. Will telling it help you understand yourself and what has happened to you in your life in new ways? Will it help you connect with a particular audience? Or maybe your narrative is meant to entertain—to get your audience laughing along with you. Whatever your purpose, keep it in mind from start to finish.

Audience. Who will read your story? Why would it interest them— or how can you get them interested? What do you want them to take away from it? What do you know about them, and how much background will you need to provide? What do you know about their age, gender, cultural heritage, basic values and beliefs, and so on? How might such factors influence the way you tell your story—and how you present yourself?

Stance. What stance will you take? How do you want to come across—as knowledgeable? thoughtful? funny? something else? Whatever stance you adopt, think about how the words you choose and the way you put them together will help establish that stance.

Context. What else has been said about your topic? Does your narrative relate to any larger social or political or economic issues (or educational ones, if you're writing a literacy narrative)—and if so, what will your audience need to know about that context? Finally, think about your own context—the requirements of an assignment, the time you have to complete your narrative, and so on.

Media and design. How will your narrative be delivered—in print? online? as an oral presentation? How does your medium affect the way your narrative is designed and the kinds of examples you can provide? Can you include visuals—photos and captions? video? audio? Would headings help readers follow the story? Your decisions about media and design should aim to help your audience follow your story and understand the major points you want to make with that story.

Try to recall details that will make your story come alive

Start by writing down everything you can remember about the event that's at the heart of your narrative—just start writing and keep going until you run out of memories and words. *What* happened? *When* and *where* did it take place? *Who* was there? What were they wearing, what did they say? Can you recall any specific sounds, smells, colors, or tastes? What vivid or quirky details can you add that will help bring your story to life so that others can experience it along with you? Can you add some dialogue—conversations or even just words that will let your audience listen in on what was happening? *Why* does this story matter?

See how Lynda Barry incorporates visual details and dialogue in her narrative essay recalling how important good teachers have been to her success as a cartoonist, author, and now a teacher herself. Here she is at age seven, sneaking out of home and in a panic about "needing to get to school":

Mark Gozonsky's narrative about making the team at age 57 is so full of juicy details that you can almost drink it. Quench your thirst on p. 801.

It was quiet outside. Stars were still out. Nothing moved and no one was in the street. It was as if someone had turned the sound off on the world.

I walked the alley, breaking thin ice over the puddles with my shoes. I didn't know why I was walking to school in the dark. . . . All I knew was a feeling of panic, like the panic that strikes kids when they realize they are lost.

That feeling eased the moment I turned the corner and saw the dark outline of my school at the top of the hill. My school was made up of about 15 nondescript portable classrooms set down on a fenced concrete lot in a rundown Seattle neighborhood, but it had the most beautiful view of the Cascade Mountains. You could see them from . . . the windows of my classroom—Room 2. . . .

"Hey there, young lady. Did you forget to go home last night?" It was Mr. Gunderson, our janitor, whom we all loved. He was nice and he was funny and he was old with white hair, thick glasses and an unbelievable number of keys. I could hear them jingling as he walked across the playfield. I felt incredibly happy to see him.

And I saw my teacher, Mrs. Claire LeSane, walking toward us in a red coat and calling my name in a very happy and surprised way, and suddenly my throat got tight and my eyes stung and I ran toward her crying. . . .

It's only thinking about it now, 28 years later, that I realize I was crying from relief. I was with my teacher, and in a while I was going to sit at my desk, with my crayons and pencils and books and class-mates all around me, and for the next six hours I was going to enjoy a thoroughly secure, warm and stable world. . . .

Mrs. LeSane asked me what was wrong and when I said "Noth-ing," she seemingly left it at that. But she asked me if I would carry her purse for her, an honor above all honors, and she asked if I wanted to come into Room 2 early and paint.

—LYNDA BARRY, "The Sanctuary of School"

Barry is a master cartoonist and storyteller, and this passage is full of colorful, quirky details. We wonder, along with her, why she is

going to school in the dark, but that thought is swept aside as she turns a corner and sees her school—her "sanctuary," even though the school is just a bunch of "nondescript portable classrooms." Then she sees the janitor, with his "unbelievable number of keys" jingling a greeting—and then her teacher, Mrs. LeSane. Note the colorful images (red coat, thin ice over puddles) and how Barry's dialogue helps make the passage more vivid and immediate, and thus carries readers along. Finally, notice how Barry's cartoon image helps tell the story: she's literally cradling her school, her sanctuary, in her arms—and with a smile on her face—as she declares, "I'm home."

Figure out how to tell your story

At this point, you should think about creating a scratch OUTLINE or STORYBOARD for your narrative. You might think of the narrative as a big arc, with a dramatic event or something else at the beginning that will get your audience's attention and then lead to other events or details or insights and eventually to some kind of conclusion. Then plot points along this arc where you'll bring in particular information.

See Chapter 22 on ways of getting and keeping attention. How can you begin in a way that will get your audience interested? How will you sequence your story and hold their interest? And how should you conclude: What do you want to leave your audience thinking?

You'll need to consider POINT OF VIEW. Will you write in the first person (*I*, *me*) throughout, or will the narrative require you to shift points of view in places as Melissa Hicks does, shifting from *I* to *we* when she refers to things her family did?

Think about how you'll represent time. Most narratives use CHRONOLOGICAL ORDER or a slight variation on it (such as adding FLASHBACKS, for example) and so use past tenses, as Hicks does:

> For my fourteenth birthday I got a cow. I did not ask for a cow. I had very clearly asked for a horse. While every girl-child wants a horse, I felt that I had earned mine. I had worked at a farm down the road.... I knew how to take care of a horse. The life my family had worked and sweated for, clearing our own little spot in the Maine woods, was as well suited to horse-raising as any of our other pursuits. The fact was, I didn't know beans about cows.
>
> —MELISSA HICKS, "The High Price of Butter"

If you want readers to experience the narrative as very immediate, you might use the present tense. Here's Hicks again, making butter: "As my arms tire, I alter the motion. Instead of shaking the jar up and down, I go side to side. My youngest sister . . . asks for the jar. My mother, setting the milk back in the fridge, tells her to wait her turn." The present tense takes readers right into the scene: we are there with her as she does the hard work of making butter.

Finally, try your hand at drafting the OPENING and CONCLUSION of your narrative. You may not use them in the end, but getting something down in print will help you build momentum. Try to start in a way that will grab your audience's attention, make them interested in reading on. There are many ways to conclude, but think about what you want them to take away from the story, what you want them to remember.

See pp. 85 and 410–12 on ways to begin; pp. 92 and 417–18 on ways to conclude.

Then work on drafting the rest of the narrative. When you've done that, see if the opening and closing still fit.

REFLECT! You probably never got a cow for a present—or maybe you did. But think about gifts you've received—or given. What gift is most memorable, and what makes it so? Write a paragraph or two that tells the story of that gift.

Indicate why the story matters

Readers expect more from a personal narrative than just a good story. We want to know why the subject of the narrative matters to the author—and why those of us reading it should care. You can't assume that readers will know why your story matters, so you need to make that clear. There's no simple formula for how to do that, other than to say what *not* to do: don't simply *say* why it matters. Let's see how some of the authors in this chapter do that.

The best arguments in the world won't change a person's mind. The only thing that can do that is a good story.
RICHARD POWERS, *The Overstory*

In her essay about how school was a "sanctuary" for her, Lynda Barry writes about more than just herself, noting that while we know that "a good education system saves lives," we are still told that "cutting the budget for public schools is necessary, that poor salaries for teachers are all we can manage." She wants to change our minds about that. Here's how she concludes her essay:

> Mrs. LeSane asked us to please stand, face the flag, place our right hands over our hearts and say the Pledge of Allegiance. Children across the country do it faithfully. I wonder now when the country will face its children and say a pledge right back.
>
> —LYNDA BARRY, "The Sanctuary of School"

Here's how Melissa Hicks shows us why her essay is about more than just the price of butter:

> To me the cost of butter is more than a price tag. The cost of butter reminds me of my childhood, and how my family struggled to be pioneers in the twentieth century. The cost of butter reminds me of the value of hard work, and how that brought my family together. . . . Yet the cost of butter is more than a symbol of hard work and quality. The fact that I buy it is an affirmation of my own choices in life. Because of my childhood, I know the cost in sweat of butter. As an adult, I choose to pay that price in cash.
>
> —MELISSA HICKS, "The High Price of Butter"

Finally, here's Michelle Obama, near the end of her memoir, *Becoming*, reflecting on her own journey and her purpose for writing that book:

> For me, becoming isn't about arriving somewhere or achieving a certain aim. I see it instead as forward motion, a means of evolving, a way to reach continuously toward a better self. The journey doesn't end. I became a mother, but I still have a lot to learn from and give to my children. I became a wife, but I continue to adapt to and be humbled by what it means to truly love and make a life with another person. I have become, by certain measures, a person of power, and yet there are moments still when I feel insecure or unheard.
>
> It's all a process, steps along a path. Becoming requires equal parts patience and rigor. Becoming is never giving up on the idea that there's more growing to be done.
>
> —MICHELLE OBAMA, *Becoming*

In all three of these examples, the writers show just why the story matters, why it's important to them and should be to us as well.

Read your draft with a critical eye, get response—and revise

Once you have a draft, ask others to read it over and talk with you about it. Ask them to be frank and open: What did they get out of your story? Was anything confusing? What did they like best? Did they find it engaging? easy to follow? Try to get response from people who represent your intended audience—and some who might not: you want to hear as many diverse perspectives as possible. Now's the time to do so!

Eventually, of course, you need to be your own best critic. After all, you know what you were aiming for. So get out your magnifying glass, and take a very close look at what you've produced.

- How will the OPENING capture the audience's attention and make them want to read on? How else could the narrative begin?

- How well has the scene for the story been DESCRIBED? Is it clear when and where the story takes place?

- If there are shifts in time in your story, are they signaled by the use of different verb tenses?

- Will readers be able to follow the narrative easily? Are there TRANSITIONS from one part of the story to the next? If not, should there be?

- What vivid details or memorable words help the story come alive?

- Does the narrative include dialogue or direct quotation? If not, should you add some?

- Are there any VISUALS—photos, maps, and so on? If so, what do they contribute to the narrative? If not, would adding some help carry the story along?

- How would you describe the TONE, and what words, visuals, or other things help establish that tone? Will the AUDIENCE you want to reach find this tone engaging?

- Is the point or significance of the story clear, both for you and others? What makes it clear? Have you stated it explicitly—and if not, should you do so?

- How does the narrative CONCLUDE? What does it leave readers thinking? How else might it end?

- Have you chosen a title? If so, how will it get your readers' attention, and are you still satisfied with it? If not, try to come up with a title that will make your readers want to read what you've written.

Now's the time to REVISE. If you've analyzed your draft and gotten advice from others, you've got a plan. You know what you need to do, and what you *want* to do. So now's your chance! But remember that you're writing a NARRATIVE: you're telling a story. And you're telling it to an AUDIENCE, and they will want to know *why* you're telling this story. Be sure to tell them why the story matters to you—and why it might matter to them.

REFLECT! "Tell me a fact and I'll learn. Tell me the truth and I'll believe. But tell me a story and it will live in my heart forever." This **Native American proverb** sets a high standard for the stories we tell. Think of a story that has stayed with you for a long time. What made it so memorable: the subject? the way the story was told? the message? Then write a paragraph or so about what makes a narrative live on "forever."

A STUDENT NARRATIVE

ISAAC LOZANO
Remote Learning Is Hard.
Losing Family Members Is Worse.

Isaac Lozano was a senior at Buena Vista High School in Chula Vista, California, when he sent this narrative to the New York Times, *where it was published on August 13, 2020. He is currently at work on a children's book.*

Last month, I learned that my uncle died of Covid-19. Not long after, his mother passed away from the virus, too. Since my parents are essential workers, I'm starting my senior year of high school worrying whether they're next.

I live in one of San Diego's <u>most infected ZIP codes</u>. And I'm a Latino in a county where Hispanics—43 percent of Covid-19 victims yet only 34 percent of the population—bear the brunt of the pandemic.

When schools went remote earlier this year, low-income students like me, who have limited access to computers and the internet, <u>faced challenges</u> keeping up with schoolwork. Trying to study in cramped quarters and without reliable connectivity was frustrating. But as schools begin this fall, I'd much rather endure the troubles of distance learning than return to campus prematurely and sacrifice my own health or that of my family.

Throughout the pandemic, my five-member family has been huddled in a 920-square-foot, two-bedroom apartment, where I share a room with my two brothers. For my parents, social distancing isn't an option. My father is a supervisor at a car distribution company, and my mother, in remission from cancer, recently resigned as a caregiver at a hospice facility. Cases in our county were rising, so she opted instead to take care of my autistic cousin through a respite care program. It's not much, but in my mother's words, the extra money will allow us to salir adelante, or get ahead.

Opens with dramatic events that make us read on: Will his parents be next?

Uses first-person point of view.

Echoes his title's contrast, which leads up to his main point.

Quotes his mother in Spanish to sum up his family's goals.

In April, when my school started distance learning, I struggled to stay focused, bouncing from room to room in search of peace and quiet. In the morning, I settled in the kitchen table to attend online meetings while my family was asleep. By the afternoon, I fled to my parents' room to finish schoolwork but only until my father came home from work and ordered me out.

Sometimes I ignored my parents or grimaced at them for no apparent reason.

Dialogue evokes tension and brings the story to life.

"Are you mad at me?" my mother would ask.

"No, I just want to stay focused," I'd retort.

Vivid details help us share his experience.

In truth, I was angry that I lived in a coronavirus hot spot; that my immigrant parents could only provide me with so much; that my middle-class peers were ensconced in their own bedrooms while I remained confined to a skinny metal chair in my kitchen.

At school, I got straight A's and was praised by English teachers for my writing. I saw myself as the poor Mexican kid who could overcome financial barriers with enough determination.

But when my uncle died of the coronavirus, I realized that gumption wasn't enough to overcome the obstacles of a pandemic. We couldn't even say goodbye.

Black and Latino children already grapple with disproportionately high rates of Covid-19 and face systemic barriers to testing and treatment. Many of us live in multigenerational homes and have parents who are essential workers. We are less likely to have access to health care. And low-income schools across the country are struggling to afford the supplies and infrastructure required to reopen safely.

Shift in tense returns us to the present.

I'm lucky that my district is postponing school reopenings until at least October. But if I am ordered back to campus prematurely, I won't do it. As difficult as distance learning was, returning to the classroom now—as cases in the U.S. break records and experts foresee the pandemic persisting until next year—would put my home and the homes of millions of low-income kids of color at greater risk of infection.

I leave my apartment not knowing if my next-door neighbors—only three feet away from my front door—could have the virus. I fear for my mother's life every time we go to our local laundromat, a cramped space where visitors don't always wear masks. Though we wash our hands and disinfect items after arriving home, I'm always left with a tingle of uneasiness—like sensing a mosquito in a dark room.

Sensory details underscore reasons for his decision.

I've lamented this to friends who, like me, live in tight quarters and have seen family members sickened: As much as we excel academically, <u>our ZIP codes still hold dominion over us and our families</u>. Living in a noisy home with domestic responsibilities during a pandemic was already a challenge, but the death of a loved one sapped my hope for the future and brought closer the difference a few digits on my address can make.

But passing the cracked sidewalks of my apartment complex, I'm reminded that others have it worse: My family is financially independent, and we've settled in a tight-knit community.

Transitions to a more hopeful view, and his mother's words.

I hear my mother's trailing words as we bring home baskets of laundry—and for a moment, I smile.

The pandemic poses unique challenges for kids like me. But if schools can offer us support—as my district is doing by providing free meals, internet hot spots and laptops to those in need—I know we can continue to learn remotely while staying safe. And with help from my teachers and hope that the quarantine subsides, I'm applying to college this fall.

Sums up the significance of this story and looks to the future.

Keeping students at home gives us—and America—the best chance to salir adelante.

Concludes by saying why keeping students at home now is so important.

Thinking about the Text

1. What is Isaac Lozano's main PURPOSE in telling the story of his uncle's death and what it represents to him?

2. Lozano wrote this text as a NARRATIVE, but it's a story with a point. What is his ARGUMENT? Do you agree with the decision he comes to? Why, or why not?

3. What details does Lozano provide to bring this narrative to life? Cite specific examples from the text.

4. What do you expect Lozano thinks it will take to *salir adelante* in the United States today?

5. Think of an event in your life (perhaps one that occurred during or was related to the pandemic of 2020) that meant a great deal to you. Then, using the guidelines provided in this chapter, write a narrative that will help others share and understand your experience.

12 Summarizing & Responding

EFFECTIVE ACADEMIC WRITING RESIDES
NOT JUST IN STATING OUR OWN IDEAS BUT IN
LISTENING TO OTHERS, SUMMARIZING THEIR VIEWS,
AND RESPONDING WITH OUR OWN IDEAS IN KIND.

—GERALD GRAFF AND CATHY BIRKENSTEIN

Your American history instructor assigns Sojourner Truth's "Ain't I a Woman?" Your job: to summarize this speech and write an essay responding to it. In your environmental science class, the instructor asks students to read the Clean Water Act of 1987 and then to summarize its major goals, followed by a response that suggests ways the act could be strengthened. And in your first-year writing class, it's presentation week! You're assigned to listen to a presentation given by two classmates and then to respond. The assignment specifies that you start by briefly summarizing what they say before responding with what you want to say.

Instructors who give these assignments know that one way to fully understand a text and remember what it says is to summarize it in our own words—and then to talk back to it, engaging with what it says and offering ideas of our own in response. That's why it's often said that such assignments are "where writing meets reading." And these moves—read-understand-respond—are fundamental to much of the work you do in college, and wherever you engage with the ideas and words of others.

A GUIDE TO SUMMARIZING AND RESPONDING

Summarizing and responding to a text is a common college assignment, a way of demonstrating that you've engaged with the text, that you understand what it says, and that you have something to say as a result. Following is some good advice on how to write effective summaries and responses, so listen up: these tips will help you!

Read the text you'll be responding to

Begin by reading the text straight through. Then reread, underlining or jotting down the major CLAIMS and ideas and the main EVIDENCE supporting those ideas. If there's an explicit THESIS, put it in brackets. And put quotation marks around any words or phrases that are written so well that you think you may want to QUOTE them.

Whatever the text says, read it with an open mind. Especially if you disagree with what it says, think about where the author is coming from and why they think differently than you do. And while you're at it, think about why *you* think the way you do. Most important, be sure that you understand exactly what the author is saying so that you'll be able to present it from their perspective rather than yours.

Write out a few sentences in your own words stating the text's main points. It can be rough—imagine you're telling a friend about what you've just read; the idea is to give the jist of what the author has said.

Think about your rhetorical situation

Once you've carefully read the text you'll be summarizing and responding to, stop and think about who your audience is and the rest of your rhetorical situation.

Purpose. If you've been assigned to write a summary/response essay, one purpose will likely be to demonstrate that you understand what the text says. But responding also gives you the opportunity to engage with what it says—and to add your own thoughts to the conversation. What do you think about what the text says, and what would you like to say back to the author?

Audience. This is a common college assignment, so your audience will likely include your instructor. But other students may read what you write—and if so, how will that affect what you write?

Genre. There are various ways you might respond. If you respond to what the text says, you'll be writing a rhetorical argument. If you respond to the way it's written, that will call for ANALYSIS. Or maybe the text just gets you thinking, in which case you might write a REFLECTION.

Stance. What is your attitude about the text? Are you a critic? a neutral reporter? something else? Think about how it will affect your response.

Context. What are the requirements of your assignment—length, due date, and so on? And what's the larger context surrounding the text you'll be writing about?

Media and design. If you get to choose, is there a medium that will work especially well for your subject? If you're writing about a film, for instance, doing so online would enable you to include audio or video clips. Whatever the medium, will your essay need headings or images or any other design elements?

Summarize accurately, fairly, and concisely

Reread the text slowly, making a list of the main ideas. Then go back and check to see that you've noted every idea that matters, ones that you'll need to account for in your summary.

Write out a sentence stating the text's main message. You could then start your summary with this sentence, and it will function as a kind of THESIS sentence.

Focus on the main ideas, leaving out unnecessary details. Keep in mind that you just need to give readers enough information so that they'll understand what you're responding to. And be sure that you capture the main ideas accurately and fairly.

Use your own words, but leave out your own opinions. This should be a SUMMARY of what the text says, not of what you think about it. (You can get to that when you *respond* to what it says!) Use neutral, non-judgmental language—say "the author's point," for example, rather than "the author's questionable point." Once you've drafted your summary, go back to the text to make sure that you haven't inadvertently copied any of the original wording or sentence structures.

If you QUOTE *any words or phrases*, be sure to enclose them in quotation marks and introduce them with a SIGNAL PHRASE to clearly distinguish what the author says from what you say. And while you could use neutral words ("X says," "according to X"), it's better to use words that reflect the author's STANCE. Here, for example, is how you might quote a line from Poet Laureate Joy Harjo's blog:

> As Poet Laureate Joy Harjo argues in a blog post about music, "The saxophone is so human. Its tendency is to be rowdy, edgy, talk too loud, bump into people."

But quote sparingly, and only when you need to use the author's exact wording for accuracy—or because the wording is so memorable that you want to call special attention to it. For example, here's a sentence you might well want to quote if you were summarizing Sojourner Truth's "Ain't I a Woman?": "Nobody ever helps me into carriages, or over mud-puddles, or gives me any best place!" This sentence is so powerful and clear in its message that it's hard to imagine how you could summarize it, so this is definitely one to quote.

Name the author and title of the text you're summarizing, usually in the first paragraph. If you're summarizing a lengthy work, you'll need to provide IN-TEXT DOCUMENTATION giving the pages you've summarized. And if you've consulted additional sources, you'll need to DOCUMENT them in a list of works cited or references.

A model summary

In the following summary, Taylor Jordan, a student at North Carolina A & T, sums up the argument about college admissions made in a *New York Times* op-ed. You can read the op-ed on page 214.

> In a *New York Times* opinion piece, "I Learned in College That Admission Has Always Been for Sale," Rainesford Stauffer argues that college bribery schemes, a huge test prep industry, and big-time donors strip opportunities from those students who actually work hard on their own. She begins with a personal narrative about a friend who had a "personalized standardized test tutor" while applying for college—and recalls her shock at realizing that some of her other friends even had professional editors and college admission coaches. She notes that the current college admissions scandal with celebrities engaging in bribery and other illegal acts is only one example of what some rich people do to help their children get into college—and that it's "no more abhorrent than what happens every day." Still, she acknowledges her own privileges as a white student with parents who went to college and says that what really makes her mad is thinking about those who have fewer privileges than she does.
>
> Stauffer seems most angry about the fact that there's a huge industry of tutors and essay writers and college admission coaches for those who can afford them—and that it's all perfectly legal.

Citing the work of a Harvard education professor, she points out that it's a system that results in "working class and poor students, black, Latino, Native American and first generation students [being] underrepresented on most campuses." To sum up, Stauffer's central argument is with the unfairness of the college admission system, and the signal it sends to students that their hard work counts for less than their parents' money.

—TAYLOR JORDAN, North Carolina A&T State University

Note that this summary begins by naming the author of the text being summarized and summing up the author's main ideas. Subsequent sentences in the first paragraph point to the author's use of her own experience and provide additional details to back up the main ideas. As she does so, Taylor Jordan includes brief quotations directly from the article, enclosed in quotation marks and integrated smoothly into her own sentences. Note also that Jordan is careful to leave her own opinions out of the summary, which focuses solely on the article she is summarizing, and that she is careful to qualify statements ("Stauffer *seems* most angry") rather than putting words in the author's mouth. Finally, note that Jordan quotes a memorable sentence from one of the article's sources, which sums up the author's central argument.

REFLECT! Choose a text that you really like—a film, an episode in a TV series, a comic book, a favorite podcast or book, whatever. Then do your best to summarize what you've chosen so that someone who isn't familiar with it will get a good sense of what it's about, and why. Keep your audience in mind as you write your summary—and then ask for their response: How well did you capture the essence of the text you summarized?

Develop your response

Responding to something you've read (or heard or seen) gives you the opportunity to speak up—to ask questions, point out details you think were overlooked, analyze the way it's written, agree, disagree. There's more than one way of responding to a text, but often you'll be assigned to respond in one of three ways:

- to respond to *what* the text says
- to respond to *how* the text is written
- to respond to the way the text affects *you*

If you're responding to what the text says

In this case you'll likely be making an ARGUMENT. You could agree or disagree with the author's ideas—or both; whatever it is, you should do so explicitly. In general, it's a good idea to provide a THESIS sentence that makes your overall response to the text clear. And then you need to give reasons and evidence to support what *you* say: facts, examples, textual evidence, data the author overlooked, and so on. Even if you agree with what the author says, you need to do more than just re-state views you share. Perhaps you could point out evidence the author didn't mention, some personal experience that's pertinent to the conversation, or counterarguments that need to be mentioned. Here are some questions that will help you think about what a text says:

See how the author of an ethics column responds to a question about hanging out with someone whose views you "hate." Read his response on p. 587.

- What's the CLAIM?
- What good REASONS and EVIDENCE support that claim? Remember that evidence can include VISUALS as well as words.
- Does the text include any COUNTERARGUMENTS or other PERSPECTIVES—and if not, are there some that should be acknowledged?
- What's *your* response? Do you agree, disagree, or both agree and disagree with the author's conclusions? Why?

If you're responding to the way the text is written

Here you'll be writing a rhetorical analysis, and you could do so in various ways. You could analyze its use of language, its sentence patterns, the way it's organized, or other elements of its style—and how these things affect the way you understand or respond to the author's message. In any case, you'll need to support your analysis with examples from the text. Here are some questions that will help you think about the way a text is written:

- How would you describe the author's STYLE—humorous? serious? conversational? passionate? logical? something else?
- What words or structures or images help to establish this style? How do they affect the way you respond? You'll need to show examples in the text that help create this style.
- Does the author use any METAPHORS, ANALOGIES, or other figures of speech—and how do they help get the point across?
- How does the way the text is written contribute to the effectiveness of its message?

If you're responding with your personal reaction

You could go in many directions. This kind of response gives you the opportunity to REFLECT on how the text affected you personally. What did it make you think about—and are you still thinking about it? Did the author make you think the subject matters or make you care about it? As with any kind of writing, you'll need to give reasons and evidence to help your audience understand your reactions—and care about what you say. Here are some questions that may help you reflect on your own reaction to a text:

- What was your first reaction to this text?
- Did anything in the text surprise you? make you laugh? annoy you? mystify you? Show some examples!
- Did it make you think or change your thinking about something? If so, in what way?

- Do you now want to learn more about the topic—and if so, what?
- What would you say about this text if you were telling a friend about it? What REASONS would you give to explain your reaction?

Begin your essay in a way that gets readers' interest

If you're responding to a text about an unusual issue, you might want to begin with a question or a dramatic statement about that subject. When you're responding to what a text says, you might begin with a sentence that first SUMMARIZES what the text says (or what others have said), before responding with what you think. If you're analyzing the way a text is written, you could start by QUOTING a line that exemplifies what you'll be writing about. Or perhaps you're responding to a text that touches on something you yourself have experienced; in that case, you might begin with a personal ANECDOTE that shows how you are connected to the topic in question. No matter how you begin, be sure to name the author and the title of the text you're responding to somewhere—ideally, in the first paragraph.

For more on ways of beginning, see pp. 85 and 410–12.

Conclude in a way that leaves readers thinking

Here's your chance to leave your audience thinking about the implications of what you've said. If you're responding to the text's argument, you could REITERATE your main point; if you're analyzing the way the text was written, you may want to remind readers about how the writer's STYLE affects the message; if your response is a personal one, you might conclude with some insight you got from reading the text.

Sometimes you might conclude by QUOTING something memorable from the text that your essay is all about. One student who summarized an interview with rapper Nipsey Hussle and responded to what he said about luck and hard work concluded by quoting a famous line from that interview: "Luck is just bein' prepared at all times, so when the door opens you're ready."

For more on ways of concluding, see pp. 92 and 417–18.

Regardless of how you conclude, you might also invite your audience to respond. Keep the conversation going!

Come up with a title

For more on coming up with a title, see pp. 92–93 and 409.

If you've written an argument, your title should indicate the topic; if you've written an analysis, your title should indicate something about what you analyzed; if you've written a reflection, the title should indicate what the text has led you to think.

Read your draft with a critical eye, get response—and revise

Now's the time to read over what you've written to see that you've summarized the text accurately, fairly, and concisely—and responded cogently and persuasively.

- Does your title make clear what the essay is about? Can you think of a better title?

- How will the OPENING make readers want to read on? Does it mention the author and title of the text you're responding to? If not, are they mentioned elsewhere?

- Is the summary written in your own words? Check to be sure. And have you provided enough detail so that readers will understand what you're responding to? Is all the detail you've included actually necessary?

- Have you SUMMARIZED the text in a fair-minded way, and without indicating your own opinion?

- If you've quoted anything, is the wording so memorable or important that it needs to be QUOTED? Is anything quoted enclosed in quotation marks?

- If you've quoted a full statement, is it introduced with a SIGNAL PHRASE—and does the verb suit the quotation? If you've used *said*, is there a more interesting or more accurate verb you might use instead—*claimed? pointed out? declared?*

- Is the point of your response clear? Have you stated it in a THESIS sentence—and if not, should you do so?
- What EVIDENCE have you provided to support your response—facts? examples from the text? personal experience? counterarguments or viewpoints the author didn't mention?
- Have you included any VISUALS? If not, is there anything that could be presented in a photo, a chart, or a graph?
- Have you provided DOCUMENTATION for any text you've summarized or quoted?
- How does the essay CONCLUDE? This is your chance to help readers engage with some ideas worth thinking about.

Now REVISE! If you've analyzed your draft and gotten advice from others, you've got a plan: you know what you need to do. But remember that you're writing a SUMMARY/RESPONSE essay, which means summing up a text succinctly and fairly and then responding in some way. Here's what *you* think about the text—and why!

AN OP-ED, AND A RESPONSE

This chapter concludes with an essay written by Julia Latrice Johnson, a student at North Carolina A&T State University. Following the guidelines in this chapter, she responded to a *New York Times* op-ed about the college admissions scandal of 2019, in which dozens of wealthy parents, celebrities, and coaches were involved in a nationwide fraud and bribery scheme that resulted in some students getting into the colleges of their dreams because of their parents' checkbooks rather than their own work or talent. As you might expect, response to this scandal was swift, especially among college students. First comes the *Times* piece, and then comes the summary/response essay.

RAINESFORD STAUFFER

I Learned in College That Admission Has Always Been for Sale

Rainesford Stauffer is a writer whose work has been published in the New York Times, *the* Atlantic, GQ, *and* Teen Vogue. *She is the author of* An Ordinary Age, *a book about the challenges of young adulthood in the United States. The piece here was first published in the* Times *in 2019.*

Shortly after my freshman year of college, when I was debating whether to transfer to another college or drop out and venture into the work force sans degree, I met with an older friend who had attended an Ivy League-adjacent school. I wanted her advice on whether to apply to her alma mater.

I'd love it there, she assured me, with one caveat: You have to be really smart, she said. It became evident that her "smart" and my "smart" were different things. She casually rattled off hours she'd logged with a personalized standardized test tutor, paid to boost her score. Her parents opted not to pay an editor to work with her on her application essay, but plenty of her classmates' families had.

I suddenly felt as though I'd failed a test I didn't know I was taking. I was even more gobsmacked when I realized how common her experience was. Asking around, I learned that a subset of my peers had been carefully groomed with tools I hadn't even known existed. I came to realize that my "A" in Literature from my freshman year and a job between classes and on weekends were not going to compete with pedigrees buffed to application perfection thanks to highly compensated college admissions coaches.

I did end up transferring, not to my friend's school but to The New School, where I finished my degree remotely while working full time, and I graduated in January 2017. Now I talk to young people, including my own sister, who agonize over the fact that no matter how hard they study, they will never compete with students who have test and application boosts. Even so, I know I've enjoyed benefits that many other students haven't because I'm white and have parents who are college graduates. I'm more angry on behalf of those with fewer resources than me who have to compete with those gaming the system.

So when news broke that celebrities, top university coaches and other ultrarich individuals were accused by the Justice Department of engaging in college admissions bribery, my initial thought was that this latest round of revelations is no more abhorrent than what happens every day.

It's obviously a scandal when rich people are accused of breaking the law to get their kids into top schools. But the bigger outrage should be that a legal version of purchasing an advantage happens every college application season and that there's an entire industry supporting it.

Anyone can see the kinds of things outlined in the indictment— bribes paid by wealthy parents in exchange for their children's admission to top universities, and accompanying schemes to secure athletics scholarships for teens who didn't even play high school sports—are unacceptable. But what about the standardized test prep industry, worth around $840 million, which involves parents forking over up to $200 an hour for Ivy League tutors tasked with increasing their children's scores. That doesn't include application essay writers, who coach students on what to write about, edit their writing and, in some cases, write for them. It doesn't include college coaching firms, which charge up to $40,000 to strategize an applicant's entire process.

Donations made to schools by the parents of legacy students can essentially buy acceptance letters. Meanwhile, there are some students who don't have a parent to skim their essay for typos or can't afford to pay to enroll in a prep course or to repeatedly take a standardized test until their score rises.

Natasha Warikoo, a professor at Harvard Graduate School of Education and the author of "The Diversity Bargain," says while there's no debate that the actions the people involved in this week's admissions scandal are accused of are reprehensible, there's actually very little agreement among Americans or admissions officers about what is and isn't O.K. in terms of application assistance.

"A fair system to me would produce an outcome in which people who are selected are representative of 18-year-olds overall in the United States," Ms. Warikoo said, noting that while wealthy students are overrepresented, working class and poor students, black, Latino, Native American and first generation students are underrepresented on most campuses. "We don't have consensus in the United States about what is a fair system of selection."

"If you had to design a system that would give rich, white kids the best odds of getting into prestigious colleges and universities, look no further than the current system," said Nikhil Goyal, author of "Schools on Trial" and a doctoral candidate at the University of Cambridge. His research has found that universities ending legacy admissions and making standardized tests optional "would boost class and racial diversity and signal to youth that their worth is less defined by test scores and more by their creativity and passions." It's no coincidence that one of these can be bought: the test scores. Creativity and passion cannot.

Perhaps it wouldn't sting so much if we scrapped the college rankings, or if we didn't bill college as the foremost experience for young people, one that sets the tone for their entire lives.

This newest admissions scandal is infuriating, but the ongoing, perfectly legal one that lets wealthy families pay for the things that lead to greater chances of admission hurts even more. It sends a message to any student who can't take advantage of the current system that no matter how hard he or she has worked, it will always be possible for someone else to buy a better life.

A STUDENT SUMMARY/RESPONSE ESSAY

JULIA LATRICE JOHNSON
Can Money Buy Almost Anything?

Julia Latrice Johnson is a student at North Carolina A&T State University, where she's majoring in English and African American Literature. After completing college, she hopes to pursue graduate study in linguistics. Her eventual goal is to help instructors learn to be more effective teachers of students who speak multiple languages and dialects.

What do you do when you desire to further your education, but your writing sucks? You know that there are better writers out there because they all have received acceptance letters from colleges where personal statements are a requirement. But how would you feel if you knew that those writers had professional tutors and editors to fix and maybe even write their work? This was the frustration described by Rainesford Stauffer in her *New York Times* op-ed, "I Learned in College That Admission Has Always Been for Sale."

Stauffer speaks distinctively about privilege—her own privilege in being white and having parents who graduated from college, and the privilege of others who have monetary advantages that essentially "buy acceptance letters." Paid tutors and admission essay editors can help "buy" college admission. Rich parents who bribe admission officers can "buy" college admission. Rich parents who donate large sums of money can "buy" college admission.

Stauffer makes it her business to talk to students who cannot "buy" admission and "who agonize over the fact that no matter how hard they study, they will never compete with students who have test and application boosts." Those boosts include essay editing, test tutoring, and admission coaching, advantages paid for by parents with money. All are common practices, and perfectly legal.

Title and opening sentence pose provocative questions that get readers' attention.

Names author and title in the first paragraph.

Summarizes major ideas in the op-ed.

Quotes a memorable statement to underscore the unfairness Stauffer is concerned with.

Lori Loughlin departing from federal court, April 2019.

Bribery, however, is not legal—but still practiced. Stauffer describes "rich people . . . breaking the law to get their kids into top schools" as an unacceptable scandal that sparked outrage. But even worse, she says, are the legal ways of buying advantages: the tutors and editors and coaches and large donations. What most enrages Stauffer is that it's an unfair system, one that privileges wealthy students but that works against "working class and poor students, black, Latino, Native American, and first generation students."

Reading Stauffer's article made me think of Lori Loughlin, Aunt Becky from *Full House*, one of the actresses currently involved in the admissions scandal. She and her husband have been accused of paying over a half million dollars to secure their daughters' admission to the University of Southern California (USC). Perhaps in response, Dr. Dre, rapper, producer, and another celebrity parent, took to *Instagram* to congratulate his daughter on her acceptance to college while also making note of the recent college scandal: "My daughter got accepted into USC all on her own. No jail time!!!" (qtd. in Amiri).

Leaving her own opinion out, focuses on what motivated Stauffer to write her op-ed.

Opens her response by giving her own first reaction to the op-ed.

And yet . . . while he may not have bribed the admissions team, his daughter still had advantages other students did not thanks to her father's $70 million donations to USC. The only difference between Lori Loughlin and Dr. Dre is that he wrote his check as a donation and she wrote hers to an organization that paid USC to admit her daughter. *Both famous parents exhibit privilege that screams for attention and response.*

Stauffer's article also puts into perspective a part of college that not many people can bring themselves to discuss. There are advantages that certain individuals have. I did not have such advantages. I did not have access to paid tutors or essay editors. I had to study and write on my own and pray that my parents were not too tired after long days at work to help me edit my essays. And I have had to focus in on what I can do myself rather than thinking about the unfair advantages others have. Despite not having any particular advantages, much less donating a million dollars, I was still able to gain admission to Coastal Carolina University and even to pursue a second degree at North Carolina A&T State University.

Offers her own experience as an example of what students without privilege do to get into college.

Dr. Dre and his daughter.

Michelle Obama speaking at North Carolina A&T State University.

Considers the op-ed in broader context, noting how others may respond to it.

This article will probably get multiple responses, depending on the readers. One response, similar to Stauffer's and my own, will most likely be shared widely among the many students who do not have access to the advantages wealthy people have, but are still working as hard as they can to get to where they hope to be. Another response may possibly come from students who are okay with the scholastic advantages they have because of their parents' money. And there will probably be a lot of privileged students who see nothing wrong with their parents using their money as a means of admission, but who still choose to work hard and go the extra mile to not have mommy or daddy's money follow them throughout life.

Introduces major claim and supports it with evidence from the op-ed.

In any case, it is not the fault of students, whether they have certain advantages or not. It's the system that is unfair in granting opportunities to some students just because their parents can "buy" them. Stauffer is right to be angry on behalf of those with fewer resources than she has "who have to compete with those gaming the system."

Reflects on what the op-ed has helped her realize about her own experience.

The system is unfair. Knowing that I may be refused admission in favor of those with rich parents or those who have essentially had the work done for them might discourage me from even applying to certain schools. Realizing that my hard work and that of my parents can be overshadowed by other people's money is disheartening, and yet it also leads me to constantly persevere in my studies.

What resonated with me the most in Stauffer's article comes at the very end when she says that the way college admission works now "sends a message to any student who can't take advantage of the current system that no matter how hard he or she has worked, it will always be possible for someone else to buy a better life." Any students who pride themselves on grasping and mastering any concept, including the college admission process, have reason to resent those who have been fortunate enough to have college and other such things gifted to them. Speaking for myself, however, knowing that anything I achieve is the result of my own hard work is highly rewarding, and that is one of the most important lessons that I learned from reading Rainesford Stauffer's op-ed.

Concludes by articulating the lesson she learned from reading this op-ed.

Works Cited

Amiri, Farnoush. "Dr. Dre Deletes Post about Daughter's Acceptance to USC after $70M Donation Resurfaces." *NBC News*, 25 Mar. 2019, www.nbcnews.com/2019 /3/25/.../dr-dre-deletes-post-about-daughter-s-acceptance -usc-after-n986906.

Stauffer, Rainesford. "I Learned in College That Admission Has Always Been for Sale." *The New York Times*, 13 Mar. 2019, www.newyorktimes.com/2019/03/13/opinion/college -admission-scandal-celebrities.html.

Thinking about the Text

1. What is the main ARGUMENT that Julia Johnson is making in response to Rainesford Stauffer's op-ed?

2. How does Johnson support that point? How does she use her own experience to support her argument?

3. What do you think makes Johnson's OPENING especially effective (or not)?

4. What do the three VISUALS add to the effectiveness of her response?

5. Write a letter responding to Johnson in which you share your own thoughts or experiences about the college admissions process.

REFLECT! Think about **Rainesford Stauffer**'s and **Julia Johnson**'s experiences with college admissions. How do your own experiences compare with theirs? What do you think about Stauffer's claim that college is always "for sale"?

13 Writing in Multiple Modes

THIS IS A TIME FOR EXPLORATION, FOR EXPERIMENTATION:
WHEN WE CAN CREATE AND RISK, WRITE GRAFFITI
ON THE WALLS AND COLOR OUTSIDE THE LINES. . . .

—ADAM BANKS

Check out an article or blog post on the web and you will probably find links to videos, databases, and other sources. Go to a sales presentation and you will no doubt encounter a speaker using slides and maybe audio or video clips—or even a print handout. Attend a poster session on campus and you'll see student presenters offering infographics that they introduce and then answer questions about. Read a film review online and you'll probably be able to click on a link to watch a trailer. Even a traditional essay assignment may call on you to use photos or drawings and to provide other information visually in pie charts or graphs. That's writing in multiple modes.

In some ways, writing in multiple modes is nothing new: just google "illustrated manuscripts and maps," for example, and you'll find pages with decorative initials and miniature drawings written over a thousand years ago. And today writers can produce texts that combine words, images, colors, sounds, and even videos—and that can be delivered through print, spoken, and digital media. This chapter will help you take advantage of the opportunities offered by writing in multiple modes—so get ready to deliver your messages as you've never delivered them before!

A GUIDE TO WRITING IN MULTIPLE MODES

Students tell me that they love doing multimodal projects. They say they're a lot of work, but a whole lot of fun. This guide will help you do the work—and have some fun!

Identify a topic

You may be assigned a topic, but if you get to choose, start by making a list of questions that really intrigue you, questions you really want to answer. Chances are one of these questions will lead you to an important topic, one that you care about and that will bring out the best in you as a thinker. Vrinda Vasavada had been reading a lot online about how much we are controlled by our phones and other devices. The more she thought about it, the more she wondered whether tech addiction was actually a problem—and if so, what we should do about it.

She decided that this topic—which was certainly timely and potentially very important—was worth investigating. But her assignment was to write using multiple modes, and so she then needed to consider what modes (and what media) she would work with. After talking with her instructor and assessing the resources available, Vasavada decided to prepare an oral presentation and assumed it would likely include print or digital materials. Her multimodal project was on the way!

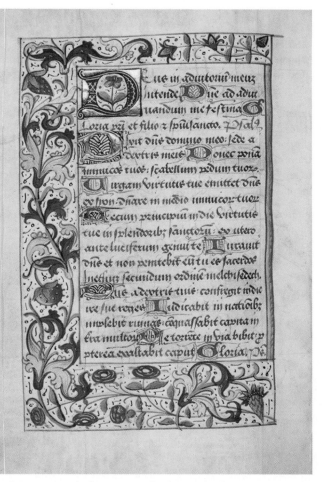

A page from a 1511 Book of Hours, a medieval prayer book.

Think about your rhetorical situation

Multimodal writing calls for the same close attention to rhetorical principles that all writing and speaking do. Whatever your topic, you need to think carefully about your purpose, audience, stance, context, and genre—in addition to modes and media.

Purpose. What are your goals for this project: To fulfill an assignment? To raise awareness about a problem? To convince others to support a cause? To provide information? Ask yourself what you want to happen as a result of your project; what actions do you want to see taken, or what ideas do you hope to convey? What modes and media will be most useful for achieving your goals?

Audience. Whom do you want to reach? What are they likely to know about your topic, and what background information will you need to provide? Will they be interested in your topic—and if not, are there certain modes that will get them interested—photos? music? a provocative title? If you want to reach students on your campus, then you might choose an online campus bulletin board or *Facebook* group. If your audience is limited to people you know, you may be able to make some assumptions about what they're likely to respond to—but most projects you put online may well be seen by people you don't know, so you can't make any such assumptions. Finally, consider how you can make your project accessible to those who have limited vision or hearing. Do you need to provide ALT TEXT?

Stance. What's your attitude toward your topic, and how do you want to present yourself to your audience—as a well-informed observer? a stern critic? a puzzled inquirer trying to figure something out? Then consider how you will reflect that stance: For an oral presentation, what facial expressions and gestures will convey your stance? What will you wear? For written projects, think about what fonts and tone will help establish your stance.

Genre. The kind of text you're writing may affect the modes you can or should use. If you're ANALYZING a scientific text or REPORTING information, you may have reason to present data visually, in graphs or pie charts. If you're writing a NARRATIVE, you may want to add photos or include some dialogue in audio. If you're making an ARGUMENT in a print essay, you might want to choose a font and write in a manner that reflects the seriousness of your subject.

Context. When is the project due, and can you manage to complete the project you have in mind in the time available? What resources will you need to complete the project? What modes would you like to use? If you plan to give an oral presentation, make sure to check out the space and equipment that will be there and find out what you will need to bring (a laptop and a particular dongle, an easel to display photographs, and so on).

Medium and design. How will your project be delivered—in print? online? as a speech? or through some combination of media? How does the medium affect the way it will be designed and the modes you can or cannot use? Will you be able to include images? audio? video? links to other sources?

Consider the modes you could use

Rhetorician Cynthia Selfe identifies five modes that writers and speakers can use to convey our messages:

>***Linguistic***—words, titles, headings, captions, ALT TEXT
>***Visual***—photos, drawings, charts, graphs, colors, fonts
>***Audio***—speech, spoken dialogue, sounds, music, tone of voice
>***Gestural***—facial expressions, body language
>***Spatial***—how text and visuals are arranged on page or screen

Your media will dictate which modes you will be able to use—you can't include audio in a print text, right?—but your AUDIENCE and PURPOSE will often determine which modes you will want to use.

Take a look at the following passage from an article about Olympic gymnast Simone Biles that depends entirely on words.

> On Sunday, during the all-around, Simone Biles, her hair trailing behind her like an exclamation point, became the first woman to perform a triple-double—two flips and three twists—in competition during a floor routine. Only a few men can do it, and the way Biles does it is better than the way most of them do. The triple-double is so difficult that U.S.A. Gymnastics has argued that a new tier needs to be added to the code of points, gymnastics' rule book, to account for it.
>
> —LOUISA THOMAS, "The Unlimited Greatness of Simone Biles"

Now let's see how this passage might be brought more fully to life by using additional modes. You could use the *visual* mode, for example, by including an image like the one shown here. As for the *audio* mode, how about an audio clip of her talking about how she learned to do a triple-double—or the roar of the audience as she does a perfect landing? And just imagine the ways you could use the *gestural* mode: you could link to a video of her doing a triple-double, showing her facial expressions as she flips and twists—or as she breaks into a big smile when she lands. Finally comes the *spatial* mode. How might you

Simone Biles warms up, 2019.

arrange the various modes? You could start with the words and then add an image or a video to illustrate what you say. Or you could do the reverse: start with an image showing Simone Biles doing a triple-double, and then describe with words what it was that she did, and what an astounding accomplishment it was.

REFLECT! Select something you've written recently that uses words only, and think about how you could use additional modes to expand, illustrate, or elaborate on what you wrote. Try doing it! And then write a paragraph or so comparing the two versions. Which one do you prefer, and why?

Choose a primary medium of delivery

Most multimodal projects have at their core one medium of delivery—oral, print, or digital. Class presentations, for example, are primarily oral, though the spoken words can be enhanced by print text (handouts) or digital ones (audio or video clips; *Power-Point* slides). An informative REPORT, on the other hand, might be primarily a print text, though one augmented with images, charts, graphs, or other visual material. A BLOG will always be delivered digitally, though it can include links to both oral and print texts. Spend some time, then, thinking about how best to deliver your message to your particular audience.

Explore your topic, do some research

Whether your primary medium is print, spoken, or digital, you'll need to immerse yourself in your topic, exploring it in various ways and likely doing some research. Your goal is to examine the topic from multiple PERSPECTIVES, not only to understand the topic but to be aware of the conversation surrounding it, of who's talking about it and what they're saying. Here too you can use various modes to explore a

"Moby Dick? Let's see ... Would you like the DVD, the podcast or the interpretive dance?"

CartoonStock.com

topic. You might start by **FREEWRITING** about the topic or even try drawing a picture of it. If your topic is a current issue, there may be a podcast about it. And there could also be some people on campus with expertise in the topic who you could interview. For her project about tech addiction, Vrinda Vasavada found information in a number of databases available through her university's library, in several blogs and podcasts, and from some interviews.

For more detail on exploring a topic, see pp. 82–83.

Come up with a working thesis

See pp. 84–89 for detail on coming up with a thesis.

Once you have some idea about what you want to say about your topic, take some time to craft a working thesis, a clear statement identifying the topic and the claim you will make about it. Keep in mind that this **THESIS** may well change (and get better and more precise!) as you continue to work.

Vrinda Vasavada began with a nagging question about whether tech addiction was real. As she researched the topic, she found more and more evidence to support the fact that such behavior is indeed evident in many people who devote a lot of time to their phones and other devices. But she dug deeper still, looking at the causes of such addiction and at ways of addressing the problem. Here's the thesis she began with:

> Tech addiction is a verifiable phenomenon, and while users can work to limit their screen time, it is the responsibility of tech companies to make design choices that prioritize user health.

Whatever media you're using, you need to make your major point very clear. Don't make your audience search for it! In a spoken presentation, you'll want to state your thesis clearly up front, at the beginning of your talk. You may want to put it on a slide so that your audience will both hear it and see it. You have more options in a print text: you may state your claim in your introduction, but sometimes you may have reason to withhold it until further into your text.

Ways of providing evidence

As with any text, a multimodal one will be only as good as the information you put in it. But a multimodal text gives you many ways to present that information. You can present data in a paragraph—or on a line graph. You can describe something with words, or with an image—or even a video. If you want to compare two things, you can do so with words alone, but you can also make the comparison easy to see and understand with a bar graph or pie chart. And think of all you can link to in a digital text. Vrinda Vasavada presented much of the evidence for her project about tech addiction in words, both written and spoken. But in her spoken presentation (and the video which was then posted online), she highlighted key questions and points on slides, making it easy for her audience to follow her thoughts.

See how an article about trees uses maps and other visuals to make its point better than words alone would do. Check it out on p. 739.

Organize carefully

Multimodal projects include a number of different elements, which must be carefully organized. In fact, you may well be organizing throughout the process of developing a multimodal project. You might start with a stack of sticky notes, jotting down major points, evidence, images, video and audio clips on each note, which you can then organize and arrange as they'll be used. One of my students likes to use 3-by-5 cards, each card with a main point or idea, and then tape them together in a chain to spread out on the floor. Going from top to bottom, one card at a time, lets this student see all the points and whether they follow logically from one to another or need to be rearranged, revised, and so on.

For a video essay, you might start out with a STORYBOARD, sketching in the parts of your project so that you can see how they fit together logically and systematically. For an audio essay, you'd likely develop a script that accounts for both words and any other sounds. For print texts, you might use a good old OUTLINE, making major points heads and supporting points subheads.

How to begin?

Whether your text is delivered in a print document, a speech, or online, it has to begin somewhere. Whatever the medium, you might begin with a provocative question or quotation, or by summarizing what's been said about your topic and then responding with what you think—and these are all strategies that work in any medium. But when you're writing with multiple modes, you have some additional options.

In a presentation, for example, you could not only begin by asking a question—you could have the question on a slide, in large type. Even better, you could then pause to give your audience a chance to respond to the question. And imagine you're writing a digital narrative about a frisky little dog. You could start by saying, "Once upon a time, I had a frisky little dog. His name was Gus." You might insert a photo of him right there—or even better, a video of him chasing a ball. And if your text lets readers decide where to begin, you'll want to have a menu with a button that says "Introduction." These are just some ideas; the point is that multiple modalities present a number of ways to get an audience's attention.

Ways of beginning are covered on pp. 85 and 410–12.

How to conclude?

Whatever your medium, you can conclude by summing up your argument, explaining what you hope your audience will take from what you've written or said, or call for some kind of action. You can also invite response. If you're giving an oral presentation, you'll probably follow that by saying thank you and then asking if there are any questions. If you're writing on the web, you can add your email address or *Twitter* handle and invite readers to respond. You can even invite response in a print document; you've had your say, so let readers know that you'd like to know what they think and would welcome their response.

Ways of ending are covered on pp. 92 and 417–18.

Don't forget transitions

While you may understand precisely how the parts of anything you write fit together, you need to make certain that those reading and especially those listening will be able to follow what you say. This means providing explicit transitions from point to point, and explicit references in your text to any images, audio or video clips, and other elements. Transitions are words like *first*, *then*, *also*, and *for example* that smooth the way for your audience to follow your argument and move from point to point.

See p. 424 for a list of common transitions.

To provide a transition from paragraph to paragraph, you can also write a sentence that links the two. For example:

If young people are too dependent on their phones for getting information, they also depend on them to stay connected to friends.

In this transition sentence, the first part refers back to what has just been discussed (dependence on phones for information) and then forecasts what is coming up next (dependence on phones for friendship).

For multimodal projects, transitions need to be even more explicit: you can't just insert an audio clip into a digital report, for example, and assume that your audience will know why the audio clip is there and what it contributes to the overall point you're making. Just as you would use a signal phrase to introduce a quotation in a print essay ("they declared," "the author responded"), you need to introduce images, audio or video clips, or other such elements explicitly ("Figure 1 shows---," "as you'll hear in the following audio clip"). You also need to explain explicitly what they add to your overall point ("this graph demonstrates my point that---," "as you can see in this brief video").

The best way to be sure that your organization works, that all the parts fit together smoothly and your transitions are explicit enough, is to try it out on a friend or classmate, asking them if they can follow what you say. And ask them directly if there's any place where they got confused, needed a clearer transition, or anything else.

Document sources

As with any academic assignment, you should document any sources you refer to or cite. For projects that are delivered in print, this means including a list of works cited (MLA) or references (APA). And for digital projects, you can simply link to the sources you've used, enabling readers who want to check them out to do so. For presentations, oral or digital, this usually means including a slide at the end that lists all sources; you might also distribute this list in print, as a handout.

REFLECT! "This is a time for exploration, for experimentation: when we can create and risk, write graffiti on the walls and color outside the lines. . . . we must expand our notion of academic discourse." That's a challenge that professor **Adam Banks** issued to an audience of college writing teachers. How would you answer his challenge? Find a piece of academic writing you have done, and then imagine how you could rewrite it using multiple modes. Describe that revised piece in a brief paragraph, and explain what you especially like about it.

A MULTIMODAL PROJECT IN THREE MEDIA

VRINDA VASAVADA

Is Addicted the New Normal?
Fighting Tech Addiction

Vrinda Vasavada, who is studying computer science and economics at Stanford, created a multimodal project for her second-year rhetoric and writing class. Her assignment began with a research-based argument, delivered as a print document that included some illustrations. She then developed an oral presentation with PowerPoint *slides on the same topic. Finally, her presentation was videotaped and posted to the web as a digital text. Here you can see excerpts from all three versions of her project.*

Print

Here is the opening of Vasavada's print essay:

According to a recent Deloitte study, the average American young adult checks their phone seventy-four times a day (Wigginton et al. 3). In total, these checks add up to about five hours of the day, and most of this use is subconscious: according to a 2015 study by British psychologists, young adults use their phones twice as much as they estimate (Andrews et al. 6). Further, our phone usage is not restricted to times of solitude: according to a recent Pew study, 89 percent of Americans report using their phones during their last social interaction, and 82 percent of those who did say that it "deteriorated the conversation" (Rainie et al. 4).

These numbers reveal the large role that technology plays in our daily lives, but also point to a more frightening trend: we are losing control over our technology usage. While we sense that using our phones during social interactions affects the quality of our conversations negatively, we are unable to change our behavior to fix this problem. Discovering such lack of control leads us to an extremely

Opens with provocative statistics.

In-text documentation follows MLA style.

Transitional sentence sums up previous paragraph and points to new topic.

important question: is excessive technology usage a form of addiction? If so, what should different stakeholders in the technology space do to curb its effects?

From both a behavioral and a biological perspective, excessive technology usage closely mirrors other forms of behavioral addiction. While users can make specific choices to limit their tech usage, research suggests that they have not been successful in limiting screen time. Instead, the responsibility and power to curb the effects of tech addiction now rest predominantly on the shoulders of technology companies, who need to make conscious design choices that prioritize user health. In order to incentivize such changes, we need to leverage existing power dynamics within the tech space, exerting pressure from both inside and outside the companies.

Connects tech addiction to other kinds of addiction.

States thesis.

Oral

Here is the opening of Vasavada's spoken presentation:

Starts by addressing audience directly and introducing her topic.

Good morning everyone. My name is Vrinda and I'm a sophomore studying computer science and economics, and I'm excited to present my research from this term to you on fighting tech addiction. I want to start us off with a couple of quick questions.

What was the first thing you did when you woke up this morning?

Questions engage audience and elicit response.

Right. If you're like 60 percent of Americans you checked your phone within five minutes of waking up. Here's another one:

Think back to the last social event you went to. Did you check your phone?

Short sentences and everyday language make presentation engaging and easy to follow.

I thought so. Eighty-nine percent of Americans reported using their phones during their last social interaction. And something that's even crazier than that: 82 percent claimed that it deteriorated the conversation. So clearly we can sense that there's something going on where our phones are getting in the way of our conversations. But we aren't able to do anything to stop it. This leads me to my main research question for today:

Is tech addiction a real problem? And if so, what should we be doing to fix it?

Announces her research question.

And here's Vasavada's conclusion:

How can we solve the problem of tech addiction? There are a few key sources of pressure that we can use.

Question signals what comes next.

First of all, pressure from within. Engaging employees in conversations about ethics is extremely important because each of those features that we just talked about was brought up by a group of employees at one of these companies. Making sure that these people are thinking about the ethics and the impact of the features they're working on can be a powerful way of forcing companies to change.

Second, pressure from where the money is coming from: the investors. So if more investors start to place their money in places that do social good, that will have impact. And we see that this is actually happening. Recently Apple's investors called on them to produce a less addictive iPhone because they'd been seeing the negative effects that iPhone usage is having on their children and grandchildren and they are not happy.

"First," "Second," "Third" help audience follow along.

Third, leveraging hardware company power. The incentives for companies like Apple and Google are actually closely aligned with their consumers. And if consumers think their phones are getting them addicted, they are less likely to buy the next generation. So in fact these big companies are very closely aligned with our incentives in making sure that we have healthy relationships with their devices. And they're in a position of power to make sure they are curbing tech addiction.

For one thing, they can cap the number of notifications that certain apps can send us. They can also make us more conscious of how we're spending our time by sending a daily report of where we've spent our time on each app.

And finally, we see that there is a surprising source of pressure from consumers themselves. Our generation, Gen-Z, born between 1995 and 2005, has been confusing the media with our tech habits. So while we have grown up with a lot of technology, 53 percent of our generation actually prefers f2f communication to digital. Not only will these companies want to develop devices that are healthier for their consumers, but in order to survive our generation, they will need to.

Concludes with a direct appeal to her audience, noting what tech companies must do to keep them.

Thank you!

Digital

The video of Vasavada's presentation was posted on her writing program's website, and you can watch it at <u>letstalklibrary.com</u>. You'll see that she uses all five modalities: linguistic (her words), audio (her voice), gestural (her movements and facial expressions), visual (her slides), and spatial (her position in the room, the elements on her slides).

Simple, uncluttered slide uses contrast to highlight key statistic.

What was the first thing you did when
you woke up this morning?

Shows key question on slide.

Thinking about the Text

1. Vrinda Vasavada began this project by drafting a print argument. Take a look at the facts and studies she mentions in the introduction to her essay: How well do you think it supports the claim she makes as her thesis? What other points might she have made in leading up to her thesis?

2. Compare the opening of Vasavada's oral presentation with the opening of her print essay. Her research question is the same in each—is excessive tech use an addiction? But note the differences in the two versions: What do you see as the strengths of each? Which one is more memorable, and why?

3. Vasavada uses questions extensively in her oral presentation. What is the effect of those questions? Why do you think she asks questions rather than simply making statements?

4. How is the conclusion of her oral presentation organized, and what transitions link one point to the next? What do you find most memorable about the conclusion—and why?

5. Write a paragraph or two about your own use or overuse of tech devices: What advice, if any, do you have for yourself about how to modify your use of these devices?

PART FOUR

RESEARCH

FIND OUT

14 Starting with Questions, Finding Sources

RESEARCH IS FORMALIZED CURIOSITY.
IT'S POKING AND PRYING WITH A PURPOSE.

—ZORA NEALE HURSTON

THE IMPORTANT THING IS NOT TO STOP QUESTIONING.
CURIOSITY HAS ITS OWN REASON FOR EXISTENCE.

—ALBERT EINSTEIN

You, it turns out, are a born questioner. In fact, research shows that humans differ from non-human primates in just this way: we ask questions! In addition, humans have evolved to spend lots of time, brain space, and brain power articulating questions—and then searching for and creating knowledge that will help provide answers. And we do so not just because of everyday needs like food and shelter but also because, well, because it's *just what we do*. This chapter recognizes the questioner and researcher in all of us and provides guidance as you engage in these distinctly human activities.

Being curious—and asking questions—is at the very heart of the "poking and prying with a purpose" that Zora Neale Hurston associates with research. So doing research calls on you to immerse yourself in new ideas and topics you want to know more about, searching out what other people have said about them, and considering a wide range of perspectives—including those that differ from any ideas about the topic you already have.

Tracking down answers to important questions (another way of saying "research") is crucial to getting and creating knowledge. While most of us grew up accepting ideas handed down to us by others, at some point we begin to question some of those ideas, to want to understand and evaluate them on our own rather than accepting them as "just the way it is." We start to think about and search for answers to questions that excite or puzzle or even frighten us. In short, we become researchers.

In fact, you are probably already a pretty experienced researcher: the reading you do and the questions you ask before buying a new smartphone; the time you spend exploring your college's website to decide what courses to take; the hours and hours you spend looking for recordings by BTS or some other K-pop group. All research. During your college years, you will have the opportunity to do research in many courses and on many topics. Take advantage of these opportunities to put your curiosity and imagination to work, to discover things you couldn't have imagined before now, and to add to your own knowledge. This chapter will help get you started on any research you set out to do.

> No one person is the authority on anything.
> —CLEO KEAHNA

> Nell Gluckman opens with a professor wondering how her salary compares with that of her school's coaches. See where that question leads on p. 796.

STARTING WITH QUESTIONS
Choose a topic that matters to you

Sometimes a topic chooses you, one you're so fascinated by that you've been thinking about it for a long time. If so, chances are good that this is a topic you should take time to explore. Other times, you may be assigned a topic to research—particularly in a class you're taking or a job you hold. But even when topics are assigned, they are often broad enough to let you focus on one aspect that seems most important or that really piques your curiosity. Still other times, the topic may be left open to you as long as it somehow relates to the course content. In each of these cases, you need to focus the topic so that its importance is absolutely clear and in some way matters to you.

In one first-year seminar on environmental science, students were assigned to write a research-based essay on some aspect of sustainability. In response, one student who lived in a dorm chose to pursue a question that had been bothering him: How many plastic straws and bottles and aluminum cans were fellow students tossing into the trash rather than recycling? So he decided to do a little field research, counting the number of straws, bottles, and cans he found in the trash cans on three floors of his dorm. The number was even higher than he had imagined; and when he thought about how many more floors there were in this one dorm, he was even more alarmed. The question he started with led him to this basic research of his own, which he then followed up with research using online databases and other sources in order to find out what others have reported about the growing amount of perfectly recyclable material that ends up in landfills and dumps and even in the ocean. This student was certain he had identified an important topic, one that mattered and that was worth researching and writing about.

How NOT to do research!

"I'm sorry, sir, but this survey does not allow for that opinion."

Think about your rhetorical situation

Once you've identified a topic to research, take time to think carefully about your purpose, audience, and the rest of your rhetorical situation. Jotting down some notes on the following elements of the rhetorical situation will come in handy when you begin shaping your topic into a RESEARCH QUESTION and eventually a THESIS.

Purpose. Why have you chosen this topic, and what do you hope to accomplish in researching and writing about it? What do you want to happen as a result of your work?

Audience. Who will read what you write, and what are they likely to know about your topic? What background information will you need to provide? What kinds of EVIDENCE or sources will they find most persuasive?

Stance. What do you know about the topic, and what do you think and believe about it? At this point, how would you describe your attitude on the topic—neutral? curious? passionate? something else? How do you want to come across to your audience—and how can you establish your credibility to write on this topic? Your tone (serious? humorous? conversational?) will be important for establishing this stance.

Context. Who is doing research on this topic, and how will their work inform what you write? Identifying this part of your rhetorical situation brings you into a conversation that's already taking place about your topic and that will be very important to you as you begin your own research. In addition, what is the context for your assignment: When is it due? Are there any requirements about the length of what you write and the kinds of sources you should consult?

Genre. Have you been assigned to write in a particular genre—an ARGUMENT? a REPORT? an ANALYSIS? a MULTIMODAL presentation of some kind? If not, what genre best suits your topic and purpose?

Media and design. Are you required to use a certain medium? If not, which media will best suit your topic and purpose and help you reach your audience? Will you need to include photos or other images? graphs or charts? Will you need headings? Does your assignment have any format requirements?

Even if you can't answer all these questions right now, they'll get you thinking about your topic. And do take notes: it's amazing what good ideas may pop into your head as you think systematically about your rhetorical situation.

Do some research to get an overview of your topic

What's up with "Latinx"? Who says it? Who doesn't? Where? When? Why? Such questions lead one writer to do research. See where the questions lead on p. 609.

At this point, it's a good idea to do a quick *Google* search, checking out a few sources on your topic just to get a sense of who has written about it and what's been said. *Wikipedia* can be a good starting point, a site where you'll encounter the various perspectives on your topic, find links to sources you may want to consult, and read about any controversies. *Wikipedia* will likely provide a snapshot of all that, which makes it a good place to start. For now, you should just be dipping into a few sources, seeing what they have to say about your topic and casting a wide net to see what good ideas you may catch in it. Make some notes about what sources you might use.

Focus your topic

Once you've gathered some basic information and have some sense of the larger conversation surrounding your topic, think about whether you need to narrow it to make it more manageable. One good way to begin is to jot down what you now know about the topic. Then highlight the points that are most interesting to you: the more the topic matters to you, the better your research and writing about it will be.

Suppose you've been following some discussions online about the pros and cons of social media. So you begin with a broad topic like "effects of social media." But you quickly realize that you can't possibly cover such a huge topic, so you begin to focus and narrow: How about "cognitive effects of social media"? Still pretty unmanageable. So you try again: "cognitive effects of social media use on middle school kids in the United States." This is still a big topic, but it is now narrowed enough that you can at least begin to gather information in a somewhat focused way.

Come up with a research question

Once you have a manageable topic, you can turn it into a question that will guide your research as you look for compelling ways to answer it. Your question should be clear and succinct, and not one that can be answered with a simple "yes" or "no." "Does climate change exist?" Well, yes it does or no it doesn't, and you're left with a one-word response that won't help you at all to engage the large body of work that exists on climate change.

Here are two ways that the topic on the effects of social media can be recast as a research question:

> What are the cognitive effects of social media use on middle school kids in the United States?

> How does the use of social media affect the cognitive abilities of middle school kids in the United States?

These are questions that can guide you as you begin to research this topic. They are also questions worth investigating, because the answers will be very important not only to you but to others as well. As you begin your research to answer this question, remember to do so with an open mind, ready to consider sources that present many different perspectives. You don't want to choose only sources that you agree with: take a look at what researchers and scholars with many varying, even conflicting opinions have to say.

Plot out a working thesis

Once you have a research question, the next step is to come up with a working thesis that can help guide your search. Keep in mind that you'll keep asking your research question, and you may well modify the thesis as you continue the research, but your working thesis will function as a HYPOTHESIS, your best guess at this point about what you will claim in writing about your topic.

See p. 84 for more on drafting a thesis.

As someone investigating the effects of social media on middle school students, you might begin with a working thesis like this:

Middle school children in the United States seem to be strongly affected by the use of social media, and excessive use has been shown to lead to troubling cognitive results.

This thesis will almost surely change as you dig into research on the topic: Will your research turn up credible evidence to support the statement that middle school children are "strongly affected" by social media use? If so, are the most troublesome effects cognitive ones? What is the correlation between the increasing use of social media and various behaviors among middle school kids? These are questions that careful and systematic research will answer and that may then lead you to further revise your thesis statement.

REFLECT! Take some time to jot down some of the things you worry about, or things you wish you knew more about. BRAINSTORM about these things for ten or so minutes, until you've identified a few ideas. Which ones are most important to you, and which ones might have the greatest impact on others? Choose one, and write a paragraph introducing this topic to a friend and explaining why you want to carry out research on it.

FINDING SOURCES

In 2018, well into the #MeToo movement, Elizabeth Winkler began musing about all the strong, resourceful, and memorable women in Shakespeare's plays. As she attended and reread these plays, she kept finding more and more instances of remarkable women characters, so much so that she decided to research the controversy over who actually wrote "Shakespeare's" plays. So she immersed herself in the arguments various scholars had put forward in favor of possible authors—an all-male cast including Francis Bacon, Christopher Marlowe, and Edward deVere—and then turned again to the plays themselves. And they led her to ask a most provocative question: What if Shakespeare was a woman? From there, she was off on the research adventure of a lifetime.

Winkler's experience shows how research often works: you start out with a focus on a topic, even with a preliminary thesis, but a simple turn of the kaleidoscope can reveal an entirely new way of looking at the topic. And that new way of looking can then lead you to consider sources that might not have seemed relevant before. In this case, Winkler's question led her to turn to primary sources—Shakespeare's own plays—with a new eye, which in turn led her to discover things in the plays that the "real" Shakespeare would have been hard-pressed to know, but that *would* have been known by a particular woman poet living at the same time: Amelia Bassano. From there, Winkler was off on a hunt for everything she could find out about Bassano. And she found a lot—enough to support her claim that "Shakespeare" may well have been a woman.

Was "Shakespeare" a woman?

In doing her research, Winkler used time-tested methods: careful, critical reading of the plays—and of secondary sources on the question of authorship. She also did some field research, interviewing one of the scholars who's theorized that Bassano was the actual author. Most important, however, she kept her mind wide open to new possibilities, and looked for sources from a very wide range of viewpoints.

Like Winkler, you may also draw on both primary and secondary materials when you conduct research—and may even gather information from field research.

What kinds of sources do you need?

Deciding on the sources that will be most helpful to you is a challenge today when there are so many to choose from, ranging from books and articles and databases to video and audio files of all kinds—all readily available in your school library. So it's wise to spend some time thinking about the kinds of sources your topic calls for. Like Winkler's, your topic might call for consulting primary sources and historical documents. But if your topic is a contemporary one—say, about the environment—you would probably need current sources from scientific and environmental journals. You might also want to schedule an interview with an environmental studies professor. Whatever your topic, look for sources that represent different perspectives on it, including ones that challenge your own thinking on the topic. Remember that research is about INQUIRY: to learn about the topic, not simply to find support for what you already think about it.

Primary and secondary sources

Primary sources are original works—like Shakespeare's plays. They are firsthand accounts, diaries, historical documents, and materials generated from FIELD RESEARCH like interviews or surveys. *Secondary sources*, in contrast, REPORT on or ANALYZE primary sources—and provide secondhand knowledge. So *Beloved* is a primary source, while a critic's analysis of that novel is a secondary source.

Sometimes your purpose determines whether a source is primary or secondary. Suppose you are writing an essay on Cardi B, who won the 2019 Grammy for best rap album of the year. That album is your primary source, while a critic who has written a review of Cardi B's album is a secondary source. But suppose you decide to write an essay on that particular critic's work: then the review of Cardi B's album would be a primary source for your research.

Don't forget about NARRATIVES. Firsthand narratives might provide good examples or evidence, as well as appealing to readers. In the same way, a personal narrative of your own—*your* story—can also serve as a source you can draw on in doing research.

Scholarly and popular sources

Scholarly sources are those written by experts for an academic audience. Whether they're journal articles, books, conference papers, or some other publication, they've usually been peer-reviewed by experts and include full documentation of their sources. *Popular sources*, in contrast, are written for a general audience; while they can be authoritative and cite scholarly research, they haven't been as fully vetted as academic sources, nor do they usually include documentation.

In the field of psychology, the journal *Psychology of Consciousness: Theory, Research, and Practice* is a scholarly source, while *Psychology Today* is a popular source. Even though both kinds of sources can provide excellent information, you'll want to be sure that the sources you use are appropriate to your PURPOSE and AUDIENCE. If you're writing about tax policy for a business class, the *Wall Street Journal* might be a useful source, but its movie reviews would not be appropriate sources in a film analysis for a history of film class.

How to determine if a source is scholarly or popular

- **What's the title?** Scholarly titles sound academic and often include subtitles. Popular titles are more likely to be catchy, sometimes provocative.

- *What are the author's credentials?* Scholarly sources are written by academics, those affiliated with a college or university. Some academic authors also write books or articles for a general audience. These would be considered popular rather than scholarly.

- *Who's the publisher or sponsor?* Look for academic presses or organizations.

- *Does it include* DOCUMENTATION? Scholarly sources cite research and document their sources, both in in-text documentation within the text and on a list of works cited or references.

- *If it's online, what's the URL?* Colleges and universities use *.edu*.

- *Does it look scholarly?* Academic sources tend to have a one-color, conservative design and often include tables and charts. Popular texts are more likely to have a colorful design and to include photos and other illustrations.

- *Are there ads?* Popular sources often include many ads; scholarly ones have few if any ads.

See examples from popular and scholarly sources on pp. 254–55. All that said, keep a very sharp eye out for sources that claim to be credible scholarly sources—and look scholarly—because they may not be. In this age of FAKE NEWS, we now have to worry about fake scholarly sources as well, especially those that pop up in a *Google* search. Such sites are written and designed to sound and look scholarly. Check to see who's sponsoring the site: Is it an academic institution or an advocacy group? And check out *Snopes.com* or another fact-checking site to see what they say about it. See Chapter 15 for advice on how to determine whether unfamiliar sources should be trusted.

Finding sources on the internet

Many of us turn to the internet whenever we need to find some kind of information. A click of a few keys and wham-o—a long list of sources!

Search engines. Many of us today begin research by using search engines like *Bing*, *DuckDuckGo*, or *Google*. These are all powerful tools for research, but they can quickly become overwhelming. Typing in "plastic in oceans" on *Google*, for example, yields over 40 million possible sources—in less than a second. Still, using *Google* or another search engine as a starting point can give you an overview of what's out there—and help you discover photographs, videos, blogs, maps, and other materials related to your topic.

Google is not a synonym for research.
—DAN BROWN

But the results you get from any search engine are affected by algorithms designed to give you what they think you want. And that is not going to help you find the multiple perspectives on your topic that you need. So don't just click on the first two or three items that appear. The "good stuff" may appear farther down in the list!

And get to know *Google Scholar*, a search engine that will direct you to scholarly literature across an array of disciplines: journal articles, books, technical reports, court opinions, and more. (What you won't find here: news and magazine articles, book reviews, or editorials.) Many of the sources available on *Google Scholar* aren't available for free, but you can access them if your college library subscribes to the databases that contain them—and most likely it does.

Running searches on the web. Whatever search engine you use or whatever you're searching for, choosing KEYWORDS will be a key to focusing your search to get the sources you need. Say you're interested in race car driving. Searching for those three words yields an unmanageable number of results, so you try "race car drivers." Still too much. Further thinking leads you to wonder about the gender of drivers—and more specifically, about women NASCAR drivers. So you narrow your search and type in "women NASCAR drivers." There are various ways of focusing what a search engine looks for, but here are a few that work with many engines:

- Use *quotation marks* to search for an exact phrase ("women NASCAR drivers"). If you enter those same words without quotation marks, you'll get sources with all three words but not only in that order.

SCHOLARLY SOURCE

Published in an academic journal.

Contents lists available at ScienceDirect

Marine Policy

journal homepage: www.elsevier.com/locate/marpol

Human footprint in the abyss: 30 year records of deep-sea plastic debris

Multiple authors who are academics.

Sanae Chiba[a,b,*], Hideaki Saito[c], Ruth Fletcher[b], Takayuki Yogi[d], Makino Kayo[d], Shin Miyagi[d], Moritaka Ogido[d], Katsunori Fujikura[e]

[a] Japan Agency for Marine-Earth Science and Technology (JAMSTEC), 3173-25 Showamachi, Kanazawaku, Yokohama 2360001, Japan
[b] UN Environment World Conservation Monitoring Centre, 219 Huntingdon Road, Cambridge CB3 0DL, UK
[c] Global Oceanographic Data Center (GODAC), Japan Agency for Marine Science and Technology (JAMSTEC), 224-3 Aza-Toyohara, Nago 9052172, Japan
[d] Marine Works Japan, Ltd., 224-3 Aza-Toyohara, Nago 9052172, Japan
[e] Department of Marine Biodiversity Research, Japan Agency for Marine-Earth Science and Technology (JAMSTEC), 2-15 Natsushimacho, Yokosuka 2370061, Japan

A R T I C L E   I N F O

Keywords:
Deep-sea debris
Marine litter, plastic pollution
Single-use plastic
Database
North Pacific

Includes an abstract.

A B S T R A C T

This study reports plastic debris pollution in the deep-sea based on the information from a recently developed database. The Global Oceanographic Data Center (GODAC) of the Japan Agency for Marine-Earth Science and Technology (JAMSTEC) launched the Deep-sea Debris Database for public use in March 2017. The database archives photographs and videos of debris that have been collected since 1983 by deep-sea submersibles and remotely operated vehicles. From the 5010 dives in the database, 3425 man-made debris items were counted. More than 33% of the debris was macro-plastic, of which 89% was single-use products, and these ratios increased to 52% and 92%, respectively, in areas deeper than 6000 m. The deepest record was a plastic bag at 10898 m in the Mariana Trench. Deep-sea organisms were observed in the 17% of plastic debris images, which include entanglement of plastic bags on chemosynthetic cold seep communities. Quantitative density analysis for the subset data in the western North Pacific showed plastic density ranging from 17 to 335 items km^{-2} at depths of 1092–5977 m. The data show that, in addition to resource exploitation and industrial development, the influence of land-based human activities has reached the deepest parts of the ocean in areas more than 1000 km from the mainland. Establishment of international frameworks on monitoring of deep-sea plastic pollution as an Essential Ocean Variable and a data sharing protocol are the keys to delivering scientific outcomes that are useful for the effective management of plastic pollution and the conservation of deep-sea ecosystems.

Table 1
Summary of the total and plastic debris occurrences during deep-sea surveys by remotely operated vehicles and submersibles of the Japan Agency for Marine-Earth Science and Technology (JAMSTEC) in the six oceanic regions for 1982-2015. The information is based on the Deep-sea Debris Database of Global Oceanographic Data Center (GODAC) of JAMSTEC (updated on July 3rd, 2017) (http://www.godac.jamstec.go.jp/dsdebris/e/). Single use plastics are plastic bags, bottles and packages.

Describes research methods, includes numerical data.

Oceanic Region	Year of observation	Geographical range (Latitude - Longitude)	Dive depth range (m)	Debris depth range (m)	Max. depth (m) of plastics	Total dive number	Total debris number	Plastic debris number	% Single use plastic
Western North Pacific	1982-2015	1°15' - 45°34'N 122°42' - 163°15'E	100- 10,899	100-10898	10,898	4552	3370	1108	89
Eastern North Pacific	1998-2002	17°12' - 24°24'N 154°14' - 159°13'W	1714-5569	3879-4684	4684	85	8	2	100
South Pacific	1990-2013	3°10' - 34°53'S 149°52'E - 112112°29'W	499-6498	1846-4460	1986	168	12	1	100
North Atlantic	1994-2013	14°44' - 36°14'N 33°54' - 81°48'W	2265-6024	2300 - 4935	–	68	17	0	N.A.
South Atlantic	2013	20°38' - 31°06'S 34°03' - 41°39'W	921-4219	2493-2721	–	16	5	0	N.A.
Indian Ocean	1998-2015	4°02'N - 32°57'S 57°04' - 105°53'E	1276-5290	1923-3264	2573	121	13	4	100
Total						5010	3425	1115	89

Cites academic research with consistent documentation style.

at maximum, and on surveys conducted in areas relatively close to the coast. There are only a few cases of long-term observation records on deep-sea plastic pollution [18,25,26] and of surveys conducted at depths greater than the abyssal zone (> 4000 m) [13–15] and in areas more than 1000 km off the coast of the mainland [13,19,27]. Information on deep-sea debris in the western North Pacific Ocean is also very limited [15,28]. Because high concentrations of plastic debris were

2. Material and methods

2.1. Data

The data used in this study were from the Deep-sea Debris Database updated on July 3rd, 2017 (http://www.godac.jamstec.go.jp/dsdebris/e/). The debris data were obtained by visually analysing video footage

Includes complete references list.

from various aspects. The Deep Ocean Observing Strategy (DOOS) (http://www.deepoceanobserving.org) is being developed under the auspices of the Global Ocean Observation System (GOOS), with the aim of promoting and integrating physical, biogeochemical, and biological observation in the deep sea (> 2000 m) of the global ocean. In accordance with the guideline of the Framework for Ocean Observation [52], agreed upon by the global ocean science community at the OceanObs'09 meeting in 2009, DOOS is preparing to identify Essential Ocean Variables (EOVs) to measure deep-sea environments globally (http://www.goosocean.org/index.php?option = com_content&view = article&id = 14&itemid = 114). The density or occurrence of plastic is one of the possible deep-sea EOVs. It is particularly recommended to

References

[1] UNEP, GRID-Arendal, Marine Litter Vital Graphics, United Nations Environment Programme and GRID-Arendal., Nairobi and Arendal, 2016.
[2] United Nations, The Sustainable Development Goals Report. doi:http://dx.doi.org/10.18356/3405dd09f-en, 2017.
[3] M. Bergmann, M.B. Tekman, L. Gutow, Marine litter: sea change for plastic pollution, Nature 544 (2017), http://dx.doi.org/10.1038/544297a (297–297).
[4] F. Galgani, G. Hanke, T. Maes, Global Distribution, Composition and Abundance of Marine Litter, Springer International Publishing, 2015, pp. 29–56, http://dx.doi.org/10.1007/978-3-319-16510-3.2 (in: Mar. Anthropog. Litter).
[5] LITTERBASE, Online Portal for Marine Litter. 〈www.litterbase.org〉.
[6] D.K.A. Barnes, F. Galgani, R.C. Thompson, M. Barlaz, Accumul. Fragm. Plast. Debris Glob. Environ. 364 (2009) 1985–1998, http://dx.doi.org/10.1098/rstb.2008.0205.

POPULAR SOURCE

Published in a general-interest periodical.

Author is a journalist.

Catchy, provocative title and photo.

Every year, an estimated <u>eight million metric tons</u> of land-based plastic enters the world's oceans. But when marine researchers have measured how much of this plastic is floating on the water's surface, swirling in offshore gyres—most notably, the so-called Great Pacific Garbage Patch, between Hawaii and California—they have only found quantities on the order of hundreds of thousands of tons, or roughly *one per cent* of all the plastic that has ever gone into the ocean. Part of the explanation for this is that all plastic eventually breaks down into microplastic, and, although this takes some polymers decades, others break down almost immediately, or enter the ocean as microplastic already (like the synthetic fibres that pill off your fleece jacket or yoga pants in the washing machine). Scientists have recently found tiny pieces of plastic falling with the rain in the high mountains, including France's <u>Pyrenees</u> and <u>the Colorado Rockies</u>. British <u>researchers</u> collected amphipods (shrimplike crustaceans) from six of the world's deepest ocean trenches and found that eighty per cent of them had microplastic in their digestive tracts. These kinds of plastic fibres and fragments are smaller than poppy seeds and "the perfect size to enter the bottom of the food web," as Jennifer Brandon, an oceanographer at the Scripps Institution of Oceanography, told me. "They have been shown to be eaten by mussels, by coral, by sea cucumbers, by barnacles, by lots of filter-feeding plankton."

Academic experts and studies cited but not documented.

- Use *and* to retrieve texts using all of these words ("women and NASCAR and drivers").
- Use *or* to retrieve texts using any of those words ("women or NASCAR or drivers").

Wikipedia is a free online encyclopedia that can give you a sense of what is being written and debated about your topic. But because virtually anyone can edit what's on *Wikipedia*, its information is always changing—which means it's a source you usually won't want to cite. Still, most of its entries include links and bibliographies that will lead you to other sources, so it can be a good starting point for researching a topic.

Government sites. Are you looking for information about AmeriCorps? the Census Bureau? the Justice Department? the Library of Congress? the National Archives? the Supreme Court? Go to *USA.gov*, where you can access sites for these and many other government departments.

News sites. Many newspapers and magazines offer free access to at least some of their content that's available online. And your college library might well subscribe to some of those that don't; if so, you'll be able to access them through the library's portal. In addition, some newspapers allow you to search their archives so you can look for articles relevant to your topic that have been published in the past.

Google News is another source of news. It offers a continuous flow of articles from thousands of publishers and magazines. According to its site, it focuses especially on diverse perspectives—and in thirty-five languages. And it allows you to search for news from a particular time period and to request email alerts about topics you're following (or researching!).

Social media sites such as *Twitter*, *Instagram*, or *Facebook*, as well as blogs and podcasts, can be useful sources—or not. I follow the work of several cognitive scientists on *Twitter*, for example, as a way of keeping up to date on the work in this field, and I also follow linguist Dennis Baron's deeply researched and informative blog, *The Web of Language*. In these cases, I know some of the writers and their expertise; I can generally trust what they say to be credible sources of information. I am much less likely to use information provided by sources whose reputation I don't know. As we all know, there's a lot of misinformation being retweeted and reposted on social media every minute of every day. So if you cannot trust or verify information you find on *Twitter*, it's wise to pass it by—and not to cite it in anything you write.

Image, video, and audio banks. Free images, audio, and even films are available in a number of sources on the web. For photos, check out *StockSnap.io*, *Unsplash*, *Reshot*, or *Shutterstock*. For videos, consult *pexels.com* and *storybook.com*. And for audio files, check out *audio jungle.net*, *audioblocks.com*, and *freesound.org*. Remember, though, that while these sources are free of charge, you still need to acknowledge and DOCUMENT any that you use in your own writing.

REFLECT! Together with a partner, do a search for the same term using the same search engine—but each on your own computer. Compare what the two searches turn up. Most likely they will be different. Why? Spend some time BRAINSTORMING about this, and how it might affect the way you think about search results.

Using your college's library

Learn how to use your school's library—the physical library on campus and the library's website that gives access to all that's in the library. Take a tour, or try to meet with a reference librarian, and come prepared with questions: Where can you find encyclopedias, almanacs, and other general reference works? What special collections (of art, film, music, audio, and video) does the library have?

How can you access library resources online? And once you've settled on a topic, see if there's a librarian who specializes in the field that you're researching.

The library catalog. The books, the encyclopedias, the films, the audios, and more: it's all accounted for in the library catalog, with information about where it's located. At most colleges, the catalog is digital; you can search by author, title, subject, and keyword. Do an *author search* if you want to find out everything in the library written by that author. Do a *title search* if you know the complete title of what you're looking for. If you don't know a specific author or title, you can do a *subject* or *keyword search* that will give an overview of all the materials in the library related to that topic. Your library probably uses the Library of Congress Subject Headings (LCSH), so you may need to experiment for a while to make sure you're using a word that LCSH also uses. For example, if you enter "American Civil War" as a subject heading, you would get a notice telling you that this is not a LCSH subject heading—but that "United States History Civil War" is. Then you'll be on the right track to do a successful subject search.

Databases. These are large digital collections of journal, magazine, and newspaper articles and other sources. Many are available by subscription, but they are likely available through your college library.

General databases that cover a wide range of fields and include both scholarly and popular sources can be a good place to start:

- *Academic Search Complete* offers access to thousands of journals and magazines, including many that are open access.

- *JSTOR* provides access to millions of academic journals, books, and primary sources in seventy-five disciplines.

- *ProQuest Central* provides access to thousands of its "most used" academic journals, newspapers, magazines, dissertations, and more. Look here for the *New York Times,* the *Wall Street Journal, The Economist,* and more.

- *Lexis/Nexis Academic* offers documents from business, government, legal, and news sources.

Subject-specific databases come in handy once you have a research question. If you are researching the effect of changing rules in pro basketball, check with a reference librarian to recommend specific subject databases, or refer to several that are often very useful:

- *AGRIS* is a public domain database for accessing millions of resources in agricultural science and technology.
- *ERIC* gives access to journals, conference papers, and other publications related to education.
- *IEEE Xplore* provides access to publications in computer science, electrical engineering, and related fields.
- *PsychINFO* provides abstracts for peer-reviewed articles in psychology and the behavioral sciences.
- *MLA International Bibliography* indexes scholarly articles and books in the fields of literature, language, linguistics, rhetoric, and folklore.

Conducting field research

You can learn a lot at the library and on the web, but some topics might lead you to do your own firsthand research: to interview someone with expertise in your topic, to conduct a survey to gather information, or to observe people in a particular place or situation. Field research that involves people may require approval; your instructor can help you determine whether you need to consult with your college's Institutional Review Board to make sure that your study will not be harmful to any of its participants.

Interviews

You can sometimes get information by interviewing someone with expertise or experience in the area you're researching. Say you're looking into the incidence of pandemics in this century. You might interview a microbiology professor on your campus to help launch your search. Here are some tips for conducting a successful interview:

- **Request and schedule the interview** well in advance, either by email or with a telephone call. Be sure to explain your PURPOSE and ask how much time the person would be willing to grant you for the interview.

- **Prepare a list of questions** in advance. You might begin with some questions about the person's work. But then move to open-ended questions that will elicit full answers. Avoid questions that can be answered with a simple "yes" or "no" ("Do you follow the Spurs?") or that prompt certain answers ("Don't you agree that student athletes should be paid?").

- **Take notes** or record the interview—or do both. Ask for permission if you wish to tape, and be sure to test all equipment in advance!

- **Write down the person's full name** and title along with the date, time, and place.

- **Say thank-you**, both at the end of the interview and later in a written note or email.

Conversations

The best primary sources are often sitting right next to us.
—CLINT SMITH,
How the Word Is Passed

While interviews are often formal and structured, you may find that more informal, unstructured conversations can sometimes be useful for gathering information. Some indigenous researchers also stress respectful, engaged silence and listening as a way of coming to understand and appreciate the information that someone is sharing with you. Here are some tips for having such conversations:

- **Try to meet in a comfortable setting** where you can do something together—sew, cook, garden, and so on.

- **Ask permission** to record or take notes.

- **Share some of your own experience** with the topic.

- *Respect the other person's silence*, and be patient waiting for response.
- *Listen carefully* and intently, letting the person know that you're paying close attention. Do not interrupt.
- *If you do ask questions*, do so only for clarification.
- *Express gratitude* for the time spent together.

Observations

Some research questions will lead you to do firsthand observation. Say you're researching how the way desks are arranged in a classroom affects participation. You might observe several classrooms—one with desks in rows, another where they're in a circle, and a third where they're in small clusters. This kind of observing calls for intense and purposeful attention, looking to catch every detail you can and recording the data accurately. Here are some tips to help you do so:

- *Think about your* PURPOSE. What do you want to find out? And how will you use what you learn?
- *Plan ahead*. What will you observe, and when? What materials will you need—a notebook? a camera or video camera? Do you need to ask permission in advance to observe, and to take photos or videos?
- *Take notes*. DESCRIBE the place, who's there, what they're doing. Don't start analyzing what you see; just record what you observe. Be sure to note the date, time, and place.
- *After the observation*, take time to jot down any additional details and to record your thoughts about what you saw, along with any questions you may have.
- *Review your notes* and any recorded material carefully, noting any recurring patterns. What have you learned? Did anything surprise you? How can you use the findings when you write up your research?

Surveys

Sometimes your research will require you to get information from a large number of people. Suppose you want to get student response to the latest hike in tuition fees. The best way to do that is with a questionnaire. Here are some tips for planning a survey and creating a questionnaire:

- *Think about your* PURPOSE. What are you trying to learn, and how will you use the results?

- *Decide who to contact*, and how. Will you email them a questionnaire? use *Survey Monkey*? conduct the survey on the phone?

- *Write out your questions*. It's best not to ask too many questions, and to make them easy to answer. Multiple-choice questions are easy to answer and then to tabulate, but you may also need to ask some open-ended questions to get the information you're seeking.

- *Begin by saying thanks* for taking the time to respond to your questions, and be sure to explain what you're trying to learn. End by again saying thank-you and saying when the survey is due.

- ANALYZE *the responses*, looking for patterns and for what they reveal about your topic. Think about how you can use the information in reporting on your research.

REFLECT! What have you learned about your topic so far? At this point in the process, which sources seem the most promising, and why? Are you finding enough sources to answer your research question? If not, might you need to revise your question? Have you looked at your topic from a number of different perspectives? If so, have they got you thinking? If not, get to work!

15 Evaluating Sources, Checking Facts

YOU MAY HAVE READ THAT I WENT TO MIT. IN 1982 I FILLED
OUT A *WHO'S WHO* SURVEY WITH JOKING RESPONSES,
AND THEY NEVER BOTHERED TO CHECK THE FACTS.

—CHEVY CHASE

When I got my first personal computer in 1985, I heard a lot about GIGO: "garbage in, garbage out," shorthand for saying if the data you put into a computer is faulty, the outcome will be equally faulty. That phrase is still used, and its warning is perhaps as timely as ever in an even broader context: if the authors and sources you rely on in your writing are "garbage"—well, then, your writing is in danger of being garbage too! And today, when distinguishing fact from fiction, truth from lies, accurate from "deep fake" is more and more difficult, writers need all the help we can get in making sure that the information we find in sources is honest and trustworthy—and that any source we cite in our own work is too.

As you begin your search for useful and credible sources, remember that all sources will have a point of view and so will inevitably reflect at least some of the assumptions and preferences of those who create them. Even the most careful authors can never be all-seeing and all-knowing: while they can aim to present information accurately and fairly, they can't possibly see the topic from every perspective. Pure objectivity is just not possible, but we can still try hard to be as accurate and truthful as possible. It's up to you then to carefully assess all the sources you consult to determine whether you can trust and believe what they say. This chapter will help you make sure the sources you rely on are worthy of your attention—and your trust.

IS THE SOURCE USEFUL?

Once you find sources that seem promising, you need to decide whether they're likely to be useful—how they'll serve your purpose, whether your audience will find them persuasive, and so on. Here are some questions to ask of sources you're considering:

How useful is the source for your research? Check out any table of contents, abstracts, or introduction to get a sense of what the source covers. Then think about what it might contribute to your research. Does it include a bibliography that would lead you to other sources on the topic? Does it include CITATIONS or links that will lead you to other sources?

What is the source's major CLAIM—and does it make sense to you? If you find it hard to believe, see if you can find any other sources that make similar claims. If the claim does seem reasonable, what kinds of EVIDENCE does it provide as support?

What's the genre? Is it REPORTING information or ARGUING a certain position? Chances are you'll need both; but if it's advocating a particular POINT OF VIEW, you'll want to find sources that provide other PERSPECTIVES as well.

When was the source published or last updated? Keep in mind that more recent does not necessarily mean more useful; the kinds of sources you need will depend on your topic. If you're writing about free speech on your campus, you'll likely need to find recent sources with up-to-date information—but you might also want to consult the US Constitution to see what it has to say about freedom of speech.

Who are the authors, and what are their qualifications for writing on the topic? Are they affiliated with a particular organization that might affect their viewpoint or goals? If the source doesn't include any information about the author, do a web search to see what you can learn.

Who's the publisher or sponsor? If it's a university press, scholarly journal, or government organization, you can assume that the information has been peer-reviewed; if it's a mainstream news publisher, it's likely been fact-checked. If it's an online source, the URL will help you determine what kind of organization is sponsoring the site: *.org* is used by non-profits, *.gov* by government agencies, *.edu* by colleges and universities, *.us* by US government offices, and *.com* by commercial enterprises. No matter who the publisher or sponsor is, do they have a point of view or an agenda you should be aware of?

How might you use this source in your own writing—for background information? as support for your claims? as a counterargument or an example of another perspective?

IS THE SOURCE RELIABLE?

Writers today need to make sure that any sources we use are trustworthy. But that's easier said than done, now that anyone with a computer can post whatever they think—and want others to think. And when entire websites and news organizations present information deliberately slanted to favor one side and denigrate another, sorting through what's accurate and what's not is often a tough call. Just take a look at the left-leaning *Media Matters for America* and the right-leaning *Accuracy in Media* and you'll find them "reporting" the same information, but often spinning it in radically different ways. That's one reason you need to check out who sponsors such sites and do enough research on them to determine whether they have any biases you need to be aware of. This section provides strategies for checking facts and determining whether—or not—a source should be trusted.

Checking facts

Trust, but verify. —RONALD REAGAN

Jackie Chan fought off a large group of people armed with melon knives at a Hong Kong restaurant. Steph Curry parted ways with Nike because they wouldn't let him write Bible verses on his shoes. Californians are no longer allowed to take a shower, do laundry, and flush the toilet on the same day. These are all stories that were once reported as facts—and were then researched and disputed by various fact-checking organizations.

If you're working with academic sources, you may not encounter too many claims as outlandish as these. But then again, you just might. And given all the misinformation, deliberately misleading news reports, and outright lies that exist these days, you'll want to check the facts if you have any doubts. Thank goodness, there are now a number of sites dedicated to investigating what's a fact—and what's not. Here are three sites dedicated to investigating what's a fact, and what's not—all nonpartisan, meaning they lean neither left nor right:

Snopes

Checking everything from facts to news stories to images, *Snopes.com* also accepts submissions if you find something you want fact-checked.

 FACTCHECK.ORG
A PROJECT OF THE ANNENBERG PUBLIC POLICY CENTER

A non-profit site run by the Annenberg Public Policy Center at the University of Pennsylvania, *FactCheck.org* monitors the factual accuracy of what is said by major US political players in ads, debates, speeches, interviews, news releases, and other statements.

A fact-checking website run by the Pointer Institute for Media Studies, *PolitiFact.com* includes a "Truth-O-Meter" that rates claims as true, mostly true, half true, mostly false, or false. In spite of its name, this site covers more than just politics. (In fact, it's where we found the story about Steph Curry's shoes!)

Sites like these can go a long way toward helping you choose sources that are credible—and be confident that any sources you cite, and thus pass on to others, are trustworthy and accurate.

REFLECT! Choose a website that you've identified as potentially useful for a topic you're researching or are interested in learning about. Using one of the fact-checking sites listed above, decide whether the information on the site is trustworthy. Write a brief paragraph summing up how reliable the site seems—or not.

Reading laterally

Researchers at Stanford asked a number of students, historians, and professional fact-checkers to study various websites to determine which ones were credible and trustworthy. What they discovered was alarming: the historians and the students were largely unable to determine which sites were credible. The professional fact-checkers, on the other hand, identified the credible sites every time. Their secret? They would quickly look over the site, but then they would open a number of additional browser tabs and search to see what others had to say about the site. As the authors of the study say:

Sam Wineburg has a lot more to say about the importance of reading laterally. Check out his report on the subject on p. 689.

> Historians and students often fell victim to easily manipulated features of websites, such as official-looking logos and domain names. They read vertically, staying within a website to evaluate its reliability. In contrast, fact checkers read laterally, leaving a site after a quick scan and opening up new browser tabs in order to judge the credibility of the original site. Compared to the other groups, fact checkers arrived at more warranted conclusions in a fraction of the time.
>
> —SAM WINEBURG and SARAH McGREW

In short, the students and historians read *vertically*, focusing on the site they were checking—its author, its sponsor, its links, its claims—whereas the professional fact-checkers read *laterally*, leaving the site to find out what other sources had to say. Specifically, they tried to verify *if* anyone else was saying what the source they were checking said—and to find out *what* if anything other sources had to say about the site or its author.

And that's what you should do. When you're researching something online and find a website you know nothing about, take a tip from the pros: open several tabs in the same browser at the top of your screen to search for information about the site or the text.

- *Enter the title of the site*, and add keywords like "sponsor" or "funding" to find out if the site has a particular agenda.

- *If you're investigating a specific article*, enter its title to see if it's discussed on other sites—and if so, what they're saying.

- *Enter the name of the author* to see what you can find out about their expertise and STANCE on the topic.

- *Enter any claims that seem questionable*. See if any other sources make similar claims—or whether it pops up on *Snopes.com* or another fact-checking site.

By studying a number of other sites on the same topic, you'll find information that you wouldn't likely spot by simply studying the site itself—and you'll find it more quickly to boot.

REFLECT! Look again at the website you evaluated on page 267. This time look beyond the source, opening several browser tabs to see what other sites claim about the same topic. Does reading laterally turn up any new information about the source's reliability?

Triangulating

Experienced researchers know to raise a caution flag when they find a source that can't be verified by other sources. That's a pretty good sign that the source may not be trustworthy. To avoid falling victim to such sources, it's always wise to "triangulate" sources—that is, to check at least three other sources that are reporting the same story. If it's accurate, you should find a number of other sources reporting on it. Likewise, if you can find only one or two pieces of evidence to back up a claim you want to make, you'd better re-evaluate your claim: you may be on shaky ground.

But triangulation is about more than validating the accuracy of a source or its claims. In addition, it will take you deeper into the topic you're exploring, leading to a richer understanding of it and helping you see the topic from several different perspectives. Finally, triangulation is one more way to uncover and counter biases, including your own.

Reading with a critical eye

Once you've determined that a source seems reliable, read it very carefully for what you can learn about your topic and how it might inform what you yourself write.

- What's the CLAIM? Is it clearly stated? Does it support your own thinking about your topic? Or does it provide a different perspective—one that might get you thinking differently?

- What REASONS and EVIDENCE support that claim: facts? expert testimony? data? personal experience? analogies? Look here for evidence that you might use in your own argument.

- Does the source acknowledge and respond to any COUNTERARGUMENTS or other PERSPECTIVES? If it cites other sources, does it provide DOCUMENTATION? Should you check out any of these other sources?

- What's motivating the author? If there's no author, who's the sponsor—and what's their interest in the issue? What are their PURPOSES for sponsoring the site, and are they clearly stated?

- Are you convinced that the argument is one to take seriously? Is this a source you'd want to CITE?

- How would it contribute to your own argument?

Finding the good stuff

The good stuff is out there if you know how to find and verify it.

—HOWARD RHEINGOLD

You've checked facts, triangulated, read carefully and laterally. You're pretty sure the information you've found is reliable. But is it good? Take it from Howard Rheingold: it's there, and we just have to know how to find it. Here are some things he says to look for:

- The authors are identified—and it's even better if they provide a way to respond or to contact them. If they're academics, check *Google Scholar* to see if their work has been cited by other scholars.

- The site is *.edu*, *.gov*, or *.org*—and the author or site is affiliated with a college or university, government agency, or some other trustworthy institution.

- The source cites or links to other sources as support for any claims.

These are all signs of information you can trust. But don't forget about your own good common sense: if a source sounds outlandish or ridiculous or too good to be true, it very well may be. Then your own good judgment can come into play—just remember that in this age of misinformation, you probably need to confirm even your own good judgment!

Checking your own firsthand research

You also need to take a good look at any FIELD RESEARCH you yourself have done. If your research has led you to conduct experiments, interviews, observations, or surveys, then you need to do some double-checking of that work, assessing it with a critical eye. Begin by checking that you have provided necessary details—exactly when and where the research took place, the instruments you used (such as questionnaires or questions for interviews), how you went about analyzing the results, and whether you have permission to conduct the research. Make sure that you have also clarified your own part in the research and taken into account how your own beliefs or assumptions might have unconsciously influenced the findings. Double-check the data you gathered to make sure your calculations are accurate and the conclusions you draw are fully supported by the data. Finally, if you have quoted the words of any participants, check to see that these are absolutely accurate.

REFLECT! Choose two websites on a topic you're exploring or want to explore. Then use the various methods provided in this chapter—fact-checking, lateral reading, and triangulating—to assess the reliability of each site. Which method works best, and why? Finally, write a paragraph describing the steps you took to assess the sites and what you learned by doing so.

16 Building an Annotated Bibliography

AN ANNOTATED BIBLIOGRAPHY CAN SOMETIMES BE
A RESEARCHER'S BEST FRIEND.

—SHIRLEY BRICE HEATH

As a researcher, you may have several reasons for compiling an annotated bibliography. Doing so can help you narrow and focus your topic, or help move you toward a thesis or major claim. Or it can help you to decide which sources will be the most useful for your particular projecton, or to compare several sources on the same topic. In addition, annotating a source will surely help you read it carefully and critically and thus understand it more fully. And the more sources you annotate, the more you will be able to understand the larger conversation surrounding your topic, the range of perspectives on it, and the way the sources relate to your own research. Finally, compiling an annotated bibliography will help separate the sources you have found into those that are credible, timely, and useful—and those that are not. In one of my classes, students decided they would "annotate" some sources and "detonate" others!

In any case, an annotated bibliography demonstrates that you've done your homework, that you are familiar with what others have had to say about your topic, and that the sources you've identified are trustworthy and credible. Unlike the student in the cartoon on this page, you will not be relying on "anonymous" sources!

There are two ways to annotate a bibliography: by describing sources and by evaluating them. *Descriptive annotations* primarily summarize the contents of a source and explain how you expect it to contribute to your research. *Evaluative annotations* do that as well, but also they explain what you see as the source's strengths and weaknesses. This chapter provides guidelines and examples for doing each one.

"I would have done a bibliography, but my sources
prefer to remain anonymous."

A GUIDE TO ANNOTATING A BIBLIOGRAPHY

Annotations vary in length, usually between 150 and 300 words in one or two paragraphs: remember that you're trying to capture the essence of the source as succinctly as possible. You will be expected to DESCRIBE each source and explain what it will contribute to your research—and you may be assigned to EVALUATE sources as well. The following tips will help you get started:

Begin your annotation with complete documentation for the source, following the style assigned by your instructor or most often used in your field—MLA, APA, or some other style. This information will help you or your readers locate the source easily, and it can also be cut and pasted into your final list of WORKS CITED, REFERENCES, or other bibliography.

Identify any authors, along with their credentials. If they have a particular STANCE, note that as well.

Briefly SUMMARIZE *or* DESCRIBE the source's main points and any details that are relevant to your research, making sure to do so accurately and fairly. Note how the source contributes to your research and informs your thinking on the topic—and how you expect to use it in what you write.

If you're writing an evaluative bibliography, consider things that matter to your project: How AUTHORITATIVE is the source? Does it consider multiple perspectives, or a particular view you need to learn about? Does it include a bibliography or CITE any sources you didn't already know about? Be sure to note both its strengths and any limitations.

Alphabetize entries in your bibliography by the lead author's name; if there is no author, use the first word of the title (excluding *a*, *an*, or *the*). And all the annotations in a bibliography should be presented consistently: if one is written in complete sentences, they should all be.

TWO KINDS OF ANNOTATIONS

Olivia Steely is a student at the University of Missouri, St. Louis, where she is majoring in English with a minor in Spanish. The following examples are from an annotated bibliography she compiled while researching the empathetic rhetoric of Dorothy Roudebush, an educator and activist for women's rights. The first is a descriptive entry she wrote for her class, and the second is an evaluative one she wrote for this book.

A descriptive annotation

Leake, Eric. "Writing Pedagogies of Empathy: As Rhetoric and
   Disposition." *Composition Forum*, vol. 34, Jan. 2016,
   compositionforum.com/issue/34/empathy.php.

   This article by a rhetoric professor at Texas State University answers the calls for the teaching of empathy and
   discusses ways that it can be taught in writing classes.
   Leake discusses two theories of empathy and how they
   can be taught—as rhetoric, and as a disposition. Rhetorical empathy, he says, focuses on the "enticements" and
   the "limitations" of empathy as a means of persuasion,
   while dispositional empathy teaches "habits of mind" aimed
   at helping students better understand and engage with
   others. Leake also reviews multiple definitions of empathy and perspectives on it, which provides much more
   context and adds to my own understanding of what empathy can and cannot do.

An evaluative annotation

Leake, Eric. "Writing Pedagogies of Empathy: As Rhetoric and
    Disposition." *Composition Forum*, vol. 34, Jan. 2016,
    compositionforum.com/issue/34/empathy.php.

> This article by a professor of rhetoric addresses the calls
> for teaching empathy and discusses ways that it can be
> taught in writing classes. Leake discusses two theories of
> empathy and how they can be taught—as rhetoric, and as a
> disposition. Rhetorical empathy, he says, focuses on what
> he calls the "enticements" and "limitations" of empathy
> as a means of persuasion, whereas dispositional empathy
> teaches "habits of mind" aimed at helping students better
> understand and engage with others. Even though the many
> detailed suggestions he offers for incorporating empathy
> in a writing class do not pertain to my project, the multiple
> perspectives and definitions he provides will broaden both
> my understanding of empathy and the way I think about
> it. In addition, he's made me aware of what Carl Rogers,
> Krista Ratcliffe, John Duffy, and other scholars have said
> about empathy—and whose work I will now pursue.

REFLECT! If you are lucky enough to find an annotated bibliography someone else has done on a topic you're researching, it can potentially save you time and lead you to important sources you might have missed. See if you can find an annotated bibliography on a topic you're researching. If you do, does it include any sources you haven't found yourself? And if it's an evaluative one, is it helpful to you, and in what ways? If you cannot find an annotated bibliography on your topic, there are quite a few on the web about empathy. Take a look at one, and see how it compares with the examples in this chapter.

17 Synthesizing Ideas

WE ARE DROWNING IN INFORMATION . . . .
THE WORLD HENCEFORTH WILL BE RUN BY SYNTHESIZERS,
PEOPLE ABLE TO PUT TOGETHER THE RIGHT INFORMATION
AT THE RIGHT TIME, THINK CRITICALLY ABOUT IT,
AND MAKE IMPORTANT CHOICES WISELY.

—E. O. WILSON

Should a college education be free? That's your research question. You get started, and your research turns up many different answers: Yes, college should be a universal right, just like K–12. College needs to be affordable, but not free. Making college free would be a "needless windfall" for affluent students; financial aid should be given only to students who really need it. It would never actually be free; the cost would be borne by taxpayers.

These are answers that reflect many different positions and present various kinds of evidence and data, giving you a lot to think about.

As a researcher, you'll need to *synthesize* what your sources say, looking for connections, patterns, ideas, examples, controversies, and more—all things that will help you figure out what you think about your topic and then to support what you say about it. This chapter will help you think about the ideas you find in your sources and then weave some of them in with your own.

Identifying patterns and themes

As a researcher, you will often need to contend with ideas and information from varying points of view—and think about how they connect to one another (or not) and inform, support, or challenge what *you* want to say. That means reading carefully and purposefully, and *with a critical eye but an open mind*. It also means taking notes as you read, noting any similarities or differences, recurring patterns, ideas, citations, or other things. Here are some tips to help you synthesize information as you read this way:

- *What do your sources have in common?* Are there any recurring facts or examples? ideas? issues or controversies? Is there any data that's cited in more than one source?

- *Are there any disagreements among your sources?* Do they take different POSITIONS? Use different methods? Serve different audiences or purposes? Present different kinds of EVIDENCE? Rely on different sources?

- *Do any of your sources cite or refer to one another?* Do they respond to one another in any way? Do any of your sources contain the same links? Are there any sources cited that you haven't seen—and that you should check out?

- *Have you encountered any surprising ideas or* EVIDENCE— things that you now need to investigate?

- *What* GENRES *are your sources?* Magazine articles? Newspaper op-eds? Scholarly arguments? Blog posts? Books? Speeches? If they're all from the same one or two genres, consider checking out other genres as well.

Moving from what your sources say to what you say

The work you do identifying common patterns, themes, and differences among your sources is the first step in synthesizing the information you've found. You may note, for example, that almost all your sources call for one particular solution to a problem—or that each source identifies a different solution to that problem. Synthesizing this information, you could say that there is general agreement (or very little agreement) on how to solve the problem. And of course you'll likely have sources that present sharply different positions. Making sense of it all is a challenge, but it will make you aware of what many others have said about your topic—and get you thinking more about your own position.

The mind's synthesizing powers at work!

In short, the work of synthesizing multiple ideas and perspectives will help you think about (or rethink) your own POSITION. Now is the time to go back to your working THESIS: in light of all you've learned from your sources, do you need to revise it—to focus on one aspect of the topic, or to QUALIFY it in some way? Here are some questions that can help you think about how your sources have affected your thinking about your topic:

- How exactly do your sources relate to your topic or THESIS?
- Are there any ideas or positions in your sources that you want to respond to?
- Do any sources present data or examples that you want to cite or challenge?

- Have your sources changed your views—and if so, how?
- Have any sources brought up questions you hadn't considered and now want to explore?

If so, yay! Good solid research is supposed to open our minds to new possibilities and lead us to see things more clearly and comprehensively. These insights can even lead you to see your topic in a new light and to have new ideas about what you want to say about it.

If, as Zora Neale Hurston says, research is "poking and prying with a purpose," such poking and prying will inevitably lead to new discoveries, to new ideas, and to new understandings. Most important, synthesizing your sources systematically will help you to discover and clarify your own ideas and to come up with your own conclusions—and then to make your own contribution to the conversation.

REFLECT! Choose one or two sources you are working with to see if they themselves have woven in any information taken from other sources. If so, look them up to see how accurately and effectively your source has used them.

Writing that synthesizes information

See how one writer synthesizes several accounts of a famous basketball game to write a lively narrative about a game she did not attend. It's on p. 779.

You will see signs of synthesis at work in much of what you read. Here, for example, is the opening of an article that synthesizes information drawn from multiple sources on the effects that vacations can have on the health of those who take them—and of the planet:

> Beyond souvenirs and suntans, the best reason to take a break may be your own health. For the Helsinki Businessman Study, a 40-year-old cardiovascular-health study... researchers treated men at risk of

heart disease. From 1974 to 2004, those men who took at least three weeks of vacation were 37 percent less likely to die than those who took fewer weeks off (Strandberg et al.).

Even if we don't view time off as a matter of life and death, people who take more of their allotted vacation time tend to find their work more meaningful (West et al.). Vacation can yield other benefits, too. People who took all or most of their paid vacation time to travel were more likely than others to report a recent raise or bonus (U.S. Travel Association).

—BEN HEALY, "Hell Is Other People's Vacations"

So far, so good. But Healy goes on to synthesize information from other sources that share another common pattern—concern for how vacation travel is affecting our planet:

Tourism's carbon footprint grew four times as much as expected from 2009 to 2013, and accounted for 8 percent of all greenhouse-gas emissions in that period (Lenzen). What's more, the travel industry is expected to consume 92 percent more water in 2050 than it did in 2010, and 189 percent more land. In other news, people are less likely to recycle while on vacation (Oliver).

The patterns and themes Healy traces from his sources and synthesizes into these paragraphs lead him to draw an ironic conclusion of his own: "So for your own health and sanity, book that vacation. But for everyone else's, please travel as sustainably as you can, and take it easy with *Instagram*." And notice that he includes IN-TEXT DOCUMENTATION for the sources he cites. You need to do that as well.

Here's one more example. Researcher Peggy Orenstein spent two years talking to more than 100 young men between the ages of 16 and 21 about what they think it means to be a man and about how they view masculinity. In the following paragraph, she synthesizes information drawn from these interviews and from a recent survey.

[W]hen asked to describe the attributes of "the ideal guy," these boys appeared to be harking back to 1955. Dominance. Aggression. Rugged good looks (with an emphasis on height). Sexual prowess. Stoicism. Athleticism. Wealth (at least some day). It's not that these qualities, properly channeled, are bad. But while a 2018 national survey of more than 1,000 10- to 19-year-olds conducted by the polling firm PerryUndem found that young women believe there were many ways to be a girl . . . young men described just one narrow route to successful masculinity. One-third said they felt compelled to suppress their feelings, to "suck it up" or "be a man" when they were sad or scared, and more than 40 percent said that when they were angry, society expected them to be combative.

—PEGGY ORENSTEIN, "The Miseducation of the American Boy"

What Orenstein has done is to study the responses of these 100 young men, looking for patterns and themes and trends—and then reporting the results of that synthesis, in this case the characteristics these young men claim make up "the ideal man." Note that she does not cite the interview sources because they are her own research. In addition, she does not cite the source of the 2018 national survey because she is publishing this article in a magazine—*The Atlantic*—that doesn't include formal documentation. In the writing you do in your academic classes, you would cite both of these sources—your own research as well as the national survey.

REFLECT! Why not take **Peggy Orenstein**'s question ("What do you think are the attributes of the 'ideal guy'?") and interview several males you know—classmates, friends, family members. With their permission, record their responses and then look for patterns, similarities, differences, themes, and so on—and synthesize these findings into one brief paragraph.

18 Quoting, Paraphrasing, Summarizing

TO QUOTE? TO PARAPHRASE? OR SUMMARIZE?
THAT IS THE QUESTION.

—CAROLE CLARK PAPPER

Good researchers are part detective, part explorer. Their sources provide clues and point to new leads; they identify new directions that delve deeper and deeper into knowledge about the topic of research. But researchers are also part conductor, gathering sources, bringing them together to make beautiful music—not in a symphony but in a compelling, eye-opening research project.

As the conductor, you are in charge of your project—the one who discovers a new way of looking at your topic, who decides what conclusions can be drawn from the evidence you consider, who moves from a challenging research question to a thorough exploration of the question and its implications, and eventually to staking your claim, developing a thesis and supporting it. And just as an orchestra's conductor decides when to bring in the string section or turn to a flute solo, so you decide when to bring in your sources for greatest effect.

The sources you bring in act like supporting players or voices, highlighting and accenting the points you are making but without drowning out or overpowering your own voice. In most instances, you will bring these supporting voices in with a quotation (the precise words of a source, enclosed in quotation marks), a paraphrase (ideas in a passage from a source, in your own words), or a summary (a brief statement of a source's major points).

A way to establish your authority

Bringing the ideas and voices of others into your writing shows that you understand the context surrounding your topic, that you know what others have said about it and the varying perspectives they bring. In other words, it helps build your credibility and trustworthiness to write on the topic: you know what you're talking about and are now a part of the conversation. And finally, judicious quoting, paraphrasing, and summarizing allow you to be the conductor, to direct the action in your research essay to the desired end.

Deciding whether to quote, paraphrase, or summarize

While there are no hard-and-fast rules for choosing whether to quote, paraphrase, or summarize, here are some guidelines that can help you decide.

Quote

- If an idea is so important and powerfully stated that rewording it might weaken or distort it
- When it's a passage you intend to analyze

- To call attention to the author's expertise in order to help establish your own credibility
- To make sure you are presenting a source fairly and accurately, especially if it's one you do not agree with

Paraphrase

- When the precise words aren't important, but there's a point or some details you want to include
- If the language will be hard for your audience to understand

Summarize

- A lengthy passage when the point is important but the details are not

QUOTING

Quoting someone's exact words helps ensure that you're representing their ideas accurately. By quoting sources directly, you show that you're being careful and respectful, letting those you quote speak for themselves rather than interpreting what they say. Be sure to use the exact words of your source, and to enclose them in quotation marks. And make sure to frame the quotation by introducing it and then explaining how it relates to your point.

In his article on rap and poetry, Adam Bradley relies heavily on quotations. See how well they work on p. 632.

Enclose short quotations in quotation marks within your text. If you're following MLA style, short quotations should be no longer than four typed lines. If you're following APA style, short means no more than forty words. The following example is in MLA style.

> Michael Lewis, author of *Moneyball* and *The Big Short*, says in the Afterword to his 2002 book *Next: The Future Just Happened* that he "began writing this book after the Internet had become a commercial joke." In raising his voice in opposition to that view, Lewis felt he was being "ridiculously brave," though in retrospect

> neither he nor those whose views he was challenging seem to
> have gotten the Internet's significance right (*Next* 237). Today,
> eighteen years after Lewis's book came out, theorists and pundits
> are still trying to determine that significance.

In this example, the short quotations are incorporated into the sentences of the text.

Set off long quotations as BLOCK QUOTATIONS, indented from the left margin. No need to enclose them in quotation marks, but you do need to indent them five spaces (or one-half inch), either MLA or APA style. What counts as long varies: it's more than four lines for MLA or forty words for APA. The following example is in APA style.

Here is Berkeley professor Jabari Mahiri using a block quotation in a study of the language used by high school coaches and their players:

> As one technique for focusing on players' accomplishments and
> improvements, coaches gave extended turns of praise both to the
> team as a whole and to individual players, as when coach LeRoy
> Crowe pulled a player to the side after a game to say:
>> You played a good game out there my man. You know that?
>> People weren't recognizing what you were doing, but the
>> coaches saw what you were doing. You were playin' that
>> point guard position. You were looking down low. You hit
>> Kendall with a nice pass down there. You remember that pass
>> he scooped up? You weren't hitting your free throws. But,
>> I mean, we recognized that you stayed under control. (p. 34)
>
> —JABARI MAHIRI, *Shooting for Excellence:*
> *African American and Youth Culture in New Century Schools*

In this passage, Mahiri uses a long quotation to let coach Crowe speak for himself, providing an example of the kind of coach-player interaction Mahiri is studying. Note too that the parenthetical documentation comes after the period at the end of the quotation.

Quoting poetry

You can quote up to three lines of poetry in your text, enclosed within quotation marks. Separate lines with slashes, leaving one space on either side of the slash.

> Appointed in 2019, Joy Harjo, a member of Mvskoke/Creek Nation, is the first Native American Poet Laureate of the United States. In "Remember," a poem about what is most important to remember in one's life, she encourages readers to "Remember you are all people and all people are you. / Remember you are this universe and this universe is you" (lines 9-10). Here Harjo suggests that our memories should encode our common humanity.

If you're quoting four or more lines of poetry, set them off in a BLOCK QUOTATION, indented five spaces from the left margin. Set the lines as they appear in the original poem.

> Alas rhetoric can be used for harmful purposes: to humiliate and belittle, to confuse and distract, to distort and mislead. In W. B. Yeats's haunting words, written amidst the horrors of the great war in 1919:
>
>> Things fall apart; the centre cannot hold;
>> Mere anarchy is loosed upon the world,
>> The blood-dimmed tide is loosed, and everywhere
>> The ceremony of innocence is drowned;
>> The best lack all conviction, while the worst
>> Are full of passionate intensity. (lines 3-8)
>
> Today it may well seem that the worst among us are the ones whose "passionate intensity" is being heard. But giving in to that vision would mean giving up on rhetoric as ethical communication. And that we cannot do.

Changing a quotation to fit into your text

Put ELLIPSES in places where you omit words from a quotation because they're unnecessary for your point. Use three dots with a space before each one and after the last dot. If, however, you omit an entire sentence or more, add a period before the ellipses.

> In 1879, the Scottish philosopher Alexander Bain wrote one of the few nineteenth-century grammars to approve of singular *they* . . . declaring, "When both genders are implied, it is allowable to use the plural. . . . Grammarians frequently call this construction an error, not reflecting that it is equally an error to apply *his* to feminine subjects. The best writers furnish examples of the use of the plural as a mode of getting out of the difficulty."
>
> —DENNIS BARON, *What's Your Pronoun?*

Put brackets around any words that you insert in a quotation to make it fit grammatically into your text, or that you add to clarify something that might otherwise be unclear.

> In 1885, the linguist Fred Newton Scott observed that pretty much everyone used the singular *they*, both people who care about good grammar, and those who don't, noting, "The word *they* is being used as a [common gender] pronoun every day by millions of persons who are not particular about their language, and every other day by several thousands who are particular" (qtd. in Baron 167).

Punctuating quotations

When a quotation is followed by other punctuation, that punctuation goes inside the final quotation mark in some cases and outside in others. Following are some guidelines on where it goes:

Commas and periods go *inside* the closing quotation marks, except when there's in-text documentation—in that case, the documentation goes after the closing quotation mark, and the end punctuation that's part of your sentence goes *after* the parentheses.

> Chelsea's mother-in-law is disappointed that she is still working. "A mother's place is in the home," she says to Chelsea. "Your kids will be ruined."
>
> —JOEY FRANKLIN, "Working at Wendy's"

> Nothing in my education had provided me with strategies for resisting certain versions of whiteness that may privilege me but oppress others. I state this lack and unearned privilege . . . simply because I want to make them visible. For "only by visualizing this privilege and incorporating it into discourse can people of good faith combat discrimination" in ways that prevent their doing "more harm than good" (Wildman and Davis 660, 661).
>
> —KRISTA RATCLIFFE, *Rhetorical Listening: Identification, Gender, Whiteness*

Exclamation points and question marks go *inside* closing quotation marks if they are part of the quoted text. But they go *outside* the closing quotation marks if they are a part of the sentence you're writing, not a part of the quotation. And if there's any parenthetical documentation, it goes after the closing quotation mark—and the end punctuation that's part of your sentence goes after the parentheses.

> Noting that most people are more likely to cheat on their taxes if they believe others are not paying a fair share of what they earn, Rene Chun asks "So why are Americans still paying?" One answer—that taxpayers now have to list a Social Security number for every dependent—has meant that "the number of dependents nationwide shrank by millions." It's worth noting, however, that "some of the disappeared had names like Fluffy"!

Colons and semicolons always go *outside* the closing quotation marks.

> "Despite deep IRS budget cuts," Chun says, "most Americans still pay their income taxes every year"; indeed, he goes on to say that "most of us feel *obliged* to pay" ("Why Americans," par. 7).

See p. 345 (MLA) and p. 388 (APA) on punctuating parenthetical documentation with long quotations.

Parenthetical documentation goes after the quotation mark—and put any end punctuation that's part of your sentence after the parentheses.

> The restaurant became the place where Rosie studied human behavior, puzzling over the problems of her regular customers and refining her ability to deal with people in a difficult world. She took pride in "being among the public," she'd say. "There isn't a day that goes by in the restaurant that you don't learn something" (451).

—MIKE ROSE, "Blue-Collar Brilliance"

Explaining how a quotation relates to your point

When you insert a quotation into a text you're writing, you need to explain what it means and how it relates to what you are saying. If you were writing an essay about how race affects college admissions, for instance, here's something you might quote—and how you'd explain it.

> Educators are now beginning to understand the degree to which schools operate on the basis of contradictory principles. Professor Carmen Kynard has pointed out that American colleges and universities have often practiced exclusionary policies while claiming to do the opposite, a move Kynard's grandmother referred to as "runnin with the rabbits but huntin with the dogs"(19). Such contradictions, in other words, are anything but accidental.

PARAPHRASING

When you paraphrase, you restate information from a source in your own words and your own sentence structures. Paraphrase when there are ideas you want to convey but the original wording is not important. Be careful not to use the same words or structures, which could be seen as plagiarism—and make sure that you represent the original text accurately. A good paraphrase demonstrates that you have read the source carefully—and that you understand what it means! And even though you're using your own words, be sure to acknowledge where the ideas came from by naming the author and including parenthetical documentation. Here's a paragraph from an article in *The Atlantic*, followed by two possible paraphrases:

> For 23 years starting in 1885, Belgium's King Leopold II was the "proprietor," as he called himself, of the misnamed Congo Free State, the territory that today is the Democratic Republic of Congo. Exasperated by the declining power of European monarchs, Leopold wanted a place where he could reign supreme, unencumbered by voters or a parliament, and in the Congo he got it. He made a fortune from his privately owned colony—well over $1.1 billion in today's dollars—chiefly by enslaving much of its male population as laborers to tap wild rubber vines. The king's soldiers would march into village after village and hold the women hostage, in order to force the men to go deep into the rain forest for weeks at a time to gather wild rubber. Hunting, fishing, and the cultivation of crops were all disrupted, and the army seized much of what food was left. The birth rate plummeted and, weakened by hunger, people succumbed to diseases they might otherwise have survived. Demographers estimate that the Congo's population may have been slashed by as much as half, or some 10 million people.
>
> —ADAM HOCHSCHILD, "When Museums Have Ugly Pasts"

UNACCEPTABLE PARAPHRASE

In 1895, Belgium's King Leopold II was the "owner" of what he called the Congo Free State, the country that's now known as the Democratic Republic of Congo. Granting himself total power, he made a fortune by enslaving most of the male population, destroying the traditional way of life, decimating the birth rate, and leading to the death of some 10 million people.

This paraphrase fails to acknowledge the author or document the source and borrows too much from the original syntax and wording, using some of it word for word and other parts barely changed: "In 1895, Belgium's King Leopold II," "by enslaving most of the male population." It also misrepresents the original, saying that 10 million people died; the original says that the population may have declined by that number, but some of that decline would have been likely because the birth rate "plummeted."

ACCEPTABLE PARAPHRASE

According to historian Adam Hochschild, Belgium's King Leopold II was once the self-proclaimed owner of the Congo Free State (now the Democratic Republic of Congo). From 1885 to 1908, he exercised total control over the Congolese people, amassing a personal fortune mostly by forcing most of the male population into the rain forest to harvest wild rubber. This policy disrupted the traditional means of food production, which led to hunger, disease, and a declining birthrate. All told, that resulted in a steep decline in the Congo's population—by 10 million people, according to some estimates ("When Museums").

This paraphrase captures the main points of the passage without relying on the original wording or sentence structures—and it identifies the author and provides parenthetical documentation to the source.

SUMMARIZING

A summary captures a source's main ideas concisely, and in your own words. Unlike a paraphrase, it leaves out the details. Your goal is to provide just enough information to sum up the point you are summarizing. When you're summarizing a source to cite in your own writing, you'll want to make it as brief as possible—maybe only a sentence or two. As with a quotation or paraphrase, you'll need to credit the author and provide parenthetical documentation. Here's a summary of the Adam Hochschild paragraph from page 291:

From 1885 to 1908, Belgium's King Leopold II claimed ownership and total control of today's Democratic Republic of Congo, disrupting the people's traditional way of life and giving rise to hunger, disease, and the death of millions of people (Hochschild).

REFLECT! Look at the passage on page 286 in which **Jabari Mahiri** quotes Coach LeRoy Crowe. Try your hand at summarizing and paraphrasing what Coach Crowe said. Then compare these with the direct quotation, and write a paragraph about why you think Mahiri chose to quote rather than summarize or paraphrase.

INCORPORATING SOURCE MATERIALS

Whether you quote, paraphrase, or summarize a source, you need to introduce it with a signal phrase and explain how the information you're citing contributes to your own ideas.

Use SIGNAL PHRASES to introduce source materials, usually identifying the author and saying something about their credentials if need be:

> New Mexico writer and teacher Andrew Schmookler *said* he cringes when grammar rules are broken. Yet he also proposed *het, hes, hem* as a new gender-neutral pronoun, *arguing*, "Language is ours to make. (This is not France!) . . . Power to the people" (241).

Note the two signal verbs in this example: *said* to simply report what he said, but *arguing* to note something he was advocating. While you can always use a neutral verb like *say* or *think*, it's better to choose a verb that reflects the speaker's STANCE. For example:

> Erma Bombeck *urges* us to "Seize the moment," reminding us to "Remember all those women on the *Titanic* who waved off the dessert cart" (*Forever Erma* 56).

We could have written that Bombeck *says* to seize the moment, but we think that *urges* is more dynamic, fun—and accurate.

And while signal phrases often come first in a sentence, putting them in the middle or at the end of a sentence works as well—and is a way of adding variety to our writing.

"How about those Chiefs!" Andy Reid *shouted* from the podium after the Kansas City Chiefs won the 2020 Superbowl. "Pat Mahomes and all of his boys, our defense taking care of business. The coaches, man, a great job of keeping things right at the right time. It was a beautiful thing."

"Knowing what you don't know is more useful than being brilliant," *advised* Berkshire Hathaway vice chair Charlie Munger (101).

SOME USEFUL SIGNAL VERBS

acknowledge	conclude	observe
add	contend	point out
advocate	declare	refute
agree	demand	report
argue	disagree	respond
assert	dispute	say
believe	imply	suggest
claim	insist	think
comment	note	urge

Verb tenses. MLA style requires the present tense (*Beyoncé asserts*) or present perfect (*Jay-Z has said*) in signal phrases that introduce source material—but the past tense (*in 2013 Pharrell urged us to "clap along"*) when you give the date when the source was written. APA recommends the past tense (*asserted*) or the present perfect (*has* or *have asserted*)—but the present tense (*asserts*) when you're citing the implications of an experiment or findings that are generally agreed on.

REFLECT! Look over something you've written with an eye for how you've incorporated the words or ideas of others. Whether you've quoted, paraphrased, or summarized, think about why you chose that way—and then, try it a different way. Then look at your signal phrases: are there any more accurate or interesting verbs you might use? And where have you put the signal phrases? If they're all at the beginning of a sentence, try some in the middle or at the end.

19 Giving Credit, Using Sources Ethically

THERE'S NOTHING NEW UNDER THE SUN.

—ECCLESIASTES 1:9

IF I HAVE SEEN FURTHER, IT IS BY
STANDING ON THE SHOULDERS OF GIANTS.

—SIR ISAAC NEWTON

Today, when "new" and "new and improved" scream at us from every direction, it's worth wondering whether King Solomon got it wrong when he said there's nothing new under the sun. But if you stop and think about every "new" technology, every "new" idea, even every "new" story, you will soon find that they all build on earlier thinking, or earlier research. The iPhone was a new kind of phone, but it was by no means the first telephone. *Frozen* was a new film in 2013, but its story is based on "The Snow Queen," a fairy tale written by Hans Christian Andersen that was first published in 1845. Just as Isaac Newton said, what's "new" is made possible only by "standing on the shoulders" of others. Think about how this applies to your own life: Can you even begin to trace all the ways you have been influenced by the words and ideas of others? Certainly you have already stood on the shoulders of a few giants. The same is true of just about anything you write, especially when you write something that is based on research. And that's just one reason that you need to give credit to anyone whose words or ideas have informed your own. This chapter will help you know which sources you need to acknowledge— and how to use them ethically and without accidentally plagiarizing.

Who owns words and ideas, anyway?

In some cultures, words and ideas are shared, not "owned" by individuals. In others, using another person's words or ideas is viewed as a compliment, a testimony to that person's wisdom that does not need to be acknowledged explicitly. Well into the Renaissance, in fact, you could own a pig or a cow or a bed—but you couldn't own words: Shakespeare borrowed right and left from prior sources without attribution and without restraint—indeed, that was part of his genius.

Following the Copyright Act of 1710, however, a complex network of copyright and patent laws developed as a means of protecting the words, images, and ideas of people and businesses. These laws increasingly gave rights of ownership of both words and ideas, as long as they were "expressed" in some medium, such as in writing or speech—and these laws form the basis for the documentation systems developed by groups such as the Modern Language Association (MLA) and the American Psychological Association (APA) and used in schools and universities today.

So what do intellectual property and copyright laws have to do with you? It turns out that the answer is "a lot"—and not everyone is happy about this fact of academic life. Law professor Lawrence Lessig argues that such laws act as a deterrent to innovation by making it harder and harder for students and others today to use some words and images, especially those found on the internet. In particular,

Lessig points to what he calls the "remix culture" (in which existing works are changed or combined to produce something new) as a source of great creativity that is being "choked" by traditional copyright laws.

Lessig was, in fact, instrumental in expanding the notion of "fair use" and in creating an alternative system of attribution known as Creative Commons (CC), which offers "copyright licenses anyone can use to mark their work with the freedoms they want it to carry." In 2019, this non-profit organization—whose motto is "When we share, everyone wins"—launched *CC Search*, a tool that lets you search for openly licensed and public domain works that anyone can use. Many but not all are available free of charge.

While Creative Commons and other open-source organizations are expanding the notion of "fair use" and providing alternative systems of attribution, and while the conventions surrounding documentation of sources will surely continue to evolve, at this moment it's still important to cite all sources you do not create yourself. And that means paying attention! Uploading and downloading files, patching things together from various sites, cutting and pasting, jumping from one site to another and another: these everyday activities call for you to put on the brakes long enough to identify every source you intend to use and record its author or sponsor, along with where you got it.

> Check out Creative Commons at search.creative commons.org/.

Why it's important to credit your sources

While we don't routinely credit others in everyday conversation, it's important to do so in academic contexts. Giving credit to others when it's due says a lot about your values, about your fairness and trustworthiness—in other words, it demonstrates your academic integrity. Acknowledging where some of your ideas come from also shows that you've done your homework, that you know what others have said about your topic and that you understand and have considered their points of view. In short, it helps to establish your own

> See how June Jordan uses and credits her students' writing in a famous essay about language on p. 647—and what power it adds to her argument.

In everyday conversation and speeches, we don't often credit those whose ideas have influenced our own.

CREDIBILITY to write on the topic. More than that, it shows you to be openhanded, crediting others for what you've gotten from them— and sharing the credit for what you yourself have written.

What sources do you need to document?

You need to DOCUMENT most ideas, texts, images, and sounds that you CITE from other sources. But there are exceptions.

Sources you do not need to document

- *Materials you've created or collected*, such as photos you took or data you collected from a survey you conducted.

- *Common knowledge*: well-known events (the twin towers collapsed on 9/11), facts (nearly 3,000 people died on 9/11), uncontroversial information (many Americans were glued to their TVs on 9/11).

- *Well-known quotations*: "Yes we can," "Houston, we have a problem."

- *Information from public documents* such as the Bill of Rights, the US Constitution, and other such texts.

Sources you do need to document

- *Any materials you did not create yourself,* including charts, tables, graphs, infographics, and images. And if you've created a chart or graph using data from another source, you need to acknowledge that source.

- *Direct quotations, paraphrases, and summaries.* The only exception is famous or widely known quotations, which do not need to be documented.

- *Controversial information.* If you cite something that's debatable, document it so that readers can check out the source for themselves.

- *Anything you have a question about!* If you're in doubt about whether or not to document a source, err on the side of caution and include formal documentation.

Asking for permission

"Fair use" laws allow college students who are using material from copyrighted sources to use passages and images without getting permission from the author—as long as you are writing for "educational purposes" and provide full documentation. But here's the catch: if your writing will be posted online, where it can be seen by everyone, you need to have explicit permission from the copyright owner.

One student I know learned this lesson the hard way when an award-winning essay she wrote was posted on the award website. Within weeks, she heard from the author of a cartoon she'd included in her essay asking her to remove the essay from the web immediately and threatening legal action if she did not comply. Another student whose essay was posted to a class website was shocked and embarrassed when his teacher received an angry email from a professor at another college, saying the student had used too much of her work in his essay—and that he had not documented it fully enough.

So if in doubt, it's best to play it very safe and to get permission (in writing) for any source material that you post online. Here is an example that will help you request permission:

From: smoller@bankstreet.edu
To: lunsford@stanford.edu
Subject: Request for permission

Dear Professor Lunsford:

I am writing to request permission to quote from your essay "Teaching Writing in an Age of Misinformation and Lies." I am working on a presentation for my writing class on the proliferation of fake news and would like to use your definition to help clarify the subject. My presentation will be posted to our class website and accessible to all. If you are willing to grant permission, I will give full credit to you and will provide complete documentation for the journal article in which it appeared, along with the URL of the site where I first discovered your work.

Thank you very much for considering this request,

Susanna Moller

Remember to credit any collaborators!

If you have collaborated with others on your research or writing, be sure to credit and thank them either in a footnote at the bottom of a page or in an endnote on a separate page. See page 315 for how to format such notes in MLA style and pages 364–65 for how to do so in APA style.

Avoiding plagiarism

Presenting someone else's words or ideas as if they were your own and without giving credit is dishonest and unethical—and is considered plagiarism. It's a masquerade, with serious consequences.

Every year, students receive failing grades or are suspended from college for plagiarizing. Journalists, professors, and public figures have lost their positions or damaged their reputations when they've been caught using someone else's words without giving credit. Plagiarism is often intentional—witness the many online "paper mills" that guarantee an A for a certain price. But it is also easy to detect: even a quick *Google* search will often reveal the source!

Often, however, it is unintentional. Especially if you are writing about an unfamiliar topic, it can be tricky to incorporate the words or ideas of others (your sources) fairly and to acknowledge them sufficiently. Instead, you may do some of what Professor Rebecca Moore Howard calls PATCHWRITING, using material from sources in ways that stick too closely to the original wording or structure.

In fact, I've made this kind of mistake myself, when I was in junior high and writing about my hero at the time, Albert Schweitzer. With no internet to search and a very small school library, I had written to my state library asking for resources and was thrilled when a package of printed articles about Schweitzer arrived. I patched pieces of those articles into what I was writing, sometimes remembering to credit a source but often not. I felt very proud of my work. Lucky for me, I had a teacher who took the time to show me how to integrate the sources into my writing, how to use quotation marks, and how to paraphrase without copying the original author's wording or syntax. Better yet, she explained why it was important to credit my sources—and how to do so. Lesson learned!

As this example suggests, patchwriting can be a useful stage for learning how to work with sources: it certainly helped me learn a lot about Albert Schweitzer and his work. And it was a stepping-stone on the path to becoming a confident researcher and to citing sources ethically.

But some instructors will see patchwriting as plagiarism, even if it's documented. So it's something you'll want to avoid. Let's take a look at how it happens, and how you can weave the ideas of others into your own writing by using your own words and sentence structure. Imagine that you want to summarize the ideas from the following passage:

> In some professions, early decline is inescapable. No one expects an Olympic athlete to remain competitive until age 60. But in many physically nondemanding occupations, we implicitly reject the inevitability of decline before very old age. Sure, our quads and hamstrings may weaken a little as we age. But as long as we retain our marbles, our quality of work as a writer, lawyer, executive, or entrepreneur should remain high up to the very end, right? Many people think so. I recently met a man a bit older than I am who told me he planned to "push it until the wheels come off." In effect, he planned to stay at the very top of his game by any means necessary, and then keel over.
>
> But the odds are he won't be able to. The data are shockingly clear that for most people, in most fields, decline starts earlier than almost anyone thinks.
>
> According to research by Dean Keith Simonton, a professor emeritus of psychology at UC Davis and one of the world's leading experts on the trajectories of creative careers, success and productivity increase for the first 20 years after the inception of a career, on average. So if you start a career in earnest at 30, expect to do your best work around 50 and go into decline soon after that.
>
> —ARTHUR C. BROOKS, "Your Professional Decline Is Coming (Much) Sooner Than You Think: Here's How to Make the Most of It"

Suppose you wanted to make sure you remember the key information in this passage for a class discussion you are going to lead. You might be tempted to patch together a summary like this:

PATCHWRITTEN SUMMARY

Arthur C. Brooks explains that while many people believe they can stay at the top of their game well into their 60s and 70s and beyond, the odds are that these people are wrong. Brooks refers to research conducted by Dean Keith Simonton, an expert on tracking creative careers who says that success usually occurs in the first 20 years after the beginning of a career, so at age 50 people who started out at 30 are hitting the time when they will start to decline.

This summary captures the gist of Brooks's argument, but it uses far too much of Brooks's own language ("stay at the top of their game," "the odds are, "in the first 20 years"). It's fine for studying, but not for writing a summary you'd submit to an instructor as your own work.

Now take a look at another summary, one that captures the main idea in the student's own words and includes a direct quotation:

ACCEPTABLE SUMMARY

While some cling to the notion that their work level will "remain high up to the very end," Arthur C. Brooks presents research that contradicts those beliefs (70). In fact, this research reveals that high-level work performance begins to decline after about 20 years into a career.

This summary relies on the writer's own language and sentence structure and uses quotation marks to enclose language taken directly from the source. It restates the main idea of the passage clearly and simply—and leaves out any details that won't be necessary for the writer's purposes. For instance, it omits information about Brooks's sources, which won't be used in the essay the student is writing on attitudes toward aging in the workplace. Finally, he documents the page where he found the original passage.

Avoiding plagiarism starts with taking meticulous notes and being very, very careful as you incorporate the words or ideas of others into your own writing. For sources you intend to use, take down all the information you'll need for a list of works cited or references, make sure that paraphrases or summaries do not use any wording or sentence structures from the original, and enclose any words you may want to include in quotation marks. And if you have concerns about how to incorporate sources into your text, get advice from your instructor or a consultant in your school's writing center.

Joining the conversation ethically

Remember: your words are the ones that count the most in what you say—they are your way of getting in on the conversation about subjects you care about, sharing what you have learned with others and listening hard to learn from them. You'll be citing sources for sure, but those sources should play second fiddle to you and the point you are making. Nevertheless, you want to give them all the credit they deserve. That's how you become part of the larger conversation—ethically!

REFLECT! Look at something you've written that relies on outside sources. Read it carefully, paying attention to how well you've integrated words or ideas from sources into your writing: how you introduced and explained them, how you credited their authors, and how they support what you say. How successfully have you used your sources, and what might you do differently next time?

20 MLA Style

DOCUMENTATION IS THE MEANS [OF RECORDING]
SCHOLARLY CONVERSATIONS, AND THE
SPECIFICS OF THOSE CONVERSATIONS MATTER.

—KATHLEEN FITZPATRICK, *MLA HANDBOOK*

W hat started out in 1951 as a 31-page style
sheet for scholars submitting articles
to the Modern Language Association's
journal soon evolved into the *MLA Handbook*, now
in its eighth edition. MLA style, recommended or
required by some disciplines in the humanities,
calls for brief IN-TEXT DOCUMENTATION and complete
documentation in a list of WORKS CITED at the end of
the text. Such documentation is important: it gives
credit where credit is due, enables your readers
to find sources you have used, and shows that you
have done your homework. This chapter provides
templates and examples to help you document the
many different sources you're likely to cite.

Formatting a research essay   345
Student essay, MLA style   347

Throughout this chapter, you'll find color-coded templates and examples to help you see how writers include source information in their texts and in their lists of works cited: orange for author, editor, translator, and other contributors; yellow for titles; blue for publication information—date of publication, page number(s), DOIs, and other location information.

TITLE	AUTHOR	PUBLICATION

In-text documentation

Whenever you quote, paraphrase, or summarize a source in your writing, you need to provide brief documentation that tells readers what you took from the source and where in the source you found that information. This brief documentation also refers readers to the full entry in your works-cited list, so begin with whatever comes first there: the author, the title, or a description of the source.

You can mention the author or title either in a signal phrase— "Toni Morrison writes," "In *Beowulf*," "According to the article 'Every Patient's Nightmare'"—or in parentheses—(Morrison). If relevant, include pages or other details about where you found the information in the parenthetical reference: (Morrison 67).

Shorten any lengthy titles or descriptions in parentheses by including the first noun with any preceding adjectives and omitting any initial articles (*Norton Field Guide* for *The Norton Field Guide to Writing*). If the title doesn't start with a noun, use the first phrase or clause (*How to Be* for *How to Be an Antiracist*). Use the full title if it's short.

The first two examples below show basic in-text documentation of a work by one author. Variations on those examples follow. The examples illustrate the MLA style of using quotation marks around titles of short works and italicizing titles of long works.

1. AUTHOR NAMED IN A SIGNAL PHRASE

If you mention the author in a signal phrase, put only the page number(s) in parentheses. Do not write *page* or *p*. The first time you mention the author, use their first and last names. You can usually omit any middle initials.

> David McCullough describes John Adams's hands as those of someone used to manual labor (18).

2. AUTHOR NAMED IN PARENTHESES

If you do not mention the author in a signal phrase, put the author's last name in parentheses along with any page number(s). Do not use punctuation between the name and the page number(s).

> Adams is said to have had "the hands of a man accustomed to pruning his own trees, cutting his own hay, and splitting his own firewood" (McCullough 18).

Whether you use a signal phrase and parentheses or parentheses only, try to put the parenthetical documentation at the end of the sentence or as close as possible to the material you've cited—without awkwardly interrupting the sentence. When a parenthetical reference comes at the end of the sentence, the period goes at the very end.

3. TWO OR MORE WORKS BY THE SAME AUTHOR

If you cite multiple works by one author, include the title of the work you are citing either in the signal phrase or in parentheses.

> Robert Kaplan insists that understanding power in the Near East requires "Western leaders who know when to intervene, and do so without illusions" (*Eastward to Tartary* 330).

Put a comma between author and title if both are in the parentheses.

> Understanding power in the Near East requires "Western leaders who know when to intervene, and do so without illusions" (Kaplan, *Eastward to Tartary* 330).

4. AUTHORS WITH THE SAME LAST NAME

Give each author's first and last names in any signal phrase, or add the author's first initial in the parenthetical reference.

> "Imaginative" applies not only to modern literature but also to writing of all periods, whereas "magical" is often used in writing about Arthurian romances (A. Wilson 25).

TITLE	AUTHOR	PUBLICATION

5. TWO OR MORE AUTHORS

For a work with two authors, name both. If you first mention them in a signal phrase, give their first and last names.

> Lori Carlson and Cynthia Ventura's stated goal is to introduce Julio Cortázar, Marjorie Agosín, and other Latin American writers to an audience of English-speaking adolescents (v).

For a work by three or more authors that you mention in a signal phrase, you can either name them all or name the first author followed by *and others* or *and colleagues*. If you mention them in a parenthetical reference, name the first author followed by *et al.*

> Phyllis Anderson and colleagues describe British literature thematically (A54-A67).

> One survey of British literature breaks the contents into thematic groupings (Anderson et al. A54-A67).

6. ORGANIZATION OR GOVERNMENT AS AUTHOR

In a signal phrase, use the full name of the organization: American Academy of Arts and Sciences. In parentheses, use the shortest noun phrase, omitting any initial articles: American Academy.

> The US government can be direct when it wants to be. For example, it sternly warns, "If you are overpaid, we will recover any payments not due you" (Social Security Administration 12).

7. AUTHOR UNKNOWN

If you don't know the author, use the work's title in a signal phrase or in a parenthetical reference.

> A powerful editorial in *The New York Times* asserts that healthy liver donor Mike Hurewitz died because of "frightening" faulty postoperative care ("Every Patient's Nightmare").

8. LITERARY WORKS

When referring to common literary works that are available in many different editions, give the page numbers from the edition you are using, followed by information that will let readers of any edition locate the text you are citing.

NOVELS AND PROSE PLAYS. Give the page number followed by a semicolon and any chapter, section, or act numbers, separated by commas.

> In *Pride and Prejudice*, Mrs. Bennet shows no warmth toward Jane when she returns from Netherfield (Austen 105; ch. 12).

VERSE PLAYS. Give act, scene, and line numbers, separated with periods.

> Shakespeare continues the vision theme when Macbeth says, "Thou hast no speculation in those eyes / Which thou dost glare with" (*Macbeth* 3.3.96-97).

POEMS. Give part and line numbers, separated by periods. If a poem has only line numbers, use *line* or *lines* only in the first reference.

> Walt Whitman sets up opposing adjectives and nouns in "Song of Myself" when he says, "I am of old and young, of the foolish as much as the wise, / ... a child as well as a man" (16.330-32).

> One description of the mere in *Beowulf* is "not a pleasant place" (line 1372). Later, it is labeled "the awful place" (1378).

9. WORK IN AN ANTHOLOGY

Name the author(s) of the work, not the editor of the anthology.

> "It is the teapots that truly shock," according to Cynthia Ozick in her essay on teapots as metaphor (70).

> In *In Short: A Collection of Creative Nonfiction*, readers will find both an essay on Scottish tea (Hiestand) and a piece on teapots as metaphors (Ozick).

10. ENCYCLOPEDIA OR DICTIONARY

Acknowledge an entry in an encyclopedia or dictionary by giving the author's name, if available. For an entry without an author, give the entry's title.

> According to *Funk and Wagnall's New World Encyclopedia,* early in his career, most of Kubrick's income came from "hustling chess games in Washington Square Park" ("Kubrick, Stanley").

11. LEGAL DOCUMENTS

For legal cases, give whatever comes first in the works-cited entry. If you are citing a government document in parentheses and multiple entries in your works-cited list start with the same government author, give as much of the name as you need to differentiate the sources.

> In 2015, for the first time, all states were required to license and recognize the marriages of same-sex couples (United States, Supreme Court).

12. SACRED TEXT

When citing a sacred text such as the Bible or the Qur'an for the first time, give the title of the edition as well as the book, chapter, and verse (or their equivalent), separated by periods. MLA recommends abbreviating the names of the books of the Bible in parenthetical references. Later citations from the same edition do not have to repeat its title.

> The wording from *The New English Bible* follows: "In the beginning of creation, when God made heaven and earth, the earth was without form and void . . ." (Gen. 1.1-2).

13. MULTIVOLUME WORK

If you cite more than one volume of a multivolume work, each time you cite one of the volumes, give the volume *and* the page number(s) in parentheses, separated by a colon and a space.

> Sandburg concludes with the following sentence about those paying last respects to Lincoln: "All day long and through the night the unbroken line moved, the home town having its farewell" (4: 413).

If you cite an entire volume of a multivolume work in parentheses, give the author's last name followed by a comma and *vol.* before the volume number: (Sandburg, vol. 4). If your works-cited list includes only a single volume of a multivolume work, give just the page number in parentheses: (413).

14. TWO OR MORE WORKS CITED TOGETHER

If you're citing two or more works closely together, you will sometimes need to provide a parenthetical reference for each one.

> Baron (182) and Dreyer (93) describe singular *they* from slightly different perspectives.

If you are citing multiple sources for the same idea in parentheses, separate the references with a semicolon.

> Many critics have examined great works of literature from a cultural perspective (Tanner 7; Smith viii).

15. SOURCE QUOTED IN ANOTHER SOURCE

When you are quoting text that you found quoted in another source, use the abbreviation *qtd. in* in the parenthetical reference.

> Charlotte Brontë wrote to G. H. Lewes, "Why do you like Miss Austen so very much? I am puzzled on that point" (qtd. in Tanner 7).

16. WORK WITHOUT PAGE NUMBERS

For works without page or part numbers, including many online sources, no number is needed in a parenthetical reference.

> Studies show that music training helps children to be better at multitasking later in life ("Hearing the Music").

If you mention the author in a signal phrase, or if you mention the title of a work with no author, no parenthetical reference is needed.

> Arthur Brooks argues that a switch to fully remote work would have a negative effect on mental and physical health.

If the source has chapter, paragraph, or section numbers, use them with the abbreviations *ch.*, *par.*, or *sec.*: ("Hearing the Music," par. 2). Don't count lines or paragraphs on your own if they aren't numbered in the source. For an ebook, use chapter numbers. For an audio or video recording, give the hours, minutes, and seconds (separated by colons) as shown on the player: (00:05:21-31).

17. AN ENTIRE WORK OR A ONE-PAGE ARTICLE

If you cite an entire work rather than a part of it, or if you cite a single-page article, there's no need to include page numbers.

> Throughout life, John Adams strove to succeed (McCullough).

Notes

Sometimes you may need to give information that doesn't fit into the text itself—to thank people who helped you, to provide additional details, to refer readers to other sources, or to add comments about sources. Such information can be given in a footnote (at the bottom of the page) or an endnote (on a separate page with the heading *Notes* or *Endnotes* just before your works-cited list). Put a superscript number at the appropriate point in your text, signaling to readers to look for the note with the corresponding number. If you have multiple notes, number them consecutively throughout your paper.

TEXT

This essay will argue that giving student athletes preferential treatment undermines educational goals.[1]

NOTE

[1] I want to thank those who contributed to my thinking on this topic, especially my teacher Vincent Yu.

List of works cited

A works-cited list provides full bibliographic information for every source cited in your text. See page 347 for guidelines on formatting this list and page 356 for a sample works-cited list.

Core elements

MLA style provides a list of core elements for documenting sources in a works-cited list. Not all sources will include each of these elements; include as much information as is available for any title you cite. For guidance about specific sources you need to document, see the templates and examples on pages 322–45, but here are some general guidelines for how to treat each of the core elements.

CORE ELEMENTS FOR ENTRIES IN A WORKS-CITED LIST

- Author
- Title of the source
- Title of any "container," a larger work in which the source is found — an anthology, a website, a journal or magazine, a database, a streaming service like *Netflix*, or a learning management system, among others
- Editor, translator, director, or other contributors
- Version
- Number of volume and issue, episode and season

TITLE	AUTHOR	PUBLICATION

- Publisher
- Date of publication
- Location of the source: page numbers, DOI, PERMALINK, URL, etc.

The above order is the general order MLA recommends, but there will be exceptions. To document a translated essay that you found in an anthology, for instance, you'd identify the translator after the title of the essay rather than after that of the anthology. You may sometimes need additional elements as well, either at the end of an entry or somewhere in the middle—for instance, a label to indicate that your source is a map, or an original year of publication. Remember that your goal is to tell readers what sources you've consulted and where they can find them. Providing this information is one way you can engage with readers—and enable them to join in the conversation with you and your sources.

AUTHORS AND CONTRIBUTORS

- An author can be any kind of creator—a writer, a musician, an artist, and so on.
- If there is one author, put the last name first, followed by a comma and the first name: Morrison, Toni.
- If there are two authors, list the first author last name first and the second one first name first: Lunsford, Andrea, and Lisa Ede. Put their names in the order given in the work. For three or more authors, give the first author's name followed by *et al.*: Greenblatt, Stephen, et al.
- Include any middle names or initials: Toklas, Alice B.
- If the author is a group or organization, use the full name, omitting any initial article: United Nations.
- If an author uses a handle that is significantly different from their name, include the handle in square brackets after the name: Ocasio-Cortez, Alexandria [@AOC].

- If there's no known author, start the entry with the title.
- If you're citing someone in addition to an author—an editor, translator, director, or other contributors—specify their role. If there are multiple contributors, put the one whose work you wish to highlight before the title, and list any others you want to mention after the title. If you don't want to highlight one particular contributor, start with the title and include any contributors after the title. For contributors named before the title, specify their role after the name: Fincher, David, director. For those named after the title, specify their role first: Directed by David Fincher.

TITLES

- Include any subtitles and capitalize all the words except for articles (*a, an, the*), prepositions (*to, at, from*, and so on), and coordinating conjunctions (*and, but, for, or, nor, so, yet*)—unless they are the first or last word of a title or subtitle.
- Italicize the titles of books, periodicals, websites, and other long works: *Pride and Prejudice, Wired.*
- Put quotation marks around the titles of articles and other short works: "Letter from Birmingham Jail."
- To document a source that has no title, describe it without italics or quotation marks: Letter to the author, Photograph of a tree. For a short, untitled email, text message, tweet, or poem, you may want to include the text itself instead: Dickinson, Emily. "Immortal is an ample word." *American Poems*, www.americanpoems.com/poets/emilydickinson /immortal-is-an-ample-word.

VERSIONS

- If you cite a source that's available in more than one version, specify the one you consulted in your works-cited entry.

Write ordinal numbers with numerals, and abbreviate *edition*: 2nd ed. Write out names of specific versions, and capitalize following a period or if the name is a proper noun: King James Version, unabridged version, director's cut.

NUMBERS

- If you cite a book that's published in multiple volumes, indicate the volume number. Abbreviate *volume*, and write the number as a numeral: vol. 2.

- Indicate volume and issue numbers of journals (if any), abbreviating both *volume* and *number*: vol. 123, no. 4.

- If you cite a TV show or podcast episode, indicate the season and episode numbers: season 1, episode 4.

PUBLISHERS

- Write publishers', studios', and networks' names in full, but omit initial articles and business words like *Inc.* or *Company*.

- For academic presses, use *U* for *University* and *P* for *Press*: Princeton UP, U of California P. Spell out *Press* if the name doesn't include *University*: MIT Press.

- If the publisher is a division of an organization, list the organization and any divisions from largest to smallest: Stanford U, Center for the Study of Language and Information, Metaphysics Research Lab.

DATES

- Whether to give just the year or to include the month and day depends on the source. In general, give the full date that you find there. If the date is unknown, simply omit it.

- Abbreviate the months except for May, June, and July: Jan., Feb., Mar., Apr., Aug., Sept., Oct., Nov., Dec.
- For books, give the publication date on the copyright page. If there's more than one date, use the most recent one.
- Periodicals may be published annually, monthly, seasonally, weekly, or daily. Give the full date that you find there: 2019, Apr. 2019, 16 Apr. 2019. Do not capitalize the names of seasons: spring 2021.
- For online sources, use the copyright date or the full publication date you find there, or a date of revision. If the source does not give a date, use the date of access: Accessed 6 June 2020. Give a date of access as well for online sources you think are likely to change, or for websites that have disappeared.

LOCATION

- For most print articles and other short works, give a page number or range of pages: p. 24, pp. 24-35. For articles that are not on consecutive pages, give the first page number with a plus sign: pp. 24+.
- If it's necessary to specify a section of a source, give the section name before the page numbers: Sunday Review sec., p. 3.
- Indicate the location of an online source by giving a DOI if one is available; if not, give a URL—and use a PERMALINK if one is available. URLs are not always reliable, so ask your instructor if you should include them. DOIs should start with *https://doi.org/*—but no need to include *https://* for a URL, unless you want the URL to be a hyperlink.
- For a geographical location, give enough information to identify it: a city (Houston), a city and state (Portland, Maine), or a city and country (Manaus, Brazil).

TITLE	AUTHOR	PUBLICATION

- For something seen in a museum, archive, or elsewhere, name the institution and its location: Maine Jewish Museum, Portland, Maine.

- For performances or other live presentations, name the venue and its location: Mark Taper Forum, Los Angeles.

PUNCTUATION

- Use a period after the author name(s) that start an entry (Morrison, Toni.) and the title of the source you're documenting (*Beloved.*).

- Use a comma between the author's last and first names: Ede, Lisa.

- Some URLs will not fit on one line. MLA does not specify where to break a URL, but we recommend breaking it before a punctuation mark. Do *not* add a hyphen or a space.

- Sometimes you'll need to provide information about more than one work for a single source—for instance, when you cite an article from a periodical that you access through a database. MLA refers to the periodical and database (or any other entity that holds a source) as "containers" and specifies certain punctuation. Use commas between elements within each container, and put a period at the end of each container. For example:

> Semuels, Alana. "The Future Will Be Quiet." *The Atlantic,* Apr. 2016, pp. 19-20. *ProQuest,* search.proquest.com /docview/1777443553?accountid+42654.

The guidelines that follow will help you document the kinds of sources you're likely to use. The first section shows how to acknowledge authors and other contributors and applies to all kinds of sources— print, online, or others. Later sections show how to treat titles, publication information, location, and access information for many specific kinds of sources. In general, provide as much information as possible for each source—enough to tell readers how to find a source if they wish to access it themselves.

SOURCES NOT COVERED

These guidelines will help you document a variety of sources, but if you're citing a source that isn't covered, consult the MLA style blog at style.mla.org, or ask them a question at style.mla.org/ask-a-question.

Authors and contributors

When you name authors and other contributors in your citations, you are crediting them for their work and letting readers know who's in on the conversation. The following guidelines for citing authors and contributors apply to all sources you cite: in print, online, or in some other media.

1. ONE AUTHOR

Author's Last Name, First Name. *Title*. Publisher, Date.

Anderson, Chris. *The Long Tail: Why the Future of Business Is Selling Less of More*. Hyperion, 2006.

2. TWO AUTHORS

1st Author's Last Name, First Name, and 2nd Author's First and Last Names. *Title*. Publisher, Date.

Lunsford, Andrea, and Lisa Ede. *Singular Texts/Plural Authors: Perspectives on Collaborative Writing*. Southern Illinois UP, 1990.

3. THREE OR MORE AUTHORS

1st Author's Last Name, First Name, et al. *Title*. Publisher, Date.

Sebranek, Patrick, et al. *Writers INC: A Guide to Writing, Thinking, and Learning*. Write Source, 1990.

TITLE	AUTHOR	PUBLICATION

4. TWO OR MORE WORKS BY THE SAME AUTHOR

Give the author's name in the first entry, and then use three hyphens in the author slot for each of the subsequent works, listing them alphabetically by the first word of each title and ignoring any initial articles.

> Author's Last Name, First Name. *Title That Comes First Alphabetically.* Publisher, Date.
> - - -. *Title That Comes Next Alphabetically.* Publisher, Date.
> Kaplan, Robert D. *The Coming Anarchy: Shattering the Dreams of the Post Cold War.* Random House, 2000.
> - - -. *Eastward to Tartary: Travels in the Balkans, the Middle East, and the Caucasus.* Random House, 2000.

5. AUTHOR AND EDITOR OR TRANSLATOR

> Author's Last Name, First Name. *Title.* Role by First and Last Names, Publisher, Date.
> Austen, Jane. *Emma.* Edited by Stephen M. Parrish, W. W. Norton, 2000.
> Dostoevsky, Fyodor. *Crime and Punishment.* Translated by Richard Pevear and Larissa Volokhonsky, Vintage Books, 1993.

Start with the editor or translator if you are focusing on that contribution rather than the author's. If there is a translator but no author, start with the title.

> Pevear, Richard, and Larissa Volokhonsky, translators. *Crime and Punishment.* By Fyodor Dostoevsky, Vintage Books, 1993.
> *Beowulf.* Translated by Stephen Mitchell, Yale UP, 2017.

6. NO AUTHOR OR EDITOR

When there's no known author or editor, start with the title.

> *The Turner Collection in the Clore Gallery.* Tate Publications, 1987.
> "Being Invisible Closer to Reality." *The Atlanta Journal-Constitution,* 11 Aug. 2008, p. A3.

7. ORGANIZATION OR GOVERNMENT AS AUTHOR

For a government publication, give the name that is shown in the source. When a nongovernment organization is both author and publisher, start with the title and list the organization only as the publisher. If a division of an organization is listed as the author, give the division as the author and the organization as the publisher.

> Organization Name. *Title.* Publisher, Date.
> Diagram Group. *The Macmillan Visual Desk Reference.* Macmillan, 1993.
> United States, Department of Health and Human Services, National Institute of Mental Health. *Autism Spectrum Disorders.* Government Printing Office, 2004.
> *Stylebook on Religion 2000: A Reference Guide and Usage Manual.* Catholic News Service, 2002.
> Center for Workforce Studies. *2005-13: Demographics of the U.S. Psychology Workforce.* American Psychological Association, July 2015.

Articles and other short works

Articles, essays, reviews, and other shorts works are found in journals, magazines, newspapers, other periodicals, and books—all of which you may find in print, online, or in a database. For most short works, you'll need to provide information about the author, the titles of both the short work and the longer work where it's found, any page numbers, and various kinds of publication information.

8. ARTICLE IN A JOURNAL

PRINT

> Author's Last Name, First Name. "Title of Article." *Name of Journal,* Volume, Issue, Date, Pages.

Cooney, Brian C. "Considering *Robinson Crusoe*'s 'Liberty of Conscience' in an Age of Terror." *College English*, vol. 69, no. 3, Jan. 2007, pp. 197-215.

ONLINE

Author's Last Name, First Name. "Title of Article." *Name of Journal*, Volume, Issue, Date, DOI *or* URL.

Schmidt, Desmond. "A Model of Versions and Layers." *Digital Humanities Quarterly*, vol. 13, no. 3, 2019, www.digital humanities.org/dhq/vol/13/3/000430/000430.html.

9. ARTICLE IN A MAGAZINE

PRINT

Author's Last Name, First Name. "Title of Article." *Name of Magazine*, Volume (if any), Issue (if any), Date, Pages.

Burt, Tequia. "Legacy of Activism: Concerned Black Students' 50-Year History at Grinnell College." *Grinnell Magazine*, vol. 48, no. 4, summer 2016, pp. 32-38.

ONLINE

Author's Last Name, First Name. "Title of Article." *Name of Magazine*, Volume (if any), Issue (if any), Date, DOI *or* URL.

Brooks, Arthur C. "The Hidden Toll of Remote Work." *The Atlantic*, 1 Apr. 2021, www.theatlantic.com/family/archive/2021/04 /zoom-remote-work-loneliness-happiness/618473.

10. ARTICLE IN A NEWS PUBLICATION

PRINT

Author's Last Name, First Name. "Title of Article." *Name of Publication*, Date, Pages.

Saulny, Susan, and Jacques Steinberg. "On College Forms, a Question of Race Can Perplex." *The New York Times*, 14 June 2011, p. A1.

Documentation Map (MLA)
Article in a Print Journal

TITLE OF ARTICLE ··········• Marge Simpson, Blue-Haired Housewife:
Defining Domesticity on *The Simpsons*

AUTHOR ··········• JESSAMYN NEUHAUS

ORE THAN TWENTY SEASONS AFTER ITS DEBUT AS A SHORT ON *THE*
Tracy Ullman Show in 1989, pundits, politicians, scholars,
journalists, and critics continue to discuss and debate the
meaning and relevance of *The Simpsons* to American society. For
academics and educators, the show offers an especially dense pop culture text, inspiring articles and anthologies examining *The Simpsons* in
light of American religious life, the representation of homosexuality in
cartoons, and the use of pop culture in the classroom, among many
other topics (Dennis; Frank; Henry "The Whole World's Gone Gay";
Hobbs; Kristiansen). Philosophers and literary theorists in particular
are intrigued by the quintessentially postmodern self-aware form and
content of *The Simpsons* and the questions about identity, spectatorship,
and consumer culture it raises (Alberti; Bybee and Overbeck; Glynn;
Henry "The Triumph of Popular Culture"; Herron; Hull; Irwin et al.;
Ott; Parisi).

Simpsons observers frequently note that this TV show begs one of the
fundamental questions in cultural studies: can pop culture ever provide
a site of individual or collective resistance or must it always ultimately
function in the interests of the capitalist dominant ideology? Is *The
Simpsons* a brilliant satire of virtually every cherished American myth
DATE ·········· about public and private life, offering dissatisfied Americans the op-
portunity to critically reflect on contemporary issues (Turner 435)? Or
ISSUE ·········· is it simply another TV show making money for the Fox Network? Is
The Simpsons an empty, cynical, even nihilistic view of the world, lull-
VOLUME ·········· ing its viewers into laughing hopelessly at the pointless futility of

NAME OF JOURNAL ··········• *The Journal of Popular Culture*, Vol. 43, No. 4, 2010, pp. 761–81
© 2010, Wiley Periodicals, Inc.
PAGES ··········

Neuhaus, Jessamyn. "Marge Simpson, Blue-Haired Housewife:
Defining Domesticity on *The Simpsons*." *The Journal of
Popular Culture*, vol. 43, no. 4, 2010, pp. 761-81.

TITLE   AUTHOR   PUBLICATION

Documentation Map (MLA)
Article in an Online Magazine

URL

NAME OF
MAGAZINE

TITLE OF
ARTICLE

AUTHOR

DATE

Segal, Michael. "The Hit Book That Came from Mars." *Nautilus*,
    8 Jan. 2015, nautil.us/issue/20/creativity/the-hit-book-that
    -came-from-mars.

To document a particular edition of a newspaper, list the edition before the date. If a section name or number is needed to locate the article, put that detail after the date.

> Burns, John F., and Miguel Helft. "Under Pressure, YouTube Withdraws Muslim Cleric's Videos." *The New York Times*, late ed., 4 Nov. 2010, sec. 1, p. 13.

ONLINE

> Author's Last Name, First Name. "Title of Article." *Name of Publication*, Date, URL.

> Banerjee, Neela. "Proposed Religion-Based Program for Federal Inmates Is Canceled." *The New York Times*, 28 Oct. 2006, www.nytimes.com/2006/10/28/us/28prison.html.

11. ARTICLE ACCESSED THROUGH A DATABASE

> Author's Last Name, First Name. "Title of Article." *Name of Periodical*, Volume, Issue, Date, Pages. *Name of Database*, DOI or URL.

> Stalter, Sunny. "Subway Ride and Subway System in Hart Crane's 'The Tunnel.'" *Journal of Modern Literature*, vol. 33, no. 2, Jan. 2010, pp. 70-91. *JSTOR*, https://doi.org/10.2979/jml.2010.33.2.70.

12. ENTRY IN A REFERENCE WORK

PRINT

> Author's Last Name, First Name (if any). "Title of Entry." *Title of Reference Book*, edited by First and Last Names (if any), Edition number, Volume (if any), Publisher, Date, Pages.

> Fritz, Jan Marie. "Clinical Sociology." *Encyclopedia of Sociology*, edited by Edgar F. Borgatta and Rhonda J. V. Montgomery, 2nd ed., vol. 1, Macmillan Reference USA, 2000, pp. 323-29.

> "California." *The New Columbia Encyclopedia*, edited by William H. Harris and Judith S. Levey, 4th ed., Columbia UP, 1975, pp. 423-24.

Documentation Map (MLA)
Journal Article Accessed through a Database

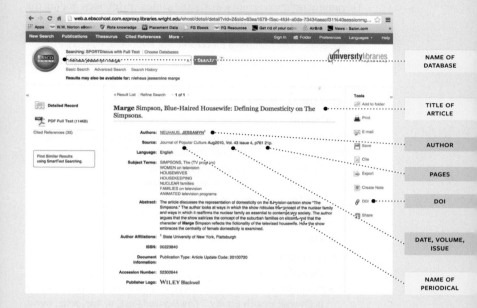

	NAME OF DATABASE
	TITLE OF ARTICLE
	AUTHOR
	PAGES
	DOI
	DATE, VOLUME, ISSUE
	NAME OF PERIODICAL

Neuhaus, Jessamyn. "Marge Simpson, Blue-Haired Housewife:
Defining Domesticity on *The Simpsons*." *Journal of Popular
Culture*, vol. 43, no. 4, Aug. 2010, pp. 761-81. *EBSCOhost*,
https://doi.org/10.1111/j.1540-5931.2010.00769.x.

ONLINE

Document online reference works the same as print ones, adding the URL after the date of publication.

"Baseball." *The Columbia Electronic Encyclopedia*, edited by Paul Lagassé, 6th ed., Columbia UP, 2012, www.infoplease .com/encyclopedia.

13. EDITORIAL OR OP-ED

EDITORIAL

Editorial Board. "Title." *Name of Periodical,* Date, Page *or* URL.

Editorial Board. "A New Look for Local News Coverage." *The Lakeville Journal*, 13 Feb. 2020, p. A8.

Editorial Board. "Editorial: Protect Reporters at Protest Scenes." *Los Angeles Times*, 11 Mar. 2021, www.latimes.com/opinion /story/2021-03-11/reporters-protest-scenes.

OP-ED

Author's Last Name, First Name. "Title." *Name of Periodical,* Date, Page *or* URL.

Okafor, Kingsley. "Opinion: The First Step to COVID Vaccine Equity Is Overall Health Equity." *The Denver Post*, 15 Apr. 2021, www .denverpost.com/2021/04/15/covid-vaccine-equity-kaiser.

If it's not clear that it's an op-ed, add a label at the end.

Balf, Todd. "Falling in Love with Swimming." *The New York Times*, 17 Apr. 2021, p. A21. Op-ed.

14. LETTER TO THE EDITOR

Author's Last Name, First Name. "Title of Letter (if any)." *Name of Periodical,* Date, Page *or* URL.

Pinker, Steven. "Language Arts." *The New Yorker*, 4 June 2012, p. 10.

If the letter has no title, include *Letter* after the author's name.

> Fleischmann, W. B. Letter. *The New York Review of Books*, 1 June 1963, www.nybooks.com/articles/1963/06/01/letter-21.

15. REVIEW

PRINT

> Reviewer's Last Name, First Name. "Title of Review." *Name of Periodical*, Date, Pages.

> Frank, Jeffrey. "Body Count." *The New Yorker*, 30 July 2007, pp. 86-87.

ONLINE

> Reviewer's Last Name, First Name. "Title of Review." *Name of Periodical*, Date, URL.

> Donadio, Rachel. "Italy's Great, Mysterious Storyteller." *The New York Review of Books*, 18 Dec. 2014, www.nybooks.com /articles/2014/12/18/italys-great-mysterious-storyteller.

If a review has no title, include the title and author of the work being reviewed after the reviewer's name.

> Lohier, Patrick. Review of *Exhalation,* by Ted Chiang. *Harvard Review Online*, 4 Oct. 2019, www.harvardreview.org/book -review/exhalation.

16. COMMENT ON AN ONLINE ARTICLE

> Commenter's Last Name, First Name *or* Username. Comment on "Title of Article." *Name of Periodical*, Date posted, Time posted, URL.

> ZeikJT. Comment on "The Post-Disaster Artist." *Polygon*, 6 May 2020, 4:33 a.m., www.polygon.com/2020/5/5/21246679/josh -trank-capone-interview-fantastic-four-chronicle.

Books and parts of books

For most books, you'll need to provide information about author, title, publisher, and year of publication. If you found the book in a larger volume, a database, or another work, be sure to specify that as well.

17. BASIC ENTRIES FOR A BOOK

PRINT

Author's Last Name, First Name. *Title*. Publisher, Year of publication.

Watson, Brad. *Miss Jane*. W. W. Norton, 2016.

EBOOK

Author's Last Name, First Name. *Title*. Ebook ed., Publisher, Year of Publication.

Watson, Brad. *Miss Jane*. Ebook ed., W. W. Norton, 2016.

ON A WEBSITE

Author's Last Name, First Name. *Title*. Publisher, Year of publication, DOI *or* URL.

Ball, Cheryl E., and Drew M. Loewe, editors. *Bad Ideas about Writing*. West Virginia U Libraries, 2017, textbooks.lib.wvu.edu/badideas/badideasaboutwriting-book.pdf.

18. ANTHOLOGY OR EDITED COLLECTION

Last Name, First Name, editor. *Title*. Publisher, Year of publication.

Kitchen, Judith, and Mary Paumier Jones, editors. *In Short: A Collection of Brief Nonfiction*. W. W. Norton, 1996.

19. WORK IN AN ANTHOLOGY

Author's Last Name, First Name. "Title of Work." *Title of Anthology*, edited by First and Last Names, Publisher, Year of publication, Pages.

Achebe, Chinua. "Uncle Ben's Choice." *The Seagull Reader: Literature*, edited by Joseph Kelly, W. W. Norton, 2005, pp. 23-27.

Documentation Map (MLA)
Print Book

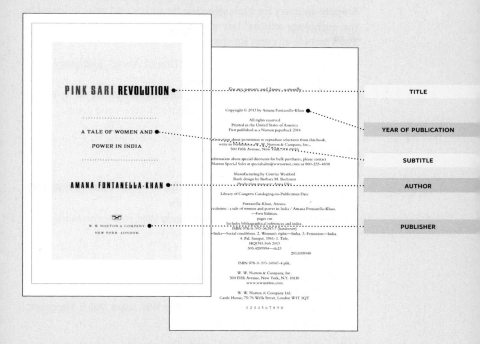

PINK SARI REVOLUTION •·· **TITLE**

A TALE OF WOMEN AND •································· **YEAR OF PUBLICATION**
POWER IN INDIA

SUBTITLE

AMANA FONTANELLA-KHAN •······················· **AUTHOR**

W. W. NORTON & COMPANY •·················· **PUBLISHER**
NEW YORK · LONDON

Fontanella-Khan, Amana. *Pink Sari Revolution: A Tale of Women and Power in India.* W. W. Norton, 2013.

TWO OR MORE WORKS FROM ONE ANTHOLOGY
Prepare an entry for each selection by author and title, followed by
the anthology editors' last names and the pages of the selection.
Then include an entry for the anthology itself (see no. 18).

> Author's Last Name, First Name. "Title of Work." Anthology
> Editors' Last Names, Pages.
> Hiestand, Emily. "Afternoon Tea." Kitchen and Jones, pp. 65-67.
> Ozick, Cynthia. "The Shock of Teapots." Kitchen and Jones,
> pp. 68-71.

20. MULTIVOLUME WORK

ALL VOLUMES

> Author's Last Name, First Name. *Title of Work.* Publisher, Year(s)
> of publication. Number of vols.
> Churchill, Winston. *The Second World War.* Houghton Mifflin,
> 1948-53. 6 vols.

SINGLE VOLUME

> Author's Last Name, First Name. *Title of Work.* Vol. number,
> Publisher, Year of publication.
> Sandburg, Carl. *Abraham Lincoln: The War Years.* Vol. 2, Harcourt,
> Brace and World, 1939.

If the volume has its own title, include it after the author's name, and
indicate the volume number and series title after the year.

> Caro, Robert A. *Means of Ascent.* Vintage Books, 1990. Vol. 2 of
> *The Years of Lyndon Johnson.*

21. BOOK IN A SERIES

> Author's Last Name, First Name. *Title of Book.* Edited by First and
> Last Names, Publisher, Year of publication. Series Title.
> Walker, Alice. *Everyday Use.* Edited by Barbara T. Christian, Rutgers
> UP, 1994. Women Writers: Texts and Contexts.

22. GRAPHIC NARRATIVE OR COMIC BOOK

Author's Last Name, First Name. *Title*. Publisher, Publication year.
Barry, Lynda. *One! Hundred! Demons!* Drawn and Quarterly, 2005.

If the work has both an author and an illustrator, start with the one you want to highlight, and label the role of the illustrator.

Pekar, Harvey. *Bob and Harv's Comics*. Illustrated by R. Crumb, Running Press, 1996.
Crumb, R., illustrator. *Bob and Harv's Comics*. By Harvey Pekar, Running Press, 1996.

If you want to cite several contributors, you can also start with the title.

Secret Invasion. By Brian Michael Bendis, illustrated by Leinil Yu, inked by Mark Morales, Marvel, 2009.

23. SACRED TEXT

If you cite a specific edition of a religious text, you need to include it in your works-cited list.

The New English Bible with the Apocrypha. Oxford UP, 1971.
The Torah: A Modern Commentary. W. Gunther Plaut, general editor, Union of American Hebrew Congregations, 1981.

24. EDITION OTHER THAN THE FIRST

Author's Last Name, First Name. *Title*. Edition name *or* number, Publisher, Year of publication.
Smart, Ninian. *The World's Religions*. 2nd ed., Cambridge UP, 1998.

25. FOREWORD, INTRODUCTION, PREFACE, OR AFTERWORD

Part Author's Last Name, First Name. Name of Part. *Title of Book*, by Author's First and Last Names, Publisher, Year of publication, Pages.
Tanner, Tony. Introduction. *Pride and Prejudice*, by Jane Austen, Penguin, 1972, pp. 7-46.

26. PUBLISHED LETTER

> Letter Writer's Last Name, First Name. "Title of letter." Day Month Year. *Title of Book,* edited by First and Last Names, Publisher, Year of publication, Pages.

White, E. B. "To Carol Angell." 28 May 1970. *Letters of E. B. White,* edited by Dorothy Guth, Harper and Row, 1976, p. 600.

27. DISSERTATION

> Author's Last Name, First Name. *Title.* Year. Institution, PhD dissertation. *Name of Database,* URL.

Simington, Maire Orav. *Chasing the American Dream Post World War II: Perspectives from Literature and Advertising.* 2003. Arizona State U, PhD dissertation. *ProQuest,* search .proquest.com/docview/305340098.

For an unpublished dissertation, end with the institution and a description of the work.

Kim, Loel. *Students Respond to Teacher Comments: A Comparison of Online Written and Voice Modalities.* 1998. Carnegie Mellon U, PhD dissertation.

Websites

Many sources are available in multiple media—for example, a print periodical that is also on the web and contained in digital databases—but some are published only on websites. A website can have an author, an editor, or neither. Some have a publisher, and some do not. Include whatever information is available. If the publisher and title of the site are the same, omit the name of the publisher.

28. ENTIRE WEBSITE

> Editor's Last Name, First Name, role. *Title of Site.* Publisher, Date, URL.

Proffitt, Michael, chief editor. *The Oxford English Dictionary.*
Oxford UP, 2021, www.oed.com.

PERSONAL WEBSITE

Author's Last Name, First Name. *Title of Site.* Date, URL.
Park, Linda Sue. *Linda Sue Park: Author and Educator.* 2021,
lindasuepark.com.

If the site is likely to change, has no date, or no longer exists, include a date of access.

Archive of Our Own. Organization for Transformative Works,
archiveofourown.org. Accessed 23 Apr. 2021.

29. WORK ON A WEBSITE

Author's Last Name, First Name (if any). "Title of Work." *Title of
Site,* Publisher (if any), Date, URL.
Cesareo, Kerry. "Moving Closer to Tackling Deforestation at Scale."
World Wildlife Fund, 20 Oct. 2020, www.worldwildlife.org
/blogs/sustainability-works/posts/moving-closer-to-tackling
-deforestation-at-scale.

30. BLOG ENTRY

Author's Last Name, First Name. "Title of Blog Entry." *Title of
Blog,* Date, URL.
Hollmichel, Stefanie. "Bring Up the Bodies." *So Many Books,*
10 Feb. 2014, somanybooksblog.com/2014/02/10/bring-up
-the-bodies.

31. WIKI

"Title of Entry." *Title of Wiki,* Publisher, Date, URL.
"Pi." *Wikipedia,* Wikimedia Foundation, 28 Aug. 2013, en.wikipedia
.org/wiki/Pi.

Documentation Map (MLA)
Work on a Website

URL

TITLE
OF SITE

TITLE
OF WORK

DATE POSTED

AUTHORS

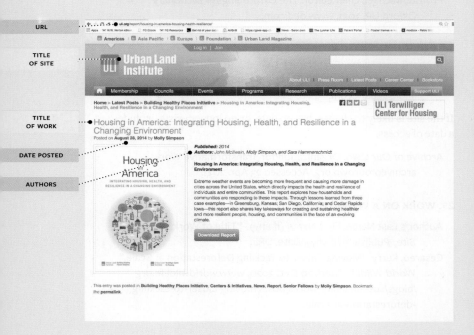

McIlwain, John, et al. "Housing in America: Integrating Housing,
Health, and Resilience in a Changing Environment." *Urban
Land Institute,* 28 Aug. 2014, uli.org/report/housing-in
-america-housing-health-resilience.

| TITLE | AUTHOR | PUBLICATION |

Personal communication and social media

32. PERSONAL LETTER

> Sender's Last Name, First Name. Letter to the author. Day
> Month Year.
> Quindlen, Anna. Letter to the author. 11 Apr. 2013.

33. EMAIL OR TEXT MESSAGE

Include the text of a short email or text message, or a concise description. If it's not clear that it's a text message or email, add a label at the end: Text message, Email. If the email or text message was sent to you, indicate that: Email to the author, Text message to the author.

> Sender's Last Name, First Name. Email *or* Text Message to First
> Name Last Name *or* "to the author." Day Month Year.
> Smith, William. Email to Richard Bullock. 19 Nov. 2013.
> Rombes, Maddy. Text message to Isaac Cohen. 4 May 2021.
> O'Malley, Kit. Text message to the author. 2 June 2020.

34. POST TO *TWITTER*, *INSTAGRAM*, OR OTHER SOCIAL MEDIA

> Author. "Title." *Title of Site,* Day Month Year, URL.
> Oregon Zoo. "Winter Wildlife Wonderland." *Facebook,* 8 Feb. 2019,
> www.facebook.com/80229441108/videos/2399570506799549.

If there's no title, you can use a concise description or the text of a short post.

> Millman, Debbie. Photos of Roxane Gay. *Instagram,* 18 Feb. 2021,
> www.instagram.com/p/CLcT_EnhnWT.
> Obama, Barack [@POTUS44]. "It's been the honor of my life
> to serve you. You made me a better leader and a better
> man." *Twitter,* 20 Jan. 2017, twitter.com/POTUS44
> /status/822445882247413761.

Audio, visual, and other sources

35. ADVERTISEMENT

PRINT

Description of ad. *Name of Periodical,* Date, Page.
Advertisement for Grey Goose. *Wine Spectator,* 18 Dec. 2020, p. 22.

VIDEO

"Title." *Title of Site,* uploaded by Company, Date, URL.
"First Visitors." *YouTube,* uploaded by Snickers, 20 Aug. 2020,
www.youtube.com/watch?v=negecoob1Lo.

36. ART

ORIGINAL

Artist's Last Name, First Name. *Title of Art.* Year created,
Location.
Van Gogh, Vincent. *The Potato Eaters.* 1885, Van Gogh Museum,
Amsterdam.

IN A BOOK

Artist's Last Name, First Name. *Title of Art.* Year created,
Location. *Title of Book,* by First and Last Names, Publisher,
Year of publication, Page.
Van Gogh, Vincent. *The Potato Eaters.* 1885, Scottish National
Gallery. *History of Art,* by H. W. Janson, Prentice Hall /
Harry N. Abrams, 1969, p. 508.

ONLINE

Artist's Last Name, First Name. *Title of Art.* Year created. *Title
of Site,* URL.
Warhol, Andy. *Self-portrait.* 1979. *J. Paul Getty Museum,* www.getty
.edu/art/collection/objects/106971/andy-warhol-self-portrait
-american-1979.

37. CARTOON

PRINT

Author's Last Name, First Name. Cartoon *or* "Title of Cartoon."
   Name of Periodical, Date, Page.
Mankoff, Robert. Cartoon. *The New Yorker,* 3 May 1993, p. 50.

ONLINE

Author's Last Name, First Name. Cartoon *or* "Title of Cartoon."
   Title of Site, Date, URL.
Munroe, Randall. "Up Goer Five." *xkcd,* 12 Nov. 2012, xkcd
   .com/1133.

38. SUPREME COURT CASE

United States, Supreme Court. *First Defendant v. Second*
   Defendant. Date of decision. *Title of Source Site,*
   Publisher, URL.
United States, Supreme Court. *District of Columbia v. Heller.*
   26 June 2008. *Legal Information Institute,* Cornell Law
   School, www.law.cornell.edu/supremecourt/text/07-290.

39. FILM

Name individuals based on the focus of your project—the director,
the screenwriter, or someone else. If your essay focuses on one
contributor, you may put their names before the title.

Title of Film. Role by First and Last Names, Production Company,
   Date.
Breakfast at Tiffany's. Directed by Blake Edwards, Paramount, 1961.
Edwards, Blake, director. *Breakfast at Tiffany's.* Paramount, 1961.

ONLINE

Title of Film. Role by First and Last Names, Production Company,
Date. *Title of Site*, URL.

Interstellar. Directed by Christopher Nolan, Paramount, 2014.
Amazon Prime Video, www.amazon.com/Interstellar
-Matthew-McConaughey/dp/B00TU9UFTS.

40. TV SHOW EPISODE

Name contributors based on the focus of your project—director,
creator, actors, or others. If you don't want to highlight anyone in
particular, don't include any contributors.

BROADCAST

"Title of Episode." *Title of Program*, role by First and Last Names
(if any), season, episode, Production Company, Date.

"The Storm." *Avatar: The Last Airbender*, created by Michael
Dante DiMartino and Bryan Konietzko, season 1, episode 12,
Nickelodeon Animation Studios, 3 June 2005.

STREAMING ONLINE

"Title of Episode." *Title of Program*, role by First and Last Names
(if any), season, episode, Production Company, Broadcast
Date. *Title of Site*, URL.

"The Storm." *Avatar: The Last Airbender*, season 1, episode 12,
Nickelodeon Animation Studios, 2005. *Netflix*, www.netflix
.com.

41. ONLINE VIDEO

"Title of Video." *Title of Site*, uploaded by Uploader's Name,
Day Month Year, URL.

"13 Severed Hands!" *YouTube*, uploaded by vlogbrothers, 30 Sept.
2009, www.youtube.com/watch?v=lDlqwbMCBg4.

42. PRESENTATION ON *ZOOM* OR OTHER VIRTUAL PLATFORM

MLA doesn't give guidance on how to cite a virtual presentation, but this is what we recommend.

> Author's Last Name, First Name. "Title." Sponsoring Institution, Day Month Year, *Name of Platform*.
>
> Budhathoki, Thir. "Cross-Cultural Perceptions of Literacies in Student Writing." Conference on College Composition and Communication, 9 Apr. 2021, *Zoom*.

43. INTERVIEW

If it's not clear that it's an interview, add a label at the end. If you are citing a transcript of an interview, indicate that at the end as well.

PUBLISHED

> Subject's Last Name, First Name. "Title of Interview." Interview by First Name Last Name (if given). *Title of Publication*, Date, Pages *or* URL.
>
> Whitehead, Colson. "Colson Whitehead: By the Book." *The New York Times*, 15 May 2014, www.nytimes.com/2014/05/18/books /review/colson-whitehead-by-the-book.html. Interview.

PERSONAL

> Subject's Last Name, First Name. Concise description. Day Month Year.
>
> Bazelon, L. S. Telephone interview with the author. 4 Oct. 2020.

44. MAP

If the title doesn't make clear it's a map, add a label at the end.

> *Title of Map*. Publisher, Date.
>
> *Brooklyn*. J. B. Beers, 1874. Map.

45. ORAL PRESENTATION

Presenter's Last Name, First Name. "Title of Presentation." Sponsoring Institution, Date, Location.

Cassin, Michael. "Nature in the Raw—The Art of Landscape Painting." Berkshire Institute for Lifelong Learning, 24 Mar. 2005, Clark Art Institute, Williamstown, Massachusetts.

46. PODCAST

If you accessed a podcast on the web, give the URL.

"Title of Episode." *Title of Podcast*, hosted by First Name Last Name, season, episode, Production Company, Date, URL.

"DUSTWUN." *Serial*, hosted by Sarah Koenig, season 2, episode 1, WBEZ / Serial Productions, 10 Dec. 2015, serialpodcast.org /season-two/1/dustwun.

THROUGH AN APP

"DUSTWUN." *Serial*, hosted by Sarah Koenig, season 2, episode 1, WBEZ / Serial Productions, 10 Dec. 2015. *Spotify* app.

47. SOUND RECORDING

Artist's Last Name, First Name. "Title of Work." *Title of Album*, Label, Date, URL.

Beyoncé. "Pray You Catch Me." *Lemonade*, Parkwood Entertainment / Columbia Records, 2016, www.beyonce .com/album/lemonade-visual-album/songs.

THROUGH AN APP

Simone, Nina. "To Be Young, Gifted and Black." *Black Gold*, RCA Records, 1969. *Spotify* app.

48. VIDEO GAME

Title of Game. Version, Distributor, Date of release.

Animal Crossing: New Horizons. Version 1.1.4, Nintendo, 6 Apr. 2020.

Formatting a research essay

Name, course, title. MLA does not require a separate title page, unless your paper is a group project. In the upper left-hand corner of your first page, include your name, your instructor's name, the course name and number, and the date. Center the title of your paper on the line after the date; capitalize it as you would a book title. If your paper is a group project, include all of that information on a title page instead, listing all the authors.

Page numbers. In the upper right-hand corner of each page, one-half inch below the top of the page, include your last name and the page number. If it's a group project and all the names don't fit, include only the page number. Number pages consecutively.

Font, spacing, margins, and indents. Choose a font that is easy to read (such as Times New Roman) and that provides a clear contrast between regular text and italic text. Set the font size between 11 and 13 points. Double-space the entire paper, including your works-cited list and any notes. Set one-inch margins at the top, bottom, and sides of your text; do not justify your text. The first line of each paragraph should be indented one-half inch from the left margin. End punctuation should be followed by one space.

Headings. Short essays do not generally need headings, but they can be useful in longer works. Use a large, bold font for the first level of heading, and smaller fonts and italics to signal lower-level headings. MLA requires that headings all be flush with the left margin.

First-Level Heading

Second-Level Heading

Third-Level Heading

Long quotations. When quoting more than three lines of poetry, more than four lines of prose, or dialogue between characters in a drama, set off the quotation from the rest of your text, indenting it one-half inch (or five spaces) from the left margin. Do not use quotation marks, and put any parenthetical documentation *after* the final punctuation.

> In *Eastward to Tartary*, Robert Kaplan captures ancient and contemporary Antioch for us:
>> At the height of its glory in the Roman-Byzantine age, when it had an amphitheater, public baths, aqueducts, and sewage pipes, half a million people lived in Antioch. Today the population is only 125,000. With sour relations between Turkey and Syria, and unstable politics throughout the Middle East, Antioch is now a backwater—seedy and tumbledown, with relatively few tourists. I found it altogether charming. (123)

> In the first stanza of Matthew Arnold's "Dover Beach," the exclamations make clear that the speaker is addressing someone who is also present in the scene:
>> Come to the window, sweet is the night air!
>> Only, from the long line of spray
>> Where the sea meets the moon-blanched land,
>> Listen! You hear the grating roar
>> Of pebbles which the waves draw back, and fling. (lines 6-10)

Be careful to maintain the poet's line breaks. If a line does not fit on one line of your paper, put the extra words on the next line. Indent that line an additional quarter inch (or two spaces). If a citation doesn't fit, put it on the next line, flush with the right margin.

Tables and illustrations. Insert illustrations and tables close to the text that discusses them, and be sure to make clear how they relate to your point. For tables, provide a number (*Table 1*) and a title on separate lines above the table and a caption with source information and any notes below. Notes should be indicated with lowercase letters. For graphs, photos, and other figures, provide a figure number

(*fig. 1*) and caption, with source information below the figure. If you give full source information in the caption, you don't have to include the source in your list of works cited. Punctuate as you would in the works-cited list, but don't invert the author's name: Berenice Sydney. *Fast Rhythm*. 1972, Tate Britain, London.

List of works cited. Start your list on a new page, following any notes. Center the title, Works Cited, and double-space the entire list. Begin each entry at the left margin, and indent subsequent lines one-half inch (or five spaces). Alphabetize the list by authors' last names (or by editors' or translators' names, if appropriate). Alphabetize works with no author or editor by title, disregarding *A*, *An*, and *The*. To document more than one work by a single author, list them as in no. 4 on page 323.

Student essay, MLA style

The following essay was written by Jackson Parell for a first-year writing course. It was awarded the Boothe Prize for outstanding expository and argumentative writing by first-year students at Stanford University in 2018. It's formatted according to the guidelines of the *MLA Handbook* (style.mla.org).

A STUDENT RESEARCH ESSAY, MLA STYLE

Jackson Parell

Professor Hammann

Writing and Rhetoric 1

21 May 2018

Free at Last, Free at Last:

Civil War Memory and Civil Rights Rhetoric

When Martin Luther King, Jr., addressed the huge crowd in Washington, DC, on August 28, 1963, he did so on the steps of the Lincoln Memorial, in Lincoln's symbolic shadow (Sundquist 146). Using the words and legacy of the Great Emancipator, King intended to make an appeal to the moral conscience of America to rid itself of the vestiges of slavery and to realize Lincoln's new birth of freedom one hundred years after it was first proposed. On this day, and throughout the Civil War Centennial years (1961-65), African American leaders, including King, successfully accessed the language of the Civil War's promise of racial justice to shape a compelling message for future progress. As historian Robert Cook writes, "The advent of the Centennial furnished [African Americans] with powerful leverage in their intensifying efforts to close the gap between the promise and the reality of American community life" (96).

However, the rhetoric of the Civil War could only serve as an appeal for racial equality if Americans commonly understood its history in the context of social justice and equal rights. Unfortunately, for many Americans in the 1960s, this was not the case (Blight 3). Northerners and Southerners alike, looking to mend sectional strife after the war, were willing to adopt a memory of reconciliation that focused on the shared honor of battle as opposed to the racial issues over which those battles were fought. Civil War valor, bravery, and brotherhood shaped American wartime memory into a "shared

Title centered.

Double-spaced throughout.

Author named in signal phrase; page number in parentheses.

No signal phrase; author and page number in parentheses.

TITLE   AUTHOR   PUBLICATION

experience"—one that would remain a potent source of nationalism well into the civil rights era (Cook 4). "For the majority, especially of white Americans," as historian David Blight writes, "emancipation in Civil War memory was still an awkward kind of politeness at best and heresy at worst.... In 1963, the national temper and mythology still preferred a story of the mutual valor of the Blue and Gray to the disruptive problem of black and white" (3). Therefore, civil rights leaders, including King, attempted to remind Americans of the war's cause and enduring racial legacies. Through pen and podium, he leveraged that history in a powerful appeal for racial justice one hundred years after Lee's surrender at Appomattox.

In October 1961, President John F. Kennedy invited King to the White House for lunch. The meeting was unofficial—it was not recorded in the secretary's docket, nor was there any official business set to be discussed (Branch 27). After lunch, Kennedy led King on a tour of the residence. Hung outside the door of Lincoln's bedroom was a copy of the original Emancipation Proclamation. It gave King the opportunity to bring up, ever so gently, the issue of civil rights (27). Already, the Montgomery bus boycotts, the Greensboro sit-ins, and the Freedom Rides had brought racial tensions to the forefront of American culture. King believed he had a solution. "Mr. President," he said, "I would like to see you stand in this room and sign a [second] Emancipation Proclamation outlawing segregation 100 years after Lincoln's. You could base it on the Fourteenth Amendment" (qtd. in Sundquist 34). In the summer of 1962, King and his associates delivered the first copy of this second Proclamation to the White House, bound in leather. This document serves as an important example of the ways in which King reshaped the memory of the Civil War and leveraged its rhetoric to advance claims for equality in civil rights. The proclamation directly engages in the battle between white

Embeds signal phrase in the middle of the quotation.

Brackets indicate the quotation has been altered for clarity.

1″

Last name and
page number.

reconciliationist memory and the memory of racial justice. In it, King
pushes back on traditional narratives of mutual valor and bravery
by instead placing emphasis on the guarantees of equality embodied
in Civil War documents. But before King could make the revisions
to Civil War history necessary to frame his plea for racial justice, he
needed to provide Kennedy with a compelling reason for doing so.
By 1962, racial tensions in the United States had come to a head.
Politicians, including Kennedy, wished to deescalate the problem as
fast as possible (Branch 52), so in his preamble, King cites increasing
racial tensions as well as the Centennial of the Civil War as impetus
to dive into the "wellsprings of history" from which the civil rights
movement began ("Appeal" 3):

2 works cited within
the same sentence.

> Mr. President, sometimes there occur moments in the history
> of our nation when it becomes necessary to pause and reflect
> upon the heritage of the past in order to determine the most
> meaningful course for the present and the future. America
> today in the field of race relations is such a moment. We believe
> the Centennial of the Emancipation Proclamation is a
> particularly important time for all our citizens to rededicate
> themselves to those early precepts and principles of equality
> before the law. ("Appeal" 1)

Uses block format for
quotation longer than
4 lines. Indents ½ inch
or 5 spaces.

Parenthetical
documentation follows
punctuation in a block
quotation.

With his first words, therefore, King encourages the president to think
about Civil War history as a tool for addressing modern issues.

After establishing the importance of looking to the past to
resolve the racial tensions of the present, King proposes the version of
Civil War history upon which he believes Kennedy should reflect. It is
a version that promotes the war's promises of racial equality over the
valor and bravery of its veterans. He references the Gettysburg
Address and the Emancipation Proclamation as the war's defining
documents, both of which place the issue of slavery as the central

Parell 4

cause of the Civil War and uphold concepts of equal justice for all
("Appeal" 1-2). King engages here with a larger historical movement
to remind Americans of the documents and narratives from their
past that support claims for racial equality. In the 1960s, historians
and researchers alike looked to rewrite Civil War memory in a way
that neither disregarded the importance of slavery as the agent of
conflict in the Civil War nor portrayed African Americans as naturally
inferior—a people without agency in the struggle for their own
freedom (Snyder 1-2, 36). By reshaping the narratives of the past to
reflect a nuanced version of the Civil War, these historians attempted
to break down the justifications for the racial hierarchy that
structured the white status quo.

By reshaping Civil War memory to focus on its promises of
equality, King develops a strong appeal for change on the grounds that
those promises had not yet been fulfilled. He draws compelling
parallels between the past and present, which framed the Civil War as
a battle unfinished, one fought today by the civil rights movement:

> The struggle for freedom, Mr. President, of which our Civil War
> was but a bloody chapter, continues throughout our land today.
> The courage and heroism of Negro citizens . . . is only further
> effort to affirm the democratic heritage so painfully won, in
> part, upon the grassy battlefields of Antietam, Lookout
> Mountain, and Gettysburg. ("Appeal" 3)

The metaphor of a modern Civil War presents Kennedy with
the moral imperative to follow in the footsteps of Lincoln, his
forebearer, and to help finally end the battle for equality begun one
hundred years before. "The time has come, Mr. President, to let those
dawn-like rays of freedom, first glimpsed in 1863, fill the heavens with
noonday sunlight of complete human decency" ("Appeal" 4). King
believed that the present situation demanded more than legislative

Includes short title because there's more than 1 source from that author.

Paragraphs indent ½ inch or 5 spaces.

action—it demanded from Kennedy an executive order that appealed to the "moral conscience of America." ("Appeal" 4)

But Kennedy never responded, and King found his ambivalence very disheartening. Without Kennedy, King felt that the civil rights movement would stall. He needed to re-create the conditions under which a document like the first Emancipation Proclamation came about—to foster the same tensions that brought to light the deep moral flaws of racism and propelled them to a national stage (Ward and Badger 141). Time was running out. The eyes of the world were focused on the civil rights movement, and King intended to capitalize. At midnight on June 1, he called his aides with an urgent message: in August, the civil rights movement would descend on the capital (Branch 53).

If King could not convince the president to change the moral conscience of America, he would attempt to do it himself. Two months later, King began to outline the speech that would conclude the ceremonies of the March on Washington. In essence, it reflected the same historical appeal he had made to the president in the Second Emancipation Proclamation. He intended to shift predominant public memory from one that highlighted the mutual sacrifice of the Blue and Gray to one that focused on the Civil War's guarantees of equality. These guarantees served as the grounds on which King would build his argument for modern civil rights progress. Evoking the language of past Republican leaders, including Lincoln, he appealed to the American public to adopt a policy of inclusion, one with a vision for the future that was, in many ways, shaped in stark contrast to America's oppressive past.

On the morning of August 28, the turnout was slim, estimated at 25,000. Soon, however, protesters began arriving in swarms. At Union Station, trains pulled in first from Baltimore, then Georgia, the

Names both authors in a work with 2 authors.

Parell   6

Carolinas, Maryland, and further north (Hansen 33-35). By the time
King took the podium, he spoke before a crowd of nearly 250,000.
"Five score years ago," King began, "a great American in whose symbolic
shadow we stand today signed the Emancipation Proclamation"
("Dream" 1). This first sentence of King's "Dream" speech refers both
to Lincoln's Gettysburg Address and to the Emancipation Proclamation,
placing both documents at the forefront of America's Civil War
consciousness (Sundquist 145). As in the Second Emancipation
Proclamation, King intended to divert the predominant reconciliationist
memory of the Civil War to one that memorialized the guarantees of
racial justice embodied in the war's documents. Although his remarks
on those documents were brief, the broader, more inclusive historical
narratives toward which they gesture—those in which slavery is
accepted as the cause of the Civil War and African Americans are
acknowledged for their strategic contributions to military efforts—
gave further justification to uphold the guarantees of equality
memorialized in the documents themselves.

    These guarantees served as the moral structure of King's
national appeal for racial justice. If, as King argues, equality was a
right ensured by the course of American history, then segregation was
simply a breach of contract between the American government and its
African American constituents. He employs the metaphor of a "bad
check" to explain the chasm between historical promises of racial
equality and the realities faced in 1960s culture:

    In a sense we've come to our nation's capital to cash a check. . . .
    This note was a promise that all men—yes, black men as well as
    white men—would be guaranteed the unalienable rights of life,
    liberty and the pursuit of happiness. It is obvious today that
    America has defaulted on this promissory note insofar as her
    citizens of color are concerned. ("Dream" 1)

Includes page range because the information cited spans multiple pages.

Uses past tense ("began") to describe the scene—and present tense ("refers") to describe the text.

Ellipses indicate that some words are left out.

For a nation that claimed to uphold basic precepts of justice, the "bad check" metaphor was particularly compelling. Americans were posed with a moral imperative to rid themselves of the modern vestiges of slavery or else risk contradicting the principles of equality upon which the nation was founded.

King's powerful appeal to the moral conscience of America was only made possible by shaping a new narrative in Civil War memory that upheld equality as a basic right for all: "Many of our white brothers . . . have come to realize that their freedom is inextricably bound to our freedom ("Dream" 3). King begins here the process of linking the fulfillment of the civil rights cause to the betterment of the nation as a whole, a process necessary to garner the support of white moderates, partial to their own self-interest and thus indifferent to historical appeals for racial justice.

The incentive for civil rights progress was only strengthened by King's final moments at the podium, from which his speech gains its name. The appeal of King's utopian dream serves as a powerful motive to pursue civil rights equality. He dreams that "sons of former slaves and the sons of former slave-owners will be able to sit down together at the table of brotherhood" ("Dream" 4). He dreams that freedom will ring from "Stone Mountains of Georgia"—where the faces of Confederate generals are etched in rock—to "Lookout Mountain of Tennessee," the site of one of the Civil War's most famous battles (6). In essence, King's dream is that America will finally live up to the principles of freedom espoused at the time of its origin and live out "the true meaning of its creed" (4). Only then, King believes, will the battle for freedom begun at Fort Sumter finally reach its conclusion. King's direct references to the issue of slavery and to the battlegrounds on which the Civil War was fought serve as anchors in history that shape a clearer vision of future progress for all Americans. The moral

Parell   8

imperative that King presents to white individuals in order to tender
the check of racial justice is thus only made more pressing by the
collective will to realize King's dream—a dream rooted in the rhetoric
of the Civil War.

　　Ultimately, therefore, King's "Dream" speech promoted a
memory that prioritized the war's promises of equality as opposed to
the honor of its many battles. Historian David Blight explains:

> As Lincoln implied in that brief address at Gettysburg, the Civil
> War necessitated a redefinition of the United States, rooted
> somehow in the destruction of slavery and the . . . principle of
> human equality. In the "Dream" speech, King argued the same
> for his own era: the civil rights movement heralded yet another
> re-founding in the same principle, one hundred . . . years after
> Lincoln's promise. (2)

　　Throughout the Centennial years, civil rights leaders, including
King, waged war not only over modern policies and ideals, but over
historical truth as well. African American activists pushed back on the
predominant Civil War memory of the 1960s, promoting the war's
guarantees of equality over those of reconciliation. Such guarantees
became the grounds on which King and others shaped a compelling
appeal for civil rights progress in the modern era. "Just as abolitionists
had sought to exploit the promises enshrined in the Declaration of
Independence," historian Robert Cook writes, "their intellectual
successors had used the events of the Centennial to raise the
conscience of the American public in the 1960s" (qtd. in Ward and
Badger 144). Ultimately, therefore, civil rights leaders molded the
rhetoric of the Civil War to inspire a nation to throw off its shackles of
oppression and to breathe new life into the old slave hymn: "Free at
last, Free at last, Great God a-mighty, We are free at last" (King,
"Dream" 6).

*Source quoted in
another source.*

1″

Works Cited

Blight, David W. *American Oracle: The Civil War in the Civil Rights Era.*
Belknap Press of Harvard UP, 2013.

Branch, Taylor. "A Second Emancipation." *Washington Monthly*, Jan.-
Feb. 2013, pp. 27-52.

Cook, Robert. *Troubled Commemoration: The American Civil War
Centennial, 1961-1965.* Louisiana State UP, 2011.

Hansen, Drew. *The Dream: Martin Luther King, Jr., and the Speech That
Inspired a Nation.* HarperCollins, 2003.

King, Martin Luther, Jr. "An Appeal to the Honorable John F.
Kennedy President of the United States." 17 May 1962.
Civil Rights Movement Archive, www.crmvet.org/info/eman
cip2.pdf.

---. "I Have a Dream . . . Speech by the Rev. Martin Luther King Jr. at
the 'March on Washington.' " 28 Aug. 1963. *National Archives*,
www.archives.gov/files/press/exhibits/dream-speech.pdf.
Accessed 14 May 2019.

Snyder, Jeffrey Aaron. *Making Black History: The Color Line, Culture,
and Race in the Age of Jim Crow.* U of Georgia P, 2018.

Sundquist, Eric. *King's Dream.* Yale UP, 2009.

Ward, Brian, and Tony Badger. *The Making of Martin Luther King and
the Civil Rights Movement.* Macmillan, 1996.

Heading centered.

The list is alphabetized by authors' last names.

Double-spaced.

Each entry begins at the left margin; subsequent lines are indented ½ inch or 5 spaces.

Multiple works by a single author are listed alphabetically by title. After first entry, the author's name is replaced with three hyphens.

Every source used is in the Works Cited.

21 APA Style

WRITE WITH CLARITY, PRECISION, AND INCLUSION.
—*PUBLICATION MANUAL OF THE AMERICAN PSYCHOLOGICAL ASSOCIATION*

In 1929, a group of anthropologists and psychologists and business writers got together to come up with guidelines that would standardize the way scholars documented sources, assuming that such standards would make articles easier to read and understand. That short guide expanded into the *Publication Manual of the American Psychological Association*, published in its 7th edition in 2020. Almost all the disciplines in the social sciences now recommend following this style. This chapter provides guidelines for formatting and documenting an essay in APA style, along with an essay written by a college student that demonstrates that style.

A DIRECTORY TO APA STYLE
In-text documentation   360

Notes   364

Reference list   365

TITLE	AUTHOR	PUBLICATION

This chapter provides models and examples that are color-coded to help you see how to include source information in a text: orange for author or editor, yellow for title, blue for publication information— publisher, date of publication, page number(s), DOI or URL, and so on.

In-text documentation

Brief documentation in your text makes clear to your reader precisely what you took from a source. If you are quoting, provide the page number(s) or other text that will help readers find the quotation in the source. You're not required to give the page number(s) with a paraphrase or summary, but you may want to do so if you are citing a long or complex work.

PARAPHRASES and SUMMARIES are more common than QUOTATIONS in APA projects. As you cite each source, you will need to decide whether to name the author in a signal phrase— "as Duffy (2020) wrote"—or in parentheses—"(Duffy, 2020)." Note that APA requires the past tense when there's a date or present perfect tense when there's no date in SIGNAL PHRASES: "Moss (2019) argued," "Moss has argued."

TITLE	AUTHOR	PUBLICATION

1. AUTHOR NAMED IN A SIGNAL PHRASE

Put the date in parentheses after the author's last name, unless the year is mentioned in the sentence. Put any page number(s) you're including in parentheses after the quotation, paraphrase, or summary. Parenthetical documentation should come *before* the period at the end of the sentence and *after* any quotation marks.

> McCullough (2020) described John Adams as having "the hands of a man accustomed to pruning his own trees, cutting his own hay, and splitting his own firewood" (p. 18).

> In 2020, McCullough noted that John Adams's hands were those of a laborer (p. 18).

If the author is named after a quotation, put the page number(s) after the date.

> John Adams had "the hands of a man accustomed to pruning his own trees," according to McCullough (2020, p. 18).

2. AUTHOR NAMED IN PARENTHESES

If you do not mention an author in a signal phrase, put the name, the year of publication, and any page numbers in parentheses at the end of the sentence or right after the quotation, paraphrase, or summary.

> John Adams had "the hands of a man accustomed to pruning his own trees, cutting his own hay, and splitting his own firewood" (McCullough, 2020, p. 18).

3. AUTHORS WITH THE SAME LAST NAME

If your reference list includes more than one first author with the same last name, include initials to distinguish the authors from one another.

> Eclecticism is common in modern criticism (J. M. Smith, 1992, p. vii).

4. TWO AUTHORS

Always mention both authors. Use *and* in a signal phrase, but use an ampersand (&) in parentheses.

> Carlson and Ventura (1990) wanted to introduce Julio Cortázar, Marjorie Agosín, and other Latin American writers to an audience of English-speaking adolescents (p. v).
>
> According to the Peter Principle, "In a hierarchy, every employee tends to rise to his level of incompetence" (Peter & Hull, 1969, p. 26).

5. THREE OR MORE AUTHORS

When you refer to a work by three or more contributors, name only the first author followed by *et al.*, Latin for "and others."

> Peilen et al. (1990) supported their claims about corporate corruption with startling anecdotal evidence (p. 75).

6. ORGANIZATION OR GOVERNMENT AS AUTHOR

If an organization name has a familiar abbreviation, give the full name and the abbreviation in brackets the first time you cite the source. In subsequent references, use only the abbreviation. If the organization does not have a familiar abbreviation, always use its full name.

FIRST REFERENCE

(American Psychological Association [APA], 2020)

SUBSEQUENT REFERENCES

(APA, 2020)

7. AUTHOR UNKNOWN

Use the complete title if it's short; if it's long, use the first few words of the title under which the work appears in the reference list. Italicize the title if it's italicized in the reference list; if it isn't italicized there, enclose the title in quotation marks.

| TITLE | AUTHOR | PUBLICATION |

According to *Feeding Habits of Rams* (2000), a ram's diet often changes from one season to the next (p. 29).

The article noted that one healthy liver donor died because of "frightening" postoperative care ("Every Patient's Nightmare," 2007).

8. TWO OR MORE WORKS TOGETHER

If you document multiple works in the same parentheses, place the source information in alphabetical order, separated by semicolons.

Many researchers have argued that what counts as "literacy" is not necessarily learned at school (Heath, 1983; Moss, 2003).

9. TWO OR MORE WORKS BY ONE AUTHOR IN THE SAME YEAR

If your list of references includes more than one work by the same author published in the same year, order them alphabetically by title, adding lowercase letters (*a*, *b*, and so on) to the year.

Kaplan (2000a) described orderly shantytowns in Turkey that did not resemble the other slums he visited.

10. SOURCE QUOTED IN ANOTHER SOURCE

When you cite a source that was quoted in another source, add the words *as cited in*.

Thus, Modern Standard Arabic was expected to serve as the "moral glue" holding the Arab world together (Choueri, 2000, as cited in Walters, 2019, p. 475).

11. WORK WITHOUT PAGE NUMBERS

Instead of page numbers, some works have paragraph numbers, which you should include (preceded by the abbreviation *para.*) if you are referring to a specific part of such a source.

Russell's dismissals from Trinity College at Cambridge and from City College in New York City have been seen as examples of the controversy that marked his life (Irvine, 2006, para. 2).

In sources with neither page nor paragraph numbers, refer readers to a particular part of the source if possible, perhaps indicating a heading: (Brody, 2020, Introduction, para. 2).

12. AN ENTIRE WORK

You do not need to give a page number if you are directing readers' attention to an entire work.

> Kaplan (2000) considered Turkey and Central Asia explosive.

When you're citing an entire website, give the URL in the text. You do not need to include the website in your reference list. To document a webpage, see number 18 on page 374.

> Beyond providing diagnostic information, the website for the Alzheimer's Association (http://www.alz.org) includes a variety of resources for the families of patients.

13. PERSONAL COMMUNICATION

Document emails, telephone conversations, interviews, personal letters, messages from nonarchived online discussion sources, and other personal texts as *personal communication*, along with the person's initial(s), last name, and the date. You do not need to include such personal communications in your reference list.

> L. Strauss (personal communication, December 6, 2013) told about visiting Yogi Berra when they both lived in Montclair, New Jersey.

Notes

You may need to use footnotes to give an explanation or information that doesn't fit into your text. To signal a content footnote, place a superscript numeral at the appropriate point in your text. Include this information as a footnote, either at the bottom of that page or on a separate page with the heading **Footnotes** centered and in bold, after your reference list. If you have multiple notes, number them consecutively throughout your text. Here is an example from *In Search of Solutions: A New Direction in Psychotherapy* (2003).

TEXT WITH SUPERSCRIPT

An important part of working with teams and one-way mirrors is taking the consultation break, as at Milan, BFTC, and MRI.[1]

FOOTNOTE

[1] It is crucial to note here that while working with a team is fun, stimulating, and revitalizing, it is not necessary for successful outcomes. Solution-oriented therapy works equally well solo.

Reference list

A reference list provides full bibliographic information for every source cited in your text with the exception of entire websites, common computer software and mobile apps, and personal communications. See page 388 for guidelines on preparing such a list; for a sample reference list, see page 402.

Key elements for documenting sources

To document a source in APA style, you need to provide information about the author, the date, the title of the work you're citing, and the source itself (who published it; volume, issue, and page numbers; any DOI or URL). The following guidelines explain how to handle each of these elements generally, but there will be exceptions. For that reason, you'll want to consult the entries for the specific kinds of sources you're documenting; these entries provide templates showing which details you need to include. Be aware, though, that sometimes the templates will show elements that your source doesn't have; if that's the case, just omit those elements.

AUTHORS

Most entries begin with the author's last name, followed by the first and any middle initials: Smith, Z. for Zadie Smith; Kinder, D. R. for Donald R. Kinder.

- If the author is a group or organization, use its full name: Black Lives Matter, American Historical Association.
- If there is no author, put the title of the work first, followed by the date.
- If the author uses a screen name, first give their real name, followed by the screen name in brackets: Scott, B. [@BostonScott2]. If only the screen name is known, leave off the brackets: AvalonGirl1990.

DATES

Include the date of publication, in parentheses right after the author. Some sources require only the year; others require the year, month, and day; and still others require something else. Consult the entry in this chapter for the specific source you're documenting.

- For a book, use the copyright year, which you'll find on the copyright page. If more than one year is given, use the most recent one.
- For most magazine or newspaper articles, use the full date that appears on the work, usually the year followed by the month and day.
- For a journal article, use the year of the volume.
- Give the volume and issue for journals and magazines that include that information. No need to give that information for newspapers.
- For a work you found on a website, use the date when the work was last updated. If that information is not available, use the date when the work was published.
- If a work has no date, use *n.d.* for "no date."
- For online content that is likely to change, include the month, day, and year when you retrieved it. No need to do so for materials that are unlikely to change.

| TITLE | AUTHOR | PUBLICATION |

TITLES

Capitalize only the first word and any PROPER NOUNS and adjectives in the title and subtitle of the work you're citing. But sometimes you'll also need to provide the title of a periodical or website where a source was found, and those are done differently: capitalize all the principal words (excluding articles and prepositions).

- **For books, reports, webpages, podcasts**, and other works that stand on their own, italicize the title—*White fragility, Radiolab, The 9/11 report*. Do not italicize the titles of the sources where you found them, however: NPR, ProQuest.

- **For journal articles, book chapters, TV series episodes**, and other works that are part of a larger work, do not italicize the title: The snowball effect, Not your average Joe. But do italicize the title of the larger work: *The Atlantic, Game of thrones*.

- **If a work has no title**, include a description in square brackets after the date: [Painting of sheep on a hill].

- **If the title includes another title**, italicize it: *Frog and Toad* and the self. If the title you're documenting is itself in italics, do not italicize the title within it: *Stay, illusion!: The* Hamlet *doctrine*.

- **For untitled social media posts** or comments, include the first twenty words as the title, in italics and followed by a bracketed description: *TIL pigeons can fly up to 700 miles in one day* [Tweet].

SOURCE INFORMATION

This indicates where the work can be found (in a database or on a website, for example) and includes information about the publisher; any volume, issue, and page numbers; and, for some sources, a DOI or URL. For books, films, and other works that stand on their own, the source might be a publisher, a database, or a website. For articles, essays, and works that are part of larger works, the source might be a magazine, an anthology, or a TV series.

DOIS OR URLS

Include a DOI (digital object identifier, a string of letters and numbers that identifies an online document) for any work that has one, whether you accessed the source in print or online. For an online work with no DOI, include a URL unless the work is from an academic database. You can use a short DOI (which you can find at shortdoi.org) or a short URL (using tinyURL.com or another URL shortener) as long as it leads to the right source. Please note that all the documentation templates include DOIs; if the work you are documenting does not have one, just leave it off.

Authors and other contributors

Most entries begin with authors—one author, two authors, or twenty-five. And some include editors, translators, or others who've contributed. The following nine templates show you how to document the various kinds of authors and other contributors.

1. ONE AUTHOR

Author's Last Name, Initials. (Year of publication). *Title*. Publisher. DOI *or* URL

Lewis, M. (2003). *Moneyball: The art of winning an unfair game*. W. W. Norton.

2. TWO AUTHORS

First Author's Last Name, Initials, & Second Author's Last Name, Initials. (Year of publication). *Title*. Publisher. DOI *or* URL

Montefiore, S., & Montefiore, S. S. (2016). *The royal rabbits of London*. Aladdin.

TITLE	AUTHOR	PUBLICATION

3. THREE OR MORE AUTHORS

For three to twenty authors, include all names.

First Author's Last Name, Initials, Next Author's Last Name, Initials, & Final Author's Last Name, Initials. (Year of publication). *Title*. Publisher. DOI *or* URL

Greig, A., Taylor, J., & MacKay, T. (2013). *Doing research with children: A practical guide*. (3rd ed.). Sage.

For a work by twenty-one or more authors, name the first nineteen, followed by three ellipsis points, and end with the final author.

4. TWO OR MORE WORKS BY THE SAME AUTHOR

List works published in different years chronologically.

Lewis, B. (1995). *The Middle East: A brief history of the last 2,000 years*. Scribner.

Lewis, B. (2003). *The crisis of Islam: Holy war and unholy terror*. Modern Library.

If the works were published in the same year, list them alphabetically by title, adding *a*, *b*, and so on to the year.

Kaplan, R. D. (2000a). *The coming anarchy: Shattering the dreams of the post Cold War*. Random House.

Kaplan, R. D. (2000b). *Eastward to Tartary: Travels in the Balkans, the Middle East, and the Caucasus*. Random House.

5. AUTHOR AND EDITOR

If a book has an author and an editor who is credited on the cover, include the editor in parentheses after the title.

Author's Last Name, Initials. (Year of publication). *Title*. (Editor's Initials Last Name, Ed.). Publisher. DOI *or* URL (Original work published Year)

Dick, P. F. (2008). *Five novels of the 1960s and 70s*. (J. Lethem, Ed.). Library of America. (Original works published 1964–1977)

6. AUTHOR AND TRANSLATOR

Author's Last Name, Initials. (Year of publication). *Title*
(Translator's Initials Last Name, Trans.). Publisher. DOI
or URL (Original work published Year)

Hugo, V. (2008). *Les misérables* (J. Rose, Trans.). Modern Library.
(Original work published 1862)

7. EDITOR

Editor's Last Name, Initials (Ed.). (Year of publication). *Title*.
Publisher. DOI *or* URL

Jones, D. (Ed.). (2007). *Modern love: 50 true and extraordinary
tales of desire, deceit, and devotion*. Three Rivers Press.

8. UNKNOWN OR NO AUTHOR OR EDITOR

Title. (Year of Publication). Publisher. DOI *or* URL

Feeding habits of rams. (2000). Land's Point Press.

Clues in salmonella outbreak. (2008, June 21). *The New York
Times*, A13.

If the author is listed as Anonymous, use that as the author's name.

9. ORGANIZATION OR GOVERNMENT AS AUTHOR

Sometimes an organization or a government agency is both author
and publisher. If so, omit the publisher.

Organization Name *or* Government Agency. (Year of publication).
Title. DOI *or* URL

Catholic News Service. (2002). *Stylebook on religion 2000: A
reference guide*.

National Institute of Mental Health. (2004). *Autism spectrum
disorders*.

Articles and other short works

Articles, essays, reviews, and other short works are found in periodicals and books—in print, online, or in a database. For most short works, provide information about the author, the date, the titles of both the short work and the longer work, plus any volume and issue numbers, page numbers, and DOI or URL if there is one.

10. ARTICLE IN A JOURNAL

Author's Last Name, Initials. (Year). Title of article. *Title of Journal, volume*(issue), page(s). DOI *or* URL

Gremer, J. R., Sala, A., & Crone, E. E. (2010). Disappearing plants: Why they hide and how they return. *Ecology, 91*(11), 3407–3413. https://doi.org/10.1890/09-1864.1

11. ARTICLE IN A MAGAZINE

If a magazine is published weekly, include the year, month, and day. Put any volume number and issue number after the title.

Author's Last Name, Initials. (Year, Month Day). Title of article. *Title of Magazine, volume*(issue), page(s). DOI *or* URL

Klump, B. (2019, November 22). Of crows and tools. *Science, 366*(6468), 965. https://doi.org/10.1126/science.aaz7775

12. ARTICLE IN A NEWSPAPER

If page numbers are consecutive, separate them with an en dash. If not, separate them with a comma.

Author's Last Name, Initials. (Year, Month Day). Title of article. *Title of Newspaper,* page(s). URL

Spencer, A. (2021, February 15). Backlash for film about autism. *The New York Times,* C1–C2.

Schneider, G. (2005, March 13). Fashion sense on wheels. *The Washington Post,* F1, F6.

13. ARTICLE ON A NEWS WEBSITE

Italicize the titles of articles on *CNN, HuffPost, Salon, Vox,* and other news websites. Do not italicize the name of the website.

Author's Last Name, Initials. (Year, Month Day). *Title of article.* Name of Site. URL

Travers, C. (2019, December 3). *Here's why you keep waking up at the same time every night.* HuffPost. https://bit.ly/3drSwAR

14. JOURNAL ARTICLE FROM A DATABASE

Author's Last Name, Initials. (Year). Title of article. *Title of Journal, volume*(issue), pages. DOI

Simpson, M. (1972). Authoritarianism and education: A comparative approach. *Sociometry, 35*(2), 223–234. https://doi.org/10.2307/2786619

15. EDITORIAL

Editorials can appear in journals, magazines, and newspapers. If the editorial is unsigned, put the title in the author position.

Author's Last Name, Initials. (Year, Month Day). Title of editorial [Editorial]. *Title of Periodical.* DOI or URL

The Guardian view on local theatres: The shows must go on [Editorial]. (2019, December 6). *The Guardian.* https://bit.ly/2VZHIUg

16. REVIEW

Reviewer's Last Name, Initials. (Year, Month Day). Title of review [Review of the work *Title,* by Author's Initials Last Name]. *Name of Periodical* or *Blog.* DOI or URL

Johnson, S. (2017, December 15). Mysteries unfold in a land of minarets and magic carpets [Review of the book *The city of brass,* by S. A. Chakraborty]. *The New York Times.* https://nyti.ms/2kvwHFP

TITLE   AUTHOR   PUBLICATION

Documentation Map (APA)

Article in a Journal with a DOI

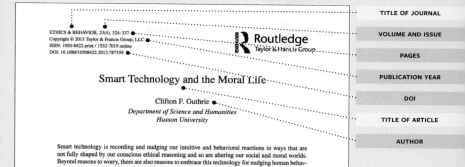

ETHICS & BEHAVIOR, 23(4), 324–337
Copyright © 2013 Taylor & Francis Group, LLC
ISSN: 1050-8422 print / 1532-7019 online
DOI: 10.1080/10508422.2013.787359

Routledge
Taylor & Francis Group

TITLE OF JOURNAL

VOLUME AND ISSUE

PAGES

PUBLICATION YEAR

DOI

TITLE OF ARTICLE

AUTHOR

Smart Technology and the Moral Life

Clifton F. Guthrie
Department of Science and Humanities
Husson University

Smart technology is recording and nudging our intuitive and behavioral reactions in ways that are not fully shaped by our conscious ethical reasoning and so are altering our social and moral worlds. Beyond reasons to worry, there are also reasons to embrace this technology for nudging human behavior toward prosocial activity. This article inquires about four ways that smart technology is shaping the individual moral life: the persuasive effect of promptware, our newly evolving experiences of embodiment, our negotiations with privacy, and our experiences of risk and serendipity.

Keywords: persuasive technology, morality, ethics, virtue

PERSUASIVE TECHNOLOGY

For some time, cars have worked to shape our behaviors, beeping to warn us when a door is unlocked or a seat belt unfastened, or giving us fuel efficiency feedback. These straightforward but persuasive sensor systems nudge us toward a repertoire of safe driving behaviors, and we often cannot override them even if we want to. Newer cars include an increasing number of smart technologies that interact with us more intelligently. Some detect the presence of electronic keys and make it impossible for drivers to lock themselves out. Others use sensors to monitor approaching obstacles or lane boundaries and give warnings or even apply the brakes. We are seeing the emergence of street intersections that communicate directly with cars and cars that can communicate with one another (Dean, Fletcher, Porges, & Ulrich, 2012). These are so-called smart technologies because they draw data from the environment and from us, and often make decisions on our behalf. A leading researcher in automated driving noted, "The driver is still in control. But if the driver is not doing the right thing, the technology takes over" (Markoff & Sengupta, 2013).

As cars become smarter they are helping to lead us into what technologists describe as a pervasive, ambient, or calm computing environment. In 1991, Mark Weiser of the Palo Alto Research Center presciently called it "ubiquitous computing" or "ubicomp" in a much-quoted article from *Scientific American*, in which he outlined what has come to be accepted as a standard interpretation of the history of human interaction with computers. This is the age in which computers are increasingly liberated from manual input devices like laptops and cell phones to become an invisible, interactive, computational sensorium. Early examples include motion sensors, smart

Correspondence should be addressed to Clifton F. Guthrie, Department of Science and Humanities, Husson University, 1 College Circle, Bangor, ME 04401. E-mail: cfguthrie@gmail.com

Guthrie, C. F. (2013). Smart technology and the moral life. *Ethics & Behavior, 23*(4), 324–337. https://doi.org/10.1080 /10508422.2013.787359

17. COMMENT ON AN ONLINE PERIODICAL ARTICLE OR BLOG POST

Writer's Last Name, Initials. [username]. (Year, Month Day).
Text of comment up to 20 words [Comment on the work
"Title of work"]. *Title of Publication*. DOI or URL

PhyllisSpecial. (2020, May 10). How about we go all the way
again? It's about time . . . [Comment on the article "2020
Eagles schedule: Picking wins and losses for all 16 games"].
The Philadelphia Inquirer. https://rb.gy/iduabz

If the author of the comment does not provide a real name, use the
username without brackets.

Simon. (2019, August 28). I've never read him, maybe I should?
[Comment on the blog post "H. P. Lovecraft. What am I
doing wrong?"]. *Reader Witch*. https://readerwitch.com
/2019/08/26/lovecraft/

18. WEBPAGE

Author's Last Name, Initials. (Year, Month Day). *Title of work*.
Title of Site. URL

Pleasant, B. (n.d.). *Annual bluegrass*. The National Gardening
Association. https://garden.org/learn/articles/view/2936/

If the author and the website name are the same, use the website
name as the author. If the content of the webpage is likely to change
and no archived version exists, use *n.d.* as the date and include a
retrieval date.

Centers for Disease Control and Prevention. (2019, December 2).
When and how to wash your hands. https://www.cdc.gov
/handwashing/when-how-handwashing.html

Worldometer. (n.d.). *World population*. Retrieved February 2,
2020, from https://www.worldometers.info/world-population/

TITLE   AUTHOR   PUBLICATION

Documentation Map (APA)
Webpage

URL

TITLE OF SITE

TITLE OF WORK

DATE OF PUBLICATION

AUTHOR

Lazette, M. P. (2015, February 24). *A hurricane's hit to households*.
Federal Reserve Bank of Cleveland. https://www.cleveland
fed .org/en/newsroom-and-events/publications/forefront
/ff-v6n01/ff-20150224-v6n0107-a-hurricanes-hit-to
-households.aspx

Books, parts of books, and reports

19. BASIC ENTRY FOR A BOOK

Author's Last Name, Initials. (Year of publication). *Title*.
Publisher. DOI *or* URL

PRINT BOOK

Penny, L. (2008). *A rule against murder*. Minotaur Books.

EBOOK

Jemisin, N. K. (2017). *The stone sky*. Orbit. https://amzn.com
/B01N7EQOFA

AUDIOBOOK

Obama, M. (2018). *Becoming* (M. Obama, Narr.) [Audiobook].
Random House Audio. http://amzn.com/B07B3JQZCL

Include the word *Audiobook* in brackets and the name of the narrator
only if you've mentioned the format and the narrator in what you've
written.

20. EDITION OTHER THAN THE FIRST

Author's Last Name, Initials. (Year). *Title* (Name *or* number ed.).
Publisher. DOI *or* URL

Rowling, J. K. (2015). *Harry Potter and the sorcerer's stone*
(Illustrated ed.). Arthur A. Levine Books.

Burch, D. (2008). *Emergency navigation: Find your position
and shape your course at sea even if your instruments fail*
(2nd ed.). International Marine/McGraw-Hill.

Documentation Map (APA)
Book

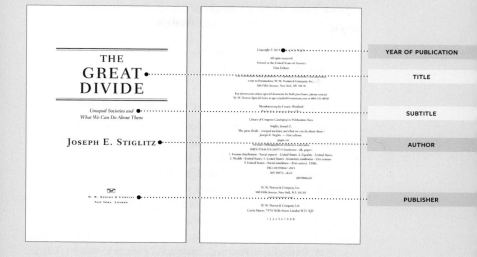

YEAR OF PUBLICATION

TITLE

SUBTITLE

AUTHOR

PUBLISHER

Stiglitz, J. E. (2015). *The great divide: Unequal societies and what we can do about them.* W. W. Norton.

21. EDITED COLLECTION OR ANTHOLOGY

Editor's Last Name, Initials (Ed.). (Year). *Title* (Name *or* number ed., Vol. number). Publisher. DOI *or* URL

Gilbert, S. M., & Gubar, S. (Eds.). (2003). *The Norton anthology of literature by women: The traditions in English* (3rd ed., Vol. 2). W. W. Norton.

22. WORK IN AN EDITED COLLECTION OR ANTHOLOGY

Author's Last Name, Initials. (Year of edited edition). Title of work. In Editor's Initials Last Name (Ed.), *Title of collection* (Name *or* number ed., Vol. number, pp. pages). Publisher. DOI *or* URL (Original work published Year)

Choi, Y. (2018). The art of losing. In H. Pitlor & R. Gay (Eds.), *The best American short stories 2018* (pp. 38–61). Houghton Mifflin. (Original work published 2017)

Baldwin, J. (2018). Notes of a native son. In M. Puchner, S. Akbari, W. Denecke, B. Fuchs, C. Levine, P. Lewis, & E. Wilson (Eds.), *The Norton anthology of world literature* (4th ed., Vol. F, pp. 728–743). W. W. Norton. (Original work published 1955)

23. CHAPTER IN AN EDITED BOOK

Author's Last Name, Initials. (Year). Title of chapter. In Editor's Initials Last Name (Ed.), *Title of book* (pp. pages). Publisher. DOI *or* URL

Amarnick, S. (2009). Trollope at fuller length: Lord Silverbridge and the manuscript of *The duke's children*. In M. Markwick, D. Denenholz Morse, & R. Gagnier (Eds.), *The politics of gender in Anthony Trollope's novels: New readings for the twenty-first century* (pp. 193–206). Routledge.

TITLE   AUTHOR   PUBLICATION

24. ENTRY IN A REFERENCE WORK

If the entry has no author, use the name of the publisher as the author. If the reference work has an editor, include their name after the title of the entry. If the entry is archived or is not likely to change, use the publication date and do not include a retrieval date.

Author's Last Name, Initials. (Year). Title of entry. In Editor's Initials Last Name (Ed.), *Title of reference work* (Name or number ed., Vol. number, pp. pages). Publisher. URL

Merriam-Webster. (n.d.). Epoxy. In *Merriam-Webster.com dictionary*. Retrieved January 29, 2020, from https://www.merriam-webster.com/dictionary/epoxy

25. BOOK IN A LANGUAGE OTHER THAN ENGLISH

Author's Last Name, Initials. (Year). *Title of book* [English translation of title]. Publisher. DOI *or* URL

Ferrante, E. (2011). *L'amica geniale* [My brilliant friend]. Edizione E/O.

26. ONE VOLUME OF A MULTIVOLUME WORK

Author's Last Name, Initials. (Year). *Title of entire work* (Vol. number). Publisher. DOI *or* URL

Spiegelman, A. (1986). *Maus* (Vol. 1). Random House.

If the volume has a separate title, include the volume number and title in italics after the main title.

27. RELIGIOUS WORK

If the date of the original publication is known, include it at the end.

Title. (Year of publication). Publisher. URL (Original work published Year)

New American Bible. (2002). United States Conference of Catholic Bishops. http://www.vatican.va/archive/ENG0839/_INDEX.HTM (Original work published 1970)

28. REPORT BY AN ORGANIZATION OR GOVERNMENT AGENCY

Author's Last Name, Initials. (Year). *Title* (Report No. number if
there is one). Publisher. DOI *or* URL

Centers for Disease Control and Prevention. (2009). *Fourth
national report on human exposure to environmental
chemicals.* US Department of Health and Human Services.
https://www.cdc.gov/exposurereport/pdf/fourthreport.pdf

Include the year, month, and day if the report you're documenting
includes that information. If more than one government department
is listed as the publisher, list the most specific department as the
author and the larger department as the publisher.

29. DISSERTATION

Author's Last Name, Initials. (Year). *Title* (Publication No.
number if there is one) [Doctoral dissertation, Name
of School]. Database or Archive Name. URL

Martin-Brualla, R. (2016). *Exploring the world's visual history*
[Doctoral dissertation, University of Washington]. Research
Works. https://digital.lib.washington.edu/researchworks
/handle/1773/37075

If the dissertation is in a database, do not include a URL.

Solomon, M. (2016). *Social media and self-examination:
The examination of social media use on identity, social
comparison, and self-esteem in young female adults*
(Publication No. 10188962) [Doctoral dissertation, William
James College]. ProQuest Dissertations & Theses Global.

30. PAPER OR POSTER PRESENTED AT A CONFERENCE

Presenter's Last Name, Initials. (Year, Month First Day–Last Day). *Title* [Paper or Poster presentation]. Name of Conference, City, State, Country. URL

Dolatian, H., & Heinz, J. (2018, May 25–27). *Reduplication and finite-state technology* [Paper presentation]. The 53rd Annual Meeting of the Chicago Linguistic Society, Chicago, United States. http://chicagolinguisticsociety.org/public/CLS53 _Booklet.pdf

Audio, visual, and other sources

If you are citing an entire website, do not include it in your reference list; simply mention the website's name in the body of your paper and include the URL in parentheses. Email, personal communication, or other unarchived discussions also do not need to be included in your list of references.

31. *WIKIPEDIA* ENTRY

Wikipedia archives its pages so give the date when you accessed the page and the URL of the version you're citing.

Title of entry. (Year, Month Day). In *Wikipedia.* URL

List of sheep breeds. (2019, September 9). In *Wikipedia.* https://en.wikipedia .org/w/index.php?title=List_of_sheep _breeds&oldid=914884262

32. ONLINE FORUM POST

Author's Last Name, Initials [username]. (Year, Month Day). *Content of the post up to 20 words* [Online forum post]. Name of Site. URL

Hanzus, D. [DanHanzus]. (2019, October 23). *GETCHA DAN HANZUS. ASK ME ANYTHING!* [Online forum post]. Reddit. https://bit.ly/38WgmSF

33. BLOG POST

Author's Last Name, Initials [username]. (Year, Month Day). Title of post. Name of Blog. URL

gcrepps. (2017, March 28). Shania Sanders. *Women@NASA*. https://blogs.nasa.gov/womenatnasa/2017/03/28/shania-sanders/

If only the username is known, use it without brackets.

34. ONLINE STREAMING VIDEO

Uploader's Last Name, Initials [username]. (Year, Month Day). *Title* [Video]. Name of Video Platform. URL

CinemaSins. (2014, August 21). *Everything wrong with* National Treasure *in 13 minutes or less* [Video]. YouTube. https://www.youtube.com/watch?v=1ul-_ZWvXTs

Whoever uploaded the video is considered the author, even if someone else created the content. If only a username is known, use it without brackets.

35. PODCAST

Host's Last Name, Initials (Host). (First Year–Last Year). *Podcast name* [Audio podcast]. Production Company. URL

Poor, N., Woods, E., & Thomas, R. (Hosts). (2017–present). *Ear hustle* [Audio podcast). PRX. https://www.earhustlesq.com/

36. PODCAST EPISODE

Host's Last Name, Initials (Host). (Year, Month Day). Episode title (No. episode number if any) [Audio podcast episode]. In *Podcast name*. Production Company. URL

Tamposi, E., & Samocki, E. (Hosts). (2020, January 8). The year of the broads [Audio podcast episode]. In *The broadcast podcast*. Podcast One. https://podcastone.com/episode/the-year-of-the-broads

37. FILM

Director's Last Name, Initials (Director). (Year). *Title* [Film].
Production Company. URL

Cuarón, A. (Director). (2016). *Harry Potter and the prisoner
of Azkaban* [Film; two-disc special ed. on DVD]. Warner
Brothers.

Jenkins, B. (Director). (2016). *Moonlight* [Film]. A24; Plan B;
PASTEL.

Indicate how you watched the film only if the format is relevant to
what you've written.

38. TELEVISION SERIES

Executive Producer's Last Name, Initials (Executive Producer).
(First Year–Last Year). *Title of series* [TV series].
Production Company. URL

Iungerich, L., Gonzalez, E., & Haft, J. (Executive Producers).
(2018–present). *On my block* [TV series]. Crazy Cat Lady
Productions.

Indicate how you watched the TV series (2-disc DVD set, for example)
only if the format is relevant to what you've written.

39. TELEVISION SERIES EPISODE

Last Name, Initials (Writer), & Last Name, Initials (Director).
(Year, Month Day). Title of episode (Season number,
Episode number) [TV series episode]. In Initials Last
Name (Executive Producer), *Title of series*. Production
Company. URL

Siegal, J. (Writer), Morgan, D. (Writer), & Sackett, M. (Director).
(2018, December 6). Janet(s) (Season 3, Episode 10)
[TV series episode]. In M. Schur, D. Miner, M. Sackett, &
D. Goddard (Executive Producers), *The good place*.
Fremulon; 3 Arts Entertainment; Universal Television.

40. MUSIC ALBUM

Artist's Last Name, Initials. (Year). *Title of album* [Album]. Label.

Lennox, A. (1995). *Medusa* [Album]. Arista.

41. SONG

Artist's Last Name, Initials. (Year). Name of song [Song]. On *Title of album*. Label.

Giddens, R. (2015). Shake sugaree [Song]. On *Tomorrow is my turn*. Nonesuch.

42. POWERPOINT SLIDES

Author's Last Name, Initials. (Year, Month Day). *Title of presentation* [PowerPoint slides]. Publisher. URL

Pavliscak, P. (2016, February 21). *Finding our happy place in the internet of things* [PowerPoint slides]. Slideshare. https://bit.ly/3aOcfs7

43. RECORDING OF A SPEECH OR WEBINAR

Author's Last Name, Initials. (Year, Month Day *or* Year). *Title* [Speech audio recording *or* Webinar]. Publisher. URL

Kennedy, J. F. (1961, January 20). *Inaugural address* [Speech audio recording]. American Rhetoric. https://bit.ly/339Gc3e

For a webinar, include only the year.

Rodrigo, S. (2020). *Keep calm (and compassionate) & move everything online* [Webinar]. W. W. Norton. https://seagull .wwnorton.com/CompositionTeachingOnline

44. MAP

Mapmaker's Last Name, Initials. (Year). *Title of map* [Map]. Publisher. URL

Daniels, M. (2018). *Human terrain: Visualizing the world's population, in 3D* [Map]. The Pudding. https://pudding .cool/2018/10/city_3d/

45. SOCIAL MEDIA POSTS

If only the username or organization is known, provide it without brackets. List any attachments (e.g., videos, images, or links) in brackets. Replicate any emoji or include a bracketed description. Do not change spelling or capitalization in a social media reference, even if it looks wrong.

Author's Last Name, Initials [@username]. (Year, Month Day). *Content of post up to 20 words* [Description of any attachments] [Type of post]. Platform. URL

TWEET

Baron, D. [@DrGrammar]. (2019, November 11). *Gender conceal: Did you know that pronouns can also hide someone's gender?* [Thumbnail with link attached] [Tweet]. Twitter. https://bit.ly/2vaCcDc

INSTAGRAM PHOTOGRAPH OR VIDEO

Jamil, J. [@jameelajamilofficial]. (2018, July 18). *Happy Birthday to our leader. I steal all my acting faces from you. @kristenanniebell* [Face with smile and sunglasses emoji] [Photograph]. Instagram. https://www.instagram.com/p/BlYX5F9FuGL/

FACEBOOK POST

Black Lives Matter. (2015, October 23). *Rise and grind! Did you sign this petition yet? We now have a sign on for ORGANIZATIONS to lend their* [Image attached]. Facebook. www.facebook.com/BlackLivesMatter/photos/a.29480720 4023865.1073741829.180212755483311/504711973033386 /?type=3&theater

46. DATA SET

> Author's Last Name, Initials. (Year). *Title of data set* (Version number if there is one) [Data set]. Publisher. DOI *or* URL
> Pew Research Center. (2019). *Core trends survey* [Data set]. https://www.pewresearch.org/internet/dataset/core-trends -survey/

If the publisher is the author, no need to list it twice.

47. SUPREME COURT CASE

> Name of Case, volume US pages (year). URL
> Plessy v. Ferguson, 163 US 537 (1896). https://www.oyez.org /cases/1850-1900/163us537
> Obergefell v. Hodges, 576 US ___ (2015). https://www.oyez.org /cases/2014/14-556

The source for most Supreme Court cases is United States Reports, which is abbreviated *US* in the reference list entry. If the case does not yet have a page number, use three underscores instead.

Sources not covered by APA

To document a source for which APA does not provide guidelines, look at models similar to the source you have cited. Give any information readers will need in order to find the source themselves— author; date of publication; title; and information about the source itself (including who published it; volume, issue, and page numbers; and a DOI or URL). You might want to check your reference note to be sure it will lead others to your source.

Formatting a research essay

Title page. APA generally requires a title page. The page number should go in the upper right-hand corner. Center the full title of the paper in bold in the top half of the page. Center your name, the name

| TITLE | AUTHOR | PUBLICATION |

of your department and school, the course number and name, the instructor's name, and the due date on separate lines below the title. Leave one line between the title and your name.

Page numbers. Place the page number in the upper right-hand corner. Number pages consecutively throughout.

Fonts, spacing, margins, and indents. Use a legible font that will be accessible to everyone, either a serif font (such as Times New Roman or Bookman) or a sans serif font (such as Calibri or Verdana). Use a sans serif font within figure images. Double-space the entire paper, including any notes and your list of references; the only exception is footnotes at the bottom of a page, which should be single-spaced, and tables and images, where the spacing will vary. Leave one-inch margins at the top, bottom, and sides of your text; do not justify the text. The first line of each paragraph should be indented one-half inch (or five to seven spaces) from the left margin. APA recommends using one space after end-of-sentence punctuation.

Headings. Though they are not required in APA style, headings can help readers follow your text. The first level of heading should be bold and centered; the second level should be bold and flush with the left margin; the third level should be bold, italicized, and flush left. Capitalize the first word and all other important words; do not capitalize *a, an, the,* or PREPOSITIONS.

First Level Heading

Second Level Heading

Third Level Heading.

Abstract. An abstract is a concise summary of your paper that introduces readers to your topic and main points. Most scholarly journals require an abstract; an abstract is not typically required for student papers, so check your instructor's preference. Put your abstract on the second page, with the word *Abstract* centered and in bold at the top. Unless your instructor specifies a length, limit your abstract to 250 words or fewer.

Long quotations. Indent quotations of forty or more words one-half inch (or five to seven spaces) from the left margin. Do not use quotation marks, and place the page number(s) or documentation information in parentheses *after* the end punctuation. If there are paragraphs in the quotation, indent the first line of each paragraph another one-half inch.

> Kaplan (2000) captured ancient and contemporary Antioch:
>> At the height of its glory in the Roman-Byzantine age, when it had an amphitheater, public baths, aqueducts, and sewage pipes, half a million people lived in Antioch. Today the population is only 125,000. With sour relations between Turkey and Syria, and unstable politics throughout the Middle East, Antioch is now a backwater—seedy and tumbledown, with relatively few tourists. (p. 123)
>
> Antioch's decline serves as a reminder that the fortunes of cities can change drastically over time.

List of references. Start your list on a new page after the text but before any endnotes. Title the page *References*, centered and in bold, and double-space the entire list. Each entry should begin at the left margin, and subsequent lines should be indented one-half inch (or five to seven spaces). Alphabetize the list by authors' last names (or by editors' names, if appropriate). Alphabetize works that have no author or editor by title, disregarding *a*, *an*, and *the*. Be sure every source listed is cited in the text; do not include sources that you consulted but did not cite.

Tables and figures. Above each table or figure (charts, diagrams, graphs, photos, and so on), write *Table* or *Figure* and a number, flush left and in bold (e.g., **Table 1**). On the following line, give a descriptive title, flush left and italicized. Below the table or figure, include a note with any necessary explanation and source information.

Table 1

Hours of Instruction Delivered per Week

	American classrooms	Japanese classrooms	Chinese classrooms
First grade			
Language arts	10.5	8.7	10.4
Mathematics	2.7	5.8	4.0
Fifth grade			
Language arts	7.9	8.0	11.1
Mathematics	3.4	7.8	11.7

Note. Adapted from *Peeking Out from Under the Blinders: Some Factors We Shouldn't Forget in Studying Writing,* by J. R. Hayes, 1991, National Center for the Study of Writing and Literacy (https://archive.nwp.org/cs/public/print/resource/720).

Number tables and figures separately, and be sure to discuss them in your text so that readers know how they relate.

Student research essay, APA style

Eli Vale is a student at Texas A & M University, San Antonio, where he is majoring in kinesiology. He wrote this essay for his Composition 2 course, one in which students spent the entire semester researching and writing about a topic of their choice. Vale wrote about the challenges that nurses in San Antonio face—and he then revised the essay for this book in order to address how a situation that did not exist when he first wrote it affected those nurses: the coronavirus pandemic. In addition to being a full-time student, Vale works as a rehab aide at a hospital in San Antonio, so his essay is based in part on his own firsthand observations and interviews.

Student Research Essay, APA Style

1

Page number appears in upper right corner.

Title is bold and centered.

Name is centered below the title, with 1 double-spaced line in between.

**The Causes of Burnout in San Antonio Nurses—
And Some Possible Solutions**

Eli Nicholas Vale

Department of Language, Literature, and Arts

Texas A&M University, San Antonio

English 1302: Composition 2

Professor Sarah Dwyer

May 22, 2020

2

Abstract

The COVID-19 pandemic has led to widespread recognition of the heroic actions that nurses take every day. It has also shed light on the many stressors that nurses face even under the best circumstances— stressors that can lead to burnout. Nurses experience burnout due to problematic nurse-to-patient ratios, intense physical and mental demands, and a lack of necessary breaks. This paper explores these causes of burnout in nurses and suggests solutions based on leading research in the field. The demands of caring for many patients at one time affects the physical and emotional health of nurses, long shifts with few breaks even to sit and eat can cause other physical strain including musculoskeletal disorders, and the nature of the medical field can leave nurses in complicated and stressful legal situations without clear legal protection. Burnout can appear as exhaustion, depersonalization, and frequent illness. Once burnout is recognized and acknowledged, a crucial first step, hospitals can start to consider solutions. These solutions include mandatory breaks from work, better staffing regulation, discounted therapy, and an increase in physical and legal protection. A damaged healthcare system has created the burnout experienced routinely by nurses, which is harmful to the nurses themselves and to their patients, and contributes to high turnover rates. Implementing solutions to nurse burnout is key in providing the best possible care for both patients and hospital employees.

Abstract begins a new page. Heading is bold and centered.

Abstract text does not need a paragraph indent.

3

**The Causes of Burnout in San Antonio Nurses—
And Some Possible Solutions**

Title is bold and centered.

Hospitals today are facing challenges never seen prior to the COVID-19 outbreak. Of all medical personnel, nurses are at the forefront of the battle against this virus. Consider the experiences, for example, of one nurse working in the coronavirus unit at Methodist Hospital in San Antonio, Texas. Here's how this nurse (who wished to remain anonymous and will be referred to as "Nurse A") described her work with COVID-19 patients: "As a COVID nurse, you become everything the patient could possibly need. You are the phlebotomist, physical therapist, respiratory therapist, patient care tech, and housekeeper. But most importantly, you become their family in this time of need" (personal communication, May 12, 2020). This is because family members are not allowed to visit loved ones who are in isolation, even if they are dying; as a result, a nurse is their last comforter, holding their hand as they pass away. Such experiences take a large emotional toll on COVID nurses.

Personal communications are documented in-text but are not included on the references list.

In fact, Nurse A (personal communication, May 12, 2020) said that the mental stress is greater than the physical stress. Even the process of gowning up and making sure all personal protective equipment (PPE) is clean and worn securely can be nerve wracking. Changing out of her clothes and then putting on the gown, mask, face shield, and gloves takes time and mental energy, even before she enters the patient's room. And when she leaves the room, she has to make sure all PPE are taken off in a way that does not contaminate other surfaces. And then she must repeat this process each time she enters and exits a patient's room.

Because of the increased responsibilities and stressful conditions, however, Nurse A (personal communication, May 12, 2020) reported that the nurses in her unit are being treated better than they were before

1″

4

the pandemic. COVID nurses have meals provided throughout the day and have ready access to bathrooms, both hard to come by in regular shifts. She pointed out that it took a global pandemic to recognize the need for safer nurse-to-patient ratios, lunch breaks, and bathroom breaks—and to finally recognize the heroic work being done by nurses, work they have always done every single day.

These improved conditions have diminished since the virus surged, and in later communication Nurse A (personal communication, August 4, 2020) said the situation in the COVID unit was vastly different than it had been prior to the surge, with nurses responsible for as many as five patients at a time. A single nurse caring for so many patients in serious condition creates a dangerous amount of stress. However, stress is something these nurses are familiar with: they have dealt with exhaustion for a long time.

1″   1″

In fact, while nurses are finally being recognized as heroes during this pandemic, they have always played an essential though often unappreciated role in the Bexar County healthcare system. According to the Texas Board of Nursing (2018), there are 11,161 registered nurses employed at inpatient and outpatient facilities in Bexar County. Nurses who work in hospital settings are likely to deal with many more daily stressors than nurses at other facilities. Many of these nurses are employed at some of the most well-known healthcare systems in San Antonio, including Methodist Hospital, Baptist Medical Center, University Hospital, and Christus Santa Rosa Medical Center (Hernandez, 2018). Unfortunately, in spite of some improvements like those described by Nurse A, the working conditions at these well-known hospitals continue to undermine their nurses' ability to provide optimal care to patients.

In San Antonio, a damaged healthcare system has created an epidemic of dangerous nursing conditions. In many cases, the ratio of

In-text documentation that includes only the date goes right after the author.

5

nurses to patients is problematic, and nurses have to take on more patients than they should. This can affect patient care, and the demands of caring for too many patients at one time can also impact nurses' own physical, emotional, and mental health. Together, these conditions put nurses at risk of experiencing burnout. Signs of such burnout include exhaustion, a lack of interest in personal interaction with others, and frequent illness (Nursing.org, n.d.). In sum, problematic nurse-to-patient ratios, intense physical demands, insufficient breaks, and mental health issues create dangerous stress, which can lead to burnout. The city of San Antonio needs to recognize these issues and come up with solutions to prevent them. Potential solutions include a permanently lowered nurse-to-patient ratio, mandatory lunch breaks, increased security, and discounted physical and mental health therapy for nurses.

For a closer look at how damaging such burnout can be, Nursing .org (n.d.) provided a succinct description of its signs and symptoms:

> Nurse burnout is caused by many different work-related issues. Nurses deal with death on a regular basis, and the emotional strain of losing patients and assisting grieving family members may become overwhelming. In addition, long shifts of 12 or more hours often lead to exhaustion and stress. ("Causes of Nursing Burnout")

Nursing.org (n.d.) went on to suggest the need to recognize those symptoms:

> The most important thing is to recognize symptoms as early as possible before they become overwhelming. No matter how minute warning signs may seem at the time, it's crucial to listen to your body and mind. All healthcare professionals should be familiar with potential burnout symptoms and should be

Signal phrases are in past tense.

1″

6

prepared to deal with them as quickly as possible. ("Warning Signs and Symptoms of Nursing Burnout")

Parenthetical documentation follows the punctuation in a block quote.

The first step toward solving the issue of nurse burnout, as Nursing .org (n.d.) pointed out, is to recognize the signs of burnout and start to combat their causes in the workplace. As Reineck and Furino (2005) concluded in a study on nursing careers: "Not only does workload take a toll on the nurse, but also affects the quality of care" (p. 30). Recognizing and reducing nurse burnout is crucial for the well-being of both the nurses and their patients.

Year follows authors' names, and page number follows direct quote.

Insufficient Staffing

Insufficient staffing is one of the primary causes of burnout, including shortages of registered nurses on overnight shifts and of supporting staff such as certified nursing assistants and patient care assistants in all shifts (Reineck & Furino, 2005). To provide some context for the situation in San Antonio, consider how many nurses there are (20,972) relative to the overall population (1,988,364). Keep in mind that the entire population of nurses—20,972—is not employed at hospitals. This total includes nurses who work in schools, home health agencies, and other settings that are less strenuous than hospitals. Table 1 compares the nurse-to-patient ratio in Bexar County (all of it in San Antonio) with that in another county in Texas and calculates how many nurses there are per 100,000 people.

2 authors in parenthetical documentation are linked with ampersand.

Table 1 shows that nurses in Bexar County have to care for many more patients than those in Bastrop County. In other words, Bastrop County is more equipped to give patients the care they need; if 100,000 people were to become ill in Bastrop County, each nurse would need to care for 2.369% of those patients. On the other hand, if 100,000 people were to fall ill in Bexar County (San Antonio), each nurse would have to care for 10.54% of them, creating a dangerous ratio of nurses to population in San Antonio.

7

Table 1

Ratio of Nurses to Population in Bastrop and Bexar Counties

Table number is bold and left justified.

Descriptive title is italicized and appears below table number.

	2018 Population	2018 RN Total	Ratio of RNs to 100,000 Population
Bastrop	94,545 citizens	224 nurses	224 nurses caring for 94,545 citizens

$$\frac{224 \text{ nurses}}{94,545 \text{ citizens}} = \frac{236.9 \text{ nurses}}{100,000 \text{ citizens}} = 2.369\%$$

Bastrop Ratio   Comparison Ratio

Based on the number of nurses in Bastrop County, each nurse would have to care for 2.369% of a population of 100,000.

The higher the percentage, the more patients each nurse needs to care for. Therefore, as the percentage increases, there is a lower number of nurses available to sufficiently care for the population.

	2018 Population	2018 RN Total	Ratio of RNs to 100,000 Population
Bexar	1,988,364 citizens	20,972 nurses	20,972 nurses caring for 1,988,364 citizens

$$\frac{20,972 \text{ nurses}}{1,988,364 \text{ citizens}} = \frac{1,054 \text{ nurses}}{100,000 \text{ citizens}} = 10.54\%$$

Bexar Ratio   Comparison Ratio

Based on the number of nurses in Bastrop County, each nurse would have to care for 10.54% of a population of 100,000.

These statistics indicate that Bexar County, which San Antonio encompasses, faces dangerous nurse-to-patient ratios due to a high population and a proportionately low number of nurses.

Note. Data from the Texas Department of State Health Services (2018).

Source information is given in table note.

8

Potential staffing solutions could include a set nurse-to-patient ratio of 1:3. Hospitals could also have a staff of on-call nurses, which would help maintain the nurse-to-patient ratio even when patient admissions increase.

When presented with evidence of insufficient staffing, people outside the nursing profession might argue that measuring the nursing population relative to the general population is misleading, given that not every person in Bexar County seeks treatment at the same time. Others might note that most nurses chose to pursue a career in a fast-paced work environment despite the risks and challenges. The shortage of nurses in San Antonio could also be attributed to factors outside of a hospital administration's control, such as a lack of younger nurses to take the place of the many older nurses in San Antonio who regularly go into retirement (Pelayo, 2013).

Notes what others might think.

We might address the need for more young nurses by encouraging students to go into hospital nursing as a way to gain hands-on experience, rather than going straight into non-clinical nursing roles. But many potential nurses may look at the job description and feel that the paycheck is not worth the intense work demands. And increasing the base pay might then impact the number of nurses hired, as the hospital would have to distribute costs.

Another option is to promote bridge programs, in which student nurses take classes at a community college or university while completing their clinical work at an affiliated hospital, which then hires the nurses upon graduation. This would offer young nurses guaranteed employment once they graduate while also helping to solve the hospital's staffing shortage.

9

Intense Physical and Mental Demands

Headings help
organize the essay.

Another major cause of burnout is the intense physical and mental demands of nursing. A significant part of a nurse's everyday regimen includes standing for prolonged periods, lifting patients, and pushing wheelchairs and gurneys, all of which can harm a nurse's physical health. The most common nursing injury is a strained back, but other physical stress points include sore shoulders from pushing wheelchairs and gurneys and injuries from falling while they work (Fohn, 2014). Nurses typically stand for most of their shift, leading to foot and knee complications and foot pain. Regardless of their fitness level, they are required to lift and transport immobile patients. As a result of this continuous lifting and bending, nurses are at a high risk of developing musculoskeletal disorders (Fohn, 2014).

While hospitals cannot eliminate the heavy physical demands of the job, they can help nurses manage such complications by providing discounted physical therapy sessions. A physical therapist can treat the aches, strains, and injuries that accumulate over long shifts, helping alleviate the fatigue and pain and other physical symptoms of burnout. Providing this kind of help would increase nurses' productivity.

Mental health issues also contribute to burnout. While many nurses in San Antonio are passionate about the care they provide to patients, that care sometimes presents life-and-death choices. As a result, nurses can become excessively worried and anxious about their work. Across the country, the nursing profession has been shown to be incredibly taxing on the mental well-being of employees. In a study conducted on 332 hospital nurses in Colorado, 86% showed symptoms of burnout (Mealer et al., 2009). And burnout was not the only mental health concern found; other psychological conditions included PTSD, depression, and anxiety (Mealer et al., 2009).

Past tense is used to
discuss the results of
a study.

10

Hospital administrators also need to respond to the psychological effects this profession can have. To ensure the mental health of nursing staff, hospitals should offer a healthcare-worker hotline. Nurses struggling with the death of a patient would be able to call this hotline for support. As with physical therapy, nurses should be offered discounted psychiatric therapy sessions. Helping nurses take care of their mental health would help prevent psychological symptoms of burnout such as irritability, dissociation, or depression.

Some of the most stressful situations are when patients become violent. And nurses who are threatened or assaulted by a patient cannot engage in self-defense without risk of losing their licenses. It wasn't until 2013 that a nurse assaulted by a patient could expect any legal defense at all. In that year, Governor Rick Perry signed a bill stating that assaulting a nurse will result in punishment ranging from a Class A misdemeanor to a third-degree felony (Emergency Nurses Association, 2013)—a welcome, if somewhat late, protection for nurses.

Parenthetical documentation goes right after the information cited, so it is not always at the end of a sentence.

Especially when life-and-death choices are on the line, emotions take over, leading to a patient confronting the caregiver or the patient's family expressing anger toward hospital staff. Some of those observing such confrontations may point out that it is reasonable for people to become aggressive when there are serious choices to be made. Families might feel worried or scared for their loved one. Or the patient might be very frightened and exhausted from treatment. However, not every such confrontation is fueled by legitimate emotions, and sometimes nurses are confronted by irrational verbal and even physical violence.

Preventing such dangerous confrontations calls for increased security in hospital units, which should be based on patient capacity. Using the same strategy as for nurse-to-patient ratios to maintain

11

optimum patient care, hospitals should adopt a reasonable security-to-patient ratio in each hospital unit of 1:50. Having one officer present for every 50 patients in a hospital unit would provide nurses with increased safety in the event of an assault. Additional officers should also be present in any unit housing hostile patients. For example, once any patients have threatened to harm themselves or others, an officer should remain in their rooms so that nurses can continue providing care without risking their own safety. Hospitals also need to regulate visitors. First, patients must approve all visitors. This requirement will help prevent abusive family members from assaulting patients or staff. In addition, no one with a record of violence, assault, or abuse should be allowed to visit. Not admitting visitors who have a history of confrontation and aggression will help decrease the frequency of violence in hospitals. Nurses in San Antonio will then be able to trust that they are safe and can put all their focus on patient care.

Skipping Necessary Breaks

Skipping meals and even bathroom breaks is a third cause of burnout among nurses. To alleviate the stress of long shifts, hospitals should require nurses to take a lunch break. An uninterrupted lunch break would not only enable nurses to take care of their own basic needs, but would also help prevent fatigue and low blood sugar levels by allowing them to rehydrate. Depending on the patient load, a nurse should have a minimum break of 30 minutes and a maximum of one hour. Nurses working 12-hour shifts should have an hour break. Unfortunately, nurses in Texas are not legally entitled to take lunch breaks (Texas Workforce Commission, n.d.). Medical employers take advantage of the fine print, which is why many nurses go without any breaks at all and administrators face few if any penalties.

We all know that in this time of pandemic, COVID nurses in San Antonio (and everywhere) are working heroically in unbelievably

12

stressful conditions. But all nurses, even those working in non-COVID units, are experiencing burnout due to problematic nurse-to-patient ratios, intense physical and mental demands, and the lack of necessary breaks. To help prevent nurse burnout, hospital administrators need to consider more staffing, discounted therapy sessions, and mandatory lunch breaks. San Antonio's nurses are taking on more patients than they can handle, which affects the quality of care they can provide. In order to deliver the best care to patients in the Bexar County area, we need to deliver the best care to those who look after them—remembering that they are our lifelines, the heroes we cannot do without.

List of references begins a new page.

Entries are arranged alphabetically by author's last name.

Entries flush left; subsequent lines indent ½″ or 5 spaces.

DOI is provided when one is available.

Retrieval date is included when the content of an online source may change.

References

Emergency Nurses Association. (2013). *Emergency Nurses Association applauds Texas legislation that raises assaults against emergency department personnel to third degree felony.* https://prnewswire .com/news-releases/emergency-nurses-association-applauds -texas-legislation-that-raises-assaults-against-emergency -department-personnel-to-third-degree-felony-212198351.html

Fohn, R. (2014, December 4). Stress test: Researchers studying soaring stress levels among nurses. *Mission.* uthscsa.edu /mission/stress-test-researchers-studying-soaring-stress -levels-among-nurses/

Hernandez, K. (2018, July 27). Largest San Antonio hospitals by beds. *San Antonio Business Journal.* https://www.bizjournals.com /sanantonio/subscriber-only/2018/07/27/hospitals-by-beds.html

Mealer, M., Burnham, E. L., Goode, C. J., Rothbaum, B., & Moss, M. (2009). The prevalence and impact of post traumatic stress disorder and burnout syndrome in nurses. *Depression & Anxiety, 26*(12), 1118–1126. http://doi.org.10.1002/da.20631

Nursing.org. (n.d.). *Nurse burnout.* Retrieved April 18, 2019, from https://www.nursing.org/resources/nurse-burnout/

Pelayo, L. W. (2013). Responding to the nursing shortage: Collaborations in an innovative paradigm for nursing education. *Nursing Education Perspectives, 34*(5), 351–352.

Reineck, C., & Furino, A. (2005, January–February). Nursing career fulfillment: Statistics and statements from registered nurses. *Nursing Economic$, 23*(1).

Texas Board of Nursing. (2018). *Practice—Peer review: Incident-based or safe harbor.* Retrieved January 24, 2019, from https://www .bon.texas.gov/practice_peer_review.asp

14

Texas Department of State Health Services. (2018, November 29). *Registered nurses, 2018*. Texas Health and Human Services. https://www.dshs.texas.gov/chs/hprc/tables/2018/RN18.aspx

Texas Workforce Commission. (n.d.). *Fair Labor Standards Act—What it does and does not do*. Retrieved April 18, 2019, from https://twc .texas.gov/news/efte/flsa_does_and_ doesnt_do.html

PART FIVE

LANGUAGE & STYLE

GET ATTENTION

22 Getting & Keeping Attention

GOOD WRITING IS . . . STILL ONE OF THE BEST TOOLS WE
HAVE TO GET AND CAPTURE PEOPLE'S ATTENTION.

—ROBIN SLOAN

Once upon a time—and for a very long time, too—style in writing meant ornamentation, "dressing up" your language the way you might dress up for a fancy party. In fact, ancient images often show rhetoric as a woman, Dame Rhetorica, in a gaudy, flowing gown covered with figures of speech—metaphors, similes, alliteration, hyperbole, and so on: her "stylish" ornaments. This view eventually led many writers to view style as mere decoration.

But not today. Not in a time of instantaneous communication, of being inundated with messages of all kinds—news, posts, notifications, ads—all of them coming at us with the force of a fire hose.

Dame Rhetorica, from Gregor Reisch's *Margarita Philosophica* (1504).

In such a time, how can we get others to pay attention to what we say or write? I believe the best answer to this question is by attending carefully to our use of language and style. And by style I mean *how* a message is presented, not simply what it says. In this view, style isn't just the use of pretty language. Rather, it is a crucial element in making a message effective, memorable, compelling—and heard.

Today, then, style and substance are inseparable, and style is more important than ever before for getting and holding an audience's attention. Rhetorician Richard Lanham argues that the most important task facing writers and speakers today is not learning as much as possible about a subject or presenting the most convincing evidence to support a claim about that subject. Rather, the most important task today is *getting the attention of those we want to address!*

For a dramatic example, think of CLICKBAIT, those provocative headlines or subject lines that are intended solely to grab readers' attention and pull them into an article, regardless of whether they are accurate or not:

> "Man tries to hug mountain lion: guess what happens next!"
>
> "She changed her name for a horrible reason. Now she tells why."
>
> "Was Amelia Earhart eaten by coconut crabs?"

These headlines fairly shout "click on me!" Marketers tell us that shocking readers is an effective way of getting their attention, though perhaps not always in holding it. And these days, getting and holding attention is sometimes a pretty desperate business. Lady Gaga recalls a time before she was well known and was singing in jazz bars in New York. One evening she faced a crowd of loud college students who would not be quiet; she just couldn't seem to get their attention. What did she do? Undressed down to her underwear, singing all the time—and getting, in short order, a very attentive audience. Later she said that night marked a kind of turning point for her, when she learned the importance of being able to "command attention."

Commanding attention is definitely a challenge in a time when we are so frequently drowning in information. This chapter provides some time-tested strategies for doing so—without taking your clothes off!

GETTING ATTENTION

In ancient Rome, orators often spoke in large outdoor amphitheaters, without the aid of microphones or visual aids. The technology they used was the human voice, which they trained to perfection so that they could project and be heard by thousands of people. Researchers are still trying to figure out how they did it, but we can assume that these speakers commanded attention through the sounds and rhythms of their voices as well as of the words they chose to use. So it's important to remember that these words count: getting attention will usually backfire if you don't have anything important, meaningful, or entertaining to say. Fortunately, speakers and writers today have many more tools available for drawing an audience's attention. Here are some that you may want to take advantage of.

Attention-getting titles

While you'll want to avoid the kind of exaggerated titles that are not followed up with substance, choosing provocative and memorable titles is a good way to command attention. One student writing about the architecture of her hometown began with a title that was less than inspired: "A Brief Look at Chicago's Architecture." That title was certainly clear, but it didn't do much to attract attention. After some thought and response from friends, she came up with a revision: "Sweet Home Chicago: Preserving the Past and Protecting the Future of the Windy City." This title refers to the blues song "Sweet Home Chicago," as well as to the well-known saying "home sweet home." And the subtitle fills in details of what the essay will be about.

See pp. 92–93 for more examples of effective titles.

Here are several other ways that titles can get an audience's attention:

- *A **puzzling statement*** can interest readers in finding out what it means. A science student writing about the need for additional research on Lyme disease chose "The Mystery of Post-Lyme Disease Syndrome," thinking that readers might be attracted to the mysterious aspect of her topic.

- *A **provocative question*** can call out to readers. One student writing about clubs at her university chose "Minority Clubs: Integration or Segregation?" Here the title states the subject, while the subtitle poses an unexpected question.

- *An **intriguing allusion*** can make readers want to read on. The title of an article in *Wired* caught my attention with an allusion: "Dr. Elon and Mr. Musk" recalls "Dr. Jekyll and Mr. Hyde" and made me want to find out how the author would connect the two.

Start strong, get readers interested

The OPENING sentences in your writing carry big responsibilities when it comes to drawing your readers in by arousing their interest and curiosity. Whether you're writing a college essay or a business report, the way it begins has a lot to do with whether your audience will stay with you. Georgina Kleege opens the introduction to a collection of essays entitled *Sight Unseen* with this enigmatic and arresting statement: "Writing this book made me blind." Readers immediately want to ask "why?" Kleege goes on to explain that while she is "just as blind" as she was before writing these essays, the process of composing them brought her to accept the label "blind." Since she began these essays, she says, "I have learned to use braille and started to carry a white cane."

The way you begin an essay can grab an audience's attention, or not. Here are some ways of making them interested in what you've got to say—and wanting to read on.

WITH A DECEPTIVELY SIMPLE STATEMENT

I was 7 years old the first time I snuck out of the house in the dark.

—LYNDA BARRY, "The Sanctuary of School"

WITH A PROVOCATIVE QUESTION

Have you ever thought about whether to have a child?

—PETER SINGER, "Should This Be the Last Generation?"

WITH A SURPRISING STATEMENT

I was transported recently to a place that is as enchanting to me as any winter wonderland: my local post office.

—ZEYNEP TUFEKCI, "Why the Post Office Makes America Great"

WITH AN AMUSING IMAGE

The seven deadly sins—avarice, sloth, envy, lust, gluttony, pride, and wrath—were all committed Sunday during the twice-annual bake sale at St. Mary's of the Immaculate Conception Church.

—*THE ONION*, "All Seven Deadly Sins Committed at Church Bake Sale"

Each of these sentences is startling, prompting us to read on in order to find out more. And each is brief, leaving us waiting for what is to come. And of course they all make powerful statements, ones that get readers' attention.

It usually takes more than a single sentence to open an essay. Consider, for example, this opening paragraph of an essay on animal rights:

The first time I opened Peter Singer's *Animal Liberation,* I was dining alone at the Palm, trying to enjoy a rib-eye steak cooked medium-rare. If this sounds like a good recipe for cognitive dissonance (if not indigestion), that was sort of the idea. Preposterous as it might seem to supporters of animal rights, what I was doing was tanta-mount to reading *Uncle Tom's Cabin* on a plantation in the Deep South in 1852.

—MICHAEL POLLAN, "An Animal's Place"

The first sentence presents an incongruous image that holds our attention: he's eating a steak while reading about animal liberation. Then the rest of the paragraph makes this incongruity even more pronounced, comparing the situation to reading an antislavery novel while on a slave-owning plantation. It's an opening that makes us want to read on. For more on opening sentences see p. 85.

Since the title and opening lines are the first things your audience will see or hear, it's well worth the effort to make sure they'll draw readers in. And it might be good to keep in mind the admonition of one reader who doesn't have a lot of patience: "I give the writer one paragraph, maybe two; if I'm not hooked by then, I stop reading." Your goal is to write openings so compelling that even impatient readers will want to keep going.

KEEPING ATTENTION

Once you've gotten your audience's attention, you need to think about how you can keep them with you. Fortunately, there are a number of strategies and techniques that will help you to do so. Take a look at how writers use some of these techniques.

Tell a story

Just as a story or ANECDOTE can draw an audience in, they can enliven much of what you write and keep them with you. Surgeon and author Atul Gawande is well known for his use of stories in the articles and books he has written about how to improve medical care in this country. In speaking about his special interest in improving end-of-life care, matching it more closely to what patients really want than to "keep alive at all cost" policies and procedures, Gawande paused to tell a story about one particular patient who, when asked his preferences for end-of-life care, said that he "wanted to stay alive as long as he could enjoy chocolate ice cream and watch football on television." This brief narrative brought home the point Gawande was making in concrete, human terms—and kept his audience interested in what he was saying.

See pp. 87–89 for more on narrative.

Offer good examples

"A single good example is often worth a dozen lengthy explanations," says English professor Thomas Cooley. That's for sure: there's no better way to support a generalization or to bring an abstraction to life. It's also a good way to help readers understand and be interested in what you're saying. In a fairly critical review of the Freddie Mercury

Rami Malek as Freddie Mercury.

biopic *Bohemian Rhapsody* ("*Bohemian Rhapsody* is a bad movie. But— boy is it entertaining."), Ann Hornaday details the ways in which the film is "bad." But then she uses one memorable **EXAMPLE** to show why, in spite of it being "trite" and "unforgivably conventional," Rami Malek, the actor who plays Freddie, makes it "captivating":

> If anyone doubted that cinema is an actor's medium, *Bohemian Rhapsody* arrives as indisputable proof. Even behind a set of distracting prosthetic teeth simulating Freddie's famous overbite, Malek delivers a committed, thoroughly inhabited performance, which winds up transcending the regrettably thin material at hand. Somewhat shorter than his character, Malek nonetheless masters the muscular swagger and captivating stage presence of a man who, when he sings in front of his first big crowd, announces that he's finally discovered his life's calling. Even at his most fey and alien-looking, Malek makes that statement utterly credible.
>
> —ANN HORNADAY, Review of *Bohemian Rhapsody*

The vivid language in this passage ("muscular swagger," "captivating stage presence," "alien-looking") makes it a persuasive example that holds the reader's attention just as Malek's performance held the attention of filmgoers.

See pp. 88–90 for more on examples.

Use an analogy

You can use ANALOGIES to help explain an unfamiliar subject by comparing it to a more familiar one. They're one more way to make abstract ideas more concrete, and even to help an audience visualize what you're saying. As such, they're a good way to hold readers' attention when you're writing about something abstract or complicated. See how Warren Buffett uses an analogy in his annual letter to stockholders to keep their attention on the point he is making:

> Investors who evaluate Berkshire sometimes obsess on the details of our many and diverse businesses—our economic "trees," so to speak. Analysis of that type can be mind-numbing, given that we own a vast array of specimens, from twigs to redwoods. A few of our trees are diseased and unlikely to be around a decade from now. Many others, though, are destined to grow in size and beauty. Fortunately, it's not necessary to evaluate each tree individually to make a rough estimate of Berkshire's intrinsic business value. That's because our forest contains five "groves" of major importance, each of which can be appraised, with reasonable accuracy, in its entirety. Four of these groves are differentiated clusters of businesses and financial assets that are easy to understand. The fifth—our huge and diverse insurance operation—delivers great value to Berkshire in a less obvious manner, one I will explain later in this letter.
>
> —WARREN BUFFETT, Letter to Stockholders

Here Buffett uses a simple analogy between a forest and his very large company, introducing readers to the "groves" and individual "trees" that make it up. The analogy helps readers visualize the company in a concrete way and paves the way for data that will support Buffett's claim that the fifth "grove" delivers "great value to Berkshire."

Appeal to emotion

Appealing to an audience's emotions can be a very effective way to both get and keep attention. Here's Joe Biden in a speech he delivered in 2020 making an appeal that reaches across party lines, noting that despite our differences, we all share certain truths, such as the right to life, liberty, and the pursuit of happiness:

> All of us. The moms and dads in Scranton, where I grew up, who have worked and scraped for everything they've ever gotten in life. The auto worker in Michigan, who still makes the best automobile in the world, the single mom in Ohio, working three jobs just to stay afloat who'll do anything for her child. Retired veteran in Florida who gave everything he had to this country. . . . White, Black, Latino, Asian American, Native American, everybody. I'm in this campaign for you. No matter your color, no matter your zip code, no matter your politics.
>
> —JOE BIDEN, Speech in Pittsburgh

Biden begins this summation with three words: "all of us." The examples that follow draw his audience in to the everyday stories of people across many different states and professions and backgrounds. Then, in the last two sentences, he shifts to *you* and *your*, speaking directly to his audience, demonstrating that he understands and cares about them. In short, he makes them feel like they matter.

As a writer and speaker, you will need to determine how much you want to stir people's emotions, remembering that too much of a good thing is—too much. So think about your audience and their expectations as you decide when and where to appeal to their emotions.

Use a startling contrast

Contrasts, especially sharp or startling ones, can create images in readers' minds that capture and hold attention. Consider how columnist Frank Bruni uses such a contrast in a headline—"She Went Blind. Then She Danced."—and then builds on that contrast as he introduces readers to Marion Sheppard:

Marion Sheppard may be blind, but she can dance!

She pitied herself. . . . She raged. . . . She trembled. . . . She spent months wrestling with those emotions, until she realized that they had pinned her in place. Time was marching on and she wasn't moving at all. Her choice was clear: She could surrender to the darkness, or she could dance. She danced.

—FRANK BRUNI, "She Went Blind. Then She Danced."

Use reiteration

A kind of repetition, reiteration provides emphasis: like a drumbeat, the repetition of a keyword, phrase, or image can help drive home a point. And it's a good way to command attention. REITERATION is especially powerful in spoken texts—think "I Have a Dream" and "Yes we can!" At the March for Our Lives rally in Washington, DC, following the killing of students and staff members at a Florida high school, student Emma González provided a powerful example of how reiteration can command an audience's attention. Telling her audience that among the students and staff at school that day, "no one understood" what had happened, "no one could comprehend the devastating aftermath," or where it would go. Here's the beginning of González's answer to that question; note the chillingly effective use of repetition:

> Six minutes and 20 seconds with an AR-15, and my friend Carmen would never complain to me about piano practice. Aaron Feis would never call Kyra "miss sunshine" . . . Alyssa Alhadeff would never, Jamie Guttenberg would never, Meadow Pollack would never.
>
> —EMMA GONZÁLEZ, March for Our Lives

Consider the power of silence

Sometimes silence can be extremely powerful, startling an audience and helping them focus on you and your lack of words. Emma González provides an example of the power of silence. Once her riveting repetitions of "would never" came to a halt, she stood there, silently, for six minutes and twenty seconds: the amount of time it had taken a killer to take the lives of seventeen innocent people. That silence held the crowd captivated, stunned, and very, very attentive.

Conclude strong, leave readers thinking

Your CONCLUSION is a chance to leave readers thinking about what you've said. You might simply restate your main point, but here are some other ways to conclude:

WITH A WITTY STATEMENT THAT MAKES YOUR POINT

Anyone who believes emoji are having even the slightest effect on English syntax is an utter 😖.

—GEOFFREY PULLUM,
"Emoji Are Ruining English, Says Dumbest Story of the Week"

Carl Zimmer tells us more than we ever wanted to know about the virus that causes the common cold—but see how his conclusion gets our attention. His essay is on p. 753.

WITH A STARTLING IMAGE

The next time we go to war, we should truly understand the sacrifices that our service members will have to make. Which is why, when my colleagues start beating the drums of war, I want to be there, standing on my artificial legs under the great Capitol dome, to remind them what the true costs of war are.

—TAMMY DUCKWORTH, "What I Learned at War"

WITH A STATEMENT THAT SHOWS WHY THEY SHOULD CARE

The closer we get to mass incarceration and extreme levels of punishment, the more I believe it is necessary to recognize that we all need mercy, we all need justice, and—perhaps—we all need some measure of unmerited grace.

—BRYAN STEVENSON, *Just Mercy*

WITH A CALL FOR ACTION

It's time, it's past time, to pay our Black citizens what they are owed.

—JANE SEARLE, "On Reparations"

See p. 92 for more ways of concluding.

You can probably think of several other very effective strategies for getting and holding the attention of your audience. It's worth taking the time to do so—and to study the examples we've offered here: we don't see any let-up in the oceans of information and data washing over us 24/7. In such an atmosphere, the one who can command attention is the one whose words will count.

REFLECT! Think about something you've read or seen recently that really held your attention: a book you couldn't put down, an op-ed piece you're still thinking about, something you saw on *Facebook* or *YouTube*. Study it now to see if you can figure out *how* it did that, and then write a short paragraph about how you can do that yourself in your own writing.

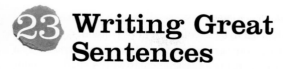

23 Writing Great Sentences

A LOT OF CRITICS THINK I'M STUPID BECAUSE MY SENTENCES
ARE SO SIMPLE . . . THEY THINK THESE ARE DEFECTS. NO.

—KURT VONNEGUT

I LIKE SENTENCES THAT DON'T BUDGE THOUGH ARMIES
CROSS THEM.

—VIRGINIA WOOLF

When a student asked author Annie Dillard, "Do you think I could become a writer?" Dillard replied with a question of her own: "Do you like sentences?" Liking or not liking sentences might not be something you've ever thought about—but we're willing to bet that you know something about how important sentences are. Anyone who has ever tried to write the perfect tweet or, better yet, the perfect love letter knows about choosing just the right words for each sentence and about the power of the three-word sentence "I love you"—or the even shorter sentence that sometimes follows from such declarations: "I do."

In his book *How to Write a Sentence*, English professor Stanley Fish declares himself to be a "connoisseur of sentences" and offers some particularly noteworthy examples. Here's one, written by a fourth grader in response to an assignment to write something about a mysterious large box that had been delivered to a school:

> I was already on the second floor when I heard about the box.

This sentence reminded my of a favorite sentence of my own, this one the beginning of a story written by a third grader:

> Today, the monster goes where no monster has gone before: Cincinnati.

Here the student manages to allude to the famous line from *Star Trek*—"to boldly go where no man has gone before"—while suggesting that Cincinnati is the most exotic place on earth and even using a colon effectively. It's quite a sentence.

Finally, here's a sentence that opens a chapter from a PhD dissertation on literacy among young people today:

> Hazel Hernandez struck me as an honest thief.

Clint Smith uses simple sentences that "startle us a bit" and "make us want to read more" in his narrative about Juneteenth. Check it out on p. 543.

Such sentences are memorable: They startle us a bit and demand attention. They make us want to read more. Who's Hazel Hernandez? What's an honest thief, and what makes her one?

As these examples suggest, you don't have to be a famous author to write a great sentence. In fact, crafting effective and memorable sentences is a skill everyone can master with careful attention and practice. Sometimes a brilliant sentence comes to you like a bolt of lightning, and all you have to do is type it out. More often, though, the perfect sentence is a result of tweaking and tinkering during your revision stages. Either way, crafting good sentences is worth the effort it may take. You may not come up with a zinger like the famous sentence John Updike wrote about Ted Williams's fabled home run in his last at bat at Fenway Park—"It was in the books while it was still in the sky."—but you can come close.

Just as certain effects in film—music, close-ups—enhance the story, a well-crafted sentence can bring power to a piece of writing.

So think about the kind of effect you want to create in what you're writing—and then look for the type of sentence that will fit the bill. Though much of the power of the examples above comes from being short and simple, remember that some rhetorical situations call for longer, complex sentences—and that the kind of sentence you write also depends on its context, such as whether it's opening an essay, summing up what's already been said, or something else. This chapter looks at some common English sentence patterns and provides some good examples for producing them in your own work.

FOUR COMMON SENTENCE PATTERNS

We make sentences with words—and we arrange those words into patterns. If a sentence is defined as a group of words that expresses a complete thought, then we can identify four basic sentence structures: a SIMPLE SENTENCE (expressing one idea); a COMPOUND SENTENCE (expressing more than one idea, with the ideas being of equal importance); a COMPLEX SENTENCE (expressing more than one idea, with one of the ideas more important than the others); and a COMPOUND-COMPLEX SENTENCE (with more than one idea of equal importance and at least one idea of less importance).

Simple sentences: one main idea

Let's take a look at some simple sentences:

- Resist!
- Consumers revolted.
- Angry consumers revolted against new debit-card fees.
- Protests from angry consumers forced banks to rescind the new fees.
- The internet's capacity to mobilize people instantly all over the world has done everything from forcing companies to rescind debit-card fees in the United States to bringing down oppressive governments in the Middle East.

As these examples illustrate, simple sentences can be as short as a single word—or they can be much longer. Each is a simple sentence, however, because it contains a single main idea or thought; in grammatical terms, each contains one and only one MAIN CLAUSE. As the name suggests, a simple sentence is often the simplest, most direct way of saying what you want to say—but not always. And often you want a sentence to include more than one idea. In that case, you need to use a compound sentence, a complex sentence, or a compound-complex sentence.

Compound sentences: joining ideas that are equally important

Sometimes you'll want to write a sentence that joins two or more ideas that are equally important, like this one attributed to former president Bill Clinton:

> You can put wings on a pig, but you don't make it an eagle.

In grammatical terms, this is a compound sentence with two MAIN CLAUSES, each of which expresses one of two independent and equally important ideas. In this case, Clinton joined the ideas with a comma and the COORDINATING CONJUNCTION *but*. But he had several other options for joining these ideas. For example, he could have joined them with only a semicolon:

> You can put wings on a pig; you don't make it an eagle.

Or he could have joined them with a semicolon, a TRANSITION like *however*, and a comma:

> You can put wings on a pig; however, you don't make it an eagle.

All of these compound sentences are perfectly acceptable—but which one seems most effective? In this case, I think Clinton's choice is: it is clear and very direct, and if you read it aloud you'll hear that the words on each side of *but* have the same number of syllables, creating a pleasing, balanced rhythm—and one that balances the two equally important ideas. It also makes the logical relationship between the two ideas explicit: *but* indicates a contrast. The version with only a semicolon, by contrast, indicates that the ideas are somehow related but doesn't show how.

Using *and*, *but*, and other coordinating conjunctions

In writing a compound sentence, keep in mind that different coordinating conjunctions carry meanings that signal different logical relationships between the main ideas in the sentence. There are only seven coordinating conjunctions.

COORDINATING CONJUNCTIONS

and	for	or	yet
but	nor	so	

China's one-child policy slowed population growth, *but* it helped create a serious gender imbalance in the country's population.

Most of us bike to the office, *so* many of us stop at the gym to shower before work.

The first two batters struck out, *yet* the Cubs went on to win the game on back-to-back homers.

See how the following sentences express different meanings depending on which coordinating conjunction is used:

You could apply to graduate school, *or* you could start looking for a job.

You could apply to graduate school, *and* you could start looking for a job.

Using a semicolon

Joining clauses with a semicolon only is a way of signaling that they are closely related without saying explicitly how. Often the second clause will expand on an idea expressed in the first clause.

My first year of college was a little bumpy; it took me a few months to get comfortable at a large university far from home.

The Wassaic Project is an arts organization in Dutchess County, New York; artists go there to engage in "art, music, and everything else."

Adding a TRANSITION can make the logical relationship between the ideas more explicit:

My first year of college was a little bumpy; *indeed*, it took me a few months to get comfortable at a large university far from home.

Note that the transition in this sentence, *indeed*, cannot join the two main clauses on its own—it requires a semicolon before it. If you use a transition between two clauses with only a comma before it, you've made a mistake called a COMMA SPLICE.

SOME COMMON TRANSITIONS

also	indeed	otherwise
certainly	likewise	similarly
furthermore	nevertheless	therefore
however	next	thus

REFLECT! Look over something you've written to see if there are any compound sentences joined by *and*. If so, does *and* express the relationship between the two parts of the sentence that you intend? Would *but, or, so, nor,* or *yet* work better?

Complex sentences:
when one idea is more important than another

Many of the sentences you write will contain two or more ideas, with one that you want to emphasize more than the other(s). You can do so by putting the idea you wish to emphasize in the MAIN CLAUSE, and those that are less important in SUBORDINATE CLAUSES.

Mendocino County is a place in California *where you can dive for abalone.*

Because the species has become scarce, abalone diving is strictly regulated.

Fish and Wildlife Department agents *who patrol the coast* use sophisticated methods to catch poachers.

As these examples show, the ideas in the subordinate clauses (italicized here) can't stand alone as sentences: when we read "where you can dive for abalone" or "who patrol the coast," we know that something's missing. Subordinate clauses begin with words such as *if* or *because*, SUBORDINATING WORDS that signal the logical relationship between the subordinate clause and the rest of the sentence.

SOME SUBORDINATING WORDS

after	even though	until
although	if	when
as	since	where
because	that	while
before	though	who

Notice that a subordinate clause can come at the beginning of a sentence, in the middle, or at the end. When it comes at the beginning, it is usually followed by a comma, as in the second example. If the opening clause in that sentence were moved to the end, a comma would not be necessary: "Abalone diving is strictly regulated because the species has become scarce."

Grammatically, each of the three examples above is a complex sentence, with one main idea and one other idea of less importance. In writing you will often have to decide whether to combine ideas in a compound sentence, which gives the ideas equal importance, or in a complex sentence, which makes one idea more important than the other(s). Looking once more at our sentence about the pig and the eagle, for example, Bill Clinton could also have made it a complex sentence:

Even though you can put wings on a pig, you don't make it an eagle.

Looking at this sentence, though, I think Clinton made a good choice in giving the two ideas equal weight because doing so balances the sentence perfectly—and tells us that both parts are equally important. In fact, neither part of this sentence is very interesting in itself: it's the balancing and the contrast that make it interesting and memorable.

Compound-complex sentences: multiple ideas—some more important, some less

When you are expressing three or more ideas in a single sentence, you'll sometimes want to use a compound-complex sentence, which gives some of the ideas more prominence and others less. Grammatically, such sentences have at least two MAIN CLAUSES and one SUBORDINATE CLAUSE.

MAIN CLAUSE

- We have experienced unparalleled natural disasters that have

SUBORDINATE CLAUSE — MAIN CLAUSE

devastated entire countries, yet identifying global warming as the

cause of these disasters is difficult.

SUBORDINATE CLAUSE

- Even after distinguished scientists issued a series of reports, critics

MAIN CLAUSE — SUBORDINATE CLAUSE

continued to question the findings because they claimed results

MAIN CLAUSE

were falsified; nothing would convince them.

As these examples show, English sentence structure is flexible, allowing you to combine groups of words in different ways in order to get your ideas across to your audience most appropriately and effectively. There's seldom only one way to write a sentence to get an idea

across: as the author, you must decide which way works best for your
RHETORICAL SITUATION.

WAYS OF EMPHASIZING THE MAIN IDEA

Sometimes you will want to lead off a sentence with the main point;
at other times you might want to hold it in reserve until the end.
CUMULATIVE SENTENCES start with a main clause and then add on to
it, "accumulating" details. PERIODIC SENTENCES start with a series
of phrases or subordinate clauses, saving the main clause for last.

Cumulative sentences: starting with the main point

This kind of sentence starts off with a MAIN CLAUSE and then adds
details in phrases and SUBORDINATE CLAUSES, extending or explaining the thought. Cumulative sentences can be useful for describing
a place or an event, operating almost like a camera panning across
a room or a landscape. The sentences below create such an effect:

> The San Bernardino Valley lies only an hour east of Los Angeles by
> the San Bernardino Freeway but is in certain ways an alien place: not
> the coastal California of the subtropical twilights and the soft west-
> erlies off the Pacific but a harsher California, haunted by the Mojave
> just beyond the mountains, devastated by the hot dry Santa Ana wind
> that comes down through the passes at 100 miles an hour and whines
> through the eucalyptus windbreaks and works on the nerves.
>
> —JOAN DIDION, "Some Dreamers of the Golden Dream"

> Public transportation in Cebu City was provided by jeepneys: refur-
> bished military jeeps with metal roofs for shade, decorated with horns
> and mirrors and fenders and flaps; painted with names, dedications,
> quotations, religious icons, logos—and much, much more.

> She hit the brakes, swearing fiercely, as the deer leapt over the hood
> and crashed into the dark woods beyond.

> The celebrated Russian pianist gave his hands a shake, a quick shake, fingers pointed down at his sides, before taking his seat and lifting them imperiously above the keys.

These cumulative sentences add details in a way that makes each sentence more emphatic. Keep this principle in mind as you write—and also when you revise. See if there are times when you might revise a sentence or sentences to add emphasis in the same way. Take a look at the following sentences, for instance:

> In 1979, China initiated free-market reforms that transformed its economy from a struggling one to an industrial powerhouse. As a result, it became the world's fastest-growing major economy. Its growth rates averaged almost 10 percent over the next four decades.

These three sentences are clearly related, with each one adding detail about the growth of China's economy. Now look what happens when the writer eliminates a little bit of repetition, adds a memorable metaphor, and combines them as a cumulative—and more emphatic—sentence:

> China's free-market reforms led to almost 10 percent average growth from 1979 to 2018, transforming it from a paper tiger to an industrial dragon that is still one of the world's fastest-growing major economies.

Periodic sentences: delaying the main point until the end

In contrast to sentences that open with the main idea, periodic sentences delay the main idea until the very end. Periodic sentences are sometimes fairly long, and withholding the main point until the end is a way of adding emphasis. It can also create suspense or build up to a surprise or inspirational ending.

> In spite of everything, in spite of the dark and twisting path he saw stretching ahead for himself, in spite of the final meeting with Voldemort he knew must come, whether in a month, in a year, or in ten,

he felt his heart lift at the thought that there was still one last golden day of peace left to enjoy with Ron and Hermione.

—J. K. ROWLING, *Harry Potter and the Half-Blood Prince*

Unprovided with original learning, uninformed in the habits of thinking, unskilled in the arts of composition, I resolved to write a book.

—EDWARD GIBBON, *Memoirs of My Life*

In the week before finals, when my studying and memorizing reached a fever pitch, came a sudden, comforting thought: I have never failed.

Here are three periodic sentences in a row about Whitney Houston, each of which withholds the main point until the end:

When her smiling brown face, complete with a close-cropped Afro, appeared on the cover of *Seventeen* in 1981, she was one of the first African-Americans to grace the cover, and the industry took notice. When she belted out a chilling and soulful version of the "Star-Spangled Banner" at the 1991 Super Bowl, the world sat back in awe of her poise and calm. And in an era when African-American actresses are often given film roles portraying them as destitute, unloving, unlovable, or just "the help," Houston played the love interest of Kevin Costner, a white Hollywood superstar.

—ALLISON SAMUELS, "A Hard Climb for the Girl Next Door"

These three periodic sentences create a drumlike effect that builds in intensity as they move through the stages in Houston's career; in all, they suggest that Houston was, even more than Kevin Costner, a "superstar."

Samuels takes a chance when she uses three sentences in a row that withhold the main point until the end: readers may get tired of waiting for that point. And readers may also find the use of too many such sentences to be, well, too much. But as the example above shows, when used carefully a sentence that puts off the main idea just long enough can keep readers' interest, making them want to reach the ending with its payoff.

You may find in your own work that periodic sentences can make your writing more emphatic. Take a look at the following sentence from an essay on the use of animals in circuses:

> The big cat took him down with one swat, just as the trainer, dressed in khakis and boots, his whip raised and his other arm extended in welcome to the cheering crowd, stepped into the ring.

This sentence paints a vivid picture, but it gives away the main action in the first six words. By withholding that action until the end, the writer builds anticipation and adds emphasis:

> Just as the trainer stepped into the ring, dressed in khakis and boots, his whip raised and his other arm extended in welcome to the cheering crowd, the big cat took him down with one swat.

VARYING YOUR SENTENCES

Read a paragraph or two of your writing out loud, and listen for its rhythm. Is it quick and abrupt? slow and leisurely? singsong? stately? rolling? Whatever it is, does the rhythm you hear match what you had in mind when you were writing? And does it put the emphasis where you want it? One way to establish the emphasis you intend and a rhythm that will keep readers reading is by varying the length of your sentences and the way those sentences flow from one to the other.

A string of sentences that are too much alike is almost certain to be boring. While you can create effective rhythms in many ways, one of the simplest and most effective is by breaking up a series of long sentences with a shorter one that gives your readers a chance to pause and absorb what you've written.

Take a look at the following passage, from an article in the *Atlantic* about the finale of the *Oprah Winfrey Show*. See how the author uses a mix of long and short sentences to describe one of the tributes to Oprah, this one highlighting her support of Black men:

Oprah's friend Tyler Perry announced that some of the "Morehouse Men," each a beneficiary of the $12 million endowment she has established at their university, had come to honor her for the scholarships she gave them. The lights were lowered, a Broadway star began singing an inspirational song, and a dozen or so black men began to walk slowly to the front of the stage. Then more came, and soon there were a score, then 100, then the huge stage was filled with men, 300 of them. They stood there, solemnly, in a tableau stage-managed in such a way that it might have robbed them of their dignity—the person serenading them (or, rather, serenading Oprah on their behalf) was Kristin Chenoweth, tiniest and whitest of all tiny white women; the song was from *Wicked*, most feminine of all musicals; and each man carried a white candle, an emblem that lent them the aspect of Norman Rockwell Christmas carolers. But they were not robbed of their dignity. They looked, all together, like a miracle. A video shown before the procession revealed that some of these men had been in gangs before going to Morehouse, some had fathers in prison, many had been living in poverty. Now they were doctors, lawyers, bankers, a Rhodes Scholar—and philanthropists, establishing their own Morehouse endowment.

—CAITLIN FLANAGAN, "The Glory of Oprah"

The passage begins with three medium-length sentences—and then one very long one (seventy-two words!) that points up the strong contrast between the 300 Black men filling the stage and the "whitest of white" singer performing a song from the "most feminine" of musicals. Then come two little sentences (the first one eight words long and the second one, seven) that give readers a chance to pause and absorb what has been said while also making an important point: that the men "looked, all together, like a miracle." The remainder of the passage moves back toward longer sentences, each of which explains just what this "miracle" is. Try reading this passage aloud, and listen for how the variation in sentences creates both emphasis and a pleasing and effective rhythm.

Morehouse Men surprise Oprah.

In addition to varying the lengths of your sentences, you can also improve your writing by making sure that they don't all use the same structure or begin in the same way. You can be pretty sure, for example, that a passage in which every sentence is a simple sentence that opens with the subject of a main clause will not read smoothly at all but rather will move along awkwardly. Take a look at this passage, for example:

> The sunset was especially beautiful today. I was on top of Table Mountain in Cape Town. I looked down and saw the sun touch the sea and sink into it. The evening shadows crept up the mountain. I got my backpack and walked over to the rest of my group. We started on the long hike down the mountain and back to the city.

There's nothing wrong with these sentences as such. Each one is grammatically correct. But if you read the passage aloud, you'll hear how it moves abruptly from sentence to sentence, lurching along rather than flowing smoothly. The problem is that the sentences are all the same: each one is a simple sentence that begins with the subject of a main clause (*sunset, I, I, evening shadows, I, We*). In addition, the use of personal pronouns at the beginning of the sentences (three *I*'s in only six sentences!) makes for dull reading. Finally, these are all fairly short sentences, and the sameness of the sentence length adds to the abrupt rhythm of the passage—and doesn't keep readers reading. Now look at how this passage can be revised by working on sentence variation:

> From the top of Cape Town's Table Mountain, the sunset was especially beautiful. I looked down just as the fiery orb touched and then sank into the sea; shadows began to creep slowly up the mountain. Picking up my backpack, I joined the rest of my group, and we started the long hike down the mountain.

This revision reduces the number of sentences in the passage from six to three (the first simple, the second compound-complex, the third compound) and varies their length. Equally important, the revision eliminates all but one of the subject openings. The first sentence now begins with the prepositional phrase ("From the top"); the second with the subject of a main clause ("I"); and the third with a participial phrase ("Picking up my backpack"). Finally, the revision varies the diction a bit, replacing the repeated word "sun" with a vivid image ("fiery orb"). Read the revised passage aloud, and you'll hear how varying the sentences creates a stronger rhythm that makes it easier to read.

This brief chapter has only scratched the surface of sentence style. But I hope it says enough to show how good sentences can be your allies, helping you get your ideas out there and connect with audiences as successfully as possible. Remember: authors are only as good as the sentences we write!

REFLECT! Read an essay you've written aloud, listening for rhythm and emphasis. If you find a passage that doesn't read well or have the emphasis you want, analyze its sentences for length (count the words) and emphasis (how does each sentence begin?). Revise them using the strategies discussed in this chapter.

Mixing Languages & Dialects

A LANGUAGE IS A DIALECT WITH AN ARMY AND NAVY.

—MAX WEINREICH

H ow many languages do you know well enough to speak or write? Which languages would you like to know? The United States is often said to be a monolingual country, one where English is the only language needed. In fact, that's never been accurate. Languages other than English have always been present here. Today the US Census Bureau estimates that 25 percent of Americans speak a language other than English at home—Spanish, Chinese, and Tagalog are the three most common; and American Sign Language is probably number four. So the United States is a country of many languages. It is also a nation of multiple dialects and registers. *Dialects* are varieties of language spoken by people in particular regions, ethnic groups, or social classes—like the English spoken in Appalachia, the Chicano English spoken primarily by Mexican Americans in the US Southwest, and the Queen's English spoken by the upper classes in the United Kingdom. *Registers* are the ways we speak in various situations—like the formal register used in much academic writing, the legalese used by lawyers, or the way certain words are used in tennis (where *love* means "zero" and *deuce* is a 40–40 score).

No matter how many languages you speak, you probably use a number of different dialects and registers. Is the way you speak with close friends different from the way you speak in class or at work? Is the way you text a friend different from the way you write an email to an instructor? We bet that it is.

I also bet that you probably mix whatever varieties of languages you use, consciously or unconsciously. Language scholars have

Notice all the languages, dialects, and registers you encounter in a day—on signs, in conversations, wherever.

identified two ways that people do so. *Code switching* is the practice of shifting from one language or dialect to another, whereas *code meshing* is a way of weaving together languages and dialects. Both are ways of mixing varieties of language for various purposes—to reflect a particular STANCE, for example, or to establish a connection with a certain AUDIENCE. This chapter provides examples and guidelines to help you mix languages, dialects, and registers for various rhetorical situations.

REFLECT! Think about the varieties of language you speak—your home language(s), and the way you speak at school or at work. And do you belong to any teams or other groups that use special words? Write a paragraph describing what influences the way you speak; include specific examples.

Using Englishes

What some call standardized English has been taught prescriptively in schools and recognized as the language of power throughout US history. As the dominant mode of discourse, standardized English has privileged some while silencing others. Yet it is itself just one of many valid and powerful dialects and languages used in the United States.

Today, many writers are pushing against the boundaries of standardized English, and against its claim to primary importance and power. In fact, throughout history many so-called standard languages have been challenged by other dialects and languages. English itself once edged out Latin as the language of power. So it's no surprise that in the United States, some have challenged or even rejected standardized English.

This chapter provides a number of examples of writers mixing varieties of language in ways that speak powerfully. Such moves are increasingly common, but doing so well requires that you keep your RHETORICAL SITUATION front and center. What's your PURPOSE, and what's at stake? Who's your AUDIENCE, and what languages and dialects will they understand and respond to?

Using languages and dialects

Some who are bilingual (or multilingual) mix languages or dialects routinely, especially when they're speaking with others who speak the same languages. But even those who are not bilingual will use one or more dialects on occasion. Sometimes doing so can help you connect with your audience, or simply get their attention. It can also be a way of illustrating a point or evoking a particular place or community. Following are some good examples demonstrating how to use different varieties of language for these purposes.

To connect with an audience

If you listen to popular music today, you can probably think of examples of lyricists mixing languages to powerful effect. Here are some lyrics from Kenyan rapper Bamboo's remix of the song "Mama Africa," first written and sung by Jamaican reggae artist Peter Tosh. A love song to the African continent, which has in Bamboo's view too often been represented negatively, his remix connects to his international audience of hip-hop and pop music fans by moving back and forth between Swahili and English:

> tunaishi vizuri
> check out the way we be livin
> na tunakula vizuri
> we always eating the best
> poteza yako kwa nini
> why should you settle for less
> TV haiwezi kuambia
> they never show on your screen

> kwa hivyo mi ntawaambia
> so you can see what I mean
> Africa maridadi
> Africa's beautiful baby
>
> —BAMBOO, "Mama Africa"

Bamboo uses hip-hop rhythms and dialects to connect with the audiences he wants to reach. By using both Swahili and English, he reaches more people than if he'd used just one language—and exposes those who speak just one of these languages to the other.

Sandra Cisneros, a Mexican American writer who's fluent in both English and Spanish, makes similar choices in a collection of short stories inspired by her experience growing up in the United States surrounded by Mexican culture. See how she mixes languages to speak to an audience that's likely to include both English and Spanish speakers:

> "¡Ay!" The true test of a native Spanish speaker. ¡Ay! To make love in Spanish, in a manner as intricate and devout as la Alhambra. To have a lover sigh mi vida, mi preciosa, mi chiquitita, and whisper things in that language crooned to babies, that language murmured by grandmothers, those words that smelled like your house, like flour tortillas.
>
> —SANDRA CISNEROS, "Bien Pretty"

As writers and speakers, we have to think carefully about when mixing different varieties of language will help us connect with our audiences—and when it won't. In most cases, writers have a kind of informal contract with readers: while readers may need to work some to understand what a writer is saying, the writer in turn promises to consider the audience's expectations and abilities. The end goal is usually accessibility: Will your message be understood by those you are trying to reach? If some members of your audience aren't likely to understand, should you provide a translation? Unless you're choosing not to translate so that your readers experience what it's like not to understand, you'll usually want to be sure they understand what you've written.

To illustrate a point

Sometimes you'll want to insert words from a different variety of language in order to illustrate a point. Professor Jamila Lyiscott mixes dialects to illustrate her point in a TED Talk titled "3 Ways to Speak English" in which she celebrates—and challenges—"the three distinct flavors of English" she speaks. Prompted by a "baffled lady" who seemed surprised to find that Lyiscott was "articulate," Lyiscott says:

> Pay attention
> 'Cause I'm "articulate"
> So when my father asks, "Wha' kinda ting is dis?"
> My "articulate" answer never goes amiss
> I say "Father, this is the impending problem at hand"
> And when I'm on the block I switch it up just because I can
> So when my boy says, "What's good with you son?"
> I just say, "I jus' fall out wit dem people but I done!"
> And sometimes in class
> I might pause the intellectual sounding flow to ask
> "Yo! Why dese books neva be about my peoples"
> Yes, I have decided to treat all three of my languages as equals
> Because I'm "articulate"
>
> —JAMILA LYISCOTT, "Broken English"

In her performance, which has more than 4 million views online, Lyiscott uses what she calls "three tongues"—one each for "home, school, and friends"—to make the point that there are many different ways to be "articulate." And she's articulate, all right, in three different dialects.

And here is Buthainah, a Saudi Arabian student writing a literacy narrative for an education class at an American college:

Watch the video of Jamila Lyiscott's TED Talk at letstalklibrary.com.

ومن يتهيّب صعود الجبال ~~~ يعش ابد الدّهر بين الحفر

"I don't want to" was my response to my parents' request of enrolling me in a nearby preschool. I did not like school. I feared it. I feared the aspect of departing my comfort zone, my home, to an unknown and unpredictable zone. . . . To encourage me, they recited a poetic line that I did not comprehend as a child but live by it as an adult. They said, "Who fears climbing the mountains ~~~ Lives forever between the holes." As I grew up, knowledge became my key to freedom; freedom of thought, freedom of doing, and freedom of beliefs.

—BUTHAINAH, "Who Fears Climbing the Mountains
Lives Forever between the Holes"

Reciting the Arabic proverb (which also serves as the title of her essay) draws readers' attention and illustrates the importance of Arabic in her journey to become the writer she is while also letting non-Arabic speakers feel a bit of what it's like to encounter a foreign language they don't understand. At the same time, she makes a point of translating the proverb for her readers as the essay progresses—"They said, 'Who fears climbing the mountains ~~~ Lives forever between the holes.'" Buthainah's essay illustrates how mixing languages can grab attention and show—instead of tell—your audience something that's important to you.

To evoke a place or community

Using the language of a specific community or group is a good way to evoke their character. In the following passage, journalist David Thompson is interviewing Lee Tonouchi, author of *Living Pidgin: Contemplations on Pidgin Culture*. Responding to a question about his work, Tonouchi uses Hawaiian Pidgin, now one of Hawaii's official languages, to evoke family relationships in his community:

[This book is] about finding humor in tragedy. It's about da relationship between one son and his uncommunicative faddah in da wake of da maddah's early passing. An den, it's also about da son's relationship with his grandmas as he discovers what it means for be Okinawan in Hawaii.

—DAVID THOMPSON, "Lee Tonouchi: Pidgin Poet"

Notice that Tonouchi mixes more academic English and Hawaiian Pidgin within sentences and not just between them, bringing the two into even closer contact. When using the language of a community you don't belong to yourself, take care to do so with respect. When possible, ask someone who does speak the language to look over what you've drafted to ensure that it's accurate and respectful.

Quoting people directly and respectfully

If you're writing about someone you've interviewed, you will want to let them speak for themself. From 1927 to 1931, Zora Neale Hurston, the famed Black anthropologist, interviewed Cudjo Lewis, one of the last living slaves to have made the journey across the Atlantic. Lewis's story, told from Hurston's perspective, appears in *Barracoon: The Story of the Last "Black Cargo."* Hurston takes care to let him speak his mind, and in his own words. She begins by telling us, "I hailed him by his African name," Oluale Kossula, which she had learned from prior research. In the next paragraph, Lewis speaks:

Oh Lor', I kno it you call my name. Nobody don't callee me my name from cross de water but you. You always callee me Kossula, jus' lak I in de Affica soil!

—ZORA NEALE HURSTON, *Barracoon: The Story of the Last "Black Cargo"*

Notice how Hurston alternates between standardized English and the actual speech of the person whose words she quotes. Quoting him helps establish her credibility as a careful researcher. Finally, the use of quotations appeals to her audience's emotions; we can hear Lewis's surprise and delight. Readers familiar with the dialect Lewis speaks might sense kinship with him, while those who are not will be reminded that Hurston is writing about a context different from their experience.

When you're quoting others, let them speak for themselves not only in their own words but also in their own language. And whenever possible, ask your subjects to review any quotations you use to ensure that they're accurate.

Providing translation

Gloria Anzaldúa sprinkles a lot of Spanish into her work. Some of it is translated; some is not. Why do you think she did that? Read her essay on p. 594.

One way to stay true to a language or dialect you identify with while still reaching readers who may not understand is to provide a translation. Bamboo's example, which invites English speakers to think about Africa's rich culture in part by including Swahili, demonstrates how translation helps when you're mixing languages.

When translating, you will usually want to introduce the term in its original language, followed by the translation, as is done on the poster on the following page announcing a conference taking place in the Navajo Nation. Note that the designer places the Navajo title first—and in slightly larger and bolder text—to underscore the importance of the Navajo language at this conference.

See how linguist Guadalupe Valdés uses translation in an ethnographic study of a family of Mexican origin:

> During his kindergarten year, . . . winning was important to Saúl. Of all the cousins who played together, it was he who ran the fastest and pushed the hardest. *"Yo gané, yo gané"* (I won, I won), he would say enthusiastically. . . . Saúl's mother, Velma, wished that he would win just a bit more quietly. . . . *"No seas peleonero"* (Don't be so quarrelsome), she would say. *"Es importante llevarse bien con todos"* (It's important to get along with everyone).
>
> —GUADALUPE VALDÉS, *"Con Respeto*: Bridging the Distances between Culturally Diverse Families and Schools"

Note especially that Valdés always puts the Spanish words first, as they were spoken, and only then gives the English translation. She

Conference poster announcing in both Navajo and English a gathering of writers in Window Rock, the capital of the Navajo Nation.

could have chosen to put the translation first, or to write only in English, but giving the Spanish first puts the spotlight on her subjects' voices and their own words. By including the English translation at all, Valdés acknowledges readers who don't speak Spanish and makes sure they can understand what she's written. Like Bamboo and the Navajo conference poster, she translates to make sure her message is accessible to as many people as possible. Notice too that Valdés italicizes words that are in a language other than English, which is a common academic convention when mixing languages.

Thinking about your rhetorical situation

Whether you're mixing standardized English with another dialect, from formal language to informal, or from one language to another, you need to think about how doing so suits your purpose and audience and the rest of your rhetorical situation.

Purpose. What do you want to accomplish: to bring attention to something you're saying? to let someone you're writing about speak for themselves? to illustrate an important point?

Audience. Will mixing different registers or dialects—or languages— help you connect with your audience? If you weave in a language they don't understand, will you need to translate? How likely are they to find your language choices engaging? Is anything at risk, like clarity?

Stance. How do you want to come across to your audience, and how will mixing registers, dialects, or languages affect that? How would it affect your credibility?

Genre. If you're writing a NARRATIVE, quoting someone in their own dialect will let readers hear that person's voice; if you're making an ARGUMENT, mixing registers or dialects or languages can help to emphasize what you're saying. If you're making a serious PROPOSAL, however, will doing so detract from your goals?

Context. If you're writing in response to an assignment, will it be appropriate to mix languages or dialects? Do you have the knowledge to do so accurately and respectfully? Are you writing or speaking in a field that is likely to welcome this kind of language use?

Medium. Mixing dialects or registers can help get an audience's attention in a spoken presentation—provided that fits well with the occasion and the audience.

REFLECT! Have you ever used language in any of the ways this chapter demonstrates? If not, find something you've written, think about its intended audience, and see if mixing dialects, registers, or languages would help to get their attention or connect with them in some way. Try it!

PART SIX

DESIGN

MAKE AN IMPRESSION

STRATEGIES

25. DESIGNING WHAT YOU WRITE

26. USING VISUALS

25 Designing What You Write

FONTS, COLORS, CONTRAST, CAPITALIZATION, SPACING, PROXIMITY—ALL THESE AFFECT WHETHER OR NOT PEOPLE READ YOUR WORDS.

—JOHN SAITO, "HOW TO DESIGN WORDS"

DESIGN IS ALL ABOUT STORYTELLING.... ABOUT COMMUNICATING WITH AN AUDIENCE THROUGH IMAGES AND LANGUAGE AND COLOR AND TYPE AND SCALE AND NUANCE AND SUBTLETY AND TEXTURE.

—STEPHEN DOYLE

Once upon a time writers had little control over the way their texts were designed: black type on white paper was pretty much it. But that was then. Today we can choose from hundreds of fonts, use color, add images of all kinds. So you need to know something about design. Whether you're drafting an essay, creating slides for a presentation, or writing up a lab report, you'll need to think about how you can design them so that readers will be able to follow, understand, and remember what you say. What fonts should you choose? Do you need headings? Is there anything you want to highlight? This chapter is here to help.

THINKING RHETORICALLY ABOUT DESIGN

The way you design a text plays a big role in how well you reach your audience and whether your text achieves its purpose. And the fact that you *can* design what you write gives you a lot of control over how effectively you present your message. In short, you have more than black ink and white paper at your disposal.

Let's take a look at two McDonald's images to see the difference that design can make. The one on the left is an ad run in the United States in the 1950s; the one on the right is a sign seen recently in the Czech Republic. The ad provides information that might make someone think of McDonald's when they're looking for a quick meal: 15 cents, "speedee" service, over 100 million sold. The focus is on the words, especially the largest one: HAMBURGERS. But nowadays the McDonald's brand is so well known that the recent sign consists simply of the famous golden arches with two words: *Máš hlad*—in English, are you hungry?—and an arrow pointing the way. The colors, image, and two-word message work to conjure up the brand.

Of course, the designers' rhetorical situations were drastically different. Those designing the ad were probably limited to black and white and could assume an audience of readers, whereas those who designed the sign could use colors—and were able to be much more playful, knowing that the golden arches would be familiar to anyone passing by.

You may not be called on to design a McDonald's ad, but you too will need to think carefully about how to design the texts you write so that they capture your audience's attention and deliver your message effectively. In short, you'll need to think *rhetorically* about how to design what you write.

Think about your rhetorical situation

Purpose. What are you trying to accomplish—provide information? persuade readers to do something? record a memory?—and what design elements will help you to do that? If you're writing a NARRATIVE about a soccer match, you might include photos. But if you're creating a poster to publicize a concert, you'll need to make the name of the group large enough to be seen from a distance and put the time and place in one place on the poster.

Audience. Are there any design elements they are likely to need, or expect? If you're writing a market ANALYSIS for a business class, will it include data that readers will expect to see in a graph or chart?

Stance. How do you want to come across to readers: as serious? objective? outraged? What fonts or colors might help establish such a stance? Bright red words might signal outrage on a poster for a protest, but that would not be appropriate on a résumé.

Genre. Does your genre have any design requirements? A lengthy REPORT, for instance, may require headings to label its parts.

Medium. For a print text, you might use black type on white paper and include headings in a bold font. But if you're planning a video for a **VLOG**, you'll need to think about what you'll wear and what you'll have in the background.

Context. Does your assignment specify any design requirements? And when is it due? Do you have time to find or create visuals?

What do you want readers to focus on, and how can design help?

Your message may start with words, but it doesn't end there. Whether you write out your words by hand or put them in a certain font, whether you arrange them on a page or a screen, the way you design your text focuses your message in a certain way and gives it a certain look. It also affects how easy your message is to read—and sometimes whether it gets read at all.

    So give some thought to what you want readers to focus on, and how you can design your text to help them do that. What do you want them to look at first? What do you want them to look at next? And after that? Is there anything you want to highlight? How do you want readers to move through the text—and how can you help them to do so? And what goes with what? Following are some principles from graphic designer Robin Williams that can help you design your texts so that they're easy to read and navigate.

Jasmine Lane's blog post begins with 3 memes that we couldn't reproduce in the text, so we faced a design quandary. See how we resolved it on p. 622.

FOUR BASIC PRINCIPLES OF DESIGN

Contrast draws our eyes to certain parts of a page or screen. A contrasting color, a **bold font**, a larger type size: these are all ways of getting readers to focus on something. The first letter of each chapter in this book, for example, is gigantic, as if to say "start here!" The bold heading on this page does the same: it's larger and bolder than most of the words on this page, so it gets your attention. And later in this chapter you'll find a **Reflect!** prompt, highlighted with a pale blue background to make it easy to spot.

Repetition of key words, images, fonts, and colors can help readers move through a text—as the bold italics do on this page.

Alignment refers to where text and images are positioned on a page. Most of the text in this book is aligned flush with the left-hand margin; the examples and bulleted lists, however, are indented, making them easier to spot on the page.

Proximity involves putting ideas, images, or text that are related close, or "proximate," to one another. Images need to be near to where they're discussed in the text, and captions need to be next to the images they label. And of course closely related ideas need to be connected visually, as the four basic design principles are here.

DESIGN ELEMENTS
Fonts

The fonts you use affect how easy your text is to read—and they also contribute to the look of what you write. You'll want to choose fonts that suit your genre and purpose, and that reflect your stance: academic, playful, businesslike, informal, whatever.

There are two basic kinds of fonts: *serif* fonts such as Times New Roman, Garamond, and Century Schoolbook, which have short cross lines at the ends of letters; and *sans serif* fonts such as Calibri, Helvetica, and Futura, which do not have such cross lines. This book is set in three different fonts: what you're reading here is set in Freight Text Book, the examples in the book are set in Freight Sans, and the blue headings are set in Clarendon.

Most fonts have **bold**, *italic*, and <u>underlined</u> versions. You might use bold for headings in an academic text or for getting attention on posters or other texts that will be read from a distance, and italic to emphasize or highlight certain words. Italics are also used for titles of books, magazines, movies, and other full-length works (*Don Quixote, The Atlantic, Mamma Mia!*).

Sometimes you'll be required or expected to use certain fonts. MLA specifies only that you use a font that's easy to read, whereas APA recommends several specific fonts, including Calibri, Arial, Times New Roman, and others.

Whatever fonts you decide to use, make sure that they are legible: depending on the font, anything smaller than 11 or 12 point will be difficult to read.

Color and white space

Color can help highlight certain things and guide your readers. You might use one color for all the headings, for example, which would make them easy for readers to spot. In digital texts, you might use color to signal that certain words are links. Notice the use of color in this book, for instance: the parts are color-coded (note the gold band at the top of this page), the main headings are blue and the secondary ones are **black**, and key terms are in red—all designed that way for the purpose of helping you find your way through the book.

Choose colors that are easy to see, and remember that contrast is key. Dark type on a light background—or light type on a dark background—will provide the kind of contrast that makes the text easy to read and that can highlight something you want to emphasize. Remember, however, that some members of your audience may not be able to see certain colors (especially green and red), so it's best not to use these colors together.

If you use more than one color in a text, be careful to choose colors that complement one another. Take a look at the color wheel on the next page, which shows colors that work well together. But remember that too many colors jousting for the reader's attention can be a distraction. And be sure as well that any color you use has a purpose—and is not there as mere decoration.

A color wheel.

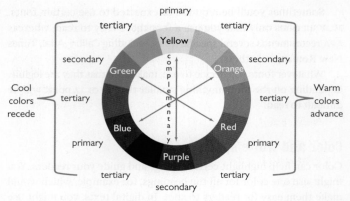

Finally, don't forget white space. Leave a one-inch margin around your text, and add some space above headings, above and below lists, and around any visuals.

Layout

No matter how many different elements a text has, they all have to be arranged in some way—and elements that are related need to be near to one another.

Paragraphs, lists, graphs, and charts If you're writing a print text that's organized in paragraphs, you'll generally want to double-space the text and indent each paragraph five spaces. Online, however, you should single-space your text, skip a line between paragraphs, and begin each paragraph flush left, without indenting. If there's anything that you want to set off as a list, use bullets to make it easy to see—or numbers if you want to put items in a certain sequence. If you're including numerical data, would it be easier for readers to understand if you presented it in a graph or chart?

For more on creating graphs and charts, see Chapter 26.

Headings can help guide readers through a written text, and sometimes on slides with an oral presentation. You may not need them for very brief texts, but they can be very helpful in long or complex texts.

Make sure that your headings are parallel in structure. They might be noun phrases: **The Dangers of Vaping**. They could also be gerund phrases: **Assessing the Dangers of Vaping**. Or even questions: **Why Has Vaping Hooked So Many Teens?** But whatever form you choose, use it consistently: all noun phrases, all gerunds, and so on.

If you have both headings and subheadings, you can distinguish them by using bold, italics, underlining, or all caps. For example:

FIRST-LEVEL HEADING

Second-Level Heading

Third-Level Heading

If you're following a particular documentation style, check to see if it has any requirements about headings. Both MLA and APA require that you use the same font for headings that you do in the rest of the text—APA requires that headings be boldface.

Visuals Putting them at the top or bottom of a print page will make it easy to lay out pages. If your text is online, however, you'll have more flexibility to put visuals wherever you wish. Be careful, though, that image files not be too large; save them as JPEGs or GIGs, compressed files that readers will be able to download.

See Chapter 26 for more on creating visual texts.

REFLECT! Look over this book's use of fonts, color, and headings. How do they help you follow the text? Now look at something you've written that's fairly lengthy. How have you used those same elements? If you did not use headings or color or more than one font, how do you think doing so might help readers follow your text more easily?

DESIGNING VISUAL TEXTS

The basic design principles of contrast, repetition, alignment, and proximity apply to all kinds of texts, visual ones included. Take a look at the two ads that follow, and consider how these principles are put to good use—and how they help us read each one.

Cause an effect.

In this poster, the subtle color contrast draws our eyes to the large, all-caps word VOTE, which ripples out beneath the water's surface. In this case, the repeated rippling draws our eyes down, where the color smooths out to match the darker blue of "VOTE" and then further down, from cause (voting) to effect: "Cause an effect." This phrase, presented in sharply contrasting white letters in the classic Century Schoolbook font, also plays on the familiar phrase "cause and effect" in ways that make readers stop and pay attention to the difference between a familiar three-word phrase and a somewhat unexpected three-word command! This poster was created by award-winning designer **Stephen Doyle** for the American Institute of Graphic Arts, a professional design association, so we can assume it had two purposes: to persuade viewers to vote, and to demonstrate design at its very best. How well do you think he succeeded?

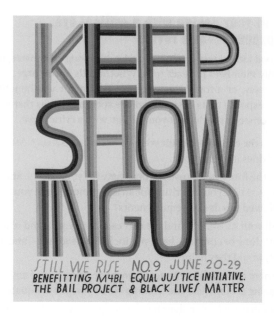

Created by **Lisa Congdon**, an award-winning artist and author of books about drawing and art, this poster also urges viewers to "cause an effect." The design choices, however, are very different from Stephen Doyle's. Here the large, sharply contrasting candy-stripe letters in all caps leap out at us. These colors are repeated—red, blue, red, blue—as our eyes are drawn down the poster, focusing on the central message: we need to show up. At first glance you may focus on the imperative—SHOW UP—since "SHOW" is in the middle, and "ING" is on the next line. Clustered at the bottom of the poster is the pertinent information inviting viewers to show up at a particular fund-raising event (No. 9) sponsored by Still We Rise supporting the work of four specific groups. The quirky, hand-drawn font also gets our attention, suggesting that this is something out of the box and important, something viewers will want to show up for.

Look at your design with a critical eye, get response—and revise

It's a good idea to test-drive your design by asking classmates, friends, or family members to react to it. Whether it's a web page, an illustrated essay, or a formal report, your document will benefit from getting response to its design. Here are some questions that will help you or someone else look at your design with a critical eye.

- Does the overall look suit your RHETORICAL SITUATION— and does it reflect your STANCE?

- Are the fonts you've used appropriate for your GENRE and PURPOSE? If you're writing for an assignment, have you followed any design requirements?

- Will your AUDIENCE find the text easy to navigate and read? If it's long or complex, have you included headings—and if not, would they help?

- Is there enough white space? Check the margins and any spacing around lists and headings to be sure it's adequate.

- If you've used color, does it suit your purpose, and have you used it to provide emphasis where it's needed?

- Is there any information that would be easier to understand if it were set off in a list?

- If you've included any statistics or other data, should it be presented in a chart or graph?

- If your text includes any VISUALS, what do they contribute to your point? If they are mostly decorative, consider deleting them.

26 Using Visuals

USE A PICTURE. IT'S WORTH A THOUSAND WORDS.
—ARTHUR BRISBANE

I'M A VISUAL THINKER. WITH ALMOST ALL MY WRITING,
I START WITH SOMETHING VISUAL.
—GERALD VIZENOR

Many of the texts we write include visuals of various kinds—photos, maps, tables, charts and graphs, still or moving images—all of which can help draw readers in and support what we have to say. In some cases, visuals can make information much easier to understand than it would be with words alone. You'll likely have reason to include visuals in some of your academic writing: paintings or drawings in an art history essay, bar graphs or pie charts in a business proposal, historical documents and maps in a history presentation. Whatever visuals you include, make sure that they support what you're saying— and that you use them both carefully and ethically.

KINDS OF VISUALS

Photos can help readers visualize what you are describing or explaining. Imagine describing with words alone this scene from *Akhnaten*, an opera by Philip Glass, in which jugglers visually represent the rhythms of Glass's music. You could do it—but the photo lets readers *see* what you're describing.

Maps can help orient readers to a place you refer to in your text. The map here is one you might include in a literary analysis of J. R. R. Tolkien's *The Return of the King*, showing Gondor, where much of the story takes place.

Table 1

US College Degrees by Males and Females, 2020

	Class of 2020		
	Percentage		Female per 100 Males
Degrees	Male	Female	
Associate's	39.1%	60.9%	**156**
Bachelor's	42.6%	57.4%	**135**
Master's	40.1%	59.9%	**149**
Doctor's	46.2%	53.8%	**116**
All Degrees	41.4%	58.6%	**142**

Source: US Department of Education

Tables are a way of presenting data in columns, which makes it easier to see than it would be in a paragraph—and are especially useful for comparing data. The table here compares college degree data for US college graduates in 2020. See page 346 on setting up tables MLA style, and pages 388–89 for APA style.

Bar graphs are useful for comparing quantitative data. In this example, the bars make it easy to see at a glance what a sample of US adults thought about the widespread use of driverless cars expected to operate on their own.

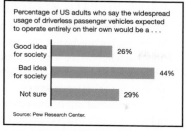

Percentage of US adults who say the widespread usage of driverless passenger vehicles expected to operate entirely on their own would be a . . .

Good idea for society	26%
Bad idea for society	44%
Not sure	29%

Source: Pew Research Center.

Line graphs are useful for showing changes in data that occur over time. One data set can be shown with a single line—as in the example here. Two or more data sets show how they compare over time.

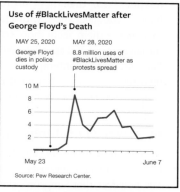

Use of #BlackLivesMatter after George Floyd's Death

MAY 25, 2020
George Floyd dies in police custody

MAY 28, 2020
8.8 million uses of #BlackLivesMatter as protests spread

May 23 — June 7

Source: Pew Research Center.

Pie charts provide a broad overview of how parts of a whole relate to one another—for example, how much of a family's earnings go for food, housing, transportation, savings, charity, and so on. Each part needs to be clearly labeled, and it's best to have no more than six or seven parts, because if the slices are too small, they can be hard to see or interpret.

Percentage of US Adults Who Say They Have Read Books in the Last 12 Months

Don't know/Refused 1%
27% No books
37% Print books only
7% Digital books only
28% Both print and digital books

Note: "Digital books" include both ebooks and audiobooks.
Source: Pew Research Center, survey conducted Jan. 8–Feb. 7, 2019.

And keep in mind cartoons! They can say a lot in a small space. See what we mean on p. 695.

USING VISUALS ETHICALLY

What you see is what you get. A picture is worth a thousand words. Maybe so, but maybe not. These familiar sayings rest on the assumption that what we see with our own eyes is real and true, unmediated, while words somehow come between us and reality, shaping and altering it, for better or worse.

It's true that our brains process images much faster than words: in fact, our eyes will recognize a familiar image in 100 milliseconds, 60 times faster than they can process the words for that image. Perhaps it's the sheer speed with which images enter our consciousness that makes them seem more trustworthy: "seeing is believing," as the saying goes. But speed doesn't equal accuracy, much less truth or fairness. And as contemporary technology has made achingly clear, pictures are just as constructed as sentences or paragraphs. Not only constructed: they can be manipulated, even falsified.

Be aware of doctored photos

You can see these two magazine covers at letstalklibrary.com.

In June 1994, both *Time* and *Newsweek* featured the same photo of O. J. Simpson on their covers. Sharp-eyed readers were quick to point out, however, that Simpson's skin color was decidedly darker on the *Time* cover. When questioned, the photo artist for *Time* said that he simply wanted to "give the image a dramatic tone" and that no deception or racial implication was intended. Maybe so, maybe not, but the altered image caused a huge public outcry against such practices.

So images and especially photographs can be problematic, to say the least. Over two decades ago, environmentalist Kenneth Brower raised an alarm in an essay titled "Photography in the Age of Falsification," in which he pointed out that even well-established magazines like *National Geographic* had been known to "doctor" photographs to make them more appealing. Noting that while the wildlife images we see in movies and magazines are often "stunning," they may well be "fake, enhanced, or manufactured by . . . digital technologies that have transformed—some say contaminated—the photography landscape." In Brower's view, such alterations raise serious ethical questions.

A leopard can't change his spots, but the modern photographer can easily do it for him.

—KENNETH BROWER

President Trump addressing a Turning Point USA conference in 2019.

Faking a sunset or moving animals around in a photo is deceptive, but some altered images go beyond deception and cause harm or embarrassment. This happened to President Trump in 2019, when he spoke at conference hosted by the conservative organization Turning Point USA. As he walked onto the stage, a large presidential seal went up on a screen. But the seal had been altered. The eagle had two heads, much like the one on the national emblem of Russia. And rather than arrows and olive branches, the bird was clutching a set of golf clubs and a wad of dollar bills. And then there was the banner: in place of "E Pluribus Unum" (Latin for "Out of Many, One"), it said "45 Es un Títere": Spanish for "45 Is a Puppet." It turned out that someone from Turning Point had to find an image of the presidential seal in a hurry and found this one on the internet—and no one checked to be sure it was the actual seal rather than a fake seal aiming to criticize "45."

Think before taking and sharing photos

President Trump's experience is all too common today, as Photoshop and other tools make it easier than ever to alter images. So the warning Kenneth Brower sounded over two decades ago is more pertinent than ever. In fact, the easy manipulation of images has led to a new field of study, visual ethics, that explores the way in which images, altered or unaltered, always reflect a particular point of view and hence have ethical dimensions. Think for a moment of the highly unflattering photos of politicians used in ads against them—or of ones that have been enhanced to make them look flawless: Are those photos fair? And think of your own experience: Has a photo ever represented you in ways you felt were unfair, especially if it was taken without your knowledge? That's what leads scholars of visual ethics to argue that both "the production and reception of images always have ethical dimensions" and to ask that photographers especially consider when it is morally acceptable to photograph people who may be highly vulnerable.

Take the case of an image of a father and daughter who drowned while trying to cross the Rio Grande that circulated widely in the summer of 2019. Some felt that it helped raise awareness of the dire circumstances leading refugees to seek asylum in the United States;

Óscar Martínez Ramírez and his daughter, Salvadoran migrants who drowned trying to cross the Rio Grande.

others found it to be insensitive and demeaning—in short, unethical. What's your take?

Certainly, Paul Martin Lester wishes he had thought more carefully when as a young reporter he was sent to an airport on assignment to photograph the reunion of two brothers who'd been separated for forty years. A ho-hum assignment, he thought, but as he waited for the brothers to emerge, something unexpected happened: Faye Dunaway, a very big star back then, exited the plane— and when she saw Lester and all his cameras, she screamed and turned her face to the wall. Lester was frozen in place for a moment, realizing that he hadn't been sent there to photograph her. But when, still badly shaken, she pulled herself together enough to walk toward him, he automatically took a flash photo. He says that this was the most unethical photo he's ever taken, so much so that he now begins every photography class he teaches with this story and his realization that he had acted in a selfish, intrusive, and unethical way. In short, he made a bad choice he doesn't want his students to replicate!

You may never have such challenging decisions to make, but even so you need to be aware of the issues involved in taking and sharing photos—and to think critically and carefully before you post or repost images, as well as when you yourself take photos. Consider this advice from one professional photographer:

> If you are taking a photograph, ask yourself why you are doing it. Try to imagine yourself on the other side of the camera. Would you want that picture taken, maybe published in blogs or magazines? Would you want this particular [image to represent you] or your community? If you can answer with an informed yes, then you are good to go.
>
> —GRAHAM MacINDOE

Get permission, credit sources

It's likely that you will use photos and other visuals drawn from other sources. In such cases, remember that the legal doctrine of fair use allows you to use images without explicit permission in your college writing—IF that writing is not going to be published. Today, some online works may be published under a CREATIVE COMMONS license, which grants permission to use the work as long as you credit the person who created the work. In such cases, you'll need to send an email asking for permission, explaining why you want to use the image, saying where it will appear, and saying that full credit will be given and documented. If it is for educational use and will not be for sale, you may receive permission.

Add alt text

Alt text is a way of describing images in digital texts for readers who are visually impaired or when computers do not load images. The goal is to describe the image in enough detail that readers who cannot see the image will be able to understand what it shows. That said, it needs to be succinct, generally no more than 125 characters.

What detail you provide depends on the RHETORICAL SITUATION. If readers need to know only what or who is in the image, your description might be just what you'd see at a glance. Say you were writing about a specific couple and needed to describe a photo of them. You might write "Susanna and Jeremy holding their dog Gus." If, however, you were writing about the gentrification of neighborhoods in Brooklyn, New York, you might describe the same photo differently: "A young white couple in front of a modest wooden house in Brooklyn. She holds a little dog; he's holding boxes from Amazon." And some images need to be named but do not need to be described: a McDonald's hamburger, for instance, or the Nike swoosh.

The way you provide alt text will depend on where the text will be read. *Word* has a built-in tool for inserting alt text, but any text that will be read on the internet needs to be embedded using HTML. Some social media programs allow you to include alt text with any images that you post. On *Twitter*, for example, you can add descriptions of up to 1,000 characters when posting a photo by clicking the "alt" button. *Instagram* uses object recognition technology to provide alt text for images posted there—and lets you write your own alt text if you prefer.

Think about your own use of visuals

- Consider whether any visuals you use will speak to your AUDIENCE. Will they understand any charts or graphs you want to use?

- Be sure that any photos you take or use represent your subjects accurately and fairly. Avoid stereotyping; be aware of your own biases, and don't let them influence images you take or use.

- Provide any necessary visual CONTEXT. Editing out essential contextual detail can make a photo misleading or hard to understand.

- Treat everything and everyone you photograph with RESPECT. Give special consideration to vulnerable subjects.

- Be sure to include a CAPTION with every visual you include.

- Remember that visuals do not speak for themselves; introduce every visual before it appears in your text, and explain how it supports your point ("as the following pie chart demonstrates, . . .").

- DOCUMENT any visuals you don't create yourself.

- In academic writing, provide a number (Figure 1, Table 1) and a descriptive title above each visual, and an explanatory caption and source note below.

See Chapter 20 on **MLA** style and Chapter 21 on **APA** style for advice on documenting sources and setting up figures and tables.

REFLECT! Choose an essay or something else you've written for a class, and read it over with an eye for how visuals might help support your point. Is there something you describe where a photo would help? Do you include any numerical data that would be easier to understand in a line or bar graph? If so, give it a try. Ask a friend to read the before and after and tell you which version is more persuasive.

MEDIA

A PORTFOLIO

 # Print

ALL I NEED IS A SHEET OF PAPER AND SOMETHING TO WRITE
WITH, AND I CAN TURN THE WORLD UPSIDE DOWN.

—FRIEDRICH NIETZSCHE

THE HUMBLE PRINT PIECE OFTEN DOES EXACTLY
WHAT THE NEW TECHNOLOGIES AIM FOR,
WITH FAR LESS COST AND EFFORT.

—TONY AGUERO

Have you seen the *YouTube* video of a "medieval helpdesk," where a puzzled patron sits in front of a printed book and just stares at it, unable to imagine what to do with it since he has never seen one before? He doesn't even know to open it up! Today, when books and other print texts are everywhere, it's hard to imagine a time when they didn't exist. But when Johannes Gutenberg invented the printing press nearly 600 years ago, he set off a communication revolution that is still unfolding. Rather than the months and months it took for scribes to copy out a text onto goatskin or parchment, Gutenberg's

Check out the medieval helpdesk video at letstalklibrary.com.

press could turn out multiple copies of a page at one time, greatly increasing the availability of books and reducing their cost. The culture of the book was born—and it held sway for hundreds of years.

Fast-forward to the twenty-first century, however, to a time when print texts are no longer the only ones we have available. Today's technologies enable readers to access digital texts with the click of a button—so much so that some pundits argue that print texts are going the way of the dodo bird and other extinct species.

But not so fast. While digital texts offer many advantages, print texts are still holding their own. Some people say they're easier to read and that it's easier to find something you're looking for in a print text—and the fact is sometimes they're really needed. You'll surely have some assignments that require you to turn in hard copy. Think too of posters, handouts, grocery lists, letters to elderly grandparents who may not be on email. And even if you read and write on a computer, there's a reason that all computers include a Print function.

Perhaps most important, you can count on good old paper to be there for you when the technology fails. Consider what happened last year when we were all working from home and Stephen Colbert was broadcasting *The Late Show* from his house in New Jersey. The guest one night was Daniel Radcliffe (yes, Harry Potter himself), who joined the show via video link from his home. We could see Radcliffe, but we couldn't hear him—and no one was able to fix the problem (even

Print can have a downside. One Vietnamese author's name causes no problems in speech—but in writing, it has complicated her life. Read why on p. 626.

Stephen Colbert and Daniel Radcliffe on *The Late Show*, March 31, 2020.

Harry didn't have his wand handy). So what did he do? He reached for pen and paper, wrote out what he wanted to say, and held it up for viewers to read. In short, print text saved the day.

So it seems likely that print texts will be with us for some time. Here are a few tips to get you thinking about how to make those that you create visually compelling and easy to read:

- What kind of print text will serve your PURPOSE? To publicize a concert, it might be a poster, or maybe a postcard. To express an opinion, it could be an essay—or that too might be a poster: think Black Lives Matter.

- But is a print text the best way to reach your AUDIENCE? If they don't use email or social media, it will need to be print. But if it's time-sensitive, better to use email or *Twitter*.

- How should your text be organized? Will it be all or mainly in paragraphs, or is there some detail that will be easier to present or understand in a list? Would headings help you to organize the text—and also help readers to follow it?

- Would VISUALS help you make or illustrate a point? If so, what kind: photos? charts or graphs? maps? Remember that you'll need to introduce any visual, add a caption, and explain how it relates to your point.

- Think about what FONTS will be suitable for your purpose—and reflect your STANCE. For most academic writing, you can't go wrong with a serif font such as Times New Roman or Bookman. But you can be more adventurous with a poster or infographic.

- And what about color? Will you need to use more than one color—and if so, what for?

Following are three print texts that demonstrate some of these elements in an illustrated essay, an infographic, and a poster.

AN ILLUSTRATED ESSAY

Following is part of an essay that Henry Tsai wrote for a composition course on the rhetoric of the graphic narratives. He graduated from Stanford with a degree in comparative studies in race and ethnicity and is now a product manager at Facebook. Go to <u>letstalklibrary.com</u> to read the full essay.

Imag(in)ed and Imposed Identities:

Illustrated Representations of Chinese Immigrants

in San Francisco, 1865–1900

In 1848, when newsman Sam Brannon ran into San Francisco shouting, "Gold! Gold! From the American River!" merchant Chum Ming wrote to his cousin in China ("Gold Rush"). Word spread quickly, and soon images of *gam saan*—"Gold Mountain"—entered the collective imagination of Chinese families impoverished by waves of famine, peasant uprisings, and rebellions (Joe). Scraping together money for a trip to the land of opportunities, poor families sent their men to the United States to work in the mines, on the railroad, or as common laborers ("Chinese Immigration").

However, life in America was harsher and more complicated than the men had imagined. Despite being welcomed as cheap laborers for the Central Pacific Railroad, Chinese immigrants became a threat when the American economy weakened (Joe) and sparked more jealousy when they discovered gold in mines that white Americans thought barren. Such anti-immigrant sentiments spread: from 1865 to 1900, negative newspaper editorials, congressional testimonies, and illustrations of Chinese immigrant men helped foster an atmosphere of fear and distrust. In this essay, I explore how these drawings imposed an identity upon Chinese immigrants, how some of these images still affect Asian Americans today, and how this historical context relates to today's immigration debate.

***

Title announces a broad theme; subtitle states the specific focus.

Starts with background information.

States the thesis.

Introduces a cartoon
and describes it
in detail.

Discusses the
implications of what
the cartoon shows.

The theme of Chinese immigrants monopolizing American industries is a prevalent one. In fig. 3, a *Harper's Weekly* cartoon titled "Another Field of American Industry Invaded by the Chinese," a Chinese man with a smirk on his face is playfully holding a baseball bat in a laundry shop. Next to him, a clothing iron weighs down a piece of paper that reads "Wanted: Chinamen to Play Base-ball. $20.00 per week." The caption relays fear of appropriation of a beloved American tradition with an undertone of racist stereotyping: "No more Washee! Playee Base-balee! Sellee out Game, alee same Melican man!" If letting the Chinese play baseball is selling out the American sport, then letting the Chinese work and live in this country is selling out the American dream. The threat to the economy is not only an influx of cheap labor, but also an "invasion" of the perceived Chinese immigrants' values intertwined with irreverence for American values. The caption also plays to the intolerant fear of foreigners. The Chinese cannot just participate in American society; they have to invade it.

ANOTHER FIELD OF AMERICAN INDUSTRY INVADED BY THE CHINESE.
"No more Washee! Playee Base-balee! Sellee out Game, alee same Melican man?"

Caption includes a
figure number and
source information.

Fig. 3. "Another Field of American Industry Invaded by the Chinese," *Harper's Weekly*, cartoon, 1883, p. 27.

AN INFOGRAPHIC

This infographic was created by Giorgia Lupi and a team at Pentagram Design, a firm that does graphics, packaging, exhibitions, advertising, websites, and more. It's one of several works from the Happy Data Project, infographics containing "small but mighty numbers" that present hopeful views of the world. The project began in 2020 as a response to the COVID-19 pandemic and the killings of George Floyd, Breonna Taylor, and so many other Black people; go to <u>happy-data.co</u> to see more examples.

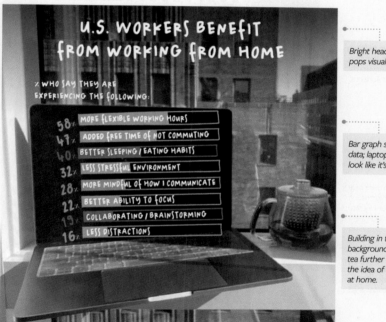

Bright heading pops visually.

Bar graph shows the data; laptop makes it look like it's at home.

Building in the background, pot of tea further emphasize the idea of working at home.

A POSTER

This poster is a call for auditions for Talisman, a student a capella group dedicated to sharing cross-cultural stories through song. Founded in 1990 at Stanford with the goal of bringing underrepresented music to campus, the group has now expanded its repertoire to include cross-cultural music from around the world. Go to <u>stanfordtalisman.com</u> to hear them sing.

Large red font draws attention to 2 keywords: Talisman and Auditions.

Smaller dark blue font gives information about when to audition and where to sign up.

The yellow sun in the background is the Talisman logo.

 # 28 Oral

WORDS CAN INSPIRE. AND WORDS CAN DESTROY.
CHOOSE YOURS WELL.

—PETER ECONOMY

YOU CAN'T REALLY NAME A MOVEMENT THAT DIDN'T START
WITH THE SPOKEN WORD.

—NANCY DUARTE

Before the rise of print texts, the spoken word was king, and queen: orators worked long and hard to make their words unforgettable and their voices audible, even to very large crowds—and with no amplification. Then came the rise of writing, and of print texts, which, ironically, seemed to drown out speech: we began to say we wanted to "see it in writing" before accepting a message; written documentation became paramount in legal proceedings; and writing was more authoritative than "just talk."

Today, however, the spoken word is again of major importance in delivering information: from town halls devoted to speeches and conversation, to public lectures, to the rise of rap and spoken word poetry, to TED Talks, to the resurgence of radio, to televised newscasts, to countless podcasts—live human voices speak to us around the clock.

Writing and speaking are both major ways to communicate, to deliver messages, and they are similar in some ways: both use language, both convey information, both address audiences. But there are significant differences too. In general, written texts are more precise, stable, and permanent than spoken texts; they are also often more formal. In addition, readers can exert some control over written texts, rereading, for instance, or going at a slower or faster pace.

Spoken texts are considerably more dynamic, allowing for more immediacy and more interaction; they are often able to engage audiences more personally and quickly. Moreover, speakers can make use of many kinds of nonverbal communication: tone and volume, pacing and inflection, gestures, movement, and more. But unless the spoken text is digitized, listeners can't go back and check on something they hear in a speech, or slow it down. As speakers, then, we need to pay very careful attention to our audiences, and be on the lookout for cues that will tell us whether the audience is following along (or not). In other words, we need to learn to "read" an audience, to be aware of puzzled looks, nods, smiles, and eye contact.

You will surely have opportunities to give oral presentations and work with other spoken texts during your college years. Whether it's a presentation in a class, a report to a group you belong to, or an oral history, you will want to make your words count. And while it's impossible to provide guidelines for every kind of spoken text you may need to produce, here are some tips that can help.

- Think about your AUDIENCE. What will they expect to hear from you? What will they need to know to follow your thoughts? How can you engage their interest?

- What's the CONTEXT? If it's a presentation, you'll need to draft a script or notes. If you're hosting a podcast or conducting an interview for an oral history, you'll need to draft some questions.

- Work especially hard on your OPENING, and about how you can get your audience interested in what you're about to say.

- NARRATIVE is a tried and true way to engage listeners and to get your points across memorably, and you can use a story to frame an entire presentation or to support a point you are making. But be careful that any story you tell has a point.

- In speaking, less is often more. As one public-speaking coach says, "trying to put too much in" is the biggest mistake inexperienced speakers make. Keep it simple; keep it clear. Rely on relatively brief sentences whenever you can.

- Keep your overall structure simple and clear as well, with explicit TRANSITIONS to guide listeners from point to point. Pausing to sum up major points can also help keep them focused on your message.

- Use vivid language, ACTIVE VOICE, and concrete nouns. But keep in mind what Mark Twain once said: "Don't use a five-dollar word when a fifty-cent word will do."

- If you're preparing a presentation, draft a script that is marked up for pauses and emphasis; a partial script that contains major points and keywords; or note cards. Think as well about how you can use gestures for emphasis.

- Your CONCLUSION is your chance to leave your audience thinking about what you've said. Think hard about what they will consider most memorable.

- Are there any VISUALS that might help get your message across—graphs or charts? Maps? Photographs or other images? If you use any visuals, make sure that every single one illustrates a point you are making.

- Remember the old saying that "practice makes perfect." Practice until you are completely comfortable with your message—and with how you'll be delivering it!

See how Greta Thunberg uses short sentences and everyday language to add power to her angry message in a speech at the UN. Read it on p. 759.

In the pages that follow, you'll find examples of three kinds of spoken texts: presentations, podcasts, and oral histories. In each case, there's no substitute for knowing your topic and knowing it well—so that you are comfortable enough to speak directly to an audience about it and to answer questions with ease and accuracy.

Oral presentations

Many oral presentations follow one common structure: beginning by describing "what is" and then suggesting what "could (or should) be." Then in the middle of the speech, the presenter moves back and forth between discussing that status quo and what it could or should be. And the conclusion evokes what could be and calls for some kind of action. In fact, this is a classic storytelling technique, setting up a conflict that needs to be resolved. And presenting your main point as a story works well in a spoken presentation because stories are easy to follow—and to remember. As you'll see, this is the way Trey Connelly structured his presentation about modes of instruction in video games, reprinted here on pages 482–87.

Podcasts

Podcasts are spoken-word audio files that can be listened to on a digital device. Some focus on the news, others tell stories, still others feature people discussing or explaining a certain topic. You may be familiar with some of the most popular podcasts—*Radiolab*, *The Daily*, *Stuff You Should Know*—or some of the political ones—*Pod Save America*, *Everything's Going to Be Alright*. And some colleges now produce podcasts, from Longwood University's *Day after Graduation* to the Stanford engineering school's *The Future of Everything*. So podcasts are a good way to stay informed about what's going on in the world—and to learn about things you know nothing about.

And if you have a smartphone and a computer and a quiet place to record, it's something you can do. We won't say it's simple, and it's beyond the scope of this little book to teach you how, but we can offer a little advice about some basic features of a podcast. They usually have a host, who introduces the topic and interviews guests or leads discussion. Some podcasts are scripted in advance, but some are organized more like a Q & A, with questions prepared in advance that guests answer. Any questions should be open-ended, eliciting more than a yes or no. Most podcasts strike an informal, conversational TONE.

Most of all, the best podcasts are both informative and entertaining. The best podcasters know their subject thoroughly and are at ease talking about it. And the better the guests, the better the podcast. In short, doing a podcast calls on you to come up with a topic that matters, to RESEARCH your topic and find knowledgeable, engaging guests—and to think hard about how you can make the discussion one that will interest *and engage* others. On pages 488–91 you'll find a transcript of Jack Long's podcast featuring two first-generation college students, along with a link to the podcast itself.

Oral histories

Oral histories are recorded interviews with people who have firsthand knowledge of significant events or places. Historians, anthropologists, and others collect oral histories as a way of recording the memories of many different people—and of learning about an event from many different perspectives. One oral history project you may be familiar with is *StoryCorps*, whose mission is "to record, preserve, and share the stories of Americans from all backgrounds and beliefs."

In interviewing someone for an oral history, then, your goal is to get them to tell their stories. Ask open-ended questions, ones that call for more than a yes or no; ask why, how, where, when. Don't interrupt: your goal is to capture your subject's memories and stories in their own words. Let them speak! And if you transcribe the recording, be sure to show it to the person interviewed to be sure you've captured what they said accurately. You will find a partial transcript of an oral history of Levi Strauss & Co. on pages 492–93, featuring its president reminiscing about the early days of the company and about one employee who became a hero to his fellow workers.

AN ORAL PRESENTATION

Sign and Design: Modes of Instruction in Digital Games

Trey Connelly gave this oral presentation for his sophomore writing class, one that focused on the theme of "How We Got Schooled: The Rhetoric of Literacy and Education." Now a junior majoring in computer science, Connelly still enjoys the study of gaming. He will graduate from Stanford University in 2021. In the following pages, you will see the script that Connelly worked from in making this presentation, along with eight of the 158 slides he prepared to accompany it.

Opening engages audience directly, including them with use of we.

Hi, I'm Trey Connelly, and I'm here to talk about games.

Games are fun! We all know that. But what's not fun is not knowing how to play.

Everyday language ("gonna be") sets informal tone.

Scrabble, baseball, karate, all of these activities can be very fun. But if you don't know how to play—if you don't know the rules—then you're just gonna be confused and frustrated, and not have a good time.

Now normally, though, this isn't much of a problem, because these are all social activities, so there's bound to be someone around who can show you the ropes.

Describes "what is"— the current state of gaming.

Except when we get to video games. Video games are unique in that they're primarily solo activities, so the job of teaching the player falls not on another person but rather on the game itself. Combine that with the fact that games, systems, and controls have gotten more, and more, and more, complicated over time, and you'll see that the job of the game designer is not an easy one.

Introduces his research project.

So my research project was about Sign and Design: Modes of Instruction in Digital Games, and what that can tell us about instruction in other contexts.

Simple, uncluttered slide announces the topic.

For this presentation, we'll be stepping into the role of the game designer in order to answer one question: How do you teach players how to play your game?

Now you might think, why not just tell them how to play? What else *would* you do? Well let's see how this works out with a case study, of *Final Fantasy X*, one of the most popular game franchises of all time. So it's gotta be good, right? And by the time you get to the tenth in the series, most fans are gonna buy it no matter what. But it introduces a few new mechanics, like this thing called a sphere grid.

Use of questions helps keep audience's attention.

So let's see how the game teaches players how to use the sphere grid system: First, you select "Sphere Grid" from the main menu. The cursor appears at the selected character's current position. Use the d-pad to move the cursor. So far so good. Information on the upgrades is displayed at the top of the screen... defense upgrades... learn an ability... nodes... press X... <yawn, click through slides>

Explains how "just telling how to play" currently works.

Slide shows how one game explains how it works.

How are you all doing? Oh! Hey, we're done. Did you get all that? Because the game isn't gonna tell you that information ever again. Not great.

So the problem with explicit instructions is that when someone who wants to play a game instead encounters a wall of text, they're not likely to pay attention. And even if they do, the chances they'd actually retain all that information by the time they get into the *game* part where it matters are essentially zero. <pause>

And this has been verified by cognitive science. Learning theorist James Gee of Arizona State explains that "Human beings are quite poor at using verbal information when given lots of it out of context and before they can see how it applies in actual situations." If this sounds like too much verbal information out of context for you, let me restate that: When it comes to games, words are bad. Or better yet, <slide>

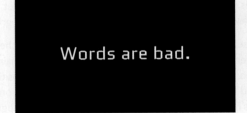

All that is to say, it seems like just telling players how to play is not the way to go.

So what if we just . . . *don't* tell them how to play? I mean, think about it. There's tons of things we do all the time without being explicitly told how to do so. Think of a toaster, for example. Sure, it comes with an instruction manual, but has anyone ever read it? We can just figure it out.

So maybe that's what we should do with games too. One game that does this is *Dwarf Fortress*. It's a bit of a cult classic, but you may

Use of short direct sentences to show failure of explicit instruction.

Slide underscores his main point with 3 words that will grab his audience's attention.

Uses an analogy to make his point.

Describes one alternative of what "could be."

know it was the inspiration behind *Minecraft*. Here's a little taste of *my* first hour trying to figure out how to play *Dwarf Fortress*:

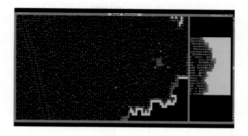

Um. Huh. Am I in a field? Is that blue thing a river? What do all these symbols mean? What should I do here? Maybe I'll just press these buttons? Oh no, am I in a cave? Is it night? I have no idea.

Points out that this alternative is no better than explicit instruction.

Yeah. In fact, *Dwarf Fortress* is so hard to understand that people have written entire books on how to *get started*, which brings us right back where we started with that same verbal information out of context that Professor Gee warned us against.

So going back to our main question, it seems like we can't just tell players how to play, but we can't *not* tell them either. But there's actually a third option. Think back to toasters. Yes, we can easily figure out how to use it—and that's no accident. It's by design. Here's what a toaster *really* looks like.

Returns to toaster analogy.

If this was your toaster, you might need an instruction manual to figure out what to do with it. But the toaster we see hides all the stuff that we don't need to see in order to understand, and leaves us with this sleek model with two visual elements: slots at the top that are just the size and shape of a slice of bread, and a lever on the side that almost screams "push me down."

This use of intentional design to convey information without words is what game designers Anna Anthropy and Naomi Clark call a "communicative visual vocabulary." And it can be incredibly effective.

In games as in toasters, Anthropy and Clark argue that we shouldn't tell the player explicitly how to play using words they won't read or remember, but nor should we abandon them to their own devices in a way that makes things incredibly hard to figure out. Instead, they say, the best way to teach a player *is* to tell them how to play, but do so *implicitly*, using visual vocabulary and intentional design that makes it easy for them to figure out what to do.

To see what I'm talking about here, let's look at one more game: *The Witness*, my personal favorite. Here's the opening segment of the game. The player starts off in a long, dark hallway that's got a brightly lit door at the other end that clearly indicates that they should move forward to get to it. Once there, there's a door with an orange panel. And actually . . . it kind of looks familiar. If we just . . . and then . . . yeah! It looks a little like a toaster! It's got the same knob and track.

Toaster analogy shows the importance of intentional design to instruction.

Proposes a better alternative to explicit instruction: implicit instruction.

Use of vivid description language evokes the experience of the game.

Points out intentional design—as easy as using a toaster!

So let's see if this visual vocabulary matches what actually happens in the game: the player comes up to the door, grabs the knob, slides it across the track, lets go—and pop, the door opens!

The designers of *The Witness* could have put a big block of instruction text next to the door saying, "When you approach an orange panel, click the circle and navigate your mouse to the end of the track."

Or they could have just thrown you right into one of the later puzzles like this one, and let you struggle to figure it out. But instead they went the way of the toaster, making it visually clear what to do without needing to be told. And the game is much better for it.

Now, as we wrap up here, you might be wondering, *Who cares? We're just talking about video games*. But really, we're talking about more than just games. The principles of instruction we've seen here are relevant in pretty much any instructional context.

No matter the situation, one of the best ways to teach someone is not just to tell them what to do or what to know, but rather to let them figure it out for themselves in an environment designed to make that easy.

Hmm. Makes you wonder, then, why so much of the instruction we get in school is still so tied to textbooks. That's a question for another time, but for now I want to leave you thinking like a game designer. So today, try to notice something in your life that uses a visual vocabulary to tell you what to do without *telling* you what to do. Appreciate the toasters in your life. Thank you.

Returns to what explicit verbal instruction would look like.

Transition signals that the presentation is coming to a close.

Notes the implications of intentional design beyond video games.

Sums up his argument.

Poses a provocative question.

Closes by asking his audience to take action.

Go to letstalk library.com to watch a video of this presentation. Notice how he ad-libbed as he spoke, adapting on the spot to connect with his audience.

Works Cited

[reference list illegible]

A PODCAST

On Being First-Gen Students

The podcast that follows was produced by Jack Long, a student who created a series of podcasts called The Third Chair *as part of his work with* The Lantern, *Ohio State's student newspaper. The podcast here features two interviews with OSU students about their experiences as first-generation students. Jack Long is a second-year student at Ohio State majoring in journalism.*

Host introduces himself, the topic of this podcast, and his 2 guests.

Jack Long: This week, you're going to hear a few stories from first-generation students. In fact, they're first-generation students who are in their first semester. I'm Jack Long, and you're listening to *The Third Chair*.

First guest gives background information.

Colin Flanagan: So I grew up in this suburb on the east side of Toledo called Oregon. Just, you know, a typical American residential suburb. Really not a whole lot to do unless you cross the river into the actual city of Toledo. We have this state park, Maumee Bay—it has a nice lodge if you're looking to stay there for, you know, a wedding or something, but other than that, you know, metro parks, but really you have to cross into Toledo. I'm Colin Flanagan, I'm a first-generation student at The Ohio State University studying political science, economics, and public policy.

Colloquial language ("yeah") establishes an informal tone.

Yeah, so my family. . . . I live in a typical 1950s American household. It's me, my mom, my dad, and my younger brother, who is currently a sophomore in high school where I went to school, named Chase. My dad is . . . he was an auto mechanic for 23 years and now he works for the city of Oregon as a street department employee, so he, you know, he'll crack seal or fix potholes in the roads, he'll plow snow or cut the grass in public areas. And right now my mom is a waitress.

My family raised me to go to college, so I would say, yeah, it was expected of me to go to college. I know that various extended family members from, say, more rural areas didn't really care if I went to college, and they warned me about the debt that I was going to endure and encouraged me to go to trade school, but I didn't think twice about going to college. I feel like college provides the most opportunity to me. I want to go into politics and hopefully attend law school before doing that and I really wasn't going to do that unless I went to college, so that's why I'm here now.

Host does not interrupt, giving the guest time and space to speak.

I come from a lower-middle-class family, maybe you could have guessed that from my parents' occupations. The government seems to think [*laughter*] that we can fork out a lot of money to pay for my education and, well, I'm not getting any of that. My expected family contribution is upward of $8,000, so I knew we really couldn't afford that. My parents' interaction with me was, I think, not all that common, although it could be. They told me from the get-go, even before senior year of high school started—start looking for scholarships, start looking for scholarships.

A touch of humor regarding college costs helps connect with his audience.

Being a first-generation student is just... a lot of the time, people are going to tell you that you don't know what to do ... and you know, maybe you don't have a really good direction about where you're going. But I think that people who aren't first-generation students fall into this category of certainty when they go away to school, go away to college or university, that they know exactly what's going to happen. And I think in some ways first-generation students have an advantage because they don't fall into that track, they don't fall into that. I think you run the line of, you really get to find things out for yourself and learn on your own. You know, you don't learn things unless you do it on your own. Like when you're a little kid and they say—cliché example—when you're a little kid and they say don't touch the stove, and you touch the stove. Well you're really not going to touch it after you do that.

Points out one advantage of being a first-gen student.

Uses an analogy to underscore doing things "on your own."

Host chooses to have second guest introduce himself directly to audience.

Brandon Hernandez: I believe my dad was fifteen when he first came to the United States, but he stayed in California and that's where he, you know, did the typical work, he worked on farms and stuff like that. He told me how he used to pick lettuce. My name's Brandon Hernandez. I'm studying political science and economics here at The Ohio State University.

Tells something about his background and upbringing.

My dad works for the city of Hamilton, he works in waste-water treatment, and my mom is a quality control specialist at a Tyson food factory. Both of my parents never finished high school, but they've always strongly emphasized and pushed for education because they believe education is kind of like a tool for success and it opens up so many doors and gives you so many opportunities that it's just necessary to have in today's day and age.

Subject of college costs comes up again, something on the minds of many students.

You know, I usually don't get like stressed out over things, but the whole aspect of the finances has taken a little bit of its toll, because I know at the end of the day it's an investment, like you're investing in your future. And as long as you find the career path that you know you'll make money, I mean it'll be worth it. But just seeing all those big numbers . . . I would say I went through a mini panic attack. If it wasn't for one of my high school teachers, whose name was Mr. Stebbins, he really helped me out throughout the process because I was really worried once I saw, you know, I didn't get a full ride.

Shift to second-person ("And you know") helps connect with his audience.

And you know, growing up and things like that, you're predicting your path and you're like, "All right, I'm going to do this, this and that, and it's just all going to work out." And then adulthood and reality hits you and you're just like, "Well, okay, that didn't work out . . . how am I going to go about this and solve it?" And I was really worried for a time in my senior year, like that was like the main thing occupying my mind, and I would say I kind of lost sleep sometimes about it, just thinking about it.

Advice helps him get beyond "lost sleep."

But Mr. Stebbins reassured me, you know: "Don't worry about it *too* much. If you let it consume you, you're going to start slacking on your sleep, which will impact your grades, which will impact all that." And he just said, "It's going to be a domino effect. It's going to affect you that way, so what you need to do is, you need to relax, don't be afraid too much about loans and the huge sums that there are, just, you go out there, you prove to them through your effort and your grades and all that that you belong here, and eventually you'll be able to pay it off."

Colin Flanagan: One more thing I want to add: I think a lot of people come in being a first-generation student and they're really afraid because they don't know what to expect. But there's a certain comfortableness in the chaos of it. Because it's just . . . you don't know what to expect. And so, with that, there's no expectations. And I think that's a lot better than having expectations not being met.

First guest sums up the message he wants to leave listeners with.

Jack Long: *The Third Chair* is produced and written by *Lantern* reporters and myself. We're published by *The Lantern* at The Ohio State University. Special thanks to Brandon Hernandez and Colin Flanagan. You can find other great podcasts from *The Lantern* on thelantern.com.

Host returns to close the session, thank his guests, and note the podcast website.

You can listen to the full podcast at letstalklibrary.com.

AN ORAL HISTORY

A Lesson about Empathy

The text that follows comes from the transcript of an oral history of Levi Strauss & Co., the fabled firm that invented Levi's jeans in 1873. It's an excerpt from an interview with Walter Haas Jr. about his years as president of the company. The interview was conducted in 1994 by Ann Lage, associate director of the Regional Oral History Office of the Bancroft Library at the University of California, Berkeley. In the following excerpt, Haas shares some stories about his first years with the firm.

Stories help capture important memories.

Haas: There are several stories: the first one didn't have to do with me, but it gave me a lesson. Milton G was an elevator operator on Battery Street. One day he went to my grandfather and said, "This is a family business. I know that a member of the family is always going to be the head of it. I want to rise to the top, and I obviously can't do it here. I'd like to go out to the factory because maybe I can someday be the factory manager." He was just a little elevator operator.

Direct quotation lets Milton G speak for himself.

Lage: And young, I would presume.

Question helps keep the narrative going.

Haas: Very young. [But some years later] Milton G became the factory manager. It was wonderful. At the end of the year, my grandfather called this young man in and said that he had done a remarkable job and they had bonuses they gave to the executives in a good year, and they wanted to give Milton G a bonus. And he said, "Mr. Stern, I am poor, I'm supporting my mother, I really need the money. But I can't take a bonus unless you give a bonus to all the factory employees as well."

More direct quotations bring Milton G to life.

Use of dialogue makes the story more immediate and personal.

This was an unheard of thing in those days. My grandfather said, "I have to think about it overnight." The next day he said, "All right, we'll do it." And Milton said, "Well, you can only do it if you come out when I give out the checks." My grandfather did, and apparently it was a scene of utter chaos and elation, that these mostly foreign-born women, mostly of Italian extraction at that time, were recognized as human beings instead of numbers on a sewing machine. They cried, and they laughed, and they hugged everybody.... I think that's a wonderful lesson, and Milton G was a remarkable man.

Explains why this story matters: the lesson it teaches.

Note that the interviewer does not interrupt the speaker.

Empathy for the Employees

Another lesson I learned from Milton. They had a cafeteria in those days, and they had a couple of ex-sewing machine operators who were along in years who washed the dishes. One day I went to Milton, and I said, "You know, I think it'd be better to buy a dishwasher. It'd save money, be more sanitary." Instead of discouraging me, he said, "Well, that's a good idea. Why don't you make a little study of the costs."

Transition leads to a second story—and another lesson.

Well, I had gone to the Harvard Business School, so I made a very detailed little study and pointed out that it would save money and be more sanitary if we in fact got a dishwasher. And he said, "Well, that's fine, but there are two ladies who've spent over thirty years in the company. What would I do with them?" And I realized that there's more than just money involved in any decision. And that was a lesson that stuck with me.

Contrasts (ironically?) what he learned at school with something he learned on the job.

Concludes his story by reiterating the lesson learned.

Milton G dancing with a colleague at a factory party—wearing Levi's, like most everyone there.

29 Digital

WE TEXT. WE ZOOM. WE SEND ONE ANOTHER
LINKS ABOUT VIROLOGY.

—DAVID REMNICK

IF I COULD COME BACK AS ANYTHING, I'D BE A BIRD—
BUT DEFINITELY THE COMMAND KEY
IS MY SECOND CHOICE

—NIKKI GIOVANNI

Where do you do most of your work? Online. Where do you go for news or information? Online. Where do you go for meetings? Increasingly, online. Where do you go for entertainment? Especially during a pandemic—online! Anytime you visit a website, play a video game, open an app, read an ebook, write an email, or attend a video conference, you're doing so via digital media. In short, the world we know today is in large part a digital world, and we are its citizens.

J. K. Rowling tapped into the magic of digital media in 2020 when many students were learning from home, launching *Harry Potter at Home*, a website that provides games, quizzes, chapters read by Daniel Ratcliffe and others—all based on the wizarding world of the Harry Potter books. It's not quite Hogwarts, but it's something that only digital media could pull off.

You may not be assigned to create a digital Hufflepuff site, but chances are that much of the work you do in college will be done online. This chapter provides tips for working with digital sites and includes a small portfolio of three of our favorite digital texts: a blog, a *YouTube* video, and a website.

Providing guidelines for every kind of digital text you might want to create isn't possible in this small book—or in any book, since technology is constantly changing—but here are some tips that can help:

- Whatever platform you're using, think about what features it offers that will help you achieve your PURPOSE and appeal to the AUDIENCE you wish to reach: images? visual data? audio? links to sources your readers are likely to trust?

- Think about how you can attract readers and viewers. Titles are especially important in digital media, both for describing what your text is about and for making it one that someone doing a *Google* search will want to click on.

- What's your STANCE toward your topic? How do you want to come across to readers? What TONE do you want to project: conversational? businesslike? earnest? something else? Be sure that the words you use convey that tone.

- Be sure to add CAPTIONS to any visuals that you include—and to credit the sources of any that you yourself have not created.

- Whether you're creating a BLOG, a *YouTube* video, or a website, think about the "look" you want. What FONTS, colors, and VISUALS will produce that look? If you're filming yourself in a video, think about what you'll wear and what will be in the background. Whatever your text, its DESIGN will affect the way it comes across—and is received.

BLOGS

Blogs (from *web* + *log*) are sites that focus on topics of all kinds. Think food blogs. Tech blogs. Mom blogs. Fitness blogs. Grammar blogs! If there's something you're interested in, chances are there's a blog about that. And if not, you might want to start one.

Most blogs follow a simple organization. A homepage describes what the site is about and lists its posts in reverse chronological order, the most recent one on top. Then comes the main content, which may include images and links. And almost always there's a place to comment.

Like a lot of writing on the web, most blogs strike an informal tone and are written in conversational language. And at their best, blogs generate conversations. Write about something you care a lot about, creating a blog of your own about that topic—and if you work at it, you can build an audience who will join you in conversation. Here are some tips to get you started:

Jane Coaston's essay on whether sports matter was originally published in a *New York Times* newsletter—a kind of blog for subscribers. Check out what she says on p. 764.

- Come up with a good name. Make it one that's easy to remember and that gives some idea of what the blog is about. *Serious Eats*, *TechCrunch*, *NASCARista*, and *Barefoot Nurse* are a few of our favorites.

- Follow other blogs on related topics, and make a point of responding to what they say. That's one way others will find you.

- Tag those blogs in your blog, and make an effort to refer to them occasionally.

- Include links to other info that may interest your readers.

- Include a Comments section on your blog, and invite response. Simply posing a question can help prompt response. And be sure to respond to any comments. Keep the conversation going.

- Update your blog regularly!

A BLOG POST

Erin Hawley is the creator, writer, and editor of The Geeky Gimp, *a blog that focuses on disability in comics, games, and TV shows. A graduate of East Carolina University, she is now an accessibility consultant for analog and digital gaming. She adores* Star Trek, Spock, *and Maria Carey. Visit her blog at* <u>geekygimp.com</u>.

Writing While Disabled: The Damage of Ableism

June 1, 2018

Share this post:

Erin Hawley

"Are people telling me this thing I wrote is good because it's actually good, or are they praising it because they have such low expectations of me?"

Being a writer is hard. I'm a perfectionist, which makes me dislike everything I produce. That's not necessarily a bad thing, as my perfectionism makes me a decent writer and an even better editor.

But as a disabled writer, I question other people's reactions to my work. The opening quote is something I ask myself every time I share my writing with others.

Some people name that thought process "imposter syndrome," but that doesn't cover it. My insecurities around people's reactions stem from ableism, specifically the way abled folks assume so little of me. It stems from inspiration porn, where **every action of a disabled person is praised**, including mundane, ordinary things like going food shopping or having friends. I grew up defying expectations from an ableist society by simply existing. Anything beyond that, like graduating from college or being in a romantic relationship, blows people's minds—and it shouldn't.

The title makes a provocative claim that draws readers in.

Date the blog was posted.

Opens with a question that announces the theme of the post.

Short paragraphs focus on the key points and make the post easy to read.

Boldface type highlights important points.

Words highlighted in blue link to definitions.

Conversational language connects with readers.

While much of my work is aimed at dismantling ableism, I understand this -ism, like all oppression, is far too ingrained in society to change overnight, or within my lifetime. That means I must learn to live within this structure. I value my writing—I need to make that clear. **This isn't about my talents**, but more about how abled and some disabled people view my talent, and how those views negatively impact my craft. I would write more if I felt secure that my work was valued and critiqued by others the same way I view and critique myself. I wouldn't hesitate to publish if I knew my writing was not seen as a miracle, or met with a patronizing "good for you!"

So when I release a blog post into the wild and receive praise for it, I can't tell if it's genuine. **And I'm certain some of it isn't genuine**, but rather a manifestation of ableism—even if well-meaning and unrealized. I want abled people to read my work knowing I am a disabled woman because I am proud of who I am, but I also want them to read it **without the framework of ableism**. That isn't possible, though, so I internalize and dissect my writing to an unhealthy degree. I can't accept praise even if I also think my blog post or poem or marketing pitch for work is good.

I've thought about ways to dismantle this thought process. What I'm trying to do is write for a small audience. I don't mean the number of people who read my posts; what I mean is, when I write, I only have myself in mind. Or I only have other disabled people in mind if I'm writing specifically about disability. I am telling myself that abled people's opinions of my writing do not affect or control my writing. Some people will view everything I do through the lens of ableism, and I **can't let that hinder my words**. Disassociating is not an easy process, but it's a necessary one to keep my powerful voice intact.

Specifies a particular audience she's addressing.

I am curious if other disabled writers experience similar thoughts, or have any tips on how to keep writing while disabled. Please let me know in the comments!

Concludes by inviting comments and response—in italics to emphasize the request.

VLOGS

Vlogs (from *video* + *log*) are blogs that are delivered in video. There are thousands of them on *YouTube*, and like blogs, they are about any number of things: travel, family reunions, how to make face masks. Many of them are by college students—and many of those are *about* being college students. Some of these provide information: how to find "the best" classes, how to juggle work and school. Many others simply tell about the vlogger's everyday routines: a day in their life at college, a stroll across campus, writing an essay at midnight that's due the next day.

In fact, it's now an option in some composition classes to produce a short vlog. Students have composed NARRATIVES about their first (or last!) day at college, REPORTS on something they're researching, ARGUMENTS for candidates they support. Even if it's not an assignment, maybe there's just something you want to tell others about.

Planning a vlog is not all that different from anything else you write, but usually you'll want to keep it casual. Start by jotting down the main points you want to cover. Some vloggers write out a script; others just make a list of keywords to keep them on track as they speak. But think about how you'll begin: you'll need to introduce yourself as well as your topic, and in a way that will make your audience want to listen to what you have to say. And keep it conversational—you'll be doing the talking, but remember that you'll have an audience, so speak directly to them and acknowledge them in some way.

It's possible to film a vlog on a simple smartphone. In fact, many of the best vlogs are appealing *because* they keep it simple. Here are some tips to help you get started:

- Watch a few vlogs to see how it's done. You could start with Brandon Hayden's vlog on page 501.

- Create a *YouTube* channel. If you've not done this before, take advantage of the QuickStart guidelines that *YouTube* provides.

- Decide on a background, but make sure it doesn't distract from YOU: you're the star of this show! If you'll be walking around, decide on your route.

- Try out your options for lighting. It's best to use natural light, with the light on you and not behind you. But avoid filming in direct sunlight.

- Get comfortable with whatever camera you use—and remember that the quality of the camera is not as important as the content of what you say.

- Consider getting an inexpensive tripod, and if you'll be seated in the vlog, position the camera at eye level. Remember to look directly at the camera.

- Practice, practice, practice.

- Press Record and start talking. Be yourself! Say what you have to say!

BRANDON HAYDEN

College101: Choosing a Major!

Brandon Hayden is a student at Georgia State, where he's majoring in sociology. The piece on the following pages comes from a vlog he runs on YouTube called College 101: A Helpful College Series! *He has another YouTube channel called* Happily Dressed, *a name he also uses for his Instagram account, @happilydressed. It's a label that reflects his belief that being ourselves is "effortless and 100% worth it"—and that "trying to fit in is old news." It's a message with an audience: Hayden now has 2.8K YouTube subscribers!*

We cannot include an actual vlog on the pages of this book, but as you'll see on the following pages, we've included several screenshots along with a partial transcript of Hayden's spirited and wise advice about choosing a major. The transcript shows his introduction and conclusion— but go to letstalklibrary.com *to see the full vlog. If you haven't yet chosen your major, Brandon Hayden is here to help.*

A *YOUTUBE* VLOG

COLLEGE 101: A Helpful College Series!
Brandon Hayden · 3 / 3   ⌃

🔁   ⤬   ☰+

1   COLLEGE 101: The Application Process
     | Brandon Hayden
     5:29   Brandon Hayden

2   COLLEGE 101: Making New Friends! |
     Brandon Hayden
     5:20   Brandon Hayden

▶   COLLEGE 101: Choosing a Major! |
     Brandon Hayden
     5:45   Brandon Hayden

▶ ▶❘ 🔊 0:01 / 5:44   CC ⚙ ⬓ ⬜ ⛶

COLLEGE 101: Choosing a Major! | Brandon Hayden

2,452 views · Mar 28, 2016   👍 82   👎 1   ➔ SHARE   ☰+ SAVE   ...

Clear title of series attracts intended audience.

List of episodes.

Simple, uncluttered background doesn't distract from the speaker.

Title of episode, number of views, date posted.

COLLEGE 101: Choosing a Major! | Brandon Hayden

2,445 views • Mar 28, 2016   👍 82   👎 1   ➤ SHARE   ≡+ SAVE   •••

Makes eye contact and crosses fingers for good luck—connecting to viewers.

Hello guys! So, we are back. I fixed my microphone, I got a new battery for it, so we're back on the nice camera. But, I'm here for another installment of the College 101 series, and today we are talking about choosing a major.

Here's a transcript of the start of Hayden's vlog.

Introduction explains the glitch and introduces a current topic.

Now this can be extremely difficult, and sometimes you just don't get it—actually, most of the time, people don't get it right on the first try. I know when I applied to Georgia State, I went under a marketing major, then I got here, changed to a communications major, then added a journalism minor, and then now I've just changed completely to sociology.

Uses his own experience to connect to the audience.

So basically, it's hard to get what you want to do right the first time. You have assumptions, you take the classes, and then you realize, you know what, maybe this is not for me—I think I have a passion somewhere else. So then you just change it. And it's okay to change majors between freshman and sophomore year. Once you get to junior and senior year, you get kind of like "uugh" if you change your major again—you kind of have to stay an extra year

Conversational tone and everyday vocabulary are used throughout.

or extra two years, so definitely try to make a decision before sophomore year is over.

But hopefully, with this video, I can help you kind of dissect what
you really want to do. To do this, I'm going to go through the process of me choosing my own major.

And here is the conclusion to Brandon Hayden's vlog.

*Explains what is to
come in the rest
of the vlog.*

I hope you guys enjoyed this video. I did a lot of talking like I always
do in all of my videos so I shouldn't be surprised. If you want more
of me and this college series and the college vlogs and just the random videos here and there, you can subscribe down below. I post
every Monday. And yeah, don't take picking a major so, so seriously.
Because once you get here, you might decide you don't want to do
it anymore, you'll choose maybe two different other ones, you can
even pick a minor. So yeah, you have time, so please, don't stress out
about picking a major. Pick what you think you want to do now, you'll
get here, and if you don't like it you can switch. And if you do, then
great on you! You're ahead of the game. But you don't necessarily
have to be.

I hope this helped you in any way, shape, or form, and if it did, and
any of your other friends are worried about picking a major, please
send them this video. And I'll see you guys next Monday! See you
guys later.

WEBSITES

Chances are, when you're online, you're on a website: looking something up on <u>wikipedia.org</u>, checking news on <u>politico.com</u> or <u>foxnews</u><u>.com</u>, reading reviews of a new film on <u>rottentomatoes.com</u>, ordering takeout from a local diner, doing schoolwork on one of your college's many sites. And that's just for starters: if you take time to jot down every website you visit in a day, you'll see just how much a part of our everyday lives these digital conveyors of information are.

The links are a key component, one that affects the way you write something on the web. For example, you can link to the definition of a term rather than defining it yourself in your text—and you can quote from a source and link to the full text rather than summarizing or paraphrasing it. If there's a chart or graph you'd like to include in your text, you can cut and paste it into your text—or you can simply link to it. Same goes for videos. The links also work for readers, letting them decide what they want to see, and not.

Whether you're creating links or clicking on them, you are using websites all the time. As former President Bill Clinton has said, "Twenty years ago only astrophysicists knew about websites. Today my cat has a website." Maybe so, but I bet the cat had some help building its site. Fortunately, free website builders like *Wix* or *GoDaddy* provide templates to help you get started. In the meantime, it's likely that you'll be posting a project or presentation to a site that already exists, much like the article on the following pages.

ROSA GUEVARA

Jailene M.: The Future of Tech, with Enthusiasm

Rosa Guevara wrote the following article when she was at LaGuardia Community College in Long Island City, New York, and was a staff writer for The Bridge, *LaGuardia's student newspaper. She's now at Baruch College, majoring in business communication—and reporting on social justice issues for* The Ticker, *their student newspaper.*

AN ARTICLE ON A WEBSITE

Subscribe: RSS

Search...

Home   News   Features   Arts and Culture   Sports   Opinion

Newspaper banner includes a photo of the Queensboro Bridge between Manhattan and Queens, home of LaGuardia Community College.

Search bar allows readers to search the site.

Main menu includes links to 6 parts of the site.

Jailene M.: The Future of Tech, with Enthusiasm

by Rosa Guevara
on October 9, 2019
in Features, Home

The title uses a key word—tech—that makes this article searchable.

Learning various English skills along with the principles of journalism to become the next great reporter providing truth and facts to citizens takes a toll on many journalism students. Jailene M. is working on all that and more, studying both journalism and digital technology. She has already closed the tech gender gap in various ways—and she hopes to empower the next generation of tech leadership by succeeding in school while also learning the basics of the digital era.

Short paragraphs make newspaper articles easier to read.

It was 5:30 pm on a Sunday when I met Jailene for a cup of coffee in Elmhurst, Queens. She was on her laptop, drinking coffee and rubbing her eyes, probably because of the brightness of the screen. I tapped on the door while she looked and enthusiastically waved at me—I opened it, and in an instant, she gave me a hug. She mentioned how she had already ordered exactly what I wanted, and as I sat down, she was already telling me how grateful she was about being interviewed—this was her first time.

Everyday language strikes a pleasing, conversational tone.

Born in Queens of Mexican descent, Jailene is not only an aspiring journalist, but also a technology enthusiast, a coder, a babysitter, a first-generation and full-time college student at LaGuardia. She is proud of her roots and where they're leading her and for what the future looks like it has in store for her. She's been studying the basics of coding with an eye toward creating her own website and publishing articles along with other first-generation students. Her main goal is to close the gender gap and become the next tech leader.

Jailene is majoring in New Media Technology with a concentration in Digital Journalism, and she says another major goal is to become as digitally adept as possible while also providing truthful informa-tion to citizens on apps or websites. In her free time, Jailene enjoys coding and teaching others, one of her strongest skills.

"I like seeing how just typing codes can turn into beautiful websites—and seeing what that can turn into has attracted me more to it, and made me want to learn more," she told me while sipping her large hot latte.

Surrounded by video games when she was growing up, Jailene developed her interest in technology at a young age. She now has the chance of making something virtual into her own masterpiece, a website that can get the recognition she hopes to attain.

While learning the ways of coding, she has noticed that she is the only Hispanic woman in her class. "I thought this only happened in Mexico!" she said, "I guess this stereotype will continuously follow me even in the United States!" When she realized that, she decided to go against the stereotype where men are usually the only ones involved in technology, to familiarize herself with coding and break the misconception about women not being able to master this computer language. During this time, she has also practiced blogging, reporting, and interviewing—in addition to attending web design classes.

"Look, I'm more focused on learning HTML coding, JavaScript, jQuery, CSS, Bootstrap and so much more. I would show you, but I think I'd confuse you so much. Maybe we can stop!" She laughed while closing her laptop and again sipping her latte.

The many direct quotations let Jailene speak for herself—and let readers hear her voice.

Jailene is a shy woman who is very passionate about her studies. But more than that, she cares about the people who want her to pursue her dreams, particularly her little brother. Her everyday motivation is to become part of the next generation of top talent in technology, to promote diversity, and to support innovation.

She also gets her inspiration from her little brother, who has been diagnosed with Attention Deficit Hyperactivity Disorder (ADHD), a neurological disorder that causes those who develop it to have difficulty paying attention and to become excessively active.

Links in this column take readers to other recent feature stories and to archives of previous issues of the newspaper.

"My brother is 10 years old and has ADHD," Jailene said. "This really does motivate me to accomplish my academic and personal goals because I want him to know that he can accomplish anything he wants no matter what his condition. I want him to know that his disorder does not define him and does not limit what he can do."

Her family back in Mexico wants the best for her, especially since she is the first granddaughter and is seen as an example. Many first-generation college students say they must go to college to help their families because they are viewed as saviors, family representatives, and a way out of poverty. She is dedicated to doing well this term while also remembering to take care of herself.

Part of the graduating class of 2019, she hopes to see the day when gender stereotypes no longer exist, in technology or any field. "Sometimes it is women competing against women or men against men. I just do not understand it—and it continues to frustrate me. We can all just help each other succeed. But that's not how it works here in America."

This powerful quotation lets Jailene have the last word.

Digital Journalism, Laguardia student feature, Slider
ABOUT ROSA GUEVARA

Link takes readers to information about the author.

View all posts by Rosa Guevara

Another link takes readers to other articles by Guevara.

30 Social

IT'S A DIALOGUE, NOT A MONOLOGUE. . . .
SOCIAL MEDIA IS MORE LIKE A TELEPHONE THAN A
TELEVISION.

—AMY JO MARTIN

ANYONE CAN BE A REPORTER OR A CULTURAL CRITIC ON
TWITTER, AND THAT'S LED TO A UNIVERSE OF DIVERSE
VIEWPOINTS, ALL AMPLIFIED ORGANICALLY.

—WIRED

ONLY CONNECT. . . . LIVE IN FRAGMENTS NO LONGER.

—E. M. FORSTER

Where do you most often get news or information these days? And how do you most often communicate with others? If you're like most people now, your answer will involve social media. A 2019 Pew Research study reports that 74 percent of adults in the United States turn to *Facebook* daily, while 63 percent turn to *Instagram* and 40 percent to *Twitter*. Again, that's *daily*.

And it very likely includes you. So this chapter is not going to tell you how to log on to *Facebook* or post a photo on *Instagram*. But it will get you thinking about how you can use social media to connect with others—and to do so carefully, effectively, and ethically.

It might be useful to stop and think about what makes social media "social." In short, it enables us to meet up with others. To talk and to listen. To think about what they say, and why. To engage with others, and with their ideas. In other words, social media is about dialogue and conversation, "more like a telephone than a television." They help us "connect." With people. With ideas. With the world.

But how exactly do social media help us connect?

- *They're interactive.* Social media sites are designed to invite response. As a writer, you can respond to what someone else posts, join a conversation, or initiate one yourself.

- *They help us find audiences—and communities.* Social media sites give you some control over who sees what you write, and they even provide ways for you to build an audience. You can use privacy settings to decide who can see your posts, and you can @mention people you *want* to see them. You can also choose who to follow.

- *They enable us to share and follow ideas—and discover new ones.* You can add tag (#) keywords to add your own thoughts to conversations on a certain topic—and to make your own posts searchable by others. Say you post something about social distancing, for instance: adding #stayhome, #sixfeet, and #washyourhands will help others interested in that topic find your posts.

- *They're driven by algorithms, which amplify the spread of information*—actual information, misinformation, and totally false information. Algorithms are designed to track clicks and "likes" and then to feed us content that's in line with our preferences; the fact that shocking, disturbing, and angry content is apparently most engaging drives the spread of such information.

- *Because they're online and instantly accessible, social media messages are amplified*—for both good and ill. Like a giant megaphone or microphone, social media blast out messages: some are truthful and fact based; others are exactly the opposite. That's why ethical users of social media take special care with the messages they send—and do not retweet or repost messages they cannot verify.

FACEBOOK

Created in 2004, *Facebook* began as an online directory of the first-year class at Harvard. It included nothing but each student's name, photo, dorm, and high school. The content was nothing new. But something else was new: students could edit their profiles, adding details about their relationships, their classes, their favorite bands or movies or teams, whatever. And they could then see who else was in their classes, who else was in Expos 20, or rooted for the Celtics. In other words, it prompted students to think about how to present themselves, and it made it easy to find communities who shared their interests. The rest is history. Today, more than 1.5 billion people log in to *Facebook* each day: primarily to stay in touch with friends and family, but also to get the news, show off vacation photos, watch videos, and more.

IT'S ALL HERE ON YOUR FACEBOOK ACCOUNT.

STAHLER.
1/14

©Jeff Stahler/Distributed by Universal Uclick for UFS via CartoonStock.com

Facebook can be a good source of news, but Elaine Godfrey argues that it's no substitute for a local newspaper. See what she says on p. 669.

As a college student, you may well use *Facebook* to learn about school events, collaborate with classmates, write to your grandparents.

Remember that your *Facebook* profile is one way that you present yourself to the world, so you'll want to think hard about what you put there. Unless you make your account private, it could reach a pretty wide audience, including future employers—who have been known to cancel interviews or reject job candidates after looking at their *Facebook* pages. Be careful not to post anything you wouldn't want a future employer to see.

INSTAGRAM ◉

A free photo-sharing app, *Instagram* allows you to upload photos and videos, and to write something about them. It will feed you posts based on what you yourself post, and you can "like" or comment on them if you wish, follow anyone whose work interests you, and forward them to others. These are all ways that *Instagram*'s algorithms will then send you other posts tailored to your interests. You can respond to what they post, and they can respond to what you post; you can follow them, they can follow you. In other words, *Instagram* can connect you with others who share your interests.

TWITTER ◪

Brevity is the soul of wit.
—WILLIAM SHAKESPEARE

A social networking service where you can post tweets and share links, photos, GIFs, and videos, *Twitter* is a site for following news and ideas—and for connecting with others who follow the same things. Unlike *Facebook* and *Instagram*, it limits what you write to 280 characters. In fact, the average tweet is around 28 characters—a challenge, but one that can really help you focus what you say, literally making every word count. You can follow topics that interest you—*The Iliad*, the Supreme Court, women's soccer, whatever. Say you're a fan of Ohio State football; doing a search for #ohiostatefootball will lead you to tweets on that topic—and a number of different perspectives on it as well. And if you yourself tweet about the team—and tag your tweets #ohiostatefootball—they will pop up whenever someone else does a search for Ohio State football or clicks on #ohiostatefootball.

That's how *Twitter* lets you find conversations on topics you want to learn about, add your own opinions, and build an audience for what you have to say. And once you specify what you're interested in, *Twitter* will suggest other accounts you might want to follow. As with all social media, *Twitter* can be misused to spread misinformation, or worse. Be careful about retweeting unless you can verify that the information is truthful.

Facebook, *Instagram*, and *Twitter* are all places where you can find many different perspectives—and where you can seek ideas different from your own. As such, they're places where you need to practice RHETORICAL LISTENING, working to understand and really ENGAGE with people whose lives and viewpoints are not the same as yours. But because these are also sites where you can actually choose those you interact with, there's also a real danger of building an information silo—that is, following and attracting only like-minded people, whose ideas and opinions are similar to yours. Be careful not to do that.

You are what you share.

—CHARLES LEADBEATER

At their best, social media can help people connect across time and space like never before. As this book goes to press, we're all working at home in order to curb the spread of COVID-19, and we're using *Zoom*, and other social platforms to attend meetings, classes, and even happy hours. But as you know, social media sites are not always at their best, and all too often they have been used not to connect but to divide, to confuse, to deceive—and to spread misinformation or lies. As an *ethical* user of social media, your job is to make sure that anything you post or share is honest, based on verifiable information, and offered in the best interests of your audience.

Writing effectively and ethically on social media

- Think carefully about the AUDIENCE who will see what you write—and whom you want to reach. Tag (#) KEYWORDS to share a post with people who are likely to be interested (#kingjames, #washyourhands); and @mention people you want to see your post (@epeters, @scolbert). Speak directly to your audience, using a friendly, conversational tone.

- Consider your PURPOSE. What do you want to happen as a result of what you write? Are you voicing an opinion?

- What's the larger CONTEXT? Are you writing for an assignment? If you're responding to a conversation that's already begun, what's being said about the topic?

- Make sure that any sources you link to or forward are reliable and that any information you share is accurate.

- Credit anything that you did not create yourself. On *Facebook*, clicking the Share button gives credit and makes a link. On *Instagram*, use an @ tag to credit the creator (@sdunn). On *Twitter*, give an HT, short for "hat tip" (HT@sdunn).

- It's usually best to keep posts short and to the point. Link to any longer text you wish to include.

- What TONE do you want to convey? Think about how you want to come across: serious? playful? frustrated? something else? You can probably be pretty casual if you're sure your readers are friends. But if you're writing about a serious topic, you'll want to establish a serious tone.

- Remember to add captions to any images. And if you haven't created the image yourself, be sure to credit whoever did.

- If you want readers to engage with what you post, try to be direct: ask a question, or issue an explicit call for action.

- Don't forget that you're interacting with real people. Don't say anything on social media that you wouldn't say to them in person.

FACEBOOK

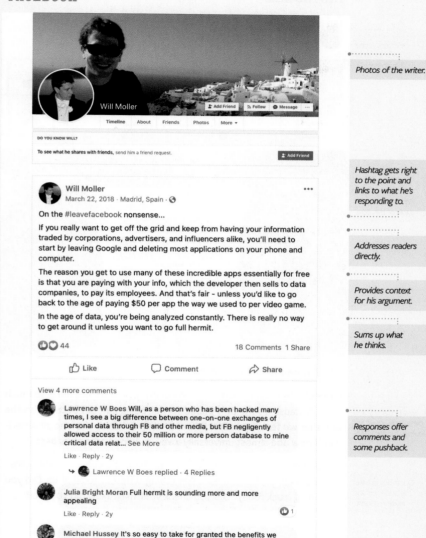

Will Moller

Timeline About Friends Photos More ▾

DO YOU KNOW WILL?

To see what he shares with friends, send him a friend request.   ✚ Add Friend

---

Will Moller
March 22, 2018 · Madrid, Spain · 🌐   •••

On the #leavefacebook nonsense...

If you really want to get off the grid and keep from having your information traded by corporations, advertisers, and influencers alike, you'll need to start by leaving Google and deleting most applications on your phone and computer.

The reason you get to use many of these incredible apps essentially for free is that you are paying with your info, which the developer then sells to data companies, to pay its employees. And that's fair - unless you'd like to go back to the age of paying $50 per app the way we used to per video game.

In the age of data, you're being analyzed constantly. There is really no way to get around it unless you want to go full hermit.

👍❤ 44   18 Comments 1 Share

👍 Like   💬 Comment   ↪ Share

View 4 more comments

Lawrence W Boes Will, as a person who has been hacked many times, I see a big difference between one-on-one exchanges of personal data through FB and other media, but FB negligently allowed access to their 50 million or more person database to mine critical data relat... See More

Like · Reply · 2y

   ↳ Lawrence W Boes replied · 4 Replies

Julia Bright Moran Full hermit is sounding more and more appealing

Like · Reply · 2y   👍 1

Michael Hussey It's so easy to take for granted the benefits we receive every single day from these network effects -- http://www.alaskahighwaynews.ca/.../charlie-lake-student...

Photos of the writer.

Hashtag gets right to the point and links to what he's responding to.

Addresses readers directly.

Provides context for his argument.

Sums up what he thinks.

Responses offer comments and some pushback.

INSTAGRAM

ianjmck
48207

Writer's name and location (his zip code!).

Photo announces topic of this post.

Liked by **emmahilldore** and **212 others**

Speaks directly and personally about her feelings for the USPS.

ianjmck The reason the destruction of our postal service hurts so much is not because it's the only public service being cut, but because it's the one that we feel most directly in our daily lives. It's the one all Americans know and almost universally love—public service at its best!

Questions draw in the audience and invite response.

Postal cuts hurt because the USPS is perhaps the only constant across all American life, but it means something different to all of us. Did you see a mail truck today? Did you check your mail? How did you feel?

To me, USPS is the remarkable consistency of Holland (49423) mail carriers that meant I could intercept bad report cards with surgical precision as a kid. Those same mail carriers brought my college acceptance letter bang on time the day before Thanksgiving years later.

Zip codes help make the point.

It's the clerk in Trenton (48183) who helped me choose the right box to mail Caroline's Christmas present.

In Holland (49423), the MSU fan clerk who, when he ran my grandparents' Ann Arbor (48108) ZIP code, remarked "the evil empire!" without missing a beat.

In Washington (20002) the clerk who made sure I got my study abroad visa application in just before the deadline.

In Detroit (48233) the clerk who went out of her way to give stamp recommendations and told me about her sister's side gig sewing masks.

Uses personal experience in every example.

It's the post office in Brooklyn (11237) that I will insist on visiting the next time I am in NYC because I am told they have a vintage Mr. ZIP floor mat.

The Chicago (60604) post office by my favorite architect.

Our USPS delivered stacks of thank you notes after I graduated from high school and again after I graduated from college.

Our USPS is the reason that I check my mail every day with great anticipation even if I'm not expecting anything—you never know!

Photo and name identifies the person posting.

Single image—of Fearless Girl sculpture on Wall Street wearing a Ruth Bader Ginsburg lace collar.

Simple caption says it all: RIP RBG.

emmahilldore

❤ 💬 ✈   🔖

emmahilldore RIP RBG

Profile photo and name arouse audience interest.

Photo engages viewers.

Caption asks a question that prompts viewers to think about visiting a national park themselves.

grandmajoysroadtrip
Cuyahoga Valley National Park

❤ 💬 ✈   🔖

1,419 likes

grandmajoysroadtrip Which National Parks are in your backyard?

Tags will make others interested in related topics aware of this post.

#GrandmaJoysRoadTrip
#CuyahogaValley
#CuyahogaValleyNationalPark
#GoParks #NPS
#NationalParkService

TWITTER

Jay Van Bavel
@jayvanbavel

I had to teach my Introduction to Psychology class today to 300+ students from my cell phone while I was trapped in my apartment building elevator with my two young kids.

This has to go down as my most surreal and stressful teaching experience.

9:30 PM · Sep 23, 2020 · TweetDeck

3.6K Retweets   **1.4K** Quote Tweets   **28.2K** Likes

Jay Van Bavel @jayvanbavel · Sep 23
Replying to @jayvanbavel
For context, I'm teaching a huge Intro Psych class this fall. It's totally remote and was massively overenrolled so I'm. trying to teach 360 students from around the world in the pandemic.

But others have it worse and the students are great so it's been fun thus far.

♡ 7   ⟲ 49   ♡ 1.7K

Jay Van Bavel @jayvanbavel · Sep 23
The first problem is that the local schools are closed and I have limited child care.

So I have to get my kids from day care at 3pm and race back to my apartment by 3:30pm. My son crashes my course and likes to share his thoughts, but the students find it funny so I don't mind.

♡ 3   ⟲ 29   ♡ 1.5K

Writer's photo, name, and Twitter handle.

Begins telling a first-person story about a "surreal" experience; pulls in readers.

Provides context, setting scene and suggesting this may be a long story.

Highlights the challenge and appeals to readers' empathy.

Go to
letstalklibrary.com
for the rest of this
Twitter thread.

Tongue-in-cheek tweet gives Alexa, Amazon's AI assistant, a command.

Alexx
@Astoyyy

Alexa

Bring back Big10 football

1:03 PM · Aug 19, 2020 · Twitter for iPhone

8 Retweets   **36** Likes

Tweet from an organization rather than an individual.

Question points to hashtag.

Tags another Twitter account.

Includes photo—fat bear winner 2019!

US Department of the Interior ✔ @Interior · Sep 23
Are you ready for #FatBearWeek? Next week, @KatmaiNPS holds its annual competition so you can judge which chubby cubby takes this year's title. Pic of last year's winner: 435 Holly #Alaska

💬 690   ♻ 14.3K   ♡ 34.5K   ⬆

Vincent Yu
@vincent_yu5

Stomper is the best mascot in all of sports! #RootedInOakland

2:53 PM · 6/16/22 · Twitter Web App

1 Like

Tags Oakland A's fan slogan.

Emma Peters @StEmmasFire · 5m
Replying to @vincent_yu5

Can I draft Stomper to my fantasy baseball team??? I don't care who I have to trade...

Playful tone, fun conversation.

WallaceWagon @wallacewago... · 36s
um I love Stomper as much as the next person...but have you seen Split, aka the World's Largest Banana? Savannah Bananas coming in strong. #thesavbananas

Tags Savannah Bananas fans.

PART EIGHT

READINGS

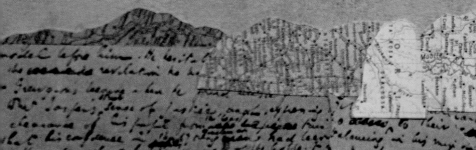

LET'S READ!

31 The Inequities That Bedevil Us

AS LONG AS POVERTY, INJUSTICE, AND GROSS INEQUALITY
PERSIST IN OUR WORLD, NONE OF US CAN TRULY REST.

—NELSON MANDELA

I f you have ever been treated unfairly or seen others experiencing unfairness, then you are aware of at least some of the inequities that bedevil us—the injustices or unfair practices at work in our society. These inequities affect every one of us every single day of our lives, even if we aren't always aware of it. By *inequities* we have in mind the many injustices or unfair practices at work in our society, one or more of which affects every one of us every single day of our lives. By *us*, we mean everyone who lives with and among other people. And since these readings are grounded primarily in the here and now, in the twenty-first-century United States, if you're here now, that *us* includes *you*. And that's where *bedevil* comes in. It's undeniably an old-school word whose use has declined in recent decades. But the decrease is more than a little ironic given its meaning: to torment or distress in a persistent and ongoing manner. In short, it's a word that seems all too relevant to our lives today.

While these readings touch on abstract concepts, such as equality itself, they also offer some concrete advice for everyday situations that many of us wrestle with. In this chapter, you'll read about race, gender, labor, disability, and more. Readings cover a range of genres, too—including argument, analysis, narrative, and more. Here's a brief synopsis of the readings you'll find in this chapter, plus several more from other chapters that touch on other troublesome inequities.

Equality: We all know what that is, right? But maybe not. Ask any five people what equality means and you'll almost certainly get five different answers. Why is that? **Joshua Rothman** puts the idea of equality under a microscope in order to determine why it's so very complicated.

On race, **Michael Gerson** addresses conservatism and systemic racism in the United States today in an op-ed, and what he says may surprise you. **Clint Smith** reports on a Juneteenth ceremony in Galveston, Texas, that includes a deep dive into the history of slavery, how that history gets shaped and told, and how that resulting history has, in turn, shaped the last century and a half of Black life in the United States.

Jodi Kantor, Karen Weise, and **Grace Ashford** team up to present a detailed account of the successes and challenges of working in an Amazon fulfillment center in New York City during the first year of the pandemic. **Richard Thompson Ford** examines how the clothes we wear serve to mark gender and enforce gendered norms. Whatever you're wearing right now, Ford has you, um, covered. An essay by **Heather Lanier** explores the worth of human life itself, asking whose life is worth living and who gets to decide. She reflects on those painful questions through the lens of her experience as the parent of a severely disabled child.

And here's a practical question: Should we hang out with someone whose political views we strongly disagree with, or even despise? You may have faced this question yourself; almost certainly, you've talked about it with someone who is facing it. It's a bedeviling question if ever there was one. One answer here comes from **Kwame Anthony Appiah**, a philosophy professor and author of a popular weekly ethics column.

We hope that the readings in this chapter and throughout the book will give you ideas to contemplate. Our goal is to give you plenty to read about, think about, talk about, and write about.

Readings in Other Chapters

Readings on <u>letstalklibrary.com</u>

JOSHUA ROTHMAN

The Equality Conundrum

MICHAEL AND ANGELA HAVE JUST TURNED FIFTY-FIVE. They know two people who have died in the past few years—one from cancer, another in a car accident. It occurs to them that they should make a plan for their kids. They have some money in the bank. Suppose they were both killed in a plane crash—what would happen to it?

They have four children, who range in age from their late teens to their late twenties. Chloe, the oldest, is a math wiz with a coding job at Google; she hopes to start her own company soon. Will, who has a degree in social work, is paying off his student debt while working at a halfway house for recovering addicts. The twins, James and Alexis, are both in college. James, a perpetually stoned underachiever, is convinced that he can make it as a YouTuber. (He's already been suspended twice, for on-campus pranks.) Alexis, who hopes to become a poet, has a congenital condition that could leave her blind by middle age.

At first, Michael and Angela plan to divide their money equally. Then they start to think about it. Chloe is on the fast track to remunerative Silicon Valley success; Will is burdened by debt in his quest to help the vulnerable. If James were to come into an inheritance, he'd likely grow even lazier, spending it on streetwear and edibles; Alexis, with her medical situation, might need help later in life. Maybe, Michael and Angela think, it doesn't make sense to divide the money into equal portions after all. Something more sophisticated might be required. What matters to them is that their children flourish equally, and this might mean giving the kids unequal amounts—an unappealing prospect.

Joshua Rothman is the ideas editor for the New Yorker *magazine, where he writes about philosophy, technology, cultural criticism, and more. This essay was published in that magazine in January 2020.*

The philosopher Ronald Dworkin considered this type of parental conundrum in an essay called "What Is Equality?" from 1981. The parents in such a family, he wrote, confront a trade-off between two worthy egalitarian goals. One goal, "equality of resources," might be achieved by dividing the inheritance evenly, but it has the downside of failing to recognize important differences among the parties involved. Another goal, "equality of welfare," tries to take account of those differences by means of twisty calculations. Take the first path, and you willfully ignore meaningful facts about your children. Take the second, and you risk dividing the inheritance both unevenly and incorrectly....

5   The complexities of egalitarianism are especially frustrating because inequalities are so easy to grasp. C.E.O.s, on average, make almost three hundred times what their employees make; billionaire donors shape our politics; automation favors owners over workers; urban economies grow while rural areas stagnate; the best health care goes to the richest. Across the political spectrum, we grieve the loss of what Alexis de Tocqueville called the "general equality of conditions," which, with the grievous exception of slavery, once shaped American society. It's not just about money. Tocqueville, writing in 1835, noted that our "ordinary practices of life" were egalitarian, too: we behaved as if there weren't many differences among us. Today, there are "premiere" lines for popcorn at the movies and five tiers of Uber; we still struggle to address obvious inequalities of all kinds based on race, gender, sexual orientation, and other aspects of identity. Inequality is everywhere, and unignorable. We've diagnosed the disease. Why can't we agree on a cure?

ACCORDING TO THE DECLARATION OF INDEPENDENCE, it is "self-evident" that all men are created equal. But, from a certain perspective, it's our inequality that's self-evident. A decade ago, the writer Deborah Solomon asked Donald Trump what he thought of the idea that "all men are created equal." "It's not true," Trump reportedly said. "Some people are born very smart. Some people are born not so smart. Some people are born very beautiful, and some people are not, so you can't say they're all created equal." Trump acknowledged that everyone is entitled to equal treatment under the law but concluded that "All men are created equal" is "a very confusing phrase to a lot of people." More than twenty percent of Americans, according to a 2015 poll, agree: they believe that the statement "All men are created equal" is false.

In political philosopher Jeremy Waldron's view, though, it's not a binary choice; it's possible to see people as equal and unequal simultaneously. A society can sort its members into various categories—lawful and criminal, brilliant and not—while also allowing some principle of basic equality to circumscribe its judgments and, in some contexts, override them. Egalitarians like Dworkin and Waldron call this principle "deep equality." It's because of deep equality that even those people who acquire additional, justified worth through their actions—heroes, senators, pop stars—can still be considered fundamentally no better than anyone else. By the same token, Waldron says, deep equality insures that even the most heinous murderer can be seen as a member of the human race, "with all the worth and status that this implies." Deep equality—among other principles—ought to tell us that it's wrong to sequester the small children of migrants in squalid prisons, whatever their legal status. Waldron wants to find its source....

In the end, Waldron concludes that there is no "small polished unitary soul-like substance" that makes us equal; there's only a patchwork of arguments for our deep equality, collectively compelling but individually limited. Equality is a composite idea—a nexus of complementary and competing intuitions.

THE BLURRY NATURE OF EQUALITY makes it hard to solve egalitarian dilemmas from first principles. In each situation, we must feel our way forward, reconciling our conflicting intuitions about what "equal" means. Deep equality is still an important idea—it tells us, among other things, that discrimination and bigotry are wrong. But it isn't, in itself, fine-grained enough to answer thorny questions about how a community should divide up what it has. To answer those questions, it must be augmented by other, narrower tenets.

> Rothman cites numerous sources, using quotations, paraphrases, and summaries to distinguish his ideas from those of his sources. Learn how to do that in Chapter 18.

10   The communities that have the easiest time doing that tend to have some clearly defined, shared purpose. Sprinters competing in a hundred-meter dash have varied endowments and train in different conditions; from a certain perspective, those differences make every race unfair. (How can you compete with someone who has better genes?) But runners form an egalitarian community with a common goal—finding out who's fastest—and so they have invented rules and procedures (qualifying heats, drug bans) that allow them to consider a race valid as long as no one jumps the gun. By embracing an agreed-upon theory of equality before the race, the sprinters can find collective meaning in the ranked inequalities that emerge when it ends. A hospital, similarly, might find an egalitarian way to do the necessary work of giving some patients priority over others, perhaps by adopting a theory of equality that ignores certain kinds of differences (some patients are rich, others poor) while acknowledging others (some patients are in urgent trouble, others less so). What matters, above all, is that the scheme makes sense to those involved.

        Because maintaining such agreements takes constant work, egalitarian communities are always in danger of disintegrating. Nevertheless, the egalitarian landscape is dotted with islands of agreement: communes, co-ops, and well-organized competitions in which a shared theory of equality is used for some practical purpose. An individual family might divide up its chores by agreeing on a theory of equality that balances quick, unpleasant tasks, such as bathroom-cleaning, with slower, more enjoyable ones, such as dog-walking. This sort of artisanal egalitarianism is comparatively easy to arrange. Mass-producing it is what's hard. A whole society can't get together in a room to hash things out. Instead, consensus must coalesce slowly around broad egalitarian principles.

        No principle is perfect; each contains hidden dangers that emerge with time. Many people, in contemplating the division of goods, invoke the principle of necessity: the idea that our first priority should be the equal fulfillment of fundamental needs. The hidden danger here becomes apparent once we go past a certain point of subsistence, creating a situation philosophers call "the problem of expensive tastes."

The problem—what feels like a necessity to one person seems like a luxury to another—is familiar to anyone who's argued with a foodie spouse or roommate about the grocery bill. It applies not just to material goods but to societal ones. To an environmentalist, protecting the spotted owl is a necessity; to a logger who stands to lose his job, it's a luxury. The problem is so insistent that a whole body of political philosophy—"prioritarianism"—is devoted to the challenge of sorting people with needs from people with wants. It's difficult in part because the line shifts as the years pass. Medical procedures that seem optional today become necessities tomorrow; educational attainments that were once unusual, such as college degrees, become increasingly indispensable with time. In a study for the National Bureau of Economic Research, four economists evaluated the success of President Lyndon Johnson's War on Poverty. They found that, judging by a modernized version of the definition of "poverty" which Johnson used, the poverty rate in America fell from 19.5 percent in 1963 to 2.3 percent in 2017. Still, they note in their paper, "expectations for minimum living standards evolve." Today, taking advantage of the social safety net that the War on Poverty put in place—food stamps, Medicaid, and so on—is itself a sign of poverty. A new, more robust safety net—free college, Medicare for All—becomes, for some, an egalitarian necessity.

Some thinkers try to tame the problem of expensive tastes by asking what a "normal" or "typical" person might find necessary. But it's easy to define "typical" too narrowly, letting unfair assumptions influence our judgments. In an influential 1999 article called "What Is the Point of Equality?," the philosopher Elizabeth Anderson pointed out an odd feature of our social contract: if you're fired from your job, unemployment benefits help keep you afloat, while if you stop working to have a child you must deal with the loss of income yourself. This contradiction, she writes, reveals an assumption that "the desire to procreate is just another expensive taste"; it reflects, she argues, the sexist presumption that "atomistic egoism and self-sufficiency" are the human norm. The word "necessity" suggests the idea of a bare minimum. In fact, it sets a high bar. Clearing it may require rethinking how society functions.

15 PERHAPS BECAUSE NECESSITY IS SO DEMANDING, our egalitarian commitments tend to rest on a different principle: luck. The philosopher Richard Arneson explained the idea a couple of decades ago: "Some people are blessed with good luck, some are cursed with bad luck, and it is the responsibility of society—all of us regarded collectively—to alter the distribution of goods and evils that arises from the jumble of lotteries that constitutes human life as we know it." Anderson, in an influential coinage, calls this outlook "luck egalitarianism."

Instead of dividing things up by asking what people need, a luck-egalitarian system tries to equalize the distribution of misfortune. If you're born on the wrong side of the tracks, or if your house is destroyed in an unpredictable natural disaster, luck egalitarianism suggests that you deserve help. If you screw up—by squandering your savings, launching a failed business, and so on—you're on your own. It's to luck egalitarianism that we owe the metaphors of the "level playing field" and the "social safety net." The first equalizes the bad luck we're born with; the second, the bad luck that finds us as adults.

As Americans, we are charged with recognizing two conflicting values: individualism and egalitarianism. By smoothing out the unlucky differences while accepting those for which people are responsible, luck egalitarianism promises to help us be individualists and egalitarians simultaneously. But, as Anderson and others have argued, doing this is harder than it sounds. One problem, Anderson writes, is that luck egalitarianism condescends to those it helps: by seeing them as hapless victims of circumstance, it denies them the "equal respect" they're due as citizens of a democracy. (It's perhaps for this reason that the people who might benefit from the extension of government programs so often vote against them.)

Another problem, which the political theorist Yascha Mounk explores in "The Age of Responsibility: Luck, Choice, and the Welfare State," is that the distinction between choice and luck is hard to sustain. If you sleep in instead of coming to work every day and then get fired, you're clearly making bad choices. But what if you're born into a family with an income just north of the poverty line, then drop out of high school to get a dead-end job? In all likelihood, you've suffered from bad luck and made bad choices. Suppose you turn down a place at your state university to take a job at the auto plant where your parents work, and the plant then closes. The closing of the plant was out of your control, but the decision to work there rather than go to college was yours to make. If you'd acquired more skills, would you be more employable? Or would the forces of globalization that led to the closure of the plant have narrowed your job prospects no matter your training? You might lie awake night after night mulling such questions without settling on answers; it's absurd, Mounk writes, to expect "a real-world state bureaucracy to answer such intricate hypothetical questions about millions of citizens."

The distinction between choice and luck, he argues, is a matter not of fact but of perspective. Explanations of human behavior have traditionally been divided into two groups: those which focus on the forces that push us around and those which emphasize how, as individuals, we can choose to resist them. The same phenomenon can be viewed from either side of the so-called structure-agency distinction....

Mounk thinks that most people understand, intuitively, that the distinction between structure and agency is—like the distinction between "nature" and "nurture"—an artifact of explanation, not a part of reality. All explanations are limited, we know, and tell only part of the story. This, he writes, is why we are so ambivalent about luck egalitarianism and the politicians who see the world through its lens. Conservatives, hoping to constrain the size of the welfare state, overstate how much control people have over their lives; liberals, hoping to expand it, overstate our powerlessness. But both positions are unconvincing. "While voters are receptive to the idea that it is deeply unjust for some public schools to have better funding than others, they balk when they are told that students who do well in school are merely lucky," Mounk writes. "And while they recognize that the explanation for the stagnating living standards of average people lies in larger structural transformations of the world economy, they are skeptical when they are told

20

that the choices of specific individuals don't play any role in determining their particular economic fate."

THERE'S A PROBLEM WITH FINDING PROBLEMS with egalitarianism. The head fights the gut; complexities can't drown out the moral law within. Reading Waldron, Anderson, Mounk, and other thinkers on egalitarianism, I found myself remembering a time that started when I was eleven or twelve years old. My parents were divorced and rarely spoke; I went to three middle schools in three years, one bad, one middling, one good. The bad school was near my mother's house, where we lived in the basement, having rented out the main floor. The good school was in a wealthy suburb. I attended it by claiming to live at the address of a family friend who had a small apartment, above a commercial space, on its edge. (So-called enrollment fraud is common across the country, especially in places where rich and poor school districts border each other.)

For a while, I took the bus home to the apartment, hanging out there until late in the evening. When this arrangement grew untenable, my mother devised a plan. She'd struck up a conversation with a cabdriver and taken his card; she called him and asked if, for a flat monthly fee, he'd pick me up at school each day and drop me at my father's house, a short drive away. There weren't many fares at two-thirty in the afternoon in the Maryland suburbs, and he said yes.

Peter, the cabdriver, began picking me up from a hidden spot past the soccer fields, under some trees. He was from West Africa, with an accent I sometimes struggled with. We talked about his home town, his girlfriend, the books I was reading—Stephen King, for the most part—in which he sweetly expressed an interest. Eventually, two of my friends, who were also picked up after school, discovered my secret spot and joined me there. As Peter and I drove away, everyone waved.

One day, Peter was agitated when he arrived. "I have to make a detour, O.K.?" he said. "Don't tell your mom." He didn't wave to my friends, and we took a left instead of a right, eventually entering a neighborhood of small, unkempt row houses. As we drove, Peter told me how the taxi business worked. He didn't own his cab; he rented it from the cab company, in a rent-to-own arrangement. If he missed his monthly payment, the company took the cab back. The payment was extremely high. "I drive and I drive and I drive," he said. "But I can't make it. I can't make it!" As we pulled up in front of his cousin's house, he sobbed. I watched from the back seat as he returned to the cab, weeping, with borrowed cash in his hand.

I wasn't a sheltered kid; I knew about economic hardship. A few   25
times that year, my mother had fallen behind on our bills, and our power had been cut off; we'd showered and eaten dinner in the dark. She'd hidden her despair, but Peter had shared his. For him, the bottom could fall out faster and more completely. More than a decade later, in a Dickensian coincidence, Peter, who was still driving cabs, picked my father up from the airport and gave him a business card. Peter started driving him, too; that year, on a trip with my dad and his family, Peter and I were reunited, to our great delight. But not long afterward he died. He suffered from diabetes and hypertension, and had no health insurance; he went too long before seeking treatment for an infection in his toe. It got into his bloodstream, and he died of septic shock.

Injustice isn't cerebral. Peter and I were two equal people on the same earth. What's so complicated about that?

THE GAP BETWEEN INTUITION AND ARGUMENT—between outrage and the best response to that outrage—is the subject of Robert Tsai's "Practical Equality: Forging Justice in a Divided Nation." Tsai, a law professor at American University, places great weight on the intuition that we are "one another's equals"—and yet, he writes, it's inevitable that, "in a diverse democracy, people will disagree about what equality means." Hashing out questions of equality, he concludes, can be so fraught, so confusing, that the wisest course is sometimes to circumvent them. Inequality can be resisted, and equality pursued, by other, less tangled means....

The US Supreme Court used such an approach in some equality-enhancing decisions. In *United States v. Virginia*, from 1996, a female high-school student filed a complaint against the Virginia Military Institute (the so-called West Point of the South), which excluded women.

The arguments on her behalf, which leaned heavily on equality, soon got bogged down in the question of what it might mean for the Institute to treat male and female cadets equally. Instead of weighing in on that issue, the Court ruled that there was no rational basis for denying women admission.

This case and many others, Tsai believes, show that it's often more practical to pursue "equality by other means" than to sail into the crosscurrents of egalitarian debate. Reasonableness, or rationality, is one test to which we can subject inegalitarian systems or rules. One can also ask whether they are fair, whether their specific consequences are cruel, whether all relevant voices have been heard. Answering these questions isn't always easy, but it's easier than generating consensus about what "equal" means. We make more progress, Tsai argues, when we "shift the focus of moral outrage."

30   LANGUAGE ITSELF MAY BE MISLEADING US. Appalled by inequality, our minds turn immediately to its opposite. Sidestepping that impulse, as Tsai advocates, requires giving up a satisfying rhetorical clarity, but it may bring us closer to our moral common sense. The philosopher David Schmidtz explains why in a 2006 book titled *Elements of Justice*. Schmidtz begins by asking us to contemplate what makes a neighborhood a good place to live: a thriving community might have a grocery store, a fire station, a library, a playground. Similarly, a system of justice must have a few different structures to be livable. It's easy to imagine justice as a unitary thing—a single, imposing building, a Supreme Court. But it's more like a collection of buildings, each with its own function.

In the neighborhood of justice, Schmidtz identifies four structures: equality, desert, reciprocity, and need. We consult these in different contexts, to solve different kinds of problems. Citizens are owed equality before the law. Workers, by contrast, should be compensated differently, depending on what they have accomplished. In relationships with our partners, we favor reciprocity. In trying to do right by our children, we ask what they need. (Michael and Angela, in considering their will, might focus on necessity more than the other concepts: instead of asking "What do they deserve?" or "What have they done for us lately?," they might ask, "What do our kids need?") None of these principles are capacious enough to serve in every situation; in fact, they are often in tension with one another. And they can be used inappropriately. No one wants a merit-based marriage. A workplace that operates by reciprocity is a dysfunctional one.

In real life, therefore, we amble around the neighborhood of justice. A coach doesn't run her team on egalitarian principles alone; to win, she must field the best players more often. But she doesn't run a ruthless meritocracy, either. On a good team, players get the help they need, they assist one another reciprocally, they're rewarded for their individual accomplishments, and they are treated similarly enough that they feel connected in a common enterprise.

The frustrations and complexities of egalitarianism reflect the hidden complexity of equality. It looks simple and self-evident, as though one could proclaim it into existence. But achieving it requires a willingness to recognize, and to shift among, many different conceptions of what's right—a kind of moral egalitarianism. Even equality itself, as an ideal, is insufficient. No one version of the good can rule the rest.

Thinking about the Text

1. Joshua Rothman ARGUES that equality is clearly desirable but tremendously difficult and complicated to accomplish. Why is that the case? He shows us why, summarizing the principles that seven philosophers propose for dealing with the inequalities that he says are "everywhere, and unignorable" (5). Which of these principles do you find most persuasive, and why?

2. What do you make of the detailed ANECDOTE about Peter, the taxi driver from West Africa? What is Rothman's point in telling us about him? How does it support what he is saying about equality and inequality?

3. In paragraph 32, Rothman gives the example of how coaches don't run their teams "on egalitarian principles alone"—that to

win, they "must field the best players more often," but that on good teams, players "are treated similarly enough that they feel connected in a common enterprise." Think about how such egalitarian principles play out in a club, committee, or some other group you belong to. Are some members of the group better than others in some way, or do they think they are? Do you help one another? Do you think everyone feels relatively equal—and if not, why not?

4. LET'S TALK. Rothman DESCRIBES "the problem of expensive tastes" (12), where something that is a necessity for some people is considered a luxury by others, and he mentions several examples. BRAINSTORM with a few classmates to come up with some other examples of something that could be either a luxury or a necessity; then, choose one and explore together how to solve the problem in a way that is as equitable and satisfactory as possible for everyone concerned.

5. AND NOW WRITE. Rothman begins his essay with the anecdote about a married couple who are drafting their will and trying to decide how to divide their assets among their four very different children. Put yourself in their place: How would you distribute the assets to those four children? Why? (Let's assume that the assets would be a helpful amount but not a fortune.) Write an essay ANALYZING how you arrived at your decision and citing how Rothman or any of the philosophers whose ideas he mentions helped you think about the situation.

MICHAEL GERSON

I'm a Conservative Who Believes Systemic Racism Is Real

THE PHRASE "systemic racism," like "climate change" and "gun control," has been sucked into the vortex of the culture war. The emotional reaction to these words seems to preclude reasoned debate on their meaning.

But a divisive concept can be clarifying. I know it has been for me: I don't think it's possible to be a conservative without believing that racism is, in part, structural.

Most on the American right have dug into a very different position. They tend to view racism as an individual act of immorality. And they regard the progressive imputation of racism to be an attack on their character. In a free society, they reason, the responsibility for success and failure is largely personal. They're proud of the productive life choices they've made and refuse to feel guilty for self-destructive life choices made by others.

It's an argument that sounds convincing—until it's tested against the experience of our own lives.

I grew up in a middle-class neighborhood of a middle-class suburb 5 in a Midwestern city. I went to a middle-class high school, with middle-class friends, eating middle-class fried bologna sandwiches. And for most of my upbringing, this seemed not only normal but normative. I assumed this was a typical American childhood.

Michael Gerson *is a syndicated columnist whose work appears in numerous US newspapers; he also appears frequently on televised news programs such as* Face the Nation. *He served as a speech writer and policy adviser to President George W. Bush and is the author of* Heroic Conservatism *(2007). This piece was first published in 2021 in the* Washington Post. *Gerson tweets from @MJGerson.*

Michael Gerson uses a narrative about his own upbringing as evidence for his argument. Learn about how to do that yourself on pp. 86–87.

Only later did I begin to see that my normality was actually a social construction. By the time I was growing up in the 1970s, St. Louis no longer had legal segregation. But my suburb, my neighborhood and my private high school were all outcomes of White flight. The systems of policing, zoning and education I grew up with had been created to ensure one result: to keep certain communities safe, orderly and pale.

I had little hint of this as a child. It seemed natural that I hardly ever met a person of color in a racially diverse city or seldom met a poor person in a place with some of the worst poverty in the country. All I knew was that I shouldn't get lost in certain neighborhoods or invite Black people to the private pool where we were members. (My brother did once, and there was suddenly a problem with processing our membership card.)

But none of this was neutral or normal. Systems had been carefully created to ensure I went to an all-White church, in an all-White neighborhood, while attending an all-White Christian school and shopping in all-White stores. I now realize I grew up in one of the most segregated cities in the United States.

Was this my fault? Not in the strictest sense. I didn't create these systems. But I wish I had realized earlier that these systems had created me.

10   This is what I mean by systemic racism. If, on my 13th birthday, all the country's laws had been suddenly, perfectly and equally enforced, my community would still have had a massive hangover of history. The structures and attitudes shaped during decades and centuries of oppression would still have existed. Legal equality in theory does not mean a society is justly constituted.

For me, part of being a conservative means taking history seriously. We do not, as Tom Paine foolishly claimed, "have it in our power to begin the world over again." We live in an imperfect world we did not create and have duties that flow from our story.

There is an important moral distinction between "guilt" and "responsibility." It is not useful, and perhaps not fair, to say that most White people are guilty of creating social systems shaped by white supremacy.

Demonstrators at a Juneteenth protest against systemic racism. Chicago, June 19, 2020.

But they do have a responsibility as citizens, and as moral creatures, to seek a society where equal opportunity is a reality for all.

It is true that "wokeness" can be used as a political weapon. It is true that shame culture can be cruel and misdirected. And, as a conservative, I believe that equal opportunity, rather than mandated economic equality, is the proper goal of a free society. But what if we are (to employ a football analogy) not 30 yards away from the goal of equal opportunity in the United States, but 70 yards? What if equal opportunity is a cruel joke to a significant portion of the country? Shouldn't that create an outrage and urgency that we rarely see, and even more rarely feel?

Though our nation is beset with systemic racism, we also have the advantage of what a friend calls "systemic anti-racism." We have documents—the Declaration of Independence, the Bill of Rights, the 14th Amendment—that call us to our better selves. We are a country that has exploited and oppressed Black Americans. But we are also the country that has risen up in mass movements, made up of Blacks and Whites, to confront those evils. The response to systemic racism is the determined, systematic application of our highest ideals.

Thinking about the Text

1. Michael Gerson draws a distinction between "guilt" and "responsibility." What is that distinction? Why does he insist that the distinction is important when considering systemic racism? Do you find his explanation persuasive? Why or why not?

2. Gerson wants us to know very clearly that he is a conservative. Why is his conservatism so important to his ARGUMENT? In what ways might his essay be interpreted differently if he hadn't announced his political views so explicitly? Explain your thinking.

3. Though Gerson is a White person and a conservative, he uses "they" when he refers to those two groups. He switches to "we," however, in sentences referring to Americans. Why do you think he uses pronouns in this way?

4. LET'S TALK. In his conclusion, Gerson encourages a "determined, systematic application of our highest ideals" (14) but he offers no concrete suggestions for how we might put those words into action. What are some possible remedies for achieving the equal opportunity that he advocates? Who should do this work? Individuals? Community organizations? The federal government? Discuss these questions with a few classmates. Keep in mind that these are complex questions and that your goal is not to argue or persuade. You don't have to all agree on a single plan. Listen to one another in good faith and explore the possibilities together.

5. AND NOW WRITE. As children, our worlds are very small; we only know what we can observe in our immediate environments. How and when did you find out that the whole world wasn't the same as the world you knew? Gerson describes how he came to realize that "systems had been carefully created" to control his environment and how he wishes he "had realized earlier that these systems had created me" (9). Think about your own experiences, write an essay DESCRIBING what you remember about the world you knew as a child and REFLECTING on the systems that have "created" you and your ideas about the world.

CLINT SMITH

Juneteenth, Galveston Island

T HE LONG-HELD MYTH that on June 19, 1865, Union general Gordon Granger stood on the balcony of Ashton Villa in Galveston,
Texas, and read the order that announced the end of slavery. Though
no contemporaneous evidence exists to specifically support the claim,
the story of General Granger reading from the balcony embedded itself
into local folklore. On this day each year, as part of Galveston's Juneteenth program, a reenactor from the Sons of Union Veterans reads
the proclamation at Ashton Villa while an audience looks on. It is an
annual moment that has taken a myth and turned it into tradition.

Galveston is a small island that sits off the coast of Southeast
Texas, and in years past this event has taken place outside. But given
the summer heat, the island's humidity, and the average age of the
attendees, the organizers moved the event inside. A man named Stephen Duncan, dressed as General Granger, stood at the base of the
stairwell, with other men dressed as Union soldiers on either side of
him. Stephen looked down at the parchment, appraising the words as
if he had never seen them before. He looked back down at the crowd,
which was looking back up at him. He cleared his throat, approached
the microphone, and lifted the yellowed parchment to eye level.

"The people of Texas are informed that, in accordance with a
proclamation from the Executive of the United States, all slaves are
free. This involves an absolute equality of personal rights and rights
of property between former masters and slaves, and the connection

---

Clint Smith *is a staff writer at the* Atlantic *and a poet who was a*
National Poetry Slam champion in 2014. This selection comes from
his book How the Word Is Passed: A Reckoning with the History
of Slavery across America, *which won a Natinal Book Critics Choice*
award in 2021. His Twitter *handle is @ClintSmithIII.*

Stephen Duncan, portraying Union general Gordon Granger, holds up the proclamation ending slavery at the Al Edwards Juneteenth Prayer Breakfast. Galveston, June 19, 2019.

heretofore existing between them becomes that between employer and hired labor. The freedmen are advised to remain quietly at their present homes and work for wages. They are informed that they will not be allowed to collect at military posts and that they will not be supported in idleness either there or elsewhere.""[1]

All slaves are free. The four words circled the room like birds that had been separated from their flock. I watched people's faces as Stephen said these words. Some closed their eyes. Some were physically shaking. Some clasped hands with the person next to them. Some simply smiled, soaking in the words that their ancestors may have heard more than a century and a half ago.

5   Being in this place, standing on the same small island where the freedom of a quarter million people was proclaimed, I felt the history pulse through my body.

General Granger and his forces arrived in Galveston more than two years after Lincoln signed the Emancipation Proclamation and more than two months after Robert E. Lee's famous surrender. A document that is widely misunderstood, Lincoln's proclamation was a military strategy with multiple aims. It prevented European countries from supporting the Confederacy by framing the war in moral terms and making it explicitly about slavery, something Lincoln had previously backed away from. As a result, France and Britain, which had contemplated supporting the Confederacy, ultimately refused to do so because of both countries' anti-slavery positions. The proclamation allowed the Union Army to recruit Black soldiers (nearly two hundred thousand would fight for the Union Army by the war's end), and it also threatened to disrupt the South's social order, which depended on the work and caste position of enslaved people.

The Emancipation Proclamation was not the sweeping, all-encompassing document that it is often remembered as. It applied only to the eleven Confederate states and did not include the border states that had remained loyal to the US, where it was still legal to own enslaved people. Despite the order of the proclamation, Texas was one of the Confederate states that ignored what it demanded. And even though many enslaved people escaped behind Union lines and enlisted

Felix Haywood.

in the Federal Army themselves, enslavers throughout the Confederacy continued to hold Black people in bondage throughout the rest of the war. General Lee surrendered on April 9, 1865, in Appomattox County, Virginia, effectively signaling that the Confederacy had lost the war, but many enslavers in Texas did not share this news with their human property. It was on June 19, 1865, soon after arriving in Galveston, that Granger issued the announcement, known as General Order Number 3, that all slaves were free and word began to spread throughout Texas, from plantation to plantation, farmstead to farmstead, person to person.

A ninety-two-year-old formerly enslaved man named Felix Haywood recalled with nostalgic jubilation what that day meant to him and so many others: "The end of the war, it come jus' like that—like you snap your fingers.... Hallelujah broke out.... Soldiers, all of a sudden, was everywhere—comin' in bunches, crossin' and walkin' and ridin'. Everyone was a-singin'. We was all walkin' on golden clouds.... We was free. Just like that we was free."[2] ...

OVER THE COURSE of the rest of the program a procession of community leaders, local politicians, and event organizers came up to the podium at the front of the room to speak about why Juneteenth is important and what it means to them.

10   One of the speeches that stood out was given by Grant Mitchell a tall middle-aged white man whose family has sponsored the program for several years.

"Today is a day for jubilation," Grant said, leaning on the podium. "We celebrate this day as the day word reached Galveston and then spread throughout the region and into other Southern states that freedom had come to millions and a great injustice had been undone.

A Juneteenth parade float.

We celebrate the day we got word our great nation, torn apart, but once again united, had taken one bold and decisive step toward fulfilling a promise at the core of its creed that all people are created equal. But this is not just a celebration. The path toward justice is long and uncertain. It sometimes moves forward and sometimes winds its way back. So today is also a day of reflection. It is a day to look around and ask ourselves, 'Where are we on the path?'"

It is not enough to study history. It is not enough to celebrate singular moments of our past or to lift up the legacy of victories that have been won without understanding the effects of those victories—and those losses—on the world around us today. The state of Texas currently has a larger Black population than any other state in the country—about 3.5 million Black people call the state home—but as is the case across the country, the Black community experiences profound disparities across income, wealth, education, and criminal justice.* Galveston, and the state of Texas as a whole, extols its history as the origin point of our greatest celebration of emancipation. It is, however, worth interrogating the past century and a half to understand what led to such wide racial chasms in a state that prides itself on its history of freedom. . . .

*Per the 2010 census, Black Texans represented 12 percent of the state's population and 32 percent of the prison and jail population, whereas white Texans made up 45 percent of the state's population and 33 percent of the prison and jail population. Of Black Texans, more than 20 percent live in poverty, compared to 15 percent of white Texans. The infant mortality rate of Black women in Texas is more than twice that of white women. The high school graduation rate is 87 percent for Black Texans and 94 percent for white Texans. The list goes on like this across almost every metric. [Data sources for footnote: "Texas Profile," Prison Policy Initiative, www.prisonpolicy.org/TXhtml; US Census Bureau, "Poverty Status in the Past 12 Months," American Community Survey 5-year estimates, 2018; "Infant Mortality Rate by Race," in *2019 Healthy Texas Mothers and Babies Data Book*, B-2, Texas Department of State Health Services website, www.dshs.texas.gov/; "Public High School Graduation Rates," in *The Condition of Education*, National Center for Education Statistics, last updated May 2020, https://nces.ed.gov/pubs2020/2020144.pdf.]

PEOPLE IN GALVESTON repeatedly asked me if I had been to "the park." If I wanted to understand what Juneteenth meant in Texas, they said, I had to go there. So on a warm September day in Houston, as summer was collecting its things and autumn was peeking around the corner, I went to Emancipation Park, an historic landmark in the city's Third Ward.

In 1872, this piece of land was purchased by a group of formerly enslaved people in the hopes of providing Houston's Black community with a place to celebrate Juneteenth. Today it is the site of one of the oldest annual Juneteenth celebrations in the country. The leader of that original group of formerly enslaved people was a man named Jack Yates, a minister and community leader who was central to the social and political landscape of Black Houston life in the late nineteenth century. I went to Emancipation Park to meet his great-granddaughter, Jackie Bostic, who lived just a few minutes away from the park and who has worked diligently to keep her great-grandfather's legacy alive.

15   I met Mrs. Bostic in a conference room of the building that was once the park's gym. She moved with a dexterity that belied her eight decades, her curly white hair coiled around her head and her eyes as calm as dusk. Her memories were lucid, and her voice was slow and smooth. Her eyes crinkled at the edges as she spoke.

Bostic grew up in Houston and remembered clearly the days when segregation animated every part of Black people's lives. Her activist sensibilities had been apparent since she was young. "You know, I always challenged what I thought was not right or unfair," she said. "And I couldn't understand how, in many places in the South—in Texas, in Louisiana, in Mississippi, and others—the population, in some areas, was totally Black, but yet you were being forced to abide by rules that were made by somebody else. And that you could not believe that you could overcome that, that you could change that situation. And I could understand the fear, because during the time there were many people being lynched. . . . But there was just always something in me that knew *No, I don't have to live like this, and I'm not going to.*" . . .

EMANCIPATION PARK served as a centerpiece of Houston's Black community for decades moving into the twentieth century. But by the 1970s, the park had become a dilapidated, fractured shadow of its former self, and ceased hosting Juneteenth celebrations altogether in 2007. The cessation served as a wake-up call to community members, and a group called Friends of Emancipation Park dedicated itself to restoring the space. That same year the Houston City Council designated the park a historic landmark, which paved the way for its revitalization....

One thing that Bostic is especially committed to is ensuring that while Emancipation Park provides a place for people to celebrate Juneteenth, these celebrations don't come at the expense of people understanding what the history of Juneteenth actually is....

"I think my generation," she said, "many getting killed, and beaten, and spit on, and dogs, and hoses, did not understand that you have to keep telling the story in order for people to understand. Each generation has to know the story of how we got where we are today, because if you don't understand, then you are in the position to go back to it."

Her voice began shaking. "I watched so much turned around, that people I know fought for... And I'm watching here, in real time, watching other people not turn it around, because we're not understanding what's happening. 20

"They may discuss in the school system that you were a slave, but they're not going to talk about what happened after slavery." Her face sank. "How you were emancipated, how others came and took your land... if you got anything at all—how you weren't given anything."

She continued: "They're not going to tell you the real story of how you went and you fought in every war that this country has ever fought, including the Civil War, where the most people have died in this country than in every war we've fought in. They're not going to tell you those things...."

The responsibility of passing on this history falls to both the community and the schools. Texas, the home of one in ten public school students in the country, has experienced a number of high-profile embarrassments with regard to how schools in the state have taught

By quoting Bostic's exact words, Smith represents her ideas accurately—and lets her speak for herself. See pp. 285–90 for tips on using quotations in your writing.

Black history, particularly slavery.[3] In 2015, the State Board of Education and publisher McGraw-Hill Education came under fire for providing students with a textbook that described how the transatlantic slave trade brought "millions of workers from Africa to the southern United States to work on agricultural plantations."[4] It seemed to many to be a deliberate obfuscation of the fact that Africans were forcibly and violently stripped from their homelands, not people who were just "workers" who simply agreed to come help cultivate North American land. . . .

The Texas State Board of Education has since revised the standards so that, across the state, slavery is understood to have played a "central role" in causing the Civil War.[5]

25   "It's a subject that nobody wants to touch, because nobody wants to really talk about it," Bostic said. She leaned toward me, and her eyes locked on mine. "But it's what is going to continue to tear our country apart, until we're willing to understand it happened. It really happened."

Notes

1. "Texas Remembers Juneteenth," Texas State Library and Archives Commission, June 19, 2020, https://www.tsl.texas.gov/ref/abouttx/juneteenth.html.

2. Ira Berlin, Marc Favreau, and Steven E. Miller, eds., *Remember Slavery: African Americans Talk about Their Personal Experiences of Slavery and Emancipation* (New York: New Press, 2000), 266; and Elizabeth H. Turner, "Juneteenth: Emancipation and Memory," in *Lone Star Pasts: Memory and History in Texas*, ed. Gregg Cantrell and Elizabeth H. Turner (Texas A & M UP, 2007), 143–75.

3. https://tea.texas.gov/sites/default/files/enroll_2019-20.pdf.

4. Laura Isensee, "Why Calling Slaves 'Workers' Is More Than an Editing Error," Houston Public Media 88.7, NPR, October 23, 2015.

5. www.npr.org/2018/11/16/668557179/texas-students-will-soon-learn-slavery-played-a-central-role-in-the-civil-war.

Thinking about the Text

1. Clint Smith takes us to a Juneteenth celebration, which starts with the reading of the order ending slavery in the state of Texas. Here's how he describes the reaction in the room: "Some closed their eyes. Some were physically shaking. Some clasped hands with the person next to them. Some simply smiled." He then notes his own reaction: "I felt the history pulse through my body" (5). A few paragraphs later he quotes Grant Mitchell, another speaker, who says that Juneteenth was not just about celebration, but that it is "also a day of reflection" (11). Why does Mitchell say that, and why does Smith then say it is not enough to celebrate extraordinary events from the past?

2. At the center of this essay is a NARRATIVE about a Juneteenth celebration in Galveston, Texas. But it's also an ARGUMENT: Smith is telling this story to make a point. What do you think that point is, and how do you know? Point to places in the essay to support your answer.

3. In addition to focusing on the history of slavery in the United States, Smith addresses the ways in which that history is taught and understood. What, if anything, do you remember learning as a child about the centuries of legal slavery in the United States? What, if anything, have you learned since then that calls your previous understanding into question?

4. LET'S TALK. Jackie Bostic tells Smith that while she wants people to celebrate Juneteenth, she hopes the celebrations do not prevent them from "understanding what the history of Juneteenth actually is" (18). Think about how Juneteenth is celebrated at your school—or about other holidays that are celebrated in the United States: Memorial Day, Martin Luther King Jr. Day, Veterans Day, Labor Day, Thanksgiving. How are they celebrated and how do the festivities reflect the significance of the days— or not? Get together with some classmates and compare notes about how you each celebrate (or just observe) some of these holidays. What do you know about the events or people that they actually celebrate and how much do you REFLECT on what they mean for us today? How could you do better?

5.   AND NOW WRITE. Smith is the author of this piece, but he incorporates the words and opinions of several others in his text. He could have paraphrased or summarized what each of them said, but he chose to quote them directly instead. Why would he have made that decision? Here's Felix Haywood, a ninety-two-year-old formerly enslaved man, recalling what the announcement that all slaves were free meant to him and many others:

> The end of the war, it come jus' like that—like you snap your fingers. . . . Hallelujah broke out. . . . Soldiers, all of a sudden, was everywhere—comin' in bunches, crossin' and walkin' and ridin'. Everyone was a-singin'. We was all walkin' on golden clouds. . . . We was free. Just like that we was free. (8)

Try PARAPHRASING this passage using your own words and sentence structures. How accurately are you able to convey what Haywood said using your words rather than his? Imagine that Smith had paraphrased or summarized what Haywood and everyone else he quotes said: How would that have affected his argument? Would it have changed his message in any way?

JODI KANTOR, KAREN WEISE
& GRACE ASHFORD

The Amazon That Customers Don't See

L AST SEPTEMBER, Ann Castillo saw an email from Amazon that made no sense. Her husband had worked for the company for five years, most recently at the supersize warehouse on Staten Island that served as the retailer's critical pipeline to New York City. Now it wanted him back on the night shift.

"We notified your manager and H.R. about your return to work on Oct. 1, 2020," the message said.

Ms. Castillo was incredulous. While working mandatory overtime in the spring, her 42-year-old husband, Alberto, had been among the first wave of employees at the site to test positive for the coronavirus. Ravaged by fevers and infections, he suffered extensive brain damage. On tests of responsiveness, Ms. Castillo said, "his score was almost nothing."

For months, Ms. Castillo, a polite, get-it-done physical therapist, had been alerting the company that her husband, who had been proud to work for the retail giant, was severely ill. The responses were disjointed and confusing. Emails and calls to Amazon's automated systems often dead-ended. The company's benefits were generous, but she had been left panicking as disability payments mysteriously halted. She managed to speak to several human resources workers, one of whom reinstated the payments, but after that, the dialogue mostly reverted to phone

This disconcerting opening grabs our attention. See Chapter 22 for tips on getting and keeping attention in what you write.

Jodi Kantor, Karen Weise, and Grace Ashford are staff journalists with the New York Times. *Kantor is an investigative reporter, Weise is a Seattle-based technology correspondent, and Ashford works on the New York metro desk. This reading comes from a multimodal investigative report that was published in the* Times *in June 2021. Kantor tweets from @JodiKantor, Weise from @KYWeise, and Ashford from @gr_ashford.*

trees, autoreplies and voice mail messages on her husband's phone asking if he was coming back.

5   The return-to-work summons deepened her suspicion that Amazon didn't fully register his situation. "Haven't they kept track of what happened to him?" she said. She wanted to ask the company: "Are your workers disposable? Can you just replace them?"

Mr. Castillo's workplace, the only Amazon fulfillment center in America's largest city, was achieving the impossible during the pandemic. With New York's classic industries suffering mass collapse, the warehouse, called JFK8, absorbed hotel workers, actors, bartenders and dancers, paying nearly $18 an hour. Driven by a new sense of mission to serve customers afraid to shop in person, JFK8 helped Amazon smash shipping records, reach stratospheric sales and book the equivalent of the previous three years' profits rolled into one.

That success, speed and agility were possible because Amazon and its founder, Jeff Bezos, had pioneered new ways of mass-managing people through technology, relying on a maze of systems that minimized human contact to grow unconstrained.

But the company was faltering in ways outsiders could not see, according to a *New York Times* examination of JFK8 over the last year.

In contrast to its precise, sophisticated processing of packages, Amazon's model for managing people—heavily reliant on metrics, apps and chatbots—was uneven and strained even before the coronavirus arrived, with employees often having to act as their own caseworkers, interviews and records show. Amid the pandemic, Amazon's system burned through workers, resulted in inadvertent firings and stalled benefits, and impeded communication, casting a shadow over a business success story for the ages.

10   Amazon took steps unprecedented at the company to offer leniency, but then at times contradicted or ended them. Workers like Mr. Castillo at JFK8 were told to take as much unpaid time off as they needed, then hit with mandatory overtime. When Amazon offered employees flexible personal leaves, the system handling them jammed, issuing a blizzard of job-abandonment notices to workers and send-

ing staff scrambling to save them, according to human resources and warehouse employees.

After absences initially soared and disrupted shipping, Amazon left employees mostly in the dark about the toll of the virus. The company did not tell workers at JFK8 or other warehouses the number of cases, causing them to worry whether notifications about "individuals" testing positive meant two or 22. While Amazon said publicly that it was disclosing confirmed cases to health officials, New York City records show no reported cases until November. The company and city officials dispute what happened.

Amazon continued to track every minute of most warehouse workers' shifts, from how fast they packed merchandise to how long they paused—the kind of monitoring that spurred a failed unionization drive led by frustrated Black employees at an Alabama warehouse this spring. If productivity flagged, Amazon's computers assumed the worker was to blame. Early in the pandemic, the online retailer paused its firing of employees for low output, but that change was not announced clearly at JFK8, so some workers still feared that moving too slowly would cost them their livelihoods.

"It is very important that area managers understand that associates are more than just numbers," an employee wrote on JFK8's internal feedback board last fall, adding: "We are human beings. We are not tools used to make their daily/weekly goals and rates."

The company touted breathtaking job-creation numbers: From July to October 2020 alone, it scooped up 350,000 new workers, more than the population of St. Louis. Many recruits—hired through a computer screening, with little conversation or vetting—lasted just days or weeks.

Even before the pandemic, previously unreported data shows, 15 Amazon lost about 3 percent of its hourly associates each week, meaning the turnover among its work force was roughly 150 percent a year. That rate, almost double that of the retail and logistics industries, has made some executives worry about running out of workers across America. . . .

This April, Mr. Bezos said he was proud of the company's work culture, the "achievable" productivity goals, the pay and benefits. In interviews, the head of human resources for warehouses and the general manager of JFK8 said that the company prioritized employee welfare, noted that it had expanded its H.R. staff and cited internal surveys showing high worker satisfaction. Some managers from JFK8 and beyond described building deep relationships with their teams.

Amazon acknowledged some issues with inadvertent firings, loss of benefits, job abandonment notices and leaves, but declined to disclose how many people were affected. Kelly Nantel, a spokeswoman, suggested that those problems and some others chronicled in this article were outliers.

Ofori Agboka, the H.R. leader, noted that social distancing and masking had made it harder to engage employees in personal ways during the pandemic. Still, he said, "98 percent of everything's going great—people are having the right experiences," getting the help they need when they want it.

But several former executives who helped design Amazon's systems, and still call themselves admirers of the company, said the high turnover, pressure over productivity and consequences of scaling up have become too critical to ignore. The company has not ambitiously addressed those issues, said Paul Stroup, who until recently led corporate teams devoted to understanding warehouse workers. . . .

20   David Niekerk, a former Amazon vice president who built the warehouse human resources operations, said that some problems stemmed from ideas the company had developed when it was much smaller. Mr. Bezos did not want an entrenched work force, calling it "a march to mediocrity," Mr. Niekerk recalled, and saw low-skilled jobs as relatively short-term. As Amazon rapidly grew, Mr. Niekerk said, its policies were harder to implement with fairness and care. "It is just a numbers game in many ways," he said. "The culture gets lost.". . .

Amazon is also on pace to become the nation's largest private employer within a year or two, as it continues expanding. About a million people in the United States, most of them hourly workers, now rely on the company's wages and benefits. Many describe the job as rewarding. Adama Ndoye had supported her family on her JFK8 pay while attending college remotely. "Lights on, food, clothes, everything," she said. Dawn George, a chef, said she was grateful to JFK8 for taking her in after hotel kitchen jobs disappeared last spring. "I'm willing to work my socks off just for an hourly income," she said.

Some admire Amazon's ambition. "It was like being a pitcher on a team that had a game every night," said Dan Cavagnaro, who started at JFK8 when it opened in 2018 and worked with Mr. Castillo.

But Mr. Cavagnaro was mistakenly fired in July while trying to return from leave, and could not reach anyone to help.

"Please note the following," he wrote in his final, unanswered email plea. "I WISH TO REMAIN EMPLOYED WITH AMAZON."

"Like a Ghost Town"

In late March 2020, Traci Weishalla walked the length of JFK8, forgo- 25
ing the fluorescent vest that marked her as a manager. She wanted an unfiltered look at what she would soon be helping to oversee: a warehouse the size of 15 football fields, serving America's largest metropolis just as it was becoming the national epicenter of the pandemic.

Traci Weishalla at Amazon's JFK8 warehouse. Staten Island, New York.

The noise, from conveyor belts whipping around packages, was like the roar of an oncoming subway train. Built to conquer the most lucrative market in the country, the facility ran almost 24 hours a day, seven days a week.

Ms. Weishalla had helped open the warehouse a year and a half earlier, and now—as homebound customers across the nation clamored for thermometers, disinfectant and puzzles—she saw opportunity and purpose in her return as assistant general manager. For an organization that dealt in logistical miracles, the coronavirus was just another obstacle to overcome, she said.

"That's what we do," Ms. Weishalla, 38, explained later. "We work to figure out the impossible problems."

But Amazon's mighty system was lurching. Semi trucks sat at warehouses around the country, without enough workers to unload them. Customers discovered that items the company had deemed nonessential might take a month to arrive—an eternity for a business that had routinely delivered within two days.

30   One critical reason: Warehouse laborers were not showing up.

To lure them back, Amazon offered a temporary $2-an-hour raise, double pay for overtime and, for the first time, unlimited unpaid time off. Executives thought that workers should be able to stay home without fear of being fired, and that with greater flexibility, some might still come in for part of a shift, according to two people familiar with the decision. (Like some other senior leaders in this article, they spoke on the condition of anonymity because they were not authorized to comment.)

Across the country, almost a third of Amazon's 500,000 workers were staying home. Some new hires abandoned jobs before they even began, according to former recruiters. JFK8 "was like a ghost town," recalled Arthur Turner, a worker who remained.

Even Alberto Castillo considered staying home. The numbers on the news were unfathomable: at least 20,000 New Yorkers already infected, city hospitals jammed, as many as 1.7 million deaths projected nationwide.

But this was no time to go without his income: The Castillos, immigrants from the Philippines, yearned to buy a house. He worked nights, troubleshooting and training with gentle mastery, frequent jokes and *Star Wars* references, colleagues said, and he had just applied for a promotion.

JFK8 was also giving contradictory instructions: Despite Amazon's 35 promise of unpaid time off, workers were alerted that every department would be on mandatory overtime.

When Mr. Castillo arrived on March 24, he heard the warehouse had its first positive case. He messaged his boss, who replied, "Yes, forgot to bring that up," and added that everyone who worked with the employee had been notified. Mr. Castillo called his wife to discuss whether to head home. They decided he would finish out his shift.

On the dawn drive back to New Jersey, his throat began itching.

Organized Labor

That morning, two workers drove in the opposite direction, beelined to JFK8's break room and told dozens of colleagues: The virus had breached the warehouse, Amazon could not be trusted to tell them the truth and the facility should be shut down.

Derrick Palmer and Chris Smalls, Amazon teammates and best friends, weren't part of any formal effort . . . Both men had been at Amazon since 2015 and knew the company from the lowest rungs. Mr. Palmer, then 31, was observant and deliberate, so fit that he often headed to the gym after a 10-hour shift. After dropping out of community college, he worked in a string of warehouses, joined Amazon and was now a "picker" at JFK8, pulling products off robotic shelves. He often produced top numbers on the software that tracked productivity, and had been selected to train others and help open a warehouse in Illinois.

He also felt let down, believing that Amazon's towering success 40 didn't accrue to workers like him. Employees felt managed largely by app, algorithm and strict but poorly explained rules, he said. When he met Ms. Weishalla at a 2019 session for workers to share feedback, he said, he requested more human interaction from management and told her he aspired to a job like hers. But he saw no changes. "If we go beyond the requirements, there's no reward," he said in an interview.

When Mr. Palmer last sought a promotion, in early 2020, he was among 382 people who applied for the position. Though he didn't know it, the odds were steep by design, an outgrowth of Mr. Bezos' management philosophies.

Amazon intentionally limited upward mobility for hourly workers, said Mr. Niekerk, the former H.R. vice president who retired in 2016 after nearly 17 years at the company. Dave Clark, then head of operations, had shot down his proposal around 2014 to create more leadership roles for hourly employees, similar to noncommissioned officers in the military, he recalled.

Instead, Mr. Clark, who is now chief executive of Amazon's consumer business, wanted to double down on hiring "wicked smart" frontline managers straight out of college, Mr. Niekerk said. By contrast, more than 75 percent of managers in Walmart's U.S. stores started as hourly employees. Following a pattern across Amazon, JFK8 promoted 220 people last year among its more than 5,000 employees, a rate that is less than half of Walmart's.

Amazon's founder didn't want hourly workers to stick around for long, viewing "a large, disgruntled" work force as a threat, Mr. Niekerk recalled. Company data showed that most employees became less eager over time, he said, and Mr. Bezos believed that people were inherently lazy. "What he would say is that our nature as humans is to expend as little energy as possible to get what we want or need." That conviction was embedded throughout the business, from the ease of instant ordering to the pervasive use of data to get the most out of employees.

45   So guaranteed wage increases stopped after three years, and Amazon provided incentives for low-skilled employees to leave. Every year, Mr. Palmer saw signs go up offering associates thousands of dollars to resign, and as he entered JFK8 each morning, he passed a classroom for free courses to train them in other fields....

As the virus arrived at JFK8, Mr. Palmer worried about how Amazon would protect and communicate with workers. Notification about the warehouse's first positive case had been uneven. A colleague working near Mr. Smalls had appeared sick, her eyes bloodshot as she struggled through her shift.

The two men saw only one solution: for JFK8 to pause, clean and reassess, as an Amazon facility in Queens had briefly done. Unpaid leave wasn't enough, they said—a company run by the richest man on earth shouldn't force workers to choose between safety and a paycheck. . . .

Nearly all the workers in the group were Black, like Mr. Palmer and Mr. Smalls, or Latino. So were more than 60 percent of associates at JFK8, according to internal Amazon records from 2019. Management, the documents show, was more than 70 percent white or Asian. Black associates at JFK8 were almost 50 percent more likely to be fired— whether for productivity, misconduct, or not showing up for work— than their white peers, the records show. (Amazon said it could not confirm the data without knowing more specifics about its source.)

Between the constant monitoring, the assumption that many workers are slackers, and the lack of advancement opportunity, "a lot of minority workers just felt like we were being used," Mr. Palmer said later.

"We're the heart and soul of that building," he wrote in the chat. 50 "Nothing gets done without us."

The two men continued their break-room warnings for several more days, and confronted JFK8 managers. "If, God forbid, somebody in this building passes away, or somebody's loved one passes away, that's going to be on your hands, not mine," Mr. Smalls, the firecracker of the pair, told the warehouse's top leader, according to an audio recording of one conversation.

On March 30, they demonstrated in the parking lot with a small group of other employees. Mr. Palmer carried a sign that read, "Treat your workers like your customers."

In Seattle, executives still grappling with cratering attendance sought to minimize the protest but instead drew more attention to it. Amazon

Chris Smalls at a demonstration outside the JFK8 warehouse protesting Amazon's failure to provide adequate protections from the coronavirus, May 1, 2020.

fired Mr. Smalls, saying his demonstration had violated a quarantine order based on his contact with the sick co-worker. (Mr. Palmer received a warning for violating social-distancing rules.) Meeting notes taken the next day by the company's top lawyer and leaked to *Vice News* called Mr. Smalls "not smart or articulate."

Though the lawyer soon said he didn't know Mr. Smalls's race, a group of Black corporate employees wrote a letter calling the smear part of "a systemic pattern of racial bias that permeates Amazon." The New York attorney general's office and Senator Elizabeth Warren asked if the firing was retaliation, which Amazon denied. . . .

Summoning Workers Back

55 With so many employees staying home—because of family needs, fear of contracting the coronavirus and reluctance to use public transit—the unthinkable was happening to Amazon: Its customers were turning to competitors.

By mid-April, Walmart, Target and other retailers were clearly gaining ground. To reverse the trend and serve its customers, Amazon would have to find a way to bring back workers. Any decision the company made would affect the lives of hundreds of thousands of employees.

The task of sweating out the scenarios fell to Paul Stroup, who ran data science teams in Seattle. Mr. Stroup had been a veteran of what he described as "the brain" of Amazon operations—a division of thousands of employees finding tiny efficiencies to optimize for cheaper, faster and more predictable deliveries—when, in 2019, he made an unusual switch to Human Resources. Some shocked colleagues teased that joining H.R. would be like going on sabbatical....

As he evaluated the return-to-work options, he felt confident that Amazon's warehouses were growing safer, thanks to billions of dollars spent on virus safeguards....

Mr. Stroup worried how Amazon would summon workers back. The company needed to know who didn't intend to return so that it could replace them. But forcing employees too abruptly could result in firing tens of thousands of people. Mr. Stroup knew the work offered a lifeline: "The cleanliness, the procedure, the pay, the benefits—all of that is very competitive," he said.

He prepared surveys and data for Mr. Clark, the operations chief, 60 who would make the final decision. "I'd heard Dave was saying: 'Let's just move faster. This isn't helping people not knowing if they are coming back to work or not. We've created a safe place to work—we've proven that people aren't getting Covid at work—so let's just find out if they want to come back or not,'" he said.

In a virtual meeting, Mr. Stroup told Mr. Clark that if employees were brought back gradually, over a month or two, only 5 to 10 percent were projected to stay home and lose their jobs. Under the faster plan, many more were likely to be fired for not showing up. "The cold-turkey example was pretty bad," Mr. Stroup said, "like it was 20 to 30 percent of people would be let go in the month."

Within days, he heard Mr. Clark had chosen that route. "My team took it hard," Mr. Stroup said....

Ms. Nantel, the spokeswoman, said the decision was about supporting customers and communities in a time of need while providing safe jobs for people who wanted them....

In late April, Amazon told workers that unlimited unpaid time off would not be extended into May. The company eased requirements for personal leaves; to remain home without penalty, workers had a week left to apply. That decision created chaos.

Human Resources by App

65 Immediately, leave applications flooded into an Amazon back office in San José, Costa Rica. The system couldn't keep up.

Dangelo Padilla, a Costa Rican case manager who started at Amazon in 2016, woke up every morning to confront what he described as insurmountable tasks before him and his colleagues. They had already been overwhelmed by a backlog of almost 18,000 cases in early March, emails show, and over the last week in April got 13,500 more requests.

Panicked workers trying to take leaves found phone lines busy and got auto-replies warning of delayed responses. Some who applied for leaves were being penalized for missing work, triggering warning notices and then terminations. When their messages reached Mr. Padilla and his colleagues, workers were distraught.

"This is impacting the employees and impacting us," Mr. Padilla said he entreated their managers. "You have to fix this."

The team that vetted leaves had long struggled with rickety technology, according to Mr. Padilla and eight other current and former employees in Costa Rica. Right before the pandemic, they started using a new case-management system called Dali to address the problems and provide flexibility, but it was buggy. Staff members were constantly encountering problems. "We were lost," Mr. Padilla said. "Not even our managers knew how to handle it."

70 Faxes and emails that were supposed to be automatically sorted ended up in a massive inbox that had to be manually triaged. Approved leaves that were supposed to be directly reflected in worker atten-

dance programs instead had to be input by hand at another back office, in Pune, India.

When that wasn't done on time, warehouse employees with approved leaves got notices warning that they would be fired for abandoning their jobs. "I saw those situations every day—people getting U.P.T. deducted for no reason, people being terminated for no reasons," Mr. Padilla said.

In interviews, more than 25 current and former Amazon employees who dealt with the disability and leave system—executives, human resources personnel from JFK8 and other warehouses, and back office staff in the United States and abroad—bemoaned its inadequacy, calling it a source of frustration and panic. For years, they said, it had been prone to the kinds of errors Mr. Padilla described. Amazon catches many of the mistakes; some employees fight their own cases and prevail. Others give up and quit.

Ms. Nantel, the spokeswoman, said that the company quickly approved personal leaves during this period, hiring 500 people to help

An Amazon employee at the JFK8 warehouse, November 2020.

process the increased volume. She said Amazon received more than a million leave requests in the first year of the pandemic, twice its forecast, and worked hard to contact employees before they were fired to see if they wanted to keep their jobs.

Workers turned to H.R. teams in the warehouses for help, though they weren't primarily responsible for leaves. Even under normal circumstances, they were stretched thin. In interviews, veterans from Staten Island and across the country described long hours trying to fix errors, enforce Amazon's rules fairly and respond to the problems that plague any low-income work force—transportation breakdowns, lack of child care. At JFK8, some employees said they had spent an entire 30-minute break waiting in line for H.R. without getting to speak to anyone....

75   At JFK8, the human resources team for the more than 5,000 employees has increased from 25 to 34 staff members since the start of the pandemic....

Record Profits, Halted Raises

On Staten Island, workers began getting the dreaded warnings.

Mr. Cavagnaro, who had worked with Alberto Castillo, had taken a leave from Amazon. He suggested a June return date on a doctor's note, but couldn't reach the company to ask questions or discuss coming back. Amazon's attendance systems recorded him as a no-show, and he began getting job-abandonment notices. Unable to get a reply, he threw his hands up and allowed himself to be fired.

After *The Times* asked Amazon about his situation, the company offered him his job back.

By the time Mr. Cavagnaro was struggling in late spring to return to JFK8, Mr. Castillo had severely declined. Doctors told his wife that he would never again speak, eat or work.

80   Health insurance that Amazon provided covered most of the medical bills, but Ms. Castillo discovered that her husband's short-term disability payments had stopped. "I kept sending in medical forms but couldn't tell if anyone on the other end was actually receiving them,"

she said. The house they had hoped to buy was a vanished dream; now she was counting every penny and accepting donations from friends.

JFK8's human resources manager apologized and set the 10 weeks of missed payments right. Amazon said the documents Ms. Castillo had submitted never made it to his case manager, a systems issue that had affected others as well.

As workers returned, Amazon informed employees nationwide that it was ending the $2-an-hour raise and double overtime pay. The extra wages had not been "hazard" pay, officials said, but an incentive to show up.

The decision to force workers back ushered the company into the most profitable era in its history. By late May, JFK8 was a top-performing warehouse, bringing in 1.68 million items in a single week, Christine Hernandez, who worked in human resources, boasted on *Twitter*. "Yasss!!!" she cheered.

In July, Amazon announced $5.2 billion in earnings for the quarter— a record, until the next quarter brought $6.3 billion.

Amazon had been "running pretty much full out" since the beginning of May when more people were back at work, Brian Olsavsky, the company's finance chief, explained on a call with reporters. That let the online retailer meet the enormous demand more efficiently, working at full capacity around the clock. It was like Black Friday every single day. 85

The Power of the Metrics

For Traci Weishalla and her peers, a key to boosting thousands of employees to that level of performance was setting the pace....

Two measurements dominated most hourly employees' shifts. Rate gauged how fast they worked, a constantly fluctuating number displayed at their station. Time off task, or T.O.T., tracked every moment they strayed from their assignment—whether trekking to the bathroom, troubleshooting broken machinery or talking to a co-worker. The company pioneered new ways to calculate both metrics in the mid-2000s, when a smaller, scrappier Amazon set out to revolutionize warehouses....

A worker whose rate was too slow, or whose time off task climbed too high, risked being disciplined or fired. If a worker was off task, the system assumed the worker was to blame. Managers were told to ask workers what happened, and manually code in what they deemed legitimate excuses, like broken machinery, to override the default.

Internal documents show that managers were instructed to address only the "top offender" for time off task in each department per shift....

90   But workers didn't know that. The goal, JFK8's internal guidelines state, "is to create an environment not where we are writing everyone up, but that associates know that we are auditing for T.O.T." Workers could not readily see their T.O.T. totals, increasing anxiety. Word spread that Amazonians couldn't take bathroom breaks—a misperception rooted in real apprehension. Some employees chronicled their work-day down to the minute in a notebook, just in case....

Burning Through the Work Force

On Oct. 13, the bus stop outside JFK8 was flooded with workers hired in a surge without parallel in American corporate history. It was Prime Day, the invented Amazon shopping holiday that kicked off the Christmas season. To meet the moment, the warehouse was absorbing entire friend and family units without job interviews, and in most cases, little to no conversation between employer and applicants....

Kevin Michelus, 60, and retired after a lifetime of odd jobs, had been drawn in by a postcard advertising work. "No résumé, no job experience required," he said. "I've never heard of a job like that." He and the other newcomers had been hired after only a quick online screening. Internally, some describe the company's automated employment process as "lights-out hiring," with algorithms making decisions, and limited sense on Amazon's part of whom it is bringing in.

Mr. Niekerk said Mr. Bezos drove the push to remove humans from the hiring process, saying Amazon's need for workers would be so great, the applications had to be "a check-the-box screen." Mr. Bezos also saw automated assessments as a consistent, unbiased way to find motivated workers, Mr. Niekerk said.

Amazon boasted about the jobs it created, calling itself a force for growth and sustenance. What the numbers masked was that many workers cycled out of Amazon within months or even days.

Amazon is so large, and its churn so high, it affects the industry turnover rate where it operates, according to a *Times* analysis. In the two years after Amazon opened a new facility, the county turnover rate of warehousing and storage employees rose an average of 30 percentage points compared with two years prior.

As the weeks wore on, hints of trouble were cropping up, according to interviews and posts on JFK8's internal feedback board viewed by *The Times*. Several said workers should get more warning about mandatory overtime, that schedules changed "with no call, no text, no email, nothing." H.R. representatives were "hard to find," "not trained," and "not able to handle genuine complaints." Others wondered why they had to go find an H.R. representative to fix errors in unpaid time off deducted by the A to Z app. "Look at all the technology we have now," one employee wrote. "I'm sure this can be corrected." ...

In 2019, Amazon hired more than 770,000 hourly workers, even though the company, including corporate staff, grew by just 150,000 that year, John Phillips, the former head of mass hiring, wrote on *LinkedIn*. That meant the equivalent of Amazon's entire work force— roughly 650,000 people at the start of the year—left and were replaced that year. The company declined to provide numbers for 2020. ...

With the high churn, multiple current and former Amazon executives fear there simply will not be enough workers. In the more remote towns where Amazon based its early U.S. operations, it burned through local labor pools and needed to bus people in.

"Six to seven people who apply equals one person showing up and actually doing work," Mr. Stroup explained. If Amazon is churning through its entire work force once or twice a year, he said, "You need to have eight, nine, 10 million people apply each year." That's about 5 percent of the entire American work force. ...

Mr. Stroup says he is forever "an Amazon fanboy." But over time in human resources there, he became disappointed that he "didn't hear long-term thinking" about the company's quick cycling through work-ers. He likened it to using fossil fuels despite climate change.

"We keep using them," he said, "even though we know we're slowly cooking ourselves." ...

Ann Castillo stood outside her New Jersey apartment complex in early December, about to take on the responsibility of a lifetime. She had decided to bring her husband, now on hospice care, home and tend to him herself. Even with Amazon's long-term disability insur-ance, she might have to move into low-income housing.

"If he's going to go, then at least he's with us," she said.

She saw no sign that anyone in charge at JFK8 knew what was going on. "They never called and asked to follow up on how he's doing," she said. ...

105   Months later, after inquiries from *The Times*, an H.R. official and a JFK8 staff member reached out to Ms. Castillo. A spokeswoman expressed regret that Ms. Castillo did not feel properly supported. Mr. Agboka, the H.R. leader, said in a statement, "We have her, her hus-band, and their loved ones in our thoughts and prayers." ...

For months, Amazon had said publicly that it was reporting con-firmed cases at JFK8 and other warehouses to local health authori-ties, as required of employers. But New York City health department records show no reports until November. ...

Looking for Signs of Change

... In the final months of Jeff Bezos' tenure as chief executive, his high-turnover model looked riskier, and the concerns about how Amazon treated the workers who powered its rise were tarnishing his legacy. During the pandemic, Mr. Bezos' personal wealth exploded from $110 bil-lion to more than $190 billion. He had also been building a $500 mil-lion superyacht, according to the new book "Amazon Unbound." ...

Mr. Bezos' commitment in April to become "Earth's best employer" raised questions—about what exactly that meant, and how far he and his successors would go. ...

But it wasn't clear how much the company was willing to reconsider the sacrosanct systems of productivity, automation and high turnover that propelled it to dominance. "Are they going to address the issue of an expendable work force?" asked Mr. Cavagnaro, the fired worker who was returning to JFK8. "Are there going to be any changes?" . . .

Thinking about the Text

1. Jodi Kantor, Karen Weise, and Grace Ashford identify Amazon's many successes as well as its many problems, noting that "in contrast to its precise, sophisticated processing of packages, Amazon's model for managing people—heavily reliant on metrics, apps, and chatbots—was uneven and strained even before the coronavirus arrived" (9). What do they say are the greatest challenges faced by Amazon's hourly workers? What do they describe as the most challenging problems faced by Amazon as a company? What solutions do they suggest for any of these problems?

2. This article opens with a NARRATIVE about Ana and Alberto Castillo in 2020, after Alberto suffered brain damage from COVID. The Castillos appear a number of other times in this article—in a flashback to the day Alberto contracted the virus, for instance (33–37). Read through the report noting every mention of the Castillos. Why do you think the authors began with their story, and how does it inform their implicit ARGUMENT? How does it affect the way you read the report?

3. This piece is a REPORT, presenting information about both problems and successes at JFK8. Does it treat Amazon fairly? Do you think the authors offer a balanced representation of what both workers and management say? If not, what additional PERSPECTIVES might they have included? Do they consider any COUNTERARGUMENTS? Be prepared to point to examples in the report to support your response.

4. LET'S TALK. According to one former HR executive, Jeff Bezos believes that people are "inherently lazy . . . that our nature as humans is to expend as little energy as possible to get what we want or need." It's a belief that is central to the Amazon business, "from the ease of instant ordering to the pervasive use of data to get the most out of employees" (44). Do you agree with Bezos's implied DEFINITION of "lazy"? Why or why not? If not, what other definition might you offer? What words might you use instead of "lazy," and why? Get together with some classmates to explore how Bezos's belief may be affecting how Amazon functions as a business and how you imagine it affects the hourly workers there. Cite some examples, both from this article and from your own work experiences.

5. AND NOW WRITE. Suppose that you are participating in a community forum organized to explore the possibility of bringing an Amazon facility to your area. Each forum member is tasked with gathering specific information relevant to the issue that will be presented at a meeting. Your task is to give a four-minute spoken summary of Kantor, Weise, and Ashford's report. Write a SUMMARY that is clear and thorough—and represents fairly all the points that the report covers.

See Chapter 12 for help writing such a summary.

RICHARD THOMPSON FORD

Dress Codes and Gender

FROM ANCIENT TIMES UNTIL THE PRESENT DAY, dress codes have required that clothing serve as a visible symbol of sex. . . . Even as changing norms and ideals have weakened the symbolic links between clothing and most types of social status, law and custom have steadfastly ensured that the symbolic link between clothing and sex remains. But because fashions change, there is no specific type of clothing that inherently "belongs" to the male or female sex; moreover, these changes always threaten to erode any working distinction between masculine and feminine attire. The central purpose of gendered dress codes is not to ensure that people of each sex wear or refrain from wearing any specific type of clothing; instead it is to ensure that clothing clearly identifies the wearer as either male or female.

Occasionally, gender symbolism can be almost mimetic, as in the case of the phallic codpiece of the late Middle Ages and Renaissance era or, arguably, the long necktie, which one might interpret as a literal phallic symbol, both pointing to and mirroring the penis. But most sartorial sex symbols are more arbitrary, such as the idea that blue is a masculine color and pink a feminine one. This commonplace convention does not reflect any inherent masculinity or femininity in the respective colors; in fact, less than a century ago, this color symbolism was the reverse. A 1918 retail trade article insisted that "[t]he generally accepted rule is pink for the boys and blue for the girls," explaining that "pink, being a more decided and stronger color, is more suitable for the boy, while blue, which is more delicate and dainty, is prettier

---

Richard Thompson Ford, professor of law at Stanford, specializes in civil rights and antidiscrimination law. He writes about cultural issues and race for the Washington Post, Esquire, Slate, *and other periodicals. This selection is from* Dress Codes: How the Laws of Fashion Made History *(2021). He tweets from @Richard_T_Ford.*

for the girl."[1] What was important was—as it still is today—that boys wore *different* clothing from girls. Indeed, while the significance of a gender divide is ancient, the precise location of the dividing line has changed over time: in the late nineteenth and early twentieth centuries, infants and small children of both sexes wore white gowns, and young boys and girls alike wore long curls in their hair, pumps on their feet, lacy collars around their necks, and bonnets on their heads. Boys received their first haircut and graduated to men's clothing only when they achieved sufficient physical maturity—around age six or seven.[2] Masculine attire wasn't linked to male sex per se but to male virility; children of either sex were considered delicate, innocent, and for those reasons were associated with domestic femininity.

The arbitrariness of such symbolism demonstrates that most gendered clothing doesn't refer to human biology; instead it reflects a social convention. "Women's clothing" isn't clothing that is especially suited to female bodies—it is simply any clothing that women typically wear. This means that every transgression of gender norms is also a potential revision of those norms: if enough women wear pants, then pants will become women's clothing.

Dress codes ensure that such changes don't erode the distinction in gendered clothing altogether. For instance, in the mid-twentieth

How long will "blue for boys and pink for girls" persist?

century, hundreds of American cities had laws on the books specifically prohibiting cross-dressing, and many others used more general prohibitions against public indecency to ban it. Typically, these dress codes didn't enforce any *specific* type of gendered attire at all. Instead, they enforced a regime of *gendered symbolism*. Because the definition of gendered attire is both unclear and in flux, these cross-dressing bans were unavoidably vague. In practice, unlawful "cross-dressing" meant either intentional transgression of gender norms or a violation of certain well-established conventions. Both of these approaches to cross-dressing were problematic, and in the 1970s, people accused of cross-dressing began to challenge these laws as violations of civil rights.

HISTORICALLY, a primary function of gendered clothing was to signal the reproductive role of the wearer. This explains not only attire designed to symbolize genital difference but also why prepubescent boys were dressed in gowns similar to those worn by girls, why unmarried women wore different clothing than married women, and why older women dressed differently than women of childbearing age. In monarchical and aristocratic societies where social status was transmitted through bloodlines, an important function of gendered attire was to symbolize the reproductive role on which the fate of dynasties, kingdoms, and empires depended. That doesn't mean that cross-dressing was ever "deceptive," but it did challenge social roles that had profound economic and in some cases geopolitical stakes.

5

Ford writes with a great deal of confidence and authority, doesn't he? Learn about how to do that yourself on pp. 167–68.

But today, political power typically is not inherited and many people lead happy and fulfilled lives without producing offspring. Pleasure has eclipsed reproduction as the primary motivation for sex and at the same time, technology has made sexless reproduction possible. Our attire reflects these changes. Fashion historian Anne Hollander noticed this trend toward asexual dress:

> [T]rue parity of the sexes . . . has . . . been found in dressing everyone like children. A crowd of adults at a museum or park now looks just like a school trip. Everyone is in the same colorful zipper jackets,

sweaters, pants and shirts worn by kids. . . . [These are] costumes connoting absolute bodily freedom and no responsibilities outside the self . . . an adult adaption of the former privilege of carefree children. . . . [Moreover they represent] freedom from the burdens of adult sexuality. . . . [M]en and women . . . dress exactly alike in versions of sand-box gear. . . . [They dress like] little boys and girls . . . at an age when their clothes need not differentiate the sexes because their activities are not supposed to, and neither are their thoughts.[3] . . .

In contrast to desexualized, juvenile attire, deliberate transgression of gendered dress codes emphasizes the mature, sexual body. Cross-dressing and transgender identification (a distinct if related phenomenon) remixes conventional gender signifiers through a variety of novel, inventive uses. It's unsurprising that people will want to combine gendered symbolism in new—and, to some, disconcerting—ways. Indeed it is—dare I say?—natural that some people will psychologically identify with the symbolism of a gender that does not "belong" to their genital sex. The use of artifice in service of a gendered ideal does not in and of itself distinguish cross-dressers or transgender people: most of us deliberately exaggerate biological sex characteristics through clothing, and many do so through other interventions, such as cosmetic surgery or extreme bodybuilding. If this is "unnatural," then so is gendered clothing generally. As the famous drag queen RuPaul puts it: "[W]e're all born naked—the rest is drag, baby."

RuPaul, host of *RuPaul's Drag Race.*

Danielle Cooper wearing a Tailory New York suit during Fashion Week, 2016.

Today, a growing number of people—some who are transgender and many who are not—use the symbolism of gendered attire unconventionally. For instance, dancer Sara Geffrard favors stylish menswear and authors a blog called *A Dapper Chick* that features interviews with inspirational women and photos highlighting her own unique fashion sense. Geffrard finds the classic suit gives her self-confidence: "I'm a very, very shy person, but if I'm in a suit, I feel very confident.... Otherwise, I would walk in feeling sort of small." For Geffrard, the most important sartorial transition was from sportswear to tailored attire: "I used to wear more... urban streetwear, and I would get certain looks that I didn't really like ... I would go into a store and someone would follow me. When I started dressing the way I do now, I didn't get that anymore." Geffrard isn't transgender and she doesn't think her suits are in tension with her gender. "These suits are actually womenswear," she says. Similarly, Danielle Cooper, author of the blog *She's a Gent*, who favors men's suits, says, "I don't want to be a guy. I want to be a woman in menswear."[4]

Jaden Smith, 2015.

In 2015, Jaden Smith—son of Will Smith and Jada Pinkett Smith—was the toast of the fashion scene when he wore a Louis Vuitton skirt for the designer's women's wear ad campaign. Smith is known for his unconventional style: *GQ* noted, admiringly, that "leopard print tights are his everyday jeans. Dresses are his T-shirts."[5] *The New York Times* chief fashion critic Vanessa Friedman pointed out that Smith's style was notable precisely because "he's not a man in transition . . . or a man wearing clothing that looks as if it could be worn by either gender. . . . He is a man who happens to be wearing obviously female clothes. And while he doesn't look like a girl in them, he actually looks pretty good. It's not about the hairy legs in a skirt bro cliché."[6] This is a harbinger, perhaps, of a future in which the dress codes of gender are more readily mixed and recombined. These new uses of gendered attire are among the many ways of imagining gender in today's world, suggesting novel social roles and new types of erotic fantasy.

10　　Despite this unsettled equilibrium—or perhaps because of it—the efforts to control and regulate gendered attire are as numerous as ever. Gendered dress codes are changing to reflect new social norms, and new technologies, but they still shape our relationship to our bodies, our social encounters, our personalities, and ourselves.

Notes

1. Jo B. Paoletti, *Pink and Blue: Telling Boys from the Girls in America* (Bloomington: Indiana University Press, 2013).

2. Jeanne Magiaty, "When Did Girls Start Wearing Pink?" Smithsonian.com, April 7, 2011.

3. Anne Hollander, *Sex and Suits: The Evolution of Modern Dress* (London: Bloomsbury Academic, 2016), 171–72.

4. Valeriya Friedman, "Jaden Smith for Louis Vuitton: The New Man in a Skirt," *New York Times*, January 6, 2016.

5. Jake Woolf, "Jaden Smith Tells Us Why He Wore a Batman Suit to KimYe's Wedding," *GQ*, June 23, 2015.

6. Friedman, "Jaden Smith."

Thinking about the Text

1. Richard Thompson Ford CLAIMS that clothing is symbolic and that "the arbitrariness of such symbolism demonstrates that most gendered clothing doesn't refer to human biology; instead it reflects a social convention." What does that statement mean? Symbolic of what? SUMMARIZE Ford's ARGUMENT, pointing to one or more of the examples he provides to support his claim.

2. Ford quotes RuPaul saying, "We're all born naked—the rest is drag, baby" (7). What do you think RuPaul means by "the rest is drag"—and do you agree?

3. Ford quotes Anne Hollander, who claims that "parity of the sexes . . . has . . . been found in dressing everyone like children" (6). Reread that passage and think about your own experience and observations—and then decide whether her claim seems accurate to you. What EXAMPLES can you provide to support or reject this claim?

4. LET'S TALK. If you've lived in the United States for a while, you can probably tell if a garment came from the women's or men's department. What are the features of clothing that signal a specific gender? Work with a few classmates to list all the features you can think of that signal men's or women's clothing, considering color, shape, fabric, contour and fit, decorative details, placement of buttons and zippers, pockets—and anything else you find relevant. What garments can you find that have no gendering signals? Does your analysis support Ford's argument that gendered dress codes "still shape our relationship to our bodies, our social encounters, our personalities, and ourselves" (10)—or not?

5. AND NOW WRITE. Take some time to analyze what's in your closet or clothing drawers. Does your analysis support Ford's argument that our clothing signals something about our gender identity—or other markers of our identity? Write an essay ANALYZING how your clothing matches (or does not match) your gender identity.

HEATHER LANIER

Out There I Have to Smile

A FEW YEARS AGO ON A GORGEOUS JUNE DAY, I found myself in a windowless bathroom with forget-me-not wallpaper, my butt on a toilet, without any good reason to be there. It was a standard mothering move. Beyond the door, I could hear my two small kids laughing and eating cereal, so I stayed in this little space, smartphone in hand. In an hour, I was headed to a bowling alley with my kids, both of whom could now walk through a doorway on their own. And this was a brilliant new development, not just for the 2-year-old who'd learned to walk at the standard age, but for the 4-year-old, Fiona, who'd spent the past three and a half years in physical therapy striving toward this lofty goal. *Forty-five percent of people with Wolf-Hirschhorn syndrome walk,* said the report when I first got her diagnosis. Her ability to walk meant I no longer had to consider wheelchair or stroller accessibility. Her ability to walk *independently* meant she could navigate the tight turns around a bowling ball return without having to steer a clunky walker. So I was taking my kids bowling, as soon as I stopped pretend-peeing and reading on my phone.

I was reading a friend's blog post about a recent appointment with her counselor. As soon as she mentioned her son, who has the same chromosomal syndrome as my daughter, she began to cry.

The therapist asked, "Why do you always cry when you talk about him in here?"

In here was the therapist's office, maybe a subdued room with sage walls and elephant statuettes. *Out there,* my friend pushed her 4-year-old son in a wheelchair.

Heather Lanier is an essayist and poet who teaches creative writing at Rowan University. Her writing has appeared in the Atlantic, Salon, *and other periodicals. This essay was first published in* Longreads *in 2019. She posts on* Twitter *and* Instagram *from @heatherklanier.*

My friend looked up at the ceiling a moment and thought. *Why 5 do I always cry when I talk about him in here?* The answer hit her, and she sobbed. She managed this sentence, eked out between heaving breaths: "Because . . . out there . . . when I'm talking . . . about him . . . I have to smile."

I put my hand over my mouth. The windowless bathroom. The forget-me-not wallpaper. I burst into tears.

FOR BODIES THAT DON'T FIT into a certain mold, for bodies we call disabled, out there can be a treacherous space. Out there has steps where you need a ramp. Out there has strobe lighting that could make you seize. Out there writes stories over your body (she's sad, broken, wrong) when you just need toilet paper.

For parents of kids with disabled bodies, out there can be exhausting. It maintains chipper myths about babies that your child breaks. What's with that feeding tube? It tosses questions at your feet like it's throwing you something between flowers and rotten fruit. Why's she so small? What happened? What's wrong? You answer with a smile, or you answer with fatigue, or you turn your head because it's none of your business.

Out there is risky. Your son might sit in a classroom led by a teacher who doesn't believe he can learn. Or your daughter might need medical care from a doctor who thinks she's a tragedy.

Out there is inconvenient. The doorway isn't wide enough for your 10 adaptive stroller. The wood chips of the town's only playground are terrible for wheelchairs. The librarian concludes public story time with a craft that requires scissors, and you must now serve as your child's occupational therapist, back hunched, palms sweaty, enabling the arduous work of cutting paper.

Out there is not exactly designed for your kind.

As a white, straight, cisgender, non-disabled woman, I must imagine how this sentiment holds true for other bodies. My experience as a caregiver to a kid with disabilities* has put me in the closest relationship to this truth. Out there is not designed for many.

*I use both person-first and identity-first language in this essay. As a non-disabled person, I don't have a right to claim an identity for someone, so I err

Lanier's topic has built-in emotional appeal, but she doesn't overdo it. Learn about using emotional appeals in your own work on p. 415.

Which is why in here spaces are so delightful. And it's why, especially in early parenting, I often lingered in them for longer than I needed. Idling in the bathroom. Struggling to leave the house. In here applies little pressure. In here asks no questions. In here often lets you and your kin be as you are. . . .

What I didn't realize until having Fiona is that if a person is intellectually disabled, a parent's feelings often become a barometer for their kid's worth. What my friend and I have known, without ever knowing we've known, is that our culture judges the worth of our kids by judging our contentment. I hadn't named this until I sat in the bathroom and read my friend's blog post on my phone, but along with all the obstacles to surmount or circumnavigate or abandon, out there obliges us to offer our cheer. Are we happy? If so, then maybe the lives of our children aren't tragic. Out there I have to smile. . . .

15   HAPPINESS IS AN ENCOURAGED PERFORMANCE in America whether you're disabled or not. By analyzing photographs, Stanford psychology professor Jeanne Tsai found that U.S. leaders are over six times more likely to display "open, toothy smiles" than Chinese leaders. This same smile, what Tsai calls "the sign of American happiness," also appears more frequently in American children's stories and women's magazines than in East Asian counterparts. "A lot of immigrants have talked to me about how exhausting it is being in the United States," she told NPR reporter Maiken Scott of *The Pulse*, "because you have to smile all the time."

But the stakes of that performance are higher for disabled people and their caregivers. Princeton ethicist Peter Singer has kept his job even after arguing that parents of disabled babies should have the

---

on the side of identity-first language until I know a person's preference—and my daughter hasn't indicated one. I also use identity-first language to stand with disability activists who argue that linguistic acrobatics to avoid the word *disabled* are a manifestation of our culture's ableism. We do not say, for instance, "I am a person with femaleness." #saytheword

right to kill their kids. Because people with disabilities cause too much suffering, he says. . . .

Singer, whose book *Practical Ethics* is in its third edition, at one point suggests that his argument about murdering babies applies to disabilities that make a child's life "so bleak" that it's "not worth living." (How would anyone determine a life "not worth living"? And who gets to decide such a thing?) But then he argues that hemophiliacs too could be justifiably killed in infancy because a woman will only have so many children, and the hemophiliac child might prevent her from having another, healthier baby. "It is . . . plausible to suppose that the prospects of a happy life are better for a normal child" than for a hemophiliac, he writes.

I think of my college roommate, a gregarious extroverted gay man who competitively roller skated and also had hemophilia. While he blasted Latin pop through our kitchen and danced with joie de vivre and sang into a spatula, I, the "normal" non-hemophiliac person, brooded in my room to the tune of melancholy female artists like Tori Amos, while writing poems about romantic angst. Certainly, disability doesn't determine happiness. . . .

But the bigger issue is this: Why should a person's happiness—or lack thereof—be used in proving their right to live? And it's not just Singer who delivers this message. Here's disabled writer Nancy Mairs on the subject, from "On Being a Cripple": "In our society, anyone who deviates from the norm had better find some way to compensate. Like fat people, who are expected to be jolly, cripples must bear their lot meekly and cheerfully. A grumpy cripple isn't playing by the rules. Early on I vowed that, if I had to have MS, by God I was going to do it well. This is a class act, ladies and gentlemen. No tears, no recriminations, no faint-heartedness."

You'll hear parents of kids with disabilities negotiate this pressure to be happy all the time when they describe their children. "He has Down syndrome, and he's nonverbal," a father will say, "but he's happy!" Or a mother will say, "She has cerebral palsy, and she doesn't walk, but she's brought us so much joy!" We can't fault the parents.   20

They add this caveat of happiness because they know it carries necessary currency.

But this can be exhausting. It turns happiness into a rhetorical strategy, and makes the faces of disabled people and their caregivers a walking argument that should never have to exist in the first place....

[A]N ARTICLE PUBLISHED.... [by]the advocacy website Ollibean... [addresses] challenges of parenting a disabled child—"the prejudice and ableism, fighting systems for an equal education, equal and accessible medical care, accessibility, insurance coverage for a new wheelchair or communication device,..."—are injustices built into a system that needs to change. This is 100% true. But the quote fell under the subheading, "It's Not Your Disabled Child, It's the System." In other words, parenting a kid with disabilities isn't ever hard because of the inherent difficulties of a disability.

It was not hard, for instance, taking my infant daughter to a swallow study (to make sure she wasn't dying from her own spit) and two kidney reflux exams (to make sure these vital organs weren't at immediate risk of failure). It was not hard spending four years helping her learn to walk, or three years helping her tiny, fine-motor-limited fingers navigate a robust communication device so she could tell us what she wanted to eat. Likewise, it was not hard when my husband and I hovered over her body as she jerked in convulsions, her eyes pried open by erratic brain synapses, and it was not hard to check the clock while we did this. More than five minutes, and a seizure can cause brain damage.

Of course it was hard....

25   But if we can't say it was hard, then how can we affect any change that would help people in power understand what kind of support we might need?

And yet, if I do say it was hard, then I am fueling, as [blogger Savannah] Logsdon-Breakstone put it, "a dangerous narrative." I'm risking the chance that people will see my kid, my glorious beautiful curly-haired feisty stubborn rascal of a kid, and think, That mom's unhappy; that kid's life is tragic.

My facial expressions out there are territory over which ideologies are fighting. My emotions out there have rhetorical power. And I will use everything I have to argue that my kid's life has equal value to anyone else's.

So I've smiled. Especially in those early years, I smiled at the nurse who called my kid's name in the waiting room. I smiled as she led us to a room for X-rays. How cute, she said to my 38-inch 5-year-old in purple hospital jammies. I smiled after I unfolded Fiona's walker with a loud click at the library, eliciting stares, and I smiled while the teacher talked me through Fiona's low report card scores.

It wasn't a conscious thing, the smiling, until I read my friend's story while sitting in the forget-me-not-wallpapered bathroom. But when happiness becomes a rhetorical move, it's a lot less fun than regular happiness. "The freedom to be happy," writes Sara Ahmed in *The Promise of Happiness*, "restricts human freedom if you are not free to be not happy." ...

YOU ASK: AM I HAPPY? I say, sometimes less than before. Because she 30 wakes six times a night. Because regular trips to pediatric specialists are no strolls through the park. Because special educators sometimes see her as broken, in need of fixing. Because her needs often exceed my energy. Because every time I've hovered above her convulsing body at night, counting the minutes, I might have gained something like courage or "life experience," but I also felt gashed in a bodily place that I can't find, I can't name.

Because loving someone has never been so hard....

What I ask is that my answer doesn't matter in determining her worth.

Thinking about the Text

1. Heather Lanier states very clearly that raising Fiona has not been easy and that sometimes she is less happy "than before" (30)—but that "out there" she has to "smile" (14). Why is that the case? What point is she trying to make in this essay?

2. When Lanier describes the challenges of being "out there," she shifts pronouns, from *I* and *my* to *you* and *your* (7–11). Why do you think she changed pronouns that way? How does it affect what she's saying and the way you understand her ARGUMENT?

3. Lanier mentions the "forget-me-not wallpaper" three times in this essay. Reread the essay to find all three mentions: Why do you think she chose to repeat this phrase? What significance might that wallpaper hold for Lanier and for her argument about "in here" and "out there"?

4. LET'S TALK. Lanier says that admitting how hard it is to raise a child with disabilities could well contribute to a "dangerous narrative" (26). What could such a narrative be? Why would it be dangerous? And whom would it affect? Talk these questions over with a few classmates and then try to think of other things that you think are hard but necessary to say and how saying them might also fuel dangerous narratives.

5. AND NOW WRITE. In writing about the obligation she feels to smile, Lanier describes how prevalent smiling is in the United States—and how it sometimes becomes a RHETORICAL strategy. Most of us smile instinctively when something amuses or pleases us, and since smiling is so often done unconsciously, you may not be aware of how often you do (or don't) smile. Pay attention for a couple of days to when you smile and when you observe others smiling. Do you ever get explicitly asked to smile? Do you ask others to smile? Does gender (or race, or age, or anything else) play a role? How about nervousness or some other emotional state? Write an essay ANALYZING when and why you smile. Do you sometimes use it as a rhetorical strategy—and if so, for what PURPOSE? Provide examples from your own experience.

Should I Hang Out with Someone Whose Political Views I Hate?

I am a liberal in a blue city in a red state. One of my friends is married to a man who has become increasingly conservative over the past year (an "anti-Black Lives Matter, anti-abortion, Democrats are all idiots and socialists are taking over the country" mind-set), and his posts on social media are becoming more and more extreme. We occasionally socialize as couples. When we are together, I am friendly with him, and we avoid overt political talk, but as his social media becomes more and more extreme, I feel conflicted about continuing to accept invitations to socialize with them. Is it hypocritical of me to socialize with them when I find his personal political views so abhorrent? Name Withheld.

W HEN I WAS FIFTEEN and in Britain for school, I came to know a neighbor of my English grandmother's. Then in his 60s, he was a right-wing member of Parliament whose views on the major issues of the day were utterly remote from mine. All the same, we enjoyed spending time together—when he took me trout fishing, it always involved more talk than trout—and though politics was far from the only thing we discussed, it wasn't a topic we avoided. Once, when he drove me to visit the college he had attended (and that I would too, just as he hoped), I spent two full hours trying to persuade him to support an

Kwame Anthony Appiah *is a British-Ghanaian philosopher who teaches at New York University. He has written numerous books and academic articles dealing with politics, ethics, and identity, including* Cosmopolitanism: Ethics in a World of Strangers (2007) *and* The Lies That Bind (2018). *He writes a weekly ethics column for the* New York Times, *where this selection was published in 2021. He tweets from* @KAnthonyAppiah.

upcoming resolution to maintain the abolition of capital punishment for murder. We must have made an odd pair—a reactionary M.P. with the strapping build of the heavyweight boxing champion he was as an undergraduate; a willowy brown teenager who kept up with what was then known as *The Peking Review*. Still, as we whizzed past the hedge-rows and incurious sheep of the Cotswolds, we carried on a vigorous debate over an issue we both cared a great deal about.

I do understand why people prefer to limit their socializing to people who share their view of the world and to steer clear of the maddeningly misguided. In recent years, certainly, America has reshaped itself in ways that accommodate the tendency. With the rise of "assortative mating," bankers—to paint in broad strokes—no longer marry secretaries; they marry other bankers. Doctors no longer marry nurses; they marry other doctors. And so on, up and down the lines of income and class. (Although social scientists have argued that this trend has deepened economic inequality, it also reflects substantial and welcome gains in gender equality in the workplace.) More to the point, the United States has become politically sorted: Increasingly, your neighborhood will be predominantly red or blue, not mixed. If racial segregation has diminished somewhat over the past generation, partisan segregation has risen.

And so have partisan identities. Your friend's husband, that is, has the political views of his tribe. These views, as with any tribal shibboleths, will often matter to him because they are signs of his membership. Maybe a few of his views were arrived at by careful reflection, but he probably couldn't argue effectively for most of his opinions before an open-minded audience. The trouble is that the same is almost certainly true of you. You have the liberal tribal beliefs and commitments. And—as a substantial body of social-science research suggests—you probably did not acquire them by deep and thoughtful analysis, because you are like most of us. Identity precedes ideology: Who you are determines what you believe.

5   I'm happy to stipulate that your views are enlightened and his benighted. Still, it's possible that you and this fellow are in one respect

allied—that you are both committed, as citizens, to participating together in the governance of this battered republic of ours. Despite the forces that would keep us socially and even geographically isolated from one another, you each have a reason to try to understand the other tribe; to figure out what its members believe and (to the extent that there are arguments involved) why they believe it. Democracy falters not when we disagree about things but when we lose interest in trying to make sense of the other person's point of view and in trying to persuade that person of the merits of our own.

If you took no pleasure in hanging out with this person, you wouldn't be asking me whether you can go on doing so. And yet you write as if there are only two options here—tolerating his views in silence or cutting him off. Here's a third option: Stick with this fellow but speak up for your politics. Encourage him to do the same. When we stop talking even to people we know and like because of political disagreements, we've abandoned the deliberative-democratic project of governing the republic together.

Not that we should delude ourselves about our prospects for shifting the other person's shibboleths. At the end of that car trip, my burly interlocutor got out of the car, stretched his legs and told me, almost ruefully: "You may have won all the arguments today. I'm still voting against the resolution." It passed anyway. And there were many other topics to discuss, from village gossip to high politics, the next time we went fishing.

And don't forget to listen! Chapter 1 provides tips for listening with the goal of understanding what others think, especially those whose views differ from yours.

Thinking about the Text

1. Kwame Anthony Appiah responds to a simple yes/no question from a reader with an extended explanation of partisan behavior along with a broad suggestion for how to proceed. What exactly does Appiah suggest? SUMMARIZE his response. Do you think the reader found his response satisfactory? Why or why not? How about you: Did you find Appiah's advice helpful? Why or why not?

2. How does Appiah go about appealing to the reader? How does he demonstrate that he RESPECTS the reader's views? In what ways

does he show that he knows what he's talking about and thus add to his CREDIBILITY? What REASONS and EVIDENCE does he provide to support the advice he offers? How does he establish COMMON GROUND?

3. Appiah begins his response in the first person (*I* and *my*), speaking of his own experience. In the next paragraph, he shifts to the third person (*they* and *their*), speaking of people in general until the next to last sentence, when he shifts again, referring to "your neighborhood." He continues with *your* in paragraph 3, directly addressing the person who sent in the question. Does the word *your* in paragraphs 2 and 3 refer to the same person? How do you know—and what difference does it make in what Appiah says? Finally, in the last paragraph, he shifts again, to *we*. Why do you think he makes this shift at the end, and how does it affect his ARGUMENT?

4. LET'S TALK. Appiah CLAIMS that "identity precedes ideology" and that "who you are determines what you believe" (4). And yet we all know of cases where siblings who grew up with the same family in the same household have vastly different beliefs. In what ways do you think *your* identity has determined your beliefs—or not? Discuss Appiah's claims and your own observations about identity and ideology with a few classmates. Consider how your beliefs might be different if some parts of your identity (such as age, religion, or sexual orientation) were different. What new insights emerge from this conversation?

5. AND NOW WRITE. We all know people whose political or other ideas differ significantly from ours. How have you dealt with encounters with the people in your life whose ideas you disagree with—or even "hate," as Appiah's title says? What strategies have you used in the past? What worked well? What didn't? How might you try to proceed with them going forward? Have Appiah's suggestions given you any new ideas or directions? Write an essay DESCRIBING a situation in which you negotiated a difficult encounter with someone you strongly disagreed with and ANALYZING the ways in which your negotiation strategies worked well—or did not. Conclude by noting what you have learned from this analysis.

32 What's Language Got to Do with It?

LANGUAGE EXERTS HIDDEN POWER,
LIKE THE MOON ON THE TIDES.

—RITA MAE BROWN

hat's language got to do with it? Well, considering the starring role that language plays in just about everything that we do, the short answer would be *plenty*. Yet despite its central role in human activity, we tend not to think about language very much. Its use is so automatic, so unconscious, that it often escapes notice. It's as invisible as air—and like air, we wouldn't get too far without it.

It would be easy to say that language—any language—is simply a collection of words that fit together according to predictable patterns in order to create meaning. That wouldn't be wrong exactly, but it would be deceptively incomplete.

Language—and all languages—carries nuances and subtleties not just in the words themselves but in the ways they work in combination; in the ways they are pronounced, embellished, said, written, or punctuated. In short, language is about more than just making "meaning." Our language use tells the world who we are, and it establishes the customs and boundaries of all kinds of human relationships, from legal codes to casual greetings on the street. Language enables us to make art that lifts the human spirit, but it can also be used to cruelly oppress it. In short, language exerts enormous power—like the moon exerts on the tide. And every day, each of us participates in its endless shaping and reshaping.

The readings in this chapter examine a broad range of language issues in both speech and writing. The English language, like all languages with a robust written tradition, has a standardized variety with norms and customs that are in widespread use. **Missy Watson** takes a critical look at standardized English, calling out its role in perpetuating harmful social practices—ones that **Jasmine Lane** acknowledges in an essay explaining why she continues to teach standard English to her highschool students.

Challenging the reality that standard English is "compulsory" in American schools, **June Jordan** writes about the exuberance of Black language in a classic essay in which the everyday realities of racial violence become part of the story. The artistry of Black language is also explored by **Adam Bradley**, who writes about rap and poetry—and the classical literary devices they share.

The chapter also looks at language and identity from several angles. **Gloria Anzaldúa** writes about how the several varieties of English and Spanish that she speaks have shaped her being, **Fernanda Zamudio-Suarez** zeros in on a single word, *Latinx*, and the controversies surrounding its ability to adequately represent the identities of people of Latin American descent. Identity also plays a central role in **Beth Nguyen's** narrative, which also focuses on a single word: in this case, her given name, Bich.

Readings in Other Chapters

- **Robin Kimmerer**, On Animacy: Learning the Grammar of Living Things   731

Readings on <u>letstalklibrary.com</u>

- **Kwame Anthony Appiah**, The Case for Capitalizing the B in Black
- **Deborah Cameron**, Women of Letters
- **Gabriel Lesser**, G Is for Gabi: Finding My Name and Language
- **Tracy Moore**, How COVID-19 Gave Me Back My Southern Accent
- **Shira Telushkin**, Making Gender-Neutral Emojis Is More Complicated Than You Think

GLORIA ANZALDÚA

How to Tame a Wild Tongue

"WE'RE GOING TO HAVE TO CONTROL YOUR TONGUE," the dentist says, pulling out all the metal from my mouth. Silver bits plop and tinkle into the basin. My mouth is a motherlode.

The dentist is cleaning out my roots. I get a whiff of the stench when I gasp. "I can't cap that tooth yet, you're still draining," he says.

"We're going to have to do something about your tongue," I hear the anger rising in his voice. My tongue keeps pushing out the wads of cotton, pushing back the drills, the long thin needles. "I've never seen anything as strong or as stubborn," he says. And I think, how do you tame a wild tongue, train it to be quiet, how do you bridle and saddle it? How do you make it lie down?

> "Who is to say that robbing a people
> of its language is less violent than war?"
> —RAY GWYN SMITH[1]

I remember being caught speaking Spanish at recess—that was good for three licks on the knuckles with a sharp ruler. I remember being sent to the corner of the classroom for "talking back" to the Anglo teacher when all I was trying to do was tell her how to pronounce my name. "If you want to be American, speak 'American.' If you don't like it, go back to Mexico where you belong."

Gloria Anzaldúa (1942–2004) *was a poet, artist, and scholar of Chicana, feminist, and queer cultures; she earned a doctoral degree in literature at the University of California, Santa Cruz, where she taught in the Women's Studies Department. Her work has received numerous awards, including the National Endowment for the Arts fiction award and the Lambda Lesbian Small Press book award. This essay is from her 1987 book,* Borderlands/La Frontera: The New Mestiza.

"I want you to speak English. *Pa' hallar buen trabajo tienes que* 5
*saber hablar el inglés bien. Qué vale toda tu educación si todavía hablas
inglés con un* 'accent,'" my mother would say, mortified that I spoke
English like a Mexican. At Pan American University, I and all Chicano
students were required to take two speech classes. Their purpose: to
get rid of our accents.

Attacks on one's form of expression with the intent to censor are
a violation of the First Amendment. *El Anglo con cara de inocente
nos arrancó la lengua.* Wild tongues can't be tamed, they can only be
cut out.

Overcoming the Tradition of Silence

> *Ahogadas, escupimos el oscuro.*
> *Peleando con nuestra propia sombra*
> *el silencio nos sepulta.*

En boca cerrada no entran moscas. "Flies don't enter a closed mouth"
is a saying I kept hearing when I was a child. *Ser habladora* was to be
a gossip and a liar, to talk too much. *Muchachitas bien criadas*, well-
bred girls don't answer back. *Es una falta de respeto* to talk back to
one's mother or father. I remember one of the sins I'd recite to the
priest in the confession box the few times I went to confession: talking
back to my mother, *hablar pa' 'tras, repelar. Hocicona, repelona, chis-
mosa*, having a big mouth, questioning, carrying tales are all signs of
being *mal criada*. In my culture they are all words that are derogatory
if applied to women—I've never heard them applied to men.

THE FIRST TIME I heard two women, a Puerto Rican and a Cuban,
say the word "*nosotras*," I was shocked. I had not known the word
existed. Chicanas use *nostros* whether we're male or female. We are
robbed of our female being by the masculine plural. Language is a
male discourse.

And our tongues have become
dry the wilderness has
dried out our tongues and
we have forgotten speech.
—IRENA KLEPFISZ[2]

Even our own people, other Spanish speakers *nos quieren poner candados en la boca.* They would hold us back with their bag of *reglas de academia.*

Oyé como ladra: El lenguaje de la frontera

Quien tiene boca se equivoca.
—MEXICAN SAYING

10   "*Pocho,* cultural traitor, you're speaking the oppressor's language by speaking English, you're ruining the Spanish language," I have been accused by various Latinos and Latinas. Chicano Spanish is considered by the purist and by most Latinos deficient, a mutilation of Spanish.

But Chicano Spanish is a border tongue which developed naturally. Change, *evolución, enriquecimiento de palabras nuevas por invención o adopción* have created variants of Chicano Spanish, *un nuevo lenguaje. Un lenguaje que corresponde a un modo de vivir.* Chicano Spanish is not incorrect, it is a living language.

For a people who are neither Spanish nor live in a country in which Spanish is the first language; for a people who live in a country in which English is the reigning tongue but who are not Anglo; for a people who cannot entirely identify with either standard (formal, Castillian) Spanish nor standard English, what recourse is left to them but to create their own language? A language which they can connect their identity to, one capable of communicating the realities and values true to themselves—a language with terms that are neither *español ni inglés,* but both. We speak a patois, a forked tongue, a variation of two languages.

Chicano Spanish sprang out of the Chicanos' need to identify ourselves as a distinct people. We needed a language with which we could communicate with ourselves, a secret language. For some of us, language is a homeland closer than the Southwest—for many Chicanos today live in the Midwest and the East. And because we are a complex, heterogeneous people, we speak many languages. Some of the languages we speak are:

1. Standard English
2. Working class and slang English
3. Standard Spanish
4. Standard Mexican Spanish
5. North Mexican Spanish dialect
6. Chicano Spanish (Texas, New Mexico, Arizona, and California have regional variations)
7. Tex-Mex
8. *Pachuco* (called *caló*)

My "home" tongues are the languages I speak with my sister and brothers, with my friends. They are the last five listed, with 6 and 7 being closest to my heart. From school, the media, and job situations, I've picked up standard and working class English. From Mamagrande Locha and from reading Spanish and Mexican literature, I've picked up Standard Spanish and Standard Mexican Spanish. From *los recién llegados*, Mexican immigrants, and *braceros*, I learned the North Mexican dialect. With Mexicans I'll try to speak either Standard Mexican Spanish or the North Mexican dialect. From my parents and Chicanos living in the Valley, I picked up Chicano Texas Spanish, and I speak it with my mom, younger brother (who married a Mexican and who rarely mixes Spanish with English), aunts, and older relatives.

With Chicanas from *Nuevo México* or *Arizona* I will speak Chicano Spanish a little, but often they don't understand what I'm saying. With most California Chicanas I speak entirely in English (unless I forget). When I first moved to San Francisco, I'd rattle off something in Spanish, unintentionally embarrassing them. Often it is only with another Chicana *tejana* that I can talk freely.

15 WORDS DISTORTED BY ENGLISH are known as anglicisms or *pochismos*. The *pocho* is an anglicized Mexican or American of Mexican origin who speaks Spanish with an accent characteristic of North Americans and who distorts and reconstructs the language according to the influence of English.[3] Tex-Mex, or Spanglish, comes most naturally to me. I may switch back and forth from English to Spanish in the same sentence or in the same word. With my sister and my brother Nune and with Chicano *tejano* contemporaries I speak in Tex-Mex.

From kids and people my own age I picked up *Pachuco. Pachuco* (the language of the zoot suiters) is a language of rebellion, both against Standard Spanish and Standard English. It is a secret language. Adults of the culture and outsiders cannot understand it. It is made up of slang words from both English and Spanish. *Ruca* means girl or woman, *vato* means guy or dude, *chale* means no, *simón* means yes, *churro* is sure, talk is *periquiar, pigionear* means petting, *que gacho* means how nerdy, *ponte águila* means watch out, death is called *la pelona*. Through lack of practice and not having others who can speak it, I've lost most of the *Pachuco* tongue.

Chicano Spanish

Chicanos, after 250 years of Spanish/Anglo colonization, have developed significant differences in the Spanish we speak. We collapse two adjacent vowels into a single syllable and sometimes shift the stress in certain words such as *maíz/maiz, cohete/cuete*. We leave out certain consonants when they appear between vowels: *lado/lao, mojado/ mojao*. Chicanos from South Texas pronounce *f* as *j* as in *jue (fue)*. Chicanos use "archaisms," words that are no longer in the Spanish language, words that have been evolved out. We say *semos, truje, haiga, ansina*, and *naiden*. We retain the "archaic" *j*, as in *jalar*, that derives from an earlier *h*, (the French *halar* or the Germanic *halon* which was lost to standard Spanish in the 16th century), but which is still found in several regional dialects such as the one spoken in South Texas. (Due to geography, Chicanos from the Valley of South Texas were cut off linguistically from other Spanish speakers. We tend to use words that the Spaniards brought over from Medieval Spain. The majority of the Spanish colonizers in Mexico and the Southwest came from Extremadura—Hernán Cortés was of them—and Andalucía. Andalucians pronounce *ll* like a *y*, and their *d*'s tend to be absorbed by adjacent vowels: *tirado* becomes *tirao*. They brought *el lenguaje popular, dialectos y regionalismos.*[4])

Chicanos and other Spanish speakers also shift *ll* to *y* and *z* to *s*.[5] We leave out initial syllables, saying *tar* for *estar, toy* for *estoy, hora* for *ahora* (*cubanos* and *puertorriqueños* also leave out initial letters of some words). We also leave out the final syllable such as *pa* for *para*. The intervocalic *y*, the *ll* as in *tortilla, ella, botella*, gets replaced by *tortia* or *tortiya, ea, botea*. We add an additional syllable at the beginning of certain words: *atocar* for *tocar, agastar* for *gastar*. Sometimes we'll say *lavaste las vacijas*, other times *lavates* (substituting the *ates* verb endings for the *aste*).

We use anglicisms, words borrowed from English: *bola* from ball, *carpeta* from carpet, *máchina de lavar* (instead of *lavadora*) from washing machine. Tex-Mex argot, created by adding a Spanish sound at the beginning or end of an English word such as *cookiar* for cook, *watchar* for watch, *parkiar* for park, and *rapiar* for rape, is the result of the pressures on Spanish speakers to adapt to English.

We don't use the word *vosotros/as* or its accompanying verb form. 20 We don't say *claro* (to mean yes), *imagínate*, or *me emociona*, unless we picked up Spanish from Latinas, out of a book, or in a classroom. Other Spanish-speaking groups are going through the same, or similar, development in their Spanish.

Linguistic Terrorism

Deslenguadas. Somos los del español deficiente. We are your linguistic nightmare, your linguistic aberration, your linguistic *mestisaje*, the subject of your *burla*. Because we speak with tongues of fire we are culturally crucified. Racially, culturally, and linguistically *somos huérfanos*—we speak an orphan tongue.

Chicanas who grew up speaking Chicano Spanish have internalized the belief that we speak poor Spanish. It is illegitimate, a bastard language. And because we internalize how our language has been used against us by the dominant culture, we use our language differences against each other.

Chicana feminists often skirt around each other with suspicion and hesitation. For the longest time I couldn't figure it out. Then it dawned on me. To be close to another Chicana is like looking into the mirror. We are afraid of what we'll see there. *Pena.* Shame. Low estimation of self. In childhood we are told that our language is wrong. Repeated attacks on our native tongue diminish our sense of self. The attacks continue throughout our lives.

Chicanas feel uncomfortable talking in Spanish to Latinas, afraid of their censure. Their language was not outlawed in their countries. They had a whole lifetime of being immersed in their native tongue; generations, centuries in which Spanish was a first language, taught in school, heard on radio and TV, and read in the newspaper.

If a person, Chicana or Latina, has a low estimation of my native tongue, she also has a low estimation of me. Often with *mexicanas y latinas* we'll speak English as a neutral language. Even among Chicanas we tend to speak English at parties or conferences. Yet, at the same time, we're afraid the other will think we're *agringadas* because we don't speak Chicano Spanish. We oppress each other trying to out-Chicano each other, vying to be the "real" Chicanas, to speak like Chicanos. There is no one Chicano language just as there is no one Chicano experience. A monolingual Chicana whose first language is English or Spanish is just as much a Chicana as one who speaks several variants of Spanish. A Chicana from Michigan or Chicago or Detroit is just as much a Chicana as one from the Southwest. Chicano Spanish is as diverse linguistically as it is regionally.

25   By the end of this century, Spanish speakers will comprise the biggest minority group in the U.S., a country where students in high schools and colleges are encouraged to take French classes because French is considered more "cultured." But for a language to remain

alive it must be used.[6] By the end of this century English, and not Spanish, will be the mother tongue of most Chicanos and Latinos.

SO, IF YOU WANT TO REALLY HURT ME, talk badly about my language. Ethnic identity is twin skin to linguistic identity—I am my language. Until I can take pride in my language, I cannot take pride in myself. Until I can accept as legitimate Chicano Texas Spanish, Tex-Mex, and all the other languages I speak, I cannot accept the legitimacy of myself. Until I am free to write bilingually and to switch codes without having always to translate, while I still have to speak English or Spanish when I would rather speak Spanglish, and as long as I have to accommodate the English speakers rather than having them accommodate me, my tongue will be illegitimate.

I will no longer be made to feel ashamed of existing. I will have my voice: Indian, Spanish, white. I will have my serpent's tongue—my woman's voice, my sexual voice, my poet's voice. I will overcome the tradition of silence.

> My fingers
> move sly against your palm
> Like women everywhere, we speak in code.
> —MELANIE KAYE/KANTROWITZ[7]

"Vistas," corridos, y comida: My native tongue

In the 1960s, I read my first Chicano novel. It was *City of Night* by John Rechy, a gay Texan, son of a Scottish father and a Mexican mother. For days I walked around in stunned amazement that a Chicano could write and could get published. When I read *I Am Joaquín*[8] I was surprised to see a bilingual book by a Chicano in print. When I saw poetry written in Tex-Mex for the first time, a feeling of pure joy flashed through me. I felt like we really existed as a people. In 1971, when I started teaching High School English to Chicano students, I tried to supplement the required texts with works by Chicanos, only to be reprimanded and forbidden to do so by the principal. He claimed that I was supposed to teach "American" and English literature. At the risk of being fired, I swore my students to secrecy and slipped in Chicano short stories, poems, a play. In graduate school, while working toward a Ph.D., I had to "argue" with one advisor after the other, semester after semester, before I was allowed to make Chicano literature an area of focus.

Even before I read books by Chicanos or Mexicans, it was the Mexican movies I saw at the drive-in—the Thursday night special of $1.00 a carload—that gave me a sense of belonging. "*Vámonos a las vistas,*" my mother would call out and we'd all—grandmother, brothers, sister, and cousins—squeeze into the car. We'd wolf down cheese and bologna white bread sandwiches while watching Pedro Infante in melodramatic tearjerkers like *Nosotros los pobres*, the first "real" Mexican movie (that was not an imitation of European movies). I remember seeing *Cuando los hijos se van* and surmising that all Mexican movies played up the love a mother has for her children and what ungrateful sons and daughters suffer when they are not devoted to their mothers. I remember the singing-type "westerns" of Jorge Negrete and Miquel Aceves Mejía. When watching Mexican movies, I felt a sense of homecoming as well as alienation. People who were to amount to something didn't go to Mexican movies, or *bailes*, or tune their radios to *bolero, rancherita*, and *corrido* music.

30 THE WHOLE TIME I WAS GROWING UP, there was *norteño* music sometimes called North Mexican border music, or Tex-Mex music, or Chicano music, or *cantina* (bar) music. I grew up listening to *conjuntos*, three- or four-piece bands made up of folk musicians playing guitar, *bajo sexto*, drums, and button accordion, which Chicanos had borrowed from the German immigrants who had come to Central Texas and Mexico to farm and build breweries. In the Rio Grande Valley, Steve Jordan and Little Joe Hernández were popular, and Flaco Jiménez was the accordion king. The rhythms of Tex-Mex music are those of the polka, also adapted from the Germans, who in turn had borrowed the polka from the Czechs and Bohemians.

I remember the hot, sultry evenings when *corridos*—songs of love and death on the Texas-Mexican borderlands—reverberated out of cheap amplifiers from the local *cantinas* and wafted in through my bedroom window.

Corridos first became widely used along the South Texas/Mexican border during the early conflict between Chicanos and Anglos. The *corridos* are usually about Mexican heroes who do valiant deeds against the Anglo oppressors. Pancho Villa's song, "*La cucaracha*," is the most famous one. *Corridos* of John F. Kennedy and his death are still very popular in the Valley. Older Chicanos remember Lydia Mendoza, one of the great border *corrido* singers who was called *la Gloria de Tejas*. Her "*El tango negro*," sung during the Great Depression, made her a singer of the people. The everpresent *corridos* narrated one hundred years of border history, bringing news of events as well as entertaining. These folk musicians and folk songs are our chief cultural mythmakers, and they made our hard lives seem bearable.

I grew up feeling ambivalent about our music. Country-western and rock-and-roll had more status. In the 50s and 60s, for the slightly educated and *agringado* Chicanos, there existed a sense of shame at being caught listening to our music. Yet I couldn't stop my feet from thumping to the music, could not stop humming the words, nor hide from myself the exhilaration I felt when I heard it.

Anzaldúa uses many vivid examples, and this one is especially evocative. See pp. 88–90 for more about using examples in your work.

THERE ARE MORE SUBTLE WAYS that we internalize identification, especially in the forms of images and emotions. For me food and certain smells are tied to my identity, to my homeland. Woodsmoke curling up to an immense blue sky; woodsmoke perfuming my grandmother's clothes, her skin. The stench of cow manure and the yellow patches on the ground; the crack of a .22 rifle and the reek of cordite. Home-made white cheese sizzling in a pan, melting inside a folded *tortilla*. My sister Hilda's hot, spicy *menudo, chile colorado* making it deep red, pieces of *panza* and hominy floating on top. My brother Carito barbequing *fajitas* in the backyard. Even now and 3,000 miles away, I can see my mother spicing the ground beef, pork, and venison with *chile*. My mouth salivates at the thought of the hot steaming *tamales* I would be eating if I were home.

Si le preguntas a mi mamá, "¿Qué eres?"

> Identity is the essential core of who
> we are as individuals, the conscious
> experience of the self inside.
> —GERSHEN KAUFMAN[9]

35   *Nosotros los* Chicanos straddle the borderlands. On one side of us, we are constantly exposed to the Spanish of the Mexicans, on the other side we hear the Anglos' incessant clamoring so that we forget our language. Among ourselves we don't say *nosotros los americanos, o nosotros los españoles, o nosotros los hispanos*. We say *nosotros los mexicanos* (by *mexicanos* we do not mean citizens of Mexico; we do not mean a national identity, but a racial one). We distinguish between *mexicanos del otro lado* and *mexicanos de este lado*. Deep in our hearts we believe that being Mexican has nothing to do with which country one lives in. Being Mexican is a state of soul—not one of mind, not one of citizenship. Neither eagle nor serpent, but both. And like the ocean, neither animal respects borders.

> *Dime con quien andas y te diré quien eres.*
> (Tell me who your friends are and I'll tell you who you are.)
> —MEXICAN SAYING

Si le preguntas a mi mamá, "¿Qué eres?" te dirá, "Soy mexicana." My brothers and sister say the same. I sometimes will answer *"soy mexicana"* and at others will say *"soy Chicana" o "soy tejana."* But I identified as *"Raza"* before I ever identified as *"mexicana"* or "Chicana."

   As a culture, we call ourselves Spanish when referring to ourselves as a linguistic group and when copping out. It is then that we forget our predominant Indian genes. We are 70–80 percent Indian.[10] We call ourselves Hispanic[11] or Spanish-American or Latin American or Latin when linking ourselves to other Spanish-speaking peoples of the Western hemisphere and when copping out. We call ourselves Mexican-American[12] to signify we are neither Mexican nor American, but more the noun "American" than the adjective "Mexican" (and when copping out).

Chicanos and other people of color suffer economically for not acculturating. This voluntary (yet forced) alienation makes for psychological conflict, a kind of dual identity—we don't identify with the Anglo-American cultural values and we don't totally identify with the Mexican cultural values. We are a synergy of two cultures with various degrees of Mexicanness or Angloness. I have so internalized the borderland conflict that sometimes I feel like one cancels out the other and we are zero, nothing, no one. *A veces no soy nada ni nadie. Pero hasta cuando no lo soy, lo soy.*

When not copping out, when we know we are more than nothing, we call ourselves Mexican, referring to race and ancestry; *mestizo* when affirming both our Indian and Spanish (but we hardly ever own our Black ancestry); Chicano when referring to a politically aware people born and/or raised in the U.S.; *Raza* when referring to Chicanos; *tejanos* when we are Chicanos from Texas.

Chicanos did not know we were a people until 1965 when Ceasar   40 Chavez and the farmworkers united and *I Am Joaquín* was published and *la Raza Unida* party was formed in Texas. With that recognition, we became a distinct people. Something momentous happened to the Chicano soul—we became aware of our reality and acquired a name and a language (Chicano Spanish) that reflected that reality. Now that we had a name, some of the fragmented pieces began to fall together— who we were, what we were, how we had evolved. We began to get glimpses of what we might eventually become.

Yet the struggle of identities continues, the struggle of borders is our reality still. One day the inner struggle will cease and a true integration take place. In the meantime, *tenémos que hacer la lucha. ¿Quién está protegiendo los ranchos de mi gente? ¿Quién está tratando de cerrar la fisura entre la india y el blanco en nuestra sangre? El Chicano, sí, el Chicano que anda como un ladrón en su propia casa.*

LOS CHICANOS, how patient we seem, how very patient. There is the quiet of the Indian about us.[13] We know how to survive. When other races have given up their tongue, we've kept ours. We know what it is to live under the hammer blow of the dominant *norte americano* culture. But more than we count the blows, we count the days the weeks the years the centuries the eons until the white laws and commerce and customs will rot in the deserts they've created, lie bleached. *Humildes* yet proud, *quietos* yet wild, *nosotros losmexicanos-Chicanos* will walk by the crumbling ashes as we go about our business. Stubborn, persevering, impenetrable as stone, yet possessing a malleability that renders us unbreakable, we, the *mestizas* and *mestizos*, will remain.

Notes

1. Ray Gwyn Smith, *Moorland Is Cold Country*, unpublished book.

2. Irena Klepfisz, "*Di rayze aheym*/The Journey Home," in *The Tribe of Dina: A Jewish Women's Anthology*, Melanie Kaye/Kantrowitz and Irena Klepfisz, eds. (Montpelier, VT: Sinister Wisdom Books, 1986), 49.

3. R. C. Ortega, *Dialectología Del Barrio*, trans. Hortencia S. Alwan (Los Angeles, CA: R. C. Ortega Publisher & Bookseller, 1977), 132.

4. Eduardo Hernandéz-Chávez, Andrew D. Cohen, and Anthony F. Beltramo, *El Lenguaje de los Chicanos: Regional and Social Characteristics of Language Used by Mexican Americans* (Arlington, VA: Center for Applied Linguistics, 1975), 39.

5. Hernandéz-Chávez, xvii.

6. Irena Klepfisz, "Secular Jewish Identity: Yidishkayt in America," in *The Tribe of Dina*, Kaye/Kantrowitz and Klepfisz, eds., 43.

7. Melanie Kaye/Kantrowitz, "Sign," in *We Speak in Code: Poems and Other Writings* (Pittsburgh, PA: Motheroot Publications, Inc., 1980), 85.

8. Rodolfo Gonzales, *I Am Joaquín/Yo Soy Joaquín* (New York, NY: Bantam Books, 1972). It was first published in 1967.

9. Gershen Kaufman, *Shame: The Power of Caring* (Cambridge, MA: Schenkman Books, Inc., 1980), 68.

10. John R. Chávez, *The Lost Land: The Chicago Images of the Southwest* (Albuquerque, NM: University of New Mexico Press, 1984), 88–90.

11. "Hispanic" is derived from *Hispanis* (*España*, a name given to the Iberian Peninsula in ancient times when it was a part of the Roman Empire) and is a term designated by the U.S. government to make it easier to handle us on paper.

12. The Treaty of Guadalupe Hidalgo created the Mexican-American in 1848.

13. Anglos, in order to alleviate their guilt for dispossessing the Chicano, stressed the Spanish part of us and perpetrated the myth of the Spanish Southwest. We have accepted the fiction that we are Hispanic, that is Spanish, in order to accommodate ourselves to the dominant culture and its abhorrence of Indians. Chávez, 88–91.

Thinking about the Text

1. Gloria Anzaldúa, playing here on the double meaning of *tongue*, does not, in fact, give readers instructions for taming a wild tongue. What is she actually saying about her wild tongue, and why does she say it's "wild"? She has a lot to say about a lot of languages, but what do you think her primary ARGUMENT is?

2. Although Anzaldúa surely knew that her AUDIENCE would include many readers who do not understand Spanish, she uses a lot of Spanish in this essay, some with a translation and some without. Why do you think she left so much of it untranslated? And how did it affect you as a reader—did you find it frustrating? interesting? Do you wish she had translated everything?

3. Anzaldúa uses *many* different terms to refer to languages and people in this essay: Chicana, Chicano; Latino, Latina; Mexican, Mexicana; Tejana, Tejano; Latin American, Spanish American; Hispanic; English—and more! If she were alive today, what might she think of *Latinx*? What do you think she'd say if Fernanda Zamudio-Suarez asked her opinion about that? (Read Zamudio-Suarez's essay on p. 609.)

4. LET'S TALK. In one of the most famous passages in this essay, Anzaldúa says, "If you want to really hurt me, talk badly about my language.... I am my language" (26). Revisit that paragraph, reading it aloud with several classmates. Then consider how that passage applies to you and your life: In what ways are you your language (or not?) How does your language (or as in Anzaldúa's case, your multiple languages) shape and/or reflect your identity?

5. AND NOW WRITE. Anzaldúa lovingly describes the Mexican movies she saw at the drive-in as a child that gave her "a sense of belonging" (29). And she describes other things as well: *bolero, rancherita, corrido*, and other genres of music; *menudo, tamales*, and other favorite foods. What are some things that you remember fondly from your childhood—movies? music? food? games? Whatever! Write a NARRATIVE about such things, explaining why they were important to you.

FERNANDA ZAMUDIO-SUAREZ

The Debate over "Latinx"

COLLEGE CAMPUSES HELP DRIVE CULTURAL CHANGE, including in the language we use. This [article explores] how academics and students are pushing the term "Latinx" into the lexicon. And don't worry: There are also practical tips about when and how to use the term.

The Debate over "Latinx"

You've probably heard the word "Latinx." It's used on diplomas to name majors, it's emblazoned on campus cultural centers, and it's how some students and instructors identify their ethnicity.

Spanish, like other Romance languages, is gendered, meaning that some words, like the commonly used "Latino" and "Latina," are considered masculine or feminine. The term "Latinx" (pronounced Latin-EX or La-TEEN-ex) refers to Latin American people or those of Latin American descent without specifying gender, and it's used instead of "Latino" or "Latina." ("Hispanic" is often seen as an inadequate term because it's tied to Spanish colonizers.) Using an "x" instead of an "a" or an "o" includes those who identify as transgender, gender-fluid, or non-binary, proponents say.

But the term, which emerged in the early 2000s, is not universally embraced. Some critics in South America say that the word is "Mexicanized," because the "x" is often used in Nahuatl and other Native Mexican languages. Others say it phonetically excludes Portuguese speakers, who pronounce "x" in at least four different ways. And some people just don't like change.

Fernanda Zamudio-Suarez writes for the Chronicle of Higher Education, *a daily periodical that covers diverse topics of interest to faculty and administrators at US colleges and universities. This article was published in the* Chronicle's newsletter, Race on Campus, *in March 2021. Zamudio-Suarez tweets from @FernandaZamudio.*

5   Academics, students, and activists are often the tectonic plates that drive these lexical shifts. New words start as oddities. Blink once, and they're everywhere. "Latinx" and its use are evolving as you read this newsletter. How do you keep up?

A Gradual Adoption

This author likely knew a lot about her subject, but she listened to many others before writing. Chapter 1 explains how to listen in order to learn something.

Don't debate whether you or your institution should or shouldn't use "Latinx." Instead, try to understand why people use the word, says Nelson Flores, an associate professor of educational linguistics at the University of Pennsylvania. The words we choose are political, he says. Sometimes a language can seem to invalidate certain people, such as those who identify as nonbinary or transgender. In an email, Flores writes that using "Latinx" acknowledges debates that challenge the gender binary and shows solidarity with nonbinary and transgender individuals in Latin America who lead such political struggles in the community.

Flores started using the term a few years ago, he says, thanks to his students, who were connecting their vocabulary to their broader political experiences and beliefs. Slowly, he began to use "Latinx" to identify himself.

He likened the gradual adoption of "Latinx" to his use of the word "queer." When Flores was in college, "queer," describing sexual orientation or gender, was mostly used in academic and activist circles, but was considered on the lexical fringe. Fast-forward several years, and in 2016 the word "genderqueer" was added to *Merriam-Webster's Unabridged Dictionary*. The verdict is still out on whether "Latinx" will become just as popular, Flores says.

Cristobal Salinas Jr., an associate professor of higher-education leadership at Florida Atlantic University, began to notice in 2015 that other scholars at conferences would refer to him as "Latinx." But people used the word without defining it. Salinas says he specifies that he uses the pronouns "he" and "him," and so he was confused at being labeled "Latinx" instead of "Latino."

10   When he researched the term, he found that some people use "Latinx" to make a political statement. He also found that some stu-

dents instead use "Latine" or "Latinu" to resist "Latinx" in their communities. Those who rejected "Latinx" said it was a term used by academics to colonize Latin American people.

When Can You Use "Latinx"?

In a paper published in the *Journal of Hispanic Higher Education*, Salinas wrote that the definition of "Latinx" depends on how an individual understands and uses it. That's why it's important for people to define "Latinx," especially in academic settings such as a presentation or a paper, he says.

Want to use "Latinx" with students or colleagues, but don't want to catch someone off guard or misuse the word? Just ask how the people you're talking about identify and what words they prefer, Salinas says.

But going back and forth over whether to use the word can get you only so far. Roberto Orozco, a doctoral candidate in higher education at Rutgers University at New Brunswick, says he understands the questions about using the term but notes there are bigger issues at stake than debates over terminology.

"We're such a multifaceted community, in terms of the Latinx community, that we're never going to get to a place where this is a term that we're all using," Orozco says. "What's important is for folks to name why they're choosing to use that."

Using "Latinx" is a starting point to call out homophobia and transphobia in Latin American communities, and in society at large, Orozco says. It also acknowledges queer and trans voices that have historically been silenced. On his social-media profiles and in his writing, he identifies as "Latinx/a/o," putting the letters for gender-nonbinary people and women before the "o" that signifies men.

When colleges want to use "Latinx" for a degree program or a cultural center, there are a few things to consider. A big one: intersectionality.

Ángel Gonzalez, an Ed.D. candidate in community-college leadership at San Diego State University and a graduate research associate at the American Council on Education, says that if colleges want to replace a degree-program or campus-center name with "Latinx," instead of "Hispanic" or "Latino/a," administrators should first listen to students to see if they want such a change.

The switch can't be in name only, Gonzalez says. Centers and programs that use "Latinx" should offer intersectional courses or resources that cover, among other topics, race, ethnicity, gender, sexual orientation, and different abilities, he says.

Last year the Hispanic/Latinx Student Union at Florida State University changed its name from the Hispanic/Latino Student Union, says Adela Larramendi, a biomedical-engineering junior and director of the organization. At the time, many of the group's board members were already using the word "Latinx" unofficially in its name, she says. The organization serves the entire student body, including those who don't identify with a gender and students of Latin American descent who don't speak fluent Spanish, Larramendi says.

20   The "x" serves as a catchall. "Latinx" is easier to pronounce in English than "Latine," "Latinu," or other alternatives, she says. And dropping the masculine form, "Latino," takes a stand against machismo, or masculine pride, in Latin American culture.

There was some pushback from alumni about the change, she says, but for many members, that didn't matter. The word stuck, and Larramendi says she's starting to hear it outside the academy.

"The more we use it in official spaces," she says, "the more people will adopt it."

Thinking about the Text

1. Fernanda Zamudio-Suarez explores some of the arguments in favor of using "Latinx" rather than *Latino* or *Latina*, along with some of the objections. What are the REASONS given for each perspective? Can you tell what she thinks? If so, what is her position?

2. Zamudio-Suarez wrote this article for an audience of college faculty and administrators, and in the first paragraph she provides "practical tips about when and how to use the term" (1). Do you think she has accomplished this goal? If not, what other advice might she have given?

3. Zamudio-Suarez defines "Latinx" as a word that "refers to Latin American people or those of Latin American descent." What is gained—and what if anything is lost—by using *Latinx*?

4. LET'S TALK. "Latinx" is only one of many language issues that we need to be thinking about now, and Zamudio-Suarez notes that students often "drive these lexical shifts" (5). Talk about this or other language issues that people on your campus are discussing. Pronoun choices? Whether to capitalize "Black" or "White"? Whether to change the name of the school mascot? Your goal is to share opinions and ideas and to listen carefully with one another.

You might want to read "The Case for Capitalizing the *B* in *Black*" on letstalklibrary.com.

5. AND NOW WRITE. Zamudio-Suarez notes that the use of "'Latinx" was evolving as she wrote this article. How have its usage and acceptance changed since her 2021 column was published? Do some research on the question and write a brief REPORT detailing your findings. This is a topic that might call for field research—consider interviewing a composition or Spanish professor, or even just talking it over with friends.

MISSY WATSON

Contesting Standardized English

CONSIDER ALL THAT WE MISS when we require just one variety of a language, just one set of discourse conventions, when we stop listening or stop reading because listening or reading takes too much work. And consider which communities such exclusion benefits and which communities it hurts.

For nearly half a century, fields like applied linguistics, sociolinguistics, teaching English as a second language, second language writing, new literacy studies, composition and rhetoric, and education have revealed a wealth of research on the nature of language and literacy, discoveries that help expose just how nonsensical, fundamentally impossible, and downright unjust it is to exclude all other language varieties from public and academic discourse in order to safeguard and perpetuate standardized English. (I have intentionally used *standardized English* rather than *Standard English* throughout this article in order to indicate that there isn't actually a language we might call "Standard English" so much as there is a version of English that we actively standardize.)

All dialects are linguistically equal and capable of meeting communicative needs. Languages and dialects spoken by individuals are multiple, intermingling, and (thus) always changing. Despite our instinct to preserve, homogenize, and standardize just one variety, no single variety is *actually* superior, we don't *actually* need a single homogeneous

Missy Watson is an assistant professor of composition and rhetoric at the City University of New York, where her research focuses on composition pedagogies, translingual writing, and language ideologies. This 2018 essay was published in Academe, *the magazine of the American Association of University Professors. Watson tweets from @MissyMayWatson.*

variety of language in order to communicate effectively, and, even if we wanted to (and we shouldn't), we can't *actually* stop languages, including standardized English, from changing.

We teachers and scholars have observed that our students are already linguistically diverse. Indeed, our students bring with them an abundance of useful and sophisticated linguistic and rhetorical resources that we should be tapping into, supporting, and strengthening. However, some of us have yet to recognize that the linguistic and rhetorical repertoires of some students are indeed useful and sophisticated; these students' lack of fluency in standardized English is the measurement by which we deem them deficient instead.

Meanwhile, we know that our students' linguistic and educational 5 backgrounds continue to expand and that acquiring English as an additional language and standardized English as an additional dialect can take years or a lifetime, not semesters. It is nearly impossible for some individuals to gain native-like proficiency in another language (especially when they have learned the language after what linguists call the "critical period" in childhood). We are also acutely aware that language and identity are inextricably linked and that societal attitudes about language (especially about which languages are to be considered inferior) affect the lived experiences and material realities of language communities. We understand that errors in speech and writing are inevitable in many native and nonnative English speakers, no matter how many years of instruction and practice they've had. Many people across our nation and globe will not or cannot attain proficiency in standardized English; their choice to pursue—or not to pursue—mastery of standardized English, however, is not indicative of the inherent superiority of standardized English or the intellectual capabilities (or lack thereof) of speakers.

Research tells us that standardized English was historically (and continues to be) modeled after the speech of privileged white communities and that it remains one of many tools used to maintain social and racial hierarchies. We've learned that our preferences for standardized English, and for any language variety for that matter, are socially constructed. And we understand that standardized English undeniably harms individuals in emotional, psychological, social, and material ways.

Scholars have traced how standardized English works to exclude groups from public discourse, education, and employment opportunities. We've come to recognize that assimilation and eradication efforts have not succeeded in leveling the playing field. We're now well aware of the potentially devastating effects of demanding that so-called non-traditional students assimilate to standardized English and "standard" academic discourse, especially at the expense of their home languages, discourses, and identities. Yet, even when we respect their language differences and encourage them to preserve their full linguistic repertoires in contexts beyond our classroom walls, we, as teachers, harm students' senses of identity and community by telling them their other languages are not welcome in academic spaces.

We can no longer justify resorting to enforcing this oppressive variety (in composition courses and beyond) with claims that it's in our students' best interest for us to teach and assess only standardized English. The myth that standardized English will save students becomes especially apparent when we examine research in sociology and critical race studies that demonstrates how race, not the learning of standardized English, is the biggest factor in determining one's socio-economic status and employment opportunities. Race—not employability, not intellect, not educability—determines stratification in rates of literacy and educational achievement.

Composition and Standardized English

I certainly play my part in perpetuating standardized English and the harms that come with it. I'm doing it right now with my use of standardized English in the writing of this essay. I regularly preach to my graduate students the need to adopt more informed and more inclusive views of language and literacy, and while I have much to say about how I do infuse different approaches and dispositions into my composition classrooms, I find myself, semester after semester, struggling to combat, reimagine, and revise my implicit and explicit enforcements and endorsements of standardized English.

And of course I'm struggling. There are lots of pragmatic reasons 10 why. Historically, that's what composition classes like the ones I teach are typically centered around: teaching and assessing standardized English. And, after all, fostering mastery of standardized English has long been one of the expected outcomes of higher education at large, which systematizes standardized English's superiority in our institutional structures, presenting relentless roadblocks to those who push back. It's difficult enough to raise awareness and persuade others that a problem actually exists (which, of course, many have tried to do for nearly fifty years).

Making the situation more complicated, most students are already accustomed to the expectation that they learn standardized English, and many are comfortable with that expectation and want such instruction. Employers and everyday citizens across the globe will continue to judge and discriminate against those who do not successfully use standardized English; students know this, and we're expert at reminding them of it. And, truth be told, we enforce standardized English partly because we ourselves are steeped in and benefit from the tradition of doing so: standardized English is what we learned in school and is what we've been trained to use and teach.

Some of my fellow composition teachers have other concerns. I've heard objections such as, "I barely have time to cover the curriculum at my college, much less infuse new approaches to language diversity," or "I myself don't have time to learn about how to treat writing and language differently, and my institution doesn't support professional development," or "Taking such radical approaches in my classroom could cost me my job." These are reasonable stances, highlighting the varied costs for teachers who work against the tide. Yet they are all the more reason for all of academe to begin taking a closer look at the prospect of—and, indeed, to begin taking more responsibility for—contesting the precedence of standardized English. No single teacher or discipline should alone bear the weight of this complicated dilemma. This should be a professional concern, across disciplines and campuses.

Standard Language Ideology

Perhaps the reality that standardized English works to oppress as well as to empower is still news to some professionals in higher education. Collectively, we've certainly been far better at focusing only on the benefits of learning and using standardized English. And perhaps that is one reason why we have not yet faced this issue in solidarity.

But what of those teacher-scholars like me, who have long known the reality of standardized English and still enforce it? Why do we do it? Why do we hesitate to fight standardized English even though we have long known of the damages such enforcement can cause? Of the fact that it only exists because it is tied to, authorized by, and serves people in power? Of the ways it more often serves as a *gate* rather than a *key* to success?

15   We do it because standard language ideology is massive and feels impenetrable. Drawing on scholarship by linguists James Milroy and Rosina Lippi-Green, I have come to a working definition of *standard language ideology* as the unquestioned belief system that assigns the written language variety of a privileged group as standard (and superior) and all others nonstandard (and inferior), a worldview uncritically assumed neutral and commonsensical but used as an instrument for social stratification and maintaining the interests of privileged groups.

Standard language ideology is deeply entrenched in the perspectives of the masses in the United States. For the most part, those individuals and groups who are the most subjugated through its dominance subscribe to it just as much as the privileged white groups who most benefit from it. Until standard language ideology is combatted on a large scale across public settings and our students' future employers come to accept other varieties of language, we reason, we had better just help our students learn the language of power.

We wouldn't say such things if we were talking about racism, class-ism, sexism, ableism, homophobia, or xenophobia—that these ideolo-gies are just too big to overcome, that they're too ingrained in the worldviews of our citizens and in the structures of society, that we ought to just settle for working *with them* rather than *against them*.

We wouldn't say, at least not in modern times, that it's in the best interest of every woman, person of color, LGBTQ person, immigrant, and working-class individual to just assimilate to the ways of upper-middle-class, hetero, able-bodied white men in power.

Of course, we know that many marginalized groups have long had to work within the constraints of such norms and dominant discourses. But, no, we don't make such demands in the face of such exclusion and oppression. Instead, we fight it, in ways big and small.

Yet, most of us across the disciplines are inclined to say, without 20 pause or hesitation, that it's in our students' best interest to master standardized English. We say that diverse groups of people should either eradicate their language differences or get darn good at switch-ing them off in order to function in public settings without having to face discrimination.

The Politics of English

Why do we see language as a more acceptable basis for discrimination than characteristics such as race, class, gender, sexuality, and ability? Is it because language is considered a mere habit or practice that can be learned and reshaped rather than a part of our physiology, psychol-ogy, and identity? Are our pragmatic concerns more powerful than the harms caused by standard language ideology?

Are we too steeped in standard language ideology ourselves? As authorities on standardized English who, frankly, make our living per-petuating standard language ideologies, are we in too deep to reimag-ine our professional identities, to redefine the substance of what we do? And why are we so uncomfortable with even pondering these ques-tions? Is it simply too unbelievable, too painful to consider that our best intentions for improving the lives and opportunities available to our students by enforcing standardized English may be, in a larger scheme, part of a problem we now must face?

To be fair, in today's globalized world, where occasions for cross-cultural communication increase daily, awareness of standard language ideology has widened, and larger communities of scholars and teachers across the globe work more explicitly to address and combat it. Many have already begun chipping away at standard language ideology, and we can and will continue to do just that.

I also believe, though, that we must continue working toward more unity on this as a problem facing higher education. The full politics of English, including standard language ideology, is an issue with which all professionals in academe must contend. We must join forces in revising the purposes of higher education, redefining the role standardized English plays within it, redesigning course outcomes and curricula, reimagining pedagogy, and retraining our community of professionals across the disciplines about how to better address the linguistic diversity at all of our campuses.

25   We must also disseminate our knowledge about standard language ideology and the harms it causes as widely as we can. We must share with the public, all educators, and all students what we have come to know about the politics of standardized English. And we must further examine how standard language ideology manifests itself in individuals, classrooms, colleges and universities, and other public spaces across and beyond our communities and nation so that we'll be better equipped to combat it.

To start, we must confront our own privileging of standardized English and the judgments we ourselves make about the language differences of our students, our colleagues, our neighbors.

We have for too long remained complacent, turning a blind eye to the harms caused by the very language variety we're compelled to uphold. Let's get busy undoing that.

Thinking about the Text

1. Missy Watson argues that standard language ideology is so "deeply entrenched" in the United States that even those who are most harmed by it are as likely to subscribe to it as the people who benefit from it most (16). Why, then—and how—does she "contest" the teaching of standardized English?

2. Watson provides many REASONS for contesting standardized English, even as she acknowledges the reasons that it continues to be taught. What are those reasons, and exactly what does she say teachers need to do in response to this complicated situation?

3. Missy Watson and June Jordan are both highly critical of standardized English. But what differences do you find in comparing their essays? Consider their PURPOSES for writing and how they address their AUDIENCES. How do you each establish their authority to write on this topic? Which of the two essays do you find most persuasive, and why? (June Jordan's essay is on p. 647.)

4. LET'S TALK. Throughout your schooling, you've likely been told that standardized English is "proper" English, which is required for your academic work and necessary for your future success. So what do you think about Watson's ARGUMENT? Do you agree with what she says? Disagree? Both agree and disagree? Talk this over with a few classmates. Remember that the point is to explore and exchange ideas: listen with an open mind and the goal of understanding what others think—and why.

5. AND NOW WRITE. How might your writing be different if you didn't have to be concerned about following the norms and conventions of standardized English? Would you be able to express yourself more clearly if you could write more like you speak? Try it: REVISE something you've written for a class using language that more closely resembles your usual way of talking or thinking. Then compare the original and the revision: Which version do you think is more effective, and for which AUDIENCES and CONTEXTS?

JASMINE LANE

Do We Have to Teach Standard English in the Classroom?

"Ain't nobody got time for dat!"   **"Hide yo kids, hide yo wife . . ."**   **"It went from worse to worser!"**

KIMBERLY WILKINS, April Williams, and Antoine Dodson. You probably don't know their names, but have likely laughed at their expense. [They're the authors of the three memes pictured above.*] The stories behind the memes are important, but instead of [telling] those stories, [I want to focus on how] *the value* of what they said was negated because they [said it in] a dialect other than Standard American English (SAE).

Standard American English. Dominant American English. "Proper" English.

These terms have become synonymous with what we called "talking white" where I grew up; talking white meant that you were trying to be something that you weren't. As a poor, Black girl from the north side of Minneapolis with two working-class parents and one who didn't

---

*From left to right, the first meme originated from a TV interview with Kimberly Wilkins, an actor who had just escaped from a fire in her apartment in Oklahoma City; the second one originated from a TV interview with Antoine Dodson about a break-in in his sister's apartment in Huntsville, Alabama; and the third one originated from a TV interview about bus service in Baton Rouge, Louisiana [*editor's note*].

Jasmine Lane *is a high school English teacher in Minneapolis who also writes for* Education Week. *This essay was posted in 2020 on* Forever Free, *a blog by and for educators and parents. Lane blogs at* jasmine teaches.wordpress.com *and tweets from @MsJasmineMN.*

finish the 9th grade (all while having this far-fetched dream of college), I guess they had a point. I didn't view myself as trying to be something that I wasn't; I was just trying to be something more than I was. I saw my language as something that could either hold me back or be used to my advancement.

This brings me to the point we debated in my graduate class a few years ago, and that was reprised when an academic said that those who teach Standard American English are "policing" their students: Is African-American Vernacular English (AAVE) a valid language? That all depends on how you define valid. It has rules, so linguistically speaking, yes it is. Is it valid such that I can feel comfortable speaking AAVE and not worry about having my intelligence dissected? Absolutely not. The truth is that when you come from where I do, whether it be for an interview with a potential employer or in the courtroom, there are so many barriers to cross for our advancement—and language is a big one.

About two years ago, the BBC wrote about a study that showed it 5 takes just thirty milliseconds of hearing someone speak before forming thoughts about their background. It's not a secret that the southern accent is perceived to be dumber than the northern one, just like it's not a secret that AAVE (often called ebonics) is perceived to be inferior to SAE. In the classroom, validating AAVE as a dialect of English is one very important concept for self-realization, but telling your Black students (or those who speak another dialect) that conventions of standard English don't matter is a misguided, dangerous, and patronizing attempt at cultural relevancy. There is a standard for "professional" English no matter how we try to spin it. If my students can read and write proficiently in academic language, then I have done a small part in making sure that they can have access to a future beyond what society tells them they can achieve. In this way, I subvert the dominant narrative of Standard American English being a marker of intelligence through a critical pedagogy.

If you're not a person of color, you have probably never had to really internally grapple with what it means to speak a non-standard dialect of English because the way you speak at home is more than likely the same as those in positions of power. Just like you can discount the importance of standardized tests because you've never had to worry about passing them, you can also purport, in essence, that "all language matters" because the reality is that speaking another dialect of English will never directly impact your future.

This is why I focus on the quality of my instruction and ensure that what and how I teach my students will give them access to spaces where there aren't many people that look like us; I can provide them with an education that allows them to change the narrative. I can't achieve this if I ignore the conventions of written English. I can't push along a 9th grade student who reads at a 3rd grade level by giving them a graphic novel, thereby allowing them to interpret images instead of grappling with a written text. When young Black girls are being strip-searched for laughing and Black boys are being forced to cut their hair because it violates a dress code, I have to give them a chance in a world that gives them no chances. And right now, what the majority of schools are giving them—that ain't it.

Lane seeks common ground with those who criticize standard English, and her argument is stronger for it. Learn more about this technique on pp. 37–40.

To be clear, I'm not advocating that "proper English" not be seen as a social construct. I'm advocating that we really dissect what we think it takes (and what we know it actually takes) to break through barriers for Black students and other students of color. When someone tells me it's unfortunate that I grew up in North Minneapolis, or they laugh at me when I let my guard down and say "finna," every day I am faced with the reality of what is expected from people that look like me. I refuse to discount the impact that my command of standard English had on my success, and I won't discount it for my students, either.

Thinking about the Text

1. Jasmine Lane highlights two words in her first paragraph, saying that *"the value"* of what the three memes said "negated" because they said it "in a dialect other than Standard American English." Elsewhere in the essay she uses the words *valid* and *validating*. How does she DEFINE *valid*, and how does her definition contribute to her ARGUMENT? In a sentence or two, what is her argument?

2. Pay attention to Lane's use of the pronouns *you* and *your*, and *we* and *us*. Who is she referring to with those pronouns, and what do they tell us about who her intended AUDIENCE is in each case?

3. Not everyone agrees with Lane's views on teaching standard English. Where in her essay does she address PERSPECTIVES other than her own? Do you think she represents those views accurately and respectfully? And how well does she answer objections that others might have to her views?

4. LET'S TALK. Speaking from her own experience as a "poor Black girl," Lane says that she saw her language "as something that could either hold me back or be used to my advancement" (3). What would Missy Watson say to that? At first glance, they appear to be taking two completely different positions, with Watson arguing for contesting standard English and Lane arguing for teaching it. But is that really the case? Work with a few classmates to look for ways that the two authors might agree. Where might they find COMMON GROUND? Where do they diverge? Do they share the same ultimate goals? (Missy Watson's essay is on p. 614.)

5. AND NOW WRITE. In her brief essay, Lane deftly conveys many nuances of a complicated situation. Write a SUMMARY/ RESPONSE essay of her arguments. For your response, you may wish to focus on what the text says or on the way it is written.

BETH NGUYEN

America Ruined My Name for Me

PEOPLE HAVE ALWAYS TOLD ME not to change my name. Some insisted that they liked it: Bich, a Vietnamese name, given to me in Saigon, where I was born and where the name is quite ordinary. When my family named me, they didn't know that we would become refugees eight months later and that I would grow up in Michigan in the nineteen-eighties, in the conservative, mostly white, west side of the state, where girls had names like Jennifer, Amy, and Stacy. A name like Bich (pronounced "Bic") didn't just make me stand out—it made me miserably visible. "Your name is what?" people would ask. "How do you spell that?" Sometimes they would laugh in my face. "You know what your name looks like, right? Did your parents really name you that?"

I have always envied Asian kids whose parents let them change their names or have separate "American" names. Phuoc at home could be Phil at school. But my parents refused to let me change my name. They said that I should be proud of who I was, and they weren't wrong, but they were so angry about it that I knew I should keep my worries to myself. I didn't want to reject my family's Vietnamese culture, replacing it with all that TV commercials promised. And so I stuck with Bich, or let it stick with me.

My earliest memories of school include the tension of roll call, when I would try to volunteer my name to stop the teacher from attempting a pronunciation. The kindest teachers were the ones who asked me directly how to say my name—in classes of almost all white kids, it wasn't difficult to figure out who would be named Bich. I was a shy

---

*Beth (**Bich Minh**) **Nguyen** is the author of the memoir* Stealing Buddha's Dinner *and two novels; she teaches creative writing at the University of Wisconsin. Her work has also appeared in* Time, Paris Review, *and other magazines. This 2021 narrative is from the* New Yorker. *Nguyen posts on* Twitter *and* Instagram *from @bichminhnguyen.*

child who then became shyer; I avoided meeting people so I could avoid saying my name. And I took on the shame of not being strong enough to handle the shame of the American gaze.

Names are deeply personal and deeply public. We have to see our names all the time. Every form, every post, every e-mail. "Your name here" at the top of every assignment in elementary school. The other kids would decorate their names with stars and hearts; they would try to make their names look bigger than everyone else's. The sight of their names gave them pleasure and satisfaction. I have never felt this pleasure, not once. Not even with publications. To me, my name has been a taunt. I'm always trying not to look at it.

The word *bich* means a kind of jade. Growing up, I knew that Vietnamese girls were supposed to wear jade bracelets and grow into them so that one day the bracelets would be permanent. The stone is meant to protect, to heal—and the greener the jade, the better. In a different country, in a different life, my given name would be just as beautiful. In truth, I could never wear a bracelet very long. In truth, most of the people who have claimed to like the name Bich, or who have been outraged and horrified at the idea of changing it, have been white women. They are the ones who told me the name was cool, was interesting, was unique, was being true to myself, was an important part of my heritage and cultural identity. They said that they liked the name, that it would break their hearts if I changed it. They did not say that they wished to have the name themselves. I wanted to believe them; for a long time, I made a choice to believe them. But I knew, too, that they liked the exotic so long as they didn't have to deal with its complications. They liked the idea of the exotic, not thinking about how *exotic* might benefit the person deciding what exotic is. Sometimes I wondered whether they also liked feeling bad for me.

I've tried to inhabit the name Bich. I used to add the accent over the "i" to show the correct spelling: Bích. The sound is somewhere between a question and an exclamation. But how can I get away from the gaze? It is one of my historical facts that the name is steeped in shame, because living in the United States as a refugee and a child of refugees was steeped in shame. America made sure I knew that,

"Deeply personal and deeply public." With those 5 words, Nguyen lets us know why her story matters. Check out pp. 195–97 for tips on telling why *your* story matters.

5

felt that, from my earliest moments of awareness. I cannot detach the name Bich from my childhood, cannot detach it from the experience of people laughing at me, calling me a bitch, letting me know that I'm the punch line of my own joke, too stupid or afraid to do anything but take it. When I see the letters that spell out Bich, I see a version of self I've had to create, to hide from trauma. Even now, typing the letters, I want to turn away. America has ruined the name Bich for me, and I have let it.

I CAN'T WRITE about my name without writing about racism, and I can't write about racism without writing about violence. I remember being a kid and hearing my dad and uncles whispering about the murder of Vincent Chin, in Detroit, in 1982. Today, I talk to my kids about the murder of six Asian women in Atlanta. I'm teaching them about colonization, Orientalism, and anti-Asian immigration laws. About what happens when Asians and Asian-Americans are made invisible except as targets of derision or as ideals of behavior—as ways to create fear, enforce compliance, and shore up racism against Black, Latinx, and indigenous people. Of course, my children worry. We've all been worried for years. These days, we are extra careful when we leave the house.

Yet, all my life, America has told me that I'm overreacting. That it is still O.K. to laugh at Asian names, still O.K. to make fun of Asian people—those weird foreigners who all look the same and have those hilarious, ugly accents. I know that it's still O.K. because it keeps happening, in media and in real life. And, when it does, and Asian people express anger about it, they are countered with "you're too sensitive; it's just a joke." I get it—the joke is more important than our existence.

My first book was published under my given name because it was a memoir and I thought one had to do that, to publish a true thing with one's given name. (I didn't have another name idea at that point, anyway.) I was then told that one should not change their name after publishing. Sure, T. C. Boyle, who used to publish as T. Coraghessan Boyle, could get away with that, but someone such as myself could not. Once, at a literary party, I overheard another writer laughing at my name. She didn't know that I was standing right there, listening, as she said to someone else, "Can you believe anyone would have a name like that?" I wonder whether she remembers that moment that I cannot forget, and have kept to myself for years. When my second book was published, it was reviewed in the *Times* along with a couple of other books under the subheading "International." My book was not international. It was a novel set in the American Midwest, released by a big American publisher. The most international-seeming thing about the book was the author's name: Bich Minh Nguyen.

Nguyen, because it's the most common Vietnamese surname, has 10 gone from suspiciously foreign and unpronounceable to acceptably different and only somewhat unpronounceable in America. Bich is still waiting for this turn. Is changing it now strategic, safe, self-care, selling out? I've been trying to figure this out, trying to write this down, for years. What I know is that being Bich, and growing up as Bich in a mostly white town in the eighties, has felt like a test that I was constantly failing. It was a double bind: the people who made me uncomfortable with my given name also thought that I'd be betraying my heritage by changing it. What I have always wanted is impossible: to be nameless, free from the gaze.

I HAD ALWAYS given fake names at restaurants, often going with Rose, Sophia, or Beatrice. One day, a few years ago, at the Shake Shack in Madison Square Park, a woman behind the counter took my order and asked the dreaded question of my name, and I said, "Beth." She nodded. She did not doubt my answer. And, in that moment, it felt real: I wasn't just saying Beth—I *was* Beth. So I started to say it more. To salespeople. To babysitters, electricians, new acquaintances, new colleagues. I'd say Beth, and a tiny blast of joy, like cool air from the refrigerator on a hot day, would come over me. Like a secret self. Like another life.

Beth is a social experiment, a hypothesis that life in America is easier with a name that no one ever gets wrong. And it's true. I am seen as less Asian and more American with the name Beth. Experiencing that difference, glimpsing a bit of that yellow peril, has been insightful and painful. As Bich, I am a foreigner who makes people uncomfortable. As Beth, I am never complimented on my English.

My closest friends accepted this name automatically. Others expressed surprise and disapproval. Some informed me that they will continue to call me by my given name, no matter what. I sort of understand this. But, if you refuse to accept someone's chosen name, aren't you refusing to accept who they are or what they have decided for themselves? I am not Beth to make life easier for everyone else; I am Beth to make life easier for me.

Still, because I haven't gone to the trouble of legally changing my name, I remain Bich on all my documents. Once, at a store with one of my kids, I had to show my driver's license. The woman behind the counter started laughing. "Is that really your name?" she asked. I think that a former self would have gone along with the laughter to avoid discomfort. I am so used to apologizing, saying, "Yeah, it is a difficult name." But my child was with me, so I stared back at the woman until she was the one who was uncomfortable. As we left, my kid said to me, "That lady was making fun of your name. That was mean." It was the first time, I think, he had experienced this. He and his brother have simple, straightforward names that, in America, no one ever questions.

15   Lately, they have been learning about ancient languages. They are trying to understand how words and sounds evolve. How, sometimes, a word—for example, *cleave*—becomes its own opposite, both definitions retaining meaning. I think that they are trying to understand the loss of a language as it turns into something else: Is it always a loss? Or does it always feel that way? Did people know that their language was changing from ancient to modern? I tell them that sometimes the shifts are so slow that they're recognized only a tiny bit at a time. That language changes all around us, and we are part of that. Like slang, like idioms, new words, new pronunciations. Words don't shift on their own. We must do the shifting. Sometimes we, too, are our own opposites.

Right now, Beth is where I have shifted. It is comfortable because it's neutral, unremarkable. It doesn't change my past, my family, our lives as refugees in the United States. It may not be forever. It just feels like a bit of space, where I can direct how I am seen rather than be directed. I realize that, my whole life, I have been waiting for some kind of permission—my own permission—to be this person.

Thinking about the Text

1. This piece is a NARRATIVE, a story about Nguyen's name, but it's a story that makes a point. What is that point? Refer to sentences in the text where she makes that clear.

2. Beth Nguyen refers to the English word *cleave* as an example of how words evolve, noting that it's a word with two meanings that are exact opposites (15). What are the meanings of *cleave*, and why does she mention it? And why do you think she does not define it?

3. What do you think Nguyen's PURPOSE was for writing this piece, and who is the AUDIENCE that will likely read it? How would you characterize her TONE, and how does that tone suit her purpose and audience?

4. LET'S TALK. How do you feel about *your* name—your given name or your last name? To what extent has your name affected your identity? Have your feelings about your name been affected by the way others react to it—and if so, how? Would you choose a new name if you could—and then, what name would you like, and why? Discuss these questions with a few classmates.

5. AND NOW WRITE. What is the story behind your name? Are you named for an elder relative or an ancestor, or perhaps a historic or mythic figure who meant something to those who named you? Does your name represent something that was happening on the day you were born? Is it relatively common? Uncommon? Downright unusual? You may not be able to learn how or why your name was chosen, but you've had a lifetime of experience with it. Write a NARRATIVE about your name and how it has (or has not) shaped who you are.

ADAM BRADLEY

Dismantling the Barriers between Rap and Poetry

THE ATLANTA-BASED RAPPER Mulatto collects scraps of language on her iPhone, words and phrases that come to her suddenly, or that she's picked up while performing online during the pandemic. Not surprisingly, one of the words that has come to mind during the past year is "pandemic"; the 22-year-old M.C. has used it twice on record so far: once last summer during a cipher—a competitive and collaborative freestyle session with other rappers—when the hip-hop magazine XXL named Latto (as she's known) to its 2020 "freshman class" of breakout stars; and again on the opening track from her major-label debut, "Queen of Da Souf," released last year.

"I just dropped a hundred on jewelry during a pandemic," she raps, give or take a word. It's standard-issue braggadocio, in praise of her newfound wealth. But boasting about spending $100,000 on a diamond-encrusted chain and watch amid a global health crisis also rates as particularly brazen, even in a musical genre that often centers the self and celebrates conspicuous consumption. Latto is aware of this. A few bars later, in her cipher verse, she adds: "I donated, too, so don't mock me!"

Listen to Latto perform and you understand what she heard in that word. On the XXL freestyle, she raps "pandemic" fluidly over a

Adam Bradley is a professor of English and director of the Lab for Race and Popular Culture at the University of California, Los Angeles. His books include the Book of Rhymes: The Poetics of Hip Hop (2009), The Poetry of Pop (2017), *and* Someday It'll All Make Sense, *a memoir about rapper Common (2012). This article was published in* T, *the style magazine of the* New York Times, *in 2021. Bradley tweets from* @adamfbradley.

lazy instrumental, so the word sounds like urgent speech. On "Youngest N Richest," she raps it more deliberately atop a frenetic track fretted with a tense violin sample. "Pandemic" becomes "PAN-demic," the stress displaced from its natural position. In reaccenting the word, Latto charges it with her Southern drawl. She puts Atlanta on it. She also does the very thing that makes rappers poets: She works the language. "Rap is definitely poetry," Latto tells me. "We just do it on top of a beat."

Many poets would agree with her. Nonetheless, a line of demarcation persists between rap and poetry, born of outmoded assumptions about both forms: that poetry only exists on the page and rap only lives in the music, that poetry is refined and rap is raw, that poetry is art and rap is entertainment. These opinions are rife with bias—against the young, the poor, the Black and brown, the self-educated, the outspoken and sometimes impolite voices that, across five decades, have carried a local tradition from the South Bronx to nearly every part of the world.

Yet today, a new generation of artists, both rappers and poets, 5 are consciously forging closer kinship between the genres. They draw

Latto, at the BET Awards, 2021.

from a common toolbox of language, use the same social media platforms to reach their audiences and respond to the same economic and political provocations to create public art. In doing so, rappers and the poets who claim affinity with them are resuscitating a body of literary practices mostly neglected in poetry during the 20th century. These ghost appendages of form—repetition, patterned rhythm and, above all, rhyme—thrive in song, especially in rap.

But the story of rap and poetry's reunion is as much about people as it is about language. Many of the artists in both realms who have come to prominence between 2010 and 2020 were raised during hip-hop's golden age, from the mid-1980s to the early 1990s. The poets Reginald Dwayne Betts and Kyle Dargan were born in 1980, the same year as T.I. and Gucci Mane. The poet Saeed Jones and the rapper J. Cole were both born in 1985. The best-selling poet alive, Rupi Kaur, born in 1992, is the same age as Cardi B. By the time they all reached elementary school, and well before they published a single line, hip-hop had gifted them a rich cultural inheritance. Earlier generations of rappers had won major battles for artistic legitimacy, established—though certainly not maximized—rap's profitability and produced a catalog of music and lyrics that a new generation could revere and revile, remix and reject.

Through its first four decades, rap was defined by bravura performances that embraced the qualities print-based poetry neglected, whether it was Gift of Gab's artful exercise in alliteration on Black-alicious's "Alphabet Aerobics" (1999) or Nicki Minaj's shape-shifting voice in her breakout verse on Kanye West's "Monster" (2010). The last decade, however, has challenged and changed rap's aesthetics: Flows—the rhythmic patterns of vocal performance—have grown more melodic and more repetitive. Rap, at least in the mainstream, has become less narrative and less complex in its rhyme structures and metaphors than it was in the time of Eric B. & Rakim's "Paid in Full" (1987), Lauryn Hill's "The Miseducation of Lauryn Hill" (1998) or Jay-Z's "The Black Album" (2003).

Bradley's audience includes avid rap experts and also people who know zero. Your audiences may be less challenging, but see pp. 25–26 for tips on how to reach them.

A facile interpretation would be to mistake rap's recent turn as a decline in craft; really, though, it demonstrates an inclination on the part of artists—and their audiences—to rethink what poetic and musical qualities most resonate in tumultuous times. Pop Smoke, the 20-year-old Brooklyn rapper who was killed during a Los Angeles home invasion early last year, had a baritone that charged even unremarkable words with haunting power. On his 2019 hit "Dior," he seeks out open-ended vowel sounds, like the long "o" in the title word, stressing the syllable to showcase the low rumble of his voice. When the 25-year-old North Philadelphia rapper Tierra Whack uses the same word on her 2020 song "Dora," she playfully clusters around it a verse's worth of end rhymes: "door," "more," "Porsche," "of course," "horse," "floor," "adore." Then there's the 28-year-old New York rapper Young M.A, who in 2019's "PettyWap" plays on the percussive possibilities of the word in a line that hits like a drum fill, the pounding bass drum of strong-stress syllables and the hissing high-hat of alliteration on the "s" sounds: "DI-or my col-OGNE, she said my SCENT is her OBSESS-ion." What draws these artists to Dior is not simply the luxury associated with the brand but the texture of the word on the tongue. In contemporary rap, sound often leads sense, defining rhythm, rhyme and voice all at once.

MEANWHILE, A PARALLEL evolution is underway in poetry, spurring a renaissance of sorts. In 2012, according to the National Endowment for the Arts' Survey of Public Participation in the Arts, only 6.7 percent of adults reported having read poetry in the last year. By 2017, the number had nearly doubled, with the largest increase (from 8.2 to 17.5 percent) occurring among 18- to 24-year-olds.

Several factors have contributed to poetry's resurgence: the influ- 10 ence of *Twitter*, *Instagram* and *TikTok* as performance and promotion platforms; the proliferation of small presses and online journals publishing increasingly varied work; the pull of poetic language, as both balm and bludgeon, during periods of national struggle. Poetry's growing readership is no doubt also tied to its expanding authorship, as a diverse array of voices are now choosing to express themselves in patterned words. "Access is all you need," the poet Morgan Parker says. "People just don't know that they like poetry."

Parker's revelation came when she discovered that poetry didn't only have to sound like Robert Frost; it could speak in words and tones familiar to her, a Black woman born in Southern California in 1987. Writing in 1944, one of Frost's contemporaries, William Carlos Williams, defined a poem as "a small (or large) machine made of words," by which he meant to emphasize the precision of form over the profundity of meaning. "Prose may carry a load of ill-defined matter like a ship," he continues. "But poetry is the machine which drives it, pruned to a perfect economy." Economy of language remains one of poetry's hallmarks. By contrast, language in rap is usually abundant, functioning on the rhetorical principle of copia, which Erasmus defined in 1512 as a practice of amplifying expression through variation, adornment and play. It's no wonder that rap inspires writers like Parker to think more expansively about what their own work could be. A poem is "no longer just a nice thing to say at a wedding," she says. "We've reached cultural acceptance of a broader definition."

Still, at their most basic levels, poetry and rap are both structured on repetition and difference. Repetition functions by accretion—building up a sound or an idea until it reaches critical mass—and transformation, keeping some parts and changing others. Repetition has an indelible place in Black expressive culture: in the syncopated rhythms of jazz, the phrasal repetitions of the blues and the guttural moans of soul made meaningful by dint of remarkable vocal performances. "Repetition shapes Blackness in a lot of ways," Parker says. "For me it becomes, 'What am I going to repeat? What is not being heard the first time or the second time or the third time?'" Her most recent poetry collection, "Magical Negro" (2019), includes a poem called "'Now More Than Ever'" that opens with a 44-line near-clinical account of white guilt and the burden it imposes on Black people. In the middle of the 44th line, the language catches, like a record stuck in the groove, and the remaining 31 lines repeat "and ever" across the page, uninter-rupted save for two bracketed ellipses and a closing parenthetical, "(cont.)"—an innocuous abbreviation made metaphor for unrelent-ing Black suffering.

Another 1987 baby, Compton's Kendrick Lamar, is similarly drawn to repetition. On "FEAR.," from Lamar's fourth studio album, "DAMN." (2017), he upends assumptions about what rap virtuosity should sound like. Rather than displaying his vaunted vocabulary, he constricts his lan-guage, repeating words and shading them with new meanings through a technique called incremental repetition, a term first used to describe the practice in medieval ballads of incorporating the same phrase through shifting contexts. "Repetition foregrounds emotion without having to go out and express that emotion explicitly," says Dargan, a Washington, D.C.–based poet. Lamar puts that principle into action: On the second verse of "FEAR.," "I'll probably die"—or some slight variation of those words—starts all but two lines. With all that repe-tition at the beginning of lines, it's easy to overlook what's missing from the end: rhyme. In an art form in which end rhyme is the rule, finding a way to deliver your verse without your listeners' missing the rhyme might be the greatest poetic flex of all.

Kendrick Lamar, winner of the 2018 Pulitzer Prize in Music.

IN FINDING THEIR own words, many poets have likewise turned to hip-hop. The 31-year-old poet Nate Marshall, a prodigy of the youth slam scene of early 2000s Chicago, fell in love with language through performance, spitting rap verses in ciphers with friends and reciting spoken-word poetry onstage at competitions. Though slams emerged in the 1980s in Chicago and spread across the world through the 1990s and early 2000s, spoken word has existed in different forms for millenniums across all continents; simply put, it's poetry that even when written is intended to be performed. In his younger years, Marshall thought of his writing as little more than a script. Now the author of multiple books, he carries that declamatory approach to print: "As a poet, you want to think of your page as a place to perform. . . . I try to do something on the page so that if you can't see me, you'll still know how to approach my poetry."

15   The key strategy that Marshall borrows from hip-hop is the sample. Sampling, the practice of taking an existing recording and repurposing it, is foundational to rap's soundscape. You can hear it on Megan Thee Stallion's "Go Crazy," a track from her debut studio album, "Good News" (2020), that samples Naughty by Nature's "O.P.P." (1991), which itself samples the Jackson 5's "ABC" (1970). Sampling also informs her lyrics, as when she channels N.W.A's Eazy-E on "Girls in the Hood," borrowing elements of his delivery. In literary terms, sampling is akin to allusion—a brief, indirect reference. Sampling, however, is also born of the Black vernacular tradition that gave us chitterlings, jazz and, yes, hip-hop. The writer Ralph Ellison once described the vernacular not simply as a spoken dialect but as a "dynamic *process* in which the most refined styles from the past are continually merged with the play-it-by-eye-and-by-ear improvisations which we invent in our efforts to control our environment and entertain ourselves." Hip-hop has historically taken that which is given, discarded or even foisted upon it and turned it into something entertaining, even liberating.

For both poets and rappers, sampling can become a political act. Betts, who is 40 and lives in New Haven, Conn., used sampling as the organizing principle of his collection "Bastards of the Reagan Era" (2015). Contained within his measured lines are allusions to Homer and Public Enemy, Nas and Paul Laurence Dunbar. "I got all of these influences that are in here," he says. "'Cause hip-hop, it's like, 'Let me flex and show you how I can do this thing.'" The book received plenty of praise, but many critics missed the point, describing Betts's work as raw and gritty, when the title poem is entirely in blank verse—unrhymed iambic pentameter. "That's Shakespeare! If you didn't hear that, then I know all that you were able to see," Betts says. Hip-hop gives him license to engage in audacious amalgamations of poetic forms and traditions. "It's vigorous in that way," he says. "I get that from hip-hop."

Hip-hop is often subject to this same mismeasure: that it is artless, unmediated expression; that its first-person voice speaks for rappers alone, never other personas; that anyone can do it. But just try rapping to a beat. It requires the orchestration of lungs and vocal folds, teeth and tongue—not to mention rhythm and invention. Neuroscientific fMRIs tell us what hip-hop artists already know: "Spontaneous improvisation is a complex cognitive process that shares features with what has been characterized as a 'flow' state," researchers reported in the open-access journal *Scientific Reports* in 2012, offering a provisional understanding of the zone rappers enter when performing. Perhaps that's what it really means to flow.

"You listen to the flow first, and then you catch the lyrics," Latto says. She often starts writing by mumbling sounds, which she'll record on her phone, capturing the cadence in nonsense syllables. Later, she'll go back and fit words to the beats, but she starts with rhythm because she knows that her audience will, too. "After they get over the flow and actually listen to what I'm saying, they're like, 'Oh, wow!'" That kind of flow comes through in poets' pages as well. In "slave grammar," from Marshall's most recent collection, "Finna" (2020), he approximates the rhythms of rap, voicing in print the swagger that makes certain verses memorable: "whole time i'm bending the language / like a bow every arrow is spinning itself / a new sharp tip. whole time /

i'm writing this down its obsoleting / itself. whole time we talking we ain't got / no dictionary we guessing the spelling / we deciphering the phrases through / our slurs we slurring like we ain't sure until / we murmur a sure vow." With simile and sonic devices like assonance (the nonrhyming echo of a vowel sound), Marshall compels us to flow, whether we want to or not.

Rappers have an obvious advantage over page-born poets when it comes to rhythm. But poets can shape rhythm, too, through patterns of stress, as well as through their lines on the page. Poets differ from writers of prose in that they, not the typographer, choose where their lines should end, thus giving them the ability to play with a reader's sense of time. Enjambment, when a syntactic unit overflows from one line to the next, is a bedrock poetic practice, one that endows poets with the capacity to make and remake meaning. In "Highest," from his forthcoming collection "Somebody Else Sold the World," the 49-year-old Indianapolis-based poet Adrian Matejka riffs on Travis Scott's 2019 hit "Highest in the Room," but where Scott's lines are almost entirely end-stopped—that is, resolving in a completed phrase—Matejka's are

Travis Scott (left) at Coachella 2018; Adrian Matejka (right), whose poetry riffs on some of Scott's music.

mostly enjambed. Sometimes the effect is syncopation: "That's / Machu Picchu high." Other times, it suspends then reanimates an image with simile: "I raise up / like the highest Black hand in history class." Still other times, it allows Matejka to unfurl a complex idea across several lines: "I am risen like the blood pressure of anybody / Black mimeographed in the textbook / of this monochromatic year." In bearing witness to a year of pandemic and racist violence, Matejka's line breaks deny any effort to skim past the pain.

Moments like these reveal the reciprocity between rap and poetry, small matters of form with large impacts on meaning. "For me, it's sound," the 45-year-old Los Angeles poet Khadijah Queen says of her work's connection to hip-hop, though her poetry also makes use of silence. In her most recent collection, "Anodyne" (2020), she uses the entire page, writing not just with words but with the blank space around them. Her lines dance, yes, but they also stumble, pick themselves back up, stop and start in ways that call to mind an inventive M.C. riding a dozen different beats in succession.

Queen also understands her role and that of her fellow poets and rappers as necessarily engaged in civic work. She looks to Frances Ellen Watkins Harper, perhaps the most prominent Black woman writer of the 19th century, who used her platform to advocate for the abolition of slavery and the rights of women and children. "Our role is to capture what folks are feeling in this time of contradiction: the difficulty and the beauty together. We are called to acknowledge what is happening with clarity," Queen says. In the aftermath of the killings of Breonna Taylor, George Floyd and many others, rappers were likewise moved to speak out in song. Atlanta's Lil Baby, 26 and one of the most successful rising artists, released "The Bigger Picture" in June, in which he earnestly grapples with police brutality: "It ain't makin' sense; I'm just here to vent." Over the last year, several other songs gave voice to Americans' anger and pain: Terrace Martin's "Pig Feet," featuring Denzel Curry, Daylyt, G Perico and Kamasi Washington; Noname's "Song 33"; Meek Mill's "Otherside of America"; H.E.R.'s

20

"I Can't Breathe"; Anderson .Paak's "Lockdown." For Queen and other Black poets, hip-hop is not only beats and rhymes but something more needful. Hearing Black voices speaking on their own terms creates a refuge, particularly at a time when Blackness and Black people are under siege. "I love hip-hop because it foregrounds the use of Black speech as the default," she says. "It's a space to be who you are, unapologetically."

THE CITY GIRLS don't apologize to anybody. Childhood friends from different areas of Miami-Dade County—Yung Miami, 27, is from Opa-locka and JT, 28, is from Liberty City—they grew up with defiant hometown pride. "The Miami sound is our slang. The way I talk is the way I rap," JT says. One of their biggest hits, "Pussy Talk" (2020), featuring the fellow newcomer Doja Cat, 25, is about just what you'd expect from its title. They use the term with joyous abandon, utter-ing it 73 times in just over three-and-a-half minutes. The song might sound like an act of reclamation—taking back a word weaponized by

JT of the City Girls, 2021.

men. But mostly it's a mood, JT says: "The sounds, the fast beats, the movement, the raunchy lyrics, being real outspoken, just saying whatever we feel."

When the infamous "Access Hollywood" tape leaked just weeks before the 2016 presidential election, Donald Trump and his supporters rushed to characterize his words as "locker room banter." Claiming that slang for a part of the female anatomy belonged to an all-male space was baffling. Still, his offhand utterance projected the word into common parlance. "Donald Trump really did blow up 'pussy' in the public consciousness of the United States," says Anne H. Charity Hudley, a leading scholar of Black linguistic traditions at the University of California, Santa Barbara. Though the word has been around for generations, it had resided primarily in the intimate vocabulary of private life. Newly public, is it any wonder we now find the word topping the Billboard charts?

Charity Hudley sees shifting attitudes when it comes to profanity—not so much a coarsening of the culture as a liberalization of language. "Bad words are not going to be seen as that bad anymore. We're not in that time culturally," she says. That doesn't mean that anything goes or that words will no longer carry within them the capacity to do harm; rather, it will come down to context.

Context, in fact, explains how profanity can play such an important 25 role in the output of both rappers and the poets whom they inspire. In the poem "my mom's favorite rapper was Too Short," (2020), Marshall explores the role that explicit language served for his own emerging literary sensibility: "how / can i unlearn some of the curses / that were the first / spells i saw conjured?" In his mother's rapturous recitation of Too Short's "CussWords" (1988), Marshall learned the expressive and emotive range that profane speech can have when put to poetic work. Parker is also attuned to the impact explicit language can make, both on the page and in a song. "I love Black female sexuality being in people's faces in a lot of different ways," she says. "I get frustrated when it's just one way." She recalls as a young girl hearing the rapper Shawnna chanting the sexually explicit hook to Ludacris's 2000 breakthrough single "What's Your Fantasy": "There's something powerful about hearing a female voice being ratchet on the radio."

Ratchet and refined, puerile and profound, it's no coincidence that women's voices are the ones largely redefining rap and poetry these days. "It's deeper than just rapping explicit lyrics," Latto says. "It's empowering women. A woman doesn't have to be submissive or be polite." Last summer, she appeared in the video for the most controversial song of the year, Cardi B and Megan Thee Stallion's "WAP," whose acronym belies the lyrics' exuberant raunchiness. When *Billboard* magazine interviewed Cardi for its December 2020 Woman of the Year issue, she was characteristically candid. "I like justice. I like to work and be creative," she explained. "But I also like popping my pussy."

This choice to be explicit is particularly significant for Black women, who are regularly silenced in both private and public spaces. "Black women are taught to be quiet all the time," Parker adds. "If we're loud, we're playing ourselves and don't have to be listened to. [These artists are] undercutting so many different mores."...

THE BEAUTY of rap, like that of poetry, is in its invitation to expression. Rap's proximity to speech has always been its most democratizing element. Along with the fact that making it didn't require access to expensive instruments or conservatory training, it meant that rap could travel to places that other music could never reach—a favela in Brazil, an encampment in the West Bank, a rec room in the South Bronx. Someone once said that hip-hop requires nothing more than two turntables and a microphone, but it needs far less than that: a mind to rhyme and rhythm of any kind, from knuckles knocking on a lunchroom tabletop to the inaudible kick and snare playing inside the head of an artist as she performs a cappella....

Taken together, rap and poetry provide the means to do exactly what the events of this past year have proven we need most: to amplify the voices of people who've gone unheard—and perhaps, one day, to bring us together under a common groove.

Thinking about the Text

1. Adam Bradley declares that "a new generation of artists, both rappers and poets, are consciously forging closer kinship" (5) and then provides a detailed ANALYSIS to demonstrate that both art forms use similar literary devices. What EVIDENCE does he present to support this claim? Note two of the examples he gives, one from rap and one from poetry.

2. What does Bradley do to make his discussion accessible to an AUDIENCE that includes some people who are familiar with the many references to poetry and rap and others who are not? Did you feel you were included in Bradley's audience—and why or why not? Were you able to understand and appreciate his explanations, and what helped (or did not help) you do so?

3. Bradley concludes by saying, "Taken together, rap and poetry provide the means to do exactly what the events of this past year have proven we need most: to amplify the voices of people who've gone unheard—and perhaps, one day, to bring us together under a common groove" (28). This essay makes a strong case for amplifying unheard voices; do you think there's hope for bringing us together—and why or why not?

4. LET'S TALK. With a group of fellow students, choose a poem written before 1950, perhaps one you've read for an English class or seen quoted on social media. Without changing any of the words, how might you perform the poem using some of the techniques that Bradley describes? Would you sample a song to use as a backdrop? add instrumentation or beatbox effects? Which of the poetic devices that Bradley mentions might you try—incremental repetition? enjambment? something else? Your goal is to explore the possibilities and expand your understanding and appreciation of both the original poem and the techniques that might be used to perform it. You don't actually have to stage a performance (though it could be lots of fun if you did!).

5. AND NOW WRITE. Choose a rap or poem that you admire. Why do you like it? Listen to it and read it, looking for alliteration, repetition, sampling, and other features that Bradley discusses. Write an essay explaining your reasons for liking the rap or poem, ANALYZING what words or features you admire or find particularly effective. Be sure to QUOTE any passages that you find especially memorable and explain why.

JUNE JORDAN

Nobody Mean More to Me Than You and the Future Life of Willie Jordan

BLACK ENGLISH is not exactly a linguistic buffalo; as children, most of the thirty-five million Afro-Americans living here depend on this language for our discovery of the world. But then we approach our maturity inside a larger social body that will not support our efforts to become anything other than the clones of those who are neither our mothers nor our fathers. We begin to grow up in a house where every true mirror shows us the face of somebody who does not belong there, whose walk and whose talk will never look or sound "right," because that house was meant to shelter a family that is alien and hostile to us. As we learn our way around this environment, either we hide our original word habits, or we completely surrender our own voice, hoping to please those who will never respect anyone different from themselves: Black English is not exactly a linguistic buffalo, but we should understand its status as an endangered species, as a perishing, irreplaceable system of community intelligence, or we should expect its extinction, and, along with that, the extinguishing of much that constitutes our own proud, and singular, identity.[1]

What we casually call "English," less and less defers to England and its "gentlemen." "English" is no longer a specific matter of geography

June Jordan (1936–2002) *was a writer, activist, and feminist critic who taught Women's Studies and African American Studies at SUNY Stony Brook and the University of California, Berkeley. The author of more than twenty-five books—including a novel, a memoir, poetry, essays, children's books, and two operatic librettos—she won numerous literary honors and awards, including special recognition from the US Congress. This essay is from her 1985 collection,* On Call: Political Essays.

or an element of class privilege; more than thirty-three countries use this tool as a means of "intranational communication."[2] Countries as disparate as Zimbabwe and Malaysia, or Israel and Uganda, use it as their non-native currency of convenience. Obviously, this tool, this "English," cannot function inside thirty-three discrete societies on the basis of rules and values absolutely determined somewhere else, in a thirty-fourth other country, for example.

In addition to that staggering congeries of non-native users of English, there are five countries, or 333,746,000 people, for whom this thing called "English" serves as a native tongue.[3] Approximately 10 percent of these native speakers of "English" are Afro-American citizens of the U.S.A. I cite these numbers and varieties of human beings dependent on "English" in order, quickly, to suggest how strange and how tenuous is any concept of "Standard English." Obviously, numerous forms of English now operate inside a natural, an uncontrollable, continuum of development. I would suppose "the standard" for English in Malaysia is not the same as "the standard" in Zimbabwe. I know that standard forms of English for Black people in this country do not copy that of Whites. And, in fact, the structural differences between these two kinds of English have intensified, becoming more Black, or less White, despite the expected homogenizing effects of television"[4] and other mass media.

Nonetheless, White standards of English persist, supreme and unquestioned, in these United States. Despite our multi-lingual population, and despite the deepening Black and White cleavage within that conglomerate, White standards control our official and popular judgments of verbal proficiency and correct, or incorrect, language skills, including speech. In contrast to India, where at least fourteen languages co-exist as legitimate Indian languages, in contrast to Nicaragua, where all citizens are legally entitled to formal school instruction in their regional or tribal languages, compulsory education in America compels accommodation to exclusively White forms of "English." White English, in America, is "Standard English."

This story begins two years ago. I was teaching a new course, 5
"In Search of the Invisible Black Woman," and my rather large class
seemed evenly divided among young Black women and men. Five or
six White students also sat in attendance. With unexpected speed
and enthusiasm we had moved through historical narratives of the
19th century to literature by and about Black women, in the 20th. I had
assigned the first forty pages of Alice Walker's *The Color Purple*, and
I came, eagerly, to class that morning:

"So!" I exclaimed, aloud. "What did you think? How did you like it?"

The students studied their hands, or the floor. There was no
response. The tense, resistant feeling in the room fairly astounded me.

At last, one student, a young woman still not meeting my eyes,
muttered something in my direction:

"What did you say?" I prompted her.

"Why she have them talk so funny. It don't sound right." 10

"You mean the language?"

Another student lifted his head: "It don't look right, neither. I couldn't
hardly read it."

At this, several students dumped on the book. Just about unanimously, their criticisms targeted the language. I listened to what they
wanted to say and silently marvelled at the similarities between their
casual speech patterns and Alice Walker's written version of Black
English.

But I decided against pointing to these identical traits of syntax;
I wanted not to make them self-conscious about their own spoken
language—not while they clearly felt it was "wrong." Instead I decided
to swallow my astonishment. Here was a negative Black reaction to a
prize-winning accomplishment of Black literature that White readers
across the country had selected as a best seller. Black rejection was
aimed at the one irreducibly Black element of Walker's work: the language—Celie's Black English. I wrote the opening lines of *The Color
Purple* on the blackboard and asked the students to help me translate
these sentences into Standard English:

You better not never tell nobody but God. It'd kill your mammy.

Dear God,
I am fourteen years old. I have always been a good girl. Maybe you can give me a sign letting me know what is happening to me.

Last spring after Little Lucious come I heard them fussing. He was pulling on her arm. She say it too soon, Fonso. I aint well. Finally he leave her alone. A week go by, he pulling on her arm again. She say, Naw, I ain't gonna. Can't you see I'm already half dead, an all of the children.[5]

Our process of translation exploded with hilarity and even hysterical, shocked laughter: The Black writer, Alice Walker, knew what she was doing! If rudimentary criteria for good fiction include the manipulation of language so that the syntax and diction of sentences will tell you the identity of speakers, the probable age and sex and class of speakers, and even the locale—urban/rural/southern/western—then Walker had written, perfectly. This is the translation into Standard English that our class produced:

Absolutely, one should never confide in anybody besides God.
Your secrets could prove devastating to your mother.

Dear God,
I am fourteen years old. I have always been good. But now, could you help me to understand what is happening to me?

Last spring, after my little brother, Lucious, was born, I heard my parents fighting. My father kept pulling at my mother's arm. But she told him, "It's too soon for sex, Alfonso. I am still not feeling well." Finally, my father left her alone. A week went by, and then he began bothering my mother, again: Pulling her arm. She told him, "No, I won't! Can't you see I'm already exhausted from all of these children?"

(Our favorite line was "It's too soon for sex, Alfonso.")

15   Once we could stop laughing, once we could stop our exponentially wild improvisations on the theme of Translated Black English, the

students pushed to explain their own negative first reactions to their spoken language on the printed page. I thought it was probably akin to the shock of seeing yourself in a photograph for the first time. Most of the students had never before seen a written facsimile of the way they talk. None of the students had ever learned how to read and write their own verbal system of communication: Black English. Alternatively, this fact began to baffle or else bemuse and then infuriate my students. Why not? Was it too late? Could they learn how to do it, now? And, ultimately, the final test question, the one testing my sincerity: Could I teach them? Because I had never taught anyone Black English and, as far as I knew, no one, anywhere in the United States, had ever offered such a course, the best I could say was "I'll try."

This translation exercise shows that words reflect more than just what they "mean"—history, culture, identity, and more. Chapter 24 says more about that.

HE LOOKED LIKE A WRESTLER.

He sat dead center in the packed room and, every time our eyes met, he quickly nodded his head as though anxious to reassure, and encourage me.

Short, with strikingly broad shoulders and long arms, he spoke with a surprisingly high, soft voice that matched the soft bright movement of his eyes. His name was Willie Jordan. He would have seemed even more unlikely in the context of Contemporary Women's Poetry, except that ten or twelve other Black men were taking the course, as well. Still, Willie was conspicuous. His extreme fitness, the muscular density of his presence underscored the riveted, gentle attention that he gave to anything anyone said. Generally, he did not join the loud and rowdy dialogue flying back and forth, but there could be no doubt about his interest in our discussions. And, when he stood to present an argument he'd prepared, overnight, that nervous smile of his vanished and an irregular stammering replaced it, as he spoke with visceral sincerity, word by word.

That was how I met Willie Jordan. It was in between "In Search of the Invisible Black Women" and "The Art of Black English." I was waiting for departmental approval and I supposed that Willie might be, so to speak, killing time until he, too, could study Black English. But Willie really did want to explore contemporary women's poetry and, to that end, volunteered for extra research and never missed a class.

20   Towards the end of that semester, Willie approached me for an independent study project on South Africa. It would commence the next semester. I thought Willie's writing needed the kind of improvement only intense practice will yield. I knew his intelligence was outstanding. But he'd wholeheartedly opted for "Standard English" at a rather late age, and the results were stilted and frequently polysyllabic, simply for the sake of having more syllables. Willie's unnatural formality of language seemed to me consistent with the formality of his research into South African apartheid. As he projected his studies, he would have little time, indeed, for newspapers. Instead, more than 90 percent of his research would mean saturation in strictly historical, if not archival, material. I was certainly interested. It would be tricky to guide him into a more confident and spontaneous relationship both with language and apartheid. It was going to be wonderful to see what happened when he could catch up with himself, entirely, and talk back to the world.

September, 1984: Breezy fall weather and much excitement! My class, "The Art of Black English," was full to the limit of the fire laws. And in Independent Study, Willie Jordan showed up weekly, fifteen minutes early for each of our sessions. I was pretty happy to be teaching, altogether!

I remember an early class when a young brother, replete with his ever-present porkpie hat, raised his hand and then told us that most of what he'd heard was "all right" except it was "too clean." "The brothers on the street," he continued, "they mix it up more. Like 'fuck' and 'motherfuck'? Or like 'shit'?" He waited. I waited. Then all of us laughed a good while, and we got into a brawl about "correct" and "realistic" Black English that led to Rule 1.

Rule 1: *Black English is about a whole lot more than mothafuckin.*

As a criterion, we decided, "realistic" could take you anywhere you want to go. Artful places. Angry places. Eloquent and sweetalkin places. Polemical places. Church. And the local Bar & Grill. We were checking out a language, not a mood or a scene or one guy's forgettable mouthing off.

It was hard. For most of the students, learning Black English required a fallback to patterns and rhythms of speech that many of their parents had beaten out of them. I mean *beaten*. And, in a majority of cases, correct Black English could be achieved only by striving for *incorrect* Standard English, something they were still pushing at, quite uncertainly. This state of affairs led to Rule 2.

Rule 2: *If it's wrong in Standard English it's probably right in Black English, or, at least, you're hot.*

It was hard. Roommates and family members ridiculed their studies, or remained incredulous, "You *studying* that shit? At school?" But we were beginning to feel the companionship of pioneers. And we decided that we needed another rule that would establish each one of us as equally important to our success. This was Rule 3.

Rule 3: If *it don't sound like something that come out somebody mouth then it don't sound right*. If *it dont sound right then it aint hardly right. Period.*

This rule produced two weeks of compositions in which the students agonizingly tried to spell the sound of the Black English sentence they wanted to convey. But Black English is, preeminently, an oral/ spoken means of communication. *And spelling don't talk.* So we needed Rule 4.

Rule 4: *Forget about the spelling. Let the syntax carry you.*

Once we arrived at Rule 4 we started to fly, because syntax, the structure of an idea, leads you to the world view of the speaker and reveals her values. The syntax of a sentence equals the structure of your consciousness. If we insisted that the language of Black English adheres to a distinctive Black syntax, then we were postulating a profound difference between White and Black people, *per se*. Was it a difference to prize or to obliterate?

There are three qualities of Black English—the presence of life, voice, and clarity—that intensify to a distinctive Black value system that we became excited about and self-consciously tried to maintain.

1. Black English has been produced by a pre-technocratic, if not anti-technological, culture. More, our culture has been constantly threatened by annihilation or, at least, the swallowed blurring of assimilation. Therefore, our language is a system constructed by people constantly needing to insist that we exist, that we are present. Our language devolves from a culture that abhors all abstraction, or anything tending to obscure or delete the fact of the human being who is here and now/the truth of the person who is speaking or listening. Consequently, *there is no passive voice construction possible in Black English*. For example, you cannot say, "Black English is being eliminated." You must say, instead, "White people eliminating Black English." The assumption of the presence of life governs all of Black English. Therefore, overwhelmingly, *all action takes place in the language of the present indicative*. And every sentence assumes the living and active participation of at least two human beings, the speaker and the listener.

2. A primary consequence of the person-centered values of Black English is the delivery of voice. If you speak or write Black English, your ideas will necessarily possess that otherwise elusive attribute, *voice*.

3. One main benefit following from the person-centered values of Black English is that of *clarity*. If your idea, your sentence, assumes the presence of at least two living and active people, you will make it understandable, because the motivation behind every sentence is the wish to say something real to somebody real.

As the weeks piled up, translation from Standard English into Black English or vice versa occupied a hefty part of our course work.

> Standard English (hereafter S.E.): "In considering the idea of studying Black English those questioned suggested—"

(What's the subject? Where's the person? Is anybody alive in here, in that idea?)

> Black English (hereafter B.E.): "I been asking people what you think about somebody studying Black English and they answer me like this:"

But there were interesting limits. You cannot "translate" instances of Standard English preoccupied with abstraction or with nothing/nobody evidently alive, into Black English. That would warp the language into uses antithetical to the guiding perspective of its community of users. Rather you must first change those Standard English sentences, them-selves, into ideas consistent with the person-centered assumptions of Black English.

Guidelines for Black English

1. Minimal number of words for every idea: This is the source for the aphoristic and/or poetic force of the language; eliminate every possible word.
2. Clarity: If the sentence is not clear it's not Black English.
3. Eliminate use of the verb *to be* whenever possible. This leads to the deployment of more descriptive and, therefore, more precise verbs.
4. Use *be* or *been* only when you want to describe a chronic, ongoing state of things.
   > He *be* at the office, by 9. (He is always at the office by 9.)
   > He *been* with her since forever.
5. Zero copula: Always eliminate the verb *to be* whenever it would combine with another verb, in Standard English.
   > S.E.: She is going out with him.
   > B.E.: She going out with him.
6. Eliminate *do* as in:
   > S.E.: What do you think? What do you want?
   > B.E.: What you think? What you want?

Rules number 3, 4, 5, and 6 provide for the use of the minimal number of verbs per idea and, therefore, greater accuracy in the choice of verb.

7. In general, if you wish to say something really positive, try to formulate the idea using emphatic negative structure.

   S.E.: He's fabulous.

   B.E.: He bad.

8. Use double or triple negatives for dramatic emphasis.

   S.E.: Tina Turner sings out of this world.

   B.E.: Ain nobody sing like Tina.

9. Never use the *-ed* suffix to indicate the past tense of a verb.

   S.E.: She closed the door.

   B.E.: She close the door. Or, she have close the door.

10. Regardless of intentional verb time, only use the third person singular, present indicative, for use of the verb *to have*, as an auxiliary.

    S.E.: He had his wallet then he lost it.

    B.E.: He have him wallet then he lose it.

    S.E.: We had seen that movie.

    B.E.: We seen that movie. Or, we have see that movie.

11. Observe a minimal inflection of verbs. Particularly, never change from the first person singular forms to the third person singular.

    S.E.: Present Tense Forms: He goes to the store.

    B.E.: He go to the store.

    S.E.: Past Tense Forms: He went to the store.

    B.E.: He go to the store. Or, he gone to the store. Or, he been to the store.

12. The possessive case scarcely ever appears in Black English. Never use an apostrophe ('s) construction. If you wander into a possessive case component of an idea, then keep logically consistent: *ours, his, theirs, mines.* But, most likely, if you bump into such a component, you have wandered outside the underlying world view of Black English.

    S.E.: He will take their car tomorrow.

    B.E.: He taking they car tomorrow.

13. Plurality: Logical consistency, continued: If the modifier indicates plurality then the noun remains in the singular case.

    S.E.: He ate twelve doughnuts.

    B.E.: He eat twelve doughnut.

    S.E.: She has many books.

    B.E.: She have many book.

14. Listen for, or invent, special Black English forms of the past tense, such as: "He losted it. That what she felted." If they are clear and readily understood, then use them.

15. Do not hesitate to play with words, sometimes inventing them: e.g. "astropotomous" means huge like a hippo plus astronomical and, therefore, signifies real big.

16. In Black English, unless you keenly want to underscore the past tense nature of an action, stay in the present tense and rely on the overall context of your ideas for the conveyance of time and sequence.

17. Never use the suffix -*ly* form of an adverb in Black English.

> S.E.: The rain came down rather quickly.
>
> B.E.: The rain come down pretty quick.

18. Never use the indefinite article *an* in Black English.

> S.E.: He wanted to ride an elephant.
>
> B.E.: He wanted to ride him a elephant.

19. Invariant syntax: in correct Black English it is possible to formulate an imperative, an interrogative, and a simple declarative idea with the same syntax:

> You going to the store?
>
> You going to the store.
>
> You going to the store!

Where was Willie Jordan? We'd reached the mid-term of the semester. Students had formulated Black English guidelines, by consensus, and they were now writing with remarkable beauty, purpose, and enjoyment:

> *I ain hardly speakin for everybody but myself so understan that.*
> —KIM PARKS

Samples from student writings:

> Janie have a great big ole hole inside her. Tea Cake the only thing that fit that hole....

> That pear tree beautiful to Janie, especial when bees fiddlin with the blossomin pear there growin large and lovely. But personal speakin, the love she get from starin at that tree ain the love what starin back at her in them relationship. (Monica Morris)

> Love a big theme in, They Eye Was Watching God. Love show people new corners inside theyself. It pull out good stuff and stuff back bad stuff.... Joe worship the doing uh his own hand and need other people to worship him too. But he ain't think about Janie that she a person and ought to live like anybody common do. Queen life not for Janie. (Monica Morris)
>
> In both life and writin, Black womens have varietous experience of love that be cold like a iceberg or fiery like a inferno. Passion got for the other partner involve, man or women, seem as shallow, ankle-deep water or the most profoundest abyss. (Constance Evans)
>
> Family love another bond that ain't never break under no pressure. (Constance Evans)
>
> You know it really cold / When the friend you / Always get out the fire / Act like they don't know you / When you in the heat. (Constance Evans)
>
> Big classroom discussion bout love at this time. I never take no class where us have any long arguin for and against for two or three day. New to me and great. I find the class time talkin a million time more interestin than detail bout the book. (Kathy Esseks)

As these examples suggest, Black English no longer limited the students, in any way. In fact, one of them, Philip Garfield, would shortly "translate" a pivotal scene from Ibsen's *A Doll's House*, as his final term paper:

> *Nora*: I didn't gived no shit. I thinked you a asshole back then, too, you make it so hard for me save mines husband life.
> *Krogstad*: Girl, it clear you ain't any idea what you done. You done exact what I once done, and I losed my reputation over it.
> *Nora*: You asks me believe you once act brave save you wife life?
> *Krogstad*: Law care less why you done it.
> *Nora*: Law must suck.
> *Krogstad*: Suck or no, if I wants, judge screw you wid dis paper.
> *Nora*: No way, man. (Philip Garfield)

But where was Willie? Compulsively punctual, and always thoroughly prepared with neat typed compositions, he had disappeared. He failed to show up for our regularly scheduled conference, and I received neither a note nor a phone call of explanation. A whole week went by. I wondered if Willie had finally been captured by the extremely current happenings in South Africa: passage of a new constitution that did not enfranchise the Black majority, and militant Black South African reaction to that affront. I wondered if he'd been hurt, somewhere. I wondered if the serious workload of weekly readings and writings had overwhelmed him and changed his mind about independent study. Where was Willie Jordan?

One week after the first conference that Willie missed, he called: "Hello, Professor Jordan? This is Willie. I'm sorry I wasn't there last week. But something has come up and I'm pretty upset. I'm sorry but I really can't deal right now."   25

I asked Willie to drop by my office and just let me see that he was okay. He agreed to do that. When I saw him I knew something hideous had happened. Something had hurt him and scared him to the marrow. He was all agitated and stammering and terse and incoherent. At last, his sadly jumbled account let me surmise, as follows: Brooklyn police had murdered his unarmed, twenty-five-year-old brother, Reggie Jordan. Neither Willie nor his elderly parents knew what to do about it. Nobody from the press was interested. His folks had no money. Police ran his family around and around, to no point. And Reggie was really dead. And Willie wanted to fight, but he felt helpless.

With Willie's permission I began to try to secure legal counsel for the Jordan family. Unfortunately, Black victims of police violence are truly numerous, while the resources available to prosecute their killers are truly scarce. A friend of mine at the Center for Constitutional Rights estimated that just the preparatory costs for bringing the cops into court normally approaches $180,000. Unless the execution of Reggie Jordan became a major community cause for organizing and protest, his murder would simply become a statistical item.

Again, with Willie's permission, I contacted every newspaper and media person I could think of. But the Bastone feature article in *The Village Voice* was the only result from that canvassing.

Again, with Willie's permission, I presented the case to my class in Black English. We had talked about the politics of language. We had talked about love and sex and child abuse and men and women. But the murder of Reggie Jordan broke like a hurricane across the room.

30   There are few "issues" as endemic to Black life as police violence. Most of the students knew and respected and liked Jordan. Many of them came from the very neighborhood where the murder had occurred. All of the students had known somebody close to them who had been killed by police, or had known frightening moments of gratuitous confrontation with the cops. They wanted to do everything at once to avenge death. Number one: They decided to compose a personal statement of condolence to Willie Jordan and his family, written in Black English. Number two: They decided to compose individual messages to the police, in Black English. These should be prefaced by an explanatory paragraph composed by the entire group. Number three: These individual messages, with their lead paragraph, should be sent to *Newsday*.

The morning after we agreed on these objectives, one of the young women students appeared with an unidentified visitor, who sat through the class, smiling in a peculiar, comfortable way.

Now we had to make more tactical decisions. Because we wanted the messages published, and because we thought it imperative that our outrage be known by the police, the tactical question was this: Should the opening, group paragraph be written in Black English or Standard English?

I have seldom been privy to a discussion with so much heart at the dead heat of it. I will never forget the eloquence, the sudden haltings of speech, the fierce struggle against tears, the furious throwaway, and useless explosions that this question elicited.

That one question contained several others, each of them extraordinarily painful to even contemplate. How best to serve the memory of Reggie Jordan? Should we use the language of the killer—Standard English—in order to make our ideas acceptable to those controlling the killers? But wouldn't what we had to say be rejected, summarily, if we said it in our own language, the language of the victim, Reggie Jordan? But if we sought to express ourselves by abandoning our language wouldn't that mean our suicide on top of Reggie's murder? But if we expressed ourselves in our own language wouldn't that be suicidal to the wish to communicate with those who, evidently, did not give a damn about us/Reggie/police violence in the Black community?

At the end of one of the longest, most difficult hours of my own 35 life, the students voted, unanimously, to preface their individual messages with a paragraph composed in the language of Reggie Jordan. *"At least we don't give up nothing else. At least we stick to the truth: Be who we been. And stay all the way with Reggie."*

It was heartbreaking to proceed, from that point. Everyone in the room realized that our decision in favor of Black English had doomed our writings, even as the distinctive reality of our Black lives always has doomed our efforts to "be who we been" in this country.

I went to the blackboard and took down this paragraph dictated by the class:

YOU COPS!

WE THE BROTHER AND SISTER OF WILLIE JORDAN, A FELLOW STONY BROOK STUDENT WHO THE BROTHER OF THE DEAD REGGIE JORDAN. REGGIE, LIKE MANY BROTHER AND SISTER, HE A VICTIM OF BRUTAL RACIST POLICE, OCTOBER 25, 1984. US APPALL, FED UP, BECAUSE THAT ANOTHER SENSELESS DEATH WHAT OCCUR IN OUR COMMUNITY. THIS WHAT WE FEEL, THIS, FROM OUR HEART, FOR WE AIN'T STAYIN' SILENT NO MORE:

With the completion of this introduction, nobody said anything. I asked for comments. At this invitation, the unidentified visitor, a young Black man, ceaselessly smiling, raised his hand. He was, it so happens, a rookie cop. He had just joined the force in September and, he said, he thought he should clarify a few things. So he came forward and sprawled easily into a posture of barroom, or fireside, nostalgia:

"See," Officer Charles enlightened us, "Most times when you out on the street and something come down you do one of two things.

Over-react or under-react. Now, if you under-react then you can get yourself kilt. And if you over-react then maybe you kill somebody. Fortunately it's about nine times out of ten and you will over-react. So the brother got kilt. And I'm sorry about that, believe me. But what you have to understand is what kilt him: Over-reaction. That's all. Now you talk about Black people and White police but see, now, I'm a cop myself. And (big smile) I'm Black. And just a couple months ago I was on the other side. But it's the same for me. You a cop, you the ultimate authority: the Ultimate Authority. And you on the street, most of the time you can only do one of two things: over-react or under-react. That's all it is with the brother. Over-reaction. Didn't have nothing to do with race."

That morning Officer Charles had the good fortune to escape without being boiled alive. But barely. And I remember the pride of his smile when I read about the fate of Black policemen and other collaborators, in South Africa. I remember him, and I remember the shock and palpable feeling of shame that filled the room. It was as though that foolish, and deadly, young man had just relieved himself of his foolish, and deadly, explanation, face to face with the grief of Reggie Jordan's father and Reggie Jordan's mother. Class ended quietly. I copied the paragraph from the blackboard, collected the individual messages and left to type them up.

40   *Newsday* rejected the piece.

The Village Voice could not find room in their "Letters" section to print the individual messages from the students to the police.

None of the TV news reporters picked up the story.

Nobody raised $180,000 to prosecute the murder of Reggie Jordan.

Reggie Jordan is really dead.

45   I asked Willie Jordan to write an essay pulling together everything important to him from that semester. He was still deeply beside himself with frustration and amazement and loss. This is what he wrote, un-edited, and in its entirety:

Throughout the course of this semester I have been researching the effects of oppression and exploitation along racial lines in South

America and its neighboring countries. I have become aware of South African police brutalization of native Africans beyond the extent of the law, even though the laws themselves are catalyst affliction upon Black men, women and children. Many Africans die each year as a result of the deliberate use of police force to protect the white power structure.

Social control agents in South Africa, such as policemen, are also used to force compliance among citizens through both overt and covert tactics. It is not uncommon to find bold-faced coercion and cold-blooded killings of Blacks by South African police for undetermined and/or inadequate reasons. Perhaps the truth is that the only reasons for this heinous treatment of Blacks rests in racial differences. We should also understand that what is conveyed through the media is not always accurate and may sometimes be construed as the tip of the iceberg at best.

I recently received a painful reminder that racism, poverty, and the abuse of power are global problems which are by no means unique to South Africa. On October 25, 1984 at approximately 3:00 p.m. my brother, Mr. Reginald Jordan, was shot and killed by two New York City policemen from the 75th precinct in the East New York section of Brooklyn. His life ended at the age of twenty-five. Even up to this current point in time the Police Department has failed to provide my family, which consists of five brothers, eight sisters, and two parents, with a plausible reason for Reggie's death. Out of the many stories that were given to my family by the Police Department, not one of them seems to hold water. In fact, I honestly believe that the Police Department's assessment of my brother's murder is nothing short of absolute bullshit, and thus far no evidence had been produced to alter perception of the situation.

Furthermore, I believe that one of three cases may have occurred in this incident. First, Reggie's death may have been the desired outcome of the police officer's action, in which case the killing was premeditated. Or, it was a case of mistaken identity, which clarifies the fact that the two officers who killed my brother and their commanding parties are all grossly incompetent. Or, both of the above cases are correct, i.e., Reggie's murderers intended to kill him and the Police Department behaved insubordinately.

Part of the argument of the officers who shot Reggie was that he had attacked one of them and took his gun. This was their major claim. They also said that only one of them had actually shot Reggie. The facts, however, speak for themselves. According to the Death Certificate and autopsy report, Reggie was shot eight times from pointblank range. The Doctor who performed the autopsy told me himself that two bullets entered the side of my brother's head, four bullets were sprayed into his back, and two bullets struck him in the back of his legs. It is obvious that unnecessary force was used by the police and that it is extremely difficult to shoot someone in his back when he is attacking or approaching you.

After experiencing a situation like this and researching South Africa I believe that to a large degree, justice may only exist as rhetoric. I find it difficult to talk of true justice when the oppression of my people both at home and abroad attests to the fact that inequality and injustice are serious problems whereby Blacks and Third World people are perpetually short-changed by society. Something has to be done about the way in which this world is set up. Although it is a difficult task, we do have the power to make a change.

—Willie J. Jordan Jr.
EGL 487, Section 58, November 14, 1984

It is my privilege to dedicate this book to the future life of Willie J. Jordan Jr. August 8, 1985.

Notes

1. Black English aphorisms crafted by Monica Morris, a junior at S.U.N.Y., Stony Brook, October, 1984.

2. *English Is Spreading, But What Is English*. A presentation by Professor S. N. Sridhar, Department of Linguistics, S.U.N.Y., Stony Brook, April 9, 1985: Dean's Convocation among the Disciplines.

3. *English Is Spreading*.

4. *New York Times*, March 15, 1985, Section One, p. 14: Report on Study by Linguists at the University of Pennsylvania

5. Alice Walker, *The Color Purple* (New York: Harcourt Brace Jovanovich, 1982), p. 11.

Thinking about the Text

1. The TITLE of June Jordan's essay gets our attention with its unusual two-part statement. What does the title mean—and what does it lead you to expect is coming? How is the title related to the main ARGUMENT Jordan is making—and how would you sum up that argument? What other titles might she have considered?

2. Toward the end of her essay, Jordan includes a NARRATIVE about Charles, the rookie cop who visited her class. In what ways does this story contribute to Jordan's argument? Note that she quotes him directly: How does that choice, and her somewhat contradictory description of him affect your response to him?

3. Writing in 1985, Jordan said that Black English was "an endangered species" and that "we should expect its extinction." What might Jasmine Lane say in response to these claims—and what do you say? (Jasmine Lane's essay is on p. 622.)

4. LET'S TALK. Read the essay that Willie Jordan wrote "pulling together everything important to him from that semester" (45). What do you think about the points he made in his essay? Get together with some other students and talk about what he said. What have they led you to think about? If you could respond to him, what would you say?

5. AND NOW WRITE. This essay is the opening selection of a collection of June Jordan's work titled *On Call: Political Essays*,

and she concludes the essay by saying "It is my privilege to dedicate this book to the future life of Willie J. Jordan Jr." It's a powerful CONCLUSION, unexpected and thought-provoking. Why do you think she concluded that way, and what does it leave you thinking? Write a brief essay REFLECTING on your own reaction to her essay. Did it surprise you? Make you want to learn more about Black language, or June Jordan—or Willie Jordan? If you were telling a friend about this essay, what would you say?

33 What's News, and How Do We Know What to Trust?

JOURNALISTS MUST STRIVE TO FIND OUT
WHAT IS GOING ON AND TELL IT . . .

—JOE SACCO

INFORMATION WALKS. MISINFORMATION FLIES.

—RUPA MAHANTI

I t may be tempting to think about the "news" like we think about the sun or the moon—as a concrete, well-defined entity whose very nature and definition is objective and uncontroversial. But that's not quite right, is it? What makes something "news"? When is a trend important enough to be considered news? In the vast ocean of information, what is newsworthy? And once an editor or journalist has decided that something is news, how should it be presented? Perhaps most important, who gets to make these decisions? In short, who are the ones choosing and shaping what we will consume as news? In a participatory, democratic society, these are not trivial questions.

This chapter presents four essays and a cartoon about the nature of news and information. **Elaine Godfrey** argues in the *Atlantic* for the importance of small local newspapers, what is lost when they disappear, and how local *Facebook* pages "can be a useful resource" but are sometimes "chaotic" in comparison. **Lewis Raven Wallace** looks at the responsibilities of those who report on the news, arguing that too many journalists today treat the people they write about as "objects" to be mined for a good story—and that they have the responsibility to write *for* those people, not simply *about* them.

Education professor **Sam Wineburg** explores an especially challenging aspect of the onslaught of news today: the need to know what to read critically—and what to ignore. And a cartoon by syndicated cartoonist **Joel Pett** agrees, reminding us on World Press Freedom Day of the need to be on the lookout for fake news.

Savannah Jacobson takes a broader look at how we get our news, focusing on the evolution of the "mainstream media" and exploring the surprisingly difficult question of what that even is.

We hope that these readings will invite you to think critically about what's in the news, what's not in the news—and how it affects all of us.

Readings in Other Chapters

- **Jemele Hill**, Naomi Osaka Is a Part of a Larger War within Sports   786
- **Emma Marris**, The Nature You See in Nature Documentaries Is Beautiful, and False   719

Readings on <u>letstalklibrary.com</u>

- **Simge Andi**, How and Why Do Consumers Access News on Social Media?
- **Nicholas Carr**, How to Fix Social Media

ELAINE GODFREY

What We Lost When Gannett Came to Town

THE GRAIN ELEVATOR EXPLODED on a cool April morning in 1987, six years before I was born. My father was testing a clay sample in a lab two miles away when suddenly the dial jumped. He ran outside, thinking that a car had smashed into the building. My mother, doing yard work at home, assumed that the nearby ammunition plant was testing a new explosive.

Dale Alison saw the blast up close. He was 32 years old, and it was his first day as the city editor of *The Hawk Eye*, a newspaper in Burlington, Iowa. From the front door of the office, he saw the train tracks outside ripple, and the air seemed to vibrate and sway. Then the windows of the newsroom blew out. Alison and his colleagues ducked under their desks, and a few looked out to see a plume of black smoke blocking the sky. The 12-story grain-storage facility—a longtime fixture on Burlington's riverfront—was wrapped in orange flames.

Alison started shouting out assignments. Matt Gallo should head to the hospital; Susan Fisher and Mike Sweet should drive downtown for man-on-the-street interviews; Steve Delaney, Tony Miller, and the photographers should go straight to the scene. Within the hour, firefighters evacuated the newsroom (train cars containing anhydrous ammonia were parked perilously close) and everyone regrouped at a nearby dive bar. Reporters made calls from the payphone and scrawled their stories on reams of paper someone had nabbed from an old typewriter shop. Photographers developed their film in a bathtub at someone's house on the northwest side of town.

Whew! The event is dramatic, but it's the details that draw us in to the action! Learn how to add lively details to your work on pp. 191–93.

Elaine Godfrey is a staff writer for the Atlantic *who investigates and writes about politics and culture. This 2021 article reports on the newspaper community of her own hometown. She tweets from @elainejgodfrey.*

669

By late afternoon, the newsroom had reopened, and the presses were rolling. Burlingtonians had their papers by 8 p.m., just three hours behind schedule, complete with a full-size photo of the fireball and aerial images from the scene. The blast had injured some workers, but miraculously no one died. It had shattered hundreds of windows downtown and sank a nearby barge.

5   Even now, veteran *Hawk Eye* staffers will tell you that the grain-elevator explosion was a career highlight. It gave them the kind of thrill that all reporters crave. But there was also a real sense of ownership to the story: This was *Burlington's* disaster—an event with an immediate impact. There was no question that *The Hawk Eye* would cover it from every possible angle.

The front page of *The Hawk Eye* from April 13, 1987, the day the grain elevator exploded.

Friday April 3, 1987

THE HAWK EYE

Iowa's Oldest Newspaper

Forecast

Explosion rips grain elevator

No one killed in blast

Throughout the next year, the newspaper published a series of follow-up stories, including investigations into the explosion's cause (a bearing had overheated and ignited a buildup of grain dust) and the company's safety standards. The blast had been just the latest in a string of elevator fires in the Midwest, and the paper's business editor, Steve Delaney, chased the story for months. By the end of the year, the Occupational Safety and Health Administration had announced new safety requirements for grain elevators.

For the people of southeastern Iowa, knowing that *The Hawk Eye* was investigating this fiasco was a source of comfort. The paper's reliable attention made us feel like our little part of Iowa mattered and that we did, too. This is what *The Hawk Eye* gave us. Back then, we took it for granted.

I grew up outside Burlington, 15 miles west on Highway 34, past alternating corn and soybean fields and past the

19,000-acre Iowa Army Ammunition Plant. But Burlington was my community—home to the nearest supermarket, the mall, the movie theater—and *The Hawk Eye* was how we kept up....

The Hawk Eye was never perfect. Readers complained about typos or misspellings. Conservatives in town called it a liberal rag, and some lefties didn't think it was progressive enough. But all the staffers at the paper lived in the area—you could call the editor on his landline and complain about a story, and you could confront Mike Sweet about his latest column in the produce section at Hy-Vee. People often did. And even *The Hawk Eye*'s most passionate detractors would still cut out the articles about their granddaughter's softball team and stick them on the fridge.

The Hawk Eye isn't dead yet, which sets it apart from many other 10 local newspapers in America. Its staff, now down to three overstretched news reporters, still produces a print edition six days a week. But the paper is dying. Its pages are smaller than they used to be, and there are fewer of them. Even so, wide margins and large fonts are used to fill space. The paper is laid out by a remote design team and printed 100 miles away in Peoria, Illinois; if a reader doesn't get her paper in the morning, she is instructed to dial a number that will connect her to a call center in the Philippines. Obituaries used to be free; now, when your uncle dies, you have to pay to publish a write-up.

These days, most of *The Hawk Eye*'s articles are ripped from other Gannett-owned Iowa publications, such as *The Des Moines Register* and *The Ames Tribune*, written for a readership three hours away. The Opinion section, once an arena for local columnists and letter writers to spar over the merits and morals of riverboat gambling and railroad jobs moving to Topeka, is dominated by syndicated national columnists.

By now, we know what happens when a community loses its newspaper. People tend to participate less often in municipal elections, and those elections are less competitive. Corruption goes unchecked, and costs sometimes go up for town governments. Disinformation becomes the norm, as people start to get their facts mainly from social media. But the decline of *The Hawk Eye* has also revealed a quieter, less quantifiable change.

When people lament the decline of small newspapers, they tend to emphasize the most important stories that will go uncovered: political corruption, school-board scandals, zoning-board hearings, police misconduct. They are right to worry about that. But often overlooked are the more quotidian stories, the ones that disappear first when a paper loses resources: stories about the annual Teddy Bear Picnic at Crapo Park, the town-hall meeting about the new swimming-pool design, and the tractor games during the Denmark Heritage Days.

These stories are the connective tissue of a community; they introduce people to their neighbors, and they encourage readers to listen to and empathize with one another. When that tissue disintegrates, something vital rots away. We don't often stop to ponder the way that a newspaper's collapse makes people feel: less connected, more alone. As local news crumbles, so does our tether to one another....

15   *The Hawk Eye* is considered the oldest newspaper in the state, but technically, it began as two separate ones, The *Wisconsin Territorial Gazette* and the *Burlington Hawk-Eye*.... During the Great Depression the two papers became one: the *Burlington Hawk-Eye Gazette*. A few years later, the Harrises, a wealthy Kansas family, added it to their collection of midwestern dailies.

The Harrises encouraged editorial independence; they didn't hover. They wanted *The Hawk Eye* to be local....

The Hawk Eye had influence: John McCormally, who edited the paper in the 1960s and '70s, was the first editor in Iowa, and probably in the country, to endorse Jimmy Carter for president, a move that contributed to Carter's victory in the Iowa caucuses. By the time my parents moved to town in the early 1980s, *The Hawk Eye* had already won Best Newspaper in Iowa three times, Alison told me. My parents took out a subscription, and followed along as *Hawk Eye* reporters covered big regional stories: the murder of Mount Pleasant Mayor Edd King; the 500-year flood of 1993; the 500-year flood of 2008; the 2015 killing of a woman named Autumn Steele, who was accidentally shot by a police officer and whose death led to a years-long fight between the newspaper and the Burlington Police Department to make police records public....

Founded in the mid-19th century, *The Hawk Eye* was initially called the *Burlington Hawk-Eye*.

As a kid, I liked the opinion pages best. I devoured Sweet's columns about global warming and the Iraq War. In sixth grade, I started writing letters to the editor about the rampant alcohol consumption at the water park, the lackadaisical recycling program at my school, the cruel treatment of the fish in the aquariums at Walmart. Each letter, printed in the op-ed section, included my name and my age: "By Elaine Godfrey, 12." ...

In late April [2021], I pulled up in my rental car to the Burlington Amtrak station, situated just off Main Street, only a few hundred yards from *The Hawk Eye*'s offices. The depot overlooks the Mississippi River. Sometimes bald eagles fly by carrying fish. Dale Alison and a few other former staffers who had been meeting at the station occasionally for coffee during the pandemic met me there, including Sweet and the onetime business editor Rex Troute. I brought a box of Casey's doughnuts and we talked about the paper's slow death while trains packed with coal and grain rattled by.

The collapse of Iowa's oldest newspaper, they told me, began with 20
a staff-wide announcement in November 2016: A publishing company

called GateHouse, run by an investment firm in New York, was the buyer. GateHouse had already bought 121 daily papers, 316 weeklies, and 117 supermarket circulars across the country. It was a good time for gobbling up newspapers: Companies could buy them cheap, centralize resources, and slash staff to make a profit. But GateHouse reassured them that things would not change much in the newsroom. "You have a great legacy here. We want to keep that going," a GateHouse editor told the staff. "GateHouse buys papers to make communities better."

After three months, Sweet retired. Steve Delaney, who had become the paper's publisher, was fired in April 2017. Alison, by then the managing editor, was let go in June, along with several others. Rex Troute retired then, too. The copy desk took buyouts that summer, and their duties were moved to Austin, Texas. Over the next two years, more reporters accepted buyouts, most of the paper's advertising roles were eliminated, the six-person press crew was dissolved, and printing operations were moved to Peoria. In 2019, GateHouse bought *USA Today* publisher Gannett and took its more well-known name. At the time, Gannett owned more than 100 daily papers, and after the merger, the company owned one out of every six newspapers in the country. *The Hawk Eye*, which started [in] 2016 with 100 people on the payroll, today has about a dozen. From the depot, the newspaper veterans and I had a decent view of the boxy brown *Hawk Eye* office. Gannett had put the building up for sale last winter.

Readers noticed the paper's sloppiness first—how there seemed to be twice as many typos as before, and how sometimes the articles would end mid-sentence instead of continuing after the jump. The newspaper's remaining reporters are overworked; there are local stories they'd like to tell but don't have the bandwidth to cover. *The Hawk Eye*'s current staff is facing the impossible task of keeping a historic newspaper alive while its owner is attempting to squeeze it dry.

None of this was inevitable: At the time of the sale to GateHouse, *The Hawk Eye* wasn't struggling financially. Far from it. In the years leading up to the sale, the paper was seeing profit margins ranging from the mid-teens to the high 20s. Gannett has dedicated much of its revenue to servicing and paying off loans associated with the merger, rather than reinvesting in local journalism. Which is to say that southeastern Iowans are losing their community paper not because it was a failing business, but because a massive media-holding company has investors to please and debts to pay. (A Gannett representative acknowledged that the company has prioritized repaying its creditors, but said that it is committed to supporting local journalism.)

I thought about the consequences of the paper's decline when I visited the cluttered archives room at the Burlington Public Library this summer. Rhonda Frevert, a librarian who writes a monthly column for *The Hawk Eye*, reminded me that the paper is more than a guide to local happenings: It's a repository of community knowledge. People come to search the archives for birth announcements, obituaries, stories about their families, and businesses that used to be in town. When those stories aren't written, they're not kept anywhere. There's no record....

In early spring, I joined a *Facebook* group called "Burlington (IOWA) Breaking News reports and MORE" and realized that many of my high-school classmates were already members. So were my mom and most of her friends. The group has more than 16,000 people in it—more than triple the number of people who subscribe to *The Hawk Eye*. It's ostensibly a site for sharing news about the community, but the page is chaotic. Scroll down and you'll find ... pictures of missing dogs, ads for rib eyes at Fareway, and comments accidentally made in all caps. I found more of the same in other *Facebook* groups, including "Greater Burlington IA Uncensored Chat" and "Greater Burlington (Iowa) Neighborhood Chatter."

The pages can be a useful resource, and a good source of community jokes and gossip. But speculation and rumor run rampant. A member might ask about a new building going up in town, and someone will guess that it will be an Olive Garden. It never is. When a member hears something that sounds like gunshots nearby, she'll post about it, and others will offer theories about the source. Once, I read a thread about an elementary-school principal suddenly skipping town. Some

The *Facebook* page for the *Burlington Breaking News.*

thought he might have behaved inappropriately with a student; one person said he'd been involved with a student's mother; another swore they'd seen security-camera footage of the principal slashing tires in a parking lot at night. I checked *The Hawk Eye* and other outlets, but I couldn't find verification of any of those stories.

Alison is a member of "Burlington Breaking News," and all of the guessing is hard for him to watch. He often interjects in the comments to correct false information. Sometimes he posts news himself. "The stop light at Gear Avenue and Agency Street isn't expected to be working until spring," he announced late last winter. People want to know what's going on, Alison told me; they just don't know how to find the answer, whom to call, where to look. That's what reporters are for.

In the absence of local coverage, all news becomes national news: Instead of reading about local policy decisions, people read about the blacklisting of Dr. Seuss books. Instead of learning about their own local candidates, they consume angry takes about Marjorie Taylor Greene. Tom Courtney, a Democrat and four-term former state senator from Burlington, made more than 10,000 phone calls to voters during his 2020 run for office. In those calls, he heard something he never had before: "People that live in small-town rural Iowa [said] they wouldn't vote for me or any Democrat because I'm in the same party as AOC," Courtney told me. "Where did they get that? Not local news!" Courtney lost in November.

It's difficult to quantify that creeping sense of disconnection, those crumbling social ties. But southeastern Iowans feel it, and they'll describe it if you ask them to. Within hours of posting in "Burlington Breaking News" to ask for people's thoughts on *The Hawk Eye*, I received dozens of comments, emails, and private *Facebook* messages. Almost everyone expressed sadness about the paper's deterioration. "We feel like we're all little islands out here," Deb Bowen, a 72-year-old Burlington resident, told me on the phone. . . .

In 2018, *Hawk Eye* alumnus Jeff Abell founded a new online news- 30
paper called the *Burlington Beacon* to help fill the void, and soon
brought on another former *Hawk Eye* reporter, William Smith. They
post articles straight to *Facebook* and have launched a weekly print
edition for subscribers. But the *Beacon* is far from profitable. Until
recently, Abell paid Smith from his own pocket. The two work out
of Abell's comic-book store in downtown Burlington. At the depot,
I asked Alison what he thought about the *Beacon*'s prospects. "Jeff
and Will are doing their best," he said. "But doggone it, it would take
150 years to build up what they had here."

Last fall, a man named Gary posted on the "Burlington Breaking
News" page, asking: "Anyone know what is going to be built at Broad-
way and Division south of the Girl Scout office?" A construction crew
had recently broken ground at the site. People in the *Facebook* group
started to weigh in: Maybe it'll be a new sandwich joint; that'd be nice.
Maybe a coffee shop, or a Dollar Tree, or another bank. Someone had
heard that it might be a dentist's office. One of the page's moderators
suggested that perhaps it was a new spec building that would soon
be put up for sale. Then the thread ended. *The Hawk Eye* never ran
a story about the new building. Soon, the post was forgotten, buried
under a mounting pile of questions from other southeastern Iowans
wondering what, exactly, was going on in town.

Thinking about the Text

1. Elaine Godfrey writes about the decline of the *Hawk Eye*, the
   daily newspaper in Burlington, Iowa, which she says had once
   given the community a sense that they and their "little part
   of Iowa mattered" (7). She then goes on to DESCRIBE things
   that were lost "when Gannett came to town." What are the
   losses she identifies and what exactly is her ARGUMENT?
   How persuasive do you find her article?

2. Godfrey quotes various people in her account and much of what
   she describes is anecdotal. What sources does she draw from
   and how many different PERSPECTIVES do they reflect? What

additional viewpoints, if any, might she have included? How well does Godfrey establish her CREDIBILITY to write on this topic?

3. Godfrey is quite critical of the "Burlington (IOWA) Breaking News Reports and More" *Facebook* group, even as she acknowledges that it has more than triple the number of subscribers that the *Hawk Eye* newspaper has. How would you describe her TONE in the way she describes this site—and how does it compare with the way she describes the *Hawk Eye*? Point to words in the text that establish her tone.

4. LET'S TALK. According to Godfrey, the everyday stories told in local newspapers are "the connective tissue of a community... introduc[ing] people to their neighbors and encourag[ing] readers to listen to and empathize with one another" (14). Think about a community you belong to—a neighborhood, a club, your college, whatever. Is there a publication, website, or some other place where members of the community share news, stories, or other information? Get together with a few classmates and talk about your experiences with such sites: Do they help you meet people? share news? discuss community issues? Why or why not?

5. AND NOW WRITE. If you had the resources to start a community newspaper or publication of some kind, what would it be? What PURPOSES and AUDIENCES would it serve? What about MEDIA: would it be print? a website? a *Facebook* page? What would you call it and what topics would it address? Write and design an ad announcing the publication of this new resource, one that would attract both attention and respect.

The View from Somewhere

IT WAS AUGUST AGAIN, HOT AND DAMP. I was back in the Midwest, this time for a ten-day reporting trip in Detroit. One of my stories was about a man, Kevin Matthews, who was killed by police, unarmed, near the border of Dearborn and Detroit just before Christmas of 2015. He had a serious psychological disability, someone his family described like a child in an adult's body.

I sat for an afternoon with Matthews's family in their suburban lawyer's office. His mother and sister and thirty-year-old younger brother eyed me suspiciously as I sat down, calmly set up my microphone, and began to ask questions, stretching my arm across the conference room table toward each of them as their great, unthinkable pain unfurled in front of me. His mother was a small woman, hunched and dark-eyed, almost unable to speak. She was a housecleaner by profession, but had barely worked since Kevin died, immobilized with grief. When Kevin's younger brother, thin and hunched like their mother, finally talked, he broke down into choking sobs. I could feel my eyes go wide trying to take in the pain of their stories, their collective grief, trying not to lose my cool. Maybe the worst part was that he'd been killed by people he had trusted. Kevin loved everybody, they said, even cops. They all wished they had done more to protect him.

This family probably met with me because they wanted desperately to have Kevin's story told to a national audience, a power I had

---

Lewis Raven Wallace is a North Carolina–based journalist who is cohost of The View from Somewhere *podcast and codirector of* Press On, *a media collective focusing on issues of social justice. He is also a poet and an accordion player. This essay is from his 2019 book,* The View from Somewhere: Undoing the Myth of Journalistic Objectivity. *Wallace tweets from @LewisPants.*

at the time. There had been protests, but they had never grown big enough to get his name in national news, to force his memory onto the world. I think I already knew then that my story on *Marketplace* probably wouldn't accomplish that. Of course, one hopes that listening and telling helps heal pain, but who knows. I didn't know, and I don't know if it felt that way for them, either. So while I absorbed this family's unbearable trauma, I remained clear with myself that I was no savior. I was there to get a story and go home.

I was also working on a series about the devastated mortgage market in the city, modern-day redlining. Since the housing crash, lenders weren't making mortgage loans in Detroit; the vast majority of transactions were happening in cash, and investors would scoop up houses for $1,000 or $5,000 a pop, speculating on which neighborhoods might "come back." In large swaths of run-down neighborhoods, unless you had cash, the only way to buy a house was through the unregulated market in land contracts. These unregulated land contract sales were often predatory—giving people homes cheap, but with high interest and hidden costs. Often enough, the buyer would fall back on the payments, and the seller would repossess the house, a few thousand bucks richer, then "sell" it again to someone else.

5   I was looking for a "character" for this story, someone who'd been sold a house in Detroit under a bad land contract. After some door-knocking and a day in eviction court, I met a lawyer from a nonprofit who connected me with a Black man in his fifties named Eddie Cave.

I rolled up to Cave's place, and at first it seemed that no one was there. It was a two-story house, blue-gray, with a pretty peaked roof on a quiet street north of downtown. There was a classic car with flat tires in the driveway, and out front, an electric wheelchair sat empty, connected to a cord that ran around to a generator in the back. I called Cave's cell over and over, and finally he picked up, apologizing profusely; he was upstairs, and he'd taken some pain pills earlier and fallen asleep. Eddie struggled down the steps on crutches and met me out front, where he collapsed into the chair. I pulled out my recording equipment and sat on the cement steps in the sun to interview him.

It turned out this house, which he'd "bought" for just $2,500 on a land contract, had no running water, no electricity, and no heat. He ran space heaters from the generator out back and cooked on a propane stove inside the dark kitchen. When his legs were feeling better, Eddie had been painting the place, beautiful blue shades that complemented the Victorian-style oak woodwork. It was a classically beautiful Detroit house, but shadowy, and marked with Eddie's obvious loneliness. Now the trouble was that the "sellers" were trying to take the house back after he fell behind on payments—he hadn't realized he would owe thousands of dollars more in back taxes that the seller had dropped into the contract, which he signed with no lawyer advising him. A local nonprofit was trying to bail him out so that he could keep the house from tax foreclosure.

Cave had wire-rimmed glasses and a giant smile, salt-and-pepper whiskers on his gaunt face. He reminded me of people I'd known, queer men (although I never asked his orientation), and he alluded to a past in which he was part of a big, active community. He'd been a DJ in New York City, where he's from, but most of his friends had died, he said, from AIDS or crack. He'd been in Detroit for a couple decades, surviving his own disability and trying to do work in his community. I listened for hours, letting Cave offer up anything he wanted to share as I prepared to create an image of him as more than just a victim of his circumstances, a full person. At some point, sitting in the sun together, he hugged me from his chair and started to sob freely. He'd bought this house because he wanted a safe haven—for himself, and for the kids on the block. He just wanted to get back to where he could DJ block parties, he said, give back to his neighborhood. He didn't want to be the one getting help. He wanted to be a journalist. "You're a beautiful person," he said, smiling into my eyes. "So are you," I said, unself-conscious about the microphone between us.

I SAT IN THE DETROIT AIRPORT later that same day, drinking hard liquor at 2 p.m. next to this fountain that sends sculptural streams of water shooting across a pool in hypnotizing patterns. . . . I had grown up with the idea of this city, forty-five minutes away, seared in my mind: it was "dangerous" and "sad." Now, the image of Eddie Cave moving slowly through his home on crutches, lighting his propane stove, eclipsed those old images. My mind filled with the sound of Kevin Matthews's younger brother, sobbing in that conference room, the sterile fluorescent lights beating down on all of us.

10   Growing up, so many white people had talked about "helping" or saving Detroit, and now there was this narrative that the city was "coming back" because white people were moving there. I hated this story. I wanted to resist any sense of white saviorism, any idea that my journalism was somehow going to save people when it wasn't. Grief-stricken as I was, I really *didn't* see myself as helping my sources—I was aware that probably they were helping me more than I was them.

I got back to the shiny high-rise where *Marketplace*'s New York studios were housed, loaded with what radio people call "good tape," powerful stories plucked from the ruins of decades of racial segregation and institutional white supremacy, tears and lonesomeness, captured with deep empathy. I tried to do stories that talked about all of this in context, put a finger on who and what is to blame, but ultimately Eddie Cave got four minutes, hardly time to explain the mortgage market and paint a quick picture of his quiet block. Kevin Matthews and his family got six minutes. Later I would use my Detroit clips to apply for jobs and fellowships.

Periodically during my years in public radio, I descended into a similar despair about what I saw as the extractive, exploitive nature of my work. I wanted to reconcile the contradictions, to believe I was doing right by people, but it called to mind one of my favorite books, Janet Malcolm's *The Journalist and the Murderer*. It's a story about a journalist covering a murder, but she also compares journalists to murderers—in that we are people whose vocation calls on us to deceive our sources, make them believe we are their friends when in fact we are just purveyors of whichever part of their story we deem the most useful, the most true. She implies that journalism is a sociopathic calling, at its root.

As journalism is taught and practiced today, I can't say I disagree. Good intentions aren't enough when you're dealing with entrenched power structures. I'd always tried to push past my own comfort zone in the search for more justice, which in this case meant abandoning the fantasy that I had truly "helped." But the version of myself that had parachuted in to Detroit, and left with a bitter picture, another sliver of poverty porn, was a version of myself I didn't really like: the journalist as murderer, or at least as miner, extracting people's pain to craft a story whose beneficiaries are the audience, the radio show, the reporter—other people, elsewhere. My empathy, no matter how deep and real, could not undo this power dynamic. I was another white person profiting off of Black people's pain. I knew there had to be another way....

WHEN I WAS WITH EDDIE CAVE and with Kevin Matthews's family, I felt wrong not because it was wrong to tell their stories. I felt wrong because I was working from a model of extraction rather than collaboration. Detroit, police violence, Blackness, poverty, and death all become products, packaged for the consumption of some other person far away.

The extractive approach to journalism treats facts like coal in a mine, using sources and places the way mining companies use land—as a resource to dig into, and then leave behind. It's the most common model for journalism today, particularly journalism about marginalized communities, and it goes hand in hand with "objectivity": the outside observer objectifies the people and places the stories are about, who become "sources" rather than human beings. It is deeply grounded in capitalist ideology: people, experiences, and events are turned into commodities, things that can be sold as "clickbait" or pushed as "shareable content." Such objectification bolsters journalists' careers, but it doesn't build trust or necessarily reflect a truer version of the world. It also limits the action and agency of the people and things we write about and claim to know, freezing them in place.... 15

FOR SARAH ALVAREZ, accountability and collaboration didn't require shared experiences or even deep empathy. Alvarez started Outlier

Media in 2016, based on the premise that low-income people in Detroit were underserved by their local outlets....

She saw that public media often talked *about* poor people but didn't often produce news that was actually *for* them, based on their needs or interests. Public radio's programming reflects its high-income audiences. The audience, in turn, is built based on programming, and then programming is further tailored to the audience, and so on in perpetuity. She thought public media lacked a vision for interrupting this cycle. But where I had seen a gaping hole I had no idea how to fill, she saw an opportunity: use data to create accountability and produce information that underserved audiences actually need.

"I don't see a lot of journalism organizations being like, 'who are we not serving.' And how do we bring them into the audience and how do we create that is of value to more people," Alvarez said in an interview.

She figured if low-income people weren't listening to public radio, it was because they didn't find it useful or interesting. So when she started Outlier Media, she used data, mostly United Way's 211 call records, to figure out what kinds of information residents were most often seeking. Housing and utilities were at the top of the list; as I had learned in my own reporting, the city is overrun with predatory landlords, shady housing transactions, tax foreclosures, and bad contracts that leave people like Eddie Cave exposed to exploitation. But instead of waiting for the Eddie Caves of the world to come out of the woodwork *after* they'd been exploited or misled, Alvarez created a news service to meet their information needs *before* they signed bad land contracts or leased homes that were in foreclosure. She built a database with public information where you can search any address for background.

20   Then, she went to her customers directly. She bought lists of phone numbers in the poorest neighborhoods and sent out automated texts inviting people to inquire about any house—their own or one they were considering buying or renting. A person could find out easily if the seller or landlord actually owned the house (deed scams are com-

mon in the city) and learn whether the house was in tax foreclosure or had other unpaid debts. This information helps tenants and prospective buyers hold landlords and owners accountable directly. After they text to receive data, they get a follow-up text encouraging them to contact Alvarez with further questions; she often answers dozens of calls a week, and the automated service is used by hundreds of people per month.

"My news consumers are very focused on accountability, as am I," she told me. "There are many people who have saved their homes with this information. There are many people who have avoided eviction with this information." . . .

Alvarez considers herself an independent journalist, but not an "objective" one.

"I definitely have an agenda," Alvarez said. "My agenda is for low-income Detroiters to have the same access to information as high-income Detroiters."

Learning about Alvarez's work in Detroit was a lightbulb moment for me: when I came to Eddie Cave to ask him to tell his story, he had already bought that house with the back taxes attached, and it wasn't even clear if the "sellers" held the deed. The story I was there to tell wasn't really for him or for people in his situation. But Alvarez's form of journalism could have shared the information that Cave needed *before* he signed a contract. And unlike models I was familiar with, this journalism didn't depend on deep and empathetic relationships with each "source"—the people usually treated as sources, low-income Detroiters like Cave, are also the *audience*. Where I had come to Detroit looking for a sad story like Cave's to extract for an outside audience, Alvarez's role in Detroit is based entirely on accountability to people like him.

She has gotten pushback from other journalists on her ideas. . . .   25

[One] criticism has been that her approach is more a charitable service than a news service; she disagrees, and to me the evidence is obvious. High-income people get reports on the stock market daily

Here Wallace uses classification to sharpen his focus— and support his argument. Learn more about using classification that strategy on pp. 89–90.

from TV news tickers and shows like *Marketplace*. Outlier Media is simply economic information for low-income people. Both the information and the delivery are different because this audience has different needs. It is news, but it's news that upends and unsettles the power dynamic of much of the mainstream media right now: in most news organizations, oppressed and marginalized people are treated as characters whose stories are there to be extracted and told, rather than as engaged audiences or community members or, god forbid, journalists themselves....

I DON'T BELIEVE IN SILVER BULLETS, and I also know journalism in the information age serves more than one purpose. For some people, it's a source of data and facts, organized in such a way that they are useful or necessary. For others, it's a source of stories to give meaning or perspective to our confusing, overstimulated lives. And for still others, journalism is a way to build community, to find connection or cohesion around an idea or an experience. So while journalists are never neutral purveyors of "just the facts," some will focus more on organizing facts while others will focus more on interpreting them or extrapolating solutions from them, and others will focus on building communities surrounding them....

In order to ensure that an equitable future is possible, I also believe media production *needs* to be paired with media activism. That means everything from working for freedom of information and protection of net neutrality, to creating robust and representative local newsrooms with clear mechanisms for accountability and feedback, to defending the free speech rights of both individual journalists and media organizations.

Building equitable, accountable organizations also inevitably means facing the power dynamics of race, class, gender, and exploitation. After all, people aren't "underrepresented" in newsrooms because they want to be, but because racism, heteropatriarchy, ableism, classism, and xenophobia are built in to the way we do journalism and the way we talk about ethics and "objectivity." And I'm afraid that until we let go of the activist/journalist divide, our hands will be tied each time we try to address inequity and power. Activism is not, and cannot be, a dirty word in journalism anymore: we need activists in our newsrooms, and activists in the street defending our newsrooms. . . .

My friend Jennifer Brandel once said that the purpose of journal- 30 ism is to show people what we are capable of—the beautiful and the bad. We have a choice about the world we depict in our stories, and that choice matters because it helps us see what is possible. Maybe the news alone can't teach imagination, curiosity, and social change, and maybe journalism alone can't end exploitation or enact justice, but it can acknowledge these values, bend toward them. We need to imagine that we are capable of changing the world just as we are capable of destroying it.

Thinking about the Text

1. Lewis Wallace notes that many journalists today, himself included, treat people as objects to be mined for a good story, particularly stories "about marginalized communities" (15). What are the characteristics of this approach, and what examples does Wallace provide? What, then, is he ARGUING in this essay?

2. Wallace uses some of his personal experience as EVIDENCE to support his argument. What other evidence does he offer, and which kind of evidence do you find most persuasive—and why?

3. Given Wallace's admission that he himself has been an exploiter, a "miner" guilty of "extracting people's pain to craft a story" (13), what does he do to gain our trust and to build CREDIBILITY as an author on this topic? What words would you substitute for *exploiter* or *miner* to describe the kind of journalism Wallace advocates?

4. LET'S TALK. The subtitle of Wallace's book is "undoing the myth of journalistic objectivity." Talk with a few classmates about this "myth" and whether it is one that you accept—and why or why not. If not objectivity, what do you think journalists should strive for? If, as Wallace argues, complete objectivity is impossible,

what can a journalist do to be fair, truthful, and empathetic—and to be a responsible journalist? How would you describe the responsibilities journalists should have toward their subjects—and their audiences? And how about you? What responsibility do you have to any people you write about?

5. AND NOW WRITE. Wallace sets forth a number of possible PURPOSES for journalism (see especially paragraph 27). Assume that you need to prepare a brief presentation for your class in which you explain what you think the major purposes of journalism in the twenty-first century should be, providing several examples of such journalism at work. Create and design a set of slides to use for this presentation.

SAM WINEBURG

Navigating the Dangers of the Web

THE WEB is a treacherous place.

A website's author may not be its author. References that confer legitimacy may have little to do with the claims they anchor. Signals of credibility like a dot-org domain can be the artful handiwork of a Washington, D.C., public relations maven.

Unless you possess multiple Ph.D.s—in virology, economics and the intricacies of immigration policy—often the wisest thing to do when landing on an unfamiliar site is to ignore it.

Learning to ignore information is not something taught in school. School teaches the opposite: to read a text thoroughly and closely before rendering judgment. Anything short of that is rash.

But on the web, where a witches' brew of advertisers, lobbyists,[1] conspiracy theorists and foreign governments[2] conspire to hijack attention, the same strategy spells doom. Online, critical ignoring is just as important as critical thinking.

That's because, like a pinball bouncing from bumper to bumper, our attention careens from notification to text message to the next vibrating thing we must check.

The cost of all this overabundance, as the late Nobel Laureate Herbert Simon observed, is scarcity. A flood of information depletes attention and fractures the ability to concentrate.

Modern society, wrote Simon, faces a challenge: to learn to "allocate attention efficiently among the overabundance of sources that might consume it."[3]

We're losing the battle between attention and information.

Sam Wineburg is a professor emeritus of education, history, and American studies at Stanford University. His research focuses on how people judge the credibility of online content. This piece first appeared in The Conversation, *an online media outlet that publishes news stories and research reports. He tweets from @samwineburg.*

We're losing the battle between attention and information.

"Glued to the Site"

10   As an applied psychologist, I study how people determine what is true online.

Notice how he slips in his academic status to demonstrate his credibility? Find out how you can establish your credibility in what you write on pp. 164–66.

My research team at Stanford University recently tested a national sample of 3,446 high school students on their ability to evaluate digital sources.[4] Armed with a live internet connection, students examined a website that claims to "disseminate factual reports" on climate science.

Students were asked to judge whether the site was reliable. A screen prompt reminded them that they could search anywhere online to reach their answer.

Instead of leaving the site, the vast majority did exactly what school teaches: They stayed glued to the site—and read. They consulted the "About" page, clicked on technical reports, and examined graphs and charts. Unless they happened to possess a master's degree in climate science, the site, filled with the trappings of academic research, looked, well, pretty good.

The few students—less than 2%—who learned the site was backed by the fossil fuel industry did so not because they applied critical thinking to its contents. They succeeded because they hopped off the website and consulted the open web. They used the web to read the web.

As a student who searched the internet for the group's name wrote: 15 "It has ties to large companies that want to purposefully mislead people when it comes to climate change. According to *USA Today*, Exxon has sponsored this nonprofit to pump out misleading information on climate change."

Instead of getting tangled up in the site's reports or suckered into its neutral-sounding language, this student did what professional fact checkers do: She evaluated the site by leaving it. Fact checkers engage in what we call lateral reading, opening up new tabs across the top of their screens to search for information about an organization or individual before diving into a site's contents.

Only after consulting the open web do they gauge whether expending attention is worth it. They know that the first step in critical thinking is knowing when to deploy it.

Critical Thinking

The good news is that students can be taught to read the internet this way.

In an online nutrition course at the University of North Texas, we embedded short instructional videos that demonstrated the dangers of dwelling on an unknown site and taught students how to evaluate it.[5]

At the beginning of the course, students were duped by features 20 that are ludicrously easy to game: a site's "look," the presence of links to established sources, strings of scientific references or the sheer quantity of information a site provides.

On the test we gave at the beginning of the semester, only three in 87 students left a site to evaluate it. By the end, over three-quarters did. Other researchers, teaching the same strategies, have found similarly hopeful results.[6]

Learning to resist the lure of dubious information demands more than a new strategy in students' digital tool box. It requires the humility that comes from facing one's vulnerability: that despite formidable intellectual powers and critical thinking skills, no one is immune to the slippery ruses plied by today's digital rogues.

By dwelling on an unfamiliar site, imagining ourselves smart enough to outsmart it, we squander attention and cede control to the site's designers.

Spending a few moments vetting the site by drawing on the awesome powers of the open web, we regain control and with it our most precious resource: Our attention.

Notes

1. Massoglia, A. (2020). "Dark money" networks hide political agendas behind fake news sites. *Open Secrets*. https://www.open secrets.org/news/2020/05/dark-money-networks-fake-news-sites/

2. Steinberg, G. (2018). Foreign-funded NGOs, political power, and democratic legitimacy. *Lawfare*. https://www.lawfareblog.com /foreign-funded-ngos-political-power-and-democratic-legitimacy

3. Simon, H. A. (1971). Designing organizations for an information-rich world. In M. Greenberg (Ed.), *Computers, Communication, and the Public Interest*. Johns Hopkins University Press.

4. Breakstone, J., Smith, M., Wineburg, S., Rapaport, A., Carle, J., Garland, M., & Saavedra, A. (in press). Students' civic online reasoning: A national portrait. *Educational Researcher*. https://purl.stanford.edu /cz440cm8408

5. Breakstone, J., Smith, M., Connors, P., Ortega, T., Kerr, D., & Wineburg, S. (2021). Lateral reading: College students learn to critically evaluate internet sources in an online course. *Harvard Kennedy School (HKS) Misinformation Review*. https://doi.org/10 .37016/mr-2020-56

6. Brodsky, J. E., Brooks, P. J., Scimeca, D., Todorova, R., Galati, P., Batson, M., Grosso, R., Matthews, M., Miller, V., Caulfield, M. (2021). Improving college students' fact-checking strategies through lateral reading instruction in a general education civics course. *Cognitive Research, 6*, 23. https://doi.org/10.1186/s41235-021-00291-4

Thinking about the Text

1. What REASONS does Sam Wineburg give for saying that "we're losing the battle between attention and information" (9)? He also says that attention is "our most precious resource" (24). How do those statements play out in your life? What problems do you face in deciding what to pay attention to—and what distracts you from doing so?

2. Wineburg wants us to read and think about what he says. What strategies does he use to get and keep our attention? Consider his OPENING sentences—saying, for example, that "foreign governments are "conspir[ing] to hijack [our] attention" (5) and even that we're "losing the battle" between attention and information (9). These are fighting words—about searching the web! See what other instances of scary or less-than-academic language you can find in this piece. Did it keep you interested in reading about a topic that may not have interested you all that much? If so, how?

3. Wineburg researches how people judge credibility. How would you assess his own CREDIBILITY in this article? What does he do to establish his own authority to write on this topic? Point to places in the text where he does so.

4. LET'S TALK. Wineburg argues that "learning to resist the lure of dubious information" demands not only critical thinking skills but also the humility to recognize that "no one is immune to the slippery ruses plied by today's digital rogues" (22). Get together with a few classmates and talk about your own experiences with "dubious information" and "digital rogues." How, where, and when have you encountered them and what have you learned from such experiences? What new strategies has this article taught you?

5. AND NOW WRITE. Wineburg echoes the suggestions given in Chapter 15 on LATERAL READING. How, and when, do you practice this kind of reading? Pay attention to your online reading habits for two days, including your browsing on social media.

What do you read quickly or briefly and what, if anything, do you skip over without pausing? What do you attend to carefully, and what, if anything, do you check on by reading laterally? After two days, review your notes and look for patterns. What topics, authors, perspectives, or kinds of sources do you seem to pay more attention to—or ignore--and why? Write a brief essay describing your findings and noting any ways you might change the way you read.

Celebrating World Press Freedom Day!

Panel 1: CELEBRATE WORLD PRESS FREEDOM!

Panel 2: CHERISH IT! *Joel Pett*

Panel 3: STOP ACCEPTING (AND SPREADING) FAKE NEWS AND LIES!

Panel 4: FIGURE OUT WHICH SOURCES SEEK OUT TRUTH... IT'S NOT THAT HARD

Panel 5: 5/2/21 LEX·HL/wy.com/#73 ...EVEN WHEN IT'S UNCOMFORTABLE!

Panel 6: *NOT* WHAT I WANTED TO HEAR!

If you want to do what the TV narrator suggests, Chapter 15 will help get you started.

Joel Pett is a cartoonist for the Lexington Herald-Leader. *His political cartoons have appeared in hundreds of newspapers and magazines, from the* Washington Post, *the* Los Angeles Times, *and the* Atlanta Journal-Constitution *to* Newsweek, Business Week, *and* Mad. *His cartoons have been published in several collections, most recently* Thinking Inside the Box (2000). *His many awards include the 2000 Pulitzer Prize for editorial cartoons and an Emmy award for TV commentary. He also does stand up and has performed at Indiana University, Ohio State, and many other colleges and universities. He sums up his philosophy this way: "Hello, God? Listen, we could use some help down here." He posts on* Instagram *from* @joelpettcartoons.

This May 2021 cartoon highlights World Press Freedom Day, an annual event sponsored by the United Nations and UNESCO to raise awareness of the importance of a free press around the world.

Thinking about the Text

1. Joel Pett packs a lot to think about into six panels of simple drawings and just a few words. How confident are you that you completely understand his message? If not, what's not quite clear to you? SUMMARIZE the cartoon's message the best you can in a few sentences.

2. Pett wrote this cartoon within a certain RHETORICAL SITUATION. Considering his AUDIENCE (readers of a newspaper in Kentucky and elsewhere) and the particular CONTEXT (the day before World Press Freedom Day), what would you say his main PURPOSE was in creating this cartoon? How can you tell— and do you think he achieved that purpose? If not, why not?

3. LET'S TALK. Who is the single character depicted in this cartoon? It's safe to say he's a man and he's not young. What else can you reasonably determine about him based on the details in the drawing? How might the message change if any of those characteristics were altered? For example, what if he were young? If his skin were dark? If he had a tattoo? If he were a woman or someone with no obvious gender markings? Work with a few classmates to imagine how the message might be understood differently if the character were different. Should Pett have chosen to depict a different character? Why or why not?

4. AND NOW WRITE. In the final panel, the character says, "*Not* what I wanted to hear!" What do you think he *does* want to hear? How would you respond to him? Write to him—agreeing with what he says, disagreeing, or both.

SAVANNAH JACOBSON

Inside the Lines

ARELIABLE WAY TO STIR UP ATTENTION is to posit that "the mainstream media" did or did not do something. Someone will invariably respond; everyone's got an opinion on the subject. That was the draw, anyway, when, to drum up business, Nick Bacon, a video producer in Chicago, named his company, which provides technical support for events, Mainstream Media LLC. He figured it would be good for search engine optimization. "We were just two guys working out of a back room in an apartment," Bacon said, "and we thought it was kind of funny to suggest that, like, this is where the mainstream media is." Bacon's strategy paid off; during the primaries in 2016 and 2020, with Trump tearing into the mainstream media on the campaign trail, people called, emailed, and tweeted at the business every week. Last year, a pair from South Carolina phoned him repeatedly for an hour. "They legitimately thought I was the mainstream media Donald Trump was talking about," Bacon said. He tried to explain what his business actually was; after an extended back-and-forth, they asked him to convey their anti-media message—which Bacon described as "impotent rage"—to the rest of us.

It's hard to blame the couple for their confusion. Everyone is constantly yelling about the mainstream media, and rarely are we referring to the same thing....

There are many ways to think about what constitutes the mainstream media, if such a thing exists at all. It can refer, simply, to any newspaper or to your local daytime talk show; at its most pernicious, the "mainstream media" represents a conspiracy of gatekeepers.... A

Savannah Jacobson *is a staff writer and editor for the* Columbia Journalism Review, *where this report was published in 2021. Jacobson tweets from @srjacobson1.*

Jacobson lays out a number of perspectives on his topic, a good way to show respect for different positions. See more about that on pp. 114–16.

popular academic argument describes the mainstream media as actors who wield "power over discourse," which conjures a certain image: wealthy, white, male. As independent local news withers, and media companies become increasingly corporatized—under the control of large conglomerates and hedge funds—that critique rings all the more true. To Sheryl Kennedy Haydel, a scholar of historically Black college and university newspapers at Louisiana State, the term "mainstream media" remains useful as long as journalism has an equity problem. "The people who are the decision-makers, or even the reporters, don't look like the nation you and I live in," she told me.

Matthew Pressman, a journalism historian at Seton Hall University, sees it differently: "I think it's a bad term," he said, "because it's so vast that it can mean anything. And is the media, you know, one random reporter who said something on *Twitter*? Or is it Mark Levin's talk radio show? Is it just the *New York Times*? Is it some local, ad-filled, flyer-type circular that is delivered in every home in a bunch of communities?" When he's teaching, Pressman often gets a firsthand look at how muddled the category can be. "Whenever my students are talking about things that the media does wrong, it's always like, '*TMZ* did this sleazy or irresponsible thing.'" ...

5   In May, the Pew Research Center released a report finding "wide agreement" among Americans surveyed that a certain set of outlets are in the mainstream: ABC News, CNN, the *New York Times*, *MSNBC*, the *Wall Street Journal*; 73 percent said that Fox News belongs to the mainstream.[1] Yet *The Sean Hannity Show* did not make the mainstream ranks. And among respondents who rely on Fox for political news, as well as those who tune in to NPR, majorities said they believe their preferred source to be mainstream yet different from most other outlets. *HuffPost* might be the mainstream media, the poll said, but *BuzzFeed* probably isn't. The more one looks at the results, the more contradictory they appear.

What is clear is that those of us who use the phrase "mainstream media" have only a loosely shared understanding of reality, at best. And yet we continue to use the same term, one weighted with history,

Four media outlets widely considered "mainstream."

to describe a phenomenon that sounds assured and entrenched but is actually amorphous and dynamic. Perhaps the ambiguity of "the mainstream media" reveals something profound about the messy information ecosystem we're in.

TO UNDERSTAND WHAT THE MEDIA IS NOW, it helps to look back at how we got here. "Certainly no one would have spoken of 'the media' in sweeping terms in the nineteenth century, when readers got their news from local papers, with all their diverse viewpoints," David Greenberg, a professor of history, journalism, and media studies at Rutgers University, wrote in a 2008 paper on liberal media.[2] Mainstreaming, if we may call it that, was a process that worked in tandem with technological advances and the professionalization of reporting. It also reflected how American media developed alongside powerful wavelengths of social discourse.

An early push toward mainstreaming came in the middle of the nineteenth century, with the invention of the telegraph. "Some journalists," Richard Allen Schwarzlose writes in *The Nation's Newsbrokers* (1989), "quickly grasped the new technologies' possibilities and pitfalls and moved to master them."[3] One of those journalists was Moses Yale Beach, the publisher of the *New York Sun*. Following the Mexican–American War, Beach helped coordinate an effort to share the costs of transmitting information among a group of New York newspapers. They called the cooperative the Harbor News Association;

eventually, it morphed into the Associated Press. The AP, which can be viewed as an early effort in mainstream journalism, helped set a standard for modern notions of "objective" reporting and newswriting, with its pithy sentences and lack of flair.

Still, newspapers remained, for the most part, highly localized, disconnected, and unflinchingly partisan. Michael Schudson, a historian and sociologist of journalism at Columbia, told me that, for most people, "if they read a newspaper at all, they read their local newspaper"; the media comprised their city's and region's outlets. That included the Black press, which wrote "with conviction against white racism, violence, and hypocrisy" and "covered the ticktock of African-American life."[4] The *Chicago Defender*, one of the most influential Black papers, encouraged families to move north during the Great Migration—a subject largely overlooked by white-owned outlets. (Isabel Wilkerson has called the Great Migration "perhaps the biggest underreported story

A newsboy selling the *Chicago Defender*, 1942.

of the twentieth century.")[5] In Haydel's view, Black newspapers defined the mainstream press, in their way, by operating outside of it. "If they referenced the papers, it would be—maybe not the term 'mainstream'— but the 'white press,'" she said. "There was that very clear distinction."

In the twentieth century, nationally distributed newspapers and 10 magazines gained prominence, as did radio. During the First and Second World Wars, the United States and its allies aimed to garner broad support for their actions, using the press as a tool. "Radio news was immensely influential in shaping public opinion because of its unique qualities as an information medium and because it was untainted by the legacies of earlier propaganda," Gerd Horten writes in *Radio Goes to War* (2002).[6] Walter Lippmann, the celebrated American journalist, coined the phrase "the manufacture of consent" to describe the influence of mass media.[7] ...

Television, and the introduction of three major news channels, marked the start of a new era, when Americans' consumption of news became a shared experience, transcending geography. By the fifties, Greenberg wrote, "the constituent parts of the national media"—the *New York Times* and other papers, *Time* and *Newsweek*, the networks— "were attracting readers on the basis of their avowedly disinterested news coverage," claiming to present unbiased, authoritative reporting to a wide audience.[8] In 1957, over two-thirds of American homes had televisions; by 1963, more Americans turned to television than any other medium to get their news. As Schudson told me, "That allows Walter Cronkite to sign off with 'And that's the way it is'"—the promise of a singular, shared truth acceptable to an American mainstream.

During the sixties and seventies, when Cronkite was the anchor of the *CBS Evening News*, he gained a reputation as "the most trusted man in America." But it was at the same time that the term "mainstream media" entered the discourse, uniting all types of journalism as one sinister entity. ... Against the backdrop of the civil rights movement, a public turn against the Vietnam War, and a broader cultural revolution, Richard Nixon entered the White House and, seeking the rhetorical upper hand against a critical press, began using "the media" to

Walter Cronkite, "the most trusted man in America in the 1960s and 70s.

obscure the valor of the Fourth Estate and set an agenda on his terms. "The press became 'the media' because the word had a manipulative, Madison Avenue, all-encompassing connotation, and the press hated it," William Safire, the columnist and former Nixon speechwriter, wrote in his memoir *Before the Fall* (1975). Or, as Schudson told me: "Nixon wanted people to hate the media."[9]

DURING THE HEIGHT of the civil rights movement—as footage of anti-Black violence aired nightly in American living rooms—the press helped sow support among white people for the cause of Black liberation. The rise of "the media," as a term, provided a conservative counterattack. "White supremacists were growing increasingly frustrated in finding themselves losing the battle for national public opinion," Greenberg wrote. "Blaming the messenger became a reflexive response."[10] The more journalists showed sympathy with civil rights activists, the more the idea became ingrained in right-wing thought: powerful media outlets, suffused with liberal bias, were operating against American interests.

That line of argument boosted a generation of conservative outlets that disingenuously, but capably, depicted themselves as operating outside the mainstream. Chief among them was the *National Review*, founded by William F. Buckley Jr. in 1955, which "cultivated doubts about the fairness of the mainstream media," as Julie B. Lane, a mass-communication historian at Boise State University, writes in *News on the Right: Studying Conservative News Cultures*.[11] The word "media" doesn't appear in the founding statement of the *National Review*, but there is discussion of "liberal orthodoxy"; mention of the *Times* as being "in place" with the United Nations, League of Women Voters, and liberal intellectuals; and ample insistence that the magazine sat outside the mainstream.[12] ...

William A. Rusher, a conservative activist who was the publisher   15
of the *National Review*, ... had a syndicated column, "The Conservative Advocate," that ran in newspapers across the country; he also appeared on radio and television. Buckley, too, wrote a column,

William F. Buckley, founder of the *National Review*.

with an even wider reach. The environment was ripe for conservative thinkers—presenting themselves as unheard and unrepresented—to take up space in major newspapers, networks, and magazines. Their platform was vastly larger than that of most civil rights activists, who remained on the fringes of public discourse.

By 1987, under Ronald Reagan, the Federal Communications Commission stopped enforcing, and effectively repealed, the Fairness Doctrine, which had required broadcasters to reflect contrasting views on matters of public interest. Talk radio and cable news shows, unhindered by speech regulations, proliferated: *The Rush Limbaugh Show* made its debut in 1988; Sean Hannity hosted his first radio program in 1989. Cable networks built out twenty-four-hour news cycles, including debate shows featuring the same talking heads who appeared in national newspapers and magazines and formed the basis of mainstream opinionating: "a tiny group," as Eric Alterman writes in *Sound and Fury* (1992), his history of punditry—but one with "a healthy dose of self-promotional talent."[13]

Fox News Channel premiered in 1996. Its founder, Rupert Murdoch, the Australian media mogul, sought to compete with the major networks; in hiring Roger Ailes, a veteran of Republican politics and conservative media, as the founding chief executive and head of the network's news division, he positioned Fox as an antidote to press coverage friendly to liberals. Ailes branded the network with a slogan that lasted twenty years: "fair and balanced." By day, Fox reported on the news; at prime time, its opinion programming spanned from moderate to deeply conservative—and shifted rightward as the years went by. "There's a whole country that elitists will never acknowledge," Ailes told the *New York Times* in 2001. "What people deeply resent out there are those in the 'blue' states thinking they're smarter. There's a touch of that in our news." He added, "If we look conservative, it's because the other guys are so far to the left."[14]

Painting the rest of the press as out of touch and elitist continues to win Fox favor, and the Buckley view—that conservatism is inherently non-mainstream, despite its occupancy of nearly all halls of power—persists. . . . I asked both a Fox News media reporter and a company spokesperson if the network considers itself part of the main-stream media, given its overwhelming popularity; neither got back to me. But in general, characters within the Fox universe, including Donald Trump, reconcile such contradictions by referring to audience members as a "silent majority"—a term that was, like "the media," borrowed from Nixon.

"WHEN PEOPLE THINK OF 'THE MEDIA' as an abstraction—and as some big, powerful, maybe malign force that's very distant from them—then they're wary and mistrustful," Pressman told me. Trust in the press is near an all-time low, but according to Gallup polling the numbers have been declining for decades. The reason is not simply political polarization. A recent study from the Media Insight Project, a collaboration between two think tanks, found a split in values espoused by the press and the public: "Rather than distrust toward the media being tied only to the perception of partisan bias, the problem at the heart of the media trust crisis may be skepticism about the underlying purpose and mission journalists are trying to fulfill in the first place."[15]

Many Americans express a desire for alternatives to the main-stream media—or at least seek to balance out their media diets. The Pew report indicates that the mainstream media is believed to be cred-ible, but individual outlets must be held in equilibrium with those of a similar caliber. Familiarity counts, in other words, but people like to perform their own degree of research. As Margaret Sullivan, of the *Washington Post*, told me, "I don't love the term 'mainstream media,' but it's somewhat useful because people seem to know what it means—the national media, including the large newspapers, the Associated Press, the broadcast networks, and the major cable networks."

What does it say about American media consumers that we swing between different half truths, that we read past one another, that we build our own miniature knowledge bubbles? With the right cable account and digital subscriptions, we can buy whatever facts we want. It's easy to conclude that we're now in a period of extreme upheaval—a collapse of consensus on the nature of reality. But there are also signs that we've swung back to the pole of the nineteenth century,

20

with one key distinction: the fractures that were once local are now individual.

Even in a marketplace with more choices, I'd argue that a mainstream media does exist. There is a collection of agenda-setting channels and publications—ABC, CBS, NBC, the *Times*, the *Washington Post*, those in the Pew report—whose coverage is influenced and reinforced by one another. Collectively, they create a mainstream point of view, to which others must react. That's not necessarily a bad thing. To Haydel, where there is a mainstream, there is always room around the edges for different kinds of expression. "As somebody who believes in alternative media, I would never want them to lose that term," she told me. "It's another access point for people who feel left out of the 'mainstream' to have a place to learn to grow. It is vital."

Notes

1. Shearer, E., & Mitchell, A. (2021). Broad agreement in U.S.—even among partisans—on which news outlets are part of the mainstream media. *Pew Research Center*. https://pewrsr.ch/2Q42UrK

2. Greenberg, D. (2008). The idea of the "liberal media" and its roots in the civil rights movement. *The Sixties, 1*, 167–186. https://www.tandfonline.com/doi/abs/10.1080/17541320802457111

3. Schwarzlose, R. A. (1989). *The nation's newsbrokers: Vol. 1. The formative years: From pretelegraph to 1865*. Northwestern University Press.

4. Neason, A. (2018). We wish to plead our own cause. *Columbia Journalism Review*. https://www.cjr.org/special_report/black-press.php

5. Wilkerson, I. (2010). *The warmth of other suns*. Vintage Books.

6. Horten, G. (2002). *Radio goes to war*. University of California Press.

7. Lippmann, W. (2010). *Public opinion*. Feather Trail Press. (Original work published 1922)

8. Greenberg, D. (2008). The idea of the "liberal media" and its roots in the civil rights movement. *The Sixties, 1*, 167–186. https://www.tandfonline.com/doi/abs/10.1080/17541320802457111

9. Safire, W. (1975). *Before the fall*. Transaction Publishers.

10. Greenberg, D. (2008). The idea of the "liberal media" and its roots in the civil rights movement. *The Sixties, 1*, 167–186. https://www.tandfonline.com/doi/abs/10.1080/17541320802457111

11. Lane, J. B. (2020). Cultivating distrust of the mainstream media: Propagandists for a liberal machine and the American establishment. In A. Nadler & A. J. Bauer (Eds.), *News on the right: Studying conservative news cultures* (pp. 157–173). Oxford.

12. Buckley, W. F., Jr. (1955). Our mission statement. *National Review.* https://www.nationalreview.com/1955/11/our-mission-statement-william-f-buckley-jr/

13. Alterman, E. (1999). *Sound and fury.* Cornell University Press.

14. Sella, M. (2001, June 24). "The red-state network." *New York Times.* https://www.nytimes.com/2001/06/24/magazine/the-red-state-network.html

15. Media Insight Project. (2021). A new way of looking at trust in media: Do Americans share journalism's core values? *American Press Institute.* https://www.americanpressinstitute.org/publications/reports/survey-research/trust-journalism-values/

Thinking about the Text

1. Throughout this article, Savannah Jacobson quotes a number of sources who offer varying definitions of "mainstream media" as well as their own takes on its usefulness. Review Jacobson's essay and then summarize how you think she defines mainstream media and what her STANCE is on it. What words and passages lead you to your answers to these questions?

2. In the next to last paragraph, Jacobson says it's easy to think that "with the right cable account and digital subscriptions, we can buy whatever facts we want." Do you agree? She doesn't offer specific examples to support this claim—but what could you point to in your own experience that might do so?

3. What strategies does Jacobson use to establish her own CREDIBILITY and ETHOS? Do the sources she relies on help establish her credentials—and if so, how? Note that Jacobson does not speak in first person "I" until the last paragraph. Why

do you think she made this choice—and what difference does using third person up until that point make?

4. LET'S TALK. What do you think constitutes the mainstream media in the United States today? How well do you trust it and the "news" it reports? Discuss these questions with a few classmates. You'll likely find that you don't have the same ideas; in what ways do you think alike, and in what ways do you differ? What advice might you offer to those who write for the media, mainstream or otherwise?

5. AND NOW WRITE. No one can follow all of the news; there's just too much of it! But we all follow *some* of it, whether it's to read about a favorite sports team, the latest celebrity gossip, the swings in the stock market, or issues facing your local community. What do you do to stay informed about things that matter to you? What kind of news do you usually follow—and where? *Twitter*? TV? *Facebook*? Radio? Podcasts? A daily or weekly newspaper? Write a brief essay DESCRIBING the way you routinely follow the news. What topics do you pay attention to, where do you look, and how reliable do you think the news you follow is? Consider everything that you ordinarily do; you may be surprised to see how much it actually is.

34 Who Owns Nature?

NATURE IS NOT A PLACE TO VISIT. IT IS HOME.

—GARY SNYDER

We hear of "mother nature," of "the call of nature," of "crimes against nature," of "going back to nature." And we are bombarded by advertisements for products that claim to be "all natural." The words "nature" and "natural" are so familiar, so all around us, that we may not have stopped to think about what they really mean and how they relate to us. What is *nature* to you? How do you define this little six-letter word? What do you think of as "natural?" Why not jot down some responses to these questions before you begin to read the essays in this chapter—and then return to your notes after reading and discussing some or all of those essays. See whether (or how) your thinking might change.

Consider wilderness and nature. Historian **William Cronon** writes about the "trouble with wilderness," challenging the common view of it as "sacred," outside time and untouched by humans. Journalist **Emma Marris** takes on this "myth of wilderness" as well, critiquing the "high-gloss version" presented in nature documentaries, which she argues are "beautiful"—but also "false." Learning to listen to trees and other natural elements led scientist and Indigenous author **Robin Kimmerer** to think about the grammar of living things, a language in which everything—rocks and rivers, mushrooms and trees—is "alive." Imagine how less lonely we would be, Kimmerer says, if we looked at the world from this perspective.

Ian Leahy and Yaryna Serkez offer another perspective on trees with a series of maps comparing the number of trees in affluent neighborhoods with the numbers in lower-income areas, arguing that "tree equity" would improve both our health and our environment. **Benji Backer** adds what he calls a "conservative case for environmentalism," calling on us, for example, to listen to and learn from people who live in coal country, whose lives depend on that resource.

Carl Zimmer takes us to the microscopic level, in an essay on how rhinoviruses—the common cold—"gently conquered the world" and proposes that such a conquest may not be a bad thing after all. Then comes the chapter's last reading, in which environmental activist **Greta Thunberg** admonishes members of the United Nations General Assembly for failing to adequately address climate change, which she believes to be a "betrayal" of all future generations.

We hope the varying perspectives and topics presented here will get you thinking hard about the issues they raise and draw you into the ongoing conversations about how best to live in what some of the authors in this chapter see as our natural home.

Readings on <u>letstalklibrary.com</u>

- **Sue Burke**, Trees of Knowledge
- **Ellen Wayland-Smith**, Natural Magic

WILLIAM CRONON

The Trouble with Wilderness

P RESERVING WILDERNESS has for decades been a fundamental
    tenet—indeed, a passion—of the environmental movement, espe-
cially in the United States. For many Americans, wilderness stands as
the last place where civilization, that all-too-human disease, has not
fully infected the earth. It is an island in the polluted sea of urban-
industrial modernity, a refuge we must somehow recover to save the
planet. As Henry David Thoreau famously declared, "In Wildness is the
preservation of the World."

But is it? The more one knows of its peculiar history, the more one
realizes that wilderness is not quite what it seems. Far from being the
one place on earth that stands apart from humanity, it is quite profoundly a human creation—indeed, the creation of very particular
human cultures at very particular moments in human history. It is not
a pristine sanctuary where the last remnant of an endangered but still
transcendent nature can be encountered without the contaminating
taint of civilization. Instead, it is a product of that civilization. As we gaze
into the mirror it holds up for us, we too easily imagine that what we
behold is nature when in fact we see the reflection of our own long-
ings and desires. Wilderness can hardly be the solution to our culture's
problematic relationship with the nonhuman world, for wilderness is
itself a part of the problem.

*William Cronon is an environmental historian and professor emeritus
of history, geography, and environmental studies at the University of
Wisconsin. Author of* Changes to the Land: Indians, Colonists, and the
Ecology of New England (1983) *and* Nature's Metropolis: Chicago
and the Great West (1991), *Cronon has been president of the American
Historical Association (2012) and serves on the board of the Trust for Public
Land. "The Trouble with Wilderness" is a chapter in his* Uncommon
Ground: Toward Reinventing Nature (1995). *He tweets from @wcronon.*

Sunset-lit saguaros in the Sonoran Desert.

To assert the unnaturalness of so natural a place may seem perverse: we can all conjure up images and sensations that seem all the more hauntingly real for having engraved themselves so indelibly on our memories. Remember this? The torrents of mist shooting out from the base of a great waterfall in the depths of a Sierra Nevada canyon, the droplets cooling your face as you listen to the roar of the water and gaze toward the sky through a rainbow that hovers just out of reach. Or this: Looking out across a desert canyon in the evening air, the only sound a lone raven calling in the distance, the rock walls dropping away into a chasm so deep that its bottom all but vanishes as you squint into the amber light of the setting sun. Remember the feelings of such moments, and you will know as well as I do that you were in the presence of something irreducibly nonhuman, something profoundly Other than yourself. Wilderness is made of that too.

And yet: what brought each of us to the places where such memories became possible is entirely a cultural invention.

5   For the Americans who first celebrated it, wilderness was tied to the myth of the frontier. The historian Frederick Jackson Turner wrote the classic academic statement of this myth in 1893, but it had been part of American thought for well over a century. As Turner described

the process, Easterners and European immigrants, in moving to the wild lands of the frontier, shed the trappings of civilization and thereby gained an energy, an independence and a creativity that were the sources of American democracy and national character. Seen this way, wilderness became a place of religious redemption and national renewal, the quintessential location for experiencing what it meant to be an American.

Those who celebrate the frontier almost always look backward, mourning an older, simpler world that has disappeared forever. That world and all its attractions, Turner said, depended on free land—on wilderness. It is no accident that the movement to set aside national parks and wilderness areas gained real momentum just as laments about the vanishing frontier reached their peak. To protect wilderness was to protect the nation's most sacred myth of origin.

THE DECADES FOLLOWING THE CIVIL WAR saw more and more of the nation's wealthiest citizens seeking out wilderness for themselves. The passion for wild land took many forms: enormous estates in the Adirondacks and elsewhere (disingenuously called "camps" despite their many servants and amenities); cattle ranches for would-be

The main lodge of Camp Sagamore, Adirondack Mountains, NY. Built in 1897 for the Vanderbilts.

Glacier National Park, Montana.

roughriders on the Great Plains; guided big-game hunting trips in the Rockies. Wilderness suddenly emerged as the landscape of choice for elite tourists. For them, it was a place of recreation.

In just this way, wilderness came to embody the frontier myth, standing for the wild freedom of America's past and seeming to represent a highly attractive natural alternative to the ugly artificiality of modern civilization. The irony, of course, was that in the process wilderness came to reflect the very civilization its devotees sought to escape. Ever since the 19th century, celebrating wilderness has been an activity mainly for well-to-do city folks. Country people generally know far too much about working the land to regard unworked land as their ideal.

There were other ironies as well. The movement to set aside national parks and wilderness areas followed hard on the heels of the final Indian wars, in which the prior human inhabitants of these regions were rounded up and moved onto reservations so that tourists could safely enjoy the illusion that they were seeing their nation in its pristine, original state—in the new morning of God's own creation. Meanwhile, its original inhabitants were kept out by dint of force, their earlier uses of the land redefined as inappropriate or even illegal. To this day, for instance, the Blackfeet continue to be accused of "poaching" on the lands of Glacier National Park, in Montana, that originally belonged to them and that were ceded by treaty only with the proviso that they be permitted to hunt there.

Members of the
Blackfeet Nation
in what is now
Glacier National
Park, 1914.

The removal of Indians to create an "uninhabited wilderness" 10
reminds us just how invented and how constructed the American wilderness really is. One of the most striking proofs of the cultural invention of wilderness is its thoroughgoing erasure of the history from which it sprang. In virtually all its manifestations, wilderness represents a flight from history. Seen as the original garden, it is a place outside time, from which human beings had to be ejected before the fallen world of history could properly begin. Seen as the frontier, it is a savage world at the dawn of civilization, whose transformation represents the very beginning of the national historical epic. Seen as sacred nature, it is the home of a God who transcends history, untouched by time's arrow. No matter what the angle from which we regard it, wilderness offers us the illusion that we can escape the cares and troubles of the world in which our past has ensnared us. It is the natural, unfallen antithesis of an unnatural civilization that has lost its soul, the place where we can see the world as it really is, and so know ourselves as we really are—or ought to be.

The trouble with wilderness is that it reproduces the very values its devotees seek to reject. It offers the illusion that we can somehow wipe clean the slate of our past and return to the tabula rasa that supposedly existed before we began to leave our marks on the world. The dream of an unworked natural landscape is very much the fantasy of people who have never themselves had to work the land to make a living—urban folk for whom food comes from a supermarket or a restaurant instead of a field, and for whom the wooden houses in which they live and work apparently have no meaningful connection to the forests in which trees grow and die. Only people whose relation to the land was already alienated could hold up wilderness as a model for human life in nature, for the romantic ideology of wilderness leaves no place in which human beings can actually make their living from the land.

We live in an urban-industrial civilization, but too often pretend to ourselves that our real home is in the wilderness. We work our nine-to-five jobs, we drive our cars (not least to reach the wilderness), we benefit from the intricate and all too invisible networks with which society shelters us, all the while pretending that these things are not an essential part of who we are. By imagining that our true home is in the wilderness, we forgive ourselves for the homes we actually inhabit. In its flight from history, in its siren song of escape, in its reproduction of the dangerous dualism that sets human beings somehow outside nature—in all these ways, wilderness poses a threat to responsible environmentalism.

"In its flight from history..." See how this sentence builds to a climax! You can craft one like it; find out how on pp. 428-30.

Do not misunderstand me. What I criticize here is not wild nature, but the alienated way we often think of ourselves in relation to it. Wilderness can still teach lessons that are hard to learn anywhere else. When we visit wild places, we find ourselves surrounded by plants and animals and landscapes whose otherness compels our attention. In forcing us to acknowledge that they are not of our making, that they have little or no need for humanity, they recall for us a creation far greater than our own. In wilderness, we need no reminder that a tree has its own reasons for being, quite apart from us—proof that ours is not the only presence in the universe.

We get into trouble only if we see the tree in the garden as wholly artificial and the tree in the wilderness as wholly natural. Both trees in some ultimate sense are wild; both in a practical sense now require our care. We need to reconcile them, to see a natural landscape that is also cultural, in which city, suburb, countryside and wilderness each has its own place. We need to discover a middle ground in which all these things, from city to wilderness, can somehow be encompassed in the word "home." Home, after all, is the place where we live. It is the place for which we take responsibility, the place we try to sustain so we can pass on what is best in it (and in ourselves) to our children.

Learning to honor the wild—learning to acknowledge the auton- 15 omy of the other—means striving for critical self-consciousness in all our actions. It means that reflection and respect must accompany each act of use, and means we must always consider the possibility of non-use. It means looking at the part of nature we intend to turn toward our own ends and asking whether we can use it again and again and again—sustainably—without diminishing it in the process. Most of all, it means practicing remembrance and gratitude for the nature, culture and history that have come together to make the world as we know it. If wildness can stop being (just) out there and start being (also) in here, if it can start being as humane as it is natural, then perhaps we can get on with the unending task of struggling to live rightly in the world—not just in the garden, not just in the wilderness, but in the home that encompasses them both.

Thinking about the Text

1. If, as William Cronon says, wilderness "is not quite what it seems," what does he say it is? He never explicitly gives his own definition, instead offering up over a dozen statements that could be viewed as definitions, beginning in the first paragraph: "wilderness stands as the last place where civilization . . . has not fully infected the earth." Re-read Cronon's essay, marking every statement that explicitly or implicitly offers a definition of what *wilderness* is—and what it is not. By the end of the essay, which DEFINITION do you think Cronon prefers, and why? Do you agree with this definition—and why (or why not)?

2. *We* is a word Cronon uses thirty-two times. That's a hint: pronouns play an important rhetorical role here. Re-read the essay with an eye for the pronouns Cronon uses as well as for how they shift.

Track the use of *we* (and *us, our, ourselves*), of *they* (and *their, them, themselves,* and of *I* or *me*. Who is Cronon referring to when he says *we* and when he says *they*? Why do you think he shifts to *you* in paragraph 3? How does paying attention to the pronouns—and to the shifts in pronouns—help you understand Cronon's own POINT OF VIEW?

3. The "wilderness myth" features prominently in another reading in this chapter, Emma Marris's "The Nature You See in Documentaries Is Beautiful and False" (see p. 719). In fact, Marris credits Cronon with "demolish[ing] the concept of wilderness" and declares that she herself is trying to continue his work. Are you persuaded that the "wilderness myth" is not only false but also damaging to conservation efforts, as Cronon and Marris both argue? In what specific ways does Marris say she is continuing Cronon's work? How has reading these arguments affected the way you think about nature?

4. LET'S TALK. Together with two or three classmates, re-read paragraph 8, in which Cronon points out a key IRONY: that the more wilderness "came to embody" a myth desired by wealthy elites, the more it "came to reflect the very civilization its devotees sought to escape." What other ironies does Cronon point out? What additional ironies might you identify about how people today see (and use the word) *wilderness*?

5. AND NOW WRITE. In the place(s) of your childhood that you called home, what counted as "nature"? It may have been a majestic forest, ants bustling about in sidewalk cracks, or birds calling at dawn, but wherever you were, there was almost certainly something "natural." Do you have any memories of nature that resemble those described in paragraph 3? Or of the place where you grew up? Cronon concludes by saying that "city, suburb, countryside and wilderness" each has its own "natural" place, "somehow... encompassed in the word 'home'" (14). It is, he notes "the place where we live." A lot to think about! Write a brief essay REFLECTING on the place you call home.

EMMA MARRIS

The Nature You See in Documentaries Is Beautiful, and False

I T'S LATE AFTERNOON, late pandemic, and I'm watching a new nature documentary in bed, after taking the daintiest of hits from a weed pen. The show is called *A Perfect Planet*, and it is narrated by Sir David Attenborough.

I am looking at the red eye of a flamingo, a molten lake surrounding a tiny black pupil. Now I am looking at drone footage of a massive colony of flamingos, the classic sweeping overhead shot, what my brother calls "POV God." Behind the images, a string orchestra sets the mood, giving the coral-pink birds an otherworldly theme in E minor.

Nature documentaries have never been more popular, in part because they offer easy escapism during a rough time, and in part because marijuana has been legalized in much of the United States. The combination is hard to resist, as my experience with *A Perfect Planet* proves. The stoned attention span perfectly matches the length of each vignette, in which Attenborough's soothing, avuncular voice guides you through a simple story about animal life. In between, you are treated to epic, empty landscapes and intense close-ups of the rich colors and textures of the nonhuman world, which pop off like

---

Emma Marris is a writer who focuses on broadening the definition of "nature," on environmentalism, and on climate justice. She's a fellow of the UCLA Institute of the Environment and Sustainability and a member of the Board of Rogue Climate, and her work has appeared in National Geographic, *the* New York Times, Wired, *the* Atlantic, *and* Nature. *Her TED Talk* "Nature Is Everywhere: We Just Need to Learn to See It" *has attracted more than 1.4 million views. The article reprinted here is part of the* Atlantic's *series* Who Owns America's Wilderness? *Marris tweets from @Emma_Marris.*

719

An intense close-up of a flamingo.

fireworks in your wide-open mind. The effect is awe-inspiring but also surprisingly chill. And there are no troublesome humans on-screen to kill the vibe.

Stoned or sober, we are streaming sharks and penguins and lions into our homes in record numbers. According to the BBC, "Over a billion people have watched Planet Earth II and Blue Planet II in the last 3 years." Those series were produced by the BBC Natural History Unit, the undisputed leader in high-polish nature documentaries since at least 2006's *Planet Earth*. The NHU is opening an office in Los Angeles this year; inking new deals with half a dozen streaming services, networks, and cable channels; and currently producing more than 20 projects, including *Planet Earth III*, set to debut in 2022. The battle royale among all the new streaming services has created "the perfect market environment for natural history," says Julian Hector, the head of the NHU.

See how smoothly Marris incorporates the quotation from her source? You'll want to learn to do that, and pp. 285–90 can help.

5   A viral sequence of a baby iguana running from menacing snakes, footage of manta rays soaring through the sea set to the strains of a Hans Zimmer score—no one does it quite like the NHU. Perhaps the greatest testament to its influence is the way it has been imitated. *A Perfect Planet* looks and sounds like an NHU series, but it was produced by Silverback Films, which is led by ex-NHU staffers. Silverback

also produced a series for Netflix, *Our Planet*, which not only has *planet* in the title but is also narrated by Attenborough.

Whether through the NHU's own films or knockoffs, the company has come to define nature for millions of people on a fast-urbanizing planet. So the stories it tells, the techniques it uses, and the world it has created are all worth examining. It is, in many respects, an altogether new world. By selecting just the most stunning shots and editing people out of the picture, the NHU creates an untouched parallel universe that's undeniably glamorous—both beautiful and inaccessible.

Back in my bedroom, I watch grizzlies swim in a transparent lake ringed by green-black conifers. If the flamingos and the bears have a thematic connection, I've already forgotten it, but I feel good. It's heartening to know that these bears are out there somewhere, living their best life. And it feels deeply satisfying to see them presented so crisply, so closely, the drops of water they shake off their fur sparkling like diamonds in the far-northern sunlight.

Something about these programs is hyper-real. Partly, this stems from the fact that the films are enhanced. It is an open secret that the long zoom lenses used to capture animals up close can make recording real-time sound nearly impossible. And so the wet crunch of lions opening up a gazelle's rib cage, the hollow clack of birds' bills closing, the groan and woosh of a calving glacier—these noises are often recorded separately or even created by sound-effect artists and added to the shots later.

These sound effects, along with the orchestral music added to nearly all of the high-end wildlife documentaries, set the emotional tone for the vignettes on-screen. Are these seabirds supposed to be majestic or comical as they enact their mating dance? The music tells us. Whom are we to root for in this interaction of predator and prey? Listen for the menacing strings.

Alenda Chang, a film and media-studies professor at UC Santa Barbara, finds the ubiquity of orchestral music in the genre "irritating." Using ambient sound, even if it has to be recorded separately or manipulated to be audible, can give viewers a truer and more complete understanding of the nonhuman world. "Using ambient sound leaves space 10

A long-exposure photo, which makes it possible to see the Milky Way.

for, not boredom exactly, but quiet contemplation," Chang says. It better replicates the experience of seeing wildlife outside, in person.

It isn't just the sounds that make these films feel more than real. They use the absolute highest-resolution cameras available, what Chang calls "military-grade lenses." The images on any modern television are thus crisp as fuck. Special techniques such as slow motion, time lapse, and underwater filming capture details that you simply can't see any other way. Most series include at least one long-exposure shot of the night sky, a technique that makes the stars and Milky Way pop in a way they never will to your naked eye, no matter how far away you get from artificial lights. I am particularly obsessed with the depth of focus in many of these films' shots. It is literally inhuman. On-screen, I can see individual feathers on the birds in the foreground and the distant mountain peaks—both sharply in focus. The effect is impossible to achieve in person with our soft, imperfect, biological eyes. What I am watching from beneath my blankets is in some measurable way *more* beautiful than real life.

Viewers reared on this high-gloss version of nature might struggle to connect to or appreciate the actual world: a place of wonder and beauty—but also mud, cold, heat, mosquito bites, and long intervals during which distant, hard-to-see animals don't really do anything. Why would I go outside and deal with all of that when I can stay tucked in bed, sipping an apricot La Croix, and get close enough to African lions to see the taste buds on their tongue?

There's a tempting analogy to porn. Frequent consumption of video of conventionally attractive people engaging in exaggerated and intense sex can turn some people off the pleasures of a roll in the hay with an imperfect, flesh-and-blood human. If the high-end documentaries are a bit like porn, then I contend that the solution to the way they might warp our expectations is the same as it is for porn—not to ban them, but to diversify them. In the case of natural-history films, we need to make more kinds of wildlife and more kinds of nature—including the nature in our cities and backyards—sexy. In the United Kingdom, the NHU's landmark series share the airwaves with NHU productions about British wildlife and working ecologists, which expands the British public's natural-history-video diet. But in the United States, we tend to stream just the landmarks. So there's an argument to include more nearby nature in them as well.

As an environmental journalist, I've had the extremely good fortune to go to some of the kinds of places where they film nature documentaries. I've been in the Amazon, days from the nearest road. I've seen humpback whales feed in groups by weaving together nets of bubbles. I've watched Tasmanian devils sunbathe, and snorkeled with sea turtles. But when I watch BBC documentaries about those places and those animals, I don't feel like I've returned to those moments. Instead, I feel like I've entered a fantasy.

It is usually a fantasyland without any humans. Chris Sandbrook 15 and Bill Adams, then conservationists at Cambridge, critiqued the 2013 NHU documentary *Africa* because, although it was stunning, it was missing something vitally important to understanding Africa: Africans. "The BBC has edited out the people of an entire continent," they wrote. They compared the lengths the filmmakers had gone to in order to exclude people from the frame to the contortions undertaken by Peter Jackson to keep New Zealand from intruding into his viewfinder while filming his *Lord of the Rings* adaptation. "Viewers are led to believe that Africa is not part of the modern world, and that Africans have no place there." The consequence is that tourists who go to Africa expect to see a pretty wilderness instead of a busy continent of 1.4 billion people. The tourism industry does what it can to oblige visitors, whisking them between cheerful eco-lodges out of sight of the farms and villages that surround most protected areas.

Nearly all of the vignettes in series such as *A Perfect Planet* take place in a vaguely specified geographical area, and all roads, fences, buildings, and traces of the camera crew have been scrupulously left out of the frame. But many of the "making of" mini-features the BBC typically releases with each episode reveal an access road, a bunch of muddy vehicles, or a park-guard office just off-screen.

Planet Earth II did have a "cities" episode, filled with roads, bicycles, and the like. It was good, though I sensed ambivalence on the part of the filmmakers. The episode sticks to animal behavior, by and large. In the few shots with humans, their faces are usually out of focus or out of the frame, and none ever speaks to the camera.

The NHU films have been taken to task before for shying away from the environmental problems that threaten the animals they feature. In recent years, Attenborough's narration has spent a bit more time on climate change and deforestation. But I'm sympathetic to the idea that not every documentary about the nonhuman world has to be about the environmental crisis. I think most people know about climate change at this point. Rather than a dour sermon about humanity's environmental sins, I just want a realistic presentation of "wild" animals as creatures embedded in a highly humanized world. Instead of showing the annual wildebeest migration through the Serengeti only via footage of the ambling ungulates, why not also show the fleets of jeeps ferrying thousands of tourists up and down the Serengeti's road network to watch the migration, or the villages and farms pressed up against the borders of the park?

By consistently presenting nature as an untouched wilderness, many nature documentaries mislead viewers into thinking that there are lots of untouched wildernesses left. I certainly thought there were, before I became an environmental journalist. This misapprehension then prompts people to build their environmental ideas around preserving untouched places and to embrace profoundly antihuman "solutions" to environmental problems, such as kicking indigenous people out of their homeland. In truth, wilderness doesn't really exist.

In his famous 1995 essay, "The Trouble with Wilderness; or, Getting Back to the Wrong Nature," the historian William Cronon demolished the concept of wilderness. Cronon argued that European settlers in North America had transformed their inherited idea of "wilderness" as worthless, scary, and unimproved land by reimagining it as a sublime, prehuman Eden. "The myth of the wilderness as 'virgin' uninhabited land had always been especially cruel when seen from the perspective of the Indians who had once called that land home," Cronon wrote. In reality, the Americas had already been thoroughly shaped by the nearly 60 million people who lived there when colonists first arrived. Agriculture and other intensive human use was widespread, covering 10 percent of the Americas' landmass; human-caused fires maintained grasslands and prairies; hunting, foraging, gathering, and replanting—sometimes in new places—regulated the populations and ranges of dozens of species.

20

Read William Cronon's essay on p. 711.

The wilderness myth is simply factually inaccurate, in the Americas and elsewhere. It has also been a real stumbling block for conservation. With wilderness set as the gold standard for nature, any human influence has come to be seen as negative by default. The myth has thus ruled out any approaches to saving nature except walling it off and keeping humans out. Trying to "save the planet" with a wilderness mindset has been all about self-exile. It offers "little hope of discovering what an ethical, sustainable, honorable human place in nature might actually look like," as Cronon wrote.

I've been trying to continue Cronon's work. I've questioned whether introduced species should be condemned simply because they weren't in an ecosystem when the first white man studied it. Sometimes, people tell me I'm attacking a straw man, that no one believes in the idea of pristine wilderness anymore. Usually, the people who say this work in fields such as conservation, restoration, and ecology, where exciting new findings in paleoecology, plus a belated but welcome interest in indigenous environmental history, have gradually changed the way they think about nature and humans' place in it. But outside that specialist world, I find that the wilderness myth lives on, 26 years after Cronon's essay. And I worry that the BBC Natural History Unit is one reason why.

Hector, the head of the NHU, says that many of the landmark series currently in production will let humans into the frame. "Virtually every title we have now will have aspects of the built environment and people in it," he told me. This is good news. The stories will still be from the animals' point of view, Hector added. This is also good news. If the NHU does one thing really well, it is showing animals as individuals in the world, making choices, taking risks, doing their best to survive and reproduce. Hector promises that more of these stories will be about animals "trying to navigate the human environment." He said his film teams are capturing "the types of decisions animals and plants have to make around the human world—and of course, the world largely is the human world."

Attenborough himself, a man who seems inseparable from the NHU, turns 95 next month. I strongly associate him with the "pristine wilderness" idea, and he seems to still see the world through that lens. Last year's *David Attenborough: A Life on Our Planet*, produced for Netflix by Silverback and the World Wide Fund for Nature, is part biography, featuring footage of the icon as a dishy young presenter, and part environmental manifesto. In it, Attenborough reminisces about the 1950s, when, he recalls, "wherever I went, there was wilderness. Sparkling coastal seas. Vast forests. Immense grasslands. You could fly for hours over the untouched wilderness." He even waxes nostalgic for the previous geologic epoch, before the rise of humans as an ecological force. "The Holocene," he says, "was our Garden of Eden."

25   The person or people who replace Attenborough when he retires will likely not see the world in such starkly dualistic terms. I hope they will present the wonders of our planet as they are, not as they might

have been in some alternative universe without humans. And I think they can do so without losing any of the fantastic close-ups, epic slow motion, or stunning underwater filming we all love. I don't think we should deny ourselves these pleasures. Most of us can't visit all the places these shows go, and even if we can, we can't see everything their cameras can show us. I once spent 10 days in the Peruvian Amazon looking at fig trees for a story. But it wasn't until *A Perfect Planet* that I got to see what the teeny-tiny wasps that pollinate them do *inside* the figs.

Models of a still-gorgeous-but-not-mythical approach exist, if you look beyond the landmark series. Take *Springwatch*, a live program produced by the NHU that has aired every spring since 2005 on BBC Two during a primetime slot. The show chronicles the gentle reawakening of life in the British countryside after the winter, and is filled with footage of butterflies, beavers, hedgehogs, and common urban birds. Signs of humanity are plentiful and not treated as eyesores. Baby foxes bounce on backyard trampolines. Honey bees drone in an apple orchard. The presenters, holding their cue cards in country lanes and narrating the action captured by nest-box cameras, sound a bit like sportscasters bantering their way through a slow-paced athletic event.

Springwatch features footage of urban birds, honey bees, and other such images submitted by viewers.

Last year, *Springwatch* came out during the scary and solitary early days of the pandemic, and the presenters explicitly promised that the program would be therapeutic for viewers. They wandered the fields and woods near their own homes with tenderness, talking about blue-bells blooming and oak leaves unfurling and listening to cuckoos call, as if these events were handholds to grasp in order to keep oneself from sliding into a pit of despair. "I am *seizing* this spring with both hands," the presenter Chris Packham says in the first episode, lean-ing against a tree in Hampshire. The connection between humans and nonhumans isn't just included in the show. It is the whole point.

My response to *Springwatch* was totally different from the slack-jawed awe I felt watching *A Perfect Planet*. I found it extremely touch-ing. I'll admit, I cried at the viewer-submitted videos of backyard birds and moths and ducks. Most of all, unlike the polished, screen-saver-esque shots of the Arctic or the Sahara in ultra-high-def, it made me want to go outside.

Springwatch is available in the United States through the Britbox streaming service, but its viewership here is undoubtedly minuscule compared with that of the flagship series. And the content is neces-

Images from the British countryside make us want to go outside.

sarily very specific to the United Kingdom. If the NHU's new Los Angeles office wants to replicate the show—and I think it should consider doing so—it would likely have to produce a dozen regional versions.

So as the NHU continues its work on *Planet Earth III*, I say let's   30
keep the dancing albatross and breaching whales and snow leopards. But let's consider skipping the music in some scenes to foreground the silence or perhaps even the enthusiastic murmurs of the camera crew. Let's linger over the charm of the house sparrow and the bumblebee. Let's remind viewers that they can likely see these creatures where they live, and maybe even give them tips for doing so. And when showing the elephants or the agouti, let's pan back and show the road or the houses or the farms that surround them. Let's see the faces and listen to the voices of the people who live near these animals. I want to hear what they say.

Thinking about the Text

1. How does Emma Marris's OPENING frame—cozy in bed during the pandemic, away from the hustle and bustle of everyday life— set the scene for what follows and illustrate and support one of her main arguments? And how did it affect you as a reader—did it get your attention and make you want to keep reading? How else might Marris have opened the article? Where in the essay does Marris return to this opening scene—and what point do you think she was trying to make by doing so?

2. In this article, Marris takes readers along on a fairly leisurely tour of some of the documentaries she has seen, DESCRIBING and commenting on them and COMPARING them to the kind of documentaries she would like to see in the future. How would you describe Marris's TONE? Does the tone shift at any point, and if so in what way? How does the tone help establish Marris's CREDIBILITY—or perhaps fail to do so?

3. While Marris seems irritated by the overuse of dramatic orchestral music rather than natural sounds, she seems less bothered by the way the filmmakers alter and "enhance" nature

and doesn't question the ethics of doing so. She does, however, point out ETHICAL issues raised when the myth of "wilderness" leads people "to embrace profoundly antihuman 'solutions' to environmental problems, such as kicking indigenous people out of their homeland" (19). What other "antihuman 'solutions'" to environmental issues can you think of—and what might be some ways to avoid or reverse them?

4. LET'S TALK. Marris provides rich DESCRIPTION of *A Perfect Planet* and other BBC nature documentaries. Have you seen any of these documentaries or any other nature documentaries—and if so, did your reactions support Marris's views that these documentaries are "undeniably glamorous" but also "false"? Get together with two or three classmates and watch one or two nature documentaries. How do you respond to these documentaries? In what ways, if any, is your response affected by Marris's argument?

The trailer for *A Perfect Planet* is available on *YouTube*.

5. AND NOW WRITE. Marris includes a mix of NARRATIVE, ANALYSIS, and DESCRIPTION—all to support an ARGUMENT. What exactly is her argument? Go through the article, noting every CLAIM Marris makes, looking for an explicit THESIS. Try making a rough outline of the article, noting the ways it builds toward a conclusion. Finally, try your hand at writing your own thesis statement for Marris's argument, and then summarize the support for that thesis.

ROBIN WALL KIMMERER

On Animacy: Learning the Grammar of Living Things

TO BE NATIVE TO A PLACE WE MUST LEARN TO SPEAK ITS LANGUAGE.

I COME HERE TO LISTEN, to nestle in the curve of the roots in a soft hollow of pine needles, to lean my bones against the column of white pine, to turn off the voice in my head until I can hear the voices outside it: the *shhh* of wind in needles, water trickling over rock, nuthatch tapping, chipmunks digging, beechnut falling, mosquito in my ear, and something more—something that is not me, for which we have no language, the wordless being of others in which we are never alone. After the drumbeat of my mother's heart, *this* was my first language....

Listening in wild places, we are audience to conversations in a language not our own. I think now that it was a longing to comprehend this language I hear in the woods that led me to science, to learn over the years to speak fluent botany. A tongue that should not, by the way, be mistaken for the language of plants. I did learn another language in science, though, one of careful observation, an intimate vocabulary

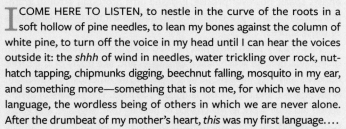

Robin Wall Kimmerer, professor of environmental and forest biology and director of the Center for Native Peoples and the Environment at the SUNY College of Environmental Science and Forestry, is a storyteller and a scientist who speaks "fluent botany." Author of award-winning books such as Gathering Moss: A Natural and Cultural History of Mosses (2003) *and* Braiding Sweetgrass: Indigenous Wisdom, Scientific Knowledge, and the Teachings of Plants (2013), *Kimmerer is a member of the Citizen Potawatomi Nation who weaves together the wisdom of science and indigenous philosophy. This essay was first published in the journal* Anthropology of Consciousness *in 2017. You can follow her at www.facebook.com/braidingsweetgrass.*

that names each little part. To name and describe you must first see, and science polishes the gift of seeing. I honor the strength of the language that has become a second tongue to me. But beneath the richness of its vocabulary and its descriptive power, something is missing, the same something that swells around you and in you when you listen to the world. Science can be a language of distance which reduces a being to its working parts; it is a language of objects. The language scientists speak, however precise, is based on a profound error in grammar, an omission, a grave loss in translation from the native languages of these shores....

Had history been different, I would likely speak Bodewadmimwin, or Potawatomi, an Anishinaabe language. But, like many of the three hundred and fifty indigenous languages of the Americas, Potawatomi is threatened, and I speak the language you read. The powers of assimilation did their work as my chance of hearing that language, and yours too, was washed from the mouths of Indian children in government boarding schools where speaking your native tongue was forbidden. Children like my grandfather, who was taken from his family when he was just a little boy of nine years old. This history scattered not only our words but also our people. Today I live far from our reservation, so even if I could speak the language, I would have no one to talk to. But a few summers ago, at our yearly tribal gathering, a language class was held and I slipped into the tent to listen.

There was a great deal of excitement about the class because, for the first time, every single fluent speaker in our tribe would be there as a teacher. When the speakers were called forward to the circle of folding chairs, they moved slowly—with canes, walkers, and wheelchairs, only a few entirely under their own power. I counted them as they filled the chairs. Nine. Nine fluent speakers. In the whole world. Our language, millennia in the making, sits in those nine chairs. The words that praised creation, told the old stories, lulled my ancestors to sleep, rests today in the tongues of nine very mortal men and women. Each in turn addresses the small group of would-be students.

5   A man with long gray braids tells how his mother hid him away when the Indian agents came to take the children.... "We're the end

of the road. We are all that is left. If you young people do not learn, the language will die. The missionaries and the U.S. government will have their victory at last."

So now my house is spangled with Post-it notes in another language, as if I were studying for a trip abroad. But I'm not going away, I'm coming home. . . .

MY SISTER'S GIFT TO ME one Christmas was a set of magnetic tiles for the refrigerator in Ojibwe, or Anishinabemowin, a language closely related to Potawatomi. I spread them out on my kitchen table looking for familiar words, but the more I looked, the more worried I got. Among the hundred or more tiles, there was but a single word that I recognized: *megwech*, thank you. The small feeling of accomplishment from months of study evaporated in a moment.

I remember paging through the Ojibwe dictionary she sent, trying to decipher the tiles, but the spellings didn't always match and the print was too small and there are way too many variations on a single word and I was feeling that this was just way too hard. The threads in my brain knotted and the harder I tried, the tighter they became. Pages blurred and my eyes settled on a word—a verb, of course: "to be a Saturday." *Pfft!* I threw down the book. Since when is *Saturday* a verb? Everyone knows it's a noun. I grabbed the dictionary and flipped more pages and all kinds of things seemed to be verbs: "to be a hill," "to be red," "to be a long sandy stretch of beach," and then my finger rested on *wiikwegamaa*: "to be a bay." "Ridiculous!" I ranted in my head. "There is no reason to make it so complicated. No wonder no one speaks it. A cumbersome language, impossible to learn, and more than that, it's all wrong. A bay is most definitely a person, place, or thing—a noun and not a verb." I was ready to give up. I'd learned a few words, done my duty to the language that was taken from my grandfather. Oh, the ghosts of the missionaries in the boarding schools must have been rubbing their hands in glee at my frustration. "She's going to surrender," they said.

And then I swear I heard the zap of synapses firing. An electric current sizzled down my arm and through my finger, and practically scorched the page where that one word lay. In that moment I could smell the water of the bay, watch it rock against the shore and hear it sift onto the sand. A bay is a noun only if water is *dead*. When *bay* is a noun, it is defined by humans, trapped between its shores and contained by the word. But the verb *wiikwegamaa*—to *be* a bay—releases the water from bondage and lets it live. "To be a bay" holds the wonder that, for this moment, the living water has decided to shelter itself between these shores, conversing with cedar roots and a flock of baby mergansers. Because it could do otherwise—become a stream or an ocean or a waterfall, and there are verbs for that, too. To be a hill, to be a sandy beach, to be a Saturday, all are possible verbs in a world where everything is alive. Water, land, and even a day, the language a mirror for seeing the animacy of the world, the life that pulses through all things, through pines and nuthatches and mushrooms.

10 *THIS* IS THE LANGUAGE I HEAR IN THE WOODS; this is the language that lets us speak of what wells up all around us. And the vestiges of boarding schools, the soap-wielding missionary wraiths, hang their heads in defeat.

Mushrooms can be a verb in the grammar of animacy.

This is the grammar of animacy. Imagine seeing your grandmother standing at the stove in her apron and then saying of her, "Look, it is making soup. It has gray hair." We might snicker at such a mistake, but we also recoil from it. In English, we never refer to a member of our family, or indeed to any person, as *it*. That would be a profound act of disrespect. *It* robs a person of selfhood and kinship, reducing a person to a mere thing. So it is that in Potawatomi and most other indigenous languages, we use the same words to address the living world as we use for our family. Because they are our family.

To whom does our language extend the grammar of animacy? Naturally, plants and animals are animate, but as I learn, I am discovering that the Potawatomi understanding of what it means to be animate diverges from the list of attributes of living beings we all learned in Biology 101. In Potawatomi 101, rocks are animate, as are mountains and water and fire and places. Beings that are imbued with spirit, our sacred medicines, our songs, drums, and even stories, are all animate. The list of the inanimate seems to be smaller, filled with objects that are made by people. Of an inanimate being, like a table, we say, "*What* is it?" And we answer *Dopwen yewe*. Table it is. But of apple, we must say, "*Who* is that being?" And reply *Mshimin yawe*. Apple that being is....

English doesn't give us many tools for incorporating respect for animacy. In English, you are either a human or a thing. Our grammar boxes us in by the choice of reducing a nonhuman being to an *it*, or it must

In Potawatomi, rocks are animate, as are mountains.

be gendered, inappropriately, as a *he* or a *she*. Where are our words for the simple existence of another living being? Where is our *yawe*? . . .

When I am in the woods with my students, teaching them the gifts of plants and how to call them by name, I try to be mindful of my language, to be bilingual between the lexicon of science and the grammar of animacy. Although they still have to learn scientific roles and Latin names, I hope I am also teaching them to know the world as a neighborhood of nonhuman residents, to know that, as ecotheologian Thomas Berry has written, "we must say of the universe that it is a communion of subjects, not a collection of objects."

15   One afternoon, I sat with my field ecology students by a *wiikwergamaa* and shared this idea of animate language. One young man, Andy, splashing his feet in the clear water, asked the big question. "Wait a second," he said as he wrapped his mind around this linguistic distinction, "doesn't this mean that speaking English, thinking in English, somehow gives us permission to disrespect nature? By denying everyone else the right to be persons? Wouldn't things be different if nothing was an *it*?"

Kimmerer didn't really have to name her student here but doing so shows respect and builds credibility. See more about that on pp. 297–98.

Swept away with the idea, he said it felt like an awakening to him. More like a remembering, I think. The animacy of the world is something we already know, but the language of animacy teeters on extinction—not just for Native peoples, but for everyone. Our toddlers speak of plants and animals as if they were people, extending to them self and intention and compassion—until we teach them not to. We quickly retrain them and make them forget. When we tell them that the tree is not a *who*, but an *it*, we make that maple an object; we put a barrier between us, absolving ourselves of moral responsibility and opening the door to exploitation. Saying *it* makes a living land into "natural resources." If a maple is an *it*, we can take up the chain saw. If a maple is a *her*, we think twice. . . .

The arrogance of English is that the only way to be animate, to be worthy of respect and moral concern, is to be a human.

A language teacher I know explained that grammar is just the way we chart relationships in language. Maybe it also reflects our relationships with each other. Maybe a grammar of animacy could lead us to whole new ways living in the world, other species a sovereign people, a world with a democracy of species, not a tyranny of one—with moral responsibility to water and wolves, and with a legal system that recognizes the standing of other species....

We Americans are reluctant to learn a foreign language of our own species, let alone another species. But imagine the possibilities. Imagine the access we would have to different perspectives, the things we might see through other eyes, the wisdom that surrounds us. We don't have to figure out everything by ourselves: there are intelligences other than our own, teachers all around us. Imagine how much less lonely the world would be....

I'm not advocating that we all learn Potawatomi or Hopi or Sem-   20
inole, even if we could. Immigrants came to these shores bearing a legacy of languages, all to be cherished. But to become native to this place, if we are to survive here, and our neighbors too, our work is to learn to speak the grammar of animacy, so that we might truly be at home.

Thinking about the Text

1. Robin Kimmerer admires the language of science, with its "careful observation" and "intimate vocabulary that names each little part." But she says that it's missing something "profound"—something we hear when we "listen to the world" (2). What is that other language, and how does Kimmerer say that we can learn it? Are you persuaded by her ARGUMENT—and why (or why not)?

2. Kimmerer's text is made up of words, and many of those words conjure up images and sounds for us. We've added a few images, but assume you have an opportunity to illustrate this essay, to make it MULTIMODAL. What would you add in the way of images (moving or still) and sounds? Where would you place them? Be ready to present your plans to the class, and to discuss which version would speak most powerfully to AUDIENCES today— and why.

3. Did you ever talk with animals you knew or had as pets—or to a special flower or tree? Did you have conversations with your beloved first bike? Or skateboard? Or—something else? Kimmerer asks, "Wouldn't things be different if nothing was an *it*?" (15). Given your own experience, how would you answer this question—and what examples or other EVIDENCE would you provide in support of your answer?

4. LET'S TALK. Kimmerer points out that in English, nouns that are human are animate—regarded as living beings—while other nouns are not. In Potawatomi and many other indigenous languages, however, rocks, mushrooms, rivers, and birds are all regarded as living beings. "Our toddlers speak of plants and animals as if they were people," Kimmerer says, "until we teach them not to" (16). Get together with two or three classmates to talk about how far you would like *animacy* to reach. If you were in charge of English, what would fall into the *animate* category and what would not? And are there nouns that you think might fall somewhere in between?

5. AND NOW WRITE. Take a tip from Kimmerer and go somewhere outside, in nature, to listen. Find a comfortable spot, settle in—still and quiet. And. Listen. For. Some. Time. What do you hear? Listen more. Then make notes on what you are hearing. Take a break and then write a paragraph DESCRIBING as best you can the sounds that you heard, sounds that Kimmerer says are "in a language not our own" (2).

IAN LEAHY & YARYNA SERKEZ

Since When Have Trees Existed Only for Rich Americans?

ACROSS THE NATION, the wealthier and whiter your neighborhood is, the greener the view from your window is likely to be. Chestnut Hill is one of the most prestigious areas in [Philadelphia]. [A house with] a median household income of about $133,000 enjoys lush greenery and cooling shade, with more than 60 percent of the surface covered in trees. Just five miles away, in a part of Nicetown-Tioga, where the median household income is roughly $37,000, trees cover only 6 percent of the area. The average temperature is more than 10 degrees higher. Decades ago, this area was "redlined" and classified as "D" by the federal government, limiting investments and economic growth because of its racial makeup. Such discriminatory practices still shape our cities and, along with income inequality, define who can enjoy a healthy tree canopy and who is surrounded by concrete.

Access to clean air and outdoor activities seems like a basic right. But in cities across the country, lower-income communities and communities of color more often live in neighborhoods with a higher share of concrete surfaces such as roads, buildings and parking lots, and a very limited number of trees and parks.

Neighborhoods with a majority of people in poverty have 25 percent less tree canopy on average than those with a minority of people in poverty, according to an analysis of income, employment, age,

---

Ian Leahy directs the Tree Equity program in the American Forests conservation organization, focusing on improving health in low-income communities through the development of tree canopies. He tweets from @iandleahy. *Yaryna Serkez* is a senior graphics editor at the New York Times, where this op-ed article was originally published in June 2021. She tweets from @iarynam.

Chestnut Hill, Philadelphia.

Nicetown-Tioga, Philadelphia.

ethnicity, health and surface temperature with tree canopy data in 486 metro areas. American Forests, a conservation organization, produced the analysis, which is called the Tree Equity Score (American Forests, 2021).

See three examples on p. 742. In the most extreme cases, wealthy areas have 65 percent more tree canopy than communities where nine out of 10 people live below the poverty line.

5   Communities with too few trees are feeling the consequences this week, as a heat wave has swept through much of the Pacific North-

High-income communities have almost 50% more greenery than low-income communities

Median share of tree cover, by income

$100k–250k	32.5%
$60k–100k	27.3%
$45k–60k	24.9%
$30k–45k	23.3%
Under $30k	22.2%

Source: American Forests

west. The average temperature can vary up to 10 degrees between places with trees and those without (Ziter et al., 2019). And where there is more heat, there is more death: Heat kills more people in the United States than any other kind of extreme weather. We can expect up to a tenfold increase in heat-related deaths in the eastern United States by the latter half of the 2050s and at least a 70 percent increase in the largest cities nationwide by 2050.

Trees today prevent approximately 1,200 more heat-related deaths annually in American cities.

Being in the vicinity of this living infrastructure provides many other benefits: Healthy trees trap air pollutants, which helps avoid 670,000 incidences of acute respiratory symptoms each year. Being in the presence of trees has also been found to improve youth educational performance, mental health, physical health and social connections. A well-maintained tree canopy may even reduce several types of crime and create economic opportunities, including careers that cannot be outsourced to plant and maintain those trees.*

So if there is no question that trees are important, why doesn't everyone have access to them? There is an emerging body of research

*The information in this paragraph and much more can be found on the website of Vibrant Cities Lab, www.vibrantcitieslab.com [*editor's note*].

Wealthy Neighborhoods Have Many More Trees Than Low-Income Neighborhoods

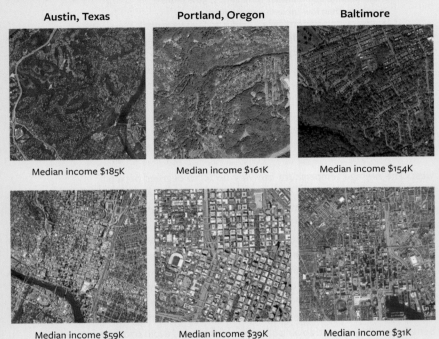

Austin, Texas	Portland, Oregon	Baltimore

Median income $185K · Median income $161K · Median income $154K

Median income $59K · Median income $39K · Median income $31K

See how these images convey a lot of information and occupy very little space? Learn how you can use visuals effectively in Chapter 26.

from the U.S. Forest Service and others that has found a direct relationship between tree canopy today and discriminatory policies of the past.

For example, from the 1930s to the 1960s and even the 1970s, a practice of discriminatory lending now known as "redlining" was carried out in cities across the country, from Los Angeles to Baltimore. Color-coded maps dissuaded not only mortgage but also health care and infrastructure investments based on where people lived. The red lines that were drawn around neighborhoods—predominantly Black as well as Catholic, Jewish and immigrant—now often line up very closely with maps showing a lack of tree canopy today.

Areas that were given an "A" grade at the time were characterized 10 by U.S.-born white populations in newer houses. Now, these same neighborhoods have nearly twice as much tree coverage as communities of color that were "redlined" by receiving the "D" grade, according to a recent paper analyzing 37 metro areas.

These disinvestments have a tangible impact on social equity issues. A University of Illinois Urbana-Champaign study of 98 Chicago public housing buildings with residents of similar socioeconomic situations found that when controlling for a number of other factors, more vegetation near a building contributed to 52 percent fewer crimes overall and 56 percent fewer violent crimes.

With temperatures rising and economic disparities widening, trees are indispensable infrastructure. However, ensuring the right tree is planted in the right place is no easy feat. It requires expertise in selecting the most resilient and beneficial species. Planners must prepare for warming climates, allow existing trees to thrive and integrate new trees with competing infrastructure. Political will and financing from the public and private sectors are needed long before a tree is planted.

Despite these challenges, opportunities can be found everywhere. Tree Equity Score shows it will take 522 million more trees to achieve an equitable balance of greenery in every neighborhood in metro areas with 50,000 people or more in the continental United States.

Getting there requires a lot more funding to both plant new and 15 maintain existing trees. Some promising tools have emerged to help boost investment, including social impact bonds (which pay investors based on such outcomes as reduced prison recidivism) and voluntary carbon markets like City Forest Credits (a registry that issues tree planting and protection credits that can be purchased by companies to offset emissions).

But an ambitious goal like 522 million new trees cannot be achieved without the public sector. There are numerous opportunities to begin addressing tree equity in cities, such as through the infrastructure legislation working through Congress, substantially increasing support for the Urban and Community Forestry program and proposals to create programs at federal agencies focused on housing, energy and transportation.

Reaching these ambitious targets would have an outsize impact on lifesaving health outcomes, quality of life and slowing climate change, all while supporting over three million jobs, especially in neighborhoods that now lack greenery.

References

American Forests. (2021). *Tree equity score*. Retrieved March 16, 2022, from https://treeequityscore.org

Ziter, C. D., Pedersen, E. J., Kucharik, C. J., & Turner, M. G. (2019). Scale-dependent interactions between tree canopy cover and impervious surfaces reduce urban heat during summer. *PNAS, 116*(15), 7575–7580. https://doi.org/10.1073/pnas.1817561116

Thinking about the Text

1. Much of the support for Ian Leahy and Yarnya Serkez's argument comes from VISUALS: graphs, photos, and maps. Try reading through the article by ignoring all visuals and paying attention only to the written text. Then read again, this time attending carefully to both the visuals and the text they accompany. What do the visuals add to your understanding? Which of the visuals do you find most compelling or persuasive, and why?

2. Much of this article is based on research done by American Forests, a nonprofit conservation organization. In fact, it's the oldest such organization in the United States, having been founded in 1875. But how reliable is their work? Do a little research on American Forests, visiting their website and also checking to see if other sources are saying what they say—and what if anything those sources have to say about American Forests. Bring your results to class and be ready to discuss how what you have learned about American Forests affects how you evaluate Leahy and Serkez's argument.

See the tips for lateral reading on pp. 267–69 for help doing this kind of research.

3. How do you think Greta Thunberg would respond to Leahy and Serkez's argument? What would she say to him? And what might they say to her? (Read Thunberg's speech on p. 759.)

4. LET'S TALK. Leahy and Serkez note that "communities with too few trees" (5) and "a higher share of concrete" (2) are "feeling the consequences" (5) of climate change. With several other classmates, examine the EVIDENCE the authors present in support of this claim. Then think about your own experience: What kinds of neighborhoods have you lived in? How many trees did those neighborhoods have—if any—and what consequences has that had on you? Do you see those consequences relating to climate change?

5. AND NOW WRITE. When this opinion piece was published in 2021, it elicited 464 comments from readers, who wrote of their own experiences in neighborhoods with trees (or with a lack of trees). Some (but not all) accepted the authors' CLAIMS about a connection between discriminatory practices of the past and the size of the tree canopy today. Write your own response to this article, REFLECTING on what you remember about trees in the neighborhood you grew up in and on how your neighborhood may compare to those described in this article. What kind of "tree equity score" do you think your home neighborhood would receive? How does your own experience support Leahy and Serkez's argument—or not?

BENJI BACKER

The Conservative Case for Environmentalism

CRADLED BENEATH THE BOOK CLIFFS MOUNTAINS is a mineral-dense expanse known as Utah's coal country. The region, encompassing Emery and Carbon counties, is home to three of the state's remaining coal power plants. It's a place few environmentalists have dared tread.

But as an environmentalist myself, I recently traveled to Utah's coal country not to finger wag or lecture about greenhouse gases; no, I went there to better understand the lives and communities that depend on coal. And what I rediscovered in the process was a pressing need for conservative environmentalism.

I agree with Ronald Reagan: "What is a conservative after all, but one who conserves, one who is committed to protecting and holding close the things by which we live."

And on a practical level, if Republicans cede questions about conservation and earth stewardship; about air quality and water; about public lands and sustainability, then it will be largely Democrats who dominate the discussion. Folks in places like Emery and Carbon counties, who desperately want to be part of the solution, will be left out.

5   When I spoke with Michael Kourianos, the mayor of Price, he notes that I was one of only a few national environmentalists to take the time to visit. The mayor describes how willing and open his citizens are to

---

Benji Backer *is founder and president of the American Conservation Coalition, a nonprofit organization dedicated to bringing more conservative voices into environmental conversations. This article was originally published in* Deseret News, *a Utah newspaper, in 2021. He tweets from @BenjiBacker and posts from @benjibacker on* Instagram.

The Intermountain Power Project. Delta, Utah.

working on environmentally focused projects. The problem, he believes, is that very few groups or politicians who are aiming to shut down the city's largest economic driver ever want to talk.

The people in the region, he says, want to utilize their knowledge and expertise in innovative ways to aid a transition away from coal. They know that their knowledge could be useful in a world where countries like China continue to increase coal production and there's still a need for them to minimize emissions. To the mayor's point, it does seem like no one even wants to listen to them.

The San Rafael Energy Research Center is just one example. While the energy research center has gained little notoriety beyond Utah, the group has coal plant workers shifting their focus toward finding innovative ways to use coal with few or no emissions. They're testing, for example, how coal might be used for nuclear power or a low-emitting gas. This is happening across the state, where some coal plants are going as far as shifting to 100% green hydrogen over the coming decades.

Yet, these communities continue to be vilified and silenced because many environmentalists refuse to consider these communities as part of the climate conversation. Hundreds of counties like Emery and Carbon are being left behind across the country, all because too many environmentalists have an ignorance of people they've never met, places they've never visited and cultures they haven't tried to understand.

The solution is for conservatives to become more involved in discussions about how to solve pressing environmental issues in the West and beyond.

10   Everyone wants clean air and fewer emissions; the debate should center on the optimal avenues to get there. Conservatives can do just that—and accurately represent these left-behind communities in the process.

The right side of the political ledger is ultimately the most compatible home for positive environmental results. Conservatism, after all, is about conserving.

From Teddy Roosevelt doubling the number of sites within the National Park System and Richard Nixon creating the Environmental Protection Agency, Clean Air and Water Acts, and the Endangered Species Act, and George H. W. Bush setting aside more public lands than any other president in recent history, the conservative environmental legacy is substantial. As presidential historian Craig Shirley has pointed out, it was Ronald Reagan who signed more "federal wilderness bills into law than any other president since the Wilderness Act was enacted in 1964."

Backer highlights a situation that's addressed on pp. 31–33—why it's so worthwhile to get to know people different from you.

But it's not just conservative government actors who advance environmental causes. Competition within the car industry to create lighter vehicles with more fuel-efficient engines has contributed to fewer emissions. This has spurred an electric car race that has General Motors planning to eliminate internal combustion engines from its new vehicles by 2035—a highly ambitious goal driven more by market forces than government action. This is one of many examples of how free enterprise and ingenuity (inherently conservative principles) have provided us with immense environmental progress.

There are strong signs that conservative elected officials are retaking their seat at the table, too. Take Utah conservatives in Congress, for example. John Curtis—who graciously toured me around his district's energy facilities—has been one of the most forward-thinking leaders on this issue. He recently launched the Conservative Climate Caucus and about one-third of the GOP House delegation is participating already. Newly elected Blake Moore has already been at the forefront of commonsense forest management policies and is a member of the Conservative Climate Caucus. Burgess Owens and Chris Stewart are also members of the caucus.

After all, conservatives often live in the areas most impacted by 15 climate change or environmental policies coming from Washington— as farmers, ranchers, energy producers, foresters and outdoors enthusiasts. We care deeply about the environment, but we've been tired of the politicization of environmentalism. The conversation has seemingly shifted from relatable, tangible environmental issues to a global conversation with solutions that come across as big government and imposing in every way.

John Kerry, President Joe Biden's "climate czar," is an example of what's wrong with this approach. Most people like Kerry (the owner of his own, oft-used private plane) don't take the time to visit traditional energy facilities, talk with relevant workers or realize how much they rely on these communities in their personal lives.

Despite the frustrations, the people of Carbon and Emery counties are some of the most passionate people I've met in discussing their love for the environment. They live and breathe immense environmental beauty surrounding them—like the San Rafael Swell.

In the purest intention of the word, these people are true "environmentalists." They care for their planet and specifically the nature in their backyards, but they also want to be able to feed their families and not be vilified for working in an industry where they've unintentionally had a negative environmental impact. They don't just want to be part of the solution, they want to help lead it.

We need more conservative people, like many in Carbon and Emery counties, to join the conversation. If not, the millions of people in conservative America will be losing their seat at the table to a few select cities—and specifically to the federal government.

20   To make matters worse, the policies that will come from that—like the Green New Deal—will harm the communities that really do care about the environment most.

    Threats to the environment are real—we are facing a dramatic increase in global carbon emissions, our air quality impacted by wildfires is making the West less hospitable, and droughts are causing immense water scarcity concerns. As we've seen these and many other issues come to fruition over the past few decades, we've learned a lot about the causes. One of the elephants in the room is the reality that carbon production has contributed in a negative way to a few of our globe's severe environmental concerns.

    But instead of vilifying vulnerable communities that had no idea that their production of affordable, abundant energy would be contributing to environmental problems, we should be utilizing their talents, background and brainpower to come up with next-generation solutions. After all, to solve complicated environmental problems, we need a diverse set of solutions and knowledgeable voices.

    That's where the needed growing environmental movement of conservatives comes into play.

    First, conservatives need to put the "environment" back into "environmentalism." We should be the movement that focuses on measuring success by what actually works, not what sounds best in a 10-second divisive soundbite.

25   Second, we need to connect and instill an authentic love for our local environment. Humans care about their own backyard more than anything—and know the most about it. As such, environmental solutions should come from locals. To do this, we can humanize the environmental conversation by understanding where people are coming from—in all geographical areas, ethnic backgrounds and political viewpoints.

    Third, we need to be the environmental movement of hope—instead of despair. Solving environmental challenges will herald from local conservation projects, exciting new technologies, job creation and an overall improvement of society. That is the conservative way: seeking innovation and solutions to tough problems rather than propagating a narrative of despair, doom and futility in a bid to shame voters into certain pro-environment policies.

Lastly, we should be the movement of putting American interests first. The United States has the most impressive environmental track record of any nation over the past few decades. We have been able to create the most innovative solutions, consistently increase the protection of our environment and lead the world in environmental progress. The more America succeeds, the more the environment does, too.

Most environmentalists have looked at the likes of Carbon and Emery counties as the enemy. That must not happen. But to change it we need a robust conservative environmental movement.

I'm a conservative who is a passionate environmentalist. Knowing the two were often at odds in our national political landscape, I founded a nonprofit organization, the American Conservation Coalition, with my peers in 2017. In late 2019, I testified before Congress with the world-renowned climate activist Greta Thunberg as the conservative alternative, which was our organization's first opportunity to show the world what conservative environmentalism looked like.

I've seen glimmers of hope that conservatives can retake the envi-   30
ronmental conversation that we once led. We are the party that lives amid nature, and it's time we take back the narrative that we are the ones who don't care about conserving it.

Thinking about the Text

1. Throughout this article, Benji Backer connects *conservation* with *conservative*, arguing that "conservatism, after all, is about conserving" (11). Reread his article, marking every point that provides evidence that the two terms are linked in the way he

suggests—as "conservative environmentalism" (2). Has he persuaded you that conservatism is in fact about "conserving"? If so, what EVIDENCE did you find most persuasive?

2. Look through Backer's article to find one or two sentences that capture what he means by "conservative environmentalism." Then look again to see how he DEFINES those who take other PERSPECTIVES. How does he characterize members of each group? Do you associate with one of these sides—and if so, why (or why not)? Can you come up with one or more other perspectives on environmental issues, or on one that perhaps combines what you see as the best parts of both sides Backer discusses?

3. This is an opinion piece. In presenting his perspective, Backer makes a number of CLAIMS and offers REASONS to back up his claims. Choose the claim you find to be most compelling and then describe the reasons Backer gives to support it. What made this particular claim most persuasive to you?

4. LET'S TALK. Backer suggests that environmentalists would make more progress by talking and listening than by lecturing or finger wagging, noting that we need to understand "where people are coming from—in all geographical areas, ethnic backgrounds and political viewpoints" (25). Who are the people Backer talks to and listens to in this article, and how many different areas, ethnicities, and viewpoints do they represent? Who else might he talk to or listen to? Work with a classmate to make a list of people or groups you think should be listened to about on environmental issues.

5. AND NOW WRITE. Backer mentions that in 2019 he testified before the US Congress with Greta Thunberg "to show the world what conservative environmentalism looked like" (29). Take Backer's advice about talking and listening to one another, and chat with another classmate about how Thunberg and Backer might have a conversation. Then write out a page or two of what you imagine that conversation might look like. (Read Thunberg's speech on p. 759.)

CARL ZIMMER

The Uncommon Cold: How Rhinoviruses Gently Conquered the World

AROUND 3,500 YEARS AGO, an Egyptian physician sat down and wrote the oldest known medical text. Among the diseases he described was something called *resh*. Even with that strange-sounding name, its symptoms—a cough and a flowing of mucus from the nose—are immediately familiar to us all. *Resh* is the common cold.

Some viruses that beset us today are new to humanity. Other viruses are obscure and exotic. But human rhinoviruses—the chief cause of the common cold—are old companions. It's been estimated that every human being on Earth will spend a year of his or her life lying in bed, sick with colds. The human rhinovirus is, in other words, one of the most successful viruses of all.

Before the discovery of rhinoviruses, doctors floundered to explain the cause of colds. Hippocrates, the ancient Greek physician, blamed an imbalance of the humors. Two thousand years later, in the early 1900s, our knowledge of colds hadn't improved much. The physiologist Leonard Hill declared that colds were caused by walking outside in the morning.

In 1914, a German microbiologist named Walther Kruse gained the first solid clue about the origin of colds by having a snuffly assistant

Carl Zimmer *is an award-winning science journalist whose work appears in* Discover, National Geographic, *and other publications. He's written many books, including* Life's Edge: The Search for What It Means to Be Alive (2021), *and* A Planet of Viruses (2021), *in which this piece was first published. He is also the only writer for whom both a species of tapeworm and an asteroid have been named. He teaches molecular biophysics and biochemistry at Yale and tweets from @carlzimmer.*

blow his nose. Kruse mixed the assistant's mucus into a salt solution, poured it through a filter, and then put a few drops of the filtered fluid into the noses of 12 colleagues. Four of them came down with colds. Later, Kruse did the same thing to 36 students, and 15 of them got sick. While he ran this experiment Kruse also kept track of 35 people who didn't get the drops. Only one of them came down with a cold on their own. Kruse's experiments made it clear that the drops from people with colds contained a tiny pathogen that was responsible for the disease.

5   At first, many experts believed it was some kind of bacteria. But the American physician Alphonse Dochez ruled that out in 1927. He filtered the mucus from people with colds, just as Beijerinck has filtered tobacco plant sap 30 years before. Even with the bacteria removed, the fluid could still make people sick. Only a virus could have slipped through Dochez's filters.

It took another three decades before scientists figured out exactly which viruses had slipped through. The most common of them are known as human rhinoviruses (*rhino* means nose). Rhinoviruses are remarkably simple. While we humans have about 20,000 genes, rhinoviruses have only 10. And yet this haiku of genetic information is enough

Human rhinovirus,
a microscopic view.

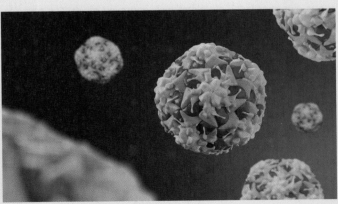

to let rhinoviruses invade our bodies, outwit our immune system, and produce new viruses that can escape to new hosts.

To get to those new hosts, rhinoviruses travel in droplets. They can get into the tiny ones that we exhale with each breath. They can get into the bigger droplets we blast out when we sneeze or cough. A careless wipe of the nose can put those droplets on our hands, and our hands can transfer them to doorknobs, elevator buttons, and other surfaces where other people can pick them up on their own hands, which can then deliver them to their own noses.

Once inside a fresh nose, rhinoviruses can latch on to the cells that line the nasal passage. They slip inside and use their host cells to make copies of their genetic material, along with protein shells to hold them. The host cell then rips apart, and the new rhinoviruses escape. In some hosts, rhinoviruses remain limited to the nose, but in others they slip into the throat and even the lungs.

Rhinoviruses infect relatively few cells, causing little real harm. So why can they cause such miserable experiences? We have only ourselves to blame. Infected cells release signaling molecules, called cytokines, which attract nearby immune cells. Those immune cells then make us feel awful. They create inflammation that triggers a scratchy feeling in the throat and leads to the production of mucus around the site of the infection. In order to recover from a cold, we have to wait not only for the immune system to wipe out the virus, but also for the immune system itself to calm down.

In ancient Egypt, physicians treated *resh* by dabbing a mixture of honey, herbs, and incense around the nose. Fifteen centuries later, the Roman scholar Pliny the Elder recommended rubbing a mouse against the nose instead. In seventeenth-century Europe, some physicians used a blend of gunpowder and eggs, others a mixture of suet and fried cow dung. Leonard Hill recommended starting the day with a cold shower.

None of these treatments worked, but even today we lack a proven cure for the common cold. In the late 1900s, some researchers got encouraged by the discovery that zinc could stop rhinoviruses from infecting cells grown in Petri dishes. Before long, drug stores were

10

Zimmer packs a lot of information in this essay. This might be a good time to practice the annotating skills that are laid out on pp. 56–58.

selling zinc tablets without a prescription, even though no one had yet shown that they worked in actual people. Some small clinical studies later hinted that zinc might cut a cold down by a couple days. But when a Finnish scientist named Harri Hemilä led a carefully designed trial 253 volunteers, he found no benefit. In fact, Hemilä reported in 2019, the volunteers who took zinc tablets took a little longer to recover from a cold than people who took sugar pills.

Other common treatments for the cold may not only be useless— they may even cause harm. Parents often give children cough syrup for colds, but studies show it doesn't make people get better faster. In fact, cough syrup poses a wide variety of rare yet serious side effects, such as convulsions, rapid heart rate, and even death. The US Food and Drug Administration warns that children under the age of two—who get colds the most often—should not take cough syrup.

It's also a mistake to treat a cold with antibiotics. Antibiotics are designed to kill bacteria and are useless against viruses. Doctors prescribe them depressingly often for colds anyway. In some cases it may be hard to tell from the symptoms patients display whether they're infected with rhinoviruses or bacteria. In other cases, doctors may respond to pressure from worried parents to do *something*. The harm that antibiotics cause in these cases isn't limited to one patient: we suffer. Our bodies are home to trillions of harmless bacteria, and antibiotics can foster the evolution of resistant strains. Those resistant bacteria can pass on their genes to disease-causing microbes. As a result, when we need antibiotics to work, they may fail us.

One reason the cold remains so hard to treat may be that we've underestimated the rhinovirus. It exists in many forms, and scientists are only starting to get a true reckoning of its genetic diversity. As a cell makes new rhinoviruses, it typically makes mistakes in copying the virus's genes. Over the generations, the virus's lineages become increasingly different. By the end of the twentieth century, scientists had identified dozens of strains of rhinovirus. They belonged to two great lineages, known as HRV-A and HRV-B.

15   In 2006, Ian Lipkin and Thomas Briese of Columbia University discovered that some New Yorkers with flu-like symptoms were infected

with rhinoviruses that did not belong to either HRV-A or HRV-B. Instead, they formed a previously unknown third lineage, which Lipkin and Briese dubbed HRV-C. Since their discovery, researchers have found HRV-C all around the world.

The more strains scientists discover, the better they come to understand the evolutionary history of rhinoviruses. Some of their genes turn out to be evolving very quickly as the viruses outrace our immune systems. One type of weapon we use to fight against viruses is antibodies—molecules that can latch on to the surface of a virus and disrupt it in all sorts of ways. Mutations can alter the surface of rhinoviruses such that those antibodies can no longer stick. Our immune systems can make new antibodies, but new mutations can allow the viruses to escape once more.

This rapid evolution has helped create a tremendous diversity of rhinoviruses. Each of us can expert to get infected by several different human rhinovirus strains every year. And just as this evolution frustrates our immune systems, it also frustrates researchers who are trying to make antivirals that can cure colds. If an antiviral works well against one strain of rhinovirus, it may fail against others. And there's always a chance that a new mutation may enable a rhinovirus to resist the drug and explode in numbers while other viruses die off.

While we don't have a cure yet for the common cold, we shouldn't give up in despair. Although some parts of rhinoviruses evolve rapidly, other parts barely change at all. In these regions of a rhinovirus, mutations may be lethal. If scientists can target these vulnerable spots in the rhinovirus, they may be able to take on every rhinovirus on Earth.

But should they? The answer is actually not clear. Human rhinoviruses impose a serious burden on public health, not just by causing colds, but by opening the way for more harmful pathogens. Yet the effects of human rhinovirus itself are relatively mild. Most colds finish in under a week, and 40 percent of people who test positive for rhinoviruses suffer no symptoms at all. In fact, human rhinoviruses may offer some benefits to their human hosts. Scientists have gathered a great deal of evidence that children who get sick with relatively harmless viruses and bacteria may be protected from immune disorders when they get older, such as allergies and Crohn's disease. Human rhinoviruses may help train our immune systems not to overreact to minor triggers, instead directing their assaults to real threats. Perhaps we should not think of colds as ancient enemies but as wise old tutors.

Thinking about the Text

1. After reviewing efforts to determine causes of the common cold, Carl Zimmer discusses the difficulty treating it and the search for a cure—before suggesting that eradicating the disease might not be the best path to take after all. Reread his essay looking for evidence of Zimmer's own STANCE on this question: What clues can you find to determine whether he leans one way or the other?

2. Notice that Zimmer refers to rhinoviruses as if they're human, saying, for example, that they're "old companions" (2), who "slip," "travel" (7), and even "outwit" (6) our immune systems. His use of such words is one way that he makes this scientific information easy to read and understand. Look closely to track other words in this piece of writing and the effect they have on you as a reader. What other STRATEGIES (ANECDOTES? DEFINITIONS? DESCRIPTION?) does Zimmer use that keep readers' attention?

3. LET'S TALK. Get together with a couple of classmates and review the remedies people in other eras used to combat the common cold (put a mouse on your nose, you say?!). Then share experiences each of you has had for treating colds: Did your families have any home remedies that you remember? Are there certain things you do now when you have a cold? During the COVID-19 pandemic, wearing a mask seems to have helped prevent the spread of common colds: What's been your experience with that?

4. AND NOW WRITE. Zimmer concludes by asking whether we should try to eliminate rhinoviruses and even suggesting that maybe "we should not think of colds as ancient enemies but as wise old tutors" (19). What do you think? Write an essay REFLECTING on that suggestion.

The World Is Waking Up

THIS IS ALL WRONG. I shouldn't be standing here.

I should be back in school on the other side of the ocean. Yet you all come to us young people for hope? How dare you!

You have taken away my dreams and my childhood with your empty words. And yet I'm one of the lucky ones.

People are suffering. People are dying. Entire ecosystems are collapsing. We are in the beginning of a mass extinction. And all you can talk about is money and fairy tales of eternal economic growth. How dare you!

For more than thirty years the science has been crystal clear. How 5 dare you continue to look away, and come here saying that you are doing enough.

When the politics and solutions needed are still nowhere in sight.

You say you "hear" us and that you understand the urgency. But no matter how sad and angry I am, I don't want to believe that. Because if you fully understood the situation and still kept on failing to act, then you would be evil.

And I refuse to believe that.

The popular idea of cutting our emissions in half in ten years only gives us a 50 percent chance of staying below 1.5°C and the risk of setting off irreversible chain reactions beyond human control.

Fifty percent may be acceptable to you. 10

Greta Thunberg launched a worldwide movement among young people calling for action on climate change when she began skipping school in August 2018 to sit outside the Swedish parliament holding a sign saying "skolstrejk för klimatet" (school strike for climate). She delivered the following remarks to the United Nations General Assembly on September 23, 2019. Thunberg tweets from @GretaThunberg.

Thunberg confidently assumes the stance of an advocate, and with a tone that conveys her anger. See pp. 26–27 for help thinking about your stance.

But since those numbers don't include tipping points, most feed-back loops, additional warming hidden by toxic air pollution, nor the aspect of equity, then a 50 percent risk is simply not acceptable to us, we who have to live with the consequences. We do not accept these odds.

To have a 67 percent chance of staying below a 1.5°C global temperature rise, the best odds given by the IPCC, the world had 420 giga-tonnes of CO_2 left to emit back on 1 January 2018.

Today, as you can see, that figure is already down to less than 350 gigatonnes. How dare you pretend that this can be solved with business as usual and some technical solutions!

With today's emission levels, that remaining CO_2 budget will be entirely gone within less than 8.5 years.

15   There will not be any solutions or plans presented in line with these figures today. Because these numbers are too uncomfortable. And you are still not mature enough to tell it like it is.

Your generation is failing us. But the young people are starting to understand your betrayal. The eyes of all future generations are upon you.

And if you choose to fail us I say we will never forgive you.

We will not let you get away with this. Right here, right now is where we draw the line.

The world is waking up.

20   And change is coming, whether you like it or not.

Thinking about the Text

1.   Greta Thunberg accuses members of the UN General Assembly of betraying her and all young people who will have to "live with the consequences" (11) of that betrayal. Exactly what is the betrayal that she refers to? Then read through her text, noting the EVIDENCE she provides to support her CLAIM. Are you persuaded that she's right? Why, or why not?

2.   Thunberg presented these remarks at a UN summit on climate change, so what you have read is a transcript of an oral presentation. Working with a classmate, read the transcript

aloud and then watch the actual presentation at www.youtube
.com/watch?v=KAJsdgTPJpU. How does Thunberg's OPENING
sentence get her audience's attention? And how about her
CONCLUSION: How does it likely keep them thinking about what
she's said? And notice her use of REITERATION: How does that
hold her audience's attention and drive home her points?

3. Obviously she's very angry, and her TONE reflects that, both
with her voice and with her words. Do you think she might have
reached more people in her audience if she'd toned down her
anger some—and why, or why not? Notice that she shifts her tone
in one place—where is that, and why do you think she did so?

4. LET'S TALK. Thunberg ends these remarks by saying that the
world "is waking up" (19) to the reality of "irreversible chain
reactions" (9) set loose by climate change. Get together with
two or three classmates to talk about whether you see evidence
today—several years after Thunberg's address—that the
world is indeed "waking up." You might do a little research to
check current predicted odds of staying below the 1.5 degrees
centigrade—or other facts that Thunberg cites. What conclusions
can you draw about the state of the planet in terms of climate
change—and about whether "change is coming," whether we like
it or not.

5. AND NOW WRITE. Take some time to reflect on how the climate
affects you, your friends and family, and your community. What
changes in the weather have you noticed over the last ten years
or so? Have they affected your day-to- day life—and if so, in what
ways? Greta Thunberg does not make specific suggestions about
what students should do, other than to protest and "never
forgive" (17) those who fail to act. Write a brief essay REFLECTING
on your own observations about the climate and recommending
what you and other students should or should not take to
respond to the situation that Thunberg describes.

35 # Do Sports Matter?

THERE IS POWER IN UNDERSTANDING THE JOURNEY OF
OTHERS TO HELP CREATE YOUR OWN.

—KOBE BRYANT

A CHAMPION IS DEFINED NOT BY THEIR WINS BUT BY HOW
THEY CAN RECOVER WHEN THEY FALL.

—SERENA WILLIAMS

As any star athlete can tell you, for every victory, there are many moments of defeat, of doubt, of despair and exhaustion. And while most of us aren't stars, sports can still do an excellent job of teaching us a lot about life. When we engage in sports as players, we have an opportunity to test ourselves and document our growth. When we engage as fans and spectators, sports offer a little escape from our daily routines, give us inspiring heroes to celebrate and emulate— and often unite us in shared knowledge and shared emotions.

The readings in this chapter touch on the powerful influence that sports have—on personal lives, on the

the business of sports, and on the social structures that shape sports as well as the social conditions that sports help to shape. **Jane Coaston** gets right to the point in her essay, "What Can Sports Teach Us?" **Mark Gozonsky**, on the other hand, explores sports as a personal challenge and struggle in a narrative about playing on a baseball team with players half his age.

Joe Drape reports on the growing popularity of e-sports and the impact that they are having on the business of sports and especially on traditional organized youth sports. **Nell Gluckman** offers another take on the business of sports in her essay on the astronomical salaries paid to many coaches at large universities.

Two other readings touch on the ways that sports affect and are affected by social issues. **Heather Gilligan** explores the racial tension that once haunted professional basketball, and how the Harlem Globetrotters changed the game forever. And **Jemele Hill** analyzes the conflicting interests of athletes, league organizers, and sports media in her look at Naomi Osaka and other high-profile athletes who are insisting on protections for their mental health.

Together, these essays can help each of us think about sports from various perspectives. Do sports matter, and if so, why—or why not?

Readings on letstalklibrary.com

- **Michael Jordan,** Eulogy for Kobe Bryant
- **Mahina Maeda,** What It Means to Be from Two Places at Once
- **Michael Rosen,** Breaking the Grass Ceiling: More Women Are Playing College Baseball Than Ever Before

JANE COASTON

What Can Sports Teach Us?

GOOD MORNING, and welcome to the first issue of my newsletter, a place where I hope to discuss the obsessions, ideas and thought processes that have shaped and guided my career.

If you subscribe to my podcast, *The Argument*, you know that I spend a lot of my time working to understand what, how and why other people think the way they do about the biggest issues of our time—from housing to critical race theory to the death penalty. A lot of that work is possible because of how I think, and because of the reading and watching that have shaped me over the past decade.

In this newsletter, I want to cover the events that may seem small or unrelated to our biggest concerns but that undergird how we think, talk and vote.

How does popular culture—or more important, our perception of popular culture—move public opinion? Why are some of the fiercest online debates not about politics, but about . . . whether fruit is good for you?

5   How has the history of alcohol and Prohibition affected the War on Drugs? How does Israel teach the Holocaust, and is there something we could learn from that to teach about slavery and Jim Crow here in the United States?

For me, much of my thought process begins with sports—so I plan to cover the subject a lot. I was not an athletic child, but I was an

---

Jane Coaston is the host of The Argument, *a podcast produced by the* New York Times *that presents strong opinions on sports, politics, and history. Her work has been published in the* National Review, *the* Washington Post, ESPN Magazine, *and other periodicals. This 2021 essay was the first entry in a newsletter Coaston writes for the* New York Times. *She tweets from @janecoaston.*

athletic-minded one. I love the context of sports—the how, the why and the how much that goes into various sports, and how they do (or don't) work.

And sports matter, even if you don't identify as a sports fan. Sports give us small, silly conduits for how a society thinks about what it values the most and what it values the least.

If sports don't matter to you, they probably matter to your neighbor, your kids or the person your favored political candidate wants to reach. And if you follow "horse race politics," or care about your political team winning (or, perhaps more accurately, your political opponents losing), you may be talking about nonsports in a very sports-like way.

I started my professional writing career covering college football and the N.F.L. Football was my first writing love, the subject of my most florid (and only slightly concerning) prose.

As you may have noticed, I'm not alone in my passion for this sport.   10
Football, specifically college football, is not just a pastime or a business. It is a culture unto itself.

The sport (or, more accurately, being competitive in the sport) requires millions of dollars in investment in order to create billions of dollars in profit, vanishingly little of which goes to the athletes who play football and endure its damages. College football coaches are the highest paid state employees in many states,[1] and the machinations of university athletic departments can alter the political tides both within their home states and nationally.

A little tale from this summer illustrates these points.

Back in August, Roger Marshall, a Republican senator from Kansas, asked the Department of Justice to investigate the country's largest sports television network to determine its involvement in the decision by two major universities to change athletic conferences.[2]

In a letter to Attorney General Merrick Garland,[3] the senator argued that ESPN may have played a part in getting Texas and Oklahoma to change conferences, asking "that the D.O.J. investigate ESPN's role in the potential destruction of the Big XII Conference and if any

By revealing her passion for college football, Coaston demonstrates both her authority and credibility. Find help establishing yours on pp. 112–13.

anti-competitive or illegal behavior occurred relating to manipulating the conference change or ESPN's contractual television rights."

15   Since 1996, the University of Texas and the University of Oklahoma have been the flagship members of the Big 12 conference,[4] which also includes schools like Texas Tech and, yes, the University of Kansas. Earlier in the summer, Texas and Oklahoma announced that they would like to leave the Big 12 conference and join the Southeastern Conference (S.E.C.), which includes athletic powerhouses like Alabama and Florida.

At the end of July, members of the S.E.C. voted unanimously to extend invitations to both Texas and Oklahoma, and both schools will join the S.E.C. in 2025. The result will be a 16-team "super-conference."

Conference realignment in college sports is nothing new. Big schools bolting conferences to make more money is a time-honored football tradition, like overestimating Notre Dame. In the grand scheme of things, this move may seem unimportant, and perhaps should not be a priority for a U.S. senator.

I am sure that Marshall is aware that the Department of Justice has absolutely no interest in investigating ESPN. And he must be aware

From left, Texas Longhorns cheerleaders; Casey Thompson about to pass against the Oklahoma Sooners at the Cotton Bowl, Dallas, Texas, 2021.

Oklahoma Sooners fans cheer as Jalen Redmond runs for a 42-yard touchdown against Iowa State. Norman, Oklahoma, 2021.

that a massive change in the sport of college football is insignificant to the lived experiences of his constituents (in comparison to Covid or climate change, for example).

But he is also aware that Texas and Oklahoma leaving the conference they helped to steer will dramatically alter the Big 12 conference. He is also aware that the swirl of conference realignment will alter how, where and when the sport of football (and, to be clear, every other college sport) is played.

I would not be shocked to learn that Marshall has received hundreds of calls and emails from voters asking him to do something, anything, to prevent this from happening. 20

For millions of Americans, from Syracuse, N.Y., to Berkeley, Calif., and everywhere in between, college football is a tether to camaraderie and shared experiences of joy and pain.

If Michigan wins a national championship in college football this season (it will not) the material difference in my life would be infinitesimal. I would not get paid more or be better at my job. And yet I would be so emotionally buoyed by a Michigan national championship in football that sometimes I dare to imagine it, just for a second, just for a hint of that feeling.

College football will not make me spiritually fulfilled or morally superior. But it can, and does, make me happy. And I've met people from across the country and around the world—people in Singapore and Australia who wake up at 2 a.m. to watch a game taking place 14 hours away—who feel very much the same, and find changes to the game as it's played now life altering.

This is the culture of college football, of the behemoth made from a game played every fall by college students who were born while I was in high school.

25   It doesn't really matter. It's not really important. But it means so very, very much.

Notes

1. Stebbins, S. (2020, September 23). *College coaches dominate list of highest-paid public employees with seven-digit salaries.* USA Today. https://www.usatoday.com/story/money/2020/09/23/these-are -the-highest-paid-public-employees-in-every-state/114091534/

2. Ward, M. (2021, August 4). *Sen. Roger Marshall calls on DOJ to investigate ESPN's role in Big 12 realignment.* Politico. https://www .politico.com/news/2021/08/04/roger-marshall-doj-investigate-espn -role-502451

3. Marshall, R. (2021, August 4). *Letter to Merrick Garland.* https:// www.marshall.senate.gov/wp-content/uploads/Letter-to-DOJ-Re -ESPN-BIG-XII-8.4.21.pdf

4. Hawkins, S. (2021, September 10). *Bigger Big 12: BYU, UCF, Cincinnati, and Houston on the way.* AP News. https://apnews.com /article/sports-college-football-football-brigham-young-cougars -football-78b828f94f6a502589d98a3545eb7d2d

Thinking about the Text

1. Jane Coaston argues that sports matter to everyone, sports fan or not. How does she support that CLAIM? What EVIDENCE does she present? What from your own experience would help to support—or perhaps refute—what she says?

2. Coaston announced that her goal for the newsletter where this piece first appeared is to cover events "that may seem small" but that "undergird how we think, talk and vote" (3). How well has she achieved her goal in this piece? Be prepared to cite examples from her text to support your answer to this question.

3. Nell Gluckman criticizes the astronomical salaries paid to the football coaches at many universities (see p. 796). What might Coaston have to say on that topic?

4. LET'S TALK. Coaston mentions that we often talk about politics and other topics in a "very sports-like way" (8). In fact, the English language is bursting with sports-based metaphors. We may call a good idea a "slam dunk" (basketball) or a "bullseye" (archery), and we talk about "low blows" (boxing), "knocking it out of the park" (baseball, softball), and many more. BRAINSTORM with a few classmates to see how many sports-based metaphors you can think of. Why do you think there are so many?

5. AND NOW WRITE. In her final paragraph, Coaston says college football "doesn't really matter. It's not really important. But it means so very, very much" (25). What in your own life experience might you say that about? Write a brief essay that DESCRIBES and explains why and how this seemingly unimportant thing means so very much to you.

JOE DRAPE

Step Aside, LeBron and Dak, and Make Room for Banjo and Kazooie

F RISCO, TEXAS—A miniature basketball hoop hangs from the bedroom door. Soccer trophies are prominent on the dresser. Each sport competes for the time and attention of David and Matthew Grimes. But both are losing ground to another staple of adolescence: the video game console.

David, 13, and Matthew, 11, are fledgling e-sports athletes.

David thumbs his controllers and listens to strategy talk from a YMCA coach on Monday nights. On Wednesday, he takes on all comers. Matthew has league play on Thursday. At least one weekend a month, they compete in a Super Smash Bros. Ultimate tournament.

David and Matthew are part of a surging migration among members of Generation Z—as those born from 1997 to 2012 are often labeled—away from the basketball courts and soccer fields built for previous generations and toward the PlayStations and Xboxes of theirs.

5 It's not a zero-sum game: Many children, including the Grimeses, enjoy sports both virtual and physical. But it's clear that the rise of e-sports has come at the expense of traditional youth sports, with implications for their future and for the way children grow up.

E-sports got a boost, especially at the grass-roots level, during the pandemic. Between at-home learning and the shutdown of youth sports, a high-tech generation found even more escape and engagement on its smartphones and consoles.

Joe Drape is a sportswriter for the New York Times, *where he reports on the intersection of sports, culture, and money. He is the author of six books, including the best seller* American Pharoah: The Untold Story of the Triple Crown Champion's Legendary Rise. *This article was published in December 2021. Drape tweets from @joedrape.*

Two brothers playing videogames with their mom.

Participation in youth sports was declining even before Covid-19: In 2018, only 38 percent of children ages 6 to 12 played team sports on a regular basis, down from 45 percent in 2008, according to the Sports & Fitness Industry Association.

In June 2020, the pandemic's early days, 19 percent of parents with kids in youth sports said their child was not interested in playing sports, according to a survey conducted by The Aspen Institute's Sports and Society Program. By September 2021, that figure was 28 percent.

On average, children play less than three years in a sport and quit by age 11, according to the survey. Why? Mostly, because it is not fun anymore.

The implications are global. There are currently more than 2.4 billion gamers—about one-third of the world's population, according to Statista, an international marketing and consumer data firm based in Germany. There are professional teams around the world that compete in tournaments for prize pools up to $34 million as well as tens of thousands of other competitions with prize money or contested in 10 school and recreational leagues, accounting for more than a $1 billion in global e-sports revenues.

The effect on traditional sports is just one of the concerns often expressed about this phenomenon. The proliferation of e-sports conjures images of children eating sugary snacks late into the night as they stare at their screens. Research, however, doesn't fully support this, with a 2019 German study finding only "a slight positive correlation" between gaming and body mass in adults, but not children.

Some youth sports coaches seem to understand the spell video games cast over their players. In 2018, a lacrosse coach in New Jersey decided if he could not beat them, he'd join them. He gave a pregame talk that demonstrated his deep knowledge of Fortnite, and it ricocheted through social media.

"This is just like Fortnite, just like Battle Royale," he said. "Twenty-four teams, there's four left. You know what? There's four left, we've got Chug Jugs, we've got the golden SCAR. Let's go! This is no different than a Fortnite battle. Let's go win this, baby!"

The waning interest in sports is hardly surprising when 87 percent of teenagers in the United States have iPhones, according to a survey of 10,000 young people by investment bank Piper Sandler, or when 26 percent of Gen Z youths named video games as their favorite entertainment activity, compared to 10 percent who chose watching television.

15   "There is a lot more stuff competing for the attention of young people—e-sports is a big one," said Dr. Travis E. Dorsch, associate professor and founding director of the Families in Sport Lab at Utah State University. "As kids get older, there is more tug at them academically and socially. We're seeing a lot of dropouts. This creates a reckoning for youth sports."

The more than $19 billion youth sports industrial complex, with its private coaching, interstate travel and $350 baseball bats, shoulders some of the blame. Ten-month seasons in pursuit of a college scholarship in a single sport can mean that kids get yelled at by overzealous coaches and parents spend thousands of dollars on team fees and travel expenses.

"We're at an inflection moment of sports in America," said Tom Cove, president and chief executive of the Sports & Fitness Industry Association, which compiles an annual report on participation in sports. "While families were at home during the pandemic, they did not have to drive their kids to practices four nights a week.

"They liked it. They decided that there must be a better way."

For Tony and Dawnita Grimes, that way led them to the YMCA of Metropolitan Dallas and a greater appreciation for e-sports.

"Let's go! This is no different than a *Fortnite* battle!"

Let the Games Begin

Frisco, a city of 200,000 about 28 miles north of Dallas, is football 20 country. It is home to The Star, the world headquarters of the Dallas Cowboys.

David Grimes wears a Cowboys T-shirt and can tell you about the team's quarterback, Dak Prescott. When The Star opened, David was chosen to carry the helmet of linebacker Leighton Vander Esch before a preseason training camp session.

Tony Grimes is a sales executive with PepsiCo. He played high school football growing up in South Los Angeles. Dawnita Grimes, a lawyer, was on dance and tennis teams growing up in Kentucky.

Tony and Dawnita Grimes steer their sons away football because of the risk of injury, but encourage soccer, swimming, basketball and golf. They want the boys to be well rounded, so David plays trumpet and Matthew piano. Sometimes the scramble of school, sports and other activities led to quick dinners or late starts on homework. The Grimeses were busy but adept at conducting the rhythms of family life.

Then came the pandemic. The cancellation of games left the boys with time on their hands.

David and Matthew Grimes play basketball with their dad.

25   "Because of Covid, I started to play video games," David Grimes said. Little brother Matthew was right behind him.

    Their mother and father were immersed in their screens, too, and in a surrender familiar to many parents, were not as disciplined as usual about clocking the amount of time their boys were on their devices.

The interview with the Grimes family nicely adds to the many facts and statistics that Drape presents. Get advice on conducting interviews on pp. 259–60.

    "Oh yeah, it was a lifeline," said Dawnita Grimes. "They were cut off from their friends. Most hadn't exchanged numbers, or they don't know each other's last names. Unless you knew their parents, it was hard to connect, and I hate to say it, except through these games."

    Tony Grimes admits that he likes picking up his boys' controllers and trying to master another universe. Beyond the peace and quiet David and Matthew's screen time afforded him, he had a new appreciation for the skills necessary to be competitive.

30   "You have to be focused, understand strategy and have good hand-eye coordination," he said.

    On a recent evening, David carried the game console downstairs so he could tell Matthew, his parents and a visitor what he had learned the previous night from the Y's online tutorial. Both boys held their controllers gently, as if they were holding a bird.

"It's not enough to watch the games, you have to actually play them," David said. "So you have to find a character that you're good with."

"Get Hero or Cloud," Matthew said as his brother clicked through characters.

E-sports let kids have fun with their friends even when they're not together. Audio headsets allow players to talk—or often scream—at one another as if they were sitting side by side. Anyone who has listened to their sons or daughters competing online has heard at least one side of conversation carried out as effortlessly as the cross talk between two basketball players on the playground during a game of HORSE.

"The hierarchy you usually find in traditional sports is gone— 35 everyone is just there," said Dorsch, who was one of the lead investigators on the Aspen Institute research. "It's more of a meritocracy."

He believes that e-sports have evolved that way because of the absence of adult influence at its introductory stage.

"You go to a soccer or basketball program and you can tell immediately the 6-year-olds who are athletic and have talent," Dorsch said. "Their parents see it and think, 'Well, he or she could be really good with better coaching.'"

For kids, that can turn a passion into a pursuit. A costly one, for parents.

In a 2016 study, Dorsch and his colleagues found many households that spent as much as 10.5 percent of their gross income annually—sometimes $20,000 or more—on personal trainers, travel costs and private teams for their children.

"Then it becomes about the adults in the room," he said. "And 40 they want a return on their investment."

In the Grimes family, the love of sports was handed down the traditional way. During one-on-one games on the miniature hoop hanging from the bedroom door, Tony Grimes was always Michael Jordan and David was LeBron James. It offered Tony an opportunity to tell the boys about a hero of his youth and how he compared to a hero of theirs.

David Grimes prefers Banjo and Koozie to LeBron and Dak.

Now, those conversations are often reversed. Tony listens to David talk about why he prefers Banjo and Kazooie, Super Smash Bros. characters, over other game avatars. Instead of shooting percentages and scoring averages, the conversation is about B-button moves or side special ones that can mean the difference between victory and defeat.

"So this is my favorite character, but I'm not great at playing him," David said, conjuring a character named Hero onto the screen. "There are some characters that you really want to get good with. I'm not. Yet."

So, Banjo and Kazooie are more important to you than LeBron and Dak?

45   "Pretty much, yeah," David said, "because those are the characters I have to play with if I want to win a match or a tournament."

A New Playing Field

He has plenty of chances to compete. In April, the YMCA of America launched a national e-sports pilot in 120 of its U.S. branches. It was an immediate hit in the Dallas area, where more than 500 middle to high school age children have participated in its programs.

"We knew how popular the games were and the fact that tournaments could be held remotely gave us a way to engage with kids during the pandemic," said Rodney Black, program director for the YMCA of

Metropolitan Dallas. "The interest was immediate and continues to grow. The plan is to have an on-site gaming lounge in 2022."

It was just the kind of mainstream recognition that persuaded Dawnita Grimes to open the online world a little wider for her boys.

"You hear the stories about predators, and you worry about how addictive these games are," she said. "Here, it is organized and supervised, and you don't have to worry about bad language and poor sportsmanship."

David has won one tournament and Matthew beat his big brother 50 in another. Still, neither has abandoned soccer and both are looking forward to tennis, golf and swimming in the spring and summer.

David, however, knows there are professionals who have sponsors and can make millions in tournament play. You can almost hear the youth league football coaches pulling their hair out when he talks about it.

"It's safer than other sports. You don't get hurt," he said. "Well, you still have to worry about hands because if your hands get messed up, that's a problem because you got to be able to play the game."

He pauses, then smiles.

"It would be awesome to get paid to play video games."

Thinking about the Text

1. Joe Drape cites many different PERSPECTIVES about the rise of e-sports, both positive and negative, but he never tells us what he thinks. Reread the article, making a list of the positives and the negatives—and looking for words or passages that might reflect what Drape himself thinks about e-sports. What do you think: Are e-sports a good thing? not so good? a little of each?

2. Drape cites many different sources in this article: the president of the Sports & Fitness Industry Association, the program director of the Dallas YMCA, a high school lacrosse coach, and more—including, of course, David and Matthew Grimes and their parents. Which among his many sources did you find the most interesting? Which ones do you think best support what Drape says about e-sports—and why?

3.   TITLES are important. They need to get an audience's attention and give them some sense of what the text is about. What did you think when you first saw the title of this piece, "Step Aside, LeBron and Dak, and Make Room for Banjo and Kazooie"? Could you tell what it was about? Did it make you want to read on—and if so, why? If not, try your hand at coming up with a different title.

4.   LET'S TALK. Can any game be a sport? Tennis is clearly a sport, but how about Pac-Man? Scrabble? Poker? Of the many kinds of video games, which ones might be considered sports, and why? What does it take to make an activity a sport? Does it need to include competition with a clear winner? Athletic skills and physical training? Talk with a few classmates and try to come up with a DEFINITION to establish what is a sport and what is not—and then decide whether e-sports fit into that definition.

5.   AND NOW WRITE. If you play e-sports, what's your opinion about what Drape says about them? Write a brief essay responding to what he says, ARGUING for what you think. You can agree, disagree, or both, but do so explicitly and provide a THESIS that makes your overall response clear. If, however, you don't play e-sports, does his article make you interested in giving them a try? Write a brief essay REFLECTING on your overall reactions to Drape's article. Whatever your response, be sure to provide REASONS and EVIDENCE to support what *you* say.

See pp. 210–11 for tips on responding to a text.

HEATHER GILLIGAN

The Black-versus-White Game That Integrated Basketball

WHEN THE HARLEM GLOBETROTTERS and the Minneapolis Lakers played an exhibition game in Chicago in 1948, critics dismissed the contest as a publicity stunt. There was no way the all-Black Globetrotters—a comedy team of sorts—could beat the Lakers, the reigning champions of the all-White National Basketball League, a precursor to today's NBA.

Instead, the match changed basketball forever.

At the time, basketball was in trouble. Despite their winning record, the Lakers, like all teams playing in the NBL, had trouble drawing an audience. The league itself was losing money.

Not so for the Harlem Globetrotters, whose antics always drew a crowd, especially in their hometown of Chicago. (The "Harlem" in their name was only a way of telling audiences the team was Black.) The matchup was the result of a friendly argument between Globetrotters owner Abe Saperstein and Lakers co-owner Max Winters about who had the best team. Around 17,000 people, Black and White, packed into Chicago Stadium on the day of the game—an unheard-of audience for the Lakers.[1]

It's unclear how many were there to see a serious contest. Globetrotters games were as much about comedy as about basketball. Players hid balls under their shirts, bounced trick passes between their teammates' legs, traveled with hugely exaggerated steps down the

5

Heather Gilligan *is a journalist and cultural critic whose work has appeared in the* Washington Post, Slate, CNN, *and other places. Her writing focuses on health and parenting, as well as on the history of race in the United States. This 2018 essay is from* Level, *a blog on* Medium. *She tweets from @HeatherGilligan.*

A Harlem
Globetrotters
poster, 1951.

length of the court without even pretending to dribble, and mimicked referees. The bits were meant to win over hostile small-town White audiences, and it earned them at least as many fans as their undeniable athletic skills.

That night, the audience waited for characteristic shenanigans from the Globetrotters, but the team was all about basketball. Goose Tatum, the Globetrotters' best physical comedian, faced Lakers star George Mikan for the tip-off. Instead of a trick, Tatum used his comically long arms to reach over the 6-foot-10-inch Mikan and tap the ball to the 'Trotters—without so much as a smile.

Tatum wasn't kidding about this game. Neither was Babe Pressley, who grabbed the tip-off and dribbled down the court before using a shovel pass to get the ball into the hands of teammate Ermer Robinson, who took the first shot and missed.

Like most cultural institutions in the United States, basketball had a long tradition of racial tension. At the time of the matchup, teams

From left, Globetrotters' Reece "Goose" Tatum, 1953; George Mikan, 1950.

were nearly always all White or all Black, but that wasn't always the case. The sport had been integrated in 1942, five years before Jackie Robinson did the same for major-league baseball—but that didn't mean the effort was going well. In one instance, a Black player lost his temper and threw a punch at a White player who'd been shoving him throughout the game; White fans swarmed the court, and the National Guard had to be called in to prevent a riot. "That scared all of the basketball promoters," the late sports writer Frank Deford explained in the 2005 PBS documentary *The Harlem Globetrotters: The Team That Changed the World*. There were just four Black players in the league at the time, and all of them were cut by the end of the year.

Cementing the segregation of the league were typical racist arguments—Black athletes did not have the intellect needed to win in a fast-paced sport like basketball; they had small lungs and heavy bones and an inability to jump; they weren't coachable. (Writer John Christgau, author of *Tricksters in the Madhouse*, a seminal book about the game, also appeared in *The Team That Changed the World*, and marveled at the thought. "Can you imagine?" he asked. "They couldn't jump.")[2]

George Mikan goes up for a shot in the Lakers-Globetrotters game. Chicago, 1948.

10   The Globetrotters, who traveled the United States playing anyone who challenged them, had won more than 100 consecutive games by the time they arrived in Chicago for the showdown with the Lakers. Still, they struggled in the first half. The Lakers were great players, and Mikan topped Tatum, the Trotters' big man, by seven inches. (As Phil Jackson once explained, Mikan was "basically Shaquille O'Neal.") The home-town team's shots would not fall. Even Robinson's opening shot, graceful as it was, hit the rim. At halftime, the Lakers led 32–23.

Gilligan's account is full of emotion. How could it not be? See p. 415 to learn more about how to use emotional appeals effectively in your work.

It wasn't until the third quarter that the Globetrotters started to shine. They started double-teaming Mikan, holding the scoring machine to nine points in the second half. With 90 seconds left in the game, the score was tied at 59–59. Globetrotter Marques Haynes dribbled for the next minute and 29 seconds. (The shot clock wouldn't be introduced until 1954.) He quickly passed to Robinson, who fired the ball from what seemed like an impossible distance of 30 feet from the basket. The shot fell at the buzzer, and fans in the multiracial crowd screamed with joy.

Although it was an exhibition game, it proved to be the beginning of the end for segregation in basketball. "All of the racist arguments for keeping [Black athletes] out of basketball began to be undone with that game," Christgau said in *The Team That Changed the World*.[3]

The sport integrated for good two years after the Globetrotters/ Lakers game, when the NBA was formed. League officials and team owners were influenced not just by the talent they would otherwise miss out on, but also by the White crowds that had turned out to see the all-Black Globetrotters in 1948, and again in a second matchup in 1949. The Globetrotters won that game, too. So it was only fitting that Globetrotter Nat "Sweetwater" Clifton became the first Black athlete to sign with an NBA team when he joined the New York Knicks in 1950.

Globetrotter Nat "Sweetwater" Clifton was the first Black athlete to sign with an NBA team, joining the New York Knicks in 1950.

The Globetrotters went on to become a worldwide sensation, playing to a crowd of 75,000 during the Berlin Olympics in 1951, making an appearance behind the Iron Curtain in 1959, and even starring in their own cartoon series in the '70s before their popularity finally waned.

15   Some argue that the Globetrotters saved the sport. Their popularity drew a cross-section of America to basketball and provided a fan base for the newly developed NBA. What had been a relatively monotonous game of men running up and down a court became a game of showmanship, cleverness, and a newer, nimbler brand of sport. The Globetrotters' flair with the ball eventually became part of the fabric of basketball. In their hands, basketball became a sport where Black and White fans alike could cheer together for a common team.

Notes

1. Howard, J. (2016, August 25). *Why Minneapolis Lakers' loss to Globetrotters was so meaningful*. ESPN. https://www.espn.com/nba/story/_/id/16211736/when-lakers-were-minneapolis-loss-globetrotters-was-blow-segregation

2. *The Harlem Globetrotters—The Team That Changed the World*. Directed by Michael Sear and Joseph Sharman. Teamworks Media, 2005. https://www.dailymotion.com/video/x34ath8

Thinking about the Text

1. This is an essay about a specific game in 1948 that Heather Gilligan claims "changed basketball forever" (2). That's no small CLAIM: In what ways does she say that this one game changed the game "forever"? What EVIDENCE does Gilligan provide— and is it sufficient to support that claim? Do you think she should have QUALIFIED her claim, and if so how?

2. In explaining the racial segregation of professional basketball in the late 1940s, Gilligan refers to "typical racist arguments" (9). What specific arguments does she list, and what TONE does she use to describe these arguments? What is her STANCE toward those arguments, and what words or phrases help you identify it? Why do you think Gilligan chose this tone and stance, and how do they affect your reading of this part of the essay?

3. Gilligan provides a detailed NARRATIVE of the game in paragraphs 6 and 7 but then interrupts the narrative to give some historical context before returning to the account of what was happening there. Why do you think she presented the contextual information in the middle of the narrative about the game itself, and how did it affect her message?

4. LET'S TALK. Gilligan's account of the Harlem Globetrotters and "the beginning of the end for segregation in basketball" (12) takes place in the late 1940s. What else was happening in the United States at that time? What do you remember learning about it in school or perhaps from movies and TV shows set in that era? What was in the news? In politics? What were the best-selling music and the most popular movies? Work with a few classmates to piece together some of this larger context for the events that Gilligan depicts. In what ways does this broader context make the Globetrotters' victory even more meaningful?

5. AND NOW WRITE. Gilligan has written about the end of segregation in US pro basketball. Choose a sport that interests you and do some research to find out when, where, and how it was desegregated. Write a brief REPORT on your findings.

JEMELE HILL

Naomi Osaka Is Part of a Larger War within Sports

CONGRATULATIONS, TENNIS. You've won neither the battle nor the war with Naomi Osaka, but you have just bullied one of the biggest stars in your sport into quitting a major tournament that could use the publicity she would have brought to it.

Osaka, the second-ranked woman in international tennis and the highest-paid female athlete in the world, withdrew from the French Open after a power struggle with tournament officials over whether she would attend obligatory press conferences. Osaka has had trouble in that tournament in the past, having never advanced out of the third round. Last week, Osaka announced on social media that she was skipping all news conferences during the event to protect her mental health. "I've often felt that people have no regard for athletes' mental health and this rings very true whenever I see a press conference or partake in one," she wrote last week. "We're often sat there and asked questions that we've been asked multiple times before or asked questions that bring doubt into our minds, and I'm just not going to subject myself to people that doubt me."

Critics quickly portrayed Osaka as shirking one of her fundamental duties: communicating with the public. In reality, the episode laid bare some of the deeper tensions in big-money athletics. Who controls a sport—the leagues that organize the competition, or the athletes who actually play? When athletes have direct access to fans via social-media platforms, what role should traditional sports media play? And

Wow! How's that for an opening? Take that, Tennis! Learn more about how you can start strong on pp. 410–12.

Jemele Hill is a staff writer for the Atlantic, *where this piece was first published; previously, she worked for ESPN, where she was one of the anchors of* SportsCenter. *She hosts the podcast* Jemele Hill Is Unbothered *and tweets from @jemelehill.*

Naomi Osaka serves at the 2020 Tokyo Olympics.

when athletes, particularly athletes of color, feel mistreated by tournaments, sports leagues, and media outlets alike, what recourse do they have?

As a sportswriter for more than 20 years, I have attended many of the postgame news conferences that so unsettle Osaka. These sessions help journalists and fans understand what we've just witnessed and why individual athletes defied expectations or failed to rise to the occasion. They also help humanize athletes whose personalities might not always come through in game footage alone. But even for seasoned journalists, the experience can be awkward. Most of us would prefer to conduct private interviews with athletes, but logistically that's not feasible. Even if athletes could spend one-on-one time with several different news outlets, they would be subjected to a lot of the same questions. Still, the reliance on press conferences means that journalists often have to ask intrusive questions in front of a crowd.

Press conferences are more crucial for journalists who report on   5
tennis than those who report on other sports. In the NBA, the NFL,

the WNBA, Major League Baseball, and the NHL, players speak with the press almost daily during their respective seasons. Tennis players, by contrast, are generally unavailable outside of tournaments. The game, although popular in America, is covered with greater intensity overseas. These factors can result in aggressive questioning of athletes during press conferences. (Although press conferences have a function in the news-gathering process, leagues have also been able to turn access to players into an additional source of revenue. Notice how many different brands and companies are on the banners behind professional athletes when they speak with the press. That placement isn't free.)

Rather than figure out a way to support Osaka or come to a workable compromise, French Open officials fined her $15,000 after she didn't participate in the mandatory news conference following her first-round win on Sunday. The fine was not a surprise. In the past, other tennis stars have skipped news conferences and received the same treatment.

But tournament leaders weren't satisfied with a fine. Officials from across the tennis world felt the need to put Osaka in her place. In a statement signed by the heads of all four Grand Slam tournaments—Wimbledon, the Australian Open, the U.S. Open, and the French Open—Osaka was warned that she could face suspension from future Grand Slam tournaments and harsher penalties if she did not fulfill her media obligations.

"We want to underline that rules are in place to ensure all players are treated exactly the same, no matter their stature, beliefs or achievement," the statement said. "As a sport there is nothing more important than ensuring no player has an unfair advantage over another, which unfortunately is the case in this situation if one player refuses to dedicate time to participate in media commitments while the others all honour their commitments."

The end result—Osaka completely out of the tournament—benefited no one. Osaka's subsequent explanation for her decision made tennis officials look all the more callous. "I never wanted to be a distraction and I accept that my timing was not ideal and my message

Naomi Osaka
at an interview
after a victory
at the US Open.
New York, 2018.

could have been clearer," she wrote. "The truth is that I have suffered long bouts of depression since the US Open in 2018 and I have had a really hard time coping with that." If the Grand Slam officials' goal was to show Osaka who's in charge, this was an enormous misstep. The sport has only further demonstrated that such tactics with today's athletes are ineffective, outdated, and likely to backfire at a time when athletes have more leverage than they've ever had.

Across all sports, top athletes are no longer willing to stay silent   10
about anything—their own personal struggles or the social and political issues they care about. They want the full scope of their humanity considered, and they are willing to confront prejudice not only in
sports but throughout society. Last year's U.S. Open took place amid
nationwide protests against racial injustice. Osaka, a 23-year-old of Japanese and Haitian ancestry, showed that her goal isn't to make other
people comfortable. She wore a succession of face masks bearing the
names of Black people who'd been killed by police and other would-be
law enforcers. After she claimed her third Grand Slam title, a reporter
asked her what message she wanted to send. Osaka responded, "Well,

what was the message that you got? [That] was more the question. I feel like the point is to make people start talking."

Osaka has received largely favorable coverage because of her performance on the court for the past two years. But she has witnessed the way two other tennis champions of color—Serena and Venus Williams—have been portrayed throughout their careers. In fact, in her Instagram post announcing that she was skipping out on media sessions at the French Open, Osaka included a clip from an interview Venus Williams did with ABC News in 1995, in which Williams's father, Richard, chastised the interviewer for continually questioning his daughter about her seemingly high confidence. "You have to understand you're dealing with the image of a 14-year-old child," he told the interviewer. "And this child is going to be out there playing when your old ass and me gonna be in the grave. . . . You're dealing with a little Black kid, and let her be a kid."

Venus Williams, age 13, on the court and being interviewed. Oakland, California, 1994.

Such scrutiny became part of an exhausting pattern for the Williams sisters. *The New York Times* once published an article about how other women in tennis don't want the kind of body Serena Williams has.

During the U.S. Open final against Osaka in 2018, Serena Williams lost her composure after being cited for multiple rule violations during

the match. Williams got into a heated argument with an umpire after he accused her of receiving coaching from the stands. The episode culminated in Williams slamming her racquet against the ground. Following her loss, an Australian newspaper published an editorial cartoon that deployed racist imagery reminiscent of the Jim Crow era to depict Williams as a poor sport. Williams's lips were overexaggerated, and her body was drawn ludicrously big.

Osaka's first major tournament victory should have been a celebratory moment, at least for her. But U.S. Open spectators booed her for beating Williams, the favorite, under acrimonious circumstances.

Notably, Osaka has cited the U.S. Open final against Williams as the starting point of her own depression and anxiety. Osaka was just as direct about her mental-health struggles when she withdrew from the French Open, drawing support from a wide array of athletes, many of whom have experienced the same anxiety about public speaking. At the French Open this week, Serena Williams told reporters: "The only thing I feel is that I feel for Naomi. I feel like I wish I could give her a hug, because I know what it's like. Like I said, I've been in those positions." The Golden State Warriors star Stephen Curry tweeted, "You shouldn't ever have to make a decision like this—but so damn impressive taking the high road when the powers that be don't protect their own. Major respect @naomiosaka." 15

That sports media in the U.S. are still overwhelmingly white and male contributes to the skepticism that many top athletes of color feel. According to the University of Central Florida's Institute for Diversity and Ethics in Sports' most recent report card for gender and racial diversity in U.S. sports media, 85 percent of sports editors are white, as are 80 percent of columnists and 82 percent of reporters. When I was a sports columnist at the *Orlando Sentinel* in 2005, a survey found that I was the only Black female sports columnist at a daily newspaper in North America. The lack of representation remains stunning—and embarrassing.

Most of the reporters I know—but not all—tread delicately when any player is having a difficult moment. But few of us dwell much on the mental health of the players we cover, the impact of nonstop scrutiny, and the emotional toll of having to explain tough losses, bad decisions, and subpar performances, as well as extraordinary success. And the possibility that people capable of athletic miracles might be in genuine emotional distress strikes many of us as incongruous.

Because of Osaka, I couldn't help but think of the former NFL player Ricky Williams. In 2004, Williams briefly retired from the NFL at 27, after testing positive for marijuana for the third time—which would have triggered a four-game suspension and a $650,000 fine. He later returned to the NFL, but he was suspended for a year after a fourth positive test. His career, which was also interrupted by a series of injuries, eventually ended with the Baltimore Ravens after the 2011 season. Williams was routinely characterized as a misfit and someone who cared more about smoking marijuana than about football. He used to do postgame interviews with a helmet on because he hated dealing with the media.

But during the third year of his pro career, Williams was diagnosed with social-anxiety disorder. He had turned to marijuana to help cope with his struggles and to help heal his body. That put Williams's entire career in a much different context. He has since become a strong advocate for cannabis use, and even started his own marijuana company. "The story was 'football player retires to go smoke pot,'" Williams told CNBC in 2018. "And part of that was true, but it was much bigger than that. I was really redefining myself and figuring out what I want to do with my life."

20   Many would look at intense media scrutiny and conflict with league officials as simply the price of being a successful professional athlete. But today's athletes aren't willing to put a happy face on their trauma just so the rest of us can be blissfully entertained.

The Brooklyn Nets star guard Kyrie Irving was fined twice this season for refusing to speak to the media, including last month. The first time was during training camp, when Irving issued a statement that read in part: "Instead of speaking to the media today, I am issuing this statement to ensure that my message is properly conveyed. I am committed to show up to work every day, ready to have fun, compete, perform, and win championships alongside my teammates and colleagues in the Nets organization. My goal this season is to let my work on and off the court speak for itself. Life hit differently this year and it requires us, it requires me, to move differently. So, this is the beginning of that change."

After being fined $25,000 by the NBA, Irving posted his response in an *Instagram* Story. "I pray we utilize the 'fine money' for the marginalized communities in need, especially seeing where our world is presently," he wrote. "[I am] here for Peace, Love and Greatness. So stop distracting me and my team, and appreciate the Art. We move different over here. I do not talk to Pawns. My attention is worth more."

When Irving did finally talk to the media, he insisted that the "pawn" comment wasn't an attack on journalists. "It's really just about how I felt about the mistreatment of certain artists when we get to a certain platform of when we make decisions within our lives to have full control and ownership.... We want to perform in a secure and protected space."

The nagging suspicion that leagues and reporters alike fundamentally misunderstand athletes of color makes these athletes still more determined to cultivate their own image with fans. That's why so many prominent athletes—including the NBA stars Russell Westbrook, LeBron James, Stephen Curry, and Kevin Durant—have opted to launch their own media companies. With their massive social-media followings, they can take their message directly to the public. Many of them don't need press conferences to promote or build their brands, and the establishment is having trouble adjusting to the new normal, in which it can't make players do what it wants simply because that's the way things have always been done.

The issues that Osaka has raised aren't going away. These days ath-   25
letes would much rather tell their own stories than let reporters do it for them. Not long ago, players couldn't win any power struggles against the media, much less their own league. Now they can.

Thinking about the Text

1. Jemele Hill comments extensively on Naomi Osaka's decision to avoid contact with the press because of the anguish such encounters have caused her. As Osaka explained, "I've often felt that people have no regard for athletes' mental health and this rings very true whenever I see a press conference or partake in one" (2). As this essay makes clear, some people have backed Osaka's decisions and her desire to protect herself from harmful encounters, while others have denigrated her for doing so. What's your take? What responsibility do you think the press has to recognize and respect the mental health concerns of athletes? What responsibility do athletes have to make themselves available to the press, no matter what?

2. Hill describes a three-way conflict of interest between players, sports leagues, and sports media. Since Hill is a long-time sports-writer and member of the media herself, we might presume that her sympathies lie primarily with the media. How fairly does she represent each of the three positions in this article and what is her STANCE toward each? What words and phrases and what examples can you point to that reflect how she feels about each position? Which one is she most sympathetic to, and why do you think so?

3. In her opening paragraph, Hill addresses tennis directly, as if it were a person, congratulating it for winning "neither the battle nor the war" and instead bullying "one of the biggest stars" (1). Here Hill adopts a sarcastic TONE to introduce her analysis of who should make the rules regarding communication between tennis and the media. Why might Hill have chosen to begin her essay this way? How did it strike you—did it draw you in? make you want to read on? put you off? or something else? Since Hill drops the sarcasm after the opening, do you think she should have chosen to open in a different way? If so, how else would you recommend that she OPEN?

4. Post-game press conferences are a staple of sports reporting. What does Hill see as the benefits and drawbacks of these events? Why, according to her, are press conferences often problematic for athletes? In paragraph 4, Hill acknowledges own her role in them as a journalist but she doesn't provide any examples of her own participation. What might such examples have added to the essay, and to Hill's CREDIBILITY to write about this topic?

5. LET'S TALK. Hill raises a tough question: Who should have control of a sport, "the leagues that organize the competition, or the athletes who actually play?" (3), and her essay aims to make us think about how this power might be more equitably shared. What do you think? Think about these issues and make some notes about your own thoughts and opinions; then talk them over with a few classmates. Your task here is to work together to deepen your understanding of a very complex problem.

6. AND NOW WRITE. Hill draws attention to the importance of considering the mental health as well as the physical health of athletes, whether major players like Naomi Osaka, the Williams sisters, and Ricky Williams or other athletes. Have you or someone you know faced situations in which mental health issues were ignored or even denied? What responsibility do we have to recognize and respect the mental health concerns of people we know? That's not an easy question to answer, but give it some thought and write a paragraph or two REFLECTING on what you might do to help address mental health issues: Would you offer specific support to someone you know who has such issues? Join a mental health club at your school? Take specific steps to raise awareness of mental health issues?

NELL GLUCKMAN

Colleges Are Paying Big Bucks for Coaches. Here's What Else They Could've Spent the Money On.

NOT LONG AGO, for a dark sort of fun, Joy Blanchard, an associate professor of higher education at Louisiana State University, calculated the difference between her salary and that of her university's head football coach at the time, Edward Orgeron.

Blanchard's base salary is "in the neighborhood" of $80,000 per year, plus she teaches three classes more than her contract stipulates, earns a stipend for being a program leader, and has a side job teaching spin classes at the university's recreation center. Orgeron made more than $9 million per year before leaving LSU this fall, according to *USA Today*. Blanchard wanted to know how long it would take him, at his salary, to earn her salary.

The answer? Just 2.6 days.

"I based it off a five-day work-week," she said. "I'm sure coaches are working seven, but I do as well."

5   Now that Orgeron is out—and Brian Kelly, until recently the University of Notre Dame coach—is in, that number is even smaller. Kelly, the university announced this week, signed a 10-year contract worth $95 million, or $9.5 million a year. For universities with top football programs, this seems to be the going rate. The University of Southern California hired Lincoln Riley from the University of Oklahoma, and though Trojans management did not make the details of the contract public and declined to share them with *The Chronicle*, they are likely

Nell Gluckman is a reporter for the Chronicle of Higher Education, *where she covers topics related to higher education, ethics, funding issues, and more. She tweets from @nellgluckman.*

From left, Brian Kelly (Notre Dame), Lincoln Riley (Oklahoma), and Mel Tucker (Michigan State)

to approach or exceed Kelly's figure. Meanwhile, Michigan State University announced last month that it had signed its head coach, Mel Tucker, to a new 10-year, $95 million contract as well.

That's a lot of money on almost any scale. But for universities still emerging from a pandemic, it's astronomical.

It's especially jarring, Blanchard noted, given how hard the NCAA has fought to prevent players from making any money beyond their scholarships and associated fees.

Aside from paying Blanchard's annual salary many times over, here's a few other things that $95 million would cover at LSU or Michigan State:

- LSU could pay for 111 assistant-professor salaries every year for 10 years, according to its posted average pay for an assistant professor in the 2018–19 academic year.
- Michigan State could pay off the student loans of 3,000 graduates, assuming those graduates had about $31,700 in loans at graduation, which the *Lansing State Journal* reported was the average for those who took out loans, as of the 2017–18 academic year.
- LSU could give all of its graduate assistant a $50,000 bonus.
- Michigan State could pay for well over a third of East Lansing's residents to attend Lansing Community College for a year.
- LSU could buy a chicken-finger sandwich combo from a Raising Cane's Chicken Fingers in Baton Rouge for every resident of Louisiana, Arkansas, and Mississippi.

Notice how this bulleted list highlights these details much more effectively than they would be in a paragraph. See more about using lists on p. 454.

LSU could use the $95 million they're paying Brian Kelly to buy a chicken-finger sandwich combo for every resident of Louisiana, Arkansas, and Mississippi.

This is not to say that administrators at Michigan State or LSU had an extra few million dollars in their budgets and decided to spend it on coaches. The most revenue-soaked athletic departments generate enough money to support themselves and are largely independent from their universities.

"It looks bad when you see those numbers being thrown around," said Willis Jones, an associate professor of higher education at the University of Miami. "The first reaction is, how many libraries could be fixed up with those coaches' salaries? But it is important to note that often those are two different pots of money."

10   In recent years, some athletics departments with Division I football programs have seen a huge increase in revenue because of the contracts their conferences have signed with television networks like ESPN and Fox Sports, Jones said. The Southeastern Conference, for example, signed a $300 million contract with ESPN last year. Athletics departments with big football and basketball programs also make money from ticket sales and donations. Boosters, particularly, can loom large. This year, two donors at Indiana University joined forces to buy the men's basketball coach out of the $10.3 million owed to him after he was fired, and to replace him.

Universities will often point to their football programs as important emblems of their brands, saying they're tools to reinforce relationships with alumni and attract new students. Jones said there's some debate about whether that's true. According to his research, a winning football team does have a positive relationship with numbers of applicants, but "it's fairly small, and it's fairly fleeting."

Jones added that though big athletic departments often generate revenue separately from the university, "there's a philosophical conversation to have about how we got to the point where there was so much value placed on athletics."

"Is that really part of the mission of the university?" he asked. "For whatever reason, this country has made college athletics this symbol for higher education."

It's hard to make the argument that the money flowing to sports teams, even though they may be financially independent, doesn't affect the university, Blanchard said. She pointed to allegations that LSU covered up sexual misconduct in order to protect the football program, reported by *USA Today*.

But she doubts she's seen the end of the ever-growing coaches' salaries. "Next year," she said, "we're going to hear about the $11 million coach." 15

Thinking about the Text

1. Nell Gluckman demonstrates that many coaches in university athletic programs are paid enormous sums of money. In addition to listing many of the ways those dollars could be put to better use, Gluckman points out other problems caused by a strong emphasis on college athletics; what are they? Which, if any, seems most problematical to you—and why?

2. In her bullet list of other ways that schools could spend $95 million— the salary of a top football coach—Gluckman includes "a chicken-finger sandwich combo" (8) for every resident of three states. (She even names a popular Baton Rouge restaurant where the sandwiches could be purchased.) Why might Gluckman have

chosen to add that bit of whimsy to her otherwise serious list of alternative ways of using $95 million? Does it strengthen her overall argument, and if so, how? What was your response to the list in general and to the chicken sandwich example in particular? How do the items in this list affect your overall assessment of the issue?

3. Gluckman notes that universities often say that their football programs are "important emblems of their brands" and that they help "attract new students" (11) (though some research questions whether this is true). How, if at all, did football or other sports figure in your choice of a college to attend—either positively or negatively? Under what circumstances might a sport have played a significant role in your decision to enroll at your school?

4. Gluckman notes that coaches' salaries are excessive, but she makes no explicit statement about her own position. What words or phrases (or anything else) in her essay suggest or signal her STANCE on the issue?

5. LET'S TALK. What problems, if any, do you see with coaches being paid vastly more money than professors and other key college workers (even if their salaries most often come from "different pots of money" [9])? Do a little research to find out the salary of top coaches at your school and compare them to the salaries given to professors. What discrepancies do you find? Share what you find with other students and ask what they think about this disparity in salaries. Then talk over your findings with several classmates. What changes, if any, might you like to recommend?

6. AND NOW WRITE. Willis Jones asks whether athletics "is really part of the mission of the university?" (13). Check out the websites of several colleges, some with prominent athletic programs and some not known for athletics. Do they connect their sports programs to the school's mission—and if so, how? Do some research to see what others have to say about this question. And see what Jane Coaston says about what sports can teach us (p. 764) and what Joe Drape says about the cognitive skills needed to succeed at e-sports (p. 770). Write an essay responding to Jones and ARGUING whether you think athletics should be part of the mission of a college or university.

MARK GOZONSKY

Gritty All Day Long

MOST OF THE OTHER BASEBALL PLAYERS at the Pacific Coast League tryouts were half my age. Nobody said the league was for guys in their twenties, but that was the deal. Some goofuses showed up in shorts and tennis shoes. Not me, though. I own four different pairs of baseball pants. I didn't have on cleats, however. I was getting by with turf shoes, because I had not yet earned the exalted status bestowed by cleats. It really makes a difference to have your feet a quarter inch off the ground. Also, the clackety-clack of cleats on concrete is clear confirmation that you are a ballplayer, not a hapless schmo just going through the motions.

I thought it was a sure thing I would be drafted, probably drafted high. Everybody needed a fifty-seven-year-old catcher who hadn't played in twenty-five years—and who, on the late-August day of tryouts, was still seeing double from brain damage in April. Not severely double right in front of me. I'd been able to teach high-school English up until the AP exam in mid-May and then take medical leave. But double, as in: Isn't it weird how the walls are intersecting twenty feet down the hallway, and the students and the lockers and the floors are all looking more than a little bit swervy?

The trick, which I learned after going back to playing tennis in early August, was to keep the ball in front of you. If you let the ball get in on you, you (a) lose power and control and (b) have to pick which one of the two balls to hit.

Mark Gozonsky is a writer and a teacher. He lives in Los Angeles, where he teaches high school English. This essay first appeared in the Sun, an independent, reader-supported magazine, and was then selected for inclusion in The Best American Sports Writing 2020. Gozonsky's blog is GzonkGzonk.com, his Instagram is @shmarkozonky, and he tweets from @MarkGozonsky.

My brain damage was not from a stroke, by the way. It was a "cavernous malformation" that leaked in my brain stem: a blob of blood-vessel cells that never quite form veins nor arteries nor capillaries; a vascular Creature from the Black Lagoon of your brain. You could have one and never know, like I did, until one day a little mutant blood vessel inside my brain stem suddenly oozed some goop. If the brain is like a computer, then this is like spilling coffee on your keyboard. I can't say what your keyboard feels, but I felt whacked by two-by-four that didn't hurt but left me seeing some

Gozonsky arranged these words to help us see more than just what the words say. Learn about ways of focusing on what you want your readers to see on p. 451.

> serious double
> and also
> a little
> wobbly, what
> with that
> numbness in
> my left
> leg

from foot to calf. For a while there, the tingling went all the way up my thigh and into my balls, which was alarming, but, still, it could have been much, much worse.

5   I slept a lot. Deeeeeep sleeeeeeep. My wife was *very upset* and demonstrated her love in both conventional and unconventional ways. For example, she went two-for-two in passing out during my initial medical exams—first in the emergency room and then again a few days later at the neurologist's office. If that's not love . . . well, it is.

She also did not yell at me one single bit when, fitted out with prism glasses, I backed my car out of the driveway and scraped her Volvo up nicely. Not a peep.

It is true that she was *very concerned* about how mean I was to her during this period. I wrote her two poems explaining that I wasn't being mean, but she wasn't buying it. For evidence of my meanness you will have to read her essay, if she ever writes one. What I felt was grateful and eager to recover so she would not feel meanness but rather l-o-v-e.

Over the course of my medical leave and summer vacation the tingling retreated back the way it came, down the quads and the calves and then around the ankle to one last holdout in my left foot, which still sometimes tingles to this day—my own personal memento mori, disconcerting but not enough to keep me sidelined. It's a reminder, if you will, to do it now, whatever *it* may be. In my case *it* was playing baseball—actual hardball, not softball—with seventeen other guys and an ump and uniforms. The real thing.

I though tryouts went great. I played catcher, just catcher. You may ask, How solid was my receiving with that lingering double vision? Well, I'm happy to report that squatting behind the plate was a miracle cure. I saw completely normal and snagged a whole lot of balls in the dirt. Each time I did, I was like: Looky here, pure gold. That whooshing hardball crashing into the grit, chaos about to explode, but no! My mitt swooped down and snagged it, and a satisfying *thunk* transmitted deep satisfaction direct from the web of the glove to the left prefrontal cortex.

Of course, plenty of balls also skipped right by me, but these were mainly wild pitches—i.e., the pitcher's fault, not mine. At least, according to me. I'm not really into whose fault it was. Let's just say a nontrivial number of pitches had destinies other than being caught. That feels like the truth. I also made no attempt whatsoever to field any pop-ups behind the plate. Too many balls lying around back there; you could break an ankle. In retrospect maybe I should have jumped up, turned around, and flung off my mask before I looked in dismay at the scattered balls and reluctantly abandoned what would have for sure been a dogged, ultimately triumphant pursuit.

To be honest, I cannot recollect ever in my entire life catching a foul pop fly as catcher, but I was in no mood to let such obvious limitations hold me back. There were about a hundred guys who needed to hit and just me and one other, obviously way-better-than-me guy taking turns behind the plate. This guy was Robo-Catcher, but perfectly friendly. He was like, Go ahead, and I was like, No, you go ahead. Me and Robo took turns. He was younger, of course, and I knew if it was just between him and me, he'd get picked first. But I could live with that. On my turn catching I was very encouraging to all the bat-ters: "Whoa, dude, you nailed that one." One batter, built like a rustic cabin, swatted a ball that dented the outfield fence. *Ka-blam!* Another guy—jitteriest person I ever saw in my entire life, a downed power line in human form—batted lefty and made plenty of contact. This guy had eye-black all over his cheeks: an impressively deranged look.

In my own at-bats I got some hits, nothing Ruthian but neverthe-less undisputed line drives to the outfield. I had no regrets. I did what I'd set out to do. Solid contact—that's my brand. When you need a line drive up the middle, call me.

After everyone had hit, it was time for the managers to pick, which was done playground style—brutal, merciless, fair: pick the best guys first, then the middle guys, and then we'll just have to see. Everybody needs a catcher who can hit, I thought. This is going to be redemptive. Watch me now.

And yet when the picking started, the coaches didn't pick me, and they didn't pick me, and they didn't pick me. Time slowed. My heart-beat amplified. All these other guys were getting picked, but not me. At first it was humbling, and then it was alarming. What if I didn't get picked at all? I had told all my students I was trying out. What would I say to them? It was too harrowing a thought to consider. The possi-bility of not getting picked blotted out everything except the green, green grass while I contemplated the question of whether to stand up straight, or lean against the fence, or gradually disappear.

15   I became full of mercy for the outcasts of the world. In the future I would treat them with compassion, show an interest, listen to their stories. In particular when kids failed in my classroom, I wouldn't secretly roll my eyes in exasperation: No! Never again. I couldn't go back and change the past, but from now on I could and would be kinder to the not-good-enough.

Then I got picked.

This tall, sad-eyed guy, who a couple of months later would hit two grand-slam home runs in the same game, approached me unnoticed (so preoccupied was I with how to stand) and said, with what in retrospect sounds like a note of apology for the long wait, "Hey, do you want to play with us?"

Whatever I actually said, what I felt was: *Whoop whoop!* I shed all trepidation like a snakeskin as I followed my new manager back to the chosen circle, leaving behind the remaining half dozen or so not-yet-and-maybe-never-picked players. One guy, as old as I am if not older, kept tossing the ball into his mitt: *thump, thump.*

I wonder even now what I would tell that guy, if I could tell him something encouraging but real. I keep thinking about that guy, who could so easily have been me; who, let's face it, *is* me in the alternative universe we all know is right there waiting for us whenever we don't catch a lucky break.

Among my instantly beloved teammates I recognized the cabin-sized guy who had hit the mightiest clout of tryouts, and the hyper guy with eye-black spread all over his cheeks. A guy with a long black beard

"As long as they let you play sometimes and you have fun, it's OK."

told me there was a pitcher on our team who could throw ninety-plus miles per hour, and I should get ready for my hand to hurt.

This was the best news I'd ever heard, although it turned out not to be true. That guy maxed out in the high seventies. Also I was our team's fourth-string catcher, which is really not a thing unless you make it one, which you must do if you are to be true to your inner game. So I hung on to that role and played maybe twenty-something innings over a fourteen-game season. I could see where things were headed early on and floated a complaint about it to my wife, who said, "As long as they let you play sometimes and you have fun, it's OK," so I went with that. I did not see a ton of action, but I also did not see none, and furthermore I made a contribution. From the dugout with the other subs I did a lot of hooraying for our side and also talked some pretty vicious trash about the other team. Everyone plays a role.

We went undefeated and won the championship by a wide margin in a game in which I did not play at all. Yet there was one midseason game where none of the other three catchers could make it. So, yeah, I caught all nine innings, ending with us up 3-2. When you win 3-2, you know the catcher had to have been doing something right, and that was me, with a hand on the ground behind home plate so I wouldn't keel over but rather maintain a steady squat. *If this is where I go from a malformed blood vessel, then bury me right here.* That was my exact thought. It kept me going through innings seven, eight, and nine.

I am not going to tell you that I was a stellar catcher. Gritty, sure. Gritty all day long. But now I know: Those balls that get by you in practice? They also get by you in a game, and while a couple of passed balls here and there is OK, more than a couple is not. I got taken out of one game, mid-inning. With the bases loaded we got the runner out at third, and the throw home was there in my mitt, then gone. That was a real gut-clencher.

I told my students about it the next day. What's the point of failure if you don't make use of it? We share personal news at the start of each class, to get off on a human note before I tell them to put their headphones away. So I told them about being taken out in the middle of the inning, and nobody said anything. The room was still. The moment lingered.

25   This was the one game where my wife was watching. The games were way out in the wilds of the San Fernando Valley, but my wife came to this game on a sunny Sunday morning with sunglasses and dimples glinting, and you know what she said?

That I looked like a ballplayer.

I think that's what I would tell that unpicked guy thumping the ball into his mitt back at tryouts. I would tell him he's a ballplayer for sure.

Thinking about the Text

1. Mark Gozonsky opens this narrative about trying out and playing for a baseball team by telling us that most of the other players at the tryouts "were half my age" (1). Why might he have chosen to OPEN his essay this way, with a focus on his age? How does this opening sentence set the scene for what is to come?

2. Like many NARRATIVES, this one makes a point. And yet while Gozonsky makes clear that playing baseball with this team mattered a lot to him, he doesn't say explicitly why it should matter to us, his readers. What larger point (or points) do you think he's trying to make? Reread the essay looking for statements that say something he wants us to think about. Be prepared to share any such statements with your class.

3. In paragraph 4, Gozonsky describes some of the physical effects of his brain damage in short, poetry-like lines that mimic what was happening to him. How does breaking the lines as he's done affect the way you read and understand what he's describing? Would the same words convey the same sense if they were written in ordinary lines, as the rest of the text is? Why or why not?

4. Gozonsky, an English teacher who obviously knows how to write academic prose, chooses in this essay to use much more INFORMAL language—"goofuses" (1), "looky here" (9), "ka-blam" (11), "clackety-clack" (1), "oozed" (4), and fragments like "Not a peep" (6). How would you describe his STYLE? How effective is it for telling his story and engaging readers—including you?

5. LET'S TALK. This essay is full of contrasts. For example, Gozonsky thought that "it was a sure thing" that he would be among the first players picked—when, in fact, he was "still seeing double from brain damage" (2). While squatting behind the plate during tryouts, he "saw completely normal and snagged a whole lot of balls" (9), but "plenty of balls also skipped right by" (10). Work with some classmates to find more such contrasts. How do you

react to these contrasts? Do you find them funny? sad? something else? What effect do they have on the way you understand Gozonsky's message?

6. AND NOW WRITE. Gozonsky never uses the word *courage*, but what he describes demonstrates very clearly that he displayed a lot of courage in going out for the team and in sticking with it until the end of the season, despite the physical and mental obstacles he was facing. Write a narrative about something you or someone you know has done that required courage, even if no one celebrated it or even recognized it.

Credits

Photographs

FRONTMATTER (BOOK ICON): Flat.Icon/Shutterstock.

CHAPTER 1: P. 5: Jesse Dittmar/Redux; **P. 6:** Ezra Shaw/Getty Images; **P. 11:** Listen First Project.

CHAPTER 2: P. 13: Tayfun Coskun/Anadolu Agency via Getty Images; **P. 22 (LEFT):** Heinz Kluetmeier/Sports Illustrated via Getty Images/Getty Images; **P. 22 (RIGHT):** Scott K. Brown/Sports Illustrated via Getty Images/Getty Images.

CHAPTER 3: P. 30: Kelly Nelson/Alamy Stock Photo; **P. 31:** Grizelda/The Spectator Magazine; **P. 34 (LEFT):** Dylan Marron and Night Vale Presents; **P. 34 (RIGHT):** Dylan Marron and Adam Cecil; **P. 36:** Don Hogan Charles/The New York Times/Redux; **P. 39:** Smallz & Raskind/Getty Images for Samsung.

CHAPTER 4: P. 45: Rovio; **P. 49:** Mike Ehrmann/Getty Images.

CHAPTER 5: P. 53: Davor Bakara Illustration; **P. 64:** Shinola.

CHAPTER 6: P. 70: WUERKER © 2016 Politico. Dist. By ANDREWS MCMEEL SYNDICATION. Reprinted with permission. All rights reserved; **P. 71:** Chainsaw suit.com by Kris Straub; **P. 75:** Anadolu Agency/Getty Images; **P. 77:** Nike.

CHAPTER 7: P. 87: Emreturanphoto/Getty Images; **P. 89:** Courtesy of Marilyn Moller; **P. 91:** TCD/Prod.DB/Alamy Stock Photo.

CHAPTER 8: P. 102: Streeter Lecka/Getty Images; **P. 107:** Photographer RM/Shutterstock; **P. 109:** Courtesy of Marilyn Moller; **P. 110:** An Rong Xu/Redux; **P. 114:** Aleppo Media/AleppoAMC/ED/CE/Camera Press/Redux; **P. 117:** Kristian Larrota/LaGuardia Community College; **P. 123:** Laurie Mastic for University of Notre Dame.

CHAPTER 9: P. 138: Tulane geographer Richard Campanella/Dan Swenson, NOLA.com/The Times-Picayune; **P. 144:** Erin Schaff/The New York Times/Redux; **P. 148:** Abbey Warner; **P. 149:** Business Wire via Getty Images; **P. 150:** Craig Barritt/Getty Images for Cosmopolitan.

CHAPTER 10: P. 163: Charley Gallay/Getty Images for Disney; **P. 172:** "The Fixer" by Joe Sacco, *Drawn and Quarterly* 2003; **P. 175:** Courtesy of Stephanie Pomales; **P. 177:** Dave Hogan/Getty Images; **P. 179:** MediaWorldImage/Alamy Stock Photo.

CHAPTER 11: P. 187: Toyota; **P. 189:** Leo Mason/Popperfoto via Getty Images; **P. 199:** Courtesy of Isaac Lozano.

CHAPTER 12: P. 217: Courtesy of Julia Johnson; **P. 218:** AP Photo/Charles Krupa; **P. 219:** Karwai Tang/WireImage/Getty Images; **P. 220:** Sara D. Davis/Getty Images.

CHAPTER 13: P. 225: National Library NZ; **P. 228:** Jamie Squire/Getty Images; **P. 230:** Clive Goddard via CartoonStock; **PP. 235–39:** Courtesy of Vrinda Devang Vasavada.

CHAPTER 14: P. 244: Gahan Wilson via Cartoon Collections; **P. 249:** Stephen Doyle; **P. 254:** Chiba, Sanae, et al. "Human Footprint in the Abyss: 30 Year Records of Deep-Sea Plastic Debris." *Marine Policy*, vol. 96, 2018, pp. 204–12, doi:10.1016/j.marpol .2018.03.022; **P. 255 (TEXT):** Carolyn Kormann, *The New Yorker*, Condé Nast; **P. 255 (PHOTO):** Paulo Oliveira/Alamy Stock Photo.

CHAPTER 15: P. 266: Snopes.com; **P. 266:** FactCheck.org; **P. 267:** Politifact.com.

CHAPTER 16: P. 273: Andertoons LLC; **P. 275:** Courtesy of Olivia Steely.

CHAPTER 17: P. 279: Marish/Shutterstock.

CHAPTER 19: P. 298: Rebeka Ryvola via Cartoon Collections.

CHAPTER 20: P. 324: Jessamyn Neuhaus, "Marge Simpson, Blue-Haired Housewife: Defining Domesticity on *The Simpsons*." *Journal of Popular Culture* 43.4 (2010); **P. 325 (TEXT):** Michael Segal, "The Hit Book That Came from Mars." *Nautilus*. Nautilus Think, 8 January 2015; **P. 325 (ILLUSTRATION):** Matt Taylor illustration; **P. 327:** ©2015 Ebsco Industries, Inc. All rights reserved; **P. 331:** Amana Fontanella-Khan, *Pink Sari Revolution: A Tale of Women and Power in India*. Norton, 2013; **P. 336:** Urban Land Institute; **P. 346:** Courtesy of Jackson Parell; **P. 352:** Central Press/Getty Images.

CHAPTER 21: P. 373: Guthrie, C. F. (2013). "Smart Technology and the Moral Life." *Ethics and Behavior*, 23(4); **P. 375:** Lazette, M. P. (2015, February 24). "A Hurricane's Hit to Households." Federal Reserve Bank of Cleveland; **P. 377:** From *The Great Divide: Unequal Societies and What We Can Do about Them* by Joseph E. Stiglitz. Copyright 2015 by Joseph E. Stiglitz. Used by permission of W. W. Norton & Company, Inc.; **P. 389:** Courtesy of Eli Vale; **P. 396:** Eli Vale.

CHAPTER 22: P. 407: Historical Views/agefotostock; **P. 413:** Alex Bailey/Twentieth Century Fox Film Corp./Courtesy Everett Collection; **P. 416:** DAMON WINTER/ The New York Times/Redux Pictures; **P. 417:** Arizzona Design/Shutterstock.

CHAPTER 23: P. 432: WENN Rights Ltd/Alamy Stock Photo.

CHAPTER 24: P. 435 (LEFT): Ron Jenkins/Getty Images; **P. 435 (RIGHT):** Miles Nelson/ Dreamstime; **P. 443:** Zunneh-bah Martin.

CHAPTER 25: P. 449 (LEFT): Pictorial Press Ltd/Alamy Stock Photo; **P. 449 (RIGHT):** Travel/Alamy Stock Photo; **P. 456:** Stephen Doyle; **P. 457:** Lisa Congdon 2020.

CHAPTER 26: P. 460 (TOP): Courtesy of Marilyn Moller; **P. 460 (CENTER):** Photo 12/ Alamy Stock Photo; **P. 463:** Alex Wong/Getty Images; **P. 464:** Stringer/Reuters/ Newscom.

CHAPTER 27: P. 471: The Late Show with Stephen Colbert/CBS; **P. 473:** Courtesy of Henry Tsai; **P. 474:** "Another Field of American Industry Invaded by the Chinese" Cartoon. *Harper's Weekly* 1883: 27; Courtesy of UC Berkeley, Bancroft Library; **P. 475:** Giorgia Lupi/Pentagram Design; **P. 476:** Stanford Talisman Publicity.

CHAPTER 28: P. 482: Courtesy of Trey Connelly; **PP. 483–87 (SLIDES):** Trey Connelly; **P. 485 (BOTTOM):** HollyHarry/Shutterstock; **P. 486:** AlexLMX/Shutterstock;

P. 488 (TOP): Courtesy of Jack Long; **P. 488 (BOTTOM):** Courtesy of Colin Flanagan; **P. 490:** Courtesy of Brandon Hernandez; **P. 493:** Marilyn Moller personal collection.

CHAPTER 29: P. 497: Erin Hawley; **PP. 501–2:** Brandon Hayden; **P. 504:** Courtesy of Rosa Guevara; **P. 505:** LaGuardia Community College, CUNY; **P. 506:** Courtesy of Jailene Maldonado.

CHAPTER 30: P. 511 (TOP): solomon7/Shutterstock; **P. 511 (BOTTOM):** Jeff Stahler/ Distributed by UniversalUclick for UFS via CartoonStock; **P. 512 (TOP):** tanuha2001/ Shutterstock; **P. 512 (BOTTOM):** solomon7/Shutterstock; **P. 513:** Lily Gellman; **P. 515:** Courtesy of Will Moller; **P. 516:** Courtesy of Ian McKnight; **P. 518 (TOP):** Courtesy of Emma Peters; **P. 518 (BOTTOM):** Brad Ryan; **P. 519:** Courtesy of Jay Van Bavel; **P. 520 (TOP):** Courtesy of Alexandria Stojovich; **P. 520 (BOTTOM):** US Department of the Interior ; **P. 521 (TOP):** Cody Glenn/Icon Sportswire via Getty Images; **P. 521 (BOTTOM):** Kent Nishimura /Los Angeles Times/Getty Images.

CHAPTER 31: P. 527: Courtesy of Joshua Rothman; **P. 539:** Scott J. Ferrell/Congressional Quarterly/Newscom; **P. 541:** AP Photo/Nam Y. Huh; **P. 543:** Paul Marotta/Getty Images; **P. 544:** AP Photo/Stuart Villanueva/The Galveston County Daily News; **P. 545:** Glasshouse Images/Alamy Stock Photo; **P. 546:** ZUMA Press, Inc./Alamy Stock Photo; **P. 557:** Chang W. Lee/The New York Times/Redux Pictures; **P. 562:** Michael Nagle/Bloomberg/Getty Images; **P. 565:** Brendan McDermid/Reuters/Alamy Stock Photo; **P. 573:** Courtesy of Richard Thompson Ford; **P. 574:** JeongMee Yoon; **P. 576:** Robin Marchant/Getty Images; **P. 577:** Matthew Sperzel/Getty Images; **P. 578:** Bauer-Griffin/Getty Images; **P. 580:** Justin Lanier; **P. 587:** Agence Opale/Alamy Stock Photo.

CHAPTER 32: P. 594: Margaret Randall; **P. 609:** *Chronicle of Higher Education*; **P. 614:** Courtesy of Missy Watson; **P. 622:** Courtesy of Jasmine Lane; **P. 626:** Henry Nguyen; **P. 632:** Jane Bradley; **P. 633:** Paras Griffin/Getty Images; **P. 637:** Lukas Maeder (13 Photo)/Redux; **P. 640 (LEFT):** Christopher Polk/Getty Images; **P. 640 (RIGHT):** Polina Osherov Photography; **P. 642:** Prince Williams/Wireimage/Getty Images; **P. 647:** Sara Miles.

CHAPTER 33: P. 669: Courtesy of The Atlantic; **P. 670:** KC McGinnis; **P. 673:** Des Moines County Historical Society; **P. 676:** Burlington Iowa Breaking News; **P. 679:** Bill Healy; **P. 689:** Courtesy of Sam Wineburg; **P. 690:** Kathrin Ziegler/Getty Images; **P. 695 (RIGHT):** Courtesy of Joel Pett; **P. 695 (LEFT):** Joel Pett Editorial Cartoon used with permission of Joel Pett and the Cartoonist Group. All rights reserved; **P. 697:** Courtesy of Savannah Jacobson; **P. 699 (RIGHT CENTER):** *The New York Times*; **P. 699 (LEFT):** Fox News; **P. 699 (RIGHT BOTTOM):** CNN; **P. 699 (RIGHT TOP):** *Washington Post*; **P. 700:** Jack Delano/Farm Security Administration/CORBIS/Corbis via Getty Images; **P. 702:** CBS Photo Archive/Getty Images; **P. 703:** Bettman Archive/Getty Images.

CHAPTER 34: P. 711: Narayan Mahon/The New York Times/Redux; **P. 712:** LHBLLC/ Shutterstock; **P. 713:** Jumping Rocks/Education Images/Getty Images; **P. 714:** Brandon

Alms/Stocksy United; **P. 715:** NPS/R.E. Marble; **P. 719:** Brian Gailey; **P. 720:** Harry Eggens/Alamy Stock Photo; **P. 722:** Todd Korol/Stocksy United; **P. 727 (LEFT):** Buiten-Beeld/Alamy Stock Photo; **P. 727 (RIGHT):** Marilyn Moller; **P. 728:** konstantinks/Getty Images; **P. 731:** Dale Kakkak; **P. 734:** Gregory Slocum/Alamy Stock Photo; **P. 735 (LEFT):** Ray49/Shutterstock; **P. 735 (RIGHT):** Everst/Alamy Stock Photo; **P. 739 (TOP):** Courtesy of Ian Leahy; **P. 739 (BOTTOM):** Courtesy of Yaryna Serkez; **P. 740:** Google Earth; **P. 742:** Google Earth; **P. 746:** Ting Shen/The New York Times/Redux; **P. 747:** Gary Whitton/Alamy Stock Photo; **P. 751:** American Conservation Coalition; **P. 753:** Courtesy of Carl Zimmer; **P. 754:** Appio studios/Alamy Stock Photo; **P. 759:** Franz Perc/Alamy Stock Photo.

CHAPTER 35: P. 764: Brad Barket/Getty Images; **P. 766 (LEFT):** John Rivera/Icon Sportswire/Getty Images; **P. 766 (RIGHT):** Tim Warner/Getty Images; **P. 767:** Brian Bahr/Getty Images; **P. 770:** Courtesy of Joe Drape; **P. 771:** Fabio Principe/Alamy Stock Photo; **P. 773:** @02Lacrosse/Instagram; **P. 774:** Jake Dockins/The New York Times/Redux; **P. 776 (LEFT):** ArcadeImages/Alamy Stock Photo; **P. 779:** Courtesy of Heather Tirado Gilligan; **P. 780:** LMPC/Getty Images; **P. 781 (LEFT):** Bettman/Getty Images; **P. 781 (RIGHT):** Everett Collection Inc/Alamy Stock Photo; **P. 782:** Wikimedia; **P. 783:** NY Daily News Archive/Getty Images; **P. 786:** Carolyn Cole/Los Angeles Times/Contour RA by Getty Images; **P. 787:** Dai Tianfang Xinhua/eyevine/Redux; **P. 789:** Tim Clayton/Corbis via Getty Images; **P. 790 (LEFT):** Al Bello/Getty Images; **P. 790 (RIGHT):** Brad Mangin/Sports Illustrated via Getty Images; **P. 796:** The Chronicle; **P. 797 (LEFT):** Michael Hickey/Getty Images; **P. 797 (CENTER):** Brett Deering/Getty Images; **P. 797 (RIGHT):** Michael Hickey/Getty Images; **P. 798:** Nick Kindelsperger/Chicago Tribune/TNS/Alamy Live News; **P. 801:** Courtesy of Mark Gozonsky; **P. 805:** Courtesy of Mark Gozonsky.

Text and illustrations

FRONTMATTER AND PART OPENERS: All collages of *Birdsong* by Stephen Doyle.

CHAPTER 5: GABRIELA MORO: "Minority Student Clubs: Segregation or Integration?" Originally published in *Fresh Writing: An Interactive Archive of Exemplary First-Year Writing Projects*, Vol. 16. Reprinted by permission of the University of Notre Dame College of Arts and Letters.

CHAPTER 8: LIFEWATER INTERNATIONAL: Excerpt from "World Water Day 2018: 10 Facts about the Water Crisis," Lifewater.org, February 10, 2020. Used by permission of Lifewater International. **BARRY MEIER:** Excerpt from "Opioid Makers Are the Big Winners in Lawsuit Settlements." From *The New York Times*, December 26, 2018. © 2018 The New York Times Company. All rights reserved. Used under license. **GAIL O. MELLOW:** Excerpt from "The Biggest Misconception about Today's College Students." From *The New York Times*, August 28, 2017. © 2017 The New York Times Company. All rights reserved. Used under license.

CHAPTER 9: WESLEY COHEN: "What's Happening Over at *Cosmo*?" originally published in *Prized Writing*, Volume 27 (2015–2016). Reprinted with permission of the author.

CHAPTER 10: SAM FORMAN: Excerpts from "The Future of Food Production." Originally published in Andrea Lunsford, *Everyone's an Author*, First Edition (W. W. Norton, 2011). Reused with permission of the author. CHRISTOPHER INGRAHAM: Excerpts from "Dog Owners Are Much Happier Than Cat Owners, Survey Finds." From *The Washington Post*, April 5, 2019. © 2019 The Washington Post. All rights reserved. Used under license. STEPHANIE POMALES: "For Better or for Worse: *Spotify* and the Music Industry," originally published in *Prized Writing*, Volume 28 (2016–2017). Reprinted with permission of the author. RESHMA SAUJANI: Excerpt from *Girls Who Code 2017 Annual Report*. Used by permission of Girls Who Code. MAJA PAWINSKA SIMS: Excerpts from "2019 Trust Barometer: Employers Emerge as Most Trusted Institution," *Holmes Report*, January 21, 2019. Used by permission of PRovoke Media. JEAN M. TWENGE: Adapted from iGEN by Jean M. Twenge, Ph.D. Copyright © 2017 by Jean M. Twenge, Ph.D. Reprinted with the permission of Atria Books, a division of Simon & Schuster, Inc. All rights reserved.

CHAPTER 11: LYNDA BARRY: "The Sanctuary of School" and "I'm Home!" written and illustrated by Lynda Barry. Originally published in *The New York Times*, January 5, 1992. Copyright © 1992 by Lynda Barry. All rights reserved. Used courtesy of Darhansoff & Verrill Literary Agents. MELISSA HICKS: Excerpts from "The High Price of Butter." Used by permission of the author. ISAAC LOZANO: "Remote Learning Is Hard. Losing a Relative Is Worse." From *The New York Times*. © 2020 The New York Times Company. All rights reserved. Used under license.

CHAPTER 12: JULIA LATRICE JOHNSON: "Can Money Buy Almost Anything?" by Julia Latrice Johnson. Reprinted with permission of the author. TAYLOR JORDAN: Summary of "I Learned in College That Admission Has Always Been for Sale" by Taylor Jordan. Reprinted with permission of the author. RAINESFORD STAUFFER: "I Learned in College That Admission Has Always Been for Sale." From *The New York Times*. © 2019 The New York Times Company. All rights reserved. Used under license.

CHAPTER 13: LOUISA THOMAS: From "The Unlimited Greatness of Simone Biles," *The New Yorker*, August 12, 2019. The New Yorker © Condé Nast. VRINDA VASAVADA: "Is Addicted the New Normal? Fighting Tech Addiction" by Vrinda Vasavada. Reprinted with permission of the author.

CHAPTER 16: OLIVIA STEELY: Annotated bibliography by Olivia Steely. Reprinted with permission of the author.

CHAPTER 17: BEN HEALY: Republished with permission of The Atlantic Monthly Group, LLC, from "Hell Is Other People's Vacations," Ben Healy, *The Atlantic Monthly*, June 2019; © 2019 The Atlantic Monthly Group, LLC; permission conveyed through Copyright Clearance Center. Courtesy of Atlantic Media.

CHAPTER 20: JACKSON PARELL: "Free at Last, Free at Last: Civil War Memory and Civil Rights Rhetoric" by Jackson Parell. Reprinted with permission of the author.

CHAPTER 21: ELI VALE: "The Causes of Burnout in San Antonio Nurses—and Some Possible Solutions" by Eli Vale. Reprinted with permission of the author.

CHAPTER 24: BAMBOO: Lyrics reprinted by permission of Bamboo from "Mama Africa Remix." **JAMILA LYISCOTT:** "3 Ways to Speak English," TED 2014. To watch the full talk, visit TED.com.

CHAPTER 26: BAR GRAPH: From "AI and Human Enhancement: Americans' Openness Is Tempered by a Range of Concerns." Pew Research Center, Washington, DC (2021). www.pewresearch.org/internet/2022/03/17/ai-and-human-enhancement-americans -openness-is-tempered-by-a-range-of-concerns/ps_2022-03-17_ai-he_00-01/. **LINE GRAPH:** From "#BlackLivesMatter Surges on *Twitter* after George Floyd's Death," Fact Tank, Pew Research Center, Washington, DC (June 10, 2020). www.pewresearch .org/fact-tank/2020/06/10/blacklivesmatter-surges-on-twitter-after-george-floyds -death/. **PIE CHART:** From "One-in-Five Americans Now Listen to Audiobooks," Fact Tank, Pew Research Center, Washington, DC (September 25, 2019). www.pew research.org/fact-tank/2019/09/25/one-in-five-americans-now-listen-to-audiobooks/. **TABLE:** US College Degrees by Gender. Used by permission of Mark J. Perry.

CHAPTER 27: HENRY TSAI: Excerpts from "Word and Image: The Rhetoric of the Graphic Narrative" by Henry Tsai. Reprinted by permission of the author.

CHAPTER 28: TREY CONNELLY: "Sign and Design: Modes of Instruction in Digital Games" by Trey Connelly. Reprinted by permission of the author. **WALTER A. HAAS, JR.:** "Levi Strauss & Co. Executive, Bay Area Philanthropist, and Owner of the Oakland Athletics: Oral History Transcript," BANC MSS 96/76, © The Regents of the University of California, The Bancroft Library, University of California, Berkeley. Reprinted with permission. **JACK LONG, COLIN FLANAGAN & BRANDON HERNANDEZ:** Excerpts from Episode 4: "First Generations," *The Third Chair*, *The Lantern*, October 22, 2018. Reprinted by permission of the contributors.

CHAPTER 29: ROSA GUEVARA: "Jailene M.: The Future of Tech with Digital Enthusiasm" from *The Bridge*, the student newspaper of LaGuardia Community College, October 9, 2019. Used with permission of the author. **ERIN HAWLEY:** "Writing While Disabled: The Damage of Ableism" from her blog *The Geeky Gimp*, June 1, 2018. Used with permission of the author. **BRANDON HAYDEN:** From "College 101: Choosing a Major!" Brandon Hayden, *YouTube*, March 28, 2016. Used with permission of the author.

CHAPTER 31: KWAME ANTHONY APPIAH: "Should I Hang Out with Someone Whose Political Views I Hate?" From *The New York Times*, June 22, 2021. © 2021 The New York Times Company. All rights reserved. Used under license. **RICHARD THOMPSON FORD:** From *Dress Codes: How the Laws of Fashion Made History* by Richard Thompson Ford. Copyright © 2021 by Richard Thompson Ford. Reprinted with the permission of Simon & Schuster, Inc. All rights reserved. **MICHAEL GERSON:** "I'm a Conservative Who Believes Systemic Racism's Real." From *The Washington Post*, June 21, 2021. © 2021 The Washington Post. All rights reserved. Used under license. **JODI KANTOR, KAREN WEISE & GRACE ASHFORD:** "The Amazon That Customers Don't See." From

The New York Times, June 15, 2021. © 2021 The New York Times Company. All rights reserved. Used under license. **HEATHER LANIER:** From "Out There I Have to Smile," Heather Lanier, *Longreads*, 2021. Used with permission of the author. **JOSHUA ROTHMAN:** From "The Equality Conundrum," *The New Yorker*, January 6, 2020. The New Yorker © Condé Nast. **CLINT SMITH:** From *How the Word Is Passed* by Clint Smith, copyright © 2021. Reprinted by permission of Little, Brown, an imprint of Hachette Book Group, Inc.

CHAPTER 32: GLORIA ANZALDÚA: From *Borderlands/La Frontera: The New Mestiza*. Copyright © 1987, 1999, 2007, 2012 by Gloria Anzaldúa. Reprinted by permission of Aunt Lute Books. **ADAM BRADLEY:** "The Artists Dismantling the Barriers between Rap and Poetry." From *The New York Times*, March 4, 2021. © 2021 The New York Times Company. All rights reserved. Used under license. **JUNE JORDAN:** "Nobody Mean More to Me Than You and the Future Life of Willie Jordan" from *On Call: Political Essays*, South End Press, 1985. Copyright 2017, 2022 June Jordan Literary Estate. Reprinted with the permission of the June M. Jordan Literary Estate. www .junejordan.com. **JASMINE LANE:** From "Here's Why I Will Teach Standardized English in My Classroom," Jasmine Lane, Ms. Jasmine's Blog, https://jasmineteaches .wordpress.com/. Used with permission of the author. **BETH NGUYEN:** From "America Ruined My Name for Me." *The New Yorker*, April 1, 2021. The New Yorker © Condé Nast. **MISSY WATSON:** From "Contesting Standardized English," *Academe*, May 2018. Reprinted by permission of the American Association of University Professors. **FERNANDA ZAMUDIO-SUAREZ:** Republished with permission of Chronicle of Higher Education, Inc., from "The Debate over 'Latinx,'" Fernanda Zamudio-Suarez, *Chronicle of Higher Education*, March 16, 2021; © 2021 Chronicle of Higher Education, Inc.; permission conveyed through Copyright Clearance Center.

CHAPTER 33: ELAINE GODFREY: Republished with permission of The Atlantic Monthly Group, LLC, from "What We Lost When Gannett Came to Town," Elaine Godfrey, *The Atlantic Monthly*, October 5, 2021; © 2021 The Atlantic Monthly Group, LLC; permission conveyed through Copyright Clearance Center. Courtesy of Atlantic Media. **SAVANNAH JACOBSON:** "Inside the Lines." From *Columbia Journalism Review* June 21, 2021. Reprinted by Permission of Columbia Journalism Review. **LEWIS RAVEN WALLACE:** Republished with permission of The University of Chicago Press; excerpted from *The View from Somewhere: Undoing the Myth of Journalistic Objectivity* by Lewis Raven Wallace. © 2019 The University of Chicago Press; permission conveyed through Copyright Clearance Center. **SAM WINEBURG:** "To Navigate the Dangers of the Web, You Need Critical Thinking—but Also Critical Ignoring" from *The Conversation*, June, 2021. Reprinted by permission of the author.

CHAPTER 34: BENJI BACKER: "The Conservative Case for Environmentalism" by Benji Backer. *DeseretNews*, September 20, 2021. Reprinted by permission. **WILLIAM CRONON:** "The Trouble with Wilderness; or, Getting Back to the Wrong Nature" by William Cronon, from *Uncommon Ground*, edited by William Cronon. Copyright © 1995 by William Cronon. Used by permission of W. W. Norton & Company, Inc.

ROBIN WALL KIMMERER: "Learning the Grammar of Animacy" from *Braiding Sweetgrass: Indigenous Wisdom, Scientific Knowledge and the Teachings of Plants.* Copyright © 2013, 2015 by Robin Wall Kimmerer. Reprinted with the permission of The Permissions Company, LLC on behalf of Milkweed Editions, www.milkweed.org. **IAN LEAHY & YARYNA SERKEZ:** "Since When Have Trees Existed Only for Rich Americans?" From *The New York Times*, June 30, 2021. © 2021 The New York Times Company. All rights reserved. Used under license. **EMMA MARRIS:** Republished with permission of The Atlantic Monthly Group, LLC, from "The Nature You See in Documentaries Is Beautiful, and False" Emma Marris, *The Atlantic Monthly*, April 2021; © 2021 The Atlantic Monthly Group, LLC; permission conveyed through Copyright Clearance Center. Courtesy of Atlantic Media. **GRETA THUNBERG:** "The World Is Waking Up (UN General Assembly, NYC 9/23/19)," *No One Is Too Small to Make a Difference* by Greta Thunberg, copyright © 2018, 2019 by Greta Thunberg. Used by permission of Penguin Books, an imprint of Penguin Publishing Group, a division of Penguin Random House LLC. Also reprinted by permission of Penguin Books Limited. **CARL ZIMMER:** Republished with permission of The University of Chicago Press; "The Uncommon Cold: How Rhinoviruses Gently Conquered the World." *A Planet of Viruses* by Carl Zimmer. © 2011 The University of Chicago Press; permission conveyed through Copyright Clearance Center.

CHAPTER 35: JANE COASTON: "What Can Sports Teach Us?" From *The New York Times*, September 11, 2021. © 2021 The New York Times Company. All rights reserved. Used under license. **JOE DRAPE:** "Step Aside, LeBron and Dak: Make Room for Banjo and Kazooie." From *The New York Times*, January 5, 2022. © 2021 The New York Times Company. All rights reserved. Used under license. **HEATHER TIRADO GILLIGAN:** "The Black-Versus-White Basketball Game That Integrated the Sport," by Heather Tirado Gilligan, from *LEVEL* (part of *Medium*), February 27, 2018. Reprinted by permission of the author. **NELL GLUCKMAN:** Republished with permission of Chronicle of Higher Education, Inc., from "Colleges Are Paying Big Bucks for Coaches: Here's How Else They Could've Spent the Money," Neil Gluckman, *Chronicle of Higher Education*, December 2, 2021; © 2021 Chronicle of Higher Education, Inc.; permission conveyed through Copyright Clearance Center. **MARK GOZONSKY:** "Gritty All Day Long" by Mark Gozonsky, from *The Sun*, November 2019. Reprinted by permission of the author. **JEMELE HILL:** Republished with permission of The Atlantic Monthly Group, LLC, from "Naomi Osaka Is Part of a Larger War within Sports" by Jemele Hill, *The Atlantic Monthly*, June 2021; © 2021 The Atlantic Monthly Group, LLC; permission conveyed through Copyright Clearance Center. Courtesy of Atlantic Media.

Submitting Papers for Publication by W. W. Norton & Company

We are interested in receiving writing from college students to consider including in our textbooks as examples of student writing. Please send this form with the work that you would like us to consider to Marilyn Moller, Student Writing, W. W. Norton & Company, 500 Fifth Avenue, New York, NY 10110. For questions, or to submit electronically, email us at composition@wwnorton.com.

Text Submission Form

Student's name _____

School _____

Address _____

Department _____

Course _____

Writing assignment the text responds to _____

_____

_____

_____

_____

_____

Instructor's name _____

Please write a few sentences about what your primary purposes were for writing this text. Also, if you wish, tell us what you learned about writing from the experience of writing it.

_____

_____

_____

_____

_____

_____

_____

_____

_____

_____

CONTACT INFORMATION

Please provide the information below so that we can contact you if your work is selected for publication.

Name_____

Permanent address_____

Email_____

Phone_____

Author/Title Index

The title of this book, *Let's Talk with Readings*, assumes that communication is a two-way street: if someone is talking, somebody else is listening, and responding. It's an assumption that goes far beyond the title, however, and this is a book of many voices—and many, many perspectives. And that turns out to be a lot of folks, of widely varying backgrounds and convictions and from widely varying places around the country and beyond. In essays and epigraphs, examples and prompts for reflection, these voices provide information, inspiration, intriguing examples, and instructive viewpoints that enliven and enrich the book before you now. Here they are—collaborators and contributors all.

Glossary/Index

This glossary/index defines key terms and concepts and directs you to pages in the book where you can find specific information on these and other topics. Please note the words set in SMALL CAPITAL LETTERS are themselves defined in the glossary / index.

A

ABSTRACT, 387–88 A GENRE of writing that summarizes a book, an article, or a paper, usually in 100–200 words. An *informative abstract* summarizes a complete report; a briefer *descriptive abstract* works more as a teaser; a stand-alone *proposal abstract* (also called a PROJECT PROPOSAL) requests permission to conduct research, write on a topic, or present a report at a scholarly conference. Key Features: a SUMMARY of basic information • an objective description • brevity

ACADEMIC HABITS OF MIND, 42–49 Practices that are essential for success in college: being curious, creative, flexible, persistent, and open to new ideas; collaborating; taking responsibility and engaging with your work; reflecting on what you're learning; and not being afraid to fail.

Academic Search Complete, 258

acknowledging multiple viewpoints, 20, 90–91
  in arguments, 114–16
  in reports, 160
acknowledging sources, 20–21, 295–304

ACTIVE VOICE When a verb is in the active voice, the subject performs the action: *Gus tripped Bodie. See also* PASSIVE VOICE

AD HOMINEM ARGUMENT A logical FALLACY that attacks someone's character rather than addresses the issues. (*Ad hominem* is Latin for "to the man.")

AGRIS, 259
algorithims, 253, 510
AllSides.com, 34, 74

ALT TEXT, 227, 466 A way of describing images in digital texts for readers who are visually impaired or whose computers do not display images.

ANALOGY, 414 A STRATEGY for COMPARISON by explaining something unfamiliar in terms of something that is more familiar. *See also* FALSE ANALOGY

APPENDIX A section at the end of a written work for supplementary material that would be distracting in the main part of the text.

ARGUMENT, 99–131 Any text that makes a CLAIM supported by REASONS and EVIDENCE. A GENRE that uses REASONS and EVIDENCE to support a CLAIM. Key Features: an explicit POSITION • a response to what others have said • appropriate background information • a clear indication of why the topic matters • good REASONS and EVIDENCE • attention to more than one POINT OF VIEW • an authoritative TONE • an appeal to readers' values

ATTRIBUTION BIAS, 70–71 The tendency to think that our motivations for believing what we believe are objectively good while thinking that those who we disagree with have objectively wrong motivations.

AUDIENCE, 25–26 Those to whom a text is directed—the people who read, listen to, or view the text. Audience is a key part of any RHETORICAL SITUATION.

AUTHORITY, 57, 112–13, 142–43 A person or text that is cited as support for an ARGUMENT. A structural engineer may be quoted as an authority on bridge construction, for example. Authority also refers to a quality conveyed by writers who are knowledgeable about their subjects.

B

BANDWAGON APPEAL A logical FALLACY that argues for thinking or acting in a certain way just because others do.

bar graphs, 170, 461

BEGGING THE QUESTION A logical FALLACY that argues in a circle, assuming as a given what the writer is trying to prove.

beginning. *See* OPENING
beliefs, 24, 70–72, 271
bias
    attribution, 70–71
    confirmation, 71–72
bibliographies, annotated, 272–76.
    See also REFERENCES
Black Lives Matter, 13
block method of comparison, 88

BLOCK QUOTATION, 286, 287 In a written work, long QUOTATIONS are indented and set without quotation marks: in MLA STYLE, set off text of more than four typed lines, indented five spaces (or one-half inch) from the left margin; in APA STYLE, set off quotes of forty or more words, indented five spaces (or one-half inch) from the left margin. *See also* QUOTE
    APA style, 388
    MLA style, 345–46

BLOG, 496–98 From *web* + *log*, blogs are sites that focus on topics of all kinds. Blogs are regularly updated, usually strike an informal TONE, and include a space where readers can respond.
    documenting APA style, 382
    documenting MLA style, 337
    student blog post, 497–98

book reviews, 253

BOT, 75 An automated program on the internet, often used to advocate ideas—and sometimes used for malicious purposes, for example, to capture email addresses for a spam mailing list.

brackets, to indicate changes in
    quotations, 288
Brady, Tom, 90

BRAINSTORMING, 45, 82 A way of GENERATING IDEAS AND TEXT by writing down everything that comes to mind about a topic, then looking for patterns or connections among the ideas.

Burke's parlor metaphor, 15

C

call for action, 92, 418

CAPTION, 346, 467 A brief explanation accompanying a photograph, diagram, chart, and screen shot, or other visual that appears in a written document.

CAUSAL ANALYSIS A kind of ANALYSIS that explains why something occurs or once occurred. *See also* FAULTY CAUSALITY

CAUSE AND EFFECT, 90 A STRATEGY for analyzing why something occurred or speculating about what its consequences will be.

charts, 461

CHRONOLOGICAL ORDER, 85, 194 A way of organizing text that proceeds from the beginning of an event to the end. Reverse chronological order proceeds in the other direction, from the end to the beginning.

CITATION, 283–94 In a text, the act of giving information from a source, for example, by QUOTING, PARAPHRASING, or SUMMARIZING. A citation and its corresponding parenthetical DOCUMENTATION, footnote, or endnote provide minimal information about the source;

complete information appears in a list of WORKS CITED or REFERENCES at the end of the text.

CLAIM, 84–85, 103–5 A statement of a belief or POSITION. In an ARGUMENT, a claim needs to be stated in a THESIS or clearly implied, and requires support by REASONS and EVIDENCE.

CLASSICAL ARGUMENT A system of ARGUMENT developed in Greece and Rome during the classical period. Key Features: an introduction that states the CLAIM; a body that includes background information, good REASONS and EVIDENCE, and attention to COUNTERARGUMENTS; and a CONCLUSION.

CLASSIFICATION, 89–90, 169–71 A STRATEGY that groups a number of items by their similarities (classifying cereal, bread, and rice as carbohydrates, for instance). Classification can serve as the organizing principle for a paragraph or whole text.

CLAUSE, 422–27 A group of words that consists of at least a SUBJECT and a VERB; a clause may be either MAIN or SUBORDINATE.

CLICKBAIT, 408 On the internet, headlines or links designed to get readers to read something or to increase page views.

CONCLUSION, 92, 211, 417–18 The way a text ends, a chance to leave an AUDIENCE thinking about what's been said. Some ways of concluding an essay: REITERATING your point, discussing the implications of your ARGUMENT, proposing some kind of action, inviting response.

CONFIRMATION BIAS, 71–72 The tendency to favor and seek out information that confirms what we already believe and to reject and ignore information that contradicts those beliefs.

CONTEXT, 17, 27–28, 59 A part of any RHETORICAL SITUATION, conditions affecting the text such as what else has been said about a topic; social, economic, and other factors; and any constants such as due date and length.

COORDINATING CONJUNCTION, 422, 423 One of these words—*and, but, or, nor, so, for,* or *yet*—used to join two elements in a way that gives equal weight to each one (*bacon and eggs; pay up or get out*).

COUNTERARGUMENT, 16, 90–91, 114, 265 In ARGUMENT, an alternative POSITION or objection to the writer's position. The writer of an argument should not only acknowledge counterarguments but also, if at all possible, accept, accommodate, or refute each counterargument.

CREATIVE COMMONS, 297, 466 A non-profit organization that licenses creative works in order to make them more accessible than they would be with traditional copyright.

CREDIBILITY, 164–66, 297–98 The sense of trustworthiness that a writer conveys through the text.

CRITERIA In an EVALUATION or a REVIEW, the standards against which something is judged.

CUBING A process for GENERATING IDEAS AND TEXT in which a writer looks at a topic in six ways—to DESCRIBE it, to COMPARE it to something else, to associate it with other things or CLASSIFY it, to ANALYZE it, to apply it, and to ARGUE for or against it.

CUMULATIVE SENTENCE, 427–28 A sentence that begins with a main idea expressed in a MAIN CLAUSE and then adds details in PHRASES and SUBORDINATE CLAUSES that follow the MAIN CLAUSE. *See also* PERIODIC SENTENCE

curiosity, 43, 81, 243–44

D

Dame Rhetorica, 407

DATA ANALYSIS A kind of ANALYSIS that looks for patterns in numbers or other data, sometimes in order to answer a stated or implied question.

DATABASES, 258–59 Digital collections of articles from journals, newspapers, and other periodicals. General databases cover a range of disciplines and topics; subject-specific databases focus on a single topic. Some databases are open-access; those that require a subscription and can usually be accessed through your campus library website.

    documenting APA style, 372
    documenting MLA style, 328
    general, 258–59
    subject-specific, 259

defensive reading, 72

DEFINITION, 88 A STRATEGY that says what something is. *Formal definitions* identify the category that something belongs to and tell what distinguishes it from other things in that category: A worm is an invertebrate (a category) with a long, rounded body and no appendages (distinguishing features). *Extended definitions* go into more detail: a paragraph or even an essay explaining why a character in a story is tragic. *Stipulative definitions* give a writer's own use of a term, one not found in a dictionary. Definition can serve as the organizing principle for a paragraph or whole text.

DESCRIPTION, 86 A STRATEGY that tells how something looks, sounds, smells, feels, or tastes. Effective description creates a clear DOMINANT IMPRESSION built from specific details. Description can be *objective, subjective,* or both. Description can serve as the organizing principle for a paragraph or whole text.

DESIGN, 27, 96–97, 448–58 The way a text is arranged and presented visually. Elements of design include FONTS, colors, visuals, LAYOUT, and white space.

color, 453–54
fonts, 452–53
getting response, 458
headings, 454–55
layout, 454–55
principles, 451–52
thinking rhetorically about, 449–51
visual texts, 455–57
white space, 454

DIALECTS, 437–41 Varieties of language that are spoken by people in a particular region, social class, or ethnic group.

dialogue, 191–93

DICTION, 433 Word choice.

digital media, 494–508
blogs, 496–98
vlogs, 499–503
websites, 504–8

DOCUMENTATION, 309–44, 360–86 Publication information about the sources cited in a text. IN-TEXT DOCUMENTATION usually appears in parentheses at the point where it's cited or in an endnote or a footnote. Complete documentation usually appears as a list of WORKS CITED or REFERENCES at the end of the text. Documentation styles vary by discipline. *See also* APA STYLE; MLA STYLE

documentation maps
APA, 373, 375, 377
MLA, 326, 327, 329, 333, 338

DOI A digital object identifier, a stable number identifying the location of a source accessed through a database.
APA style, 368
MLA style, 317

DOMINANT IMPRESSION, 86 The overall effect created by specific details in a DESCRIPTION.

DRAFTING, 85–92 The process of putting words on paper or screen. Writers often write several drafts, REVISING each until they achieve their goal or reach a deadline.

E

echo chambers, 31

EDITED ACADEMIC ENGLISH The conventions of spelling, grammar, and punctuation that have traditionally been expected in academic discourse, which tends to be more formal than conversational English. These conventions vary from country to country and change over time. *Edited* refers to the care writers are expected to take in reviewing formal written work.

EDITING, 94–96 The process of fine-tuning a text—examining each word, phrase, sentence, and paragraph—to be sure that the text is correct and precise and says exactly what the writer intends. *See also* DRAFTING; PROOFREADING; REVISING

effect. *See* CAUSE AND EFFECT

EITHER-OR ARGUMENT A logical FALLACY, also known as a false dilemma, that oversimplifies to suggest that only two possible POSITIONS exist on a complex issue.

ELLIPSES, 288 Three spaced dots (. . .) that indicate an omission or a pause.

EMOTIONAL APPEALS, 113–14, 143–44, 415 Ways of appealing to an AUDIENCE's emotions, values, and beliefs by arousing specific feelings—compassion, sympathy, anger, and so on. *See also* ETHICAL APPEALS; LOGICAL APPEALS

EMPATHY, 9, 34–35 The ability to be aware of and understand what someone else is feeling.

endings. *See* CONCLUSION
endnotes, 300, 315
engaging respectfully with others, 29–41
engaging with ideas, 44
Englishes, 436–37
ERIC, 259

ETHICAL APPEALS, 112–13 Ways that authors establish CREDIBILITY and AUTHORITY to persuade an AUDIENCE to trust their ARGUMENTS—by showing that they know what they're talking about (by citing TRUSTWORTHY SOURCES), demonstrating that they're fair (by representing opposing views accurately and even-handedly), and establishing COMMON GROUND. *See also* EMOTIONAL APPEALS; LOGICAL APPEALS

ETHICS, 14–15 Right or moral conduct, practices, or choices that guide us in life.

ETHOS From the Greek word for "character," ethos reflects the values and ideals of a person or culture.

EVALUATION A GENRE of writing that makes a judgment about something— a source, poem, film, restaurant, whatever—based on certain CRITERIA. Key Features: a description of the subject • clearly defined criteria • knowledgeable discussion of the subject • a balanced and fair assessment

EVIDENCE, 85–90 The data you present to support a CLAIM. Such data may include statistics, calculations, EXAMPLES, ANECDOTES, QUOTATIONS, case studies, or anything else that will convince your readers that your reasons are compelling. Evidence should be *sufficient* (enough to show that the reasons have merit) and *relevant* (appropriate to the argument you're making).

EXAMPLES 88–89, 108–10, 412–13 Specific things that illustrate and support a point. An essay on the best films directed by Spike Lee would cite specific examples from his work that support the ARGUMENT that they are indeed the "best."

EXPLETIVES Words such as *it* and *there* used to introduce information provided later in a sentence: *It was difficult to drive on the icy road. There is plenty of food in the refrigerator.*

F

FACT-CHECKING, 72–75, 266–69 The process of verifying the accuracy of FACTS and CLAIMS presented in a piece of writing, a speech, or elsewhere—by READING LATERALLY, TRIANGULATING, or consulting fact-checking sites.

FACTS, 69–70, 106–8 Information that can be backed up and verified by reliable evidence.

FAKE NEWS, 68–70, 252 False or misleading information designed and written to look like authentic news. *See also* MISINFORMATION

FALLACY Faulty reasoning that can mislead an AUDIENCE. Fallacies include AD HOMINEM, BANDWAGON APPEAL, BEGGING THE QUESTION, EITHER-OR ARGUMENT, FALSE ANALOGY, FAULTY CAUSALITY (also called *post hoc, ergo propter hoc*), HASTY GENERALIZATION, and SLIPPERY SLOPE.

FALSE ANALOGY A FALLACY comparing things that resemble each other but are not alike in the most important respects.

FAULTY CAUSALITY A FALLACY, also called *post hoc, ergo propter hoc* (Latin for "after this, therefore because of this"), that mistakenly assumes the first of two events causes the second.

FIELD RESEARCH, 259–62 Collecting first-hand data through observation, interviews, conversation, and surveys.

first person. *See* POINT OF VIEW

FLASHBACK, 194 In NARRATIVE, an interruption of the main story in order to show an incident that occurred at an earlier time.

FLASH-FORWARD In NARRATIVE, an interruption of the main story in order to show an incident that will occur in the future.

FONTS, 472 Typefaces, such as Calibri or Times New Roman

FORMAL WRITING Writing intended to be evaluated by someone such as an instructor or read by an audience expecting academic or businesslike argument and presentation. Formal writing should be carefully revised, edited, and proofread. *See also* INFORMAL WRITING

FRAGMENT A group of words that is capitalized and punctuated as a sentence but is not one, either because it lacks a subject, a VERB, or both, or because it begins with a word that makes it a SUBORDINATE CLAUSE.

FREEWRITING, 82 A process for GENERATING IDEAS AND TEXT by writing continuously for several minutes without pausing to read what has been written.

FUSED SENTENCE Two or more MAIN CLAUSES with no punctuation between them: *I came I saw I conquered.*

G

GENERATING IDEAS AND TEXT, 82–83 Activities for exploring and developing a topic by BRAINSTORMING, CLUSTERING, FREEWRITING, LOOPING, OUTLINING, and QUESTIONING.

GENRE, 27, 82, 245 A way of classifying things. The genres this book is concerned with are kinds of writing that writers can use to accomplish a certain goal and to reach a particular AUDIENCE. As such, they have well-established features that help guide writers, but they are flexible and change over time, and can be adapted by writers to address their own RHETORICAL SITUATIONS. Genres covered in this book include ANALYSES, ANNOTATED BIBLIOGRAPHIES, ARGUMENTS, NARRATIVES, REPORTS, SUMMARY/RESPONSE essays, and VISUAL ANALYSES.

GERUND A VERB form ending in *-ing* that functions as a NOUN: *Swimming improves muscle tone and circulation.*

GRAPH, 460–61 A diagram showing a relationship between two or more things. *Bar graphs* are useful for comparing quantitative data; *line graphs* are useful for showing changes in data over time.

H

HASHTAG, 510, 514 A metadata tag created by placing a number sign (#) in front of a word or unspaced phrase (for example, #BlackLives Matter), used in social media to mark posts by KEYWORD or theme and make them searchable by these tags. Also used to add commentary in SOCIAL MEDIA.

HASTY GENERALIZATION The FAL-LACY that reaches a conclusion based on insufficient or inappropriately qualified EVIDENCE.

HYPOTHESIS, 247-48 A supposition that's a starting point for exploration and investigation.

I

I/WE Personal pronouns that we all use frequently. Be aware, though, that they can send signals: sometimes using *I* suggests a focus on yourself, perhaps to the exclusion of others, whereas using *we* can send the opposite message, that you're one of many—or that you're including your AUDIENCE in what you say.

IMRAD A GENRE of writing scientific reports organized in four parts: an introduction (asks a question), methods (tells about experiments), results (states findings), and discussion (tries to make sense of findings in light of what was already known).

INDEFINITE PRONOUN Words such as *all, anyone, anything, everyone, everything, few, many, nobody, nothing, one, some,* and *something* that do not refer to a specific person or thing.

INFINITIVE *To* plus the base form of the verb: to come, to go. An infinitive can function as a noun (*He likes to run first thing in the morning*); an adjective (*She needs a campaign to run*); or an adverb (*He registered to run in the marathon*).

INFORMAL WRITING Writing not intended to be evaluated, sometimes not even to be read by others. Informal writing is produced primarily to explore ideas or to communicate casually with friends and acquaintances. *See also* FORMAL WRITING

A process for investigating a topic by posing questions, searching for multiple answers, and keeping an open mind.

INTERPRETATION An explanation or the process of making sense of something or explaining what you think it means. Interpretation is one goal of writing a LITERARY ANALYSIS or rhetorical analysis.

IN-TEXT DOCUMENTATION Brief documentation in a text that tells readers what the writer has taken from a source and where in the source they found that information.

introductions. *See* OPENING

INVITATIONAL ARGUMENT A system of ARGUMENT that aims for understanding and shared goals by listening carefully to everyone concerned. Invitational arguments introduce the issue, present all perspectives on it fairly, identify any commonalities among the perspectives, and conclude by seeking a resolution that is agreeable to all.

IRONY The use of words and phrases that convey a message that is opposite the literal meaning of the words, often for humorous effect, as in calling cafeteria food "delicious" when it is actually almost inedible.

J

journals, for reflecting, 48
JSTOR, 258

K

KAIROS An ancient Greek term meaning "the opportune moment"—for example, to look for just the right moment to make a particular ARGUMENT, appeal to a particular AUDIENCE, and so on.

KEYWORD, 83, 253, 258 A term that a researcher inputs when searching for information in library catalogs, databases, and elsewhere on the internet.
  about current issues, 83
  in the library catalog, 258
  on the web, 253, 256

L

LAB REPORT A GENRE of writing that covers the process of conducting an experiment. Key Features: TITLE ● ABSTRACT ● PURPOSE ● methods ● results and discussion ● REFERENCES ● APPENDIX ● appropriate format

LATERAL READING, 267–69 A process for evaluating a source by checking what others say about it. *See also* VERTICAL READING

LAYOUT, 454–55 The way text is arranged on a page or screen—for example, in paragraphs, in lists, on charts, with headings, and so on.

LITERACY NARRATIVE, 188–90 A GENRE of writing that tells about a writer's experience learning to read or write or do something else. Key Features: a well-told story • a first-hand account • an indication of the narrative's significance

LITERARY ANALYSIS A GENRE of writing that examines a literary text and argues for a particular INTERPRETATION of the text. Key Features: arguable THESIS • careful attention to the text's language • attention to patterns or themes • a clear INTERPRETATION • MLA STYLE

LITERATURE REVIEW A GENRE of writing that surveys and synthesizes the prior research on a topic. In the sciences, a literature review is a required part of the introduction to an IMRAD report. Key Features: a survey of relevant research on the topic • an objective summary of the literature • an evaluation of the literature • an organization appropriate to your assignment and PURPOSE • DOCUMENTATION

LOGICAL APPEALS, 105–12 Ways of using REASONS and EVIDENCE to persuade an AUDIENCE to accept a CLAIM: facts, images, observations, statistics, testimony, and so on. *See also* EMOTIONAL APPEALS; ETHICAL APPEALS

logos. *See* LOGICAL APPEALS

LOOPING A process for GENERATING IDEAS AND TEXT by writing about a topic quickly for several minutes and then writing a one-sentence summary of the most important or interesting idea, which becomes the beginning of another round of writing and summarizing—and repeating this process until you find a tentative topic for writing.

M

MAIN CLAUSE, 422, 424–28 A CLAUSE, containing a subject and a

VERB, that can stand alone as a sentence: *She sang. The world-famous soprano sang several arias.*

MEDIA, 27, 191, 205, 226–29 The means of delivering messages—for example, digital, oral, print, and social. The singular of *media* is "medium."

MEMOIR, 406–7 A **GENRE** of writing that focuses on something significant from the writer's past. Key Features: a good story • vivid detail • clear significance

METAPHOR A figure of speech that makes a comparison without using the word *like* or *as*: "All the world's a stage / And all the men and women merely players" (Shakespeare, *As You Like It*). *See also* **SIMILE**

MISINFORMATION, 68–70 False or inaccurate information that may or may not be intended to deceive. Lies, on the other hand, are always told deliberately.

MLA STYLE, 305–56 A system of **DOCUMENTATION** established by the Modern Language Association and used in the humanities.

MODES, 223–29 Means of conveying a message. Writers often use multiple modes: linguistic, visual, audio, spatial, and/or gestural.

MULTIMEDIA Using more than one medium to deliver a message: digital, oral, print, and social.

MULTIMODAL WRITING, 223–39 Writing that uses more than one **MODE**

N

NARRATIVE, 186–202 A GENRE that tells a story for the PURPOSE of making a point. Key Features: a clearly defined event • a clearly described setting • vivid, descriptive details • a consistent POINT OF VIEW • a clear point. Also a STRATEGY for presenting information as a story, for telling "what happened." When used in an essay, narration is used to support a point—not merely to tell an interesting story for its own sake. Narration can serve as the organizing principle for a paragraph or an entire text. *See also* LITERACY NARRATIVE

NOUN A word that refers to a person, place, animal, thing, or idea (*a justice, Ruth Bader Ginsburg, a forest, Mexico, a tree frog, a notebook, democracy*).

O

OPENING, 85, 146, 410–12 How a text begins. Some ways of beginning an essay: with a dramatic or deceptively simple statement, with something others have said about your topic, with a provocative question or a startling CLAIM, or with an ANECDOTE.

OUTLINING, 194 A process for GENERATING IDEAS AND TEXT or for examining a text. An *informal outline* simply lists ideas and then numbers them in the order that they will appear; a *working outline* distinguishes support from main ideas by indenting the former; a *formal outline* is arranged as a series of headings and indented subheadings, each on a separate line, with letters and numbers indicating relative levels of importance.

P

PARALLELISM Writing technique that puts similar items into the same grammatical structure. For example, every item on a to-do list might begin with a command: *clean, wash, iron*; or a discussion of favorite hobbies might name each as a GERUND: *running, playing basketball, writing poetry.*

editing, 97
headings, 455

PARAPHRASE, 284–85, 290–92 To reword a text in about the same number of words but without using the word order or sentence structure of the original. Paraphrasing is generally called for when you want to include the details of a passage but do not need to QUOTE it word for word. Paraphrasing a source in academic writing requires DOCUMENTATION. *See also* PATCHWRITING

avoiding patchwriting, 301–3
deciding whether to quote, paraphrase, or summarize, 284–85

parenthetical documentation. *See* IN-TEXT DOCUMENTATION

PASSIVE VOICE When a VERB is in the passive voice, the subject is acted upon: *Bodi was tripped by Gus. See also* ACTIVE VOICE

PATCHWRITING, 301–3 PARAPHRASES that lean too heavily on the words or sentence structure of the original, adding or deleting some words, replacing words with SYNONYMS, altering the syntax slightly—in other words, not restating the passage in fresh language and structure.

PERIODIC SENTENCE, 427–28 A sentence that delays the main idea, expressed in a MAIN CLAUSE, until after details given in phrases and SUBORDINATE CLAUSES. *See also* CUMULATIVE SENTENCE

PERMALINK, 316, 319 A URL that permanently links to a specific web page or BLOG post.

permission to use copyrighted materials, 299–300
persistence, 46
personal experience, 110–12

PERSONAL NARRATIVE A GENRE of writing that tells a story about a writer's personal experience. MEMOIR and autobiography are two common types of personal narratives. Key Features: a well-told story • vivid detail • some indication of the narrative's significance

PERSPECTIVES, 29–41, 90–91 Viewpoints, an important part of a writer's STANCE. As a writer and a researcher, you should always strive to seek, think about, and work to understand multiple perspectives.

in analysis, 145
in argument, 103, 114–16
in listening, 8–9
in reporting, 160

perspectives (cont.)
in research, 250, 256
in summarizing, 204
in thinking rhetorically, 15–16, 24

photos, 460
fact-checking, 75–77
using ethically, 462–65
pie charts, 461

PLAGIARISM, 300–303 The use of another person's words, SYNTAX, or ideas without giving appropriate credit and DOCUMENTATION. Plagiarism is a serious breach of ethics.
avoiding patchwriting, 301–3

podcasts, 480–81, 488–91
documenting APA style, 382
documenting MLA style, 342
poetry
analyzing, 137
quoting, 287
point-by-point comparison, 88

POINT OF VIEW, 194 The position from which something is considered: first person (*I* or *we*), second person (*you*), or third person (*he, she,* or *they*). *See also* PERSPECTIVES

PolitiFact.com, 267
popular research sources, 251–52, 255

PORTFOLIO A collection of writing selected by a writer to show their work, often with a statement assess-ing the work and explaining what it demonstrates.

POSITION, 43–44 A statement that asserts a belief or a CLAIM. In an ARGUMENT, a position needs to be stated in a THESIS or clearly implied and to be supported with REASONS and EVIDENCE.

posters, 476
post-truth, 69

PREPOSITION A word or group of words that tells about the relationship of a NOUN or a PRONOUN to another word in the sentence. Some common prepositions are *after, at, before, behind, between, by, for, from, in, of, on, to, under, until, with,* and *without.*
in APA style, 387
in MLA style, 318

previewing, 53–54

PRIMARY SOURCE, 250–51 A source such as a literary work, historical doc-ument, work of art, or performance that a researcher examines first-hand. Primary sources also include exper-iments and FIELD RESEARCH. In writ-ing about the Revolutionary War, a researcher would probably consider the Declaration of Independence a primary source, whereas a textbook's analysis of the document would be a SECONDARY SOURCE.

PROBLEM/SOLUTION A STRATEGY for supporting an ARGUMENT by framing it as a way of solving a problem, or of introducing a change of some kind. If you can first convince readers that there's a problem (and that it matters), they'll be more likely to read on to hear about how it can be solved. This is also a classic storytelling technique: setting up a conflict that needs to be resolved is a good way of getting and keeping an AUDIENCE's attention.

PROCESS ANALYSIS A kind of ANALYSIS that closely examines the steps of a process.

PROFILE, 46, 91 A REPORT about people, places, events, institutions, or other things. Key Features: a first-hand account • detailed information about the subject • an interesting angle

PROJECT PROPOSAL A GENRE of writing that describes the PURPOSE of a research project, the steps of the project, and its goal. Key Features: a discussion of the topic • an indication of a specific focus • the REASON you're interested in the topic • a research plan • a schedule

PRONOUN A word that takes the place of a NOUN or functions the way a noun does.

PRONOUN REFERENCE The way in which a PRONOUN indicates its ANTECEDENT. Pronoun reference must be clear and unambiguous in order to avoid confusing readers.

PROOFREADING, 97 The process that follows REVISING for checking surface issues: spelling, punctuation, TRANSITIONS, headings, FONTS. *See also* EDITING; REVISING

PROPER NOUN A NOUN that names a specific person, place, or thing (*Steph Curry, Brazil, Google*).

PROPOSAL A GENRE that argues for a solution to a problem or suggests some kind of action. Key Features: a precise description of the problem • a clear and compelling solution • EVIDENCE that your solution will address the problem • acknowledgment of other possible solutions • a statement of what your proposal will accomplish. *See also* PROJECT PROPOSAL

on-screen and off, 62–63
with an open mind, 55–56
to preview, 53–54
to respond, 60–61
to understand, 53–55
vertically, 268
visuals, 63–65

REASONS, 105–6 Support for a
CLAIM or a POSITION. A reason, in turn,
requires its own support.

REFERENCES, 365–86 The list of
sources at the end of a text prepared
in APA STYLE.

REFERENCE WORKS, 257 Encyclopedias, handbooks, atlases, bio-
graphical dictionaries, almanacs, and
other such sources that provide over-
views of a topic.
documenting APA style, 379
documenting MLA style, 328–30

REFLECT, 48, 98 To explore a topic
thoughtfully. Reflections are a GENRE
of writing. Key Features: a topic that
you think about • specific details • a
speculative TONE

REGISTER, 435 Ways that language
is used in particular situations, like
the *informal register* we speak with
friends, the *technical register* used by
engineers, or the language used in certain sports (think *pick-and-roll* and
layup in basketball).

REITERATION Repeating a word, a
phrase, or an image in a way that drives
home a point.
in conclusions, 92, 211
to emphasize a point, 416–17

REPORT, 157–85 A GENRE of writing
that presents information to inform
readers on a subject. Key Features: a
topic carefully focused for a specific
AUDIENCE • definitions of key terms •
TRUSTWORTHY information • appropriate organization and DESIGN • a confident TONE that informs rather than
argues. *See also* IMRAD; PROFILE
a confident stance, 167–68
credibility, 164–66
engaging tone, 167–68
read, respond, revise, 173–74
rhetorical situation, 158–59
a student essay, 175–85
a target audience, 162–64
a topic that interests you, 158
visuals, 171–73
ways of organizing, 169–71
working thesis, 160–62

RESEARCH, 83, 103, 159–60 A
process of INQUIRY—of gathering information from reliable sources to learn
about something, find an answer to
a question that interests you, understand or support an ARGUMENT, and
more. *See also* FIELD RESEARCH
annotating a bibliography, 272–76
avoiding plagiarism, 300–303

RESEARCH QUESTION, 247 A question that guides research. A good research question should be simple, focused, and require more than just a "yes" or "no" answer.

RESPECT, 29–41 The act of giving someone or something your careful attention, listening with an open mind, being polite and considerate, and according someone else the same right to speak that you wish for yourself.

REVIEW A GENRE of writing that makes a judgment about something— a film, book, product, restaurant, job performance, whatever—based on certain CRITERIA. Key Features: relevant information about the subject • criteria for the judgment • a well-supported evaluation • attention to the AUDIENCE's needs and expectations • an authoritative TONE • awareness of the ethics of reviewing. *See also* EVALUATION; LITERATURE REVIEW

REVISING, 93–94 The process of making substantive changes, including additions and deletions, to a DRAFT so that it contains all the necessary information in an appropriate organization. Revision generally moves from whole-text issues to details with the goals of sharpening the focus and strengthening the ARGUMENT. *See also* response and revision

RHETORIC, 12–28 One of the three original disciplines in the ancient world (along with grammar and logic), rhetoric has been defined in many ways through the centuries. This book

SPATIAL ORGANIZATION A way of ordering a text that mirrors the physical arrangement of the subject—for instance, from top to bottom, left to right, outside to inside.

STANCE, 17–19, 26–27 A writer's attitude toward the subject—for example, reasonable, neutral, angry, curious. Stance is conveyed through TONE and word choice.

STANDARDIZED ENGLISH, 436 The variety of English taught in schools and generally expected in most academic and professional contexts. There is now a growing recognition in the United States of the validity of other, broader ways of speaking and writing.

STASIS THEORY A simple system for identifying the crux of an ARGUMENT—what's at stake in it—by asking four questions: (1) What are the facts? (2) How can the issue be defined? (3) How much does it matter, and why? (4) What actions should be taken as a result?

STORYBOARD, 194, 232 A series of sketches used in planning a film or video essay to map out the sequence of camera shots, movement, and action.

STRATEGIES FOR SUPPORTING AN ARGUMENT, 85–90, 105–12 Patterns for organizing and providing EVIDENCE to support a POSITION: CAUSE AND EFFECT, CLASSIFICATION, COMPARISON AND CONTRAST, DEFINITION, DESCRIPTION, EXAMPLE, FACTS, NARRATIVE, personal testimony, etc.

STYLE, 210, 406–7 The particular way something is written, designed, or communicated—its sentence structure, TONE, DESIGN, and word choice—that make it distinctive and get attention.

VLOG, 499–503 A blog that's delivered in video, often on *YouTube*.

W

WIKI A website format, often consisting of many linked pages on related topics, that allows readers to add, edit, delete, or otherwise change the site's content.

WORKING BIBLIOGRAPHY A record of all sources consulted during RESEARCH. Each entry provides all the bibliographic information necessary for DOCUMENTING each source, including author, TITLE, and publication information. A working bibliography is a useful tool for recording and keeping track of sources.

WORKS CITED, 316–44 The list of full bibliographic information for all the sources cited in the text, which appears at the end of a researched text prepared in MLA STYLE.

writing in multiple modes. *See* MULTI-MODAL WRITING

WRITING PROCESSES, 80–98 Activities that writers engage in when producing a text: considering our RHETORICAL SITUATION, GENERATING IDEAS AND TEXT and doing RESEARCH, coming up with a THESIS and EVIDENCE, considering multiple PERSPECTIVES, DRAFTING, getting response and revising, thinking about DESIGN, EDITING, and PROOFREADING.

MLA DOCUMENTATION DIRECTORY

APA DOCUMENTATION DIRECTORY

A DIRECTORY OF READINGS

* Student writing ** On letstalklibrary.com